LITERARY CRITICISMS
BY FRANCIS THOMPSON

FRANCIS THOMPSON IN CHANCERY LANE

From a Pastel by the HONORABLE NEVILLE LYTTON
in the Thompson Room, Boston College

Literary Criticisms
BY FRANCIS THOMPSON

Newly Discovered and Collected

BY

Rev. Terence L. Connolly, S. J., Ph. D.

LIBRARIAN AND CURATOR
OF THE THOMPSON COLLECTION
BOSTON COLLEGE

New York
E P Dutton and Company Inc
1948

PERMISSU SUPERIORUM

S. A. JACOBS, THE GOLDEN EAGLE PRESS

MOUNT VERNON, N.Y.

meth. Pub. House
10.00
10-2-57 se
11-14-57 cdm

To

Mr. Wilfrid Meynell

The Poet's
"Father, Brother, Friend"

FOREWORD

IN his study of other poets, Francis Thompson was deeply
interested in finding·the future man in the boy. And in his
own mature work as critic, no less than poet, there is clear evidence
of the boy of whom his father once said: "I cannot imagine where
that boy has learned all that he knows." Thompson's critical work
embraces an incredible number of subjects, ranging from the
poems of Ernest Dowson to the Odes of Coventry Patmore; from
Roman empresses to the Blind Sisters of St. Paul; from Marysiencka
to St. Teresa of Avila; from the early Church to the Salvation
Army; from Astro-Physics to Mysticism. Learned, keen, and well-
balanced, these criticisms are expressed in flawless prose — witty,
racy, and, at times, sublime — that every week delighted readers
of London's most important periodicals.

Because many of these articles were unsigned, few of Thompson's contemporaries had any knowledge of the incredible amount
of work he accomplished in the field of criticism during the last
ten years of his life — the decade that bridged the close of the
nineteenth century and the beginning of the twentieth.

> 1897: End of Poet. Beginning of Journalist.
> The years of transition completed.

That simple entry in one of Thompson's notebooks records the
change that issued in the rich legacy of criticism that he has left us.

A notable description of Thompson during his days of book
reviewing, quoted by Everard Meynell in his *Life* of the poet, was
the inspiration of the Honorable Neville Lytton's pastel reproduced as frontispiece of this volume.

vii

In memory I see him one miserable November afternoon communing with the Seraphim, and frolicking with the young-eyed Cherubim in Chancery Lane. The roads were ankle-deep in slush; a thin, icy rain was falling; the yellow fog enwrapped the pedestrians squelching down the lane; and, going through them in a narrow path, I saw Francis Thompson, wet and mud-spattered. But he was not unhappy. What is a day of unpleasant weather to one who lives in eternity? His lips were moving, his head was raised, his eyes were humid with emotion, for above the roof of the Chancery Lane Safe Deposit Company, in the murk of the fog, he saw beatific visions. They were his reality, not the visible world. He was on his way to the office of the *Academy* with the manuscript of a book review, and on his damp back was slung the weather-worn satchel in which he would carry away volumes for the ensuing week.

On nearly every page of the present volume, it is clear that the vision that was Thompson's in Chancery Lane did not desert him in his lodgings near Palace Court, as he labored far into the night, over a book review or article for which an anxious editor was waiting.

It was while engaged in examining Thompson's manuscripts, letters, notebooks, and other material for a deeper appreciation of his poetry, that the present writer gradually came to a realization of the poet's importance as a critic. The best of his criticism has long been accessible in the volume of prose edited by Mr. Meynell. But in that volume, the aim was, primarily, to present Thompson as a prose-writer. The object of the following pages is, primarily, to present Thompson the critic. But in doing so, care has been taken that nothing should be included that might detract from Thompson's literary reputation.

This is scarcely the place to enter upon a discussion of the confused state of theories and principles in contemporary literary criticism. Ours is not an age of clashing *theories* in literature, art, or religion. It is an age of *action,* action in life that is often opposed to truth: action in art that is frequently in opposition to a definite aesthetic derived from truth. In such an age, in a volume of criticism such as this, there is an element of appositeness that may reasonably be expected to arouse some degree of interest.

In view of the tendency of literature in Thompson's day, it is somewhat of an enigma that his criticism was as eagerly sought and published by the *Academy* and *Athenæum*, as by *Merry England* and the *Franciscan Annals*. For English literary criticism then, as now, gave unmistakable evidence of the mentality that Thompson describes in one of the reviews here reprinted:

It was long a conviction in the mind of the average English Protestant that Catholicity exerted a stunting influence on literary development, a belief which the educational disabilities incidental to English Catholicism for some time tended to confirm. The idea in the Protestant mind was something after this fashion — that from Martin Luther came the Reformation, from the Reformation came those twin gifts of Heaven, Good Queen Bess and William Shakespeare, from Good Queen Bess came our greatness, and from William Shakespeare came our literature.   Q. E. D.

Besides the lack of appreciation consequent upon religious prejudice, Catholic literature fared ill at the hands of critics who held that form is everything, while subject-matter is of no importance. Chief among such critics was George Saintsbury. In 1895, two years before the decade of Thompson's intensive critical work, Saintsbury wrote: "Practically everything has been said. . . . the only question is whether the present sayer and thinker has shown due skill and originality in his manner of thought and expression." (*Collected Essays*, Vol. II, p. 200.) Several years earlier, in 1866, in his *Essay on Baudelaire*, he described the aim of a critic as merely to express, "in the best manner that he can, the effect produced on his own mind by a given work of art."

Thompson entered into no formal controversy with such ideas or the principle from which they were derived, "Art for Art's Sake." But in his critical work, he artlessly, firmly and effectively demonstrated the fallacy of this principle, and its melancholy effect upon English literature. As a critic, his was the art that conceals art. Never obtruding his principles unnecessarily; seldom, even, explicitly invoking them, his criticism was completely permeated with them. To borrow his own metaphor, the dry bones of philosophy and dogma were the skeleton of his work, and in criticism, as in poetry, he clothed this skeleton with the flesh and blood of his artistry, and breathed into it the living soul of Truth.

As a critic, Thompson is not a panacea for all the ills of modern criticism. But the principles of his criticism and his fearless though gentle application of them, cannot fail to impress any student, critic, or reader who opens his mind to them. The need of contemporary critics whose aim too often is merely a factual description of their own reactions, is right principles. The need of those who profess right principles, is unswerving application of them.

The chief aim of this volume, then, is to make accessible Thompson's hitherto unknown or uncollected criticism. Most of the material is here, for the first time, identified as Thompson's. Nothing here included has previously appeared in a published volume of Thompson's prose. "Sanctity and Song," as here printed, is the second of two articles under that title contributed to *Franciscan Annals*. The first article is the essay to be found in Mr. Meynell's definitive edition.

The means of identifying the material here presented was first placed at the editor's disposal by Mr. Meynell, at Greatham, during the summer of 1938. During that visit, Mr. Meynell presented the editor with many of Thompson's notebooks, letters and manuscripts which, upon more leisurely examination, at home, yielded further clues for the identification of unsigned reviews and articles. In 1945, immediately after the conclusion of World War II, the editor, through the courtesy of the State Department, was permitted to return to England. There, through Mr. Meynell's unfailing kindness, the work was completed.

With the exception of "Varia," the arrangement of material within a chapter is as follows. General articles are placed first, followed by those on particular subjects, alphabetically arranged according to the subject treated. Where there is more than one article on the same subject, they are grouped together in the order of their original publication. "Varia" is, in general, arranged according to the dates when the articles appeared. But those on Shakespeare are grouped together, and "Books That Have Influenced Me" is placed at the end, because it is not a literary criticism.

T. L. C.

CONTENTS

xi

ACKNOWLEDGMENTS

From the Foreword, it is evident that the work in the following pages was made possible, chiefly, by Mr. Wilfrid Meynell's largesse. For nearly a decade, the task of searching through endless periodical files, identifying and classifying material, could not have been accomplished without the constant cooperation of Miss Helen Carlin. For concessions in lending material, I am indebted to the British Museum, the Boston Athenæum, Mr. Milton E. Lord of the Boston Public Library, Mr. Carl B. Roden of the Chicago Public Library, and Mr. John M. O'Loughlin and his assistants in the Library at Boston College. Permission to use articles from *Merry England* adds another to many previous obligations to Mr. Wilfrid Meynell. His Eminence, Bernard Cardinal Griffin, Archbishop of Westminster, has graciously approved the inclusion of three reviews from the *Weekly Register*. His Grace, the Duke of Westminster, has granted permission to reprint material from the *New Review* and the *Outlook*. For the use of material from the *Franciscan Annals*, I am indebted to the Reverend Editor, Father Martin, O.S.F.C. Reviews from the *Tablet* (London) and the *Dublin Review* are reprinted with the permission of their respective editors, Mr. Douglas Woodruff and Mr. T. S. Gregory. From the office of the *Daily News*, successor to the *Daily Chronicle*, approval has been received for the use of a review that originally appeared in the latter publication. To Mrs. Edward C. Donnelly I am grateful for her unfailing interest and help.

LITERARY CRITICISMS
BY FRANCIS THOMPSON

Truth is a maid, whom men woo diversely;
This, as a spouse; that, as a light-o'-love,
To know, and having known, to make his brag.
But woe to him that takes the immortal kiss,
And not estates her in his housing life,
Mother of all his seed!

BIOGRAPHY

THE LIEBIG OF BIOGRAPHY *
[*Academy*, July 30, 1898]

In two reviews Thompson points out the greatness and weakness of
Stephen's versatility, and analyzes the faults and virtues of his creative and
critical work. The second of these reviews appeared more than four years
after the first, during which interval Stephen became Sir Leslie Stephen.
What Thompson most admires in Stephen is a characteristic for which
he himself was distinguished — chivalrous treatment of an adversary whose
root-principles were "the destructive opposite of his own." Thompson's
résumé of *Caleb Williams,* in the second review, must have grieved the
hearts of Victorian Philistia. His characterization of Stevenson's "mastery
of weird terror," is Thompson at his best. In 1915, the first of these reviews
was privately printed in pamphlet form by Clement Shorter.

A VARIOUS and (in its way) influential career has been
Mr. Leslie Stephen's in modern English literature. His *Hours
in a Library* have given him deserved reputation as an essayist. His
History of English Thought in the Eighteenth Century has given
him reputation in the more solid walks of literature. In Mr. John
Morley's "Men of Letters" series, his studies of Pope, Swift, and
especially his admirable Johnson, have exhibited his power as a
biographer — a biographer on the minor scale. As editor of the
Cornhill he attained success and prominence in yet another line.
Seldom does a successful *littérateur* make a good editor; but under
Mr. Leslie Stephen's direction the *Cornhill* took a new lease of
vitality such as it had not done since the days of its start by
Thackeray, though its brilliance was on different lines from those
followed by the great novelist. Under Mr. Stephen the immortal
initials R. L. S. lit up its pages; he, too, if we recollect rightly,
gave asylum to Mr. Henley, destined himself to be a famous editor.
Both these writers might have sought in vain the recognition of the
conventional editor. Homage to the man who helps others up
the ladder which he has climbed himself. But with energies

* *Studies of a Biographer*. By Leslie Stephen. Vols. I and II.

unexhausted, his last adventure was his most memorable. He became
the editor and the inspiration of that monumental work, the *Dictionary of National Biography*, and not only went through all the
labours of its editing, but contributed numbers of articles to its
first volumes. It has now been relinquished to the control of Mr.
Sidney Lee; but its inception must ever be associated with Mr.
Leslie Stephen. For he not only edited it, wrote for it, but he
impressed on it — in style and plan — his own character. The
numerous contributors who supported and continue to support the
undertaking wrote as they have written because Mr. Stephen set
them the model. And the model was his own.

What that model is may be learned from his new volumes,
Studies of a Biographer, which represent most of the characteristics
to be found in his life's work, except, perhaps, such more lengthy
and set work as the *History of Eighteenth Century Thought*.
The title, *Studies of a Biographer*, almost disclaims the name of
essayist, though we have called him essayist. Yet there are some
things in this work which justify that name, and these let us
consider first. From this aspect, among his many aspects, Mr.
Leslie Stephen is peculiar and difficult to estimate aright. Let it
be said frankly, and in general, that the essay (properly so called,
and exercising the widest latitude in the interpretation of the term)
is not Mr. Stephen's province. Yet it is impossible to refuse him
respect in it. The essay is not his province by birthright; yet he
makes it his by force of arms. In the essay on Matthew Arnold
(delivered as a lecture before the Owens College, but really an
essay) he modestly sets himself down a Philistine. "Humility is
truth," said St. Bernard. Humility here is truth. Mr. Leslie Stephen,
from the standpoint of Matthew Arnold, is a Philistine. That
reminds us how the word has shifted its meanings since the days
of Arnold. It has come to mean a man who cares nothing for
literature. Nay, its uttermost degradation has been reached by a
writer in the daily press, a writer belonging to the class of "young
barbarians" whom Arnold contemned, and who has used it to
designate those that do not dress according to the highly tailored
canons of the "Johnnies" and "Chappies." After this, the spiritual
children of Arnold have nothing left but to abandon the word, as

cast-off clothing, to the *valets* of language. Arnold intended it for those — inside or outside literature — who were natively prosaic and unimaginative. Now to these Mr. Stephen belongs. One is loath to endorse his self-claim of that ugly word "Philistine." One is loath to abandon him to the enemy — he does too much honour to them. He is a literary Panther:

> So poised, so gently he descends from high,
> It seems a soft dismissal from the sky.

Yet throughout his writing one cannot but be conscious of a certain hardness, a lack of moist light. He appreciates poetry — particularly the poetry of men such as Wordsworth and Arnold. But his appreciation is intellectual. Poetry, or the appreciation of poetry, requires in its fulness both intellect and emotion. Nevertheless one may have it without intellect, but not without emotion. Mr. Stephen does seem in a certain way to reach an intellectual appreciation even of the aesthetic side in poetry. If he does not reach it directly, he seems, by a certain strenuous fairness of mind, to reach it in a reflex way, through considering and appreciating its aesthetic effect on others. In the same manner he succeeds in forming an intellectual image of much else, in diverse directions, which has no personal appeal to him. So he becomes the most cultivated of non-aesthetic writers; of all Philistines, the one whom those of the opposite camp can read with pleasure and placidity.

All this comes out remarkably in his discourse on Arnold. It is the best essay ever written by a critic on an author with whom he was in no native sympathy. That is to say, an author whose root-principles are the destructive opposite of his own. Over and over again one exclaims: "He should have belonged to us!" Yet we are simultaneously aware that he never could have been one of us; that he is a born antagonist, with a superbly chivalrous recognition of his adversary's merit and strength. His judgment of Arnold is admirable, his sympathy refused or unwilling. That is a paradox which runs through Mr. Leslie Stephen's whole nature. His mind is that of the "scientist," but a glorified scientist. The scientist professes to examine everything without *a priori* bias; but when he confronts something alien to his own province, resting on principles other than his own, he becomes the most partisan and bigoted of critics. Mr. Stephen really tries to carry out the principles which the brethren of his cause only profess. To perceive this, compare his methods when he confronts an idealist with the methods (in a like situation) of Professor Huxley. Take as a specimen of his thoughtfully candid spirit this passage on Arnold, with which we might have some quarrel in a detail or so, but surely none in essence:

We — for I may perhaps presume that some of you belong, like me, to the prosaic faction — feel, when dealing with such a man as Arnold, at a loss. He has intuitions where we have only calculations. . . . He shows at once a type where our rough statistical and analytical tables fail to reveal more than a few tangible facts; he perceives the spirit and finer essence of an idea where it seems to slip through our coarser fingers, leaving only a residuum of sophistical paradox. In the long run, the prosaic weigher and measurer has one advantage — he is generally in the right as far as he goes. [Quite true.] His tests may be coarser, but they are more decisive, and less dependent upon his own fancies ["fancy" is an erroneous word in the case of a *true* master of intuition]; but when he tries to understand his rival, to explain how at a bound the intuitive perception has reached conclusions after which he can only hobble on limping feet, he is apt to make a bungle of it; to despise the power in which he is so deficient; and probably to suggest unreasonable doubts as to its reality and value.

Was ever such recognising criticism from an avowed demi-adversary? Throughout, Mr. Stephen admits the value of being "shaken up" by Arnold's keen assaults on the rigid Philistine position. *Fas est ab hoste doceri* is the burthen of his essay. Yet there is a suggested reason for his avowed half-protesting sympathy. Arnold and he are really one in cause. They are both Agnostics, though their Agnosticism is so diverse in pattern. And many of his strictures on Arnold would be admitted — nay, applauded — by idealists who were not Agnostics.

Mr. Stephen's limitations as essayist are better seen in his comments on the recent *Life of Tennyson*. He takes up the position which many of us take — that the later Tennyson is not equal to the earlier. He takes it up with characteristic modesty and apology, fearing that he may be "Philistine." But when he comes to the reason of the faith that is in him, he flounders. He shelters himself behind the allegory of "The Idylls," and his dislike of allegory; behind his dislike of philosophy, so shadowily and indirectly conveyed. One may almost assert with confidence that the real reason of his abated enthusiasm is one with ours. Ruskin expressed it when he said that he felt the art and finish in these poems a little more than he liked to feel it. To this Tennyson replied that "The Idylls" were really rapidly written. Mr. Stephen feels the answer to be insufficient, but goes into all manner of roundabout considerations in the endeavour to explain *why* the answer is unsatisfactory. If his strength had lain in discussion, comment, analysis, he would have struck the direct answer at once. Mr. Ruskin was right. It matters nothing at all *how* a poem was written: it matters everything what is its effect. If the effect be one of downright inspiration, it is insignificant whether the poet spent months upon it. If the effect be one of self-conscious elaboration, without fire or fervour, or spontaneous richness, it does not signify though it were written in an hour after supper. Tennyson's earlier poems were full enough of highly wrought diction (whether he actually lingered over them or not); but this was carried off by the underlying *spirit* of inspiration. In "The Idylls" this magic is apparent only in passages, in images, in lines, in phrases: the general tissue has an air of mere artistry, without magic, without inevitableness. The allegory is neither here nor there; one's tastes as to the poetic expression of philosophy are neither here nor there. One comes to perceive that Mr. Stephen's power hardly lies in criticism. Even in the case of Arnold he makes no illuminative remarks; says nothing that in substance has not been said before. Neither, most certainly, does it lie in making a subject the theme for his own flights of thought or fancy. Where does it lie?

If one had read nothing else that Mr. Leslie Stephen had written; if one had read neither his "Men of Letters" volumes nor his contributions to the *Dictionary of National Biography*, the answer would yet be apparent in the present volumes. The reader may find it writ large in the "Johnsoniana," the "Byrom," the "Gibbon's Autobiography," the "Importation of German," above all, in "Wordsworth's Youth." The "Johnsoniana" deals with Dr. Birkbeck Hill's

"Johnsonian Miscellanies," and in masterly manner impresses into its few pages a sketch of the un-Boswellian Johnson; bringing out by contrast the debt we owe Boswell, the true genius of that much-sneered-at writer. Yet with all its compression it is not dry. Even more typical is the article on Wordsworth. Mr. Stephen is here treating a book of M. Legouis — a book singularly interesting and unexpectedly excellent as coming from a French writer. With some dissent in minor matters (as he mentions), he does yet give the reader, in effect, an admirable and clear synopsis of what M. Legouis takes a book to set forth. The detailed examination by which M. Legouis brings out and enforces his conclusions is, perforce, absent; but the pith of the book is there. So that, having read Mr. Stephen, you could almost work out the French writer's demonstration for yourself.

That, in a phrase, is Mr. Leslie Stephen's peculiar function and excellence — to extract the square root of a book, or of many books. Clearly, we cannot call such a production an essay, or such a writer an essayist, in the original meaning of the terms. Not, indeed, according to any sense of these terms, with all their modern latitude of application. He does not make a book or a theme a nucleus of his own discourse; he macerates a subject; he scoops the pulp of the fruit, and throws away the skin. Essentially, no matter what he writes, at his best and most characteristic he is, in fact, a biographer. Whether writing *Johnson* for the "Men of Letters," or the "Johnsoniana" in these volumes, which is professedly more or less an essay, he is equally a biographer. A biographer, but a biographer in little. And thus all his tasks have been really an unconscious preparation for the crowning task by which he will chiefly live — the *Dictionary of National Biography*. There his gift of scholarly and felicitous compression, his power to fuse multifarious information without dulness and with perfect proportion, found its fitting exercise. It does not matter that only a certain portion of the innumerable articles in that work are actually from his pen. The credit of an architect is not lessened because the details of his work must needs be executed by subordinates. And Mr. Leslie Stephen is the architect of the Dictionary; though, like Michelangelo, he has had to leave to another architect the task of continuing and completing his conception. Every article therein is framed under laws and upon a model laid by him. And those laws, that model, are derived from his own practice; from that method of cultured, perspicuous, symmetrical condensation, exhibited in this book as in those which have gone before it. One or two papers there are, it is true, in the beginning of the book, both desultory in structure, and frequently slipshod in grammar. But the bulk of it is as well-knit in style as in substance. The Liebig of biography — that is our final verdict on Mr. Leslie Stephen.

ANALYSIS, ORDER, EXACTITUDE*
[*Academy*, December 6, 1902]

THE first two volumes of Sir Leslie Stephen's *Studies of a Biographer* were reviewed by us on their appearance: now, in a "Second Series," he gives us two more volumes. The articles which compose them are republished, with three exceptions, he tells us, from the *National Review;* but all have appeared in one periodical or another. In our review of the first series we commented on the appropriateness of the title; and noted that Sir Leslie's most essential gift was that capacity for miniature biography, for pithing a subject or a career, and presenting the complex details in a perspicuous summary, which found its fulfilment in his work in the *Dictionary of National Biography*. Analysis, order, exactitude, logical clearness and compression are his in conspicuous measure: it might be said that he applies to literature the mind of the physical scientist, a combination which has both value and rarity. It is a mere necessity that he has the limitations of such a union: we sometimes feel as if he were a literary critic made, not born; as if his taste, in some directions, were painfully grafted rather than innate. This sensation we have chiefly in regard to matters of the higher imagination, where such a mind might be expected mostly to touch its limits. It is an engaging part of his character that he is himself aware of this, and endeavours to allow for it in a manner as modest

* *Studies of a Biographer*. By Sir Leslie Stephen. Vols. III & IV.

as it is rare. For he has that fair-minded integrity which is his aim, but too seldom the attainment of the scientific mind, when it fronts matters for which it has no congenital sympathy. Withal, this modesty implies no lack of courage or firmness: he has the resolution of his judgment, but the caution to mark possible fallibility.

These volumes, as compared with those of the previous series, are more uniformly concerned with subjects of literary criticism, and less with biographical or semi-biographical studies. They do not, therefore, bring out the author's special power so well as some of the essays in the former volumes. Still, even when we are most aware of his limits, these articles do not fail to interest. A good example, and well within his scope, is the paper on that curious minor philosopher, Godwin. It is the more interesting because no one remembers Godwin nowadays. True, Sir Leslie has scant sympathy with him on the philosophic side. Indeed, he is provoked to the most sweeping departure from sobriety we have known in him, when he says that "with minds sharpened by study, young ladies will soon make their brothers' discovery, that when a man claims to be a philosopher there is a strong presumption that he must be an imposter." Such an indictment of a class which has produced the supreme intellects of humanity, from Plato downwards, seems almost inconceivable. Truly, a mediocre philosopher is an impermissible being. But so is a mediocre poet. Godwin, however, one may freely abandon to the author, who does him substantial justice, and writes with the pleasantest quiet humour about the solemn contradictions and absurdities of his life. A man of considerable ability, who by sheer one-eyed thoroughness and placid self-belief got much abler men to take him at his own valuation. Of humour Godwin was comfortably and portentously destitute. His disciple Shelley was a low comedian compared with him. We can never think of Godwin without recollections of that venerable Patriarch, Mr. Casby. Not, indeed, consciously a humbug, he was very much of an unconscious one. Sir Leslie rests his chief claim to memory on his once celebrated novel, *Caleb Williams*. Even there his solemn vacuity of humour is amusingly apparent. He held the theory (which very different men have

held) that the nature of a government affected every member of
the nation subject to it. But he held it in the most ludicrously
obvious way; and set out to demonstrate it in *Caleb Williams* after
the absurdest impossible fashion. England being ruled by a tyran-
nical oligarchy, it follows, as the day the night, that Squire Tyrrell
must be a tyrant too, and a brute and a bully and a blockhead into
the bargain. The "pure reason" which Godwin worshipped proceeds to show how, as a further consequence of a tyrannous
government, Squire Tyrrell quarrels with the virtuous and high-
minded Squire Falkland, and insults him beyond endurance. Failing to obtain redress for his injured honour, Falkland murders
Tyrrell in a fit of high-mindedness. The influence of a blighting
oligarchy then assails Falkland, causing him not only to hang two
innocent men in his own stead, but when his secretary, Caleb
Williams, is discovered discovering his crime and begs for pardon,
first to keep him captive, then when he escapes, to have him found
guilty of a false charge, and afterwards to hunt him through the
country by spies of the deepest dye. Caleb finally turns at bay,
and accuses him in language of pure reason; whereat Falkland,
overcome by remorse — and pure reason — throws himself into his
arms and shortly dies of acute high-mindedness.

In the novel our critic finds a certain power, despite its stolid
didacticism. But the charm of his essay is in the admirable relation
of Godwin's delicious absurdities; the knot of charming women
disciples who wept when he married Mary Wollstonecraft, but
declined the subsequent honour of replacing her; his successive
attempts to convince them, by pure reason, that they ought by
every principle of logic to be in love with him, and their unphilo-
sophical obduracy to logic; with the final fall of the philosopher
to the illogical methods of the ineligible widow next door, who
cried as he sat on his balcony: "Is it possible that I behold the
immortal Godwin?" So she married him, and Lamb called her "that
damned Mrs. Godwin," the "disgusting woman who wears green
spectacles." Handsome, says Sir Leslie; but could any woman be
beautiful in green spectacles? We all know how the opponent of
marriage played the outraged father when Shelley practised his
principles at his daughter's expense, and sternly refused Shelley's

cheque — unless it were made payable in another name. "How charming is divine philosophy!" Mr. Casby could not have behaved better, had Clennam run away with Flora — or Mr. F.'s Aunt.

Good, too, is the study of Stevenson; if not subtle or markedly original. But it is late days to be original on Stevenson. The author seizes, we think, the correct point of view — that Stevenson was essentially a beatific boy, with the boy's gallant spirits and the boy's insatiable love of adventurous literature — or rather the literature of adventure. In his latest years, as Sir Leslie notes, he could play with toys — brick-building, a war-game with tin soldiers, a toy-periodical, or what not. Yet there was one gift which Stevenson seems to us never to have exploited to the full — we mean his mastery of weird terror. He handled it once, in *Jekyll and Hyde*; but with that exception only touched on it incidentally. Yet wherever it appears he reveals an exceptional power. It gleams sinisterly across the pages of *Treasure Island*, in the tapping stick of the blind Pew, in casual touches of John Silver. The *Ebb Tide* starts into evil power with the stepping of Attwater over the ship's side and the gradual unhooding of Huish as his abominable protagonist. The plotting of the murder in the cabin is one of the most snaky things in literature. Sir Leslie Stephen, apparently, cannot away with Huish; because, it should seem, he feels in him merely the repulsiveness, not the malign impressiveness of the creature — as though one stirred a fusty rag in a London alley, and met the eyes of a cobra scintillating under the yellow gas-lamp. This vein, we think, Stevenson had in him to have worked as none have done since Edgar Poe, and with a strange potency all his own. But the gift lurks with fitful glimpses in his work.

Stevenson, says the essayist, is a Bohemian, touching life at many aspects in a gay, picaresque fashion, but not attempting the deeper, higher or broader things of the novel, even from the romantic standpoint. And it must surely be allowed that no novelist of equal gifts has ever been so content to skim vivaciously over the windy surfaces of life — a sea-mew of letters. It is not merely his limits that surprise, but his temperamental content in those limits. In protesting against the ascription to him of the deeper powers which he scarce coveted, Sir Leslie is right. As an artist, he was indifferent either to love or tears. When before could such a thing be said of such an artist? It would be long to enumerate the other great names on which the author alights. Such a study as the "Milton," for all its good sense, does not show him at his best. But it would be wrong to quit his book without mentioning the "Southey" as one of the very best. With this nowadays little-read author he is entirely at home, and shows his strong discriminative faculty to excellent advantage. One is glad to find him speaking a word for *The Doctor*, that mine of erudition, pedantry, clumsy jesting, kindly pleasantry, attraction and repulsion; a book to dip into, not to read. He has the boldness to say that Southey's chief right to fame is the child's tale of "The Three Bears." Shall a man write epics by the yard, and come to this? Yet perhaps it is true, and no bad thing to come to, when all's said.

THE DECADENCE OF FEMALE DECADENCE*
[*Academy*, September 23, 1899]

Thompson's critical capacity for light but not facetious treatment of the wicked heroine in literature and life makes us regret that he is not with us today. Our emancipated females in life and literature thrive on the publicity of serious criticism, but they would scarcely withstand Thompson's deadly ridicule. From his poetry we know his awesome reverence for womanhood:

> Whose spirit sure is lineal to that
> Which sang *Magnificat*.

Here, we have his reaction to women who have proved the truth of the old adage, *corruptio optimi pessima* — or should we say *optimae?*

THERE is a fashion in women, as in the dress of women. It is modish for women to be aesthetic or athletic, and forthwith we have a crop of damsels willowy and Botticelli-like, or tall as goddesses and muscular as Guardsmen. Such is the determination of woman, that she will grow in the fashion, and add the Scriptural cubit to

---

* *The Roman Empresses*. By Jacques Roergas de Serviez.
Translated from the French.

her stature if the mode demand it. These things are a mystery. There is a fashion also in female character, as evidenced in the novels of the day. The pale and pensive, the artistic, the sprightly and brilliant — all have their turn of popularity. At present, as a result of the "decadence," the wicked heroine is "in." She may be of varying patterns, but wickedness is essential — nay, had we not some while ago *The Lives of Twelve Bad Women?* Whether the fashion has affected society we are not aware; but it is writ large in literature, and has invaded the stage. The present book is therefore quite in the vogue. For the Roman empresses were most of them wicked; and several superbly, scenically wicked. A new work on such a subject would have distinct interest and value; but it is to be regretted that this is a mere reprint of an old translation of an eighteenth-century French book, by one De Serviez. It is full, faithful, not very discriminating, stilted, and dry — dry as mechanical handling and superfluous moral platitudes of the most approved fashion can make it.

A bad woman is a very bad woman. A bad man has usually some stump of a conscience left, and feels in it occasional aches and twinges which he refers automatically to the amputated organ. But a woman has none. Her wickedness comes from her with cheerfulness and comfort. The man is a strong swimmer in evil; but to the woman it becomes her element, her habitation. Drawn out (so to speak) on to the land of virtue, she could not breathe, but would plunge back with relief into her proper environment of vice. But while all are perfectly bad in an absolute sense, relatively there are degrees of perfection, as among good women we see. Perhaps the palm of perfection may be awarded to the wicked women of Italy. We say it with some hesitation. The women of the East we have hardly means for studying, or they might complicate the decision. Semiramis is too distant, too legendary; besides, she was a conqueror, and a perfect bad woman should not allow these things to divert her from the practice of her art. Catherine of Russia is in the same case, and even her badness is far from undisputed. It comes to this, that the North generally does not show up well, and England in particular makes a very poor display. We have to admit with regret that we have, perhaps, no bad women of any particular excellence. Queen Elinor enjoys a quite unfounded reputation on the strength of a mythical bowl of poison: she did not take away Rosamond's life, but in all probability merely her reputation, over the mediæval substitute for five o'clock tea. Besides, poison in a bowl — not even a phial: a thumping bowlful, as if she were going to poison a horse — and a dagger; what coarse, what primitive means! Neither of the Elinors has any solid evidence for her repute. The Castlemaines and Portsmouths of the Restoration were very poor copies of French originals — themselves not in the first rank — and one of them turned charitable, or pious, or something equally fatal to serious claims. We are driven back upon the Mrs. Brownriggs, and women who murder their babies, and suchlike types of sordid achievement. France is much better. The Mme. de Pompadours, it is true (in spite of that single fine saying about the deluge), do not come up to one's highest ideals of badness in woman: but the ladies of Catherine de Medici's "bodyguard" had undoubtedly attained no common order of excellence, though their Italian training takes from the supreme merit of originality. The same must be said of the Brinvilliers, who would otherwise have been a bad woman of real distinction; and generally, in this otherwise prolific period, there was no nationally French school of female wickedness. It derived strongly from Italy. In earlier French history there are some striking examples of native talent; but it is in the Carolingian time that we find real greatness. Brünnhilda and her rival queen were eminent examples of the true type. Nevertheless, there is a certain Teutonic coarseness and crudeness about the amours and murders of these Frankish queens which makes one adhere to Italy as the land where the bad woman has been produced in her perfection.

The mingling of softness, fire, and subtlety which makes Italy the most feminine of lands, and the Italian woman typically dear to the imagination of our poets, has caused it in all ages to produce the most arresting examples of female evil. Where woman is most woman for good she will also be most woman for evil. From Italy Webster took his "White Devil," Vittoria Corombona. Italy gave to the popular imagination its ideal type of the baleful, lovely woman in Lucrezia Borgia, though cold history avers that there have been much worse women in Italy and out of it, than Lucrezia of the wonderful hair. Where the evil-doing of men works by preference in feminine ways; where poison, the naturally feminine weapon, was used till it became an art, it is not surprising that women should become conspicuous in evil. Yet more than this is needed: there must be something in the blood itself to explain the parity in wickedness between the woman of mediæval Italy and the woman of old Rome. The Romans were a martial race; they dealt in blood and iron. Yet the history of the Roman empresses recalls strongly the worst women of Italian mediæval history. The one period may be used to illustrate the other.

There is a daring about their action which we notice also in the mediæval Italian women. It is not the Northern, but the Latin races which produce the Amazonian women. Where the men are women, the women are men; and it was when the sturdy warrior-race of Rome was past that the Roman woman began to show her potentialities in politics and crime. So we notice the same trait in Caterina Sforza, standing on the walls of her city in armour, to defy Caesar Borgia with indecorously masculine insults and in the ruthless boldness of an Agrippina. The inventions of the novelist pale before these ladies' vigorous reality. In spite of our novelists, the day of the bad woman is over; and no doubt, on the whole, it is as well.

THE NEWMAN OF HIS TIME*

[*Academy*, June 23, 1900]

Because of the parallel between St. Augustine's *Confessions* and Thompson's lyrical soul-biography, "The Hound of Heaven," this review is of double interest. The chivalrous remarks about St. Augustine's mistress are not unlike the tender tribute in "Sister Songs," to the girl of the street who befriended Thompson in the darkest days of his outcast existence in London. In his encomium on St. Augustine's sainted mother, there is an overtone of Thompson's reverential love of his own mother. Too great to be made the theme of his poetry, it merited the higher tribute of silence.

* *The Confessions of St. Augustine*. In Ten Books.

IT IS not a new translation of the famous *Confessions of St. Augustine* which Messrs. Kegan Paul have issued; but it is a new and limited edition, beautiful in letterpress and parchment binding. It is so fine an edition that we are the more tempted to regret the publishers did not depart from the bad old precedent by issuing a complete translation. For, in accordance with the usual custom, the last three books are omitted. It is true that these last three books have no personal bearing, and are not of a nature to interest the majority of readers. But that is a matter for the reader himself, not for publisher or translator. Why should this, alone of all masterpieces, be subject to arbitrary and sweeping mutilation, in an age which is seriously indignant at the omission of the smallest obscenity from any profane author? We sincerely hope that some publisher will have the enterprise to give us a complete edition of the *Confessions*, leaving the responsibility for all they contain, as it should be left, with their illustrious author.

The fact that such an iniquity can be perpetrated, and has for a number of years been perpetrated, without so much as a comment, suggests that this famous book is more familiar by name than in fact. Even Byron talked of it; but when he said that St. Augustine "in his fine *Confessions* makes us envy his transgressions," one wonders whether he had read it — as Byron was certainly the last person one would expect to read St. Augustine. For anything less voluptuous than the saint's account of those "transgressions" could not well be conceived: the romantic reader will be disposed, indeed, to complain that it is so meagre and dispassionate. In truth, the reader who approaches this book with expectations roused by the customary manner of reference to it is likely to be very considerably discomfited. Have the customary referrers themselves any firsthand knowledge of it? one is moved to speculate. They suggest to the modern reader that he will find in Augustine a classical Amiel, a religious Marie Bashkirtseff — intimate details of early profligacy, experiments on life, soul-questioning and world-questioning. But to the reader accustomed to the very open door, the extreme dishabille and unquailing "realism" of the modish autobiography, St. Augustine will seem very skimmed milk indeed. They will feel as if they had gone to a theatre and come by mistake upon a pulpit-orator. The biography has not much detail according to our ideas; it is cast in a most undramatic — we might almost say un-narrative — form; and it is soaked through with the religious spirit in such a fashion that you are not for a moment suffered to forget the intense religious preoccupation of its author. To the student of character this feature is itself a document, an integral part of the man, and therefore of the book's appeal. But to the general reader it must come as a disconcerting surprise. He will have the temerity to say that the great and lauded *Confessions* are "dry."

Yet if you will put yourself in the proper attitude they are not that: nay, if you put yourself in the proper attitude you will understand the traditional reputation of the book. Conceive yourself a Christian — or, if you will, a Pagan — in the days of Valentinian the Emperor, when Christianity was established, through the Imperial profession of it, but Paganism was the aristocratic and fashionable creed. To be a Christian still meant to draw upon yourself cold looks and obloquy from your friends, if you were a member of the higher orders, as Augustine shows us in this book. The question between Paganism and Christianity was a burning question, as full of vital appeal to the hearts and consciences of the moment as the old Tractarian controversy (let us say) in its day. But the appeal was more instant, more universal. Upon such a world came forth this book from the Newman of his time, a man who had gone through the great internal struggle through which thousands were going, and had attained high ecclesiastical rank, high reputation as a great controversial writer, in the Church of his final adoption. It was Augustine's *Apologia pro Vitâ Suâ*. This — and more. For it was a world entirely without personal literature of any kind; a world still feeding on the stately remains of the classical authors, brought up on their coldly impersonal models, imbued with their impersonal literary traditions. And this man had gone through the great struggle common to most of mankind — decide it how they will — the struggle between the higher life and the lower, between the body and the soul, the beast and the angel. In this he had gone through more than the calm recluse of Littlemore. Upon a world so without the very conception of, or precedent for, personal literature he exploded the record of that personal struggle. Related simply, truthfully, without ostentation and without suppression, in so far as he undertook to relate it at all. Exploded is the right word, for the effect was resounding. It was Newman to an age which had no precedent for a Newman; it was Rousseau to an age which had not conceived in its heart the possibility of a Rousseau. It was the mirror of what all were experiencing held up before eyes which had never seen the likeness of a mirror. All which to us seems human and charming was to them trebly so; all which to us seems pale was to them magically and startlingly frank. An added intimacy of detail was not conceivable to them. The reverberations of that first *éclatant* sensation have come down the ages to us, impressing modern criticism of the book with the stress of accumulated tradition. It is as difficult to speak independently of it as to speak independently of Homer.

Yet when all this has been deduced and allowed for, there remains an undoubted residuum of eternal appeal. It was no traditional reverence which made Shelley condense an exquisite quotation from it as a heading for *Alastor*. "I was in love with love, nor had I aught which I might love; and I sought for what I might love, being in love with love." So it runs, as far as it is possible to translate it; and it suggests the reason of the *Confessions'* perennial appeal. For the quotation might stand as the motto of the *Confessions* themselves; it represents the whole strife and quest to which Augustine finally worked out the issue which satisfied himself. It was not the issue of *Alastor;* but the quest in both was the same. So long as that is the quest of the human heart, to human hearts the *Confessions* will have their interest.

For the man is very human, and has a very human history, notably human among religious biographies. We may well believe that his sins were forgiven him because he had loved much. The brilliant boy of Tagaste, who grew into the brilliant young teacher of rhetoric, had a strong element of the poet in him. In a more propitious age we may believe he would have been a poet; but it was an age when the hearthstone of poetry was cold, and the most distinguished career open to such gifts was doubtless that of rhetoric. The *Confessions* are full of poetic flashes. "Too late," he exclaims after his conversion, "too late I learned to love Thee, O Thou Beauty of ancient days!" The outburst is lyrical; it recalls a modern poet, who laments

That life was once so low, and love arrived so late.

Poetry and philosophy make Platonism, and "Plato the divine" was a passion with Augustine; the two milestones in his conversion are Plato and Paul. The open humanity of the man shines forth at every turn. Like Newman, he had a genius for friendship, and a magnetic power of retaining it; like Newman, he carried many of his friends with him even in his change of creed. There was a natural ingenuousness and refinement in him which caused him to retain an invincible modesty of demeanour and an unstaled attraction even during the aberrations of his youth. And, indeed, his very sensuality was singularly unsensual, strikingly delicate for that age of unashamed coarseness. In his early quest for *quid amarem* he did not scruple to search for and pick up his mistress in the church itself — like that very different personage, Mr. Pepys. But, having found her, he remained absolutely faithful to her, and she to him, until the date of his conversion — an affection which he extended to the son she bore him. There must have been something unique, and uniquely fascinating, about the young rhetorician's character, for such mutual constancy, in such a period of society, and so irregular a connexion. Nor can his choice, one must surmise, have been a bad one, apart from the nature of the tie itself. Who she was or what she was Augustine never mentions: she passes from his narrative nameless and all but noteless. One regrets that it was not his conversion which at last broke the constant bond between them, but his mother's persistent treaty that he should "range himself" (as the French say) by a respectable marriage. And the immediate result of the separation was simply, alas! that Augustine took another mistress. Under the circumstances one feels a compassion for the hapless girl, and no little impatience with certain of the saint's biographers. One such, an ecclesiastic, expresses his hope that the sinning woman spent the rest of her life (in the convent to which she retired) repenting her sin in having so long kept this great servant of God from the Church to which he naturally pertained. Seeing that it was Augustine (so far as may be gathered from his own implication) who sought her, not she who sought Augustine; seeing her fidelity till she was set aside by his own decree, a more unjust attitude towards the poor child could not well be conceived. We are tempted to hope (and suppose) that the saint spent a considerable portion of *his* remaining life in repentance that he seduced a tender-hearted girl, and, after years of faithful cohabitation, abandoned the still loving mother of his child to shame. Unfair as it would be, it is less unfair than the position of the ecclesiastical biographer. We need hardly say that Augustine in no wise gives the smallest countenance to this ungenerous and iniquitous judgment. The saint was emphatically a gentleman — after the ideas of his time. If he did not marry the girl (and how many modern gentlemen would think it necessary?), he abstains from any slur upon her. He would hardly view it as an honour to him that anyone should cast on his poor victim the obloquy of enticement which he never cast; reversing their relations in a falsified zeal for his glory. He, the seducer, made the seduced; she, the betrayed, made the betrayer. It is not the attitude of the *Confessions*, nor one which could be less than abhorrent to the man who meant those *Confessions* to be a disclosure of his early flagitiousness.

How far, one may ask, has that purpose of self-humiliation caused him to exaggerate his early sins? It does not seem to have led him into any intemperance of statement. His errors, on his own showing, were very much less than those of most brilliant young men in the heyday of the senses and the passionate search for happiness which hurried him from Tagaste to Carthage, and Carthage to Rome, and Rome to Milan. But it has biased him towards intemperance of judgment. His boyish lies, thefts, and gluttonies are set forth with an ascetic rigour of condemnation. He even declares that when Christ said, "Of such is the kingdom of Heaven," He must have spoken allegorically of the low stature of children, since they are too evil for the words to be literally understood!

But the mention of Augustine's childhood recalls what is assur-

edly a main part in the undying human appeal of this book. And
that is Monica, his mother. She is one of the great and beautiful
female figures of literature, no less than of history, as she is drawn
by the tender touches of her son; she stands side by side with
Antigone, Imogen, Cordelia. The world will not forget the ideal
record of that long prayerful and patient pursuit of her child who
was gone astray, which drew from the old bishop the declaration
that the son of so many tears could not perish. *Elevaverunt
flumina voces* — the floods have lifted up their voice; those floods
of her year-long and life-long tears, the voice of which is heard
through the ages "with the sound of many waters." That scene
by night at Ostia, when she sat with the son whose conversion had
at last been yielded to her prayers, discoursing of the heaven into
which she was about to enter, remains in its unearthly beauty one
of the memorable things in literature. That alone would make the
Confessions divinely human, so long as man is born of woman.

MADAME DE KRUDENER *

[*Merry England*, May, 1893]

The portrait of the amazing lady here reviewed is by Thompson framed
in her environment. A carved frame of rather intricate detail, it would
detract from the portrait were it less skillfully wrought. It reveals the
sure insight with which Thompson grasps the significance of the externali-
ties of history and human conduct. His distinction between complexity and
disorganization in human character, is an instance of his clear thinking
and speaking. His analysis of Madame de Krudener's character is classic.
She was a bundle of contradictions — not paradoxes — incredibly audacious
in her vanity, and obviously a woman determined to *feel* holy rather than
to *be* so. She is a rare subject for any man's consideration. And Thompson
makes the most of it in this highly entertaining review.

IT IS, I apprehend, a somewhat difficult task which a Catholic
biographer has undertaken in striving to evoke the English reader's
sympathy for the once famous Julie de Krudener. In the earlier

* *Madame de Krudener*. By Clarence Ford.

part of her career she is a Marie Bashkirtseff *à la mode de Rousseau;* and she suffers as a landscape of Gainsborough suffers in the age of Monet. Both were thought terribly naturalistic in their day; both appear conventional in our day. In her later career she suffers from even more complex causes. She is a mystic and a humanitarian; yet a mystic too humanitarian for the mystic, and a humanitarian too mystic for the humanitarian. As a mystic pure and simple she can hardly find a thorough sympathiser now. She is too evangelical for the cultivated, too Catholic for the evangelical, too imbued with Swedenborg for the Catholic, and too Swedenborgian for the understander of Swedenborg. Yet Mr. Ford has done well to bring her forward in his comprehending yet discriminative biography, lightly and delicately touched. No life of her previously appeared in English; yet she is an interesting forerunner of the "emancipated female" of to-day, and it is curious to note the differentiation imposed on her by her age. It was an age more volcanic than ours, alike in its sorrows and joys; an age already feeling the inroads of disease, but not yet sunken to a confirmed invalidity; an age already tossing in the access of the *weldschmerz* (word horrible!), but not yet given over to Ecclesiastes-and-water. It was the age of Chateaubriand and *Atala*, of Victor Hugo and "*Ce qu'on entend sur la montagne.*" It had discovered that life was full of sound and fury; it had not yet discovered that life signifies nothing. So the struck eagle quivered on the plain, as he quivers in the letters and autobiography of Berlioz. The *mal du siècle* was at his heart, and he clamoured in blind rage on all the gods to tell him what the accursèd thing might be. Take the description in Berlioz of his first initiation in the malady; for though Berlioz habitually lied and exaggerated with the whole-heartedness of Cellini, he has there written a page of sheer verity — as many a sufferer may still bear witness from his own self-knowledge. The great musician was standing, a mere adolescent, in the midst of the country, listening to the distant chant of a procession, as it passed with its surpliced priest blessing the fields. All at once he was seized with a mighty exaltation towards he knew not what, a vast and boundless yearning for he knew not what, the riotous blossoming of that joy which prepares the sombre fruit of pain.

With equal brusqueness, the vivid leaves were shed: he was bitten
with unimagined and uncomprehended agony: with desire for all
impossible things, with loss of all never-possessed things, with the
ravening for an uncircumscribed love, with the starvation-pangs
of a horrible and suddenly-known isolation. He fell on the ground,
and rolled over and over, tearing up the grass by handfuls, and
sobbing for rage and grief. The fit passed, leaving him exhausted;
but the experience was thenceforth an intermittent part of his
life's malady. English men of genius may know this thing; but
happily they regard it as a thing to be subdued and lived down,
not to be indulged. They do not glory in the ignominies of their
nature. Achilles is not proud of the weak spot in his heel. Only
on the Continent can a really great man show his sores and ulcers
by the wayside —

> To beg of Hob and Dick, that do pass by,
> Their needless vouchers;

that the women may murmur pity, and the men drop a copper into
the hat his publisher holds for him. It is not surprising, therefore,
that Madame de Krudener appears, at the outset, as a becomingly
feminised René, with the addition of a hugely petty female vanity.
In the latter respect she preludes very respectably to the astound-
ing frankness of Marie Bashkirtseff's vanity; save that Madame
de Krudener's appears unconsciously betrayed, while Marie's is
not without the suspicion of being deliberately displayed in a
sensational *demi-toilette*. The woman is vain of her vanity.

The character of Julie de Krudener her English biographer
pronounces a complex one. But many characters are called complex which are only disorganised. A shifting whirl of interests,
and a capacity for persuading yourself that you are what you
wish others to think you, prove levity and sophistication, but not
complexity. We do not call a vessel complex because it is cracked
in all directions. Complexity implies an organism, not a disorganism.
As a matter of fact, she seems to have been shallow and impulsive
of nature, with a heart susceptible rather than tenacious of impressions, and an intellect of feminine receptiveness which she and

others took for creativeness. There are many such women who are human phonographs, and can be fitted with new tunes like a barrel-organ. Now De la Rochefoucauld set the tune, now Madame de Staël, now Madame de Guyon, now Swedenborg or Boehme at secondhand: she was all of these in turn, but never Madame de Krudener. Or rather it was essentially Madame de Krudener to be all of these in turn. Like all people with a weakly fertile imagination, she could convince herself of being anything she was not; and her vanity always wished to be something above what God and nature had made her. In her very conversion, sincere enough in its way, vanity was rampant at the very moment she was vaunting its subdual. In a Welsh church a local magnate has left a tablet to inform the world how he hated pride. And of such a feat Madame de Krudener was quite capable. Even before her conversion, at the time she was fresh from the desertion of her husband, though she had recently returned to him, she was persuaded that she stood in special favour with the Court of Heaven. She desired to do great things, but did only sensational things, nor was aware of the difference. For she could never learn the lesson so difficult to teach women, yet which no woman has effected anything lofty till she learned, that all great work must rise like the Temple of Solomon, without sound of axe and hammer. Precisely, however, for all these reasons, she is a representative woman — representative, that is, of a class of women; and her life is an interesting study in human entomology.

She was born of good parentage in Riga, and as a girl did nothing that was remarkable. She married an elderly baron who was a good match, and spent the next nineteen years of her life in proving that a good match means a bad marriage. Not that the Baron de Krudener was in fault. Considering that he was a double-dyed *divorcé*, he turned out a surprisingly good husband — much better than the nature of her marriage could have given the youthful Julie any right to expect. And Madame de Krudener started with every disposition to love her husband. But the fact is that Julie was — well, Julie was a goose. The Baron goes out one evening, for example, to visit some friends, and is caught in a thunderstorm. The heroic wife will sit up for him; nay, at two in the morning she will dash out in wild alarm and a chance carriage to search for him. The astonished Baron is met not far from the house, and very reasonably asks: "My dear child, how could you be so foolish? What possible harm could have happened to me? You ought to have gone to bed!" Internal tragedy-attitude — "Alas! in my place he would have gone to bed, and to sleep!" This is the kind of woman whom any man might be excused for making love to, but no man for marrying. Then there was a young private secretary attached to the Baron — and, unfortunately, also attached to the Baroness. But —

> Charlotte was a married lady,
> And a moral man was Werther;

moreover, Alexandre de Stakieff (this was Werther's name) had, it appears, "an unusual sense of honour" — let us hope not so unusual. So he kept his passion to himself, till the Baron went as Russian Ambassador to the Danish Court, and the Baroness began to flirt with the young Danish officers. Poor De Stakieff naturally felt that this was putting his self-denial to too severe a test. If the woman was resolved to go to the deuce, De Stakieff was surely as good an escort on that road as any young Danish officer, and had a prior right to the office. But the secretary, like the fine fellow he seems to have been, resolved to prevent the temptation, and threw up his post, explaining by letter to the Baron the reason of his departure from Copenhagen. His letter was worthy of his conduct. "What I cannot explain," he wrote, "but what is, nevertheless, true, is that I worship her because she loves you. If ever she were to love you less, she would be no more to me than any other woman, and I should love her no more." The Baron committed what Mr. Ford calls "the incredible imprudence" of showing this letter to his wife. Imprudence it doubtless was; but what is the exact value of a virtue which totters at the first knowledge of passion inspired in another? Madame de Krudener shortly afterwards left her husband for a time by reason of ill-health, and visited with her children Paris and the South of France. At Montpellier she made the acquaintance of the Comte de Frégeville, a young officer of Hussars, and after a period of struggle received him as her lover. He accompanied her to Paris and to Copenhagen, where she avowed matters to her husband. For two months she made a bold attempt to realise the dear Shelleian ideal; but Castor de Krudener and Pollux de Frégeville did not display a proper manageableness in their rising and setting; so the Baroness ended, at her husband's suggestion, by separating from both, and retiring to her mother at Riga. Here she became gracefully religious, found that her vanity was completely conquered, that her desires were moderate, and restricted to a simple life in harmony with nature. This last was a time for which Julie had been fitted at Paris by Bernardin de St.-Pierre, of *Paul and Virginia* fame; and it always remained a favourite with her. Then followed reconciliation with her husband, and a journey to Berlin, where she was resolved to devote her life to her husband's happiness. But at Berlin there were Court ceremonies, and Madame de Krudener did not like Court ceremonies. So she left her husband again, and wrote to St.-Pierre from Leipsic in a rapture of sentiment and moralism, imploring him to join her in a visit to Switzerland. "I make you this offer from a heart that knows how to appreciate you; I add nothing to it, for I am simple and true, and not at all eloquent." Eight years later she suddenly rejoined her husband, who had been appointed Ambassador to Berlin. But there terrible trials befell her; and she wrote to her friend, Madame Armand, after this fashion:

I have lived through terrible moments of intense regret at having condemned myself to such torture; but religion has come to my assistance, has dried the bitter tears that I shed in secret, and has shown me the hidden charm of painful sacrifice. I have said to myself: Religion will support and will save this feeble body from being utterly crushed.

And again:

You can see that daily, and indeed almost hourly, sacrifices cannot be put up with for very long. I may say that I have borne it heroically, but constant suffering would be impossible, and I hope to put an end to it all.

What could have befallen this elect soul? Divine martyr! she was bored. It was that dreadful Court ceremonial which was breaking down her health and trying religious resignation to the snapping-point. But the Emperor Paul of Russia was murdered about this time; which we cannot doubt to have been a special intervention of Providence on behalf of the Christian heroine. The Baron feared loss of favour under the new Emperor, began to reduce expenditure and pay debts. Consequently, to lighten expenses, Madame de Krudener and her children left for Töplitz; and she never met her husband again. There her health promptly returned, her religious fortitude recovered amidst theatricals and brilliant society, and she was able to write to the Comte de Tilly in her sweetest naturalistic vein:

> Will you not come and try the waters here? ... You will find the Prince de Ligne, who is as lively as ever; and besides him a whole host of German nobles, with a following of ridiculous women, who are always amusing. And finally, I trust you will find me, and that you will be very glad to see me, who am always kind and frank to my friends, always at open war with the Germans and their thirty-two quarterings; always devoted to everything that is pleasant, true, simple.

"Oh — your sentiment!" The reader perhaps finds that Josephine Surface is not "always amusing." Then she went to Switzerland, where she made the acquaintance of Madame de Staël and an epigram on the Genevese women: *"Je n'aime point les Génevoises: elles n'ont ni les charmes de l'innocence ni les grâces du péché."* And from Switzerland she followed Madame de Staël to Paris. During her residence here she formed a new *liaison* with the singer Garat, her husband died, and *Valérie* was published. *Valérie* was the novel which elicited the praise of Sainte-Beuve; and it is the one work of Madame de Krudener which is still read. But Julie did not trust solely to the merits of her work; she understood *réclame* as well as any modern Parisian, and employed it with a truly feminine originality and an unblushingness astonishing even in this graceless day. She got a physician, Dr. Gay, to write verses to her under the name of Sidonie (known as the heroine of one of her previous books), proclaiming her gifts and graces, and asking why they were buried in the provinces. (She was then temporarily staying at Lyons.) But the letter itself must be given, for it is an inimitable piece of unconscious self-satire:

Pray have some verses written by a good poet to our friend Sidonie. In these verses, which I need not describe to you and which must be in perfect taste, there must be no other *envoi* but "To Sidonie." The poet will ask her why she resides in the provinces, why we are deprived of her wit and grace? Her triumphs call her to Paris. Her talents and her charms will there be appreciated at their full value. Her enchanting dance has been described; but who can describe all that distinguishes her? *Mon ami*, I confide in your friendship; I am ashamed on behalf of Sidonie, for I know her modesty, and you know that she is not vain. But I have a reason far more important than mere vanity for begging you to have the verses written, and as soon as possible. . . . Have the lines printed in the evening paper. . . . You will greatly oblige your friend by doing this; she will explain her reasons personally for having troubled you. You know her hatred of civilisation, her love of solitude, and her indifference to praise, but in this case it will be doing her a special service.

But this was not enough; there remained a crowning triumph of female audacity. She went round the Parisian shops in her carriage — incognito, of course — asking for articles *à la Valérie.* Sometimes she would pretend to recognise the article she wanted. At others, if the *modistes* denied knowledge of any such article, she would smilingly pity them for their ignorance of the new novel. Her friends imitated her; soon the shops were filled with things *à la Valérie,* and the name of the new book was known and heard everywhere. *Valérie* came out; was an immense success; and the pious authoress referred it all to Heaven!

The success of *Valérie* is complete and unheard of, and someone remarked to me the other day that there is something supernatural in such a success. Yes, my dear friend, it is the will of Heaven that the ideas and the purer morality the book contains should be spread throughout France, where such thoughts are little known!

Yet two years later the worldly and capricious creature was converted, and converted as truly, perhaps, as a woman so constituted could be outside the Catholic Church. What was she converted to? To primitive Catholicism. And what was primitive

Catholicism? I am clear that I do not know; it seems equally clear that Julie de Krudener did not know; and still more clear that nobody else ever knew. But it sounded very well, and there is great virtue in sound. The decease of a young admirer at Riga, who fell dead in the street as he was raising his hat to her while she stood at her window, was the occasion, and a Moravian shoemaker was the instrument. She then came into connexion with the once celebrated Jung-Stilling, who was deeply permeated by Swedenborgian ideas; and the subsequent reading of Madame de Guyon completed her curious religious equipment. Her mystical enthusiasm was raised to fanaticism by an imposter named Fontaine, minister at Ste-Marie-aux-Mines in Alsace, who kept a private prophetess in the shape of a peasant woman named Maria Kummrin. He actually welcomed Madame de Krudener in a parody of Scripture: "Art thou she that should come, or look we for another?" She readily came to believe herself a prophetess; and commenced a course of preaching, public and private, which led her from place to place, and gradually drew around her a little band of zealous disciples. Of her extraordinary later career I have left myself small limits to speak. How she became the religious friend and adviser of the Czar Alexander after the Congress of Vienna; how her spiritual salon in Paris after Waterloo was one of the sensations of that sensational time; how she became the real inspirer of the Holy Alliance, which was originally a veritable religious idea in the Czar's mind — for all this I must refer the reader to Mr. Ford's striking pages. After the cooling of the Czar's friendship for her she made a kind of apostolic progress through Switzerland, gathering everywhere large crowds, and favoured by many even of the Catholic clergy. For she preached no dogma, and sent those whom she converted to the ministers of their respective religions, if they had any. Her charity, her care of the poor, her self-denial, were truly evangelic. But the authorities persecuted her, dissolved her following, and finally compelled her, with two companions, to take refuge in her native country. To this result certain political opinions which she mixed with her religious views no doubt contributed.

She died at Karasu-Basar, in the Crimea, with every sign of

spiritual self-renunciation. On the whole, the verdict passed upon this remarkable woman by her English biographer seems just and adequate. "Let it be granted, at once, that she was neither a St. Catherine, nor a St. Teresa, nor even a Madame Guyon, by whose writings she had been so frequently inspired; but let us none the less honour her as a tender-hearted, loving woman, who, having passed through fire herself, stepped down bravely from her social eminence in order to extend a warm hand of help and sympathy to those of her brothers and sisters who were groping blindly along the stony paths of life; who sacrificed much in her great love for her Divine Master, and who, in her humility, felt herself rewarded far beyond her deserts by the peace and joy which illumined her soul throughout the years of her self-imposed apostolate."

THOMAS à KEMPIS: HIS AGE AND BOOK*

[*Athenæum*, January 19, 1907]

Were it only for the concluding sentences descriptive of the *Imitation*, this review would merit inclusion here. But there is more than that to recommend it — chiefly, the instance of Thompson's recognition of the author's special pleading and the errors to which it led.

THIS is an excellent and thorough book on the famous *Imitation of Christ* and its author. Mr. de Montmorency, indeed, says it would need many books to treat the matter thoroughly; but his is sufficient for all practical purposes. He discusses in successive sections the writer's epoch, his life and personality, the disputed authorship, the manuscripts; analyses the structure of the book; and then deals with its subject and its mysticism. All is done with the sedulousness of a devout student, and with sympathetic intelligence. The value of his volume is enhanced by reproductions of illuminations, woodcuts, and specimen pages from MSS. of, or connected with, the *Imitation*. For such a book, it has, further,

* *Thomas à Kempis: His Age and Book.* By J. E. C. de Montmorency.

the merit of cheapness. Truly, it shows we have gone a long way from the day when even such a writer as De Quincey could sneer at à Kempis as a worthless author who owed his repute to the fact that he was a mediæval substitute for the Bible.

Yet the book is not one to be swallowed whole. It might have been almost a manual to à Kempis but for one circumstance. How often do we guilelessly conceive ourselves to be reading a loving and understanding treatise on a writer, when we become uneasily aware that we are cozened, that the author has an axe of his own to grind! Mr. de Montmorency has an axe to grind — and sharpens it on à Kempis. It is most evident in the section on à Kempis's age. He sets up a distinction between the visible or official Church and an invisible Church, existing within the official Church, of which it is the truly vital and Catholic part. It showed itself in a movement for social reform, leading logically to the French Revolution; and a mystical, Platonising movement, from which issued such figures as St. Catherine of Siena, St. Bridget of Sweden, and Thomas à Kempis. Curiously, the author seems to have no sympathy with the avowed Neo-Platonists of the Renaissance (if we may judge from negative signs), who were surely the logical result of the Platonic mysticism to which he refers, and with which he connects the eminent Catholic mystics mentioned. It might seem an obvious objection that the mediæval Church never lacked mystics. But Mr. de Montmorency claims them all for his invisible Church. They formed the chain by which Platonic mysticism was kept alive and handed down from St. Augustine, who in his turn absorbed it indirectly from Plotinus; and they are represented as essentially one with the Lollards and other more or less avowed rebels to Church authority. In fact, the author claims unity and a common movement for all mysticism, orthodox or unorthodox, throughout the mediæval Church, if not the Christian era, down to the mystical movement of our own day, with which, as a forerunner, he desires to identify à Kempis.

Right or wrong, this strong bias introduces an element of special pleading which requires the reader to be on his guard, to read the author's views and statements with a certain allowance. When a writer can conjoin Gerson, Fénelon, and Rousseau as precursors of the Revolution, he is evidently capable of extremes, and lacking in temperate sanity, where his pet foibles are concerned. The influence of his theory is evident in his handling of the *Imitation* itself, as when, for example, he emphasises its Platonic element absorbed from St. Augustine, who himself (Mr. de Montmorency contends) was influenced by the Plotinian philosophy of his friend Victorinus Afer more even than by Plato himself. It is a plausible contention, of course; and, with the needful caution, the reader will find Mr. de Montmorency's handling of the book full of suggestion and matter for reflection. In treating purely evidential questions, such as the authorship, he is sane and dispassionate enough. He is interested mainly in the mystical aspect of the *Imitation*, and his analysis is a defence of its mysticism, as it appears to Mr. de Montmorency, from the charges and limitations urged against it.

But had à Kempis been merely a mystic, he would have had no more readers among us than other and greater mystics. His power is in his profound humanity. His appeal to the English mind is, in a way, somewhat like the appeal of Herbert's poetry. Both, in their diverse ways, bring mysticism down to earth, or leaven daily life with mysticism: they blend the subtleties of spirituality with a homely practicality, a Teutonic common sense, which seems in other hands alien to mysticism, and is conspicuously absent from the recognised type of Teuton mystic. Hence their twofold appeal alike to the most aerial and the most practical minds. A Kempis is in more than one way a singular union of opposites. As Mr. de Montmorency shows, he rested absolutely on the past and present of Christianity, he anticipated no future developments; yet he remains quick and vital to a generation which has drifted far from the moorings of the past. His book, as Mr. de Montmorency again shows, is elaborately structural, formal, artificial, and unspontaneous in composition and plan; it is written in a cunning species of rhythmic or semi-metrical prose (whence the English copies style it *Musica Ecclesiastica*), with a kind of musical notation to show the cadence; yet it has all the effect of the simplest and most unmeditated spontaneity, of a spiritual diary straight from the heart. It is often (in this respect like most of the mediæval Doctors) almost a cento from Scripture, and draws freely on a variety of sources; yet its language has a profound impress of direct personality. In the miracle which welds these opposites to a homogeneity, in the combination of wisdom and simple practicality, meditative gravity and deep truth of emotional experience, and in the breath of humble fraternal love which gives a fragrance to it all, lies the grip of the book on all generations. It is not only a voice from the cloister, it is also the beating of a heart.

LANDOR AND ROSE – WATER*

[*Academy*, February 18, 1899]

Starting with a suppressed side of Landor, and regretting the suppression, Thompson goes far afield before the end of this review, and in the going reveals his broad knowledge of English poetry. His rollicking humor in presenting the one-sided Landor of the letters to Rose Paynter is Thompson on a reviewer's holiday.

ALL KNOW, at least by repute, the character of Walter Savage Landor; for has it not been caricatured in Dickens' Boythorn? Not for nothing did he bear the prefix "Savage." As King Hal says to mine Ancient: "It sorts well with your fierceness." And has not his descendant felt it necessary to justify that family prefix by ferocious experiences in Thibet? It is a thousand pities that to the elder Landor did not fall that terrible adventure. In the first place, his published language about the mild Thibetan would have been powerful to outlast marble monuments. Moreover, his talk on the subject would have been distinctly precious. It would have run somewhat like this: "Pain? I never felt pain in my life. I defy you to make me feel pain! Why, sir, I was tortured by a set of scoundrelly Thibetan savages — I'll be sworn, sir, within an inch of my life; and then set a-horseback with a spike, sir, a

* *Letters of Walter Savage Landor, Private and Public.* Edited by Stephen Wheeler.

rascally spike in the saddle; and so rid the whole way back to the Indian frontier — spiked, sir, like a dismountable lead soldier! And I'll be shot if I ever enjoyed a better ride in my life! I could have ridden it back again, to show the torturing miscreants what a Briton was like with such a seat."

But in vain will you look here for a touch of Boythorn. These letters to Miss Rose Paynter (now Lady Graves-Sawle) are avowedly published to show the gentler side of Landor. All the world knows that he had a youthful attachment for the Rose Aylmer whom he has immortalised in an exquisite little lyric. In later life he met at Florence Mrs. Paynter, never encountered since, as a little girl, she had run by the side of her elder sister in those tenderly remembered days of his young love. A friendship naturally arose with one to whom he could talk of the dead Rose; and it happened that of her two daughters one bore the name and some lineaments of her mother's sister. To this girl he accorded a special affection — part memory of the mouldered, part admiration of the budding, Rose. He kept up correspondence with her to the end of his life; sent her verses every birthday, and others at chance intervals. These letters, with the interspersed verses, Mr. Wheeler, with the lady's permission,now for the first time gives to the world.

It is comprehensible that the object of so faithful an attachment should cling to, and the editor (as a devotee of Landor) act on, the principle *de mortuis nil nisi bonum*. It is excusable that she should shrink from exhibiting her old friend's little asperities of temper, should think they had already been too liberally exposed to the public, and desire that nothing be allowed to roughen the little idyllic picture of Omphale and Heracles. But we would the editor had taken his courage in his hands and advised her otherwise. The very fact that Landor's character is so fully known makes suppression useless to his memory, and irritatingly flawing to the artistic effect. Nobody can be persuaded into accepting this halcyon view of the great writer. Nobody but is fretted into protest against this Landor among the Roses. What is worse, a picture is pruned and tamed into unconvincingness, which would have been really charming, left with its natural relief and contrast. Ares at the feet of Aphrodite — a very pretty scene. But let us have a growl or two, an occasional martial tang of the tongue, or rugged fling of the limbs, to convince us that we have, indeed, the god of War, and no other, bound in these rosy links and manacles. We should feel much more sensibly the poet's self-yielding gentleness, and the young lady's triumph, if her lion were allowed an occasional roar — to show us he is the real sort, and not of those who eat plum-cake and box with unicorns; if he did not always "shake a mane *en papillottes*." Furthermore — and this is the utmost verge and scope of our indictment — he would not then be dull. Landor — Landor in his frank and unconsidered moments — dull, pitiful heavens! Yet to this complexion is he come, through Mr. Wheeler's injudicious showmanship. These letters become positively languid and tedious. We yawn in sympathy with the frequent *hiatus* which disfigures these pages, and look disgustedly at the enshrouding asterisks which fill it. What could Landor have said so *very* dreadful? we ask; and whatever it was, we could suffer it gladly: yea, we would beg — "Let him roar again! Let him roar again!" as warmly as the audience of Bottom's imagining. We love not Landor with a nice clean collar and his hair combed.

Well, here is our Landor, expurgated for the use of families and suitable as a present for young ladies' schools — at least, the first half of the volume. Of course, there are interesting bits, and we see the old poet in a very pleasing and domestic light — only too much so. He writes to Rose's mother in 1838:

> Yesterday I breakfasted with Milnes. He invited a good number of his cleverest friends to meet me. I did him wrong in fancying I had lost a portion of his kind feelings. . . . Lady Blessington has persuaded me to remain a few days longer, that I and D'Orsay may be accompaniments to her in a picture. So flattering a wish is not to be denied.

This letter is from Gore House. Does the picture exist, one wonders? It would be of exceeding interest. A more curious combination for a portrait-group could scarce be conceived than Lady Blessington, D'Orsay, and Landor! He was much at Gore House about this time. Mr. Wheeler reminds us that Mr. Augustus Hare relates how Landor talked to him about the company at Gore

House, and how, while Lady Blessington and D'Orsay talked, Disraeli would sit "silently watching their conversation as if it were a display of fireworks." One does not conceive Disraeli "silently watching" anyone's conversation. He must have been taking lessons for his own future displays. But the note on this letter is more interesting than the letter itself. It quotes Crabb Robinson's note regarding Landor's breakfast with him the following day: "A great deal of rattling on the part of Landor. He maintained Blake to be the greatest of poets; that Milnes is the greatest poet now living in England." Milnes was present, it may be remarked. It is interesting to know that Landor, in 1838, saw the greatness of Blake while he was still an unknown quantity to English critics. But there was always "a great deal of rattling on the part of Landor." When he affirmed Blake to be the greatest of poets, it meant no more than that he admired him much. As for the judgment on Milnes, a graceful, quite minor poet, it is purely one of Landor's oddities — even allowing for the influence of Milnes' presence. The man could not say a thing without hyperbole. For be it remembered Tennyson was "living in England," and the *Quarterly* (as Mr. Wheeler reminds us) jeered Milnes for his worship of "such baby idols as Mr. John Keats and Mr. Alfred Tennyson." Thus contemporary criticism "wanders at its own sweet will."

We have another curious specimen of Landor's critical whims in a letter of 1843. He tells Miss Rose that certain verses want compression, "as nearly all modern poetry does, particularly Byron's. Cowper, Crabbe, and Moore run the least into this fault since the time of Goldsmith. There is much of the superfluous even in Gray's beautiful elegy." The remark is true enough regarding most poetry of that day. But fancy the exceptions! Cowper, with the interminable didactic *longueurs* of the "Task," "The Sofa," and the rest; Moore, with the gaudy facility of "Lalla Rookh" and the "Loves of the Angels," and superfluous page on page which one shrinks even from remembering! It is correct enough of Gray. But in the *Imaginary Conversations* he not only declared that the Elegy would be read as long as any work of Shakespeare, "despite the moping owl and the tin kettle of an epitaph tied to its tail"; but also said: "Expunge from his Elegy the second and third stanzas, together with all those which follow the words

> Even in our ashes live their wonted fires,

and you will leave a poem with scarcely a blemish — a poem which will always have more readers than *any* other in *any* language." The italics are ours. Of course he merely intended that it would always be a very popular poem; but superlatives were his bread of life. Why, though, did he wish away the second stanza? You know it, reader:

> Now fades the glimmering landscape on the sight,
>   And all the air a solemn stillness holds,
> Save where the beetle wheels his droning flight,
>   And drowsy tinklings lull the distant folds.

Surely it is one of the best in the poem. Or why should he have said, again, that he would sooner have written the stanza beginning

> The boast of heraldry, the pomp of power,

together with one of George Herbert's, than any other in poetry? A stanza the solemn movement of which makes it undeniably fine; but how far below the great inspired passages of poetry! It has a lapidary dignity, as of some thing carved in stone; but Landor's praise is extreme. Truth to say, he had himself a tendency to leading out by the hand spinster phrases, to personifications constructed chiefly of initial capitals, which at times recalls the eighteenth century manner. He would apostrophise his "pensive friend" (virtuous youths and maidens were apt to be "pensive" in the eighteenth century), would talk about "the pomps of regal state," and inform his pensive friend that

> Thee only Virtue can elate,
>   She only leads thy steps to Love.

Virtue, in this style, acquires corporeal substance and the right to a "she" by title of a large "V." With a small "v" poor virtue becomes a mere "it" — and quite helplessly unpoetical. There is, indeed, only one poem in this volume that is at all rememberable.

Landor seems, again, to attach a curiously overweening value to French verse compared with English. But let us acknowledge that he is entirely right about the "moping owl." Owls are the most active of birds at night. And he has the boldness — with a half-apology — to tell Miss Rose Paynter some little truths about her private verses. Then — classic poet though he was — he has a hearty enthusiasm for Gothic architecture and York Minster. And he shows a true native taste for music, though professing no knowledge of it. Here is an interesting little notice:

A German boy named Rubenstein has been playing to us [at Gore House] on the pianoforte. Never did I hear anything so wonderful and of so pure a taste at the same time. Wonder, where it exists at all, generally predominates over every other feeling; not so in him. He appears to be about eleven or twelve years old.

There is, however, a second section, of political and public letters, where we have the unwhittled Landor. The mere style often makes them interesting; and there are general remarks couched in memorable language, and worth memory. The case against Russia has never been put so well as by him and here. But in detailed politics the most striking thing is the wonderful crop of prophecies that failed, and the imperturbable confidence with which he goes on to make new ones destined to a like fate. Once he claims to have had a prophecy fulfilled (about Louis Napoleon), and on the strength of this he feels free to prophesy at large for the rest of his days. Happy, hot-headed, self-confident prophet, whose blacks to his own blest sight are for ever white! Isaiah had no such felicity, Jeremiah no such confidence. Read the book, and thank — with some permissible grumbling — the editor; for half Landor is better than no Landor at all.

THE NOVELIST AND THE APOSTLE*
[*Academy*, June 5, 1897]

Compatible with Thompson's broad sympathy and understanding, was his refusal to tolerate a writer's deliberate attempt to handle a theme admittedly beyond his powers. Although Thompson frankly points out the ludicrous incongruities of such a performance, he is at great pains to give the good points of the volume before him. But in the end, it is his conclusion that the author's zeal to avoid painting the Apostle "smug and smooth," led him to turn out a portrait in which the most unpleasant lines of the countenance are unduly marked. The result of this tendency in contemporary attempts to rewrite lives of saints and, even, of Our Lord, call for just such criticism as Thompson's, condemning the unrealistic result of a too ardently realistic effort.

To THE jaded palate of the age such an incongruity as the life of an Apostle by a popular novelist should be stimulating. If it should fail to be so, it will be because the book does not fulfil the promise held forth by the bizarre association of ideas; not because it is not an able and interesting book, with certain limitations in its ability which might easily be foreseen. Mr. Baring-Gould explains in a preface what were his intentions in undertaking a life of St. Paul. He designed to regard the Apostle solely from the standpoint of a novelist and man of the world, a man necessarily having some acquaintance with the mainsprings of human character and motive; a man, in fact, such as Mr. Baring-Gould undeniably is. But, in the first place, he cannot keep his limitations. A man is all that he thinks and writes, as well as all that he does; therefore, Mr. Baring-Gould has inevitably to devote a prominent space to St. Paul as a thinker, where the special advantages which he claims for himself avail him nothing. Moreover, he truly remarks that St. Paul the man was more than St. Paul the man; that he had a mystic side, and this mystic side is like the hidden side of the moon. In relation to a novelist and man of the world, it undeniably is. Apparently he feels only the embarrassment to which it puts

* *A Study of St. Paul*. By S. Baring-Gould.

him in his consideration of the man. But in truth it is thrice as
fatal to him in considering the writer. Nor is his aim at all so original
as he conceives, and as the reader is at first disposed to hope. It
soon becomes evident that Mr. Baring-Gould has read Renan, and
Renan's *Life of St. Paul*, and that we have here an attempt to adapt
the methods of Renan for English readers — as our playwrights
adapt the methods of the French stage for English audiences —
minus the infidelity, though with a considerable infusion of the
naturalism of Renan. Mr. Baring-Gould's announced aim, moreover, is not single and dominant enough to unify the temper of
his book. He has many sides, and they so intercross each other
as to make of his work a very mingled yarn. There is Mr. Baring-
Gould, the man of the world, and much of the book is very man-
of-the-worldly; there is Mr. Baring-Gould the novelist, and not a
little of the book smells strong of the novelist; there is Mr. Baring-
Gould, the student of Renan, and we sniff now and again a distinct
whiff of Renan. But such a phrase as "When I was a curate"
reminds us that there is also Mr. Baring-Gould the clergyman
of the Church by law established, and we are not suffered to forget
that we must allow for yet another idiosyncrasy.

When we find the subject of the "Petrine" claims insisted upon
with great cleverness and subtlety from the orthodox Anglican
standpoint; when we find the writer rejoicingly strong upon St.
Peter's wife, and St. Paul's lady-friends, and St. Paul's alleged
marriage with Lydia, we are aware of the Anglican clergyman.
The novelist comes to the front in a certain method of filling-
in recorded facts with supposed details. When St. Paul is rescued
from the Jewish rioters by the Roman soldiery, he is represented
by the author as hoisted on their shoulders. "Then the Apostle,
leaning down to the tribune, said in his ear, 'May I speak?'" Is
this a passage from an intended historical romance? It has no
foundation in fact. The same (we cannot but think) cheap manner
of imparting colour by imaginary details is carried yet farther in
the account of the riot at Ephesus. Here it is:

Alexander, thrusting, elbowing his way through the crowd, scrambled
on to the stage, signed with his hand that he desired to be heard, and gained
an audience. But no sooner did the mob recognise that he was a Jew than

their howls broke out again: "Great Artemis of Ephesus!" At last, when they had yelled themselves hoarse, a lull ensued, and the magistrates seized their opportunity to send forward the chief municipal officer, the chancellor, who kept the town archives and was treasurer for the wealth of the Temple of Artemis. He came out from behind the side-scenes, and, stepping to the front of the stage, ordered silence.

Mr. Baring-Gould's account of the speech which followed, adhering for the most part to the Biblical language, concludes with this even ludicrously incongruous piece of modernism: "Since we are wholly unable to give any rational account of this mass meeting." There are some who will admire this kind of "picturesqueness." But there is either too much of it in the book or too little. If it was to be done at all, it should have been a main feature of the style, instead of cropping up spasmodically in unexpected places. When, again, St. Paul retires to Arabia after his conversion, we are told that it is possible he retired to an Essene community. There is not a fact alleged in support of it. It seems likely to the author's imagination, for reasons he gives. That is all. This method of padding a history where facts are meagre by "It is possible," and "We may well imagine," is one which cannot be rebuked too strongly. The culmination was reached some years ago in a French ecclesiastic who gave us a Life of the Good Thief (the penitent thief crucified with Christ). It only remains for someone else to give us a "Life of Balaam's Ass," and the historical imagination will have reached its climax as a book-making faculty. Connected with this, but also with a savour of Renan, is Mr. Baring-Gould's way of emulating Falstaff's evolution of men in buckram. For instance, we have the moderate and unimpeachable statement that Christian writers have admitted certain grave disorders as having happened sometimes at the Agapes of the early Christians. But on the next page these certain grave disorders have swelled into "orgies." It looks as though his own moderation were every now and again pricked in the flanks by a resolve prepense to be original and tradition-breaking, to go as near the example of the French iconoclast as his reputable English orthodoxy would allow.

But we have done with picking of holes. This book is an interesting and valuable performance none the less. St. Paul's journeys are made vivid to us by skilfully realised descriptions of the countries and places through which he passed. Only once, in the author's desire to introduce modern vivacity, does he fall into such a slip as where he describes Corinth resounding with the voices of singers "running up and down the chromatic scales," as they no doubt would have done, only that chromatic scales were not then invented. Very felicitously he sets before us the way in which circumstances gradually forced on St. Paul the apostolate of the Gentiles. He does not repeat the common error of supposing that a great man sees his objective from the beginning, and that all his actions are dictated by a constant regard for it. In one respect, however, he ascribes a set and far-sighted plan to St. Paul; and his suggestion is at any rate original and valuable. He believes that the Apostle had conceived the design of stringing a set of Christian communities along the great trade-route between Syria and Rome, which ran through Southern Asia Minor. This, at any rate, he points out, is what the Apostle effected. Derbe, Lystra, Antioch, Colossæ, Laodicea, Ephesus, Corinth, and the communities established along the Egnatian road, followed this route, and secured the great highway for Christianity. Very clearly, also, he shows us the special nature of the difficulties with which St. Paul had to contend. He enters thoroughly into the standpoint of the orthodox Jews and Judaising Christians who formed his adversaries. This is not surprising. Their standpoint was that of a man of the world, and a man of the world Mr. Baring-Gould proclaims himself. Indeed, one feels that had he lived in the Apostolic era he would infallibly have regarded the Apostle as an imprudent fanatic. But there is room for all diversities of temper; and we can be thankful for the disposition which enables Mr. Baring-Gould to put with such sympathetic insight the case of those whom others — wise after the event — represent as stupid or purely malicious. Nor is he less successful in doing justice to the wisdom and forbearance of St. Peter and the other Apostles at Jerusalem, which allowed full scope to the fiery Paul, without disconcerting their own more centralised designs. He shows, we think truly, the vast importance at the outset of having a central body such as the Apostles at Jerusalem, influencing the Jews through their metropolitan synagogue, and sending forth, as from a heart, a constant pulsation of Christian influence to all the peripheral Jewish communities. Owing to their wise action in regard to St. Paul and the work among the Gentiles, this did not interfere with the extension of the Christian body at its peripheries. Again, Mr. Baring-Gould shows that St. Paul did not, except at Athens, preach to the heathen directly. He acted through the local Jewish community in each place he visited.

St. Paul the man is Mr. Baring-Gould's declared object of study. He presents us with a sufficiently vivid picture, in which he has thought for himself to an extent even aggressive. But because of this very determination to be original, to break through traditional modes of view, we doubt whether he quite knows the impression he creates. It is not exactly a pleasant impression — speaking for ourselves. This St. Paul of Mr. Baring-Gould's is zealous, self-devoted, absorbed in one idea — the propagation of the Gospel among the Gentiles; much-enduring, persuasive, patient with neophytes and submissive disciples; but masterful, overbearing, hot-tempered, impatient of opposition, ready to quarrel with all who thwart his will in the slightest degree, harsh and unconciliatory to all who do not see as he sees; a man more for respect and fear than love; having, moreover, a kind of pious *penchant* towards women, ripening on one occasion into a love-affair, and on another leading him to let a girl go about with him in man's clothes. It would seem that this is not the author's own view. In the close of his book he observes:

It is the humanity of Paul that meets us and makes us cling to, listen to, and love him. In his wonderful epistles he had a word for everyone in all times — a word that went deep into every heart, met every experience, comforted in every sorrow, cheered in every discouragement, that braced every tired soul.

This comes upon the reader as a surprise. One is forced to the conclusion that Mr. Baring-Gould (after a manner very familiar to critics) in his desire to protest against and make his points against the routine view, has neglected to emphasise the points in which he agrees with the routine view; determined not to paint the

Apostle smug and smooth, he has unconsciously turned out a portrait in which chiefly the unpleasant lines are marked. It remains that, having given us a study of St. Paul, he should give us an historical novel on St. Paul. We think he would develop his negative more according to his intention.

Many points in a book necessarily full of matter for controversy we have unavoidably omitted. Yet one point we must touch. Mr. Baring-Gould has been compelled to deal with St. Paul the thinker, and here his limitations become marked. The man of the world and the novelist, even with the clergyman superadded, do not form a combination adequate for this portion of the task. The good-natured scorn with which he condemns the Apostle or sets him to rights, the air of "Hannibal, sir, was a very pretty fellow in his day," remind us of the superior Britisher in foreign parts. The tendency which produces the "damned nigger" attitude is a little too manifest, accentuated, it may be, by a wish to be daring and original. St. Paul's method, he says, is Oriental, not Occidental. Most true. What was needed, then, was for Mr. Baring-Gould to have entered sympathetically into the Oriental mode of thought and interpreted it, or else to have left this side of St. Paul alone as beyond his view.

But who says "Oriental," says confused and puerile, according to Mr. Baring-Gould's idea, says "damned nigger" in fact, though in a polished and cultivated way. He criticises the intellectual side of the Epistles from the standpoint of Western dialectics, regardless of his own admission, which is the very sign-post to those who would study St. Paul the thinker. His typical Western mind has no capacity to follow the Eastern mind. In one important case, as a result, he quite misses St. Paul's meaning — following a throng of Western critics in doing so. But for the most part he simply misunderstands the Apostle's aims and methods. He looks for dialectical proof, after the Western fashion, where the Apostle intends exposition and illustration. He finds St. Paul adopting the "textual method," and thinks that it must mean the reasoned proof from Scripture which it would mean in European controversy. Whereas it is an attempt to illustrate and develop the "lie" (so to speak) of the Apostle's position, from a

mystical standpoint, by means of images and parallels from Scripture mystically interpreted.

This mystical use of Scripture was a thing universally accepted
in St. Paul's day, based on certain defined principles, and handed
down to the early Christian Church; from which it long survived
in the Roman Church, and has, of late, begun to show a curious
revival in modern sects which Mr. Baring-Gould has not, we
should think, studied. The whole method, as is characteristic of
the East and inherent in the mysticism beloved of the East, is
poetical rather than dialectic. Indeed, the profoundest admirer
of St. Paul as a thinker that we ever met was a distinguished
modern poet.

On this aspect of St. Paul Mr. Baring-Gould is an unsafe guide;
though we admire his boldness in saying so outspokenly what
most Englishmen, it is likely, have thought about these subtle,
difficult, and most un-English utterances. But, on the whole, he
has written an interesting, picturesque book, in which he has
thought for himself, often with very suggestive results. The value
of the book, we may add, is increased by two clear maps of
St. Paul's journeys, and by a complete index.

THE SEVENTEENTH CENTURY

THE PILGRIM'S PROGRESS – AFTER TWO CENTURIES*
[*Academy*, August 27, 1898]

Thompson here indulges in a good-natured laugh at the defects of Bunyan's performance, as friend laughs at friend. When the laugh is over, they are still friends. Clear thinking and precision in the use of language such as we find in this critical performance are rare in reviewing columns today.

FORTUNATE the age which permits a man to carry in his pocket such a charming edition of the *Pilgrim's Progress* as this which Messrs. Dent have added to their "Temple Classics." With this slim and attractive little pocket companion, "Let those who always read now read the more." There is no need to adjure those to read who never read before; for, we suppose, almost every man has read the immortal allegory of the Elstow tinker, and the greater part have done so in their childhood. For this latter reason it is apt to be regarded as the books that have fed our young years alone can be regarded. Such books we cannot criticise; they are set in a halo, surrounded by the glory which shines over the fields and flowers and comrades of that sweet time. How much this has had to do with modern estimates of the *Pilgrim's Progress* it would be difficult to say. A work which has stood the test of centuries, has been praised and loved by men of the people and men above the people, men of religion and men of the world, men of letters and men unlettered, men of all sects, all beliefs, and of no belief; such a work surely has a true vitality, a deserved vitality, which it were idle to question. Not idle, however, may it be to examine the nature and cause of this vitality with a more critical distinction, a less fond panegyric, a greater aloofness and detachment than have yet been brought to bear upon

* *The Pilgrim's Progress*. By John Bunyan.

47

it — than men have been capable of bringing to bear upon it. Many, because their judgment was subjected by the consentaneous verdict of ages; all (it is likely) because of those childish prepossessions from which they could not disentwine their minds.

Macaulay's panegyric heads all which has been written about the book. Most boldly partial of writers, he was confessedly dominated by the recollection of his childhood in regard to Bunyan, and was not likely thereby to become more judicial, less sweeping and impulsive, than his wont. It may be taken that he has said, picturesquely, vividly, energetically, all that a lawyer fed by affection could say in behalf of his client; a lawyer, moreover, holding a strong brief, having an imposing case. On the other side, what has there been? Censure seems to have been voiceless — even judicial and kindly censure. Yet no writer is perfect; and it may be taken there is another side to the case. Just one exception comes to mind. The late Mr. Richard Dowling, in his *Indolent Essays* (recently referred to in these columns), made a very vigorous protest against the prescriptive worship of Bunyan — one-sided, as reaction is apt to be. But the book is little known, and the protest has passed unheeded. Avoiding the one-sidedness, so far as in us lies, let us try to emphasise what was most forcible in his points, adding thereto points of our own. At the same time we shall endeavour to sum the matter with the evenness proper to a true critic; to give no unbalanced view of a performance which, we have declared, must needs have its rightful claim to renown. No literary impostor ever survived for two centuries.

We may dismiss one part of Mr. Dowling's indictment. He complains that the allegory does not hang together in detail; that its particulars are often incongruous, absurd. The idea of Christian going about with a great burden on his back, invisible to his wife and friends; the way in which the burden is at times ignored, forgotten for a time, by the author; the idea of a man being ignorant of a filthy slough but a few fields from his home; the immorality of his running away from his wife and children, leaving them to chance and, perhaps, poverty — these and other such things he dwells upon. But it is, we think, a sufficient answer that (as Macaulay elsewhere says) no one ever yet succeeded in making an allegory go upon all fours. Some discrepancies must be; some allowance must be asked from the reader. It is of much more importance when an allegory fails in propriety of spiritual application; when it is inwardly and imaginatively deficient. And Bunyan, as we shall show in due course, does sometimes trip gravely in this latter regard. He is further accused by Mr. Dowling of a low and vulgar imagination (it would have been better to say fancy); and of no less vulgarity in language. His language is a kind of degraded Biblical language; and the whole thing (says Mr. Dowling) is a horrible attempt to tinker the Bible, without appeal to an educated imagination. This is the very opposite to Macaulay's declaration that the *Pilgrim's Progress* makes singularly vivid appeal to every imagination. Let us take some of these things *seriatim*.

We can hardly agree with the attack on Bunyan's language. The genesis of that language is very frankly given by Bunyan himself:

> It seems a novelty, and yet contains
> Nothing but sound and honest Gospel-strains.

It is the homely dialect of the peasantry of his day, raised and purified by an infusion of Biblical diction. Of course, it is open to anyone to view it from the opposite side, and call it Biblical language lowered by an intermixture of peasant diction. We prefer to consider it a speech excellently adapted to Bunyan's purpose. The homely peasant element admirably fits the familiar nature of the allegory, and is racy of the soil to the most literary ear; while the Biblical model sorts well with the more solemn and directly religious portions of the work. It is chiefly where Bunyan attempts poetic conceptions that the language has an effect of meanness and incongruity. On the whole, the grafting of Biblical speech on the vernacular of Bunyan's day is accomplished happily: the result is clean-knit, idiomatic, and full of popular appeal in the worthiest sense. Strength, plainness, directness, are its character.

But as to Bunyan's imagination, we refuse to subscribe to tradition and Macaulay. He was a typical Saxon of the lower class, if a glorified type. He had vigour, forthrightness, narrative gift, a certain kind of vision, and ingenuity. But imagination he had not; a sound trotter, but no Pegasus. The quality mainly underlying the *Pilgrim's Progress* is a certain ingenuity, which may, doubtless, be considered fancy of a homely sort. A like quality gives apt and shrewd illustration to the speech of occasional rustics belonging to the old order, in the remoter country districts which have escaped the innovating whistle of the locomotive. Much, surely, of the vividness which Macaulay finds in his descriptions must be set down to the pictorial and improving mind of the childish reader, and the persistent associations left by it in later life. Take the account of the Valley of the Shadow. To an adult reader it is surely a somewhat pedestrian and matter-of-fact description. We are told, indeed, of darkness and hideous sights, dreadful sounds, and the mouth of hell agape by the way-side. But there is no attempt to realise or suggest these terrors to the reader by a single touch of fancy or magic phrase, such as the great imaginative writers would have given us in a sentence or so. Hell-mouth affects us less than an iron foundry, so poorly and barely is it rendered. Such, at least, is the impression which one reader ventures to declare. The allegory is apt, hence the name of the Valley has become famous, proverbial; but not, we think, through any singularity of power in the description. Bunyan has a rustic's inability to rise to great conceptions, to go outside the imagery of the wayside and the homestead. It is, indeed, the very limitation which accounts for much of his popularity. But it does not speak much for his force of imagination. When he does go outside these homely sources, and attempt the exalted and poetic, his imagery is purely conventional, an assemblage of hackneyed Scriptural figures which lose their original majesty in his use of them. Consider his description of the Heavenly City, for example, and the delights of the just therein. You are to wear a golden crown, to spend your time in praise and shouting, to be clothed with glory, and put into an equipage fit to ride out with the Almighty. That last touch is all Bunyan's own — a kind of celestial Lord Mayor's coach, so to say. For the rest, it is harps, and crowns, and palms, and streets paved with gold — as conventional as the angels in bedgowns that haunt tombstones.

This absence of anything deserving to be called imagination sometimes appears in the allegory itself (as we hinted before), making it inadequate and inapt, destroying its inward propriety. Take the whole episode of Giant Despair and Doubting Castle. Here is a conspicuous and interesting example of Bunyan's essentially unimaginative mind. For here we can compare him with a real master of imagination — Spenser. In this instance, at least, Spenser shows imagination, besides the fancy which is his peculiar excellence. The ground-plan of both allegories is the same: Despair endeavours to spur his victims to suicide. But how different the details! Spenser's Despair is a woe-begone, meagre wretch, laired in a cavern, wherein the armour of his intended victim makes

A little glooming light, much like a shade.

He has no apparatus, no raw-head and bloody-bones machinery; his method is terribly simple. Knife and halter he sets before the strayed wayfarer, and needs, to impel their use, nothing but his own baleful eloquence. Read his speech in Spenser, and say whether brute violence could do aught but mar its dark persuasion. The tinker's allegory is by comparison a tinker's allegory. His Despair is a schoolboy's giant — a stupid billet-head clumping about with a cudgel, so rightly distrustful of his bacon-fed bucolic eloquence that he must reinforce it with sound thumps. In spite of his feudal castle, he is a farmer-like, domestic creature, of very honest, orderly habits, and has a wife to counsel his dull brain. She is Diffidence. Despair taking counsel from Diffidence — the weaker passion strengthening the stronger! After cudgelling his prisoners, the absurd, ineffectual creation lumbers upstairs to his wife and bed. As if Despair could sleep! Despair couched between comfortable sheets, in married snugness, bestowing connubial endearments on his very practical spouse! Nay, let us laugh outright, and leave the grotesque ineptitude.

We have said enough, we need not labour to prove our point that in imagination, or anything like the higher fancy, Bunyan is completely to seek. It will be seen in what points we think the *Pilgrim's Progress* needs some abatement of the undistinguishing eulogy traditionally poured out upon it. But having said all this, its position remains virtually unaffected. That very inveterate home-liness of conception, which makes Bunyan's weakness when he attempts the higher ranges of conception, is the main strength of his work in the greater part. The familiar ingenuity of the imagery, the symbolism, the allegorical details, make them admir-ably suited to impress the daily understanding. Nor does the culti-vated mind fail to admire them, as we admire the shrewd practical instances of a clever peasant-talker. The whole allegory, with a bold originality like that of a child, to whom its surroundings are not commonplace or unromantic, flows along through the fields, and stiles, and streams, the quagmires, homesteads, and pastoral hills of familiar rural England. Even the sudden passing of Christian into undiscovered country, so soon as he begins to run across the fields adjoining his own house, is like the fancy of a child, to whom all romance-land may be hidden within a few meadows-length of its little home. The map of Christian's journey is arbitrary, neighbours and strangers exist in pleasant jumbled contiguity, the details of the allegory are allowed to crop up with a fine haphazard disregard for consistency. It matters not; we are frankly launched upon a meandering tide of reverie, where we are ready to let happen what happen will. And Bunyan has a real power of quite homely vision: he sees his persons, his places, his happenings, though not with the eye of the poet or romancer; and he makes us see them. Not for nothing has Macaulay praised the spirit and pictorial realism of the trial scene in Vanity Fair. It is a veritable transcript from scenes historic and only too com-mon at the time. It is, too, related with excellent, shrewd humour. Humour, indeed, distinguishes this religious allegory by its un-expected and welcome presence. Mme. Bubble and Mr. By-Ends and the rest, they are realised in curt downright strokes, which bring them instantly before us. It is the immortal work of a true and most original allegory-maker — perhaps the best of allegory-makers. But it is not what it has hastily been called — a work of strong imagination; unless we are to use that word in a special and unauthentic sense.

THE UNKNOWN BUTLER*

[*Academy*, September 20, 1902]

Thompson was fond of espousing lost causes, and Butler's brilliance in *Characters* was such a cause.

THE writer of the article in the *Quarterly Review* on English prose of the seventeeth century, with which we dealt in the *Academy* the other week, made special reference to the neglected *Characters* of Samuel Butler, the celebrated author of *Hudibras*. In his opinion it was a specimen of vernacular prose which he did not hesitate to compare to Swift's.

Though exaggerated in expression, the *Quarterly* reviewer's protest against the neglect of Butler's prose is just in substance. To rank the *Characters* too high would be to bring about a reaction of disappointment. But the point is that they have been overlooked completely. In the usual accounts of Butler you find it stated that one contemporary professed to have been shown by him something like *Hudibras* in prose; but that all Butler left behind him, besides the miscellaneous metrical pieces usually published with his verse, was a few prose fragments of no value. Those accounts which do notice the *Characters* represent them as exercises in a then fashionable but now obsolete kind, and not among the best specimens of that kind. Several years ago we had the curiosity to look them out; and speedily arrived at (virtually) the same conclusion as the *Quarterly* reviewer. It is unfortunately true that they belong to an obsolete order of composition. We no longer relish detached and set sketches of prominent human types—general or social — depending for effect on shrewd or witty strokes. The thing, indeed, survives in a different way. The *Sketches by Boz* are the modern form of it; diffuser, depending on picturesque external details and descriptions of habits, rather than abstract analysis of character. Above all, we do not care for what Dryden's time called "sheer wit." Butler's *Characters*,

* *Characters*. By Samuel ["Hudibras"] Butler.

like the best parts of *Hudibras* itself, are a tissue of "sheer wit."

But if the kind be obsolete, that is all which can be objected. They are head and shoulders above the other specimens of that kind. The best of these are at most shrewd: few would think to call them brilliant. We can see no just cause why that epithet should not be applied to Butler's work, granted the drawbacks of its kind. It was surely to it that the contemporary we have mentioned referred as *Hudibras* in prose. Some of the sayings have actually been transferred to *Hudibras*. Doubtless it was Butler's perception that so hackneyed a mode of composition would be at a disadvantage beside his satiric poem which withheld him from giving prominence to the *Characters* during his lifetime. But if stroke after stroke of wit, in epigram, simile, aphorism, unfailingly original, often pungent and observant, make for brilliancy, then this prose is brilliant. Every now and again you have in some sentence the condensed experience of a sardonic master of life; and always there is the unexpected comic fancy. We cannot see that the wit is anywise inferior to the wit of *Hudibras*. The obstacle is that it is too incessant, too unmingled for the modern mind, with its wandering and soon-tired attention. Also, it must be confessed, the brilliant wit is largely wasted on trivial subjects — a conjuror, a Wittol, a Host, and so forth. There is the advantage of *Hudibras*. That an age which is fatigued by the over-brilliance of Congreve's matchless *Way of the World* should read Butler's *Characters*, with all their drawbacks of theme and kind, is perhaps a hopeless expectation. Yet it may be worth while to bring them under the notice of literary students — for, even in this day, such unpopular beings surely are.

His sketch of "A Modern Politician," the longest and most elaborate performance in these mostly short and off-hand *Characters*, yields good examples of his sardonic and ironic satire. It shows that Swift did not "introduce" (as he claimed) though he may have "refined" irony:

He never speaks his own sense, but that which he finds comes nearest to the meaning of those he converses with; as birds are drawn into nets by pipes that counterfeit their own voices.

As for religion, he believes a wise man ought to possess it, only that he may not be observed to have freed himself from the obligations of it, and so teach others by his example to take the same freedom.

All regards, and civil applications, should, like true devotion, look upwards, and address to those that are above us, and from whom we may in probability expect either good or evil; but to apply to those that are our equals, or such as cannot benefit or hurt us, is a far more irrational idolatry than worshipping of images or beasts. All the good that can proceed from friendship is but this, that it puts men in a way to betray one another.

He is of opinion that no men are so fit to be employed or trusted as fools or knaves; for the first understand no right, the others regard none.

Then follows a passage on the uses of fools as political agents, from the standpoint of the Second Charles's shifty and unprincipled ministers.

The acute insight into the corruptions, weaknesses, and abounding villainies of human nature, the grimly cynical irony, the racy vernacular, are strongly suggestive of Swift, and not below him in terse, incisive scorn. But the style is less finished, tags and splinters project from the sentences. Portions of the satire even yet hold good, though the more unscrupulous ways of politicians have doubtless been bettered. Still more permanent is his satire on the "Small Poet" — the "Minor Poet" of our day. Butler does not spare to foul his own nest; and his remarks have all the keenness of inside knowledge. The "Small Poet" has not changed; his ways are persistent as those of women. It is a good example of Butler's lighter wit:

He measures other men's wits by *their* modesty, and his own by *his* confidence. He makes nothing of writing plays, because he has not wit enough to understand the difficulty. . . . He grows the unwiser by other men's harms; for the worse they write, he finds the more encouragement to do so too.

If you dislike him, it is at your own peril; he is sure to put in a *caveat* beforehand against your understanding; and, like a malefactor in wit, is always furnished with exceptions against his judges. . . . He professes to write with as great facility as if his muse was sliding down Parnassus. [The modern affectation is rather the other way. He proceeds ironically to advocate the poet's liberty to blow his own trumpet.] It is not likely that Nature gave men great parts upon such terms as the fairies use to give money, to pinch and leave them if they speak of it. They say — *Praise is but the shadow of virtue;* and sure that virtue is very foolish that is afraid of its own shadow.

Turning to poetry in general, he has a hit at the philosophers, who "will not allow poets fit to live in a commonwealth"; specially referring, of course, to the famous condemnation of poets in Plato's *Republic:*

Plato, who first banished poets from his Republic, forgot that that very Commonwealth was poetical. . . . Alexander the Great had no wiser way to secure that empire to himself by right, which he had gotten by force, than by declaring himself the son of Jupiter; and who was Jupiter but the son of a poet?

The stroke is unanswerably witty. Butler satirises some political types peculiar to the time; such as the "State-Convert," the Round-head turned Royalist with the Restoration:

He is a thrifty penitent, that never left rebellion till it left him. What he gained by serving against the King, he laid out to purchase profitable employment in his service; for he is one that will neither obey nor rebel against him for nothing. He pretends to be the only man in the world that brought in the King, which is in one sense very true; for if he had not driven him out first, it had been impossible ever to have brought him in.

Yet the type thus dexterously ridiculed is as permanent in essence as the Talleyrands and Fouchés, the Brutuses and Scævolas who slunk into Bonaparte's police, or climbed to his heterogeneous peerage after lopping the heads of their aristocratic predecessors. The *doctrinaire* "Republican" is still with us, and Butler's comments on him are fundamentally and abidingly sagacious:

While he is modelling of Governments, he forgets that no Government was ever made by model: for they are not built as houses are, but grow as trees do. And as some trees thrive best in one soil, some in another, so do Governments. . . . Most that I know of this sort are haranguers, that will hold any argument, rather than their tongues.

That is a lesson still unlearned, admirably wise and admirably put. But the trivial *Characters* which have nothing but observation and wit, are worth reading for their wit; as this of the "Wooer"—what we now call the fortune-hunter:

He has passions lying by him of all sizes proportionable to all women's fortunes. If his mistress's fortune and his do but come to an agreement, their persons are easily satisfied. He has a great desire to beget money on the body of a woman, and as for other issue is very indifferent, and cares not how old she be, so she be not past money-bearing.

The specimens we have gathered will, we hope, show lovers of literature the wisdom, not less than the wit, hidden away in these forgotten writings of a little-read author. In that hope we have culled them.

HUDIBRAS-BUTLER *

[*Academy*, February 11, 1905]

Two characteristics divorced by the Puritans whom Butler satirizes, gaiety and seriousness, are here joined in Thompson's review. He examines with common sense and right judgment such editorial defects as are sometimes left unchallenged by critics who fear to give offense where the intelligentsia are concerned.

OF THE *Hudibras* recently edited for the "Cambridge English Classics" by Mr. A. R. Waller we have only one mild complaint to make. The plan of Mr. Waller's edition excludes explanatory notes and all introductory matter except a short bibliographical note. But on the blank page opposite the title-page appears this short but disquieting legend:

SAMUEL BUTLER.
Born 1612?
Died 1680.

We cannot deny the exactitude of the question-mark. It is true we do not know that Butler was born in 1612, but research has

* *Hudibras.* By Samuel Butler. Edited by A. R. Waller.

shown that he was christened in February of that year; and if *incorrupta Fides nudaque Veritas* demanded the precautionary symbol, surely a drop of comfort might have been afforded to the curious in the form of a note.

A cynic might, indeed, find occasion for a sneer in this record of Butler's christening, being, as it is, almost the only fact of his life about which there is no doubt. For though, "according to all accounts" (says Mr. R. B. Johnson, the Aldine Editor), he "led a life of strict integrity," and though "no sneer has passed the poet's lips against religion or morality," there is singularly little of the distinctive features of Christianity in Butler's character. Perhaps to blame a satirist for uncharitableness is like finding fault with a tiger for inhumanity, or with Rabelais for grossness. He does not profess to supply the milk of human kindness, nor ask you to admire his organ of benevolence. But, for all that, "the great Butler," as "the great Doctor" calls him, gives the unpleasant impression of double-dealing and backbiting to a degree rare even among satirists. Critics are not agreed to what extent "Hudibras" is intended for a portrait of the Presbyterian, Sir Samuel Luke, "who was of an ancient family in Bedfordshire, but, to his dishonour" (says the earliest of Butler's biographers), "an eminent commander under the Usurper, Oliver Cromwell." Other Puritans, and perhaps other patrons of Butler, are laid under contribution by the satirist; and the spirit of burlesque accumulates many traits which have little to do with the Puritans at all. Butler, however, meant to make his "i's" easy to dot when he made Sir Hudibras say —

> "'Tis sung there is a valiant Mamaluke,
>   In foreign land, yclep'd ——,
>   To whom we have been oft compar'd,
>   For person, parts, address, and beard."

Rhyme and reason alike pitch upon Sir Samuel, or rather Sir Sammle Luke, to fill the gap. Anyhow, he lived in the service of this "Knight so notorious," either as secretary or steward or valet, and employed his opportunities in that situation in accumulating the materials for *Hudibras*, and probably composing a good part of the work. He kept the poison of asps well under his lips, however, until it was quite safe to launch it against the defeated party: and was then rewarded, like Horace's schoolmaster, *maiore fama quam emolumento*. Charles II, we are told, was always quoting *Hudibras*, and kept it in his pocket; but he put little or nothing into the author's pocket in its place. Perhaps he thought, or other Royalists who had better memories and fatter purses may have thought, that benevolence might be misplaced in this dull fellow — for so he appears to have been in company — who might, after all, survive them, and then let the world know what he thought of them. As a matter of fact, he was amassing the materials for such an exposure while the wits were laughing over his satire upon the Puritans. He satirised the licence, the gaming, the drunkenness, of Charles II's court; he satirised poor Sir John Denham, both for his poetry and for his madness; he satirised the newly formed Royal Society, first in octosyllabics, and then expanded these into the heroic measure to which he became more addicted in later years. All these rods, however, were laid up in pickle only when he died; they did not see the light till about eighty years after his death. Altogether, though the patrons who enjoyed his wit did not deserve well of him, it is difficult to avoid smiling at the expressions chosen by Otway, who was always overflowing with sentiment, in referring to this neglect:

> Tell them how Spenser starv'd, how Cowley mourn'd,
> How Butler's faith and service were return'd.

Mr. Waller does break through his reserve in his bibliographical note to the extent of giving us the entertaining passage from *Pepys' Diary* in which Mr. Pepys describes how, "falling into discourse" with Mr. Battersby "of a new book of drollery in use, called *Hudibras*, I would needs go find it out, and met with it at the Temple: cost me 2s. 6d. But when I came to read it, it is so silly an abuse of the Presbyter Knight going to the warrs, that I am ashamed of it; and by and by, meeting at Mr. Townsend's at dinner, I sold it to him for 18d." Six weeks later, however, he found it necessary to buy *Hudibras* again — presumably for 2s. 6d.; but later entries in the *Diary* show that he never could see the fun of it, though he once records having enjoyed having Mr. Butler and others to dinner — "a good dinner, and company that pleased me mightily, being all eminent men in their way. Spent all the afternoon in talk and mirth, and in the evening parted." Mr. Pepys was not a connoisseur in wit: Charles II was, and was undoubtedly in the right here. Whatever else Butler was, he was a prince of wits. The Restoration has a great name for wit, and, in spite of Macaulay, deserves it. But Butler is a giant among the Restoration wits, just as Milton is a giant among the Restoration poets. His is not mere verbal wit, nor the raillery of a highly artificial society. It is im- aginative and racy, not merely rippling the surface of the mind into a smile, but stirring up the depths of laughter. He is a man of exceptionally sound sense talking outrageous nonsense, a feat which always conveys the impression of great power. In this respect he deserves to be mentioned in the same breath with Aristophanes and Rabelais, and with the master to whom he owed the main idea of *Hudibras*, Cervantes, though he is wanting in the good-humour which is half the greatness of these much greater men.

A larger portion of good-humour would have made *Hudibras* more readable to remote posterity. "To-day it is not read," says Mr. R. B. Johnson, "and to a large extent would not be under- stood." The second remark is true, if the "large extent" be not pressed too hard. *Hudibras* is, of course, packed with topical allu- sions, as well as with all sorts of allusions the very reverse of topical — out-of-the-way bits of learning such as Rabelais delighted in, which we may be sure were as unintelligible to Charles II as they are to us. The latter, however, are part of the fun, now as then. And as to the topical allusions, it is true that the objects of Butler's ridicule are no longer before our eyes; while the passions which were then excited over ecclesiastical government have been succeeded by a long line of descendants, which all have a strong family likeness, but are too vigorous in each generation to feel much interest in their ancestry. But the mere fact that we cannot understand many passages without the aid of a note, and even the fact that a note is sometimes inevitably wanting, because the key to the allusion has long been lost — these facts only explain in part why *Hudibras* as a whole is not read to-day. *Don Quixote* has more allusions which are pointless to the average English reader: yet few people find *Don Quixote* difficult to read. You may say that it is because *Don Quixote* is drawn on a larger canvas, and breathes the open air of adventure for all its satire of knight-errantry. Yes, but this is much the same as saying that it is full of good-humour. Cervantes looks upon all the world, including his crazy hero, with a kindly eye. He moves with careless and jovial freedom of gait, and gives his reader time to digest his wit. Butler is like a hanging judge who is witty at the expense of the prisoner. He looks on all the world with "lidless dragon eyes," and mercilessly exposes everybody's faults and follies, without a hint that he is of the same clay as the rest of us. His scorn and contempt for the human race is like that of the only one of his imitators who is his equal: and in reading Swift we seem to be assisting at some dreadful tragedy, a man afflicted with some strange madness, cursing and uprooting his own heart; whereas Butler's satire is just heartless. And his wit gives you hardly any rest. Dr. Johnson puts this matter well in the course of his somewhat jerky and indeterminate account of Butler. "If inexhaustible wit could give perpetual pleasure, no eye would ever leave half-read the work of Butler; for what poet has ever brought so many remote images so happily together? It is scarcely possible to peruse a page without finding some association of images that was never found before. By the first paragraph the reader is amused, by the next he is delighted, and by a few more strained to astonishment; but astonishment is a toilsome pleasure; he is soon weary of wondering, and longs to be diverted."

But what wit it is! One cannot quote it to advantage. Many of his couplets have passed into proverbs too familiar to quote: but even these, to be thoroughly enjoyed, should be read in their context. It is the volubility at such a high level, the agility of the doggerel rhymes, with their ease and naturalness, the apparently uncontrolled spontaneity of the whole performance, that is so amazing every time one takes up the book. It is difficult to believe that the author amassed his material in "Commonplace Books," and wrote and re-wrote with anxious care. Certainly there never was a better illustration of the maxim which Pope paraphrased from Horace:

> Success in writing comes from art, not chance,
> As those move easiest who have learned to dance.

The only poet who has attempted the Hudibrastic manner of handling rhyme on a large scale, and as an accompaniment to his matter and not the end in itself, is Browning; but Browning never "learned to dance"; nor did he realise, apparently, that Butler's very triumph depended upon the perfect match between his manner and his matter.

A GREAT MINOR POET*

[*Academy*, December 21, 1901]

What is said in these reviews supplements the essay on Crashaw in the definitive edition of Thompson's works. His infinite pains in noting faults and excellences of editorship is illustrated in the second review.

NOT an inappropriate publication for the nearing Christmastide is this little edition of the poet who wrote the lovely song on the birth of Christ, "On the Holy Nativity." Mr. Hutton, of course, cannot, and does not, claim any original honours as an editor. The way had been cleared for him, not only by Dr. Grosart's bulky edition of the complete Crashaw, but by Mr. Tutin's complete edition of the English poems. Why, by the way, does Mr. Hutton adopt Mr. Tutin's exact title, which cannot but lead to confusion, unfair to that gentleman, who has laboured so zealously to promote the love of Crashaw? The present edition is not quite complete, even with regard to the English poems. It omits some twelve pieces from the Tanner MSS., but it contains all that the lover of Crashaw

* *The English Poems of Richard Crashaw*. Edited with Introduction and Notes by Edward Hutton.

really wants; while its cheapness and neatness make it very handy and welcome.

With the exception we have noted, this tiny volume gives the reader all but Crashaw's Latin poems, including even his translations. For, like Vaughan, and more even than Herbert, Crashaw's work is slender and exquisite. He is a Minor Poet (name "soiled with all ignoble use!") — one of those lesser jewels half-obscured in the opulent English crown of poets; his name scarce uttered but with an ignorant jeer before the day of Coleridge, who affirmed that the "Hymn to St. Teresa" in some strange way inspired "Christabel." One can half understand it, for Crashaw is an artist to the finger-tips, one of the forerunners of that elaborate modern art which diversely blossoms in Shelley and Coleridge, as Vaughan intimates Wordsworth. Had he but possessed the control of his own gift, indeed, no minor rank would have been his; for his great moments are unsurpassable in their kind. So rare an artist, he was also an unsteady artist, of the most capricious taste. Much should be pardoned to one who was an experimenter, trying paths new in English lyric verse, and who died comparatively young (Mr. Hutton, by the way, does not mention the date of his death in the introduction). His sins are virtues which have overshot their mark. He is a wonderful *virtuoso*, who will follow the most thrilling feat with a flourish of unpardonable eccentricity. Yet the comparison is unjust, in so far as it implies the desire to astonish and display. His passion is rather for close felicity of expression. But his sins are subtly different from those of the modern *virtuosi* in language. They, at their best, leave you surprised and admiring rather than thrilled: you feel they lay their imagery cold on the anvil, with whatever mastery they beat it out. But when Crashaw's shaping is most perverse, the metal, it is plain, came red from the forge. His fervour and sincerity are never doubtful when his taste is more than doubtful. And always he is the artist in purpose, though his execution for whole passages may fail. You are moved by something of the same feeling as in the childlike quaintnesses of a Pre-Raphaelite painter. Perhaps there are analogies between Crashaw and Botticelli.

His most wonderful feats with language are in "Music's Duel."

They are too wonderful, even when they succeed; too conscious in the closeness of their felicity. The nightingale

> Folds in waved notes with a trembling bill
> The pliant series of her slippery song.

The second line moves with the undulant pliancy of chain-mail in sunlight; the phrasing is miraculously complete. And again:

> Trails her plain ditty in one long-spun note
> Through the sleek passage of her open throat,
> A clear unwrinkled song.

The last words are beautiful. Yet you feel that a little of this will go far. It never ceases, and at last becomes too glutinous a sweetness for the most luxurious palate. To see Crashaw's art in a less elaborate mood, however, we need not mutilate by quotation the justly famous "Wishes to a Supposed Mistress." It will suffice to quote part of the lines "On the Death of a Gentleman":

> Now, though the blow that catched him hence
> Stopped the mouth of Eloquence;

> *   *   *   *   *   *

> Yet if at least she not denies
> The sad language of our eyes,
> We are contented; for than this
> Language none more fluent is.
> Nothing speaks our grief so well
> As to speak nothing. Come then, tell
> Thy mind in tears, whoe'er thou be
> That ow'st a name to misery:
> Eyes are vocal, tears have tongues,
> And there be words not made with lungs,
> Sententious showers, O, let them fall,
> Their cadence is rhetorical.
> Here's a theme will drink th' expense
> Of all thy watery eloquence;
> Weep, then, only be exprest
> Thus much: He's dead; and weep the rest.

A more exquisite phrasing, a more delicate poise of line and couplet, a more adroit yet reticent use of "turn" (as Dryden calls the changes rung upon a word or group of words, like the "turn" upon a note or group of notes in music), a defter point and sententious sweetness of poetry, could not well be. The versification is as exquisite in its accomplishment as the expression. Crashaw is one of the few masters of the octosyllabic couplet — a so-called "easy" metre, which a mere handful of poets has written finely, though anyone can write it mediocrely. In the art of fine compliment (of which the epitaph is usually a grave form) Crashaw is supreme, along with Dryden and a small number of others — including Donne at his best. The seventeenth century in general had the art of it, as of everything courtly and magnificent in gentlemanliness. The epitaph on Mr. John Ashton, from which Pope borrowed, is another example. And of his exquisite miniature gift, "Love's Horoscope" is an erotic example only inferior to the "Wishes to a Supposed Mistress."

But, of course, the supreme Crashaw is in those ardorous and sensuous religious poems into which he put all his strength — and weakness. There his most extraordinary conceits jostle the most triumphant imagery. And they are both of the one texture — the conceits are the images gone wrong, the images the conceits come right: while the lyric fervour is as sincere in the one case as in the other. Yet the "Nativity" hymn, to a sympathetic taste, is perhaps fine throughout. For once there are no intrusive absurdities. What shall one *not* quote from the ecstatic outburst:

> It was Thy day, Sweet, and did rise,
> Not from the East, but from Thine eyes!

It is an eclogue between two of the Shepherds, with a chorus of the rest — a felicitous scheme:

> I saw the curled drops, soft and slow,
>   Come hovering o'er the place's head;
> Offering their whitest sheets of snow
>   To furnish the fair Infant's bed:
> "Forbear," said I; "be not too bold.
>   Your fleece is white, but 'tis too cold."

> I saw the obsequious seraphim
>   Their rosy fleece of fire bestow,
> For well they now can spare their wing,
>   Since Heaven itself lies here below.
> "Well done," said I; "but are you sure
> Your down so warm will pass for pure?"
>
> No, no, your King's not yet to seek
>   Where to repose His royal head;
> See, see, how soon, his new-bloom'd cheek
>   'Twixt Mother's breasts is gone to bed.
> "Sweet choice," said we, "no way but so
> Not to lie cold, yet sleep in snow."
>
> We saw Thee in Thy balmy nest,
>   Bright dawn of our eternal day!
> We saw Thine eyes break from their East,
>   And chase the trembling shades away.
> We saw Thee, and we blest the sight,
> We saw Thee by Thine Own sweet light.

It is a triumphant poem. Still more triumphant is the conclusion of the "Flaming Heart" — too well known to quote; while the "Hymn to St. Teresa" is an acknowledged masterpiece:

> She never undertook to know
> What Death with Love should have to do;
> Nor has she e'er yet understood
> Why to show love, she should shed blood,
> Yet though she cannot tell you why,
> She can love, and she can die.

All his own are those sudden tender apostrophes, a kind of divine familiarity which take one by the heart in this, as in other poems:

> Farewell house, and farewell home!
> She's for the Moors and martyrdom.
> Sweet, not so fast!

Not his the fragrant common-sense of Herbert, nor the penetrating remoteness of Vaughan's secret magic. But a luxuriant and flaming

fancy, with a loving dexterity of expression, take one by a continual surprise. Even in his most fantastic poem, "The Weeper,"
you have such things as this:

> Sadness all the while
> She sits in such a throne as this,
> Can do nought but smile,
> Nor believes she Sadness is.
> Gladness itself would be more glad
> To be made so sweetly sad.

A poet whose very imperfections have the breath of life, the
recognition of him steadily grows; and this volume will bring him
from the library to the coat-pocket.

DANIEL AND DRAYTON*

[*Academy*, August 19, 1899]

Although Thompson admits his preference for Drayton, he is right and
just in his criticism of Daniel, and in no wise overindulgent of Drayton's
faults. In reviewing the work of both poets, he focuses his attention upon
technique and sources. In the latter consideration, we catch an occasional
glimpse of Thompson, the literary detective, identifying stolen goods. His
criticism of the technique of both poets is the criticism of one who has
experience as well as knowledge of a poet's craftsmanship.

THIS little volume could have found no better editor than Mr.
Beeching; who, at home as he is among all poets, is never more at
home than in dealing with the Elizabethans and their immediate
successors. We have had no reprint in these days of reprints, of

* *Selections from the Poetry of Samuel Daniel and Michael Drayton.*
Introduction and Notes by Rev. H. C. Beeching.

either Daniel or Drayton, save Mr. Bullen's expensive and now scarce selections from the latter poet. Needing a text-book for his Oxford pupils, Mr. Beeching was moved to undertake the present volume. His selections are judicious, and his introduction a thoroughly understanding piece of criticism. The reader of modest means may now see for himself what minor poets were like at the close of the sixteenth century. For both these poets are representative minor singers, in that terminal period of the Elizabethan school which preceded the outbreak of seventeenth century poetry, with its Donne, Crashaw, Cowley, and the Cavalier lyrists. And both are well worth better knowledge.

To indulge our own predilection, we will reverse Mr. Beeching's order, and speak first of Drayton. More fortunate than Daniel, he is known to every schoolboy (not merely him too famous in Macaulay's pages) by the rousing "Ballad of Agincourt"; yet, unfortunate enough, he is further known in literary histories chiefly as the author of that very fearsome production — the *Polyolbion*. Not twenty Charles Lambs could get any unleisured man to read it. In reality he is one of the most masculine and individual among our minor poets. Whatever he does is burly, forthright, with a true English independence. Other ways may be better, he seems to say, but he will do things his own way. And his own way is mostly worth doing.

Yet Drayton, it must grudgingly be confessed, is a clumsy workman. Like most clumsy-workmen who have something to say, he offends by awkward or downright unintelligible ellipses. Clumsy workmen who have nothing to say sin in quite other fashion. But inexpert craftsmen who are full of matter almost invariably try to bring their matter within metrical compass by the omission of connecting words — what is technically called ellipsis. It takes a great artist to use ellipsis well. Shakespeare is a master of it; yet even Shakespeare sometimes faults by excessive and crabbed ellipsis. Donne, a very pregnant writer, who, like Drayton, is not a good craftsman, is full of violent and knotty ellipses. But he has at least the palliation that his ellipses are scholarly, and result from an indiscreet imitation of the Latin, where the inflected character of the language permits bold ellipsis inadmissible to an uninflected language like the English. Drayton's ellipses are not scholarly; they are thoroughly indigenous and awkward, as well as crabbed; the mere untaught expedients of a man who finds it difficult to shepherd his thick-coming ideas into the strait pen of a defined stanza. For this reason — whether or not he be at his best poetically — he is least clumsy in expression where he employs continuous metre (as in his pastorals) which permits him to take what compass he pleases in his utterance — gives him, in fact, room to turn round in. And Drayton, like the sturdy, strong, not unbovine Anglo-Saxon he is, needs a good deal of room to turn round in. This lack of adroitness hampers him in his sonnets, which abound in lumbering and quite unclassical ellipses, making them difficult reading. He is still more clod-paced in his Odes, and other poems written in brief stanzas of curt lines. Yet he is curiously fond of such measures — doubtless from his instinctive love of pregnancy. His virile abundance of idea well qualifies him for these stern, short metres — indeed, almost calls for them. But unluckily his indexterity of execution no less disqualifies him. He is like a man of pithy temperament but thick utterance. So that most readers had better take refuge in his pastorals, with their charming simplicity and flowing expression. Those only who are willing to wrestle with maladroit and knotty expression for the sake of masculine substance — whose teeth are sound enough to crack a tough nut for the sake of a nutritious kernel — should adventure upon the sonnets and the poems in curt stanza form. He declares in one fine sonnet that his mistress has made the dumb to speak — in causing him to write. Whether he were really first urged to write by love or not, it is clear to us that he did to some extent compose *invitâ Minervâ* — driven on by an inward heat, in spite of a native obtuseness of utterance.

Yet this poet, whom we have in effect compared to a broad-shouldered Saxon farmer, needing much room to "come about" (in nautical phrase), can be delightfully dainty on occasion, full of pretty fancy — nay, even a certain arch caprice. So it was with rough old Ben, but Jonson had a classic elegance and accomplishment in his lighter moods, which is lacking to the less learned Drayton. Charming is the fancy and whimsy of "Nymphidia,"

Drayton's mock-heroic fairy poem. Hark how the very metre seems to trip along on little feet, most apt for a fay story:

> Hence shadows, seeming idle shapes,
> Of little frisking elves and apes
> To earth do make their wanton scapes,
>   As hope or pastime hastes them;
> Which maids think on the hearth they see
> When fires well-near consumèd be,
> There dancing fays by two and three,
>   Just as their fancy casts them.

He has, indeed, a happy instinct for minor metres; witness the most graceful measure of the song in "The Shepherd's Sirena." Pity it is these things are flawed at intervals by his awkward twists of expression. His pastorals have a sweet and clean rusticity about them, if they lack the downright realism of Allan Ramsay, and are full of the open air. Old Walton might have quoted his praise of fishing in the "Sixth Nymphal." There is much that is fine in the ode "To the Virginian Voyage," with its prophecy fulfilled so splendidly in later times:

> And in regions far,
> Such heroes bring ye forth
>   As those from whom we came;
>   And plant our name
> Under that star
> Not known unto our North.

One sonnet of Drayton's is famous: "Since there's no help, come let us kiss and part." But the others are by no means so vastly inferior, for all the faults we have already noted in them. We think more highly of them, indeed, than Mr. Beeching does. Manly and full-sounding is this, for example:

> Why should your fair eyes with such sovereign grace
> Disperse their rays on every vulgar spirit,
> Whilst I in darkness in the self-same place
> Get not one glance to recompense my merit?

So doth the ploughman gaze the wandering star,
And only rest contented with the light,
That never learned what constellations are,
Beyond the bent of his unknowing sight.
O, why should beauty, custom to obey,
To their gross sense apply herself so ill!
Would God I were as ignorant as they,
When I am made unhappy by my skill;
  Only compelled on this poor good to boast,
  Heavens are not kind to them that know them most.

Daniel resembles Drayton only in manliness. His style is very different, extremely clear and carefully finished. Wordsworth and Coleridge both admired the openness and simplicity of his diction. His characteristic vein is that of grave and dignified reflection. Perhaps his thought is not always so deep as Mr. Beeching would have it; there may be more than a touch of conventional moralising about it, as about Wordsworth himself. Wordsworth borrowed from the "Epistle to the Countess of Cumberland" the final couplet:

Unless above himself he can
Erect himself, how poor a thing is man!

He was fond of such borrowings, and did not always acknowledge them, as he has done in this case. That great close of a great sonnet:

Who are to judge of danger, which they fear,
And honour, which they do not understand;

is taken literally from Sir Fulke Greville, without statement of the fact. In sententiousness lies much of Daniel's merit; though in "Hymen's Triumph" we have beauty with no lack. But perhaps the finest specimen of him in this book is the chorus from "Cleopatra." Its severe and even language, its elevated thought, the stately movement and cunning structure of the verse, all leave an impression of high admiration. The final stanza may fairly be called great:

> O then, all-seeing light,
> High President of heaven,
> You Magistrates, the stars,
> Of that eternal court
> Of Providence and Right,
> Are these the bounds ye have given,
> Th' untranspassable bars
> That limit pride so short?
> Is greatness of this sort,
> That greatness greatness mars,
> And wracks itself, self-driven
> On rocks of her own might?
> Doth Order order so
> Disorder's overthrow?

The closeness of both thought and expression is here so great that it needs more than one reading to understand the lines, though the language is precise enough. And in other places a like reason makes Daniel not quite fluent reading, in spite of his clear diction and structure. But he is a worthy companion to Drayton, with whom he makes a happy contrast. We could well do with more such handy little reprints of the older poets.

BEATIFIC POT-BOILERS*

[*Academy*, July 21, 1900]

Did ever pot-boilers evoke such criticism! There is power in what Thompson has to say about the writers of his day, who, like the statesmen of our own, are satisfied with mediocre achievement, not because it squares with their ideals and consciences, but because "it pays." His apology for Dryden's stylistic *via media*, lying between the two extremes of journalism, is a classic. And his question, apropos the naval battle off the coast of England, savors somewhat of prophecy. Asked in 1900, it has twice been answered beyond Thompson's dreaming, in World War I and World War II. And the world today is asking if the time is at hand for the third world conflict. It is not difficult to understand why Thompson selected,

* *Essays of John Dryden.* Selected and Edited by W. P. Ker. 2 Vols.

as an example of Dryden's "forceful and happy manner," his apology for his Latinisms. It could be quoted verbatim in justification of Thompson's practice.

THESE essays, which Prof. Walter Ker has had the excellent idea of issuing in a detached form, are the critical prefaces to Dryden's various publications, excluding such as were purely dedicatory. Here we have two volumes of pot-boilers flagrant, unashamed, with little reason, indeed, for shame, since they have survived — and gloriously survived — near two centuries.

> Read all the prefaces of Dryden,
> For them the critics much confide in;
> Though only writ at first for filling,
> To raise the volume's price a shilling.

Byron's doggerel happily memorises a fact. Dryden, when he threw off these prefaces to gratify the demands of "the trade," had small thought of writing masterpieces, small thought that he was marking an epoch in English prose. Yet this he did. And he did it by arrant pot-boiling.

> O that the present hour would lend
> One more pot-boiler of the kind!
> Such "padding" as his we should not mind!

Byron may pardon the outrage for its appropriateness. These essays (as Prof. Ker not untruly styles them) are a monumental proof that the man of parts can gild his literary chains; that it is cowardly to say: "I wrote badly because I wrote, not of my own impulse, but for pay"; that the pot-boiler may at least be a thing of veritable merit, if not of transcendent merit. Granted that, without blame, even a man of parts might fail to wear his chains like "Glorious John" — "Glorious John," who could have made a decent poem out of *Bradshaw's Guide*. Yet do these beatific pot-boilers come as a seasonable rebuke to the slovenly work which overflows the modern press, often the work of men who could do better things, were their literary conscience not hardened as the soles of a street-Arab.

Yet further are they a rebuke, and at the same time a wholesome antidote, to the prevalent poverty of slipshod style. We do not speak of the few who write solely for literary fame: *their* disease is quite other — a too meticulous anxiety of expression, though not often of structure. We speak of the virtual or avowed pot-boiler, of what goes by the generic name of journalistic style — the style of those who must needs write *currente calamo*, with indeliberate pen. One knows this general style. With the more expert it consists in successive sentences of almost infantile brevity, turning the flank of structural difficulty — the chopped sausage-meat of composition, Macaulay done to rags. With the less expert it is a diffuse, weak-minded sentence, a labefaction of all structure, relatives wandering aimless, distressedly looking for their connexions, with an unhappy sense that the search is hopeless; there is no attempt at clause, but instead the nearest the writer can go to organism is to take several short sentences, put them end to end, and knock the heads out of them. Dryden is an admirable example for the reformation of both these kinds. He stands midway between the two. His sentences are not mere short yaps, like an excited cur. Nor yet has he the formal, *periodic* structure of Johnson, or the still somewhat formal though looser structure of Swift. A formal structure would be useless for informal writing. Succeeding to the stately writers of the seventeenth century, yet obliged by circumstances and his own temper to write fluently, he hits on a happy compromise. His sentences are direct, with a certain felicitous laxity of construction, which rids them of all pedantry, any air of deliberation; yet he dexterously avoids the dissolution of structure, and keeps them well in rein, for all the easy bravery of their pace. At the same time, there is throughout the vigorous straightness, the idiomatic, vernacular turn, fresh from and smelling of the soil, which eminently suited his genius, and must have been a joy to himself, as it is to the reader. All these characters make it an admirable influence for the reformation of modern journalistic style, in either extreme of its slovenly effeteness. Above all, Dryden is not effete. He is brimming with virility, his style is full of fight. Yet it has no taint of the vulgarity, the *rowdiness*, of what now too often passes for "vigorous English." A phrase here, of course, a construction there, a word or so elsewhere, is obsolete; but these are casual, easily eliminated.

Of his staider narrative style, a little more calculated than the thorough Drydenian writing when his blood is up, there is an excellent specimen in the opening of "The Essay on Dramatic Poesy." It has, moreover, a peculiar interest; for it is an admirable little cabinet picture of a striking historical episode as it was realised by the Londoner of that day. Not often, in those impersonal times, are we given a glimpse of events as they came home to the man in the street; but here we are allowed, for a single moment, to see London in a war experience with almost the intimacy of the present day. It concerns a battle off the English coast between the Dutch fleet and the English led by the Duke of York. We insert the proper names, instead of the fictitious ones given by Dryden:

It was that memorable day, in the first summer of the late war, when our navy engaged the Dutch — a day wherein the two most mighty and best appointed fleets which any age had ever seen disputed the command of the greater half of the globe, the commerce of nations, and the riches of the universe. While these vast floating bodies, on either side, moved against each other in parallel lines, and our countrymen, under the happy conduct of His Royal Highness, went breaking, little by little, into the line of the enemies, the noise of the cannon from both navies reached our ears about the city, so that all men, being alarmed with it, and in a dreadful suspense of the event which we knew was then deciding, every one went following the sound as his fancy led him; and, leaving the town almost empty, some took towards the park, some cross the river, others down it — all seeking the noise in the depth of silence.

Among the rest it was the fortune of Lord Buckhurst, Sir Robert Howard, Sir Charles Sedley, and Mr. Dryden to be in company together.... Taking, then, a barge which a servant of Sir Charles Sedley had provided for them, they made haste to shoot the bridge, and left behind them the great fall of waters which hindered them from hearing what they desired; after which, having disengaged themselves from many vessels which rode at anchor in the Thames, and almost blocked up the passage towards Greenwich, they ordered the watermen to let fall their oars more gently; and then, every one favouring his own curiosity with a strict silence, it was not long ere they perceived the air to break about them like the noise of distant thunder, or of swallows in a chimney: those little undulations of sound, though almost vanishing before they reached them, yet still seeming to retain somewhat of their first horror, which they had betwixt the fleets. After they had attentively listened till such time as the sound by little and little went from them, Lord Buckhurst, lifting up his head, and taking notice of it, was the first who congratulated to the rest that happy omen of our nation's victory, adding that we had but this to desire in confirmation of it, that we might hear no more of that noise which was now leaving the English coast.

Buckhurst's wish (or Dryden's in Buckhurst's mouth) has been fulfilled. For near two centuries London city has never again sat solitary, while its citizens flocked Greenwich-ward to harken anxiously that sound as of "swallows in a chimney"— the thunder of an enemy's guns. Is the time at hand when the scene described with such life-like touches may be renewed? Anyway, a more taking introduction to an essay was never contrived.

But this is not, as we have said, Dryden's more current style. Of that a quite average conception may be formed from the following passage in the "*Examen Poeticum,*" where he is treating the proper manner of translation:

> Mr. Chapman, in his translation of Homer, professes to have done it somewhat paraphrastically, and that on set purpose; his opinion being, that a good poet is to be translated in that manner. I remember not the reason which he gives for it; but I suppose it is for fear of omitting any of his excellencies. Sure I am, that if it be a fault, 'tis much more pardonable than that of those who run into the other extreme of a literal and close translation, where the poet is confined so straitly to his author's words that he wants elbow-room to express his elegancies. He leaves him obscure; he leaves him prose, where he found him verse; and no better than thus has Ovid been served by the so-much-admired Sandys. . . . But this proceeded from the wrong judgment of the age in which he lived. They neither knew good verse nor loved it; they were scholars, 'tis true, but they were pedants; and for a just reward of their pedantic pains all their translations want to be translated into English.

We may demur to that illiberal judgment on an age which produced better translations than anything the eighteenth century has given us; though Sandys, truly, was a poor specimen. But the easy directness of the style, the inartificial variety of short and long sentences; the well-knit structure, diversified with a certain agreeable laxity; the strong, clear vernacular, the English backbone of it all; these things are not only excellent in themselves, but most imitable at the present day. Here, again, is a typical specimen of his most forceful and happy manner; which has the further advantage of containing a judicious and judicial criticism on a point which still affords matter for heated and by no means always judicious discussion. It is from the "Dedication of the *Æneis*":

> I will not excuse, but justify, myself for one pretended crime with which I am liable to be charged by false critics . . . that I Latinise too much. 'Tis true that when I find an English word significant and sounding, I neither borrow from the Latin nor any other language; but when I want at home, I must seek abroad.
>
> If sounding words are not of our growth, who shall hinder me to import them from a foreign country? I carry not out the treasure of the nation, which is never to return; but what I bring from Italy I spend in England: here it remains and here it circulates; for if the coin be good, it will pass from one hand to another. I trade both with the living and the dead, for the enrichment of our native language. We have enough in England to supply our necessity; but if we will have things of magnificence and splendour, we must get them by commerce. Poetry requires ornament, and that is not to be had from our old Teuton monosyllables; therefore, if I find any elegant word in a classic author, I propose it to be naturalised by using it myself; and, if the public approve of it, the bill passes. But every man cannot distinguish between pedantry and poetry: every man, therefore, is not fit to innovate. Upon the whole matter a poet must first be certain that the word he would introduce is beautiful in the Latin, and is to consider, in the next place, whether it will agree with the English idiom. After this, he ought to take the opinion of judicious friends, such as are learned in both languages. And, lastly, since no man is infallible, let him use this licence very sparingly; for if too many foreign words are poured in upon us, it looks as if they were designed, not to assist the natives, but to conquer them.

This is Dryden's criticism at its best; sound, sensible judgment, unentangled by questions of principle, wherein he shows weak. It leaves little to be said on the matter. One notes a characteristic feature of his argumentative style — a certain lively cut-and-thrust manner, sometimes animated by interrogation, which recalls a forcible debater. Such a style is liable to be too unexceptious, to

slur nice considerations: here and there one might demand a modification of some statement too sweeping. He slips sometimes in
strict grammar: "every man is not fit to innovate" were better "not
every man is fit to innovate," for it means structurally other than
he intends. You will note his happiness of homely illustration:
Swift himself scarce betters it, though he be more fecund in it.
What joy were it if many modern *critiques* were as sane in decision,
as hardy and clean in style!

The editing is excellently done. Of course, having once decided
what class of preface to exclude, the task with regard to the
remainder became mainly a mechanical one. Yet some matters
remain for an editor's decision, even in a reprint. Should he adopt
the text of Dryden's first or Dryden's latest edition? In this case
Prof. Ker seems to us to have made an unfortunate choice. He
elects to follow the first editions, on the ground that the text of
the later editions is already accessible in other forms, while that
of the first editions is not. But is there any reason why readers
should hunger after the first edition texts? Dryden's corrections
were, as Prof. Ker says, mainly grammatical. He might have
added that Dryden (as might be expected from a man who all his
life was improving his *technique*) showed sound judgment in these
mostly grammatical corrections. It is surely a curious standard
of editorship which reprints an inferior text in preference to a
better and later text (corrected, too, by the ripe judgment of the
author himself), merely because no other editor has done it — as
why on earth should he? Moreover, this is the only separate reprint
of Dryden's prose in general — apart from his total works — and
the more reason, therefore, why the text should be the best avail-
able. Prof. Ker has seemingly been bitten by the modern mania to
reprint non-valuable things solely because they are inaccessible —
and would they remained so! On the other hand, his judgment in
using modern spelling seems well supported by the reasons he
advances. Above all, we owe him gratitude for the admirable
critical analysis of Dryden's prose — both general and particular —
with which he prefaces these volumes.

GEORGE HERBERT*

[*Athenæum*, March 16, 1907]

Thompson was in happy mood when he wrote this review, else he might have been rather devastating. He damns Mr. Hyde with very faint praise and in doing so makes us laugh, but not unkindly. The application to Herbert of Patmore's lines about the yoke of Christ, is an example of the criticism that Thompson so frequently compassed with completeness and brevity.

So LITTLE new material has been recovered, as Mr. Hyde says, that a modern biography of George Herbert can be scarcely more than a commentary on Walton. Except a jejune memoir prefixed to *The Country Parson,* and the few references of Herbert's brother, the Lord of Cherbury (with, of course, his own too scanty letters), old Izaak's *Life* of the poet remains the one source of knowledge. Mr. Hyde claims, however, the merit of correlating Herbert's life and writings with the history and life of his time — with his environment, in fact; the inevitable attempt of every such biographer since Taine. Here it amounts mainly to some chapters reviewing, from the standpoint of a moderate, but more or less High Church sympathiser, the religious movement which had Laud for its militant apostle and Herbert for its most representative singer. (Its *first* we cannot say, with Donne's later poems in view.) For the rest, Mr. Hyde as a biographer, without being in any way inspired, is careful, competent, straightforward, and not extreme. He has accumulated whatever minutiæ of information might throw light on Herbert's surroundings throughout his career, and related them in an orderly, direct fashion. He has hardly, it is true, managed to create Herbert's environment in the larger sense of the term — mainly because he is not an artist. He cannot vitalise his material. He comes, indeed, as near to being dull as may be with such a subject and his wisely close following of Walton. But such virtues as the merely careful and temperate writer, whose

* *George Herbert and His Times.* By A. G. Hyde.

gifts do not include art or style, may command, his book has.

Among these virtues cannot be reckoned grammatical precision. In one place, after referring — with a nice derangement of relatives — to a certain letter of Herbert's, he begins a new sentence by stating: "Never yet recovered, a Latin letter . . . has been preserved," and gives us the contents of the other epistle. Which means that a Latin letter never yet recovered has (by a fortunate if imperfect compensation) been preserved. On the other hand, Mr. Hyde's intention, though certainly not preserved, may yet be recovered from this curious sentence. The "never yet recovered" of course relates to the letter discussed in a previous sentence, not the Latin letter so happily "preserved" in the later sentence. But "you know what I mean" is an excuse that can only pass in talk. Nowadays, however, we have often to be thankful for technical ambiguity which (like this) leaves the sense but momentarily obscured. And this, be it said, is an extreme instance. Mr. Hyde, indeed, is moderate in all things; even his admiration of Herbert's poetry is tempered to something below scalding-point.

Herbert, without Walton's charm of style, and doomed to carry his archæology and "environment" and "such odd branches of learning" on his back, presents a slight and undiversified life. His letters scarcely lift the veil which covers most men of his time. Men had not then learnt the art of correspondence: from Herbert to Swift or Cowper is a far cry, unless perhaps we except one or two delightfully Charles-Surface-like letters of Suckling. If you are interested in that disputed influence of race on poetry to which the "Celtic Movement" has called attention, Herbert is a case to your hand. His lyrical work is a remarkable fusion of poetic fantasy and mystic imagination with strong, homely, practical sense, loving an aphoristic terseness — a blend to Mr. Hyde "curious," to some others delightful.

The poet was of mixed blood. The Herberts, in their border fastness of Montgomery, had a Cymric streak across their ancestry; while Magdalen, his mother, came from the old Princes of Powysland. No one, indeed, has observed how much that mystic or religious revival of the seventeenth century went to the Cymry for its singers. Of the brilliant five — Donne, Herbert, Crashaw,

Vaughan, Traherne — Herbert was semi-Cymric, Vaughan entirely Welsh, while Traherne, if there be any faith in names, must have been Cornish at least by descent. Even from a portrait not much better in art than the outrages on Shakespeare, one knows the delicate, valetudinarian poet. He has straight hair flowing almost to the sloping shoulders from the brow, high, narrow, and domed above well-opened eyes; and a sharp, hooked nose, the tip being an elongated appendage to the nose proper, as though it had been nipped and stretched between one's finger and thumb — nose, shall we say, as of a mortified Punch? We see a long upper lip; long, somewhat apple-shaped chin; high-boned cheek and hollow; and a well-proportioned upper face, marred by excessive elongation of all below the junction of nose and lip, and by that comma-like downward dip of the extreme nose. Set this face atop of a meagre, tallish, bottle-shouldered figure, and you have George Herbert, a man with the austere, almost Puritanic look which comes of bodily pain and effort of inward restraint, not of morose nature.

For the meagre scholar was not only a courtly gentleman, but also quick-tempered, of keen physical sensibilities, with a relish for that world which he never found it an easy matter to despise. He was among those (in Patmore's grim jibe)

> Who sing "O easy yoke of Christ!"
> But find 'tis hard to get it on.

Mr. Hyde is somewhat reluctant to admit this feature in "holy" George Herbert. But the fact is sufficiently plain, and excuse is needless. Were despising the world so easy a process, why should we admire the despising of it? Herbert, plainly, as a brilliant young man found university honours much to his taste, a career of Court ambition very attractive, the favour of kings not to be "sneezed at"; and (most humanly) having a mind to the serving of kings, he found excellent good reason why a little serving of kings was not irreconcilable with the serving of God. The flattering of them was still easier — was it not part of his official duty as Public Orator of Cambridge? — and perhaps he once stretched it a point too far.

So he finally launched on a definite, though brief Court career, satisfied that pitch need not always defile. Happily he was not brought to the trial where men as good did not keep clean hands. You could choose your circle at Court; and to please a learned king, to chat with brilliant Donne, discourse with wise Verulam, was no such giddy worldliness for a religious-minded man. Ambition itself may be exalted and grave. One guesses the dreams — serious dreams and very pleasant. But the deaths of two noblemen and the royal pedant, James, left the young courtier patronless; and so Providence decided for Master George Herbert. It took him some time to stomach that decision. Even when he had made his ecclesiastical election, and Bemerton parsonage came his way, it needed Laud to overrule his shrinking from that final step.

But then, according to Mr. Hyde, it was all over. After that, all was serene and whole-hearted saintliness. We know his life at Bemerton, touching and admirable to read — a life that reformed the neglected parish. His zealous and cheerful performance of duty amidst failing health; his charity and accessibility to the poor; the periodical music-meeting in town which was his one relaxation; his sweetness of spirit, shown in those charming stories of Walton's which bear out the idea of a soul at peace and quiet — these we know, and the death-scene, meet close for such a life. Yet the poems tell another story. They show that (however Herbert may have found peace at the last) for long the parson's life failed to yield him the anticipated content. Under that sweet and devoted external life the old conflict between worldly desires and the spiritual life was renewed and persistent. The dual nature was still at civil strife, not to be harmonised and subdued by a single act of decision; and the war was painful and keen. It is just this which gives to his poetry the human and sympathetic element — that it reflects a weakness and struggle common to all men. Both its lesson and the lesson of his life are lost if we insist on regarding him as a saint completed at a stroke, by one final act of self-abnegation. The true George Herbert is closer to us than that; and therefore secure of appeal to all generations, both as poet, and here in his life as man.

MILTON'S PROSE*

[*Academy*, September 15, 1900]

Thompson has surpassed himself in this review, although he frequently treated the theme of "Poets as Prose Writers." It is to be doubted that in the annals of English criticism this review can be matched for its completeness and brevity issuing in so just and documented an appraisal of Milton's prose. It is an excellent complement of the criticism of Milton as a poet, reprinted from the *Academy*, March 27, 1897, in Mr. Wilfrid Meynell's volume of Thompson's prose.

"THIS manner of writing," said John Milton regarding his prose, "wherein knowing myself inferior to myself, led by the genial power of nature to another task, I have the use, as I may account, but of my left hand." It is a sentence strange to encounter, in the strong and copious prose-work of the great Puritan — copious in style and diction, if not in quantity. Most poets, nevertheless, must have been ready to echo it; must have felt the new-born hesitancy of their accustomed ready handmaid, Expression, when she was called to walk with them in the dusty and frequented ways of prose. Yet not a beaten way was that when Milton adventured on it — wittingly we say *adventured*. It had for the poet an attraction which has fallen from it to-day, in that — no less than poetry — it offered him the privileges of the conqueror and explorer; a new empire to be founded, a new region to be reduced under obedience and law. And this, to some its difficulty, to the poet must have been its allurement. In poetry the great traditions had been set; in prose they remained to be set. In this medium, the language lay plastic under his hands; the whole question of its style expected his formative touch; its whole structural laws hearkened for his creative *fiat*. Such an unsullied and virgin opportunity comes not twice in a language.

Milton, whose authoritative sanction lies large over English poetry, made, it must be confessed, no equivalent use of his vast

* *Areopagitica*. Temple Classics.

chance in prose. He did fine things with it, but he estated no tradition on his successors, he laid no mandate on the language: not to him have our fathers gone for a precedent, nor can we go for a resurrecting voice in prose. It has passed as an axiom that poets' prose (when poets do write prose) is peculiarly clean, pure, forthright, and workmanly; that, in fact (contrary to probable anticipation) it has no tincture of "poetic prose," but is as distinctively prose as their verse is distinctively poetry. It would be interesting to inquire whether this be so. It is so with Byron, Cowper, and Southey, who were not imaginative poets; it is so with Wordsworth when he treats philosophically of poetic principle. But when he writes on the Cintra Convention he adopts the raised manner of Hooker and his fellows; nor does the law hold exactly good with Coleridge, still less with Rossetti or Swinburne. Dryden and Matthew Arnold can be cited for it, and the prose of Shakespeare's plays; but against it again is Sidney, and against it again is Milton. Under his large motions, the garment of prose intermittently falls aside, revealing the immortal limbs of poetry.

But this alone will not explain why he is a splendidly impossible model. Browne is full of rhetoric that hovers on the confines of poetry, yet from the grand physician of Norwich it is possible to learn, as Johnson learned, and Stevenson. Browne's sentences are admirable in structure, and (apart from diction) need little, if anything, to be quite modern — we do not say fashionably modern. Therein is the difference. Milton was Milton to the last. As he went to Virgil for the structural art of his blank verse, he went to Cicero for the structure of his prose. But the Latinisation which his genius triumphantly imposed on poetry failed against the stubborn native grain of English prose. It is true (as Professor Vaughan remarks, in this "Temple Classics" edition of the *Areopagitica*) that he is looser in structure than Hooker; his long sentences are in the main "not a synthesis of clauses, but an agglomeration." Clearly he discerned that rigid Latinisation would not work, and sought for such a successful compromise as he had carried out in verse. But the two elements of the compromise are only reined in equal yoke by his powerful hand; they must needs break loose from any other. Even in his hand the combination is often less than masterly, sometimes downright cumbersome and awkward. The *accretions* of sentence are tagged on in almost slovenly fashion. Such are the changes brought about by the fixing of a language that a child can now smile at the difficulties of the great Milton. We (so to speak) have but to touch a spring, where he had all to do with his own hand. That we may not appear to censure without giving testimony of the infelicity, consider this passage:

What if I had written as your friend the author of the aforesaid mime, *Mundus alter et idem,* to have been ravished like some young Cephalus or Hylas, by a troop of camping housewives in Viraginea, and that he was there forced to swear himself an uxorious varlet: then after a long servitude to have come into Aphrodisia, that pleasant country that gave such a sweet smell to his nostrils among the shameless courtezans of Desvergonia?

Here clause is inartificially hooked on to clause; with an unpleasant effect intensified by the changes of construction; not absolutely ungrammatical, but perplexing and inelegant.

Yet again examine another sentence, where the like faulty looseness of structure is pushed to a final obscurity of expression:

So if my name and outward demeanour be not evident enough to defend me, I must make trial if the discovery of my inmost thoughts can: wherein of two purposes, both honest and sincere, the one perhaps I shall not miss; although I fail to gain belief with others, of being such as my perpetual thoughts shall here disclose me, I may yet not fail of success in persuading some to be such really themselves, as they cannot believe me to be more than what I feign.

This, despite its intended openness of structure, is truly involved, not *evolved* after the manner of a long sentence justly builded. And such is the fault which may rightly be charged against Milton. Of occasional Latinisms we make less account. As thus:

But these frequent songs throughout the law and the prophets . . . may be easily made appear over all the kinds of lyric poetry to be incomparable.

Or, again: "The chief of learned men reputed in this land." The like may be found, much more frequently, in Hooker; and Milton is rather to be praised that they appear so seldom, than censured that they appear sometimes. The former, indeed, exemplifies a construction which we could wish Milton had succeeded in recommending, the inversion not being violent, while there is force and propriety in bringing down the close upon the emphatic word. Next to the genius of the language, the great power which fought against the splendid host of Latinising writers was doubtless the English Bible. The Bible had decided before Dryden that the language should not set in their mould.

But if not as an imitable model, yet as a magnificent study and recreation, like the hearing of grave and lofty music, the prose-work of Milton deserves to pass from the exclusive hands of scholars into those of all who care for exalted English. Though critics have dwelt on his Latinised diction, the substance is fine and virile Saxon, on which the Latin is a stately broidery, harmonised with rare art. He can pass from it at will to the most energetic simplicity, as one might conjecture in the author of "Comus."

They thought themselves gallant men, and I thought them fools; they made sport, and I laughed; they mispronounced, and I misliked; and, to make up the atticism, they were out, and I hissed.

Were ever unlucky actors assailed with more vernacular scorn? That it can exceed, at times, in too rough abuse, we might surmise from passages in the poems. But the cudgel, if too knotty, is sound English wood; and one has a laughing relish in hearing its hearty ring — the savagery of the blows deadened by a distance of two centuries. And when Milton's matter gives him scope, how those long sentences drop like a cloak all suspicion of stiffness or pedantry, and advance in sweet and noble measure! Listen to this, if you will to hear music:

Next . . . that I may tell ye whither my younger feet wandered, I betook me among those lofty fables and romances, which recount in solemn cantos the deeds of knighthood founded by our victorious kings, and from hence had in renown over all Christendom. There I read it in the oath of every knight, that he should defend to the expense of his best blood, or of his life, if so befell him, the honour and chastity of virgin or matron; from whence even then I learned what a noble virtue chastity sure must be, to the defence of which so many worthies, by such a dear adventure of themselves, had sworn. And if I found in the story afterward, any of them, by word or deed, breaking that oath, I judged it the same fault of the poet as that which is attributed to Homer, to have written indecent things of the gods. Only this my mind gave me, that every free and gentle spirit, without that oath, ought to be borne a knight, nor needed to expect the gilt spur, or the laying of a sword upon his shoulder, to stir him up both by his counsel and his arms to secure and protect the weakness of any attempted chastity. So that even those books, which to many others have been the fuel of wantonness and loose living, I cannot think how, unless by divine indulgence, proved to me so many incitements, as you have heard, to the love and steadfast observation of that virtue which abhors the society of bordelloes.

The language of this is as pure and austerely beautiful as the thought, which is (so to speak) the finest blend of chivalry and Puritanism.

There is in the above passage a certain strain of exalted declamation, which appears yet more notable in Milton's most splendid outbursts. *Outbursts* they are, so that one continually considers what an orator might have been in him. Always he seems perorating to some august assembly, like his own Satan in Pandemonium: the very rhythm seems designed to swell through resounding distances and reverberate above the multitudinous murmur of frequent congregations. This suits, also, the essential spaciousness of the man's mind, its love of large grandeurs, of massed and massive sound, of all imperial amplitudes, alike in conception, expression, and ambitions. It is in such mood and at such opportunities, therefore, that his great and entirely personal style is most completely under his control, can deploy its full resources and rejoice unafraid in its own power. At such moments his style is the prose counterpart of the supreme numbers which awe us in *Paradise Lost*, so far as the occasion and the lesser range of prose will admit. Sometimes it comes and passes in a single gust, as when he speaks of the "poet, soaring in the high region of his fancies, with his garland and singing robes about him." Or, yet more magnificent:

The Apocalypse of St. John is the majestic image of a high and stately tragedy, shutting up and intermingling her solemn scenes and acts with a sevenfold chorus of hallelujahs and harping symphonies.

To keep on such a level would be to make his prose purely lyrical; and, therefore, in the sustained passages, Milton starts from a lower stage. Take that fine passage in the *Areopagitica:*

> Books are not absolutely dead things, but do contain a potency of life in them to be as active as that soul was whose progeny they are; nay, they do preserve as in a vial the purest efficacy and extraction of that living intellect that bred them. I know they are as lively, and as vigorously productive, as those fabulous dragon's teeth; and being sown up and down, may chance to spring up armed men. And yet, on the other hand, unless wariness be used, as good, almost, kill a man as kill a good book. Who kills a man kills a reasonable creature, God's image; but he who destroys a good book, kills reason itself, kills the image of God, as it were, in the eye. Many a man lives a burthen to the earth; but a good book is the precious life-blood of a master spirit, embalmed and treasured up on purpose to a life beyond life. 'Tis true, no age can restore a life, . . . and revolutions of ages do not oft recover the loss of a rejected truth, for the want of which whole nations fare the worse.

This weighty piece of reflection is almost modern in form. From it Milton rises or descends at will, until he reaches his majestic and characteristic level, shown in the following passage:

> Good and evil we know in the field of this world grow up together almost inseparably; and the knowledge of good is so involved and inter-woven with the knowledge of evil, and in so many cunning resemblances hardly to be discerned, that those confused seeds which were imposed upon Psyche as an incessant labour to cull out, and sort asunder, were not more intermixed. It was from out the rind of one apple tasted, that the knowledge of good and evil, as two twins cleaving together, leaped forth into the world. . . . He that can apprehend and consider vice with all her baits and seeming pleasures, and yet abstain, and yet distinguish, and yet prefer that which is truly better, he is the true wayfaring Christian. I cannot praise a fugitive and cloistered virtue, unexercised and unbreathed, that never sallies out and sees her adversary, but slinks out of the race, where that immortal garland is to be run for, not without dust and heat. Assuredly we bring not innocence into the world, we bring impurity much rather; that which purifies us is trial, and trial is by what is contrary. That virtue therefore which is but a youngling in the contemplation of evil, and knows not the utmost which vice promises to her followers, and rejects it, is but a blank virtue, not a pure; her whiteness is but an excremental whiteness.

Praise is impotent before such prose as this, which only Milton could transcend. Often quoted, we must yet quote again the words in which he achieves that feat:

Methinks I see in my mind a noble and puissant nation rousing herself like a strong man after sleep, and shaking her invincible locks. Methinks I see her as an eagle mewing her mighty youth, and kindling her un-dazzled eyes at the full midday beam: purging and unscaling her long-abused sight at the fountain itself of heavenly radiance; while the whole noise of timorous and flocking birds, with those also that love the twilight, flutter about, amazed at what she means, and in their envious gabble would prognosticate a year of sects and schisms.

So puissant a passage (to use Milton's own word) is not to be found elsewhere, and could hardly be written again. We could no more build like the builders of Egypt than we could write in this colossal manner. The Miltonic prose overtops our praise, and seems framed for a larger generation. It stands with the columns of Memphis and Babylonian gardens, and all primeval survivals which have testified, or still testify, to the living little, of the spacious dead. Let us not overlay it with the parasitical growth of vain words.

A REDISCOVERED POET*

[*Academy*, April 11, 1903]

Although the major part of this review is devoted to a discussion of the editor's and Thompson's ideas on the influence Vaughan exerted upon Traherne, there is in it a discerning and authentic appraisal of Traherne's poetical performance. In the last paragraph, Thompson is more apodictical than is his wont.

Is THERE any end to the fecundity of the sixteenth and seven-teenth centuries? *The Poetical Works of Thomas Traherne*, edited and published by Mr. Bertram Dobell, add another name to those of Herbert, Vaughan, and Crashaw. The "find" is undoubtedly

---

* *The Poetical Works of Thomas Traherne.* Now First Published from the Original MS. Edited by Bertram Dobell.

a remarkable one; though Mr. Dobell, like most discoverers, is inclined to magnify his discovery beyond bounds, and assigns to his very own poet a rank which will scarce meet, we think, with final acceptance. The discovery is the more curious because the poems had never been published at all. They were picked up on a second-hand bookstall, in manuscript, by Mr. W. T. Brooke, who sold them to the late Dr. Grosart. Both men thought the poems (which were anonymous) to be by Henry Vaughan, and Grosart was actually preparing to include them in an edition of Vaughan when he died. They then passed into Mr. Dobell's hands, who soon doubted the ascription to Vaughan. Through Mr. Brooke, a likeness was discovered to some poems in a volume ultimately found to be by Thomas Traherne. Traherne, it was ascertained, had published two other books. One was prose, the other a poem; and this poem ("Christian Ethicks") was finally encountered among the MS. in a shorter form, with some variations. That completed the evidence.

Traherne was a clergyman of the middle seventeenth century; and all that here concerns us is the nature and quality of his poems. They are religious poems, modelled as to form on Herbert's "Temple." That he was acquainted with Herbert Mr. Dobell admits, but he denies that the poems show any acquaintance with Vaughan. The wish is father to the belief, we think; for to admit acquaintance with Vaughan is to rob Traherne's best poems of the complete originality which it is Mr. Dobell's object to claim for them. We have ourselves come to a quite other conclusion; even as we dissent from many other of the claims which Mr. Dobell advances on Traherne's behalf. But the first duty is to recognise that a number of the poems show fine poetic quality. There is, in fact, to our mind, a clear dividing line in the book with regard to merit. It opens with a series of poems on childhood, which fully justify enthusiasm; but in the poems which follow there is a strik-ing change — not to say diminution — of poetic quality. Now it is precisely in those poems on childhood that we cannot but perceive what seems the influence of Vaughan.

In that first section there is a strong metaphysical quality which is all Traherne's own, and distinguishes him from either Herbert or Vaughan. The poems are strenuously thoughtful. He has nothing of Herbert's fancy; there is seldom an image or an analogy. But quickening the metaphysic thought, and making the abstract concrete, there is a breath of poetic emotion which has somewhat of Herbert, somewhat of Vaughan, yet is Traherne's own, and not that of either. A beautiful example is the opening poem, which shows Traherne quite at his best. From this, "The Salutation," we quote the opening and concluding stanzas:

> These little limbs,
> These eyes and hands which here I find,
> These rosy cheeks wherewith my life begins,
> Where have ye been? Behind
> What curtain were ye from me hid so long!
> Where was, in what abyss, my speaking tongue?
>
> When silent I,
> So many thousand thousand years,
> Beneath the dust did in a chaos lie,
> How could I smiles or tears,
> Or lips, or hands, or eyes, or ears perceive?
> Welcome ye treasures which I now receive.

     *   *   *   *   *   *   *   *

> New-burnisht joys,
> Which yellow gold or pearl excel!
> Such sacred treasures are the limbs in boys,
> In which a soul doth dwell;
> Their organised joints and azure veins
> More wealth include than all the world contains.

     *   *   *   *   *   *   *   *

> A stranger here
> Strange things doth meet, strange glories see;
> Strange treasures lodg'd in this fair world appear,
> Strange all and new to me;
> But that they mine should be, who nothing was,
> That strangest is of all, yet brought to pass.

This is extremely fine; the thought strikingly bold, and winged by a certain fervour of delight. It is alone enough to show that

Mr. Dobell has had memorable good fortune, which other students
and searchers of the past well may envy. In the succeeding poem
the resemblance to Vaughan is stronger, both in occasional cast
of expression, and still more in the nature of the central idea. The
opening line, even Mr. Dobell admits, directly recalls Vaughan's
reference to —

> Those early days when I
> Shined in mine angel-infancy.

When this is so reinforced by the character of the general conception, as it is in Traherne's "Wonder," one cannot but draw
the inference:

> How like an Angel came I down!
> How bright are all things here!
> When first among His works I did appear
> O how their Glory me did crown!
> The world resembled His *Eternity*,
> In which my soul did walk;
> And everything that I did see
> Did with me talk.
>
> A native health and innocence
> Within my bones did grow,
> And while my God did all his Glories show,
> I felt a vigour in my sense
> That was all Spirit. I within did flow
> With seas of life like wine;
> I nothing in the world did know
> But 'twas divine.

*   *   *   *   *   *   *   *

> The streets were paved with golden stones,
> The boys and girls were mine,
> Oh how did all their lovely faces shine!
> The sons of men were holy ones,
> In joy and beauty they appeared to me,
> And everything which here I found,
> While like an angel I did see,
> Adorned the ground.

*   *   *   *   *   *   *   *

Cursed and devised proprieties,
    With envy, avarice,
And fraud, the fiends which spoil even Paradise,
    Flew from the splendour of mine eyes.
And so did hedges, ditches, limits, bounds,
    I dreamed not aught of those,
But wandered over all men's grounds,
    And found repose.

Proprieties themselves were mine,
    And hedges ornaments;
Walls, boxes, coffers, and their rich contents,
    Did not divide my joys, but all combine.
Clothes, ribbons, jewels, laces, I esteemed
    My joys by others worn;
For me they all to wear them seemed
    When I was born.

This, and the preceding poem from which we also cited stanzas, are (we think) Traherne's best. Such a line as "The sons of men were holy ones" suggests Vaughan at his most characteristic. On the other hand, in "Oh, how did all their lovely faces shine!" and elsewhere in these poems of childhood, there is something which curiously and strikingly anticipates the manner of Blake. Even from these chosen stanzas, however (which necessarily show the poet mostly at his best), it will be seen that Traherne does not always sustain himself at such a height. More often than Herbert himself, he lapses into flat prose, redeemed only by the thought. Nor does he seem to move quite natively in verse: too frequently, it will be noticed, there are stiff and awkward inversions, to get rhyme or metre. It is in the sequent poem, "Eden," that he most plainly builds on Vaughan:

A learned and a happy ignorance
    Divided me
    From all the vanity,
From all the sloth, care, pain, and sorrow that advance
    The madness and the misery
Of men. No error, no distraction I
Saw soil the earth or overcloud the sky.

> I knew not that there was a serpent's sting
> Whose poison shed
> On men, did overspread
> The world; nor did I dream of such a thing
> As sin, in which mankind lay dead.
> They all were brisk and living wights to me,
> Yea, pure and full of immortality.

> *   *   *   *   *   *   *   *

> Only what Adam in his first estate,
> Did I behold;
> Hard silver and dry gold
> As yet lay under ground; my blessed fate
> Was more acquainted with the old
> And innocent delights which he did see
> In his original simplicity.

The whole of the poem from which these stanzas are taken is, in truth, simply an expansion in idea of Vaughan's exquisite poem already mentioned. When it is considered along with the two previous poems and the following poem, "Innocence," it becomes difficult to evade the conclusion that throughout the series Traherne is playing variations upon the theme of this and Vaughan's other lovely poem on childhood. In a subsequent poem on a different theme, in the present book, we find —

> My contemplation dazzles in the end
> Of all I comprehend;

and we are at once reminded of Vaughan's phrase in one of those two childhood poems:

> My striving eye
> Dazzles at it, as at Eternity.

When we pass from this section of poems on childhood to the second section, there is a marked change in Traherne. Two poems, "The Preparative" and "The Vision," retain the former quality with an increase of the metaphysical element. But thereafter the metaphysical element becomes knottily predominant, while the poetic quality, the charm, the rapture, if not absent, are insufficiently present. The verse has lost its wing, exactly when the additional weight of metaphysic thought needed a stronger wing. We have not room for further quotation, but the fact must strike a careful reader. And we must needs draw the inference. It is this.

Traherne is a highly thoughtful and metaphysical poet, without corresponding emotional power — insufficiently a poet, in fact. But in one group of poems, where (apparently) he had the advantage of drawing inspiration from Vaughan, he rose beyond himself, and attained striking poetic quality. It is not (save at moments) the quality of Vaughan, but his own. He has not the supreme and passionless passion of Vaughan, like that intense motion of the blue sky which seems motionless. But he has his own emotional charm, sometimes (we have said) singularly suggesting Blake. He is unequal, he has not poetry at command, he has no technique, apart from his inspired moments. Save in moments, he lacks the great magic. But there remains a handful of poetry admirable, original, of a single and captivating sweetness, overcoming by force of inspiration the lack of native instinct for verse. And Mr. Dobell's is the most remarkable discovery of recent years.

THE ROMANTIC MOVEMENT

MR. HENLEY'S "BURNS" *
[*Academy*, October 2, 1897]

Thompson does not miss Henley's rare accomplishment, a gradually maturing judgment, without sacrifice of brilliancy and effectiveness. But he points out the exception, when Henley goes to extremes in according Burns so high a place among English poets. This excessive praise, Thompson shows, is the result of Henley's exaggerated opinion of the importance of humor and dramatic vision. In estimating Burns' absolute powers, he is correct. But in comparing him with other poets, he is wrong. Thompson especially praises Henley's courage in replacing the traditional Burns with the actual Burns who emerges from his editor's relentless and painstaking research. As a consequence of Henley's findings, Thompson acknowledges a reversal of his own opinion of Burns the poet. The review of volume III, is, in part, incorporated into "Henley's Byron and Burns," in *Essays of To-day and Yesterday*. For this reason it is not here included.

M R. HENLEY has ever been the *enfant perdu* of literature. It has always been the emprise perilous which has had attractions for him. In the achievement (essayed in company with Mr. T. F. Henderson) which he has now brought to a successful close by this fourth and final volume of the *Centenary Edition of Burns*, the old fighting instinct shows itself strong as ten or a dozen years ago. Of whatever he set his pen to, one might be sure the average man would say: "True, no doubt; but how frightfully imprudent to say it!" To speak the truth about Burns! If Mr. Henley had looked round him for what forlorn hope yet remained to lead, he could not have made a more keenly characteristic choice. When the third volume appeared, the vital and straight-spoken notes of

* *The Poetry of Robert Burns*. Vol. IV. Edited by W. E. Henley and T. F. Henderson.

Mr. Henley and Mr. Henderson showed plainly enough to what manner of issue they were leading; and that issue we indicated in our comments at the time. Now we have Mr. Henley's own summing-up of Burns's "Life, Genius, and Achievement," in an essay bold, vivid, complete with all his old mastery. We look to see how far it confirms or contradicts the summary which we based on those former notes, and find that in the main we were not far astray as to his mind. What difference there is arises mostly from the fact that we dealt with but a part of Burns, and here (of course) Mr. Henley is dealing with the whole; so that it displays Burns in a more favourable — rightly, a more favourable light. Let it be our first duty, and our pleasure, to say that we accept Mr. Henley's conclusions with an assent as complete and cordial as is well possible for two diverse minds in this world of divergence. In but a few points (which we shall come at in due course) do we feel any recalcitrance; and those are mostly things which have to do with Burns the man, not Burns the poet.

The editors tell us (in the preface) that they have already incurred violent hostility from numbers of the poet's countrymen, on account of the previous volumes; though their views were rather to be gathered than read therein. Mr. Henley's essay will not be a peace-offering; but he has too many scars of battle to care. Let him take the thanks of the few, which to-morrow will be the thanks of the many. He has uttered what none have dared to utter, and none — if they had dared — could have uttered with like weight, and faculty to compel audience. It is fortunately impossible — or impossible with any plausibility — to account for his utterance by international prejudice. He has at all times shown such liking for Scots writers, and been so connected with Scotsmen, that many have taken him to be himself a Scot. It was as editor of a Scots paper that he first acquired his present brilliant repute and authority in the world of journalism. Already, indeed, his book of prose had made him known as a master of letters, with a style of perfect individuality and insuperable *élan* — the *beau sabreur* of essayists. But it was his editing of the *Scots* — afterwards the *National* — *Observer*, which made him not merely the possessor of style in himself, but the cause of style in others, an acknowledged revolutioniser of English journalism. Therefore none can ascribe his summary of Burns to anything but a disposition which sets the truth of literature before all nationality, and before ignorant obloquy. Nor has he tripped as he might have tripped. The Mr. Henley we knew of old neither praised nor blamed by halves. He loved a writer; and he descended in avalanchine praise which often swept judgment before it. He saw grave, unnoted sins in a writer; and poured on him a glut of *mitraille* before which the hapless author's renown "reeled, shattered and sundered." Into no such trap has he fallen here. Mr. Henley seems to gain with the process of the years. Without sacrificing a jot of effectiveness, he has compassed an even balance of treatment. Seldom, indeed, can so grave a justice of matter have been fused with such brilliant *entrain* of manner.

What admirer of Burns, in good truth, could desire bolder, nay, more audacious estimate of the poet's place in literature than is given by Mr. Henley? It will not suffice the rabid Burnsian: "Think nothing gained," he cries, "while aught remains"; and allow that his poet's Muse stands next in beauty to Helen and Cleopatra, he will not be pacified unless you concede that she unites the golden tresses of the Greek with the dark riches of the Egyptian. Reason — at the name of Burns reason must bow; "there is reason in roasting of eggs," but not in toasting of Burns. His place, says Mr. Henley, is "in the first flight of English poets after Milton, Chaucer, Shakespeare." Is it not enough? "Enough, aye, and too much!" many may be inclined to cry with the reviewer; "Is this the grave judgment you talked of even now?" Well, let us look Mr. Henley's gift-horse a little in the mouth. He declares with explicit justice: "It is not for 'the love of lovely words' that we revert to Burns. He has all manner of qualities — wit, fancy, vision of a kind, nature, gaiety, the richest humour, a sort of homespun verbal magic." Nevertheless he affirms, "But for beauty we must go elsewhither." It is simple verity. What, then, does Mr. Henley mean by his first-quoted declaration? This he means: the power, the consummate power of Burns is to be sought in what we may perhaps call his poems of character. "The master-quality of Burns . . . is humour." There it is, the long-awaited truth spoken at last; directly, clearly, courageously. Therefore Mr. Henley concludes:

> The world of "Scotch morals, Scotch religion, and Scotch drink," may be ugly or not (as refracted through his temperament it is *not*). Ugly or not, however, it was the world of Burns; to paint it was part of his mission. . . . The world of realism lay broad-beaten by his ancestors . . . he followed it with vision, with humour, "inspiration and sympathy," and with art; and in the sequel he is found to have a place of his own in the first flight of English poets after Milton, Chaucer, Shakespeare.

You see now what it means. It means — not that Mr. Henley is under any delusion as to the mode of Burns's gift—but that humour and dramatic vision have for Mr. Henley a poetic value which for some of us they have not. Admit that, and Burns's latest editor is not far wrong in the place he assigns to Burns.

Wherefore, seeing that his comparative estimate in no way thickens his sight of Burns's absolute powers and their nature, we are little disposed to contend over it; we can afford to pass it by on the other side. Personally, if Shakespeare had given us Falstaffs as the sands of the sea, and plays like *Much Ado about Nothing* as the stars of the heavens, we should judge him a great dramatist, we should not judge him a great poet. But the essential thing remains, that Mr. Henley sees Burns exactly as he is, and utters his seeing without fear or flinching. The rest is a bagatelle. "The master-quality of Burns is humour." The "Address to the Deil," "The Devil and Dr. Hornbook," those irreverent, pungent, irresistible flights of satire against the gloomy spirit of Scotch Calvinism, those pictures of peasant jollity, of vagrant revelry, full of animal spirits, of shrewdness, of character—instantaneous *sgraffiti*, the Comic Muse barefoot, reckless, tossing with dishevelled laughter; these are "rantin', rovin' Robin" himself. Himself, and also — as Mr. Henley sees — his predecessors, Fergusson, and the author of *Christ's Kirk on the Green*, and the many more. In the Songs this is far more so. Mr. Henley says plainly that Burns worked best in these where "he had a lead" from some older singer; and that it is such lyrics which "show Burns the song-smith at his best." He adduces in the notes of this edition abundant proofs of the fact — some of which we quoted at length in reviewing

the third volume. In our opinion, this fact, now thoroughly established by Messrs. Henley and Henderson, must needs place Burns
somewhat below true greatness as a song-writer. This, however,
does not seem to be altogether Mr. Henley's view. It is so far true,
he says, in that "the Burns of fact differs, and differs considerably
and at many points, from the Burns of legend." But "enough
remains to Burns to keep him easily first in the first flight of singers
in the vernacular, and to secure him, outside the vernacular, the
fame of an unique artist." Our objection to this (let it pass for
what it is worth) would be that the old border singers were
"vernacular," and easily pass Burns in the serious lyric. Perhaps,
however, Mr. Henley would argue that few of their productions
are real songs, but rather belong to the class of brief ballads.

Mr. Henley is not less, but rather more outspoken, in dealing
with Burns the man. Terrible will be the flutter in the kailyards
over this section of his work. Not Don Quixote among the puppets
worked such slaughter grim and great as Mr. Henley when he lugs
out his long sword, and slices right and left among the marionettes
that have hitherto done duty in the pleasant tragedy mixed full
of lamentable mirth of "The Ploughman Poet; or, the Glasses
and the Lasses." Wood and tinsel are scattered about the stage;
even Highland Mary lies lopped and low. For that last deed let
Mr. Henley have our warmest thanks. Hateful is all sham, but
most hateful of all the sentimental sham. Let him also be thanked
that, by way of righteous compensation, he has championed poor
Jean Armour, neglected of all the sentimentalists, because Burns
took the romance out of her by giving her the tardy justice of
marriage — not that the tardiness was his fault. For the first time
we have Burns with the whitewash scraped off him — in his colours
as he lived.

Mr. Henley sums his own sketch in one chance-dropped sentence: "The lewd, amazing peasant of genius, the inspired faun."
Nay, he carries the revolt against smug unreality to excess; until
we think of Lear tearing off his "lendings," when the contemplation of Poor Tom has convicted him of being "sophisticated." He
declares it too late to apologise for the "primordial instinct," and
a particularly rank absurdity "in the case of a man who so exulted

in its manifestations and results" as Burns. Passing by the principle involved in this sentence, most people will understand from it that Mr. Henley applauds Burns for illustrating the "primordial instinct" by a life-long career of seduction; and it is not probable that Mr. Henley quite meant that. He shows clearly enough at the end what is really to be said of Burns: "a peasant of genius perverted from his peasanthood . . . constrained to live his qualities into defects." Let it be added, that, though we have talked of the poet's "career of seduction" (because, like Mr. Henley, we have a taste for calling things by their names), it was far from implying what it would imply in a higher society. The young ladies of such a community did not need much seduction. The delicate manner in which Jean Armour opened her affair with Burns is typical. Some philosophers affirm that in all love affairs the first call comes from the woman, though it is a silent call. But these maidens were articulate, and left nothing to chance.

We are not, it is true, personally acquainted with Scottish village-life, we are willing to believe that things may have bettered since Burns wrote; and there is an immense gap between Mauchline and Thrums. Yet we do not speak out of our inner consciousness only. The reviewer has lived intimately in contact with a type of peasantry strongly analogous to that described by Burns, though more dour, less streaked with gaiety, and has, therefore, a vivid realisation of what such an environment means. Even in our actual position of superiority and proud enlightenment, we do not find any stone exactly safe to throw at him. From this same experience, we doubt the heroism which Mr. Henley imputes to Jean Armour in a certain detail of conduct. He hardly, we think, realises the extent to which such girls' sensibilities are dulled in these matters. But all this is not to be pursued here. Enough that without such experience it is not possible to understand all the excuse for Burns.

In conclusion, let us hope that Mr. Henley's courage and sincerity will purify the atmosphere about Burns. As in the case of the Chinese Emperor's clothes, one has spoken, and now many may begin to speak. But, as in Andersen's story, to say that first word it needed, if not a child, what is in some ways the same — a man of genius.

THE SUN OF SCOTLAND*
[*Academy*, January 20, 1906]

Thompson's fine sense of language and the *verbum proprium* is exemplified
in his treatment of Burns's selected poems to which Andrew Lang wrote
the introduction. He gently crosses swords with Lang and after overwhelming proof of his case, suggests a reconsideration of "the traditional
belief that Burns was most excellent in his Scottish poems." It is not difficult
to understand how quick was Thompson to realize that Burns's personal
experiences in life "led him to understand the whole gamut of human
emotion." The same was true of Thompson. But he differed from Burns in
this — he was not personally defiled by his experiences, although, during
his outcast years, he lived on more intimate terms with the *bête humaine*
than did his Scots brother. And yet, contrary to the popular idea, Thompson's understanding of "the whole gamut of human emotion" was the
more profound of the two.

Before these words are in print, Scotland will once more have
celebrated the day when "a blast o' Janwar win' blew hansel in
on Robin," and *à propos* of which this little book of selections has
been issued. To our mind the chief point of interest in it is the
excellent introduction supplied by Mr. Andrew Lang. While
appreciative, it is at the same time sane, quiet, and marked by the
critic's good sense and sound judgment. There are a few points,
however, which are almost certain to lead to a little friendly argument. Some time ago we directed attention to an acute piece of
criticism from the pen of the late Canon Ainger, who maintained
that the best passages in Robert Burns were written in the purest
English. Mr. Andrew Lang probably did not notice this remark;
at any rate, he maintains the opinion that "his Scotch poems are, by
universal consent, as well as in his own opinion, infinitely his best
poems," and this he follows up with a sneer at the model of Burns,
"the divine Shenstone." Now it seems to us that this opinion is very
much open to question. It is a curious fact that the peasant, either
in England or in Scotland, when moved by strong feeling of any

* *Selected Poems of Robert Burns*. With an Introduction by Andrew Lang.

kind, has a tendency to express it, not in dialect but in pure and beautiful English. The cause, in the instance of Burns, is not far to seek. Whilst colloquial Scotch was the every-day, commonplace language of his friends and associates, and the homely *patois* of his family, we must never forget the influence of the "big ha' Bible" and the habit of closing the day with a reading from it as described in "The Cotter's Saturday Night."

> The chearfu' Supper done, wi' serious face,
>   They, round the ingle, form a circle wide:
> The Sire turns o'er, wi' patriarchal grace,
>   The big *ha'-Bible*, ance his Father's pride;
> His bonnet rev'rently is laid aside,
>   His *lyart haffets* wearing thin an' bare;
> Those strains that once did sweet in Zion glide,
>   He wales a portion with judicious care,
> "And let us worship God!" he says, with solemn air.

Now, if we examine the choicest passages in the works of Burns, we find none of those obscure dialect words which, according to Mr. Andrew Lang, puzzle the reader. Even in "Tam O'Shanter," a piece famed for the exquisite force and vividness of the native Doric, we find many of the finest lines to be set down in English that might have proceeded from Wordsworth himself.

> But pleasures are like poppies spread,
> You seize the flow'r, its bloom is shed;
> Or like the snow-falls in the river,
> A moment white—then melts for ever;
> Or like the borealis race,
> That flit ere you can point their place;
> Or like the rainbow's lovely form
> Evanishing amid the storm.

There is only, it may be observed, a single word — and that not a dialect word — here that would not be understood by a London schoolboy. Again, if we take what are generally considered to be the most tender lines ever written by the poet, the same observation holds good.

> Had we never lov'd sae kindly,
> Had we never lov'd sae blindly,
> Never met—or never parted,
> We had ne'er been broken-hearted.

In passing it may be permissible to say that the writer has ever looked upon the first line of this poem as a fine example of the instinctive good taste of Burns for the appropriate word: "Ae fond kiss, and then we sever." The English word "sever," naturally as it occurs in this context, is one that on first thoughts we would not have expected Burns to employ. However, to proceed with our argument, we find that as the poet draws to his culmination, when his emotion is worked up to its highest pitch, his language becomes ever purer and more beautiful. At first, when he is in a despondent mood, describing the humdrum tedium and despair of life, the homely dialect is delightful.

> There, lanely, by the ingle-cheek,
> I sat and ey'd the spewing reek,
> That fill'd, wi' boast-provoking smeek,
>   The auld, clay biggin;
> An' heard the restless rattons squeak
>   About the riggin.

The softness, the harmony and dignity of the last verse are expressed in language that Shakespeare could not have bettered.

> "*And wear thou this*,"—she solemn said,
> And bound the *Holly* round my head:
> The polish'd leaves, and berries red,
>   Did rustling play;
> And, like a passing thought, she fled
>   In light away.

It is, however, remarkable that in "The Jolly Beggars," while all the lesser characters use broad Scotch, some of it most idiomatic, to display their contempt for everything that is respectable and conventional, the supreme expression of the wanderers for all that genteel society holds most dear is set forth in words that might have come from the pen of Swift, if Swift had been as much a poet as Burns was. To illustrate the Scottish idiom, we cannot do better than quote the first verse of the fiddler's song:

> Let me ryke up to dight that tear,
> An' go wi' me an' be my dear,
> An' then your every care an' fear
> 　May whistle owre the lave o't;

and the conclusion of the poem will make our other point clear:

> Life is all a *variorum*,
> 　We regard not how it goes;
> Let them cant about *decorum*
> 　Who have characters to lose.
>
> Here's to budgets, bags and wallets!
> 　Here's to all the wandering train!
> Here's our ragged *brats* and *callets*!
> 　One and all cry out,—"Amen!"
>
> *A fig for those by law protected!*
> 　*Liberty's a glorious feast!*
> *Courts for cowards were erected,*
> 　*Churches built to please the priest!*

In view of these passages, which are but samples of many others that could be produced, we think that the traditional belief that Burns was most excellent in his Scottish poems deserves reconsideration. All the same, it may be frankly admitted that he showed an occasional tendency to become stilted when he wrote English, especially when he used it for ordinary purposes and occasionally when he tried his highest flight, as "To Mary in Heaven." There is an excellent criticism of this poem conveyed incidentally in Mr. Holman Hunt's history of the Pre-Raphaelite Brotherhood.

During the intercourse of this journey we were much engaged in discussions on the character of English poetry of all periods. Palgrave was a man of solid culture, and was engaged at the time on his unrivalled forthcoming selection, *The Golden Treasury*. While Burns was under review, his poem "To Mary in Heaven" was excluded from the selection, Tennyson agreeing that the refrain of "Hear'st thou the groans that rend this breast?" had the ring of hysterical insincerity and bombast in it, a rare fault in that simple poet.

While admitting that Tennyson was right, as he generally was, we refuse to believe that the comparative failure here was one of language. It would be difficult, for instance, to suggest how the third verse could be improved by a Scotch paraphrase.

> Ayr, gurgling kiss'd his pebbled shore,
>   O'erhung with wild-woods, thick'ning green;
> The fragrant birch, and hawthorn hoar,
>   Twin'd am'rous round the raptur'd scene:
> The flowers sprang wanton to be prest,
>   The birds sang love on ev'ry spray,
> Till too, too soon, the glowing west
>   Proclaim'd the speed of winged day.

Another opinion expressed by Mr. Andrew Lang is one exclusively of temperament. It is conveyed in the following sentence:

Once I ventured to say—Principal Shairp had said it before—that I wished we knew no more of Burns's life than of Shakespeare's. It was a vain thing to wish; we cannot keep his poetry, with its frequent confessions, and be ignorant of his life. But I meant no more than a natural desire to be spared sermons, scandal, tattle about a poet. I care no more to grope after the last gossip about Jean Armour, than to listen to the last "chatter about Harriet."

As far as disliking a scandal about a dead poet goes, we are in the most complete agreement with Mr. Andrew Lang; but, on the other hand, there is much to be said in favour of Carlyle's view, that it is better to see a man exactly as he really is than to behold him cloaked and posed as if awaiting a visit from the sculptor. In our opinion it tends to give a deeper insight into human nature. We see in Burns a man who was described with the utmost exactitude by himself in "A Bard's Epitaph":

The poor Inhabitant below
Was quick to learn and wise to know,
And keenly felt the friendly glow,
        And *softer flame*,
But thoughtless follies laid him low,
        And stain'd his name!

We see in Burns one who had all the finest instincts and impulses that human nature could be endowed with. If they had been accompanied by mental force he would probably have been a great saint but a very poor poet. It was because of his very weakness and lack of that "prudent, cautious self-control" which he found by bitter experience to be "wisdom's root" he fell into so many thoughtless follies; but even in doing so he was, like Sir Walter Scott under very different circumstances, "making himself." In a word, he was drinking life to the very lees, and the pathos, remorse, pity, and sadness combined with the mad gaiety of it led him to understand the whole gamut of human emotion. His example is not one to set up for imitation; and yet, looking back and comparing the fruit with the plant, we find that they are one and indivisible. It was his keen sympathy combined with experience that made him capable of fulfilling his own ambition — to become a singer of "the loves, the ways of simple swains"; or, if Mr. Andrew Lang's more grandiose phrase be preferred, even as Homer was the sun of Hellas, so was Robert Burns the sun of Scotland.

THE NEW BYRON*
[*Outlook*, May 7, 1898]

Thompson does not spare the editor who digs up the dead bones of poems suppressed by the poet himself, but with his habitual balance of judgment he sees some good in the result. The appraisal of Byron's *Juvenilia* is priceless.

THE long-expected new edition of Byron, issued by Mr. Murray, and edited by Mr. Ernest Hartley Coleridge, is at length to hand

* *The Works of Lord Byron*. A New Revised and Enlarged Edition with Illustrations. Vol. I. Edited by Ernest Hartley Coleridge.

in its first volume. Adopting what has of late become a rampant cant-word, the literary announcements have described it as "definitive." There are no "definitive" editions; there are only "latest editions." This we might describe, perhaps, as an "extra-special edition"; to be followed, no doubt, in due lapse of time, by a "second" or "third extra-special," and so *ad infinitum*. Its special "definitiveness" lies in the fact that Mr. Coleridge has had access to the Earl of Lovelace's original manuscripts; and so, no doubt, will be able to give us a text including nearly, or quite, everything which Byron wrote — and very much more than was worth publishing. For chief *bonnes-bouches* we are promised fifteen stanzas of the unfinished seventeenth canto of "Don Juan" and a considerable fragment of the third part of the "Deformed Transformed." The first may be interesting; it is more than problematical whether the second will be. Altogether we are to expect "at least thirty unpublished poems." Of what quality we can only surmise from sad experience of such raking among the dead bones of literature. This first volume seems well and sensibly edited, the poems taking the chronological order. The notes are printed at the foot of the page. They show every sign of care and industry; they are workmanlike notes; but it would be unfair to compare them with the brilliant notes in Mr. Henley's *Byron*. They do not attempt such competition. Our chief objection is that Mr. Coleridge is no artist in arranging his necessarily compressed information. Item is huddled upon item, at times, in a way which leaves us misty as to the main point — the elucidation of the poet's referential meaning; while sometimes the drift of the note appears obscure, through an attempt to pack too much collateral information into a brief compass, without proportion, perspective, symmetry. An extreme example is the note on Wellington's nephew, the "Long-Tylney-Wellesley-Long-Pole" of the "Rejected Addresses." He first appears as "Pole-Wellesley." Then, without explanation, he is referred to as "Wellesley-Pole"; and then as "Pole." Coupled with his adoption of his father-in-law's title of Tylney-Long, it becomes as intricate as the burlesque in the "Rejected Addresses" itself. A confusion of relatives winds up and complicates this perplexed and perplexing note. Mr. Coleridge, in fact, though thorough and industrious, is no master of language.

This first volume is limited to Byron's juvenile or semi-juvenile poems. Of his famous work, the only specimen it includes is "English Bards and Scotch Reviewers." Mr. Coleridge has enlarged by eleven poems the juvenile series known by the general title of "Hours of Idleness," though in reality (as he shows) composed from the contents of three distinct juvenile volumes. The first was entirely suppressed; the second (to which alone the title really belonged) was reissued in an altered form, with several poems omitted and added. All the suppressed poems are now for the first time printed. From the commercial standpoint we make our compliments to Mr. Coleridge. From the literary standpoint we are compelled to say, "*Dove diavolo, Messer Ernesto, avete pigliato tante coglionerie?*" It is of no possible interest to anyone but publishers, and the great British public, which loves to find a master writing *coglionerie* after its own heart, that these fooleries should be added to a collection already abundantly foolish. Let us use Byron's own words regarding the fate of another writer. "Certes, these rakers of 'Remains' come under the statute against 'resurrection men.' Is it so bad to unearth his bones as his blunders? 'We know what we are, but we know not what we may be'; and it is to be hoped we never shall know, if a man who has passed through life with a sort of *éclat* is to find himself a mountebank on the other side of Styx." We do not blame Mr. Coleridge: Fate, fashion, public, and publishers compel him. But the plain fact is that these Byron *Juvenilia* are the most worthless ever put forth by a man of genius. We mean the collection generally called "Hours of Idleness." They are feeble imitations of feeble imitations of feeble enough imitations; the dregs of the eighteenth century commingled with the settlings of the early nineteenth century; the lees of the "fast" hours of a fat schoolboy.

The beginnings of the true Byron are to be sought, not in the "English Bards," but in some minor poems of about the same date, and in "The Waltz." Yet the "English Bards" is so important in Byron's career that it must be dwelt upon; though it is tiro's work. That is not the conventional judgment. Mr. Coleridge, cleaving to the line of least resistance, after the fashion which makes a "safe" and popular critic, gives the conventional judgment, with exaggeration. It was, he says, "recognised at once as a work of genius. It has intercepted the popularity of its great predecessors, who are often quoted, but seldom read. It is still a popular poem, and appeals with fresh delight to readers who know the names of many of the bards only because Byron mentions them, and count others whom he ridicules among the greatest poets of the century." Now, that Dryden and Pope are more quoted than read, there is, unluckily, no doubt. But Byron's satire is seldom quoted, and we will back our opinion that it is still more seldom read — even by Byronians. Like the satires of Dryden and Pope, it is read only by students; and we are entirely sceptical that it has intercepted among them the "popularity" of its immeasurably greater predecessors. Let the truth come forth — it is an academic study in the school of Pope; weak, weak, abundantly weak, in spite of a quotable epigram here and there. Take the lines on Coleridge, which are neither better nor worse than the bulk of the satire:

> Shall gentle Coleridge pass unnoticed here,
> To turgid ode and tumid stanza dear?
> Though themes of innocence amuse him best,
> Yet still Obscurity's a welcome guest.
> If Inspiration should her aid refuse
> To him who takes a Pixy for a muse,
> Yet none in lofty numbers can surpass
> The bard who soars to elegize an ass:
> So well the subject suits his noble mind,
> He brays, the Laureate of the long-eared kind.

Is it mordant, this brilliant variant of the time-honoured epigram, "Smith is an ass"? The whole poem is the would-be terrific onslaught of an ambitious and cleverish schoolboy who has read Pope. There is not a trace of the formidable satirist who was one day to write "The Vision of Judgment." The "Hints from Horace" are just as good — or bad; and their obscurity proves what would have been the fate of "English Bards" had it been less sensationally "topical." It won its fame because it attacked by name the best-known poets of the day.

Yet in this volume there are minor poems of about the same date, in which we see the development of the true Byron. The "Lines on a Cup formed from a Skull" already have no small portion of the reckless Byronic edge. The succeeding lines to Mary Chaworth show Byron's sentimental side in process of formation, with much of its rhetorical effectiveness and directness, all of its melodramatic pose. "The Waltz" has considerable measure of his slashing mockery, and is a far stronger satire than "English Bards." The truth is that Byron's evil genius was Pope. It was a true instinct which made him impatient of the current demand for "romantic" poetry, and made him perpetually tend towards satire. It was a false instinct which led him to adopt the Pope model in satire. Pope, with his supremely feminine dexterousness of point, his swift and stinging rapier play, was the antithesis of Byron's daring masculinity. Already in the brilliant devilry of his letters Byron had found his true *métier*. He only needed to forego his ambition of the "grand style" in satire — the formal style of Pope and Dryden — and to carry the quality of his letters, polished and compacted, into verse. He only needed to look in his — want of heart, and write. The day came when he found the secret, when he wedded his native temper with his ambition. And straightway we had "Don Juan" and "Beppo," and the "Vision of Judgment"; we had a master. The real interest of this volume lies not where the British reader will seek it — in the juvenile sentimentalities, in the lines to innumerable Maries and so forth, of whom Mary Chaworth is the chosen figure taken to the great heart of the public — Byron's "Highland Mary"; not in the traditional "brilliant satire" of "English Bards"; it lies in the opportunity of gauging Byron's unconscious struggles towards completion in that *genre* whereof he was a supreme master — social satire. And Mr. Coleridge's best praise is that his arrangement for the first time enables us to trace, step by step, this growth of the poet.

A POET'S TABLE TALK*
[*Academy*, May 2, 1903]

There is sound criticism as well as originality in the characterization of "Don Juan" as "table talk." In justifying the term, Thompson shows sane, balanced judgment in appraising the literary merits of one whose philosophy was the antithesis of his own.

THE words "Poetry, Vol. VI.," on the back of Mr. Murray's new edition of "Don Juan," have more arithmetical than literary importance, for if all the poems in the preceding volumes were to perish to-morrow, Byron's reputation would stand unshaken on "Vol. VI." It is become a commonplace that "Don Juan" embraces all that he could do in literature. It conveys his best in his aptest manner. It is large, various and headstrong as himself, throbbing with those energies of love, hate, contempt, analysis, and worship to which his unsteady genius could give no perfect separate expression. He could fuse these inimitably after one fashion, the fashion of "Don Juan." This poem is not more alone among his works than it is alone among all English books. Many poets have given life and spiritual unity to a story, some have built up an argument with Orphean grace, but only Byron has maintained the warmth and tension of a giant through sixteen cantos of miscellaneous remarks. Well was that friend inspired who wrote to him: "Stick to 'Don Juan,' it is the only sincere thing you have written, and it will live after all your 'Harolds' have ceased to be 'a schoolgirl's tale, the wonder of an hour.' It is the best of all your works — the most spirited, the most straight-forward the most interesting, the most poetical." This far-seeing reader did not need to be told that Byron's fame would cease to rest on his poems and dramas of dark-souled loneliness, and would be firmly re-established on his dashed-off letters and his poetic table-talk.

For "Don Juan" is table-talk: the finest in the language. It has neither story nor purpose. Its integral form never troubled Byron.

* *Poetical Works of Lord Byron.* 7 Volumes. Edited by Ernest Hartley Coleridge. Volume VI. "DON JUAN."

He finished its first canto in Venice in 1818, and wrote to Moore: "It is called 'Don Juan,' and is meant to be a little quietly facetious upon everything." Type-writing was not, and what with his rides on the Lido, his love-making to Margarita Cogni, and his chance intrigues at opera and *ridotto*, he found the copying of his rough draft an intolerable bore. The poem struggled into being by fits and bits, and was regarded by him with mixed feelings of indifference and jealousy. "The poem will please, if it is lively," he wrote Murray with the second canto, "if it is stupid it will fail: but I will have none of your damned cutting and slashing." Three months later it is: "You ask me if I mean to continue D.J., &c. How should I know? What encouragement do you give me, all of you, with your nonsensical prudery? Publish the two Cantos, and then you will see."

The one purpose that grew in him was to write his mind into "Don Juan." "Come what may I never will flatter the million's canting in any shape." Later still, he will let Murray suppress the cantos he has in hand, aye, and burn them if he is afraid of the growing outcry, but patch and palliate he will not; he will either " 'make a spoon or spoil a horn,' and there's an end." Almost three years pass before he is on the fifth canto, but this is "hardly the beginning," and he does not know how he will go on or whether, if he lives, he will go on at all. Three months later he has promised the Countess Guiccioli to drop the work; Murray is to look upon the finished cantos as the last; the Countess's objection, he explains, "arises from the wish of all women to exalt the sentiment of the passions. . . . Now Don Juan strips off this illusion, and laughs at that and most other things." And so the see-saw of work and neglect continued. The first canto was of 1818, the sixteenth was of 1823. The length and shapelessness of the work became his own jest:

> I rattle on exactly as I'd talk
> With anybody in a ride or walk,

a statement in which there is no affectation. "His conversation," says Stanhope, "was a mixture of philosophy and slang, of everything, like his 'Don Juan.' "

We save much unprofitable discussion by accepting "Don

Juan" as the metrical table-talk of a man full of fire, sensibility, and experience. It bursts into poetry, as such talk will; it is wilfully and abundantly changeful; the white-hot outburst is cooled by a gibe; the expected climax is delayed by a caprice; and the torrent rushes headlong or whirls idly, but always with the strength or restraint of a great and whimsical whole. The one persisting poetic character is the measure. Never was verse so managed and moulded. Impassioned poetry, trivial badinage, tersest narrative, lightest reflection — all find in Byron's *ottava rima* an easy vehicle. Compare:

> Ave Maria! blessèd be the hour!
>   The time, the clime, the spot, where I so oft
> Have felt that moment in its fullest power
>   Sink o'er the earth—so beautiful and soft—
> While swung the deep bell in the distant tower,
>   On the faint dying day-hymn stole aloft,
> And not a breath crept through the rosy air,
> And yet the forest leaves seemed stirred with prayer.

with the death of the highwayman on Shooter's Hill:

> But ere they could perform this pious duty,
>   The dying man cried, "Hold! I've got my gruel!
> Oh! for a glass of max! We've missed our booty;
>   Let me die where I am!" And as the fuel
> Of Life shrunk in his heart, and thick and sooty
>   The drops fell from his death-wound, and he drew ill
> His breath,—he from his swelling throat untied
> A kerchief, crying, "Give Sal that!"—and died.

And then compare both with the description of the picture gallery at Newstead Abbey:

> But ever and anon, to soothe your vision,
>   Fatigued with these hereditary glories,
> There rose a Carlo Dolce or a Titian,
>   Or wilder group of savage Salvatore's:
> Here danced Albano's boys, and there the sea shone
>   In Vernet's ocean lights; and there the stories
> Of martyrs awed, as Spagnoletto tainted
> His brush with all the blood of all the sainted.

Here sweetly spread a landscape of Lorraine;
　　There Rembrandt made his darkness equal light,
Or gloomy Caravaggio's gloomier stain
　　Bronzed o'er some lean and stoic anchorite:—
But, lo! a Teniers woos, and not in vain,
　　Your eyes to revel in a livelier sight:
His bell-mouth'd goblet makes me feel quite Danish
Or Dutch with thirst—What, ho! a flask of Rhenish.

But the secret of "Don Juan's" appeal lies deeper. Why will men not willingly let die a poem so charged with irreverence for things above and contempt for things below? Is it not because we all savour Byron's opinions in moments and crises of our lives, and are pleased to find them finely phrased, and linked to a splendid personality? It must be remembered that "Don Juan" produces no impression of world-weariness. It is not a sigh, but a shout. Open it where you will it flashes life. The negations and nihilisms with which it abounds are uttered as roundly as other men's faiths; there is no miserable infection of the utterance; no miasma or helpless ranting. Every line reveals the cheerful yet implacable fighter. Naturally, the poem offers no regular inspiration or guidance. It is rather an armoury, to be visited on occasion.

Indeed, its mission to the individual now is not different from its mission to society eighty years ago. The collapse of Napoleon had brought every government to its feet, resolved to shut those fateful swinging doors through which men had for twenty-five years caught maddening glimpses of a new social order, wider institutions, a sunnier freedom. It was Byron's aim to keep alive these visions and the formative discontent they produced, to explode the closing mine, to probe the healing wounds. He attempted this in the only way possible to himself; he flung his own picturesque denials, his own passionate protests, broad-cast over Europe. He gave a form and a human reference to all these hesitant geyser-like aspirations, these smouldering thoughts of destruction and reconstruction; he gave them the embodiment of his own heart and career. While kingship and the old institutions and the old banalities were returning to their seats he remained convinced that their day was over, and that, though he would not like to live to see it, the breath of republicanism must soon fill the nation's lungs and bring new light to their eyes. There has been no rapid or striking fulfilment of his dream, and where the fulfilment has been greatest — in England, in France, in America — there has been re-action. The world will mend at its own pace, and largely in deviation from programmes. Yet Byron sowed the spirit of questioning, and the courage of denial, deep in the hearts of men; and without these nothing can be done. His scorn of social selfishness has made such scorn easier of attainment, and more to be dreaded. His independence has had the same result.

Nor is the appeal of "Don Juan" weakened because for a hundred years Europe has seen no upheaval of earth-shaking magnitude. The poem is not a gospel or a propaganda: it is an armoury of opinions and phrases to which men will have recourse according to their needs. Few men shape their lives by a steady compass. Faith they must have, but a secret loyalty to truth forbids them ever to lose touch of doubt. Ease they seek, but deep down in their hearts there is a response to a noble discontent. Morality they all preserve, but with a haunting conviction that the rules must be altered. Woman they worship, yet with memories of the Apple which will still be uttered. Knowledge they amass, but ever they will go behind it and say "We know nothing." Thus it is that though Byron is no man's guide, he will always have a hearing. The mere stimulus of his opinions and ejaculations is of value. He is our deputy-rebel, and he has this advantage, that he speaks not as a croaker in a corner, but, with incomparable strength of utterance, as a man who had seen the kingdoms of the world and their glory.

The permanence of "Don Juan," then, is accounted for by its almost unparalleled display of reckless intelligence warmed by poetic fervour. In it Byron meets us on no practicable plane of social or individual aspiration: he has none for his own feet; but he does help us by the abundance and courage of his ideas on man and his turbid feelings, on the world and its welter of affairs.

SAMUEL TAYLOR COLERIDGE*
[*Academy,* October 3, 1903]

The general criticism of the essay on Coleridge, included by Mr. Meynell in his definitive volume of Thompson's prose—it originally appeared in the *Academy*, February 6, 1897—is interestingly supplemented by the detailed attention which Thompson here gives to Coleridge's poetry and especially to the influence which Wordsworth exercised upon him.

THIS is a very fairly representative selection from Coleridge. Indeed, from the point of strict poetical value it is more than representative: there is a vast deal which has no poetical value at all. But the editor's aim has been to exhibit the development of Coleridge's genius; and for this purpose much which is not even poetry at all has an historical value. Even so, we would have cast the net less widely; and our sole reason for hesitating to call the book absolutely representative is that it represents too much of Coleridge's rubbish. The poems are set in chronological order, with the date — or the approximate date — prefixed to each; and we must give a special word of praise to the Notes. Not only do they give what, for so small a volume, is abundant information about the poems, but they are so handled as to form a kind of memoir, assigning to each poem its special period in Coleridge's life, and displaying the influences at work on him when it was written. The reader is thus able to view each poem in its proper relation to Coleridge's development. The editor's own critical taste is shown in casual comments; his criticisms are mostly drawn from the works of others, and are judiciously chosen.

"Five years from fifty saved!" exclaims Rossetti in his sonnet on Coleridge; and he might have shortened the period. Never has genius so illustrious been so absolutely a flash in the pan:

> He was a mighty poet, and
> A subtle-souled psychologist,

* *Select Poems of Samuel Taylor Coleridge.* Edited by Andrew J. George.

sang Shelley. A "subtle-souled psychologist" and a wonderful talker he remained to the last; a "mighty poet" he was only for a brief year or so. The most singular thing is that this brief poetic power dawned as suddenly as it set. Out of mediocrity it rose, into mediocrity it sank. That is not a customary assertion, but it is true. Why it was so sluggish to disclose is more perplexing than its premature decay, for which there is cause manifold. He is at the head of those poets whose genius was (what Nordau would have all genius to be) a disease. But the genius of disease is usually precocious; so it was with Chatterton, Keats, Shelley, Blake, Rossetti. Kit Smart, indeed, took his time before writing the "Song to David"; but Kit had the good luck to go mad, or he would never have written anything resembling poetry at all — indeed, it was only at the second attempt that he went mad to any purpose. And Coleridge was never in the least degree mad.

Yet he ought to have shown poetic precocity. Few poets are geniuses to their schoolfellows. Shelley was not, Keats was not, Wordsworth was not. But his schoolmates at Christ's Hospital swore by the genius of the "inspired charity-boy." He was a genius even to the terrible Bowyer, his master, who assailed his poetry with "Muse, boy, Muse? Your nurse's daughter, you mean!" It *was* the nurse's daughter, and he addressed her in this wise: —

> Maid of my love, sweet Genevieve,
>   In beauty's light you glide along;
> Your eye is like the star of eve,
>   And sweet your voice as seraph's song.
> Yet not your heavenly beauty gives
>   This heart with passion soft to glow:
> Within your soul a voice there lives,
>   It bids you hear the tale of woe.
> When, sinking low, the sufferer wan
>   Beholds no hand outstretched to save,
> Fair as the bosom of the swan
>   That rises graceful o'er the wave,
> I've seen your breast with pity heave,
>   And *therefore* love I you, sweet Genevieve!

Very pretty for a lad of fifteen, and in its soft melody curiously characteristic of the mature Coleridge who wrote that later and most lovely "Genevieve" — if it was not retouched in after-years, of which we have villainous doubts, knowing his ways. His school-fellows would swear to his being a poet: yet after he left school, though he was in love more than once, and had one bitter disappointment in love, neither love nor loss of love produced anything so good even as this poem. He assiduously poured out floods of rather stilted and quite mediocre verse; and though the influence of the Rev. Mr. Bowles's clergymanly muse simplified his style, it gave him no spark of the "right madness." Which is not surprising. Yet his friends continued to believe in — nay, admire — his poetry. It is a proof of what eighteenth-century poetry had come to.

Wordsworth taught him to be a poet. That is quite certain. Even in such a poem as "The Æolian Harp," the one quite fine passage was added after his encounter with Wordsworth. It was a chemical interaction between the two poets. Both wrote far better after the meeting than they had ever done before it. Wordsworth received from Coleridge his philosophic mysticism, or mystical philosophy, which became the very basis of the northern poet's verse: he gave to Coleridge the very stuff of poetry. For a time, indeed, Coleridge's manner bore the stamp of Wordsworth. Besides the four great poems, and the one or two later poems usually quoted, there is more really fine work among Coleridge's lesser poetry than is generally recognised (though, be it admitted, little enough absolutely). But it has the Wordsworthian manner so perfectly that it might well pass among Wordsworth's best work. Such is the admirable "Frost at Midnight," but that is pretty well known. Quite unknown, however, is the inserted passage of "The Æolian Harp," to which we have already referred. The preceding passage, belonging to the pre-Wordsworthian days, leads up to it excellently.

> How, by the desultory breeze caressed,
> Like some coy maid half-yielding to her lover,
> It pours such sweet upbraiding as must needs
> Tempt to repeat the wrong! And now, its strings
> Boldlier swept, the long sequacious notes
> Over delicious surges sink and rise,
> Such a soft floating witchery of sound

> As twilight Elfins make, when they at eve
> Voyage on gentle gales from Fairy-Land,
> Where Melodies round honey-dropping flowers,
> Footless and wild, like birds of Paradise,
> Nor pause, nor perch, hovering on untamed wing!

That is charming; but what follows is "of a higher mood":

> O the one life within us and abroad;
> Which meets all motion and becomes its soul,
> A light in sound, a sound-like power in light,
> Rhythm in all thought, and joyance everywhere—
> Methinks, it should have been impossible
> Not to love all things in a world so filled;
> Where the breeze warbles, and the mute still air
> Is Music slumbering on her instrument.

Is it not very Wordsworth? The metre itself changes from the soft Coleridgian to the grave Wordsworthian movement. The final image, "beautiful exceedingly," alone is pure Coleridge; the rest is very noble Wordsworth. All Wordsworth, too, is the poem written after hearing Wordsworth read his "Prelude," an echo of that poem itself. But who can care from whom it is derived, being the austere and lofty thing it is? When you have such things as the reference to the French Revolution —

> When France in all her towns lay vibrating
> Like some becalmèd bark beneath the burst
> Of Heaven's immediate thunder, when no cloud
> Is visible, or shadow on the main.

Or the description of the "Prelude" as —

>   an Orphic song indeed,
> A song divine of high and passionate thoughts
> To their own music chanted!

Then, most personal and pathetic, the cry of regret over his own shattered powers:

> Ah! as I listened with a heart forlorn,
> The pulses of my being beat anew:
> And even as life returns upon the drowned,
> Life's joy rekindling roused a throng of pains—
> Keen pangs of Love, awakening as a babe
> Turbulent, with an outcry in the heart;
> And fears self-willed, that shunned the eye of hope;
> And hope that scarce would know itself from fear;
> Sense of past youth, and manhood come in vain,
> And genius given, and knowledge won in vain;
> And all which I had culled in wood-walks wild,
> And all which patient toil had reared, and all
> Commune with thee had opened out—but flowers
> Strewed on my corse, and borne upon my bier,
> In the same coffin, for the self-same grave!

It was a lament, and a prophecy. All, indeed, was doomed to wasteful ruin. Of the consummate and uniquely individual Coleridge — of the "Ancient Mariner," "Christabel," "Kubla Khan," "Genevieve," — what should we speak? It is too late a day. These things are an unparalleled union of music and verbal magic, wherein it is hard to say whether sense or sound be the more enchanted and enchanting. Were "Kubla Khan" (for instance) mere nonsense-verse, it would still be enthralling poetry by the power of the sound alone. Even into casual and unnoted lyrics the spillings of this gift overflow; as in the trifle from "Zapolya":

> A sunny shaft did I behold,
>   From sky to earth it slanted;
> And poised therein a bird so bold—
>   Sweet bird, thou wert enchanted!
> He sank, he rose, he twinkled, he trolled,
>   Within that shaft of sunny mist;
> His eyes of fire, his beak of gold,
>   All else of amethyst!

The melody catches you; yet what is in it? Or what sense can you attach to the lark's song? On the whole, this was surely the mightiest genius since Milton. In poetry there is not his like, when he rose to his full power; he was a philosopher the immensity of whose mind cannot be gauged by anything he has left behind; a critic the subtlest and most profound of his time. Yet these vast and varied powers flowed away in the shifting sands of talk; and what remains is but what the few landlocked pools are to the receding ocean which has left them casually behind without sensible diminution of its waters. It is the saddest and costliest wreck in literary annals; an argosy of priceless freight gone down with all its treasure, save a little flotsam which is more treasurable than most vessels' whole lading.

WORDSWORTH AS PROSE WRITER*

[*Academy*, April 10, 1897]

This review is an interesting though limited expression of Thompson's ideas on Wordsworth as a prose writer. "The Prose of Poets," a subject which interested him greatly, inspired his well-known essays contributed to the *Academy* and included by Wilfrid Meynell in his volume of the poet's prose. Strangely, Wordsworth is not among the poets treated, and so this review, which illustrates Thompson's grasp of all that had previously been written about this phase of Wordsworth's work, is of special interest. Of interest, too, in view of the subsequent development of Free Verse, are Thompson's observations on De Quincey's tendency to efface the formal barrier that separates prose from poetry. In this and in other matters of prose style, the contrast drawn between Wordsworth and De Quincey is most apt.

UNTIL Dr. Grosart published his edition, in 1876, the public hardly realised that Wordsworth had left a sufficient body of prose to be described by the title of "Works." Dr. Grosart's edition included not only the poet's letters, but those of his sister Dorothy. Mr. Knight has (we think wisely) reserved the letters for subsequent publication, and confined these two volumes to what might be regarded as independent and detachable prose. A few pieces which are ostensibly letters find place in these volumes. But they are really essays cast in epistolary form; and Mr. Knight has shown

* *The Prose Works of William Wordsworth*. Edited by William Knight.

correct judgment in detaching them from the letters proper. He objects, justly enough, to Dr. Grosart's assigning of titles to some pieces which were not the poet's own, and to his inclusion of a letter by Prof. Wilson, without due notice in the body of the text that it was not by Wordsworth, but was only published to elucidate Wordsworth's answering letter. These minor errors are corrected in Mr. Knight's edition, which, moreover, contains prose writings of the poet not given by Dr. Grosart. This constitutes its independent value. For the rest, Mr. Knight confesses that some of the pieces (such as the "Letter to the Bishop of Landaff") are simply reprinted from Dr. Grosart. In the interval between the two editions, the MSS. from which Dr. Grosart drew have disappeared; so that to Dr. Grosart belongs the credit of having rescued from oblivion what, but for his timely enterprise, would have been lost to us. But there can be no doubt that Mr. Knight's additions and amendments make this edition an advance upon its predecessor.

These writings are very miscellaneous. They include, for example, a "Guide to the Lake District," the most unconventional guide-book ever published. It is full of valuable information about the Lake District in Wordsworth's time, conveyed in a characteristically Wordsworthian, but by no means popular, manner. There are observations of incidental, but far from transitory, interest. But the best-written part of it, to our mind, is a journal of a tour through some part of the Lake country, which the editor, in a footnote, ascribes to Dorothy Wordsworth. It is observant, sensitive, at once clear, pictorial, and restrained in its style; but when Mr. Knight says that it was written by Dorothy he can hardly mean more than that Dorothy was the amanuensis employed by her brother. At any rate, one finds such an expression as "when I was a boy." It would have been better if the editor had explained himself more clearly in this and one or two other footnotes. The journal reads very unlike any woman's writing; and we cannot but suppose that Mr. Knight has been loose in his statement. In fact, the writing harmonises absolutely with the descriptive portions of the rest of the "Guide," and leaves an impression that Wordsworth was an admirable master of that manner of prose description which is contented with the just and sufficient epithet, without aiming at the magical epithet. This is characteristic of all Wordsworth's prose. Our own day has seen the rise of a school which in some degree effaces the formal barriers between poetry and prose; which endeavours not only after the right, but the thrillingly right word. It may be said that a contemporary and friend of Wordsworth commenced this innovation — namely De Quincey; but Wordsworth's own writing rigidly observes the distinction between prose and poetry.

Poets, it has been said, are always good prose writers. From this rule it has been the fashion to except Wordsworth; and if there be any prose writing of Wordsworth's, which all critics and editors (until late years) described as dull and undistinguished, that writing was emphatically the pamphlet on the *Convention of Cintra* — which, thanks to some muddle between De Quincey (who saw it through the press), Wordsworth, and a third person commissioned by Wordsworth with a special revision, appeared too late, and fell utterly flat. Mr. Knight, being a Wordsworthian, of course considers the *Convention of Cintra* a masterpiece, and appeals to the authority of Rogers, the banker who once passed for a poet. The truth is, that it has some really magnificent passages, full of a grave and lofty passion unmatched in Wordsworth's prose, though easily to be paralleled in his poetry. Manifestly, in this effusion, he took for models such seventeenth-century writers as Hooker, whom Mr. Ruskin also followed in *Modern Painters*. There is the same length and involution of sentence which we find in that early work of Ruskin; but there the resemblance ends. The austere Wordsworthian mind will admit no flowers of beauty; and the sentence-structure is managed with far inferior skill. It is cumbrous, unwieldy, elephantine: it has no power, like De Quincey's equally periodic style, of accommodating itself to the variations of its subject-matter. But when the subject-matter comes into harmony with *it*, when, with puffing and snorting, the ponderous organism has got itself into motion with a clear course before it, then, indeed, we have fine and sustained examples of antique and virile eloquence. Space will not serve for extracts, or we would gladly make them. But, when all is said, the most permanent value of Wordsworth's prose lies in the essays — prefatory or supplementary — which accompanied his poems, and are here brought together. His prose-style is rootedly abstract, and therefore shows at its worst in dealing with concrete subjects. But in philosophic criticism of poetic principles its austere abstraction becomes not only justified, but meritorious. In spite of the excessive and one-sided theories about "poetic diction," at which even Coleridge smiled, these essays are full of most original and invaluable statement of principles which can never be obsolete, in language which cleaves to its subject-matter like gold-leaf.

> Read all the prefaces of Dryden,
> For them the critics much confide in,

said Byron. Whatever may be the confidence of critics, we say much more unhesitatingly, "Read all the prefaces of Wordsworth." They are stimulating, suggestive, concisely put: if you can think for yourself, they will help you to think.

KNIGHT'S "WORDSWORTH"*

[*Academy*, September 4, 1897]

Thompson's strictures on the failure of Wordsworth's poems to make an organic whole suggest a contrast, on this score, between his own poems and Wordsworth's. Thompson enthusiasts who would publish all that the poet has written will find food for thought in his remarks about the doubtful wisdom of modern editors "in reviewing trivialities which the poet himself destined to oblivion."

WITH this volume Mr. Knight brings to a close his elaborate and most complete edition of Wordsworth's poems. One admirable feature of this edition is that Wordsworth's fanciful and baffling arrangement of his poems under certain headings — such as "Poems

---

* *The Poetical Works of William Wordsworth*. Vol. VIII. Edited by William Knight.

of Sentiment and Reflection," "Poems of Fancy," "Poems of Imagination," &c., is departed from. Wordsworth, being above all things systematic and philosophical, was desirous to give a kind of symmetrical air to his poems; to make them appear an organic whole, arranged upon certain systematised lines. But, in fact, this was untrue, artificial. He was the most occasional of poets — apart from his great, but abortive, poem, "The Recluse," of which the "Prelude" and the "Excursion" were portions. His poems were composed (to their great advantage) as occasion prompted; and it was an afterthought to gather them into certain categories, and make them appear parts of an organic whole. Their only unity is that of temperament and temperamental development. Accordingly Prof. Knight has done a valuable work in reducing them to chronological order; so that we are enabled to study the development — and the decline — of a great poet. His sole departure from this arrangement is in the case of two poems. It is a departure suggested — as he tells us — by Mr. Aubrey de Vere; and we owe a debt to Mr. de Vere for the suggestion. In the first place, the great "Ode on Intimations of Immortality" is placed at the end of Wordsworth's latest work, as being the crown, both poetically and philosophically, of the poet's achievement. In the second place, Wordsworth's sole Laureate Ode is remitted to the appendix, on the ground that evidence shows it to have been the work of Edward Quillinan — at the most, touched by Wordsworth. It needs no external evidence for the fact to any understander of poetry. The ode is not the work of a poet at all — least of all Wordsworth. The abominable mockery of metre, the academic diction — half a century behind that of Wordsworth — sufficiently show that the austere poet never could have written it. With these exceptions, we have Wordsworth's poems in the order in which they were written; which is the most useful order, except where a poet has really given organic unity to a series of poems. No one would dream, for example, of resolving Rossetti's "House of Life" into chronological order. But, generally speaking, Wordsworth's were absolutely poems of occasion; and the chronological order is an immense gain. It enables us to study accurately the poet's development and decline; which is always in itself a gain, though some poets forbid it by the excellent judgment with which they have arranged their poems in vital and organic connexion.

This volume divides itself into two sections. Firstly (with the exception of the great ode), the poems of Wordsworth's later years; secondly, very early poems, and poems recovered from various sources, which Wordsworth did not include in his published works — for the most part justly. This inevitably implies that there are few treasurable things in this last volume. It shows, only too clearly, that Wordsworth, like Tennyson, in his later years declined. Nay, he declined much worse than Tennyson; for Tennyson was a careful external artist, and was able to maintain a certain level of workmanship even when his inspiration had fled from him. Whereas Wordsworth had not a particle of external art: at his best period, there was an extraordinary intermixture of superb felicity and prosy twaddle. When, owing to declining strength, his inspiration forsook him, he became altogether a vendor of goody-goody twaddle: most unimpeachably virtuous, most unendurably long-winded and commonplace. And the less of a poet he grew, the more appalling was his "he-that-heareth-not-the-prophets" air. Never was a poet more absolutely dependent on inspiration, less capable of working-up uninspired passages by means of art, so as to make them appear not unworthy companions of the inspired passages. So that he is either unapproachable or unendurable; and very often both in the compass of twenty lines. When it comes to his final period, he is "most tolerable and not to be endured." Unfortunately, this is precisely the Wordsworth that Wordsworthian poets too often imitate; because it needs no inspiration to imitate him. And it is also the Wordsworth that Wordsworthian readers too often admire; because it needs no deep poetic sense to admire him. Such readers will find in this last volume of Prof. Knight an abundant treasury. The few who love the inspired Wordsworth will be very tired over it. Nor is the second section, consisting of Wordsworthian treasure-trove from many sources, likely to recompense them. Almost the only exception is "Home at Grasmere," and another fragment, both connected with the unexecuted "Recluse." "Home at Grasmere," in particular, has many fine passages, though it is very unequal. But what shall we say of the "Sonnet on Seeing Miss Helen Maria Williams Weep at a Tale of Distress," and similar very early poems? Simply that they show how very badly Wordsworth could write in his youth. And yet it has one good idea in it, which anticipates the sonnet of Blanco White. But then the idea had already been anticipated by Sir Thomas Browne, and another writer of about the same period. Really, the most valuable of these gleanings belongs not to Wordsworth at all. It is a poem of Coleridge's, addressed to Wordsworth under the title of "Axiologus," and preserved by Mr. Dykes Campbell. Prof. Knight is careful to say that he does not know the source from which Mr. Dykes Campbell got it. But the internal evidence is abundantly sufficient. It is in hexameters; and Coleridge was fond of such experiments. There is an acknowledged poem of his to Wordsworth in hexameters. Above all, the ideas are such as could only belong to Coleridge; particularly the conclusion, with its depth of mystical philosophy (if we may use such a term). Here it is:

> This is the word of the Lord! it is spoken, and Beings Eternal
> Live and are born as an infant, the Eternal begets the Immortal—
> Love is the Spirit of Life, and Music the Life of the Spirit!

"Music," be it observed, here signifies poetry in general — song — as well as music technically so called. It is Coleridge beyond all possibility of mistake; and the last line is as deep an utterance as Coleridge ever gave vent to.

This reminds us that, in the first section, the poem "On the Death of James Hogg," for the most part poor and prosaic, contains a few not unworthy lines upon the death of Coleridge:

> Nor has the rolling year twice measured,
> From sign to sign, its steadfast course,
> Since every mortal power of Coleridge
> Was frozen at its marvellous source.
>
> The rapt One, of the godlike forehead,
> The heaven-eyed creature, sleeps in earth.

It is pleasant to read this tribute, since Wordsworth's egotism, his inability to forgive a censure, brought about a rupture with Coleridge, which lasted to the day of that weak and unfortunate poet's death. When it was too late, even the self-centred Wordsworth remembered the early days which he had better have remembered before. Alas, with how many is that the case! If we bestowed upon our friend while it could benefit him the love and regret we pour out over his grave!

In conclusion, this is an edition of Wordsworth which can never be superseded. To our mind, it errs with all modern editions in reviving trivialities which the poet himself destined to oblivion. Useless in all cases, it is peculiarly mistaken in the case of Wordsworth, who himself perpetuated too much which he should have let die. What even Wordsworth thought unsuccessful, why should any editor resuscitate? But since such is the fashion, we can only say that Prof. Knight has followed it with entire completeness. If a definitive edition must include everything which ever fell from a poet's pen, this edition is indeed definitive. And Mr. Knight's notes give every information which could be desired. It is, what Mr. Aubrey de Vere calls it in his letter to Prof. Knight, "a monumental edition."

THE VICTORIAN AGE

SOBER AND SUBSTANTIAL*
[*Academy*, January 13, 1900]

MATTHEW ARNOLD

This is one of the sprightliest of Thompson's reviews. Wisely, he does not attempt to touch upon all of Harrison's literary estimates. He centers his attention upon Matthew Arnold, after a bow to the vanishing Positivists, and gives us one of his best brief appraisals of Arnold's literary performance. It explains with finality why Thompson's work was, as he said, "in sharpest contrast with Arnold's." But it reveals a knowledge of Arnold's poetry inconsistent with Thompson's statement ten years earlier: "I have studied no poet less."

M R. FREDERIC HARRISON is a man of versatile gift, as we are aware. For years his pen has touched, in the principal reviews, various themes of the day; and his scope has not been limited, while he has always shown himself an accomplished gladiator. But it is as an intellectual gladiator that we chiefly think of him, and as the gladiator of a special cause. He stands to us for the high priest and protagonist of Positivism. Instinctively, at the sound of his name, there leaps to our memory that deft pasquinade — do the younger generation know it? — of Mortimer Collins:

> Churches and creeds are all lost in the mists,
> Truth must be sought with the Positivists.
>
> Wise are their teachers beyond all comparison,
> Comte, Huxley, Tindall, Mill, Morley, and Harrison;
> Who will adventure to enter the lists
> With such a squadron of Positivists?

The squadron, alas! is scattered; *viscerunt*. No longer, in compact ranks, do they ride the fields of literature, and bear down all before

* *Tennyson, Ruskin, Mill and Other Literary Estimates*. By Frederic Harrison.

them, as (Comte excepted) they did in the earlier times of the century. Mr. John Morley and Mr. Frederic Harrison alone survive to witness a reaction against the principles they valiantly championed, and which they still unfaintingly maintain. But it is not Mr. Harrison the gladiator who now, in this volume, confronts us. He enters the silken lists of pure literature, controversy (save incidentally) laid aside. Unarmed and pacific, he casts a backward eye upon some of the principal writers who have been his contemporaries, whom he has known in the campaigns of literature. These essays, consequently, cover no small part of the great figures in Victorian letters; and such, he tells us, was the deliberate plan of his book.

Mr. Harrison has very considerable equipment for such a task. His style is always cultivated, equable, lucid, and graceful; though it cannot claim the distinct and individualising stamp which is the token of genius. He has a tolerant appreciation of multifarious excellence; and his taste only falls short of the last and keenest edge with regard to verse. But it does so fall a little short; and also (which is well-nigh an inevitable limitation) his appreciation is confined mainly to the writers of his own youth and prime. Beyond these there is a level line of silence — not the less felt for being mostly inexplicit, *merely* indicated by reticence. In a book which covers (through successive essays) Tennyson, Ruskin, Arnold, Symonds, Lamb, Keats, Gibbon, Froude, Freeman, and John Stuart Mill, the writer can scarce narrow himself entirely to pure literary criticism. The man must show at intervals through the critic; not only his idiosyncracy, but his general views, his prejudices, his personal attitude towards life and life's problems. Therefore, as we have hinted, the veteran of Positivism emerges now and again: we are not suffered to forget under what banner Mr. Harrison fights; and the reader, after his several kind, must allow for the critic's peculiar views. For the most part, however, these are expressed with courtesy, if also at times with energy; they are offensive only in the martial sense. It is exceptional to encounter (in the fine essay on "Ruskin as Prophet") a fleer at "tender mothers adoring the divine judgment which consigns their children to hell-fire" — exceptional, and we note it with regret. Such an utterance is in hopelessly bad taste, not merely because it is crass, perverse, and unfair — a hit below the belt — but because it is calculated wantonly to wound the deepest feelings of multitudes among Mr. Harrison's fellow-citizens; and especially of the tenderest class. It is as if he had buffeted a woman. So cheap a sneer might be left to the scurrilous rank of controversialists; it is not worthy of Mr. Harrison — let us trust he will see fit to suppress or modify it. But because of its rarity we note it: Mr. Harrison is not given to hit below the belt.

Not in vain has he studied his favourite master in criticism, Matthew Arnold, whose balance and sanity he conscientiously strives to imitate. Dealing with so various a range of writers, he holds a level balance in regard to all; no easy feat, requiring a judiciality combined with catholicism of taste, not in these hasty days too common. In detail we may, and do, freely dissent from him; but there is seldom much fault to be found with the broad scope and trend of his judgment. This is high praise of essays which compass so large a field. Yet with all their merits they do not rank Mr. Harrison among the illuminative critics; there are neither flashes nor broad lights of insight, bringing to sudden view unsuspected aspects, dark recesses in the great authors analysed. We do not feel as we rise from our reading that we know substantially more of them than we did. The best which is held in solution by the better criticism of our day has been precipitated and presented to us in crystalline form; our most truthful previous impressions are pleasantly confirmed and interpreted to us; but beyond sifting and discrimination these polished essays hardly go. The best of them is perhaps the elaborate study of Ruskin, which runs through three successive essays; it is eloquent, it is enthusiastic — as in these reactionary days a study of Ruskin ought to be; it analyses his prose with understanding love; it defends his greatness as teacher with selective sense of his limits, weaknesses, perfervid extravagances, and appreciation of his power more generous than could be surmised from a rival apostle, professedly out of touch with many of Ruskin's most basic beliefs. But there is like fair-minded justice, if (on account of the subject-matter) less eloquently set forth, in the studies of those two most opposite and antagonistic historians, Froude and Freeman, in the perhaps too genially balanced notice of Addington Symonds.

Perhaps, however, we may study Mr. Harrison's defects and qualities in representative equipoise by considering the essay on Arnold. After some remarks on Arnold's admitted felicity as a *phraseur*, he proceeds to discuss his poetry, with the disputable opinion that in poetry he reached his finest vein, and by it will be longest remembered. To this succeeds the assertion that no poet in our literature, unless it be Milton, "has been so essentially saturated to the very bone with the classical genius." Much depends on the interpretation of this sentence, and one must confine it to the poets of Mr. Harrison's own prime. His remarks on the sense in which Arnold is classical — "the serene self-command, the harmony of tone, the measured fitness, the sweet reasonableness of his verse" — would need for their due discussion an essay on what is permanent, essential, universal in Greek poetry, apart from what is local, external, and externally imitable. Mr. Harrison thinks that the full acceptance of Arnold's poetry has yet to come — which we may seriously doubt, calculated as its appeal was for his special time. That Arnold's equableness is attained at the expense of height and passion Mr. Harrison perceives. Arnold is, he says, peculiarly a *gnomic* poet, a moralist on life and conduct. He credits him with seeing into the intellectual world of our age "more deeply and more surely than any contemporary poet." If this somewhat inexplicit sentence means that Arnold reproduced the tone of thought common to the cultured circles of his day, it is true. That is just what he did. But we cannot extend it further. "A resolute and pensive insight into the mystery of life and of things" we cannot discern in him, but rather a resigned pausing at the gates of the mystery. The ethical lesson of nature preoccupies him when he is not dealing directly with human conduct Mr. Harrison recognises. It is no loss to Mr. Harrison — though it is to us — that Arnold, unlike his beloved preceptor, Wordsworth, halts at the ethical lesson of nature, is insensitive to the spirit within and behind nature which was the solemnly convinced burthen of Wordsworth's song.

To this "concentration of poetry on ethics, and even

metaphysics," Mr. Harrison attributes Arnold's limitations and
"loss of charm." Yet, at the same time, he says that Arnold, unlike
Wordsworth, is "never prosaic." Here it is that we find that falling
short of the keenest poetic sense which we have attributed to
Mr. Harrison. Arnold, unfortunately, is too often prosaic — for
line after line, passage after passage. Perhaps, as a subsequent portion of the essay would suggest, Mr. Harrison is not insensible
to this; and we should take him to mean that Arnold is never *prosy*.
That is the exact truth; he is too much an artificer to *prose* like
Wordsworth, but prosaic he is frequently, to a level extent — that
is to say, his language is the language of very fine and distinguished
prose. Even when he rises higher, he too often hovers on the
doubtful border where we hesitate to pronounce it poetry, are
loath to pronounce it prose. And though it is true that the greatest
poets are seldom directly didactic, it is not this which depresses
Arnold; it is the lack of inspiration to give wings to his thought.
The greater the burthen of intellectuality, the more of sheer
inspiration is necessary.

"Dramatic passion," "tumultuous passion" — not these, as Mr.
Harrison regretfully supposes, does Arnold need. Wordsworth
had them not, and yet soared into regions of which Arnold but
desirously dreams. It is inspiring emotion, the solemn passion,
intense in its still ardour, appropriate to intellectual poetry, which
Arnold needs. It is really passion of the intensest order, deceptively
calm through its equipoise with the weight of thought. The calm
which results from the careful husbanding of effort may imitate it
with the multitude, but can never deceive the elect. In the main,
Arnold reaches only this latter calm; and that Mr. Harrison should
identify it with that inspired tranquillity and impassioned peace
of Wordsworth (at his highest), the supreme Greek poets, and
Dante, shows that Mr. Harrison — as we say — has not the keenest
edge of poetic sensitiveness.

That is why Mr. Harrison feels that Arnold, though faultless, is
"not of the highest rank." It is a misnomer, in fact, to call such
poets "faultless," whether it be Racine or Arnold, when in line
after line there is the blot of absent inspiration, when there is not
the only possible word in the only possible place. The greatest

of all faults in a poet is to lack poetry, and that is theirs. At the same time Mr. Harrison does not, perhaps, lay sufficient stress upon Arnold's occasional success in touching the mark at which he aimed. The austere and noble sonnet on Shakespeare, with other brief achievements of the kind, are worth more than long poems full of fine thought, but only now and again inevitable in expression. For they are integral; and it is that quality which makes for permanence. Mr. Harrison (in this influenced by Arnold himself) is too apt to set store by detached lines and passages, which poets of no high power can often forge in tolerable quantity, to the great comfort of reviewers who pant for "quotes." He ignores too much the supreme value of relation and organism. Thus he depreciates, justly enough, the quality of Arnold's metre; but the reason he alleges is quite unconvincing and inadequate — namely, that Arnold has lines containing harsh collocations of consonants. The same could be alleged against Shakespeare, could be — and has been — alleged against Milton. Lowell rightly replies that metre may aim either at melody or harmony; that while the former demands smoothness, the larger music of harmony not only admits but makes use of occasional roughnesses, as discords have their function in the harmonies of music proper. To cite these individual lines of Arnold's, disjoined from their relation, proves nothing. Yet Mr. Harrison is right in his judgment, though defective in his reason: Arnold was lacking in metrical power, though he could strike out fine imitative music in occasional passages.

When we leave details, and attend to Mr. Harrison's summing-up, we find, indeed, that he is mainly right, and that our objections have caught largely on side-issues.

By temperament and by training he, who at birth "was breathed on by the rural Pan," was deprived of that fountain of delight that is essential to the highest poetry, the dithyrambic glow — the ἀνήριθμον γέλασμα —

'The countless dimples of the laughing seas'

of perennial poetry. This, perhaps, more than his want of passion, of dramatic power, of rapidity of action, limits the audience of Arnold as a poet. But those who thirst for the pure Castalian spring, inspired by restrained and lofty thoughts, who care for that high seriousness of which he spoke so much as the very essence of the best poetry, have long known that they find it in Matthew Arnold more than in any of his even greater contemporaries.

That is a good specimen of Mr. Frederic Harrison's style, and it states the case for Arnold as a poet with a discrimination which leaves little to desire. Partly, indeed, it agrees with our own criticism of Mr. Harrison's criticism, or so nearly that the difference seems to become inconspicuous. And this excellently exemplifies the studiousness of balance which characterises Mr. Harrison's appreciations. Not once nor twice does he thus in his summary disarm the reviewer, and leave him half-apologetic for differences which are finally made so small. What may in the body of the essay have erred by overemphasis or omission is here usually rectified and supplied. His picture of Arnold altogether (though he gives less space than we could desire to the prose) is urbane, sympathetic, and observant of poise. If we doubt his forecast of an extended future for Arnold, it is because we think his aloofness from the many is due to more than his mere distinction and those other fastidious causes set forth by Mr. Harrison. Arnold as a teacher was pre-eminently undecided (to use an adjective thrown out by Mr. Harrison himself). A teacher of delicate incertitude, a watchman who has no word of the night, a prophet who disclaims prophecy, and

> Whose only message is that he sees nought,

is never likely to have acceptance with the many who still, as of old, ask for a sign. And even among the few his cultivated stoicism and half-complaisant, half-melancholy indecision is scarce likely to be the fashion of the future. Even the cultured and sovereign few now begin to cry for a gospel and a hand from the cloud. But that constant reference to conduct, which Mr. Harrison rightly adjudges his dominant note, will doubtless secure to him long his measure of influence with the practical Saxon mind. His spirit has done a worthy posthumous work in prompting the eminent sanity of Mr. Harrison's extremely able, though not strongly original book.

OF RALEIGH'S BREED *

[*Academy*, September 10, 1898]

This review is of equal value for its flawless evaluation of Blunt's poetic achievement, and its devastating challenge of Henley's professed fondness of "Art for Art's Sake." There is an association-interest here, as well, since Blunt was Thompson's well-meaning but scarcely successful host during those last days in Sussex just before the end.

WHEN Mr. Henley sat down to preface the excellently chosen and representative selection which Mr. George Wyndham and himself have made from the poems of Mr. Wilfrid Blunt, he had congenial work on hand. "Let us leave a saint to write the life of a saint," said Aquinas, quitting the cell where St. Bonaventure was at work on the biography of the great Assisian. "Let us leave a poet-fighter to praise the work of a poet-fighter," Mr. Wyndham might have said when he resigned to his colleague the task of penning this preface. Dissimilar enough in all other poetic qualities, Mr. Henley and Mr. Blunt are one in abounding virility, in love of the objective things of life. One wholly a writer, the other a man of the most various pursuits and energies, they are alike in this, that they have both been stout and stark fighters of the grim battle of life. Yes, Mr. Henley was the right man to appreciate the poetry of Mr. Wilfrid Blunt. Yet, in his uncompromising championship of his author, Mr. Henley has approved himself a "swallower of formulas" more doughty than any of Carlyle's heroes. The hardest of all formulas for a man to swallow are his own. Who knows not that Mr. Henley worships the formula of "Art for Art's Sake"? How long has he not taught us that the substance is nothing, the form everything; that the sublimest teaching, if the utterance be peccable, is not worth one impeccable stanza or so to a dancer's eyelash? We have heard, and bowed: for "all these things are so" — however we may quarrel with the principle which he would educe from them. But now it seems that the substance ceases to be unimportant, and acquires something like self-justification, when it is the substance which

* *The Poetry of Wilfrid Blunt*. Selected and Arranged by W. E. Henley and George Wyndham.

Mr. Henley loves — the expression of life in its activities, its external energies. Either he must slacken the bit of his dogma or bear hard on Mr. Wilfrid Blunt. Thus put to it, Mr. Henley makes a wry face, and with an audible gulp very frankly swallows his formula. We have never held the formula, therefore need not swallow it. But the importance of form we do hold, and in due place shall show how far it causes us to differ from Mr. Henley in our estimate of Mr. Blunt.

Mr. Wilfrid Blunt would possess a singular interest for one reason alone, were there no other, in that he represents a class once among the conspicuous glories of England, but now grown so regrettably rare as well-nigh to be extinct — the class of men of action who are also men of letters. Once the energies of the race so abounded and superabounded that statesmen, warriors, restless searchers for adventure on every land and sea, could spend the mere overflow of their redundant fire in poetry or prose, and the things thus casually done availed to a separate immortality, a twofold name. The great Elizabethan Age rings with the names of such. Raleigh is perhaps their chiefest type; but Sidney disputes with him the palm, greater in literature though less great in act; and on their heels come Oxford and a band of gallant courtier singers — later, Montrose, Lovelace, and the "Cavalier poets." A yet later day had Shaftesbury, Bolingbroke, Halifax, and others. In our own day we have had Beaconsfield; but the breed seems now effete. It is no longer the fashion for a young gallant to be a well-graced man of letters: it is much if he can hold his own in public life. The energies of our higher classes seem extinct; we have come to the day of "young barbarians," and the middle-class runs either to an unlettered plutocracy or to professional journalism. We can no longer live the dual life. A few there are, like Mr. George Wyndham himself, Mr. Curzon, or Mr. Wilfrid Blunt.

Mr. Blunt has been an English squire, a politician, and a traveller in many lands; he has seen the inside of diplomacy and Parliament; he has bred Arab horses, lived with Arabs, and set up his tents as an Arab and nomad himself; he has fought for unpopular causes, and braved the wrath of his countrymen as a champion of Home Rule and Arabi Pasha, the cause of Ireland and the cause of Egypt.

Thereto he has also written poetry, full of the fire and energy which he has displayed in his life. When such a man writes poetry, it is easy to be understood that it will breathe those qualities of actuality and brave masculinity which Mr. Henley loves, and which should be loved by the many, were poetry any longer read by the many. Emphatically, whatever shortcomings his verse may possess, it breathes. Its material has been wrought for, suffered for, lived for; it has pulse and blood. The best of his work is that which first made him known, the *Love-Sonnets of Proteus*. They are personal and quick with passion. The sonnet with its necessitous condensation suits him. When he writes free from bonds he tends to diffuseness, to an over-lavish outpour of himself. But within this curb he moves masterfully, and proves what the greatest poets have proved before him — that the sonnet, far from being the languidly elegant trifling it becomes in ordinary hands, is an altogether strong and masculine form, the very medium for pregnant force. The skill with which he handles it is the more striking because he does not use the pure form. His favourite form is a kind of compromise between the Shakespearean and Petrarchan model, sure of failure in other hands. Yet he contrives to attain more of the dignified Shakespearean ring than any writer we know. He is, further, fond of an occasional redundant sonnet, reaching to sixteen or eighteen lines. We refuse, indeed, to call it a sonnet; but in his hands it is, at any rate, skilful and musically moulded verse. Take this as a specimen of his impassioned vein:

> I love not thy perfections. When I hear
> Thy beauty blazoned, and the common tongue
> Cheapening with vulgar praise a lip, an ear,
> A cheek that I have prayed to;—when among
> The loud world's gods my god is noised and sung,
> Her wit applauded, even her taste, her dress,
> Her each dear hidden marvel lightly flung
> At the world's feet and stripped to nakedness—
> Then I despise thy beauty utterly,
> Crying, "Be these your gods, O Israel!"
> And I remember that on such a day
> I found thee with eyes bleared and cheeks all pale,
> And lips that trembled to a voiceless cry,
> And that thy bosom in my bosom lay.

That is fine. And the same quality of condensation which gives power and dignity to its passion appears in the forcibleness of his descriptive sonnets — though he is little given to mere description. The desert has never been described as in the following lines. Each image has the white-hot distinctness of the glaring desert's own detail:

> How the earth burns! Each pebble underfoot
> Is as a living thing with power to wound.
> The white sand quivers, and the footfall mute
> Of the slow camel strikes but gives no sound,
> As though they walked on flame, not solid ground.
> 'Tis noon, and the beasts' shadows even have fled
> Back to their feet, and there is fire around
> And fire beneath, and overhead the sun.

Lastly, to complete the range of his power in this, his most successful form of verse, take the following sonnet, "To the Bedouin Arabs":

> Children of Shem! Firstborn of Noah's race,
> But still for ever children; at the door
> Of Eden found, unconscious of disgrace,
> And loitering on while all are gone before;
> Too proud to dig; too careless to be poor;
> Taking the gifts of God in thanklessness,
> Not rendering aught, nor supplicating more,
> Nor arguing with Him when He hides His face:
> Yours is the rain and sunshine, and the way
> Of an old wisdom by our world forgot,
> The courage of a day which knew not death.
> Well may we sons of Japhet in dismay
> Pause in our vain mad fight for life and breath,
> Beholding you. I bow and reason not.

That is monumental; in its gravely carven kind as fine a sonnet as we know.

Of Mr. Blunt's power outside the sonnet there is a beautiful specimen in the lines called "On the Way to Church." Here he has curbed his tendency to overflow when not confined by set limits, and the poem has a tender restraint entirely fitting the theme. We will quote the opening portion describing the woman:

There is one I know. I see her sometimes pass
In the morning streets upon her way to Mass,
A calm, sweet woman with unearthly eyes.
Men turn to look at her, but never stop;
Reading in those blue eyes the death of hope,
And a wise chastisement for thoughts unwise.

Pure is her brow as of a marble Saint,
Her brown hair pencils it with ripples faint,
There is no shadow on it and no light.
Her cheeks are pale like lilies in eclipse,
Hardly a little redness on her lips
Paints the sad smile where all the rest is white.

Tall is she and bent forward like a reed
Which the wind toys with as she walks with speed:
Girl-like her limbs and virginal her waist.
Of the world's wonders there is none so sweet
As this, the summer lightning of her feet
Speeding her onward like a fawn in haste.

Could you have a more lovely image than that in the penultimate line? The close of the poem, which we have not quoted, is on a poignant note.

As regards the lyric in its lighter and more *cantabile* forms, Mr. Blunt is not so often successful; though there is a lovely specimen at the close of the blank verse poem called "A Rhapsody" — lovely, in spite of its echo of a certain lyric in "Endymion." But when we come to Mr. Blunt's narrative poems, such as "Esther" or "Griselda," we cannot follow Mr. Henley's admiration. Here Mr. Blunt's deficiency in artistic form seems to us accentuated; and we must also say that here we miss the breath of poetry. The title given to "Griselda," a novel in verse, might have been given also to "Esther" as regards its form. And we do not admire the novel in verse. "Esther" is well told, and has plenty of actuality; it is undoubtedly sincere. But to our mind it would have been as well, nay better, in prose. It misses the compressed passion of the sonnets; it is not song. The lyric "In the Night" is song, and strikes again the powerful note of the sonnets. On the whole, it is to the sonnets, and to an occasional lyric such as those mentioned, that we return for our estimate of Mr. Blunt's powers. He is a true poet, a very personal poet, but an unequal poet. He lacks art, as Mr. Henley regretfully admits. He comes right through sheer impulse, or not at all. But passion does often bring him right; and then, we think, Mr. Henley has no need to complain of defective form. Some of his work, particularly of the sonnets, ought to find an assured place in future anthologies. But as to how far his work will last in bulk, as Mr. Henley hopes, beside the sonnets of Sidney and Shakespeare, we do not feel like confidence. Art tells, in poetry of this kind, in spite of all actuality. And Mr. Henley lays his finger on the weak spot when he describes Mr. Blunt as descended from Byron through Owen Meredith. There is a certain morbidity, peculiar to that modern school, which it may need very consummate art to carry down the stream of time. The love is not a healthy love, it is too pessimistic; Romeo wails from the beginning his foreknowledge of Juliet's falsity. The evils and ruin of the false Eros are charged upon the head of the true. No such mistake does Shakespeare make: he is lured by the false light, but quite clearly distinguishes it from the fair light, and blames not Love, but his own weakness in error. And then — Shakespeare had the consummate art.

THOMAS EDWARD BROWN, THE MANX POET: AN APPRECIATION*
[*Athenæum*, February 23, 1907]

Besides giving a very adequate appraisal of Brown's ability as a poet, Thompson here reads a stern lesson to reviewers and critics who incline to excessive praise, to neutralize condemnation of a favorite.

T. E. BROWN is a poet so true and little known that anything which aims at increasing the knowledge of him deserves welcome;

* *Thomas Edward Brown, The Manx Poet: An Appreciation.* By Selwyn G. Simpson. Preface by Rev. J. M. Wilson.

and therefore we welcome Mr. Simpson's book, though it is scarcely, we think, adequate to its subject. It consists of a brief outline, by way of memoir, and an appreciation of Brown's poems which is at least detailed and enthusiastic. But it has the modern vice of hyperbole and indiscriminate eulogy. Mr. Simpson, indeed, is weak on the critical side, as his gratuitous *obiter dicta* on other great writers sufficiently show: some are of a perversity we would charitably ascribe to immaturity. But he does enable the reader to reach a conception of Brown for himself, by full account of the poems and quotation; and that service should earn gratitude.

Brown's life presents nothing for record beyond what could be told in a page. The son of a Manx clergyman, with Scottish blood on the mother's side, a Celt of the Celts, after a distinguished University career he took orders, and passed most of his life in the not too beloved career of a schoolmaster — first at Gloucester, and then at Clifton. What matters in it is just the fact that he had for a Gloucester pupil a lad of genius — W. E. Henley, himself a fine poet and brilliant prose-writer, who gave to the world as editor most of Brown's work. Being Brown, he was a good schoolmaster. Mr. H. F. Brown confirms Henley's account of the whiff from the greater outside world he brought into the lives of his scholars. Breadth was of the essence of the man. Not till he was forty-three did he publish in the early seventies his first poem, "Betsy Lee"; and then also his letters took that rare and mature vigour which makes them treasurable. Tennyson and George Eliot both wrote to him their recognition of "Betsy Lee." Like other neglected poets, he found in the welcome of his peers throughout his life private amends for public indifference. He was a man of letters to the marrow: had he not been so much more a poet, he might have been a great prose writer, as his letters show. But it is with his poetry that we have to do.

We shall not, for Brown's own sake, adopt Mr. Simpson's attitude towards him. To say that his descriptive passages are "unparalleled in modern poetry," that his poetry is "worthy indeed of the highest place in English literature," and the like, is not good for Brown. Nowadays, when a poet is unduly neglected, his admirers think to remedy the matter by sheer shouting. They roll up their sleeves and go into the scrimmage head down, bowling over illustrious poets, old or new, to make way for their client. The writer they champion must be wonderful, and thrice wonderful, and "past whooping" wonderful; and if whooping can do it, he shall be wonderful. Even at the close, Mr. Simpson informs us that if Brown has not Shakespeare's this, or Milton's that, or Dante's the other, he has, &c. These big comparisons are ill policy. They prejudice the sane few — not in your favour; and set up the back of every reader who, having his favourite poet, resents your intrusion on him of a *parvenu* rival. Brown has genius enough to do without hyperbole. Nor are all the poems his advocate cries up equally worthy of laudation. To have written even twenty lines of really classic poetry, said a great poet, is something not given to every man. By "classic" he intended an austere standard of righteousness, not a manner or style of poetry. It is a standard fatal to much bepraised verse, winnowing with trying severity even poetry that has pith and power. But the poet who has true mettle in him does well to face the ordeal. What comes safe out of the assay may be small in quantity, but is gold indeed, and will stand the proof of time. Brown is worth the stern compliment of that strictest standard.

Most readers — perhaps rightly — base his highest claims on the narrative "Yarns" in Manx dialect. We may be forgiven if we would rather rely on the best of the lyrics. It is not that we admire the "Yarns" less, but the lyrics more. Both, indeed, are essential parts of his complete gift as a poet. Lyrically, Brown is most often best when the effusive and impetuous Celt in him submits to limit and brevity, when the Scots side of him takes the rein of the Cymric nature. His English strain did like service for the half-Cymric George Herbert; and the Manx (we conceive) are a strip of the Cymry nipt off by the sea. In these short lyrics there is at times a notable suggestion of Herbert's way, but spiritualised beyond Herbert. The finest of them are perfect things: a single idea suggested with the tersest touch, not a word beyond the exactly needed limit — orbed and right as a drop of dew, sometimes not less delicate. The idea is original, it takes you with a surprise of freshness. Such is that garden-lyric:

My garden is a lovesome thing—God wot!
Rose plot,
Fringed pool,
Ferned grot—
The veriest school
Of peace; and yet the fool
Contends that God is not.—
Not God, in gardens! when the sun is cool?
Nay, but I have a sign!
'Tis very sure God walks in mine.

That is "the large utterance of the early gods " — of the old seventeenth-century masters; yet it is also the very Brown — the resemblance is inherent and unsought. Those ten assured and calmly beautiful lines would alone show him a master. They illustrate also, to some extent, a main source of effect in many of the shorter lyrics — a certain epigrammatic quality, a faculty of Heinesque surprise in the turn given to the close of a poem. You have it in another snatch, which exhibits the deliberately careless, half-colloquial manner of his lighter verse, but with its own grace of whim and fancy:

I bended unto me a bough of May—
That I might see and smell:
It bore it in a sort of way,
It bore it very well:
But when I let it backward sway,
Then it were hard to tell
With what a toss, with what a swing,
The dainty thing
Resumed its proper level,
And sent me to the devil.
I know it did.—You doubt it?
I turned, and saw them whispering about it.

Easy, you think? Very — for Brown. But try to do it! Nowhere does he more suggest Herbert than in some of the grave, restrained, and contained religious lyrics, such as the admirable "Planting." They are often markedly pantheistic, the immanence of God

throughout Nature being a part of his poetic creed. It is beautifully
expressed in the longer lyric "Disguises" — too long to quote.
Creed is not for judgment here: the fact itself must be noted in
any review of Brown.

Not a philosophical poet, he yet shows in all the lyrics grave
thoughtfulness, and a power at will of deep tenderness. Though
he was too sanely hearty for Celtic melancholy, pathos and sadness
are seldom far from the surface, and often overflow. The Celtic
spirituality lights the poems with sudden transfiguring flashes.
And with this, in striking contrast, is an amazingly masculine
vigour. Where strength is wanted, his language has the force of
a flail, with an idiomatic raciness that *tangs* of Brown as a sea-gust
of the brine. The poem on the foul old schooner becalmed and
transfigured out at sea brings the two qualities of startling strength
and spiritualised beauty into direct and abrupt juxtaposition.
Henley was Brown's pupil in racy vigour. The first half of this
poem might well have been written by the younger poet, but only
the master could have written the second. Of his pathos we would
quote as proof "Mater Dolorosa" (though in character it really
belongs to the "Yarns"). This dramatic lyric in dialect is more
than pathetic; the poignancy of bereaved maternity is expressed
with an intimacy that rends the heart: we scarcely feel justified
in overhearing anything so cruelly personal and feminine. But
the finest of all Brown's lyrics is perhaps that beginning "When
Jenny comes with her soft breast." Brief, beautiful, perfect,
intimately spiritual, it has in its closing turn a haunting depth of
emotional suggestion which recalls Wordsworth in his moments
of secret magic.

To turn to the "Yarns" is to step into another world. The subjective poet of the lyrics becomes an objective poet of a power
unmatched — nay, unapproached in these self-conscious days.
Brown has the gift of narrative in his bones, and therewith a
vigour, an abounding vitality, that banish the thought of art, and
make the whole matter appear as unforced and natural as the tale
of an old seaman. Yet the art is there, though it may be that best
art which is spontaneous and from within. These yarns put into
the mouth of a Manx sailor, and couched in Manx dialect, are

salty with shrewd and genial humour, salient with observation and character. Like Chaucer, Brown blends the skill of narration with that of dramatic characterization — indeed, if they suggest any poet, it is the author of *The Canterbury Tales*. But the observant humour lacks Chaucer's sly demureness; it is more gustful, racy, generous, and highly vitalised. The types presented are new to the English reader, individualised and striking as Mr. Hardy's Wessex peasantry. The descriptive touches achieve the difficult art of being poetic, yet consonant with 'the mind and vocabulary of a Manx seaman — or give the illusion of being so. For a like feat one must turn to Mr. Kipling and Tommy Atkins. But the poetry is not really in description and quotable "passages" or "extracts"; it is in the marrow and tissue of the "Yarns." It is above all in their power of dramatic emotion. For Brown has the dramatic quality in high degree. Tom Baynes's parting from his mother stirs the well-head of elemental tears, and elemental passion breaks the leash in his wrath at the loss of Betsy; while such a thing as Cain's outburst to the Almighty catches one's breath by the strength and audacity of its dramatic rightness. It is not the least of their distinctions that in a day of ultra-subtilisation these "Yarns" unseal anew the lost springs of elemental nature and humanity. Their chief fault is, perhaps, a certain tendency to expansion. But a poet who combines so individual a lyric gift with so remarkable a narrative gift has assuredly not yet received his due hearing, though it must one day come — a day we trust Mr. Simpson's volume may hasten.

ACADEMY PORTRAIT XXVI

[*Academy*, May 8, 1897]

ROBERT BROWNING

Included in this article is a discussion of one of Thompson's favorite themes, the technique of poetry. The application of his ideas to Browning's work affords one of the most interesting passages to be found among Thompson's critical writings.

BROWNING is the most hotly disputed of all indisputable poets. Such a critic as Mr. Henley will not hear of his being a poet at all; neither would such a critic as Mr. Coventry Patmore. The reason of both was the same: Browning's extreme disregard of recognised poetic form and conventions. He would, even in the midst of his most poetical poems, introduce passages of unquestionable rhymed prose; he could never proceed for long without exhibiting flagrant roughness and unmetricalness in metre. Consequently, such critics said that he lacked the most primary requisite of a singer — he could not sing. In our opinion, there are two distinct things to be separated in metre — ruggedness and roughness. Metre may be rugged and yet musical. Metre, in fact, may aim at two different things — melody and harmony. In this it corresponds to music. There is the Italian school of music, characterised by melody; there is the German school of music, characterised by harmony. Melody must be smooth, harmony admits of ruggedness. The same is the case with poetry. Swinburne is a conspicuous melodist, and is always smooth. Milton is a conspicuous harmonist, and is often rugged in detail. Coleridge stands between the two, being a harmonist whose harmonies are always melodious. So, too, are Milton's on the whole, in spite of their ruggedness in detail. But Shakespeare, in his greatest blank verse, that of his latest period, is rugged in the very nature of his harmonies. They roll with the grandeur of mountain boulders, only to be understood by a large and masculine ear. It is not so with Browning. There are in him no harmonies moving on so colossal a scale, that the individual frictions play only the part of the frictions in a male, as compared with a female voice. It is not ruggedness; it is veritable roughness, like the roughness of a harsh male voice. We must allow, therefore, that he lacks something of the quality of a singer. Yet it sometimes happens that a singer with a rough voice commands attention in despite of its roughness. And so, we think, it is with Browning. Donne is another example. Criticism has come round to the recognition of Donne, in spite of the roughest utterance ever employed by a poet of like gifts. Upon this precedent we rest our recognition of Browning as a poet. He went out of his way to be rough, apparently for roughness' sake, and without any large scale of harmonies to justify it. But his intrinsic qualities, far more than in the case of Donne, make him a poet in the teeth of this defect of execution; such is our opinion. Fineness of manner has often carried off smallness of matter. And, though to a rarer extent, we think that fineness of matter may sometimes carry off defect of manner.

Of the fineness of matter in Browning we can see no doubt. It is true that it is not invariably strictly poetical: there are whole pieces, like the famous monologue of Bishop Blougram, which can no more be called poetry than a soliloquy of Iago or Richard III. His was, in fact, a dramatic mind, though a dramatic mind of peculiar character. His special invention was the dramatic lyric. Even in his lyrics he was Robert Browning the "maker of plays," and he felt it and virtually said it. He has given us plays, and they are plays of a unique kind, coming under no previous precedent. His concern is not with action, but with the motives which lead to action, and the way in which those motives are unconsciously influenced by the varying play of circumstance. He is a verse-Meredith, indeed, so far as there can be affinity between two separate individualities. His plays turn virtually upon a single situation, which puts all the characters in a position of doubt. Their minds veer and shift under the intricate side-winds of circumstance; and at last they work out to a decision which is only half their own. With that solving of the situation the drama ends; and it is the exhibition of these intricate inward processes, conditioned by outward events and the interaction of the characters on each other, which constitutes the play. Naturally Browning has to adopt a new convention for an object so new and characteristically modern. He finds it in a daring extension of the principle of the soliloquy. The soliloquy is itself a convention, by which the characters are permitted to think aloud in solitude, after a fashion very rare in real life. But Browning's characters think aloud under all circumstances. A dialogue between two lovers, in a given difficult situation, is with him a matter in which both not only think, but feel aloud to each other, as never two lovers did or could. Yet their language is so skilfully managed, it is given so much of the form of colloquy, that we are deceived while we read into overlooking the intrinsic impossibility of the thing. Having once won from us that involuntary concession, he is able to do what he pleases, and to keep our interest on the stretch throughout a play in which nothing happens till the very last; in which we are throughout interested in the problem of what is going to happen. Needless to say such a drama is for the closet, not the stage. We can hardly conceive a Browning play being a stage success with any ordinary audience.

The dramatic lyrics, which seem to us Browning's finest contributions to poetry, are really such plays treated in brief, through the mouth of one of the people concerned. Always there is a similar problem involved, and always it is upon the working out of that problem that Browning fixes his interest. Consequently, in them, as in the dramas, pure poetry is left to come as an accident; it is not the object of the lyric. Yet there are few qualities of pure poetry which Browning is not capable of displaying as occasion arises. Music even comes, when the course of the feeling leads him into a train of pure beauty. Imagination is his at command. Take, for example, the passage in "Colombe's Birthday," where he illustrates the thesis that lost confidence is never renewed in noble natures.

> Twist off the crab's claw, wait a smarting-while,
> And something grows and grows and gets to be
> A mimic of the lost joint, just so like
> As keeps in mind, it never, never will
> Replace its predecessor! Crabs do that:
> But lop the lion's foot, and—

It is perfect, and the work of a poet undeniable. Then, for an example of emotion fused with imagination, look at such a thing as the passage where a lover hears his Spanish mistress name to him the flowers in her garden:

> Flower, you Spaniard, look that you grow not,
> Stay as you are, and be loved for ever!

His power of word-painting (abhorred but unreplaceable epithet!) partakes of his characteristic roughness, yet it is all his own and vivid:

> By the rose-flesh mushrooms, undivulged
>   Last evening—nay, in to-day's first dew
> Yon sudden coral nipple bulged,
>   While a freaked, fawn-coloured, flaky crew
> Of toad-stools peep indulged.

Then consider his occasional, but (when he exerts it) Elizabethan power of ardorous fancy. This, for instance:

> Most like the centre-spike of gold
>   Which burns deep in the bluebell's womb,
> What time, with ardours manifold,
>   The bee goes singing to her groom,
> Drunken and overbold.

The *Dramatic Lyrics*, and *Men and Women*, seem to our mind the most characteristically valuable of this virile poet's contributions to English literature. Though his whole occupation is with problems of the inner nature, and problems, moreover (as a previous critic has noted), less deep than devious, yet his sane and impartial voice, sometimes, in them, trembles with a pathos all the more effective because it is so sudden, restrained, and brief. For instance, that most deeply tender conclusion of "Two in the Campagna":

> Only I discern
> Infinite pathos, and the pain
> Of finite hearts that yearn.

He has a strange power, indeed, of distilling the moral of a coolly argued poem into a single poignant drop at the last. Sometimes, too, he accomplishes that imaginative feat of the greatest poets — the animating of external objects with human passion. So it is in "A Serenade at the Villa":

> Earth turned in her sleep with pain,
>   Sultrily suspired for proof.

> *   *   *   *   *

> Oh, how dusk your villa was,
>   Windows fast and obdurate!
> How the garden grudged me grass
>   Where I stood — the iron gate
> Ground its teeth to let me pass!

This is of the very breath of the elder poets. Then, too, the forbearing, regretful, most masculine tenderness which he can express towards women — the tenderness which can alone find utterance from supreme strength pitifully considerate of weakness, pardoning the wrong towards itself, through wise and sweet insight into the weakness and incapacity of the wronger:

> But for loving—why, you would not, sweet,
>   Though we prayed you,
>   Paid you, brayed you
> In a mortar—for you could not, sweet!

As to Browning's "message" much has been written, and many blasphemies. There are some who will have nothing of "messages" in poetry; who ask with Tennyson:

> Oh, to what uses shall we put
>   The wild-weed flower that simply blows,
> And is there any moral shut
>   Within the bosom of the rose?

Others answer that the dandelion makes excellent salad, and that the poets of the world have found morals shut within the bosom of the rose. It is a deep controversy, which is not for decision here;

but, setting it aside, we are unable to find that Browning had, or thought himself to have, any message. There are incidental utterances of wisdom in him, as in all but the slenderest poets; but, for the most part, he was essentially a questioner, who speculated upon all things, and was content to answer: "Thus men *do;* what it all means, and what is the issue of the play, I shall find out when my part in it is played." It is very strange that modern criticism should have fathered sermons upon *the* man, next to Shakespeare, who was most disinterested in his outlook upon life, and most remote from preaching them. To summarise Browning would tax any critic. Some of his points we have indicated; many we have had necessarily to leave unconsidered. He was insufficiently an artist; but he was a strong, sane, cheerful, curious poetic onlooker upon life; great we unhesitatingly think, lacking few qualities of the greatest poets but the instinct to be orderly in his greatness.

BROWNING RE-CONSIDERED *
[*Academy*, October 25, 1902]

In his critique of Stopford Brooke's study, Thompson indulges in the inevitable comparison of Browning's descriptive poetry with Tennyson's. But presently he goes to the root of the matter, describing Browning as a "psychological analyst" who was at the same time a great poet, "lofty and noble," but lacking "spirituality." Anyone familiar with Thompson's sequence, "In Dian's Lap," will find it difficult to concur in the opinion that Browning "could draw women as they have not been drawn in the poetry of our day."

MR. STOPFORD BROOKE has given us a very careful and full analysis of Browning's vast body of work. Opening with the inevitable parallel between Browning and Tennyson, he studies in detail and in successive chapters his handling of nature, his theory of life, his treatment of the passions, his poetry of art, his dramas, and so forth, illustrating each by elaborate investigation of the leading

* *The Poetry of Robert Browning.* By Stopford A. Brooke.

poems or divisions of poems. Far too full to be followed in detail, we may say in general that his study is sympathetic, intelligent, and affectionate. It is an excellent introduction to Browning. The chief fault is an excessive diffuseness; the matter could have been put adequately in almost half the space. Too fond he is, also, of not very original and very expansive imagery.

Mr. Stopford Brooke begins his study of the poet (after the first chapter on Browning compared with Tennyson) by considering Browning's treatment of Nature. It is characteristic of the modern mind that he should do so. Nature — meaning thereby the external universe — has for the present day a preponderating poetic importance which is to our thinking quite undue, which in the great poets recedes before the supreme interest of man. Browning, in this matter, was at one with the great poets rather than with his own day. Nature is to him a background — a sentient and significant background — for the drama of humanity. His touch in natural description is very peculiar, and quite his own. It has nothing of the finished beauty we expect from such poetry, it has all the rough, off-hand, impatient manner of his other work. Yet it is often beautiful in a high degree, and always strong, individual, selective, seizing the pith of what is described, having the beauty of perfect justness. He drives in the apt word with one sinewy stroke. With all this, his average description, admirable though it be, misses the magic of Wordsworth at his best, of Shelley or Tennyson, and the great poets in general; it is a purely graphic charm. For instance:

> That crimson the creeper's leaf across
>   Like a splash of blood, intense, abrupt,
> O'er a shield else gold from rim to boss,
>   And lay it for show on the fairy-cupped
> Elf-needled mat of moss,
>
> By the rose-flesh mushrooms, undivulged
>   Last evening—nay, in to-day's first dew
> Yon sudden coral nipple bulged,
>   Where a freaked, fawn-coloured, flaky crew
> Of toad-stools peep indulged.

It strikes you with deserved admiration; it has fancy, the words are precise and fresh; it could have but one thing more — the enchantment which Shelley (for example) would have given it, but which it has not; the sense of something miraculous and spiritual within the language. Perhaps in that word "spiritual" we have touched the matter: lofty and noble Browning could be, but that elusive thing we call spirituality was not in him, or at least he touched it but rarely. There was too much of Martha about him that he should have much of Mary: he was emphatically busy about many things, and it reacted injuriously even on such a matter as his description of Nature. But now and again his descriptions captured this magical quality also. Mr. Stopford Brooke quotes some:

> Mincio, in its place,
> Laughed, a broad water, in next morning's face,
> And, where the mists broke up immense and white
> I' the steady wind, burned like a spilth of light
> Out of the crashing of a million stars.

This is fine; but better still, because more condensed, is the sunset over autumnal wood in "Sordello":

> A last remains of sunset dimly burned
> O'er the far forests, like a torch-flame turned
> By the wind back upon its bearer's hand
> In one long flare of crimson; as a brand
> The woods beneath lay black.

It is splendid; the very spirit of the scene, the hour, and the season, thrills to the reader's heart. The magic quality, too, is in that passage of "James Lee's Wife," beginning:

> O good gigantic smile o' the brown old earth
> This autumn morning!

For magic, as that passage exhibits, may lie in strength as well as in beauty. Still, for this inward quality of descriptive power one has to go far afield in Browning.

Mr. Brooke dwells on the fact that Browning did not, like Tennyson, invent description; that he described from actual observation only. It is true, though perhaps Tennyson invented less than Mr. Brooke imagines. Certainly the descriptions in "Œnone" and "'Mariana in the South" were not invented, as he alleges; nor were those in the latter drawn from Italy; both were due to his Pyrenean journey. If Browning used Nature more or less incidentally, it was yet an integral element in his work; and when he ceased to use it (as Mr. Brooke observes) his poetry declined. But his primal interest was in man: "Paint man, man, whatever the issue." In man, and all things which concerned man, Mr. Brooke is assuredly not wrong in singling as his motive characteristic an immense curiousity. He wanted to know the springs of everything. Not only the inwards of man, but of all with which man busied and interested himself. It is curious that this poet, who was so careless, in his work, of poetic art or metrical music for its own sake, yet was deeply interested in Art and Music proper. It is hardly less curious that great metrical musicians, such as Coleridge in the past, have been without understanding of music. Browning has devoted whole poems to art and music, while his work shows him no less inquiring concerning his own art of poetry. But in these matters (*pace* Mr. Brooke) he pursues rather the intricacies than the depths. The same has been said by Mr. Aubrey de Vere concerning his study of men; and it is true.

As Mr. Brooke remarks, Browning was an analyst before analytic study of humanity became fashionable: it is one of the several points in which the author shows that he delayed his own acceptance by anticipating his age. What *The Ring and the Book* does on a gigantic scale, nearly all his poems do on a lesser scale: they seize some problem involving a conflict of human motives, and inquire how and why it must work out to a given conclusion. The problem is chosen so as to take the several forces engaged at their point of intersection, and thence the threads are traced outward. It is turned about on every side; the various jarring forces of passion and interest are teased out as with a needle-point; such and such allowance is carefully made for the side-currents of circumstance; and the final result is stated with such precision of demonstration that one expects the poet to add Q.E.D. The mode is scientific, almost geometrical. It is analytic, not synthetic. But analysis, a sufficiently doubtful boon in the novel, is death to the whole spirit of poetry, which is properly synthetic. And this is just the doubtful and incalculable element in the endurance of Browning's reputation. This analytic method, and yet more, this analytic temper, are responsible for half the intrusion of innumerable extra-poetic matters into Browning's work, flies in the ointment of poetry, things which weary and are like grit between the teeth. It is all curious to him, and he forgets that he is a poet, in his curiosity. But he is more concerned that his problem should be subtle, that it should bring into play sufficient intricacy of motives, than that it should go deep. We should hesitate to call Browning a profound master of the human heart. A subtle one, he undoubtedly is. He loved the obscure alleys and lanes of human conduct, and no theme was too petty, if he could spin about it a spider-web of psychological casuistry. Indeed, that were no bad word for him — "a psychological casuist."

That despite, not because of, his method he did arrive at poetry, that he united so much of genuine gold with such natively unpromising ore, is the miracle. No man ever took a stranger road to be a poet than Robert Browning, and only he could have compassed the feat. So analytic a mode would throw by the heels any imitator — as it has done; and thus happily we have not to fear the immeasurable calamity of a Browning school. It was no common central heat which even partially fused together metals so diverse; and if embedded along with the mass we find odd rubbish, we must take it as a consequence of this strange force. Passion and imagination are in the shrewd experimenter on life. It is not all unaccountable. In recalling the past, persons do naturally analyse to some extent their feelings and motives, and the process begets from recollection a present emotion. Extended by an allowable convention, here is a native groundwork for impassioned analysis (if not carried too far), which becomes, indeed, a kind of synthetic process — a recombining the disjoined bones of the past. In some such way does Browning often give nature, or the illusion of nature, and passion to his anatomisation of men's hearts.

Above all, this man, so constantly rugged, so busied with many things that his verse itself is perturbed as with the thorns and brambles of the world, had in him a great and singular power of tenderness — at times of austere beauty. He could draw women as they have not been drawn in the poetry of our day. Only the strongest poets have been able to draw women — women as they live and act among men; a noteworthy fact. In his portrait of Pompilia, Browning reaches sustained spirituality, the quality he so seldom attains. And when he does pass into pure tenderness or beauty, his utterance may stand by that of any poet. So it is also in "Balaustion's Adventure." His heroine seems to raise and purify his speech. The knotted lines lapse into untroubled movement, the "Babylonish dialect" grows suave and noble. Take one casual passage:

> The music sighed itself away, one moan
> Iphigeneia made by Aulis' strand;
> With her and music died Euripides.

Could verse be more augustly beautiful than this, in idea and utterance? As no poet has a greater command of burly and idiomatic vernacular — his sentences fall at times like the blows of a cudgel — so not any poet has given us more concentrated passages of pathos. Strength and pity are twin in poetry — with few exceptions. But to touch more than an aspect or so of this full and many-sided poet is impossible here. We have already dwelt over much on his negative side, or we should have said a word on his too facile optimism, the optimism of a man "whose sails were never to the tempest given," which by no means delights us so much as it delights Mr. Stopford Brooke.

MRS. BROWNING AS PROPHETESS*

[*Academy*, October 12, 1901]

In examining the prophecies in Mrs. Browning's poetry, Thompson detects a falsity common to the prophecies of her more famous husband. It springs from a "too facile optimism." His own prophecies were, by contrast, difficult and unpleasant but true, founded upon the real significance of contemporary happenings. Because Mrs. Browning, like her husband, was more subtle than profound—a "psychological casuist," Thompson calls him—she failed to see what was clearly visible to the keener insight of Thompson's profounder nature. Although *Casa Guidi Windows* is alone considered in the following review, enough is said about Mrs. Browning's general poetic manner to justify its inclusion here.

THIS handy little reissue of one of Mrs. Browning's later poems, *Casa Guidi Windows,* has a short preface by a fellow-poet, Mme. Duclaux, better known as Miss Mary Robinson. Mme. Duclaux briefly relates the circumstances under which the poem came to be written, and interprets its spirit with sympathetic enthusiasm. But neither here nor anywhere in the book do we find what is essentially needed in a good reissue of *Casa Guidi Windows* — explanation of its crowded references to the Italian and Florentine politics of the day; references intelligible enough at the time, but now grown dim as the political references of Dryden and Pope. An unannotated edition of "Absalom and Achitophel" were but a degree more unsatisfactory. A very little trouble would have removed this defect, and caused the book to supply a real want, which in its present form we can scarcely think it does. For the rest, it is well printed on good paper and satisfactory in all other respects.

Casa Guidi Windows shows the turn of the tide towards Mrs. Browning's final manner, fully developed in "Aurora Leigh"; which, with all respect to Mme. Duclaux's judgment, we cannot think an improvement on her previous manner. On the whole, it seems to us a decided change for the worse. In this poem it is

* *Casa Guidi Windows*. By Mrs. Browning. Preface by Miss Mary Robinson.

still tentative, and even Mme. Duclaux frankly admits its deficiency. The poem is entirely political, and not unnaturally it is in Mrs. Browning's rhetorical rather than her poetical style. Few poets can treat a political theme without falling into this style, which it were perhaps more accurate to call oratorical than rhetorical. It takes the lyric power of Shelley to write a "Hellas," and even Shelley fell from poetry in "The Masque of Anarchy," while he did not uniformly maintain it in "The Revolt of Islam." Still, this would be a mere question of species, were the eloquence good, as Mrs. Browning's sometimes is. But in this poem it is strained, tense, excited, often downright shrill. This defect of execution is not mended by the absence of construction. The poem is desultory, a string of reflections conditioned by passing events. It is a woman's meditations on the Italian politics of four years, taking for starting-point that Florentine portion of them which she witnessed from her windows. But her reflections are sufficiently divagatory to embrace the international exhibition at the Crystal Palace, which, as we know, was to inaugurate an era of peace and universal brotherhood. Of course, the poem is intentionally desultory. But to compensate the absence of definite scheme, the wilful invertebrateness of it, there needs a felicity of execution, an inspired caprice, an opulent luxuriance of impulse, which are unfortunately lacking. A voluntary [lack of definite scheme] must be very rich in detail to excuse the deliberate lack of unity.

Mme. Duclaux would palliate the shortcomings of style by having us admire Mrs. Browning in the part of prophetess. Now, it is true she prophesies the ultimate triumph of Italian unity, at a time when the cause had come to grief. But it needs no large power of prophecy to foresee that a great national movement, the chief barrier against which is a steadily decadent power like Austria, will ultimately win its way. Moreover, when one's whole hopes are bound up with the success of a cause, it is human nature, and woman's nature above all, to believe that the cause must ultimately triumph, no matter how dark its destinies may temporarily be. What forlorn hope but has had some woman to believe in it? When we come to things less vague and general than the triumph of *Italia Irredenta,* Mrs. Browning's fallacy as a prophetess seems blazoned large over *Casa Guidi Windows*. She believed that the day of universal brotherhood was nigh at hand, the era when wars should cease, and thinkers replace fighters as the peaceful warriors of the future. It is there in black and white. Are we any nearer it than when she shared these generous illusions with a crowd of others, who mistook the cravenness of the stay-at-home *bourgeois*, anxious to fill his moneybags in peace, for a change of heart in mankind?

> The poet shall look grander in the face
> Than ever he looked of old, when he began
> To sing that "Achillean wrath which slew
> So many heroes."

Yet the Poet Laureate is not noticeably a better model for a bust than Homer. Her Britannic prophecies are peculiarly belied by time:

> Send abroad thy high hopes and thy higher
> Resolves, from that most virtuous altitude,
> Till nations shall unconsciously aspire
> By looking up to thee, and learn that good
> And glory are not different.

Is that precisely the way in which the admiring nations now look up to England?

> No war!
> Disband thy captains, change thy victories,
> Be henceforth prosperous as the angels are —
> Helping, not humbling!

Which would be excellent, were earth Heaven. But even the angels (if we are rightly informed) humble demons. In other words, Mrs. Browning's prophecies represent the current enthusiasms of her age, and are no more nor less right than those enthusiasms. Had she lived, she would seemingly have been a Little Englander — unless, being the child of the enthusiasms of her age, she had been an ardent Imperialist.

But, being withal Elizabeth Barrett Browning, she could not escape frequent lapses into lofty eloquence, or even rank poetry. Ever and again they blow on us with triumphant refreshment. So in the finely summarised description of the nations meeting at the Crystal Palace Exhibition, each with her characteristic product in her hand:

> Imperial England draws
> The flowing ends of the earth, from Fez, Canton,
>   Delhi and Stockholm, Athens and Madrid,
> The Russias and the vast Americas,
>   As a queen gathers in her robes amid
> Her golden cincture. . . .
>   "I wove these stuffs so subtly, that the gold
> Swims to the surface of the silk, like cream,
>   And curdles to fair patterns. Ye behold?"

>   *   *   *   *   *

> "These carpets—you walk slow on them like kings,
>   Inaudible like spirits, while your foot
> Dips deep in velvet roses and such things."—

>   *   *   *   *   *

> "This model of a steamship moves your wonder?
>   You should behold it crushing down the brine
> Like a blind Jove who feels his way with thunder."—

>   *   *   *   *

> "Methinks you will not match this steel of ours."—
>   "Nor you this porcelain! One might think the clay
> Retained in it the larvae of the flowers,
>   They bud so, round the cup, the old spring way."

That is Mrs. Browning at her best — the large, masculine way which no other woman has compassed, and which she, ever passionately and daringly trying, only seized aright by fits and starts.

> You should behold it crushing down the brine
> Like a blind Jove who feels his way with thunder.

Of what majestic grasp is that — insolently easy, not to be disdained of Shakespeare's self! No other woman has reached her hand to such things; and Elizabeth Browning could not keep her grasp on them, but clutched desperately for them, capturing them only at moments. She was best when she was content with a lesser scope. But that she could seize such images at times, all honour to her fervid, ultra-feminine soul in a frame too weak! In this poem one sees the influence of her husband beginning, not (on the whole) to her advantage; making her careless of form (of which she was never too careful), and self-indulgent in jerkinesses of style, wherein she tries to copy his native brusqueness and abruptness. The beginning of a decline (as we think) largely induced by her husband; but with splendid flakes of the old Elizabeth Barrett still clinging about her. As, indeed, even in "Aurora Leigh," they did not abandon her.

LIVING HISTORY*
[*Academy*, April 18, 1903]

Not only as a criticism of Carlyle, but for the larger significance of contrasting the scientific and literary presentation of history, this is among the most significant of Thompson's reviews.

THE issue of a new edition of Carlyle's *French Revolution* excellently edited and commented by Mr. Holland Rose, the author of the admirable *Life of Napoleon*, awakens many reflections and recollections. Some of us can remember when it opened to our then young eyes an enchanted land of history; vitalising for us scholastic history as we vitalised for ourselves the historic figures of our childhood, or as those we saw, "sole-sitting on the shores of old romance." Mirabeau and Danton took place beside Prince Hal and Coeur-de-Lion. To make "sober history" no less living than the history of Shakespeare and Scott — that is a feat com-

* *The French Revolution*. By Thomas Carlyle. Edited by Holland Rose.

passed by but one man who writes the English tongue. And the
name of him is Carlyle. One reads again the remembered pages,
with a recollected fondness, and an associated charm. Not that
they need those associations. On the contrary, one has a regretful
pleasure in turning them over. For they speak out of the past
to us in a day when history has gone far from the Carlylean ways.
For of the many virtues and ideals possible or proper to history, it
may almost be said we have retained but one — the noblest, if
you will — truth. The noblest, the most necessary, but surely not
all. Yet we have made it well-nigh all. It was overmuch neglected,
it may be, by past historians; and the whirligig of time brings in
this revenge. We have a race of historians devoted to elaborate fairness of mind, careful research of fact, anxious sifting of detail,
judicial weighing of evidence, scrupulous consultation and painful
setting-down of first-hand authorities. It is magnificent, but is it
history? Is it more than a glorified chronicle, glorified by superior
care of veracity? Science and the scientific spirit have invaded
history, as they have invaded every department of literature;
bringing with them the letter that killeth. In history the letter is
most necessary, be it granted: unless the foundations prove sound,
there is no soundness in the edifice. But do we not think overmuch of detail, without discrimination of its importance? And is
it needful to show the scaffolding so apparently as our histories
show it? Is it necessary to thresh out the whole process in front
of the reader? Their text banked-up with references, and ob-
structed with arguments of *pro* and *con*, they resemble legal
treatises more nearly than histories. Might not some portion of
these things be relegated to appendices for the information of
the serious student and the brother-historian?

Meanwhile, all conception of history as a literary art is pushed
to the wall by this zeal for the stony fact. Nay, the philosophy of
history suffers — to a less degree. There are no entrails, no viscera
in these histories; in many there is scarce flesh on the ribs. Can
these dry bones live? We think not: they are but skeletons, nay,
fossil remains, carefully brought together for some future Owen
of history. Carlyle's biographer alone upholds Carlyle's tradition;
and with his pictorial inaccuracy is, after all, more of a Macaulay

than a Carlyle. For this Carlyle was no scorner of accurate research. Here was one who made these dry bones live; but he had first laboured severely in the collecting of them. In this *French Revolution* there are mistakes; but he had to sift and delve without predecessors in sifting and delving. And thereto he added the spirit of life, the spirit of art; the thing stands on its feet, and is clothed with flesh, and speaks, and is an organism. And with what flesh he clothed it! Not since Tacitus had man brought to history such force of the living word. The principle of life, the ancients held, was fire; and this *Revolution* is aflame — yea, and if you will, a-smoke too — fuliginous, as he would himself have said. It is a fuming and Plutonic energy, of red glare and violent shadow, an upheaval of decorous conventions and a defiance of anointed traditions in style. Only so (Coventry Patmore is reported to have said) could he have compressed so much into so brief a compass. "The style was itself a revolution." Which is most true. Germanic that style may be, in main features of its mechanical structure or defect of structure; but inwardly and substantially, in those features which cannot be squared by the grammarian's coarse analysis, it is Carlyle and reducible to no precedent beloved of the line-and-level critic. Not only does the sentence-structure, serried, bristling, scornful of flowing and precisely connective progression, make for pregnancy. The bold figures, the startling devices, which so arrest and stimulate attention, are not there merely to astonish, for Teutonic audacity of adornment: they are hieroglyphs, with the condensing power of hieroglyphs. They concentrate like a burning-lens, bring a fulness of meaning to the focal point. Here, as throughout his work, he compels the poetic method to the service of history. Might we not even say that Carlyle had anticipated Wagner? Those nicknames, and other introductory devices by which he combines the stage-light on a prominent figure as it first fronts the reader, and keeps it on him at every successive re-entry: are they not the *leit motif* in history?

Many readings but increase one's admiration for the vivid art — or rather inspiration — of the performance. These Carlylean histories are scarce narrative; they are drama. The thing unfolds like a fiery frieze, turbulent, closer to us than the happenings of Morocco or Somaliland; and the dead clamours of history are borne to us voicefully. Yet out of what rubbish-heaps is the illusion produced; with what power of holding chaotic material in simultaneous liquefaction, and fusing it with volcanic completion. The swift procession of this *French Revolution* dissembles from the reader the difficulties overcome, the organising (or, rather, organic) power put forth in the overcoming of them. Think (for an example) of that royal flight to Varennes in the "Korff berline"; how the intricate details are marshalled with utmost narrative clearness, yet made subservient to a hurrying climax of dramatic effect.

In the *French Revolution* Carlyle's style is not yet pushed to the extreme of the *Friedrich*, with its "Dryasdust" and other tricks for labelling minor matter, needlessly cumbrous and *outré;* its picturesqueness grown somewhat mechanical and taking thought to itself. A style which had its function in power of compression is applied to matter less crowded, on a larger scale, losing somewhat of its justification. All that in the *French Revolution* had made for brevity is magnified like a huge distorted shadow; nodosities pictorial on the smaller scale become unwieldy contortions in the slow-labouring amplification. But *Friedrich* remains a monumental exertion of shaggy and solitary strength. The Plutonic force of the *Revolution* has abated; the grim thoroughness is increased. And still the thing is fierily alive beside other histories. Yet more, Carlyle's history has soul and significance. He sees under all entangled factual confusions the working of transcendental powers. But does not this make for unreliability: is not this *Revolution* (as Frenchmen have said) a huge misreading? Say it be (though we are far from saying it). Such a man can hardly put forth even a mistaken view without more illuminative flashes and suggestions of truth than a colder writer's coldest precision of factual truth: having in him a divining spirit, even when its utterance is choked and perverted by stubborn conglomerate of prejudice. Amidst compilations of conscientiously strained fact, passed through a very colander of research, we still long with regret for such another historian. Innumerable articulating of dry bones; but the spirit will not blow on them, and they do not live.

A THESIS IN VERSE*
[*Daily Chronicle*, June 29, 1901]

The opposition between Thompson and Davidson was the opposition between a poet whose philosophy was Christo-centric, and one whose philosophy was ego-centric. Their views of pain were derivative — one from self; the other from Christ. But a difference in ideals in no way interfered with Thompson's power to evaluate the technical artistry of Davidson's poetry.

IT SHOULD appear that this poem is the first in a series of "Testaments" which Mr. John Davidson purposes to give the public. We do not look forward to them altogether happily, judging by this first specimen; though, like all which Mr. Davidson does, it has its power. Not once or twice only has he shown himself a true poet, resolutely himself, and unlike anyone else now writing, with a special power of seizing the lurking poetic elements in modern actuality — latent, indeed, and needing enough looking for. Yet to our mind even he is at his brightest and best when he ceases the grim wrestle with the recalcitrant ugliness of ultra-modernity, and indulges in free draughts of the immemorial poetic stimulants — country sights and sounds, or the architecture of great cities under atmospheric effects; the dome of St. Paul's rising magically under one of those special conditions frequent in London, or Romney Marsh — though in the latter case he characteristically draws beauty from the telegraph-wire, "within the wind a core of sound."

> Shrill blew the wind, and shrill the wire
> Rang out from Hythe to Romney Town.

But in this latest development of his resolved modernity he seems to us to have handicapped himself almost defiantly. It is, in effect, the *apologia* of an arch-vivisector. Apart from the native

* *The Testament of a Vivisector.* By John Davidson.

difficulties of the theme, at the outset it challenges ineludible comparisons. For though the style is Mr. Davidson's own, in conception it is Browningesque.

It is one of those dramatic monologues, all of which trace their lineage to "Lippo-Lippi" and the rest of that most Browningesque series. It is couched in blank verse which has scarcely a formal difference from prose — again the Browning way. But Browning's metre has a more sinewy cast, a more distinct movement of its own — despite the prosaic quality which makes any metrical movement a difficult matter: while Mr. Davidson's has a Tennysonian linearity and languour which, in conjunction with its purposed prosaic character, often begets a horrible semblance of *journalese* chopped in lengths, like treacly coffee or strings of molasses.

> When I began to hew the living flesh,
> I seemed to seek—I seemed: for who can tell
> The drift of aims utility distorts?—
> The mitigation of disease. Not long
> A bias of humanity deflects
> Advancement in the true Materialist!

That is not lovely. The last lines of the poem trail off into such unashamed prose that it is difficult to judge whether they are meant for blank verse or not.

> The solid bent
> Of Matter, the infinite vanity
> Of the Universe, being evermore
> Self-knowledge.

The penultimate two lines might, by forced scansion, be tormented into five-foot lines: but assuredly they read as though the poet, losing patience at the last, had thrown metre to the dogs.

The poem is, of course, the exhibition of a character, and the opinions are not to be taken as Mr. Davidson's own. But a great dramatic defect meets us on the threshold. Browning's monologues always portray a conceivable character. You may doubt sometimes of their actuality, that Browning imputes his own subtlety overmuch to his creations: you may have a conviction that the prototype of Sludge, the medium, acted from much coarser and less complex motives than Sludge; that Bishop Blougram's prototype was very unlike Bishop Blougram. But given Browning's premises, the men are thinkable. It is unthinkable that any vivisector ever felt, still less reasoned, as Mr. Davidson's vivisector feels and reasons. Granted Mr. Davidson's premises, the man is rather the phantasm of a particularly bad nightmare, than a thing believable with a sound digestion in the light of day.

He proclaims himself (and in stating this we are stating the argument of the poem, the man's *apologia*) not merely a person stripped of pity, lustful of inflicting and witnessing pain — *that* were conceivable. But he affirms himself a devotee of Pain, a man with a Pain Philosophy, as Carlyle had a Clothes Philosophy— one to whom the *norm* of the universe is Pain. Nay, one may say the very motive-power of the universe is Pain. He torments a dying horse in order to elucidate the resuscitative force of pain. Pain and ease, to him, are very nearly the same thing.

> Anguished breath and breath of healthy ease
> Differ in function by a jot, perhaps.

Therefore, in his eyes the whole of life is Pain and Knowledge; pain spurring men to knowledge, knowledge reinforcing pain. For increase of knowledge is increase of consciousness; increase of consciousness is increase of pain. With this conviction, pity becomes a futility; pity for others or pity for himself.

Such, peeled of some not very exquisite metaphysics, is the thesis of the vivisector and the poem. Can one conceive the most arch-vivisector feeling and thinking like this — even though he held the germ of such a philosophy? And we have known the germ of the philosophy held by an actual person, who yet had no dream of such fanatical application. Human nature counts for something, and we are unable to repose even imaginative belief in the monstrosity which Mr. Davidson has incarnated. Yet it is not imaginative, but reasoned and actual belief that he exacts from us, if we are to take this as a dramatic monologue.

As regards the execution, we have already hinted that we care not for Mr. Davidson as a metaphysician in verse. His expression in such matters is often singularly imprecise and *un-getatable*. Thus, he calls Thought —

> Organ of Matter's consciousness—

meaning that it makes Matter conscious. The expression is as perverse and perverting as if he called the mind "organ of the brain's consciousness"; an organ being that which is acted through, not that which acts through. But these are by-matters. If we cannot accept Mr. Davidson's conception as human, it is none the less a logical phantasy requiring an original imagination, and often of abhorrent impressiveness in his delivery of it. That he not infrequently becomes weak and prosaic we have partly implied in our remarks on the metre. He has not the unfailing nervous muscularity of utterance which carries one through *Sludge* — the *Vivisector's* nearest parallel. But when his task really gives him a chance, he can take it, and rises to a power which makes one regret that he should so have prisoned his gifts by choice of subject.

Nowhere is he stronger than in the concluding passage:

> We cannot put an end to that
> In which we live and move and have our being,
> The interstellar spaces, Matter cold
> And thin, the darksome vehicle of light.

>   *   *   *

> And I believe that they who delve the soil,
> Who reap the grain, who dig and smelt the ore,
> The girl who plucks a rose, the sweetest voice
> That thrills the air with sound, give Matter pain:
> Think you the sun is happy in his flames,
> Or that the cooling earth no anguish feels,
> Nor quails from her contraction? Rather say,
> The systems, constellations, galaxies,
> That strew the ethereal waste, are wheeling there
> In agony unutterable. Pain?
> It may be Matter in itself is pain,
> Sweetened in sexual love that so mankind,
> The medium of Matter's consciousness,
> May never cease to know.

We surmise that in the last terrible passage, on the potentiality for pain of non-animal life, Mr. Davidson is speaking his own view, as it happens fundamentally to be the reviewer's. But that is neither here nor there. The point is that the whole quotation is most excellently well expressed. Here you have Mr. Davidson at his best, strong, unforced, and himself, reaching distinguished utterance through sheer authenticity of emotion and imaginative realisation. He sees, he feels what he sees, and vents it with trained faculty of speech; the result impresses by its vital adequacy, without an image, without a phrase which you can pluck off and hold up for detached admiration as poetry. Such is the gift of the man; no poet of quotable lines (with few exceptions), ornaments stuck on or tacked together, which show better out of their place than in it — and this, of these days, is no common praise. That he should drop upon an habitual and stereotyped line like —

In which we live and move and have our being,

is also characteristic. Not an artist externally and apart from inspiration, he is always liable to juxtapose elevated with commonplace speech, and leaves the juxtaposition uncorrected, seemingly unconscious or careless of it. But passages such as this, and the imaginative homogeneity of the total conception, however alien to one's conception of actual humanity, make the poem a noticeable work, if we hesitate to think it an example of Mr. Davidson's best powers.

MR. HENLEY'S NEW POEMS*
[*Academy*, December 14, 1901]

Thompson here discusses the similarity between Henley's "irregular" ode-meter and Patmore's—a poet, surely, with whom Henley had no "spiritual troth-plight." As we read the remarks on poetasters who mistake the variations of such meter for an easy vehicle of " 'fine' lawlessness—more lawless than fine," we can imagine what Thompson's reaction would have been to the contention that Free Verse is a direct descendant of such technical perfection as Patmore's. When we recall his own lovely imaginings that coupled Spring with Our Lady,

> Who guid'st the bare and dabbled feet of May,

we realize the restraint in Thompson's questioning of Henley's imagery that makes Spring "a wild, sweet-blooded, wonderful harlot." There is indefinable pathos in the concluding paragraph of this review, and it illustrates Thompson's sure insight that detected the false note in Henley's defiance — a defiance that issued in the mournfulness of "despairing valiance."

Some of these poems have appeared in this or that periodical. The prologue was included in Mr. Henley's little collection of patriotic verse. But, taking them integrally, this is their first appearance in volume form. They are not, throughout, all that we have learned to expect from Mr. Henley. Were we to compare it with the generality of new verse, we could not but rate it exceptionally high. It is not the competition of younger poets which Mr. Henley needs to dread: it is the competition of himself. We know exactly the best he has done, and resent instinctively the slightest deflection from it. Well, here there are such deflections — that is all which can be said; and we feel them in exact proportion to our love of the poet who caught and held us of old. He still catches and holds us in his moments, but the grip is not always compulsive. Yet now and again the old mastery thrills us, and we remember. It is good so to remember.

* *"Hawthorn and Lavender," With Other Verses.* By W. E. Henley.

If you sift and select, there is a very sufficient number of such poems; and a conspicuous few which are equal to all but the greatest of Mr. Henley's previous work. When we have finally panned out these siftings, indeed, we are almost ashamed to have indulged in cavil at all. The "Hawthorn and Lavender" section is the largest in the volume; and the best of this are either descriptive or profoundly personal. The weakest, as a rule, are those which are most song-like — lyric in the narrower sense. Once, indeed, Mr. Henley becomes actually Swinburnian — a sacrifice of individuality rare exceedingly with him. Yet here is a charming lyric:

> Look down, dear eyes, look down,
>   Lest you betray her gladness.
> Dear brows, do naught but frown,
>   Lest men miscall my madness.
>
> Come not, dear hands, so near,
>   Lest all besides come nearer.
> Dear heart, hold me less dear,
>   Lest time hold nothing dearer.
>
> Keep me, dear lips, O keep
>   The last great word unspoken,
> Lest other eyes go weep,
>   Lest other lives lie broken!

And of the descriptive lyrics we may quote a couple of stanzas, with the grimmer Henley touch in them:

> The night dislimns, and breaks
>   Like snows slow thawn;
> An evil wind awakes
>   On lea and lawn;
> The low East wakes; and hark!
> Out of the kindless dark,
> A fierce protesting lark,
>   High in the horror of dawn!
>
> A shivering streak of light,
>   A scurry of rain:
> Bleak day from bleaker night
>   Creeps pinched and fain;

> The old gloom thins and dies,
> And in the wretched skies
> A new gloom, sick to rise,
>   Sprawls, like a thing in pain.

That has a fantastic and even fierce strength of imagination which we know in former days of Mr. Henley's work. If, indeed, the line about the lark be not too violent and resolved a wresting of natural fact to fit the mood of the soul. No charge of violence, however, can be brought against what is perhaps the most beautiful poem in the book.

> There was no kiss that day?
> No intimate Yea-and-Nay,
> No sweets in hand, no tender, lingering touch?
> None of those desperate, exquisite caresses,
> So instant—O, so brief—and yet so much,
> The thought of the swiftest lifts and blesses?
> Nor any one of those great royal words,
> Those sovran privacies of speech,
> Frank as the call of April birds,
> That, whispered, live a life of gold
> Among the heart's still sainted memories,
> And irk, and thrill, and ravish, and beseech,
> Even when the dream of dreams in death's a-cold?
> No, there was none of these,
> Dear one, and yet—
> O, eyes on eyes! O, voices breaking still,
> For all the watchful will,
> Into a kinder kindness than seemed due
> From you to me, and me to you!
> And that hot-eyed, close-throated, blind regret
> Of woman and man baulked and debarred the blue!
> No kiss—no kiss that day?
> Nay, rather, though we seemed to wear the rue,
> Sweet friend, how many and how goodly—say!

This nobly tender poem has a keen edge of expression, at once impassioned and restrained, such as Mr. Henley himself has rarely attained. Such lines as:

> Nor any of those great royal words,
> Those sovran privacies of speech,
> Frank as the call of April birds,

suggest Coventry Patmore, a poet with whom Mr. Henley has otherwise no spiritual troth-plight. Only a superficial reader could suppose derivation of one from the other. Nothing could be more dissimilar than their hand on that so-called "irregular" ode-metre which they use in common. It is notable that Mr. Henley generally rises to his best when he uses this metre. Very comprehensibly. Your poetaster thinks it an easy vehicle for "fine" lawlessness — more lawless than fine. Your true poet uses it only when he is touched *ad ima præcordia* — to the most intimate privacies of his heart. Of all metres, it is closest to the nerve itself, and only intense feeling can use it self-vindicatingly. Therefore, Mr. Henley uses it in a strongly personal poem:

> In Shoreham River, hurrying down
> To the live sea,
> By working, marrying, breeding Shoreham Town,
> Breaking the sunset's wistful and solemn dream,
> An old, black rotter of a boat
> Past service to the labouring, tumbling flote,
> Lay stranded in mid-stream:
> With a horrid list, a frightening lapse from the line,
> That made me think of legs and a broken spine:
> Soon, all too soon,
> Ungainly and forlorn to lie
> Full in the eye
> Of the cynical, discomfortable moon
> That, as I looked, stared from the fading sky,
> A clown's face flour'd for work. And by and by
> The wide-winged sunset wanned and waned;
> The lean night-wind crept westward, chilling and sighing;
> The poor old hulk remained,
> Stuck helpless in mid-ebb. And I knew why—
> Why, as I looked, my heart felt crying.
> For, as I looked, the good green earth seemed dying—
> Dying or dead;
> And, as I looked at the old boat, I said:—
> *"Dear God, it's I!"*

That is Mr. Henley at his sternest and strongest, every line like wrought ebony. Very fine is the "Praeludium," where he uses the same metre without rhyme in a most felicitously worded allegory between colour and music. But why does it end:

> The wild, sweet-blooded, wonderful harlot, Spring?

Why, in the name of all that is wilful, must Spring — of all the months, poor Spring — be a harlot? Even the author of "Dolores" was content to leave her "the girl-child Spring." Why commit this defloration on the most virginal of seasons?

In the other section we have "Prologues" and other occasional verses, few lacking Mr. Henley's practised skill in this kind; and "London Types" — a series of Shakespearean sonnets, recalling the "Hospital Poems." None quite equal to the best of these, all are very good, and some only short of his possible best. Take the "Sandwich-Man":

> An ill March noon; the flag-stones gray with dust;
> An all-round east wind volleying straws and grit;
> St. Martin's Steps, where every venomous gust
> Lingers to buffet, or sneap, the passing cit;
> And in the gutter, squelching a rotten boot,
> Draped in a wrap that, modish ten year syne,
> Partners, obscene with sweat and grease and soot,
> A horrible hat, that once was just as fine;
> The drunkard's mouth a-wash for something drinkable,
> The drunkard's eye alert for casual *toppers*,
> The drunkard's neck stooped to a lot scarce thinkable,
> A living, crawling blazoning of Hot Coppers,
>   He trails his mildews towards a Kingdom-Come
>   Compact of *sausage-and-mash* and *two-o'-rum!*

You see him brutally distinct. And this section is the most level of the book. Over the book at large (in conclusion) is a mournfulness; as of a pirate going grimly down beneath the enemy's guns, with the black flag nailed to the mast — consoled by the remembrance that he has drunk, and kissed, and fought, before the end came. That despairing valiance leaves the reader in a saddened mood when the final leaf is turned.

ACADEMY PORTRAIT XVI
[*Academy*, February 27, 1897]

WALTER SAVAGE LANDOR

There is here, in abundance, the patient good humor that dulls the edge of wrath, and Landor was often wrathful in his writings no less than in his life. Thompson takes him seriously, but lightly—the best way to take Landor — and in the process gives us a delightful example of playful seriousness.

LANDOR was born of good family at Ipsley Court, Warwickshire, in 1775, and was educated at Rugby and Oxford. He did not neglect his university training, for he obtained private notoriety on account of his Latin verses before his name was much known to the public, and this classical taste evidences itself strongly in the Greek character of his poetry. It was not for nothing that he bore the name of Savage. It was said of someone that if he could split himself in halves, the one half would go to buffets with the other. It might have been said of Landor. Look even at his portrait, and you see obstinacy armed in the face. He disagreed — not unreasonably — with his father, who wished to dictate his profession (did dictation, one wonders, run in the family?). Landor *père* would have Landor *fils* in the Army: Landor *fils*, being a virtuous republican, would not away with the Army. Thereupon Landor *aîné* said: "Law and four hundred a year, or your own way and a third of the sum." Landor *jeune* took his own will with that dowry, as he would doubtless have taken her with no portion at all; for his own will was the sole spouse to whom Walter Savage Landor was wedded without quarrelling. He succeeded to the family estate, sold it off, bought two others in Monmouthshire, expended some £70,000 in improvements, quarrelled with his tenants, pulled down his house, and went to Italy. He had previously joined the Spaniards in their first insurrection, raising a troop, and giving 20,000 reals towards expenses. In 1815 came the Italian journey; and several years later he returned from his Florentine villa to Bath. In 1858 he was tried for publishing grossly indecent and slanderous verses against a lady of that place, and condemned in a thousand pounds' damages. He had but a remnant of his fortune when this happened; and he had published a declaration that he would bestow it on the widow of whosoever should successfully assassinate the Emperor of the French. Having now no fortune left for such playful and amiable objects, he returned to Italy; and his friends combined to rescue him from the consequences of his indomitable perversity. His brothers gave him an annuity of £200, Browning kindly looked after its proper expenditure, and the literary Ishmael settled down at Florence. He died in 1864; having quarrelled, as consistently as human infirmity would allow, with everybody on earth — including, it is hardly necessary to say, his wife. In the intervals allowed him by this main purpose of life he published enough, in prose and verse, to fill two closely printed volumes.

His poetry consists of two long poems, "Gebir" and "Count Julian"; a collection of Hellenics, poems avowedly in the old Greek taste; and a quantity of miscellaneous verse. "Gebir" and "Count Julian" were enthusiastically admired by such men as De Quincey; but Landor's warmest admirers would hardly stake his reputation on them now. There are a few passages still worth quoting, but no more. Such is the couplet on the moonbeam:

> And the long moonbeam on the hard wet sand
> Lay like a Jasper column half upreared.

That is fine, but it stands alone. Fine, too, is the passage on Julian nursing his solitary grief:

> Wakeful he sits, and lonely and unmoved,
> Beyond the arrows, shouts, and views of men,
> As oftentimes an eagle, when the sun
> Throws o'er the varying earth his early ray,
> Stands solitary, stands immovable,
> Upon some higher cliff, and rolls his eye,
> Clear, constant, unobservant, unabased,
> In the cold light.

The miscellaneous poems are really one in character with the Hellenics. They aim at Greek brevity, form, lucidity, measure. It is usually considered that Landor was a master in this kind. Of some, such as the beautiful "Rose Aylmer," it may be admitted frankly that this is true. But, as a whole, it seems to us that the restraint has nothing to restrain; Pegasus would prove himself a most discreet ambler, even if the reins were laid upon his neck. Landor's prose is another matter. It is not, as a rule, imaginative, nor distinguished by any other extra-prose qualities; it gives one no thrill, no "shock of sweet surprise": it is most absolute prose, but also most admirable prose; lucid, structural, with an unclamorous rightness of phrase. Sometimes he goes out of his way for an epithet, with self-justifying result, as when he speaks about "the omnigenous imagery of Shakespeare." The adjective is exactly and felicitously apt, a sentence-saving adjective. But this is rare. He has, in fact, described his own style — probably not unawares.

Elegance in prose composition is mainly this: a just admission of topics and of words, neither too many nor too few of either; enough of sweetness in the sound to induce us to enter and sit still; enough of illustration and reflection to change the posture of our minds when they would tire; and enough of sound matter in the complex to repay us for our attention.

This does not describe a profound writer, nor is Landor profound. The "sound matter in the complex" is a variable quality with him. He loves paradox and paradoxical satire — for if we have called his writing "absolute prose," we by no means meant to call it prosaic. But the paradox is as likely as not to be more startling than deep; and perhaps one of the circumstances which keep the reader alert in attention is, that you never know whether the next paradox will be convincing or maddeningly perverse. He upholds, for example, the unexpected proposition that Locke is the most elegant of English writers; and to the question why Plato is so much more applauded, answers most Landorianly that it is because he is so much less read.

The difficulties we never try are no difficulties to us.... Until a short time ago, I could have conversed much more fluently about Plato than I can at present — I had read all the titles to his dialogues, and several scraps of commentary: these I have now forgotten, and am indebted to long attacks of the gout for what I have acquired instead.

It is exquisitely put, and contains just enough truth to make him unable to refrain from the falsehood. He presently caps it by declaring that without the gout he would have had less patience, which from the mouth of Landor is magnificent and unsurpassable. His dialogue on Milton is a good example of his qualities as a critic. It is full of taste and good sense, marred by rash confidence, particularly on points of metre, where Landor seems to have had a narrow ear. He can see nothing — we should rather say hear nothing — in Milton's "aggregates of proper names," and selects for condemnation —

> Knights of Logres and of Lyones,
> Lancelot, and Pelleas, and Pellenore.

To which one can best say that the last line ravished the ear of Tennyson to the extent of evoking from him a minutely careful imitation —

> Ulfius, and Brastias, and Bedivere.

By what careful study Landor gained his command of English is to be seen in the dialogue between Horne Tooke and Johnson. It deserves to be read for its acute criticism of language — mixed, of course, with Landorian crotchets and obstinacies.

"Since we are become a learned nation," he says, "not only the words we have cast aside, but also those we have substituted in the place of them, are mostly injudicious; and such others as we have taken the trouble to construct are unskilful botches."

Landor slips in expression: he does not mean that the words we have cast aside are injudicious, but that it was injudicious to cast them aside. The substance, however, is the view of all those — chiefly poets — who have striven in modern days, against a chorus of facile censure, to revive some of those cast-off pieces of the English tongue. Yet in the midst of his criticism of others he himself uses the horrible comparative "frequenter" — by way, we suppose, of being still a mutineer, and Landor. Landor he always is: the *Imaginary Conversations*, which are his classical work in prose, if (as De Quincey insists) they have many points of skilful dialogue, are not dramatic; Chatham, for instance, is not Chatham, but Landor without the smallest of masks. Mr. Coventry Patmore drew a distinction between two kinds of dogmatism: the dogmatism of the seer, and the dogmatism of the man who opines. "By their fruits ye shall know them" — which means that to discern between the two the hearer must himself have the gift of recognising, though not of divining, truth. Landor belonged emphatically to the second class. He is stiff in opinion, not because his vision of truth is so dazzling, but because he has the bull-dog's instinct of hanging-on to whatever comes between his teeth. "Mamma says so," remarked the once famous child in *Punch*; "and if Mamma says so, it *is* so, even if it isn't!" That was the opinion of Walter Savage Landor about Walter Savage Landor's opinions — even when he recommended the Greeks to fight the Turks with bows and arrows instead of firearms. Let us be thankful that a certain genius makes them not too seldom right, and that a classical style allied with a strong personality makes them always interesting. In no intellectual quality, perhaps, can he be called great; but he has written some of the best prose in the English language.

THE POETRY AND PHILOSOPHY OF GEORGE MEREDITH*
[*Athenæum*, July 7, 1906]

Thompson's criticism of one of his most important contemporaries can scarcely be omitted, although it is somewhat ponderous in style — not a common fault of Thompson.

Mr. TREVELYAN's is the most detailed and elaborate study of Mr. Meredith's poetry that has yet appeared. It is a manifest labour of

* *The Poetry and Philosophy of George Meredith.*
By George Macaulay Trevelyan.

love, the work of an enthusiastic admirer, as appreciative criticism should be. It is also mainly just and discriminating in temper, which is rarer in the case of a poet who moves most critics to extremes of panegyric or antipathy. The volume aims at being a kind of guide to Meredith the poet, a Meredith manual. It studies the poems in all their varieties, and the poet in all his aspects. It is not brilliant or subtle, and its treatment is not always exhaustive. But it is sound, understanding, and, as we have said, mostly balanced work. In the case of a poet so intricate, perhaps we should not complain that, in his zealous delving into detail, Mr. Trevelyan leaves us with a rather confused impression of perspective. He declines, as a hopeless task, to attempt a summary of his own pages, his own views. What, then, must be the plight of the reviewer? We certainly have a difficulty in seeing the wood for the trees. We are sensible that the author has covered much and various ground, that with most of his industrious and cultivated analysis we have been in sympathy, that sometimes we have tended to dissent or supplement. It is a compliment to his appreciation of this fine and strongly original poet that our remarks prove chiefly to concern Mr. Meredith's limitations.

Mr. Trevelyan takes a sane and unbiased view of the poet's obscurity — a point on which sanity and discrimination are not common. In all such cases one side sees only cloudy affectation, another declares the difficulty to rise solely from depth of thought. He admits (though a firm Meredithian) that there is obscurity of expression: partly from certain grammatical (or ungrammatical) mannerisms; partly from the peculiar use of incessant, restless, and *momentary* imagery — metaphor whizzing after metaphor, each so condensed as to need reflective attention; and partly from the poet's packed and pemmican-like style. He allows the grammatical tricks to be faulty — the docking of relatives and connexions generally, and so forth. They are all parts of Mr. Meredith's lust for compression, as he says. But he hardly notes sufficiently the poet's harassment of his readers when he says that these tricks are soon mastered and give no further trouble. For they and the quest of compression which begets them lead Mr. Meredith intermittently into sheer bad grammar. The omitted connexions land him in confused connexions. The reader, dazed and thrown off the scent, has finally to hark back and pick up in an earlier clause the antecedent of something which, according to all grammatical logic, should refer to the clause immediately preceding. The connexion is so present to the poet's mind that he forgets it will not be equally present to the mind of the reader, who can only follow the grammar, not being prescient of the author's intention. Similar obtuseness to the reader's necessary limitations in following the processes and transitions of the poet's mind (obtuseness displayed not always in grammar alone, but in wider questions of reference) studs Mr. Meredith's pages, and becomes cumulatively exasperating to readers hard tried enough by the legitimate difficulty in the nature of his style. Such things represent the kind of failing which a poet never suspects, and which his friends lack the courage to tell him.

Mr. Meredith's passion for pregnancy has other consequences, not noted by Mr. Trevelyan. The latter dismisses somewhat too lightly the thorniness of metre which this poet shares with Browning, though admitting it to be often a defect. But the mischief is that it is a constant defect. A knotty manner of thought must bring knotty metre, since without correspondence of expression between substance and versification, versification would be metrical nonsense. But even when a passage relaxes into beauty the verse does not relax with it; it remains unsoftened, and still rattles and jolts. That is indefensible. Yet this poet can write fluent verse: "Love in a Valley" is beautiful metre, "Attila" in its virile way has no uncalled-for obstructions to the metrical torrent. It would seem a poem must be altogether fluid or altogether rubbly. Commonly it is the latter. Much of this is from the hunger after compression. Beauty and fluency and spaciousness of movement demand mostly a certain proportion of polysyllables, or the lines grow cramped and frozen. Mr. Meredith knows this, and in theory reprobates the pettiness of Saxon monosyllables and dissyllables, trotting after each other like a file of pigmies. But when it comes to packing words in a line, you can edge in thrice as many of these as of their long-limbed companions. So, in practice, the Meredithian verse is largely formed of such short words, flattened on each other like a layer of sardines. For the like reason, these thick-set little vocables are often wedged into the unaccented place, where a lighter syllable had been preferable. The total result is that the lines become jammed and will not move, or only with creaking like the limbs of a Dutch doll. The poet loves his Latin and Romance words, but grudges their house-room (so to speak) in his crowded tenement. When, in fact, it is a choice between metre and compactness, metre has the wall.

Mr. Trevelyan insists much on, but cannot exaggerate, the amazing intellectual and imaginative fecundity of the poet. That generative energy is ceaseless as the productive forces of a tropical forest, and Mr. Meredith has a fiery restlessness like that of his own Attila. The imaginative without the intellectual fertility would have made him a more popular poet. But fantasy with him is wedded to the English love for definite thinking, for a "message"; and the product, under the fierce blast of his energy, is something that often makes Browning babes' meat. This sleepless generative energy is at once his strength and his undoing. His central fault, the flaw which sums up all other flaws, is precisely the obverse side of this brilliant power — it is the restlessness of his poetry. *Quandoque bonus dormitat Homerus;* but Meredith — never. Better were it if he did sometimes sleep, at the right time. The great thing lacking to his poetry is repose. Throughout this incessant germination of thoughts and images there is a lack of relief, of space. He is at constant high pressure; and so in the packed mass of brilliance there is likewise a want of breadth.

Yet we scarcely agree with Mr. Trevelyan as to the poet's wealth of thought. There is a surprising wealth of *thoughts;* everything is elaborated through a creative profusion of veritably*matted* ideas — a tangled detail of individual thoughts. But beneath this expressional thought (as we might call it) the basic thought is not of great amount. Mr. Meredith's poetry, as we think, expresses again and again, with an astonishingly perpetual variety of utterance, a few basic ideas. Yet, if we are unable to regard him as a profound or original thinker (in the deeper meaning of the words), the philosophy of life he has based on these ideas is his own; and that in a poet is what chiefly matters. Mr. Trevelyan is whole-hearted in his admiring acceptance of that philosophy, which might perhaps be summed thus: — you must not go behind Nature, but take her as she is and fit yourself to her, suffering gladly her laws of death as of birth, of winter as of spring; and to do this you must learn, like her, the correlation of forces and the conservation of energy. Which, like most summaries, conveys nothing till it is explained; so the reader had best fall back on Mr. Trevelyan. Mr. Meredith's gospel, like most modern "messages," has one chief defect: it is a gospel for the few. Under its poetic garlands and insistence on the joy of life it is more iron than Stoicism. It demands an austere strength. The limitation of so many modern evangels, poetic and other, which compel admiration, may be summed up in one sentence: *Salvatio fortibus, væ infirmis.* And of these is Mr. Meredith's. It offers strength to the strong; to him that hath it gives more. The weak must admire, and look for another prophet, unless they submit to Nietzsche's sentence that their case is hopeless. And we are few of us "supermen."

But these are details which concern chiefly (as we have said) the poet's limitations. The book remains a good and helpful book, which really expounds Mr. Meredith's strength without shirking the acknowledgment that he is more trying than a poet should be; and it should increase the number of his intelligent admirers. A hard nut, but worth the cracking, says Mr. Trevelyan in effect to hesitant readers. And he has given them (shall we say?) a pair of nut-crackers.

MR. MEREDITH'S ODE
[*Academy*, March 12, 1898]

In this brief review of Meredith's Ode on the French Revolution, Thompson's criticism of the lawlessness of Meredith's metre forms an interesting contrast with his apology for Patmore's daring metrical variations.

I HAVE read Mr. Meredith's Ode in the current *Cosmopolis* with an amazement passing words. Amazement for its power, amazement for its sins, its flagrancies, its defiant pitching to the devil of all law recognised even by the boldest, the most scornful of merely conventional tradition; amazement — for it fulfils its title, it is itself an anarchy, a turbulence, tumultuously eruptive as the Revolution in its first unchaining. To say it is not a perfect poem would be mild. It challenges all order; it has every fault within a poet's compass, except the tame faults, except lack of inspiration. On the plenitude, the undeniable plenitude, of its aggressive force, it seems to stake everything. No one can complain that Mr. Meredith fears his fate too much. I am in tune with most audacity, but Mr. Meredith leaves me gasping.

You must read the poem once, as you play a difficult fantasia once, merely to see how it goes; a second time, to begin to read it; a third time, to begin to realise it. All the arduous power and all the more repellent vices of Mr. Meredith's poetic style are here at grips, exalted by mutual antiposition and counteraction. Never has he been more intermittently careless of grammatical construction, obscuring what is already inherently difficult. He storms onward like his own France, crashing and contorting in his path the astonishing sentences, now volcanic and irresistibly thundering, now twisted and writhing or furiously splintered. The metre is likewise; lines blocked, immobile, inflexible, with needless rubble of words, or whirring all ways like snapped and disintegrated machinery; yet at times forcing their way to rightness through sheer inward heat, and leaping like a geyser-spout — magnificently impressive.

For the Ode is wonderful, though an unlawful wonder. The first nine stanzas, with all their perverse difficulties and disfeatures, are full of astonishing imagery, passages like the loosing of pent fires. The poem has a devil in it. By no other word can we describe the magnetic intensity of its repellentness and arrestingness. Those who overcome their first recoil must end in submission — if protesting submission — to its potency. No youth could rival the nether furnaces of this production of age, no young imagination conceive these images which outpour by troops and battalia. Mr. Meredith's own language can alone figure the poem:

Ravishing as red wine in woman's form,
A splendid Mænad, she of the delirious laugh,
Her body twisted flames with the smoke-cap crowned,
. . . . who sang, who sang
Intoxication to her swarm,
Resolved them, hair, voice, feet, in her carmagnole.

That splendid outburst is all for which I have room. If this Ode be not a success (as I wish I might persuade myself it is), more power has gone to such a failure than would make a score of reputations. And assuredly much, very much, it were blind to call anything but success.

MRS. MEYNELL'S POEMS *
[*Tablet*, January 21, 1893]

It were an affectation to comment upon this review, one of Thompson's greatest. Its comprehension of Mrs. Meynell's work and its unqualified praise of her poetry, illustrate the catholicity of Thompson's literary taste and critical judgment, that could so delight in poetry wherein the mode and technique were so different from his own.

THE poetry of Mrs. Meynell is of a peculiarly and indescribably evanescing quality: she deals with emotions which it might seem as impossible to communicate as to paint a wind. These, nevertheless, she conveys through a union of expression and suggestion that is absolutely adequate. It is diction rarefied to the vanishing point. She has a power quite extraordinary of uttering the many unspoken things through the one spoken thing, of stirring in the reader's mind many circles with the one pebble. The footfalls of her Muse waken not sounds, but silences. We lift a feather from the marsh and say: "This way went a heron." And so with her, the emotion sheds but a single phrase to betoken what manner of wings

* *Poems*. By Alice Meynell.

had lonely passage athwart her soul. In this respect she is a Coleridge of the feelings; she is volatilised feeling, as Coleridge is volatilised imagination. And, even as with Coleridge's imagination, her imagination is wholly of the etherealised quality; you must not look in it for ardour. Her power becomes visible from a bare two lines like these:

> I touch not this day's secret, nor the thing
> That in the silence makes thy sweet eyes wild.

They ache with their own exquisiteness, and grieve the heart with the bodilessness of the beauty which troubles them.

It would be very false, nevertheless, to suppose her only an emotional poet. On the contrary, she is penetratingly thoughtful. But feeling is the essence of her verse; it is feeling oozed through the pores of thought. And profoundly imaginative her poetry always is, even when its emotion is too instant for thought. That thought itself, at its most characteristic, is typically imaginative thought. Much poetic thought can be divorced from its poetry, and rendered with completeness into naked prose. But Mrs. Meynell's thought is as indissolubly wedded to imagination as light to colour. We may, abstractly, conceive the existence of light without colour; but, did it thus exist, we should cease to be cognizant of it. So, too, divorce her thought from its imaginative expression, and it might exist in her mind, but it would become invisible — that is, incommunicable. As a test, let anyone attempt to explain "Builders of Ruins" to a quite unimaginative person. He will soon conclude that, on the whole, it would be a more prosperous employment to translate Aquinas into Romany. And because this poem so centrally exhibits her characteristic of imaginative thought with feeling murmuring about its base, the poem is perhaps her greatest, or at least greatest of her longer poems. But it is not her most completely representative, because one quite personal note of hers is in it subduedly struck — her tenderness.

Entirely representative are "The Poet to his Childhood" and the "Letter from a Girl to her Own Old Age." The originality of their conception is quite singular. The spiritual perception of inclusions — of the blossom in the bud and the precedent bud in the blossom — which Mrs. Meynell, consciously or unconsciously, has developed from its germs in Shelley, is here carried to innovating lengths; lengths which, in fact, make the method so proper to herself, that it will be difficult henceforth for a poet to use it without arousing perilous comparisons. No extract, however, could give a just impression of these poems' quality. It is more possible to quote from the lines "To Any Poet" which tell him that Nature and her shy children flee him during life; that only in death can he win their trust. It is timorous with instinct for the lovely pity of decay, the tender cruelty of tears, the celestial compunction of the tomb, the wide and gentle kinship whereunto we are assumed by ruinous adoption:

> Silent labours of the rain
> Shall be near thee, reconciled;
> Little lives of leaves and grain,
>   All things shy and wild,
> Tell thee secrets, quiet child.
>
> Earth, set free from thy fair fancies
> And the art thou shalt resign,
> Will bring forth her rue and pansies
>   Unto more divine
> Thoughts than any thoughts of thine.
>
> Nought will fear thee, humbled creature.
> There will lie thy mortal burden
> Pressed unto the heart of Nature,
>   Songless in a garden,
> With a long embrace of pardon.
>
> Then the truth all creatures tell,
> And His will Whom thou entreatest,
> Shall absorb thee; there shall dwell
>   Silence, the completest
> Of thy poems, last, and sweetest.

To choose among the briefer poems is a task at once bewildering and futile. The little book was surely written to show that in short measures books, not less than life, may perfect be. It has no mere rhyme; it is all (in the Roman sense of the word) mere

poetry — poetry with no allaying verse, *vinum merum* of song.
"Pygmalion," like much of her work, is a poet's poem, for probably
only a poet can entirely know and feel its moving truth. Of this
order, too, is the sonnet, "The Love of Narcissus":

> Like him who met his own eyes in the river,
>   The poet trembles at his own long gaze
>   That meets him through the changing nights and days
> From out great Nature; all her waters quiver
> With his fair image facing him for ever;
>   The music that he listens to betrays
>   His own heart to his ears; by trackless ways
> His wild thoughts tend to him in long endeavour.
>
> His dreams are far among the silent hills;
>   His vague voice calls him from the darkened plain
> With winds at night; strange recognition thrills
>   His lonely heart with piercing love and pain;
> He knows again his mirth in mountain rills,
>   His weary tears that touch him with the rain.

As in a stirless evening pool, wherefrom a stake stands upright,
the stake's reflection seems but the under-water moiety of the
stake itself; so in such poetry the mirrored feeling seems one with
its original. The incommunicable melancholy remoteness drifts
down the line. "His dreams are far among the silent hills" is like
the sound of distant waters flowing under ice by night. Nevertheless the diction is so seeming innocent, that the spell might be
supposed to be resident only in the feeling and the unsought
phrases might be imagined to be destitute of art. But make essay
to change one meanest vocable. Each lightest word in lines like
these was as the single fatal hair in the head of Ariosto's giant: you
have plucked but one, yet the verse has paled, and trailed in death.

Mrs. Meynell's metre echoes her diction — shunning elaborate
form, but full of noiseless magic. Her hatred for the suspicion of
insistence keeps the versification delicately numerous in an age
whose metre tends to strong tuniness. Consequently the sweet and
still modulation of its phrasing, the intelligent and vital niceties
of its symmetry, will evade the untrained ear. "The Poet to his
Childhood," for example, is written in a metre which — in all

other hands — is by nature lilting. Yet, without destroying its melodic form, she fingers it with a numerousness that gives it newly beautiful grace. So with the anapæstic "Day to the Night"— it is almost a new rhythm in anapæsts. Its lovely elegance of movement differs wholly from the rich luxury of movement in "The Sensitive Plant"; but for the quality of variousness, so rare and difficult in anapæsts, the two poems may rank together. Whatever her metre, her numbers are truly numbers.

Mrs. Meynell's is poetry the spiritual voice of which will become audible when "the high noises" of to-day have followed the feet that made them. To have done worthy work, and to know this; leaving the work to Him who also knows this; to rest content, even in a little ignorance of how far one's work is worthy; to discern that not the spade is fashioned for honour, but the garden it tilled, and the gardener who tilled with it — this is to be more than a poet, more yet than one's poetry; this is to have compassed greatness, being oneself greater than the greatness. Foremost singer of a sex which is at last breaking the silence that followed on Mary's "Magnificat," she will leave to her successors a serener tradition than masculine poets bequeathed to men. She has reared for them an unpriced precedent, and she has given them the law of silence. That high speech must be shod with silence, that high work must be set forth with silence, that high destiny must be waited on with silence — was a lesson the age lacked much. Our own sex has heard the nobly tacit message of Mr. Coventry Patmore. But by an exception rare as beautiful, the woman's calm has been austerer-perfect than the man's.

LOUIS LE BIEN-AIMÉ*

[*Weekly Register*, January 10, 1891]

The barbed, if not bitter jesting of this criticism is to be found in no other Thompson review known to the present writer. It illustrates how roused Thompson could become at sight of a poet unworthy of his high vocation. Unfortunately, in this instance, Thompson's indignation is not expressed with his habitual restraint and unyielding gentleness, so much more forceful and convincing than the mode he here adopts.

Fidelibus. Such is the simple dedication of Mr. Morris's new book. *Fidelibus.* What "faithful" is it that the poet addresses? Surely is it not they who call upon the name of Morris, and have exalted him in the high places, even in the booksellers' windows; who have clothed him in green raiment and set him between the chiefs of the land, yea, between Matthew who is called Arnold, and Alfred surnamed Tennyson? These must be the faithful to whom Lewis the Well-Beloved so touchingly confides his latest poem. For their fidelity — is it not written in many editions, and the gates of Hades have not prevailed against it? Now he gives to the faithful a "Vision" the like whereof no man but he has visioned: it is published in the streets of London, and the daughters of the Philistines rejoice.

Nevertheless, (dropping from the lyric raptures into which our elevated theme has so excusably betrayed us) we must complain that the poet has not adequately utilised his opportunities. The Saints who have troubled his nightly trances form, we admit, a series such as it required his genius to put before us. They are the Seven Sleepers of Ephesus, St. Christopher, Antoninus Pius, SS. Perpetua and Felicitas, Cecilia, Adrian and Natalia, Phocas, Dorothea, Alexis, Marina, Francis of Assisi, Elizabeth of Hungary, Roch, Catherine of Siena, George Herbert, Bunyan, Henry Martyn, Mrs. Fry, and Father Damien. This is a fair company, and would doubtlessly bring down the house at a Drury Lane Panto-

* *A Vision of Saints.* By Lewis Morris.

mime, for which, we presume, the procession was originally designed. We can quite conceive how effective would be the allegorical spectacle of St. Christopher, with Antoninus Pius on his back, crossing the headlong torrent of the Morresque muse. Yet we must sorrowfully reiterate that the poet has failed to embody the full grandeur of his own conception. For why stop here? Why not have given us likewise Buddha, and Confucius, and Hiawatha, and Mohammed, and Joanna Southcote, and the Mahdi, and General Booth, and Madame Blavatsky, and Mr. Frederic Harrison, and the Grand Old Man? True, some of these are alive. But we cannot accept such excuse from the chief of the New Poetry. The New Poetry should not lag behind the New Journalism; and the New Journalism can not only write a man's life, but occasionally even his obituary, before his demise. In fact, Mr. Morris's selection reminds us of nothing so much as the scriptural saying: "There shall be two in a field; one shall be taken, the other shall be left." Wherefore George Herbert should be canonised, and not (for example) Henry More or Keble; wherefore Antoninus Pius should be canonised, and not (for example) Socrates: such things as these leave one a little bewildered. A hypothetical explanation regarding the origin of the poem strikes us. When we said that only Mr. Morris had visioned such a vision of Saints, we were wrong. A Prelate of the Establishment, as was lately reported in our columns, has formulated a scheme for a future Anglican hagiology, strikingly akin to the vision of the Cambrian seer. Is it possible that some wily Jesuit, learning beforehand the episcopal scheme, bribed Mr. Lewis Morris to turn devil's advocate? If so, the method is effectual. Whom Mr. Morris has once canonised, what Church would dare re-canonise? That would be to paint the lily. They are already preserved to posterity in the amber of the great Philistine poet. Nor is it lightly that we compare Mr. Morris to amber. For amber, like Mr. Morris, is in the mouths of many men, yea, frequent in the mouth of the Philistine; it is quickly seen through, it is brittle and endureth not, and what issueth from it is — smoke.

Yet is Mr. Morris a personage deserving of serious study; for, as we have already hinted, his works are published in popular form uniform with the editions of Arnold and Tennyson.

"Thou art become as one of us!" they cry.

And, in the second place, he is in one sense the most national of our singers; no less national than was Burns. All the previous poets on the illustrious English bead-roll have represented a small nation within the larger limits of the complex English race — the nation of literature. Now, at length, the nation of shopkeepers — innumerably the largest nation — speaking the English language — has produced a representative poet; and prompt has been its recognition of him. Turn to the Press notices which Lewis the Well-Beloved has modestly heaped at the end of his volume. Clearly the Philistines have profited by the experience of their neighbours the Midianites, for never since Gideon was there such a clatter in empty pitchers. The critics have lifted up their voice with the noise of many papers. What, amidst this din of the Faithful, what o' God's name is left for those who dwell *in partibus infidelium?* Let us personally conduct the elect through this land of vision, and disclose to them the beauties which we are not worthy to touch.

We will take the "Father Damien," because it has the most current interest; and in regard to excellence, it matters not which poem of Mr. Morris's you take. He is as level as the young ladies of an elder day; who, whether they saw a china shepherdess or the Jungfrau, were never betrayed into an ill-regulated emotion: they raised their hands and voices becomingly, and exclaimed: "Oh, that's *sweetly* pretty!" Mr. Morris, in effect, begins by exclaiming that Father Damien was sweetly pretty. He had "comely youth, dark kindly eyes, and broad and thoughtful brow." This is as it should be; it shows that the poet has studied that ruggedly realistic artist, Mr. Edward Clifford. In fact, it is noticeable that Mr. Morris now and again breaks the "torrent rapture" of his devoutness by a little smacking of lips over his Saints' "fair nude youthful grace," or "thick golden locks," or "white moulded breast": which must afford his chosen audience a delightful sensation of sacred brimstone in worldly treacle — such as they derive from the pious magic-lantern, where the Prodigal Son in a loin-cloth is embraced

by his father in tears and lemon-yellow. The poet proceeds to
relate how at Tremeloo

> was born
> He whom the admiring tongues of half the world
> Called Damien.

Which seems singularly *banal* in the admiring tongues of half the
world. If they had called him Jemalow, or Tchoglokoff, or Hig-
ginson —! Still, Mr. Morris does well to avoid point; he might
scratch himself with it. Thereafter he describes, in a boldly original
passage, how the boy Damien

> with the sheperds loved
> To drive afield ere now the opening morn,
> Loosed from its floodgates in the illumined east,
> O'erflowed the slumbering plains.

We remember to have seen a passage considerably like this in a
but little-read writer, thought by some (though we would not be
understood to acquiesce in such an opinion) not too far behind
Mr. Morris himself.

> Together both, ere the high lawns appeared
> Under the opening eyelids of the morn,
> We drove afield.

It is observable, too, that in the very opening of the book there is
a similar instance of borrowing from Wordsworth. We have not
to travel far, after this, for some fine descriptive lines which seem
to have suggested those in that overrated poem called "Enoch
Arden":

> From out the odorous gloom
> Of blossomed trees a myriad creepers hang
> Laden with perfume, and the feathery fronds
> Of giant ferns spring upward twice the height
> Of a man's stature, and bright birds flash by
> On jewelled wings, a thousand brilliant hues,
> Flower-like, among the flowers, *etc.*

Here we have also a superlative specimen of the far-famed Morresque music. It has been said to be imitated from the Laureate's music. But its peculiar beauty, which differentiates it from the Laureate's, is that you can learn it by heart and stamp your feet to it; and we appeal to the discerning critics who sit in the galleries of our theatres, who have made our music halls what they are, who have fostered that noble school of religious music by which Messrs. Moody and Sankey have so happily superseded the pedantries of a Tallis, a Byrd, or a Purcell — we appeal to such connoisseurs whether it be not this simple test that detects in music the note of genius? Nay, there is an authentic story recorded by a Danish writer, regarding an Emperor of China and a nightingale; which shows that the Chinese Court esteemed its laureate for a precisely similar reason. You always know what you are going to have for dinner, so to speak; which, to be sure, is most gratifying to the conservative Briton. Mr. Morris can, however, vary his music when he likes; witness the following exquisite little snatch:

Last, when, a year ago, his failing strength laid him upon his bed, keeping the use of his great Church, first would the good man make confession of his sins, and thanksgiving because the Lord had spared his life so long to do his work.

We quote in this form merely to show the remarkable affinity between Mr. Morris and another gentleman of genius — called, we think, Jourdain. But in our preoccupation with such metrical mastery, we have unaccountably passed by what is — in the present poem — perhaps the crowning specimen of the Hadean power:

There the green surge, translucent, flowered with foam,
Breaks creaming on the sand beneath the palms;
But from its tepid waters came no sound
Of rippling mirth, nor more the fair brown forms,
Half heathen, naked, joyous, crowned with flowers,
Floated as erst on the caressing waves.

Here, again, we seem to have read something about waves that break creaming on the sand in poems published under the name of "Tennyson"; and has not something concerning "moonflowers" and "foam-flowers" appeared under the signature "A. C.

Swinburne"? Can it be that Tennyson, Swinburne, *etc.*, are all but *noms de plume* of one boundless Morris? May it be that the whole Morresque series, from *Songs of Two Worlds* to this *Vision of Saints*, is but — you understand? Cryptogram — "concealed poets" —finger on lip — not a whisper! Light dawns on us. The hidden things are made plain. This supplies to the poems that depth of meaning which is one of the two things that to a *very* severe taste might have seemed lacking. In the second place it supplies a reason why they were written — which is the only other thing that seemed lacking.

While we have been occupied over this great discovery, the poet has got hopelessly beyond us. Father Damien has undergone the second martyrdom for which he was resurrected, and Mr. Morris has concluded the volume with a select assortment of tinned Saints, packed layer on layer like sardines in his demulcent numbers. Let us, therefore, in lieu of further criticism, give the reader a receipt which, with a little practise, will enable him to prepare visions of Saints for himself. You wish to describe, we will say, a Saint's youth — a female Saint for choice, because that is prettier. First you set the thing down in prose — somewhat like this:

She remained solitary, absorbed in ecstatic contemplation, while the girls of her own age were running about the fields, or dancing to rustic music.

This, however, you can, if you like, copy *verbatim* from the nearest life of your Saint; but the next process is most important. You select from the best authors two or three passages to be worked in, which must, of course, correspond to the divisions of your own prose passages — thus:

SOLITUDE

His soul was like a star, and dwelt apart. —*Wordsworth.*

MAIDENS DANCING

Or on spring-flowered lea
Spread a green kirtle to the minstrelsy. —*Keats.*

RUSTIC MUSIC

To the jocund rebeck's sound. —*Milton.*

Now chop fine, flavour slightly with Tennyson, and serve with a garnish of the same poet.

> She dwelt ecstatic, lonely as a star,
> While her girl-peers would on the flowery-lea
> Run races with the wind, or to the sound
> Of flute and rebeck blithe their kirtles flaunt
> In hue the arum, where its stem's dusk green
> Holds spousals with the white.

We really feel tempted to compete for the Morresque succession. But, perhaps, on that throne there will never be another Louis le Grand. And his motto is, or ought to be, *"la Philistie, c'est moi."*

We have written in jest: we find it difficult to conclude in jest. It appears to us a blot on English letters that this man, who performs for the Laureate the office which the organ-grinder performs for our operas, should have received a critical applause one tithe of which has never been bestowed on fine living poets. It gives us a qualm to the heart when we see the rows of heads thrust out of window at the approach of this barrel-organ Tennyson, with his apish Muse chattering on his shoulder. Yet, after all, we must needs part friends with Mr. Morris, who has surely proved himself the Britannic Dante. For has he not given us hell, Heaven, and purgatory? Hell in the *Epic*, Heaven in this *Vision*, and purgatory in the reading of them.

THE PRE-RAPHAELITE MORRIS *
[*Academy*, August 1, 1903]

In his remarks on the earlier work of William Morris, Thompson gives much valuable criticism of the early phase of the Pre-Raphaelite Movement with which Morris' name was so intimately connected.

THE NAME of William Morris as a poet is a well-known name. Mention it, and your hearer will at once say, "The Earthly Paradise." And he is satisfied that he has placed Morris, pigeon-holed

* *The Defence of Guenevere.* By William Morris.

him as men like to pigeon-hole poets, novelists, or painters. He stands for somewhat dreamy and immeasurably diffuse narrative poetry, with Chaucerian elaboration of detail. A follower of Chaucer, without Chaucerian freshness and interest in the actualities of life. Yes, he is known and placed. But there is another Morris, who is seemingly quite forgotten in these days; and of that fact the reissue of "The Defence of Guenevere" reminds us. For though it underwent some revision by the author in 1892, that revision leaves it substantially the volume of 1858; some slight alteration in the order of the poems being the chief change. It is the early William Morris; and the early William Morris is (to our mind) most undeservedly overlooked. Though doubtless more tentative, though doubtless under external influence to a greater degree than in the voluminous poem which won him fame, this early Morris is to us in many ways more attractive than the later Morris (if we except "Love Is Enough," which is only less neglected by the general reader than "The Defence of Guenevere"). It has a freshness, a fervour of a new movement embraced with all the ardour of youth, a frequent zeal of inspiration, which we find lacking in the elaborate "Earthly Paradise." It is nowise elaborated, but bears the visible token of young impulse. And it is in a style which has now become historical, and for its historic importance alone must have an interest.

For it is the Pre-Raphaelite Morris. It was written while the author was one of the young Oxford band, in which Burne-Jones, Mr. Swinburne, and himself were leaders, which gathered round the fervid inspiration of Dante Rossetti. The influence of Rossetti is writ large across it, and it bears the common character of the Pre-Raphaelite Movement. It is in love with mediæval themes, and the romance of mediæval habits and manners, as all these Pre-Raphaelites were. The minute and scrupulous detail which characterised the Pre-Raphaelite Movement alike in painting and poetry is more conspicuous in it than in Rossetti himself — if one except a few poems of Rossetti's, such as the unfinished early poem which his brother has printed in the poet-painter's collected works. All these young men, it is clear, were doing the same thing at the same time.

Yet withal it is individual. Despite the common character it shares with its inspirer, Rossetti, it is clearly the work of a separate personality in the Pre-Raphaelite band. It is Morris, not an echo of a greater poet. The association with Rossetti only lends it charm. There is, for instance, a very charming poem to Morris's future wife ("Beata Mea Domina") which we remember reading before we were aware that Mrs. William Morris was the model for Rossetti's later pictures. Yet so admirably does the poem give the character and sentiment of her peculiar beauty, that we instantly recognised in it the lady of Rossetti's painting. It is no slight feat for words thus to rival paint, though it be not the higher order of poetry. And two, at least, of the poems are suggested by early pictures of Rossetti's — one "The Blue Bower," among the best, to our mind.

The peculiar strength we find in many of these early poems — a strength which afterwards disappeared from William Morris's work — is a very vivid and cunning dramatic quality. One, indeed, "Sir Peter Harpdon's End," is cast in dramatic form; and a very successful little dramatic sketch it seems to us, in these undramatic days. The final scene only (so far as we can discern) lacks the quality of action necessary for the stage. The other narrative or lyric poems have constantly a dramatic touch, and it is always effective. Morris seizes just the little details of actuality which bring scene or action home to us. This quality does not lend itself to quotation, since it is the accumulation of such touches which produces the effect. Nor has he the descriptive magic that makes Tennyson so quotable; though he can be graphic enough. For instance:

> One kiss,
> And I should be in Avalon asleep,
> Among the poppies, and the yellow flowers;
> And they should brush my cheek, my hair being spread
> Far out among the stems; soft mice and small
> Eating and creeping all about my feet,
> Red shod and tired; and the flies should come
> Creeping o'er my broad eyelids unafraid;
> And there should be a noise of water going,
> Clear blue fresh water breaking on the slates.

*   *   *   *   *

> A trumpet? I will run fast, leap adown
> The slippery sea-stairs, where the crabs fight.

It is vivid, it pleases; but it does not enchant, there is no marvel in it. Of the dramatic quality you have a taste in this bit, where the old knight tells how, as a boy, he fought by his father in the suppression of the Jacquerie — that mediæval fore-relish of the French Revolution. They enter Beauvais Church, which the peasants had fired, after heaping it with slaughter of women and men.

> My father, who was by me, gave a shout
> Between a beast's howl and a woman's scream,
>   Then, panting, chuckled to me: "John, look! look!
> Count the dames' skeletons!" From some bad dream
>   Like a man just awaked, my father shook;
> And I, being faint with smelling the burnt bones,
>   And very hot with fighting down the street,
> And sick of such a life, fell down, with groans
>   My head went weakly nodding to my feet.

Perhaps the reader may discern a quality there; but the passage fades, torn from its context, and on the whole we find it impossible to illustrate our praise by less than the whole poem itself. In "Sir Peter Harpdon's End" there is not only drama, but characteristic dialogue — obvious character, it may be. "The Haystack in the Floods" is a finished little piece of dramatic narration; not a syllable too much or too little, and strong effect wrought by simplicity and restraint. You get imaginative realisation in such slight and casual, but intimate, touches as:

> While for rage his thumb beat fast
> Upon his sword-hilt.

Or this:

> A wicked smile
> Wrinkled her face, her lips grew thin,
> A long way out she thrust her chin.

Note the admirable pictorial touch in the last line. Or again this:

> Straightway Godmar's head,
> As though it hung on strong wires, turn'd
> Most sharply round, and his face burn'd.

The image of the second line is excellently graphic. And when the lady's lover is slain before her eyes, and she is menaced with her own final doom —

> She shook her head, and gaz'd awhile
> At her cold hands with a rueful smile,
> As though this thing had made her mad.

It is worth reams of piteous description. But the masterliness lies in the exact adequacy of the entire narrative, not in this detachable portion or that.

Much of the book, however, is occupied with poems that seek a romantic or even dream effect, which touch on what Mr. Stead would call "Borderland." Many are too little in earnest, too obvious sports of fancy, to have much appeal, or more than a superficial pleasurableness. The best, we think, is the poem suggested by Rossetti's picture, "The Blue Bower." It is over-vague, even for a class in which vagueness is a needful element of impression; yet it does to a considerable extent, and in the greater part of it, compass a real hauntingness. Especially is this so with the repeated refrain, and with the opening and final portions. Thus it begins:

THE DAMOZELS

> Lady Alice, Lady Louise,
> Between the wash of the tumbling seas
> We are ready to sing, if so ye please;
> So lay your long hands on the keys;
> Sing, *Laudate pueri.*

> *And ever the great bell overhead*
> *Boom'd in the wind a knell for the dead,*
> *Though no one toll'd it, a knell for the dead.*

LADY LOUISE

Sister, let the measure swell
Not too loud; for you sing not well
If you drown the faint boom of the bell;
    He is weary, so am I.

And ever the chevron overhead
Flapp'd on the banner of the dead;
(Was he asleep, or was he dead?)

The refrain has, indeed, a sullen and mysterious toll; and were the poem somewhat more distinctly and sufficingly motived, it might have been an addition to the few successful things of the kind. As it is, there is much that clings to the fancy. "Golden Wings" is a pure piece of romance at play; a mixture of the early Tennyson with Pre-Raphaelite mediævalism; charming enough in its irresponsible kind; and there is much like it. A lack of central substance is the fault of many things in the book: some of the ballads might well have inspired Calverley's delightful mockery, with its refrain — *"Butter and eggs and a pound of cheese."* They come to very little beyond tinkling rhyme. But as a whole, if not great poetry, this is a distinctly interesting volume, and this devotedly mediæval Morris a pleasant Morris to make acquaintance with, a fresher poet than he of the "Earthly Paradise."

A POET'S RELIGION *

[*Merry England*, September, 1893]

In the following review, Thompson gives a forthright, outspoken criticism of the reception given Patmore's essays by Victorian England and he does not hesitate to mention the reason, Patmore's uncompromising Catholicism. The danger of presenting Patmore's ideas to the spiritually unprepared, Thompson likens to "placing a sword in the hands of a child." But in his own hand, as in Patmore's, this sword was the "sword of the Spirit (which

* *Religio Poetæ*. By Coventry Patmore.

is the word of God)," wielded by those whose loins were "girt about with truth, having on the breastplate of justice . . . and in all things taking the shield of faith." As a consequence, both poets were as popular among the literary Philistines of Victorian England, as were the soldiers of Saint Paul among the sophists and false teachers of Ephesus. In his discussion of the *arcanum fidei*, the liturgy, the source and use of Catholic symbolism, and similar subjects, Thompson reveals the deep, broad knowledge that inspired some of his most gorgeous imagery and most authentic poetry. Like Patmore, he was not only learned in the symbols of the Church, but more learned in the truth they symbolize. This truth he treasured as the all-embracing principle of his life and art. Literal exegetes may not share Thompson's enthusiasm for Patmore's many-sided interpretations. But Saint Bernard, the chief source of Patmore's ideas, gives his approval to as many interpretations as are compatible with truth. In his treatise, *On the Love of God*, translated by Patmore and his first wife, we read: "To how many uses is water put for the good of our bodies? In the same way, any divinely inspired statement will not fail of its purpose if it bears different meanings adapted to the various needs and habits of souls." Thompson's right understanding of truths common to pagan myths and Catholic dogma is particularly interesting in view of the false conclusions drawn from this coincidence by such writers as David Friedrich Strauss and others among his contemporaries.

Vox clamantis in deserto is the sentence which the non-Catholic papers would probably have passed upon Mr. Coventry Patmore's new volume of Essays, *Religio Poetæ*, had it been written by a less eminent man. As it is, some of them have sub-expressed it. A man of genius, in this nineteenth century, who quotes the Fathers as living authorities; says that the "amount of substantial poetry" to be found in St. Augustine, St. Bernard, St. Thomas, St. Francis of Sales, St. John of the Cross, "is ten times greater than is to be found in all the poets of the past two thousand years put together"; declares that "Aquinas is to Dante as the Tableland of Thibet is to the Peak of Teneriffe"; and is a symbolist after another fashion than that of M. Mallarmé and his school — prodigious! "Does not life consist of the four elements?" asks Sir Toby Belch. "Faith, so they say; but I think it rather consists of eating and drinking," answers Sir Andrew. "Right!" exclaims Sir Toby: "thou art a philosopher; let us therefore eat and drink." And a good part of the nineteenth century, agreeing with Sir Toby that Sir Andrew was a philosopher, is by no means likely to think Mr. Patmore one.

We the more regret our necessity for abstaining from comment on some of Mr. Patmore's most important essays in this book, though for reasons very different from those of the Protestant press. The book itself will find only fit audience; but a magazine is read by unlearned alike and learned. And these essays deal with mysteries of spiritual experience such as those of which Clemens Alexandrinus said that there were some to which he was unwilling to allude even in words, much more in writing, lest he should be placing a sword in the hands of a child. Since then we have had the writings of the great Spanish mystic Saints; but no one, so far as we are aware, has thought a magazine the proper place for their intimate discussion, nor do we conceive that the effect would be a wholesome one upon the average simple Christian. What Mr. Patmore says is deducible from that profoundly mystic passage of St. Paul: "The husband is the head of the wife, as Christ is the head of the Church. He is the Saviour of His body. . . . So also ought men to love their wives as their own bodies. He that loveth his wife, loveth himself. For no man ever hated his own flesh, but loveth it and cherisheth it, as also Christ doth the Church." He who completely understands this passage may study Mr. Patmore's book for himself. But there are two of the more esoteric essays on which we may comment. One is "The Precursor." The other is "The Language of Religion," which appeared in these pages. In the latter Mr. Patmore is mainly concerned to enforce two things. Firstly, that the whole system of the Church's language and rites proves that there is a body of knowledge which ought not to be, and cannot be, effectually communicated to all. The language in which the Church adumbrates this knowledge, says Mr. Patmore, like the religious language both of the Jewish prophets and of the heathen mythologies, is symbolic.

No one has ventured to touch Mr. Patmore's assertions regarding the symbolic meanings of the Breviary, the Scriptures, or the mythologies; for the unfortunate reason, we fear, that symbolism in this age of Strauss and Renan has become a dead language to English Catholics. But his mention of a body of knowledge not communicable to all aroused unintelligent opposition. Read in its place among the other essays, we doubt whether it would even have excited comment. For it is clear that Mr. Patmore spoke of that science of the Saints which is hardly to be called teaching, since it is rather learned than taught. Of this science, doubtless, it was that the Alexandrian doctor spoke in the passage we quoted above; and even the most intimate of Catholic mystic writers, although writing a language hardly to be understanded of the multitude, a language of "liquefactions, exolutions, ecstasies, and the kiss of the spouse," have, it is not to be doubted, respected the "secret of the King."

The second point is that the Church has largely borrowed the language of the ancient mythologies in figuring her own mysteries; and he particularly insists on Egypt as the source to which she was of old indebted. If anybody should be scandalised at this, it merely shows how little Catholics know their own writers — the Abbé Ancessi, for example. This was a commonplace of knowledge with the early Christian writers. Egypt was used by the Almighty as a seminary for the primitive shepherd tribe which Jacob led into the land of Pharaoh. Apart from the tradition of the true God, and such fragments of traditional wisdom as it gathered from its ancestors' residence in Chaldæa and later in Canaan, Israel had only such wisdom as the Almighty directly imparted to it; and this was after all elementary, since the Israelites' capacity for the consumption of pearls was limited. With the exception of elect individuals like Jacob himself and Joseph, these nomads were a carnal race. For proof, read the story of Juda and his daughter-in-law. The naked and unashamed brutality of it forbids us to quote it here. This rude tribe went down into Egypt fine barbarians, and came out Egyptianised. Lord Beaconsfield was hardly so much, and Mr. Goschen is not more, Anglicised, than the early Jews were Egyptianised. They brought out with them Egyptian arts, Egyptian civilisation, traces of the Egyptian language (chiefly, we think, in the case of words connected with Egyptian worship), and last, but not least, the Egyptian mystic wisdom. The command to *spoil the Egyptians*, like most things connected with that mysterious exodus, was a symbolical command. It symbolised that higher spoliation which the Israelites, under the direction of Moses, committed on the sacred wisdom of Egypt. "God," says St. John Chrysostom, "for the salvation of the erring, suffered Himself to be honoured in those things which had served in the worship of idols, modifying them in some measure." And he gives the reason: "that they might never afterward hanker after the Egyptians or any of those things which they had been accustomed to in Egypt." The Abbé Ancessi has shown that the vestments of the high priest, down even to the mystic rational, were modified from the vestments of the Egyptian Pontiff-King. The Ark was a well-known feature of Egyptian worship. The sacred beetle of the sun was exhibited in an ark, overshadowed by the wings of two figures of the goddess Thmei. An instructive dissertation, did our space allow it, might be written on the meaning of Aaron's action in erecting the golden calf; which certainly was not *intended* for an idolatrous calf, though the Jews so perverted it, and Aaron was justly censured since he foreknew that they would so pervert it. In fact, when Protestants allege the First Commandment against the use of images in religious worship, they not only overlook the actual use of images in Jewish worship, but they overlook the very wording of the Commandment: "Thou shalt not make *to thyself* any graven thing." In other words, it was not a prohibition against the authorised use of images, but against their *private* use, which so carnal a nation as the Jews was certain to abuse, and did abuse.

Passing from symbols such as these to the knowledge symbolised, the most probable derivation of the mystic Urim and Thummim of the high priest's robe connects them with *aur*, "light" (whence almost to a certainty the Egyptian *uræus*, the sun-symbol), and *tum*, "hidden"—a name given by the Egyptians to one of their gods. These instruments of Jewish oracle would, therefore, appear to typify the union of diffused and mystic wisdom: "Day unto day uttereth speech, and night unto night showeth knowledge." No student of Egyptology can be ignorant how deeply rooted in the Egyptian religion were the ideas underlying this, and symbolised in their sacred colours, black and white. In the Egyptian religious books we find the Last Judgment, with the placing of the good on the right, the wicked on the left. The just enumerate among their good actions that they have given food to the hungry, drink to the thirsty, clothes to the naked. In the same books we first find used such well-known Scriptural expressions as the worm that never dies, the waters of life, the land of the living, and the second death. There also we find: "The just shall shine as stars in the firmament of Heaven." St. Jerome speaks of the "*Vineam Domini nostri, quam de Ægypto hujus sæculi transtulit.*" Now, this mystical application would lack foundation, St. Jerome's language would have no meaning, unless there had first been an actual transference of the vineyard of Divine knowledge from the literal Egypt. Let it be granted that he refers to the transplantation of the Jewish *Church* from Egypt; still something more than the mere *people* must have been transplanted before St. Jerome could thus use the image. What (in passing), unless this fact be borne in mind, can be made of the words addressed to the Bride of the Canticle: "*Assimilavi te equitatui meo in curribus Pharaonis?*" (As a matter of fact, very little *has* been made of this passage by the commentators.) But, indeed, we are urging truisms for those who know the Fathers. The time is coming — Mr. Patmore's essays are a sign of it — when Catholic writers must quit the flesh-pots of that literal and historical exegesis which Renan forced on them for the manna of mystical interpretation on which the early Doctors of the Church fed.

In "The Precursor" Mr. Patmore seeks to show that St. John the Baptist represents natural love as the precursor of Christ, the Divine Love. He is careful to add that both loves find their fulfilment in Christ; the special type of Divine love apart from natural love being St. John the Divine. Most modern Christians will certainly boggle at this. "Why do you paint the tree?" asked Rousseau's pesant; "the tree is there, is it not?" "Why do you allegorise these men?" will ask the modern Christian; "the men were real men, were they not?" To which we answer; firstly, as regards the principle. It is an established canon of Catholic Scriptural exegesis that while man allegorises only through words and things, God allegorises also through persons and events. Let it not be forgotten that the Divine Word is Himself a Person. The ideal Saint speaks no idle word; and so God cannot direct or fashion an event or person that is not charged to the full with manifold significances.

Secondly, as regards the proof of this principle. We have the testimony both of Christ and the Apostles that the leading personages of the Old Testament had a typical and allegorical significance. Thirdly, as regards the application of the principle to the personages of the New Testament. The Fathers sanction the belief that the two St. Johns and St. Peter had a deep mystic meaning, besides their direct import as historical personages. Mr. Patmore expressly disclaims the intention to exclude any other interpretations of the Baptist's mystical import: therefore we the less hesitate to express our conviction that his interpretation is *a* truth, whether or not it be the total truth. We cannot here follow him in his very subtle and detailed exposition. As an example of his manner of procedure, we may mention that he interprets the Baptist's raiment of camel's hair to "denote what is natural"; his food of locusts to "signify nutriment in the extreme natural," and of wild honey to signify natural good. We rather wonder that Mr. Patmore did not collate that strange passage in Kings, where Jonathan, contrary to Saul's rash ordinance, tastes wild honey from the trees in his pursuit of the Philistines; and immediately *his eyes were enlightened*. Informed of his father's order, Jonathan replies: "My father has troubled the land; you have seen yourselves that my eyes are enlightened, because I tasted a little of his honey." Without presuming to assert that such is the meaning of Scripture, we may draw from it the lesson that while a leader of the Church has the right to bind himself to abstinence from natural good in his warfare against the powers of evil, he has no right to make himself a rule to the generality; since for them natural good may be the appointed means whereby their eyes shall be enlightened to pursue their strife with higher insight.

The water which the Baptist drank Mr. Patmore also interprets as signifying "the life of the external senses, or nature." Let him who doubts this turn to the prayer over the mingled wine and water in the Mass. In the original Gelasian Sacramentary it ran: "Grant us, we pray, to become partakers of His Godhead, Who was pleased to share in our human nature." But this was not explicit enough for those who adapted it to the Common of the Mass. So they inserted: "Grant us, *by the secret signification of this commingling of wine with water,* to become, *etc.*" In other words, the union of water with wine means the union of natural humanity with the Divinity. The celebration of the Mass under both species, as we all know, is likewise symbolic. It typifies the union of the Body with the Divinity in Christ: bread, being the typical formative food, stands for the body; while wine, which imparts vitality, stands for the Divinity. Of course, the wine also stands for the Precious Blood; since "the blood is for the soul." That is, blood, as the vitaliser of the tissues, represents the soul, which is the vitaliser of the body. Similar is the imagery of the Marriage of Cana. The changing of water into wine signified the changing of the natural into the Divine; and its *special* significance is pointed by the circumstances under which the miracle was worked — at a marriage feast. In other words, it meant the ultimate transformation of the natural Sacrament of Marriage into the Divine Sacrament of the Marriage of the Lamb. The *ultimate,* not the *immediate* transformation; for He "kept the best wine to the last." We may add that this use of natural love as a gradual preparation for Divine love, on which Mr. Patmore insists as at least *a* meaning of the Precursor's personality, is directly alluded to in the Canticle: "Under the apple tree I raised thee up." St. Augustine's interpretation of the Baptist is that he signifies the Old Law as the forerunner of the New.

Possibly, a wider exposition than either St. Augustine's or Mr. Patmore's may prove the ultimate explanation of the profoundly mysterious symbolism embodied in the Precursor. It is, at any rate, certain that St. John the Baptist and St. John the Divine are two of the most mysterious — perhaps we might say the two most mysterious — personages in all Scripture; and their collation with the Divine Infant in Christian art is, as Mr. Patmore well urges, undoubtedly no mere matter of sentiment. "Thus will I that he remain till I come." Such is the note to which the Church constantly returns in the offices of the Evangelist's day. Whoever can reach the full explanation of that mysterious saying — so mysterious that even the Evangelist himself could not or would not interpret it — will have done much to unlock for us the unique position which he of Patmos holds in Christian mysticism. This much we may point out for any who feel inspired to study the matter; that saying is intimately connected with the words spoken to St. John in the Apocalypse: "Thou must prophesy again to many peoples, and nations, and tongues."

We have left scant space to notice the class of Mr. Patmore's Essays which deals with more literary themes. Whether he is illuminatingly supporting the decried thesis that *Bad morality is bad Art,* crushing the fallacy that poetry appeals to the emotions only (as most poetry of the day too unfortunately does), he is equally full of profound suggestion. But we the less regret our limitation, because these papers do not lend themselves to review; they require discussion. For Mr. Patmore does not aim at "appreciation," but at the elucidation of principles. We may add a word as to the style of the book. It is severely pregnant to a degree which some will call bald. But we do not call a countenance "bald" because it is rased of the "excrement" (to speak Shakespearcanly), which hides the play of facial expression. He desires exposition, not the softer graces. Indeed, his subject matter is such, that the cultivation of beauty for beauty's sake would but obscure what is in itself difficult enough. The beauty of precision is the only legitimate beauty in such a case. Accordingly, imagery is used only for illustration or deeper expression. Few would see beauty in the style of Aquinas. Yet De Quincey justly says that St. Thomas's is a style admirably fitted to its peculiar purpose. Is not this the supreme justification of all style? Let it be the justification of Mr. Patmore's. One who has had a purely literary training, and has afterwards passed to the treatment of such subjects as occupy *Religio Poetæ,* must have experienced a disagreeable surprise. He discovers that the style of literary beauty which had been the pride of his heart, is as useless for his new objects as a butterfly-net for deep-sea fishing.

PATMORE'S PHILOSOPHY
[*Academy*, November 24, 1900]

The first sentence in the following article explains that it is a continuation of the Champneys review, printed three weeks earlier in the *Academy*. Patmore's philosophy, as reported by Champneys and criticized by Thompson, whom it so profoundly influenced, will be of peculiar interest to students of both poets.

IN OUR review of Mr. Champneys's biography of Mr. Coventry Patmore, we left untouched the large section dealing with his speculative opinions and unpublished fragments. We propose now to give some view of both. Our space, indeed, will not allow us to follow Mr. Champneys in his full and very excellent account of the poet's whole system, but we may give, perhaps, an idea of its central portion.

The whole of his teaching, both in prose and poetry, was based upon the principle that "the things which are unseen are known by the things which are seen"; or, in his favourite quotation from Goethe, "God reveals himself in ultimates." The universe, no less than man, is made after the image of God. But, since things equal to the same thing are equal to one another, it follows that Nature is throughout analogous with man, as both are with God. On this, the system of the Neo-Platonists, Mr. Patmore proceeds, in verse and prose, perpetually discerning in Nature the revelation of man, in man of Nature, of God in both. For his first principles he relies on intuition, which, like all true poets and Platonists, he holds to be a higher reason. Of the ladder of symbols by which he ascends to God and the "choir invisible," the base, to him, is nuptial love. He rightly discerns the mystery of sex as the core of creation — "Which two great sexes animate the world." And nuptial love he considers the image and key of the ultimate relations between God and man. Hence he exalts the sanctity of true marriage, as not opposed to, but a heightening of chastity. Chastity lost can be regained by struggle.

There of pure Virgins none
Is fairer seen,
Save One,
Than Mary Magdalene.

he says in one Ode. True marriage is that wherein spiritual union precedes, exalts, and justifies the union of sense.

Bright with the spirit shines the sense,
As with the sun a fleecy cloud.

It is such marriage alone which is a symbol of the marriage between Creator and creature.

These views explain his life-long devotion to the single theme of sex, which, in his hands, comprises the whole scheme and philosophy of human life. He carried the analogy into literature, art, and even (as Mr. Champneys rightly judges) politics. The method of symbolical interpretation which resulted from his philosophy he applied to the ritual of his church, and to the explanation of Scripture. In this he merely revived a primitive tradition, thrust out of sight by modern Rationalism. There is an example among the fragments in this book where he applies the loss and finding of Christ in the Temple to man's spiritual loss of Christ amidst the cares of business. Finally, he says, the soul finds Him in the Temple, its own *body*. For it is a consequence of the principles we have sketched, that in the study of the analogies of the body man has a key to the knowledge of God, so far as such knowledge applies to his own needs. The poetic beauty with which he handles this method can only be understood in the reading; nor will it be relished by the average Anglo-Saxon, with his terror of imagery. It is a further result of Coventry Patmore's principles that he holds no men to have been without some truth; and therefore applies his system to the heathen myths, finding in them analogies to Christian doctrine, as did the Early Christians. Hence the abundant allusions to pagan mythology in his poems, never arbitrary, but showing true insight into analogy. The difference between his poems and his prose is strictly the difference between synthesis and analysis. What in the one is condensed in all the splendours of inclusive imagery, in the other reappears set forth with almost scholastic plainness and severity — so far as the difficult subject-matter will admit.

The fragments which are given in Mr. Champneys's biography from his papers or his letters are unequal, especially in the poetical sections, but often contain the quintessence of his spirit, for the not too many who are in sympathy with his peculiar cast of mind. Thus in verse:

> Men oft see God,
> But never know 'tis He till He has passed.

Or this very characteristic couplet:

> What little, laughing Goddess comes this way,
> Round as an O, and simple as Good-day?

Here is one of his most truculent epigrams:

> A bee upon a briar-rose hung,
> And wild with pleasure, suck'd and kiss'd;
> A flesh-fly near, with snout in dung,
> Sneer'd, "What a Transcendentalist!"

The second line of the following is in the poet's most Crashaw-like vein of exquisitely discriminated diction:

> Thou'st turned my substance all to honeycomb,
> Each atomy a cell of discrete sweet.

Lovely is the line on primroses:

> That touched mine eyes like kisses cool.

Touched with his own grave pathos is this couplet:

> Sad as a ship far off at fall of day,
> Alone upon the wide sea-way.

He speaks, with keen observation of natural contrast, about

> The baby leaves of aged elms in Spring.

And there is a very fine bit, full of ominous magic:

> A cloud-bank pale
> With phantom portent of unhappy peace.

This has the great and singular suggestiveness of his best work. Another couplet has the vignette quality which one finds in Milton's — and Coventry Patmore's — "L'Allegro":

> The sunny field of shadowy stooks
> Untied by ambush-fearing rooks.

Finally, we may cite a passage the serenely sweet felicity of which is entirely his own:

> As seen from smoky street, the thymy head
> Of some high hill alone with the sweet sun.

To quote the aphoristic and other prose fragments of Coventry Patmore, when they bear on religion, is a more difficult matter; because they are usually intimately concerned with his most recondite spiritual psychology, and are not unfrequently couched in the special terms of his own religion. Thus they would each require a commentary of some length to be made intelligible for average readers. But it is possible to adventure on a few, which shall be given without comment:

A little bone, questioned by the anatomist, remembers the whole beast, a million years deceased.

Thy love is an incessant trouble in my breast, like one of those little quiet wells where the upheaval of the sand never ceases.

Like milk from the kind, impatient breast, so willing to feed that, on the approach of the baby's mouth, it waits not to be pressed.

Good people and religious are the first to say, "He hath a devil," of any one whose way is widely different from, and may be greatly higher, than their own.

The song that *is* the thing it says.

That which is unique in the soul is its true self, which is only expressed in life or art when the false self has been surrendered wholly. In saints this surrender is continual; in poets, &c., it is only in inspired moments.

None can move this world unless he stands upon another.

As the Word of God is God's image, so the word of man is *his* image, and "a man is known by his speech."

By this you may know vision: that it is not what you expected, or even what you could have imagined, and that it is never repeated.

Then comes a selection, partly from letters, partly from writings for the press, with the difference from those already quoted that they are on secular themes — largely literary. Here there is scarce any need for commentary; yet it may be said of the two first extracts that he did actually acknowledge a power and meteoric splendour in Shelley which it would not be surmised that he confessed from what is here said. Browning, on the other hand, he would not accept as a poet — repelled by his outrages on form. This he held more essential than matter — firmly though he insisted on the latter:

I have been reading Shelley again, after never having looked at him for thirty years. My young impression of him is quite unchanged. Most of his poems — even his most celebrated, as "Prometheus Bound" [Unbound] — is all unsubstantial splendour, like the transformation scene of a pantomime or the silvered globes hung up in gin-palaces. He is least unreal when he is wicked, or representing wicked people, as in the "Cenci."

Browning has nearly every poetic faculty — except that of writing poetry — in an eminent degree. But as a pie must have a crust, and a good pie must have a good crust, so a good poem must have, not merely worthy contents, but a beautiful exterior; indeed, the external in poetry is of *more* consequence than the internal.

I have lately read again Morris's poem, "Love is Enough," which you gave me. It is a most lofty and delicate atmosphere of mystic tenderness and joy. I don't know that a poem can have higher praise. But it is one of those things which, as Lord Dundreary says, "No fellow can be expected to understand."

[By this he probably meant that it was beyond the vulgar comprehension. He always maintained his high admiration for this single poem of William Morris.]

There is a good deal [in Coleridge] which is not much worth reading, but when he is himself, that is, in about one-sixth of what he has written, he is quite beyond any modern poet in the power of expressing himself consummately and with apparent ease. Yet he, more than anyone else, always gives me the impression that poetic expression is far from having reached its last development. Language, I am sure, has latent musical powers beyond anything we at present imagine; and if I were twenty years younger, I would set about endeavouring to prove this. Perhaps I may yet do a little in that way.

[His Odes were his contribution to the experiment. But he held that only in a handful had he made adequate use of the metre; and he still cherished vague ideas of further possible refinements in versification.]

It is a common mistake of modern artists — poets, painters, musicians, and others — to think that they are intense when they are only tense. Great intensity is always calm, often gay and playful in its exterior.

I went to see the exhibition of the Blake drawings at the Burlington Club, and they quite confirmed me in my old view of Blake as artist and poet. It was nearly all utter rubbish, with here and there not so much a gleam as a trick of genius. He does not seem to me to have been mad, but only to have assumed a sort of voluntary madness of freedom from convention in order to make himself original. He is, therefore, in a measure original, as any tolerably clever and perceptive mind would become if it chose to pay so ruinous a price for originality. He reminds me a good deal of that "pet lamb" we had at Heron's Ghyll, who imperceptibly grew into a strong pet ram, and was still called the "pet lamb," until suddenly it dawned on us that it was not a lamb at all, but a very ill-behaved ram assuming the airs and privileges of his infancy. So, you remember, we sent him to the butcher's.

The synthetic eye, which is the highest and rarest faculty of the artist, is almost one and the same thing with what is called poetic imagination, and is the source of all artistic beauty. The heather is not much, and the rock is not much, but the heather and the rock, discerned in their living expressional relationship by the poetic eye, are very much indeed — a beauty which is living with the life of man, and therefore inexhaustible. The greater the number of objects that are taken in at once by the poet's or the artist's eye, the greater the beauty: but true poets and artists know that this power . . . can only be exercised, in the present state of our faculties, in a very limited way: hence there is generally . . . a great simplicity in and apparently jealousy of their subjects, strikingly in contrast with the works of those who fancy that they are describing when they are only cataloguing. The power of seeing things in their living relationships which constitutes genius is rather a virtue than a talent . . . . Simply to believe the witness of their own eyes is what few men ever dream of unless such witness happens to have the testimony of common consent. There is, perhaps, more of the innocent vision of ripe genius in English poetry than in all other poetry, ancient and modern put together; and this confers upon English poetry a rhythmical excellence which is not only scarcely ever found in the poetry of any other modern people, but which no other modern people seem to have faculties to comprehend.

The whole of this last passage, which we have abbreviated, is profound and true. Indeed — while we leave to the reader these extracts too varied and question-raising to be summed up — it may be said, in conclusion, that, if the judgments on individuals may often call for *caveat* and modification, the statements of general principle appear more sound to the roots the more they are meditated. This was characteristic of Coventry Patmore. He is not strong in "appreciation," but in philosophic analysis of artistic law his writings have a quite classic weight and permanence.

ACADEMY PORTRAIT XXXVIII
[*Academy*, October 8, 1898]

JOHN RUSKIN

This is a pencil sketch of Ruskin rather than a portrait. Despite its clarity, it lacks the color and detail that usually characterize Thompson's criticism of work important as Ruskin's. The result may, perhaps, be explained by the exigencies of space, so often a subject of complaint in his letters to editors.

As a publicly acknowledged teacher, Mr. Ruskin was, and is not, and apparently shall be again. For it is said that among the rising generation of art students his name is great. The sale of his books has never ceased, and with the continually extending circle of his readers his time is bound to come again. Ruskin, for most people, means *Modern Painters*. When Ruskin is praised, or Ruskin's style, it is the Ruskin of those first volumes to whom men turn as typical. Yet if there be but one Ruskin, he has more than one style, and more than one style which is worth considering. We say advisedly "worth considering." For while it is understood that there is a later Ruskin with a different style, it is usually supposed that the later deteriorated from the earlier, partly in substance, but still more in style. Against this idea it is full time to enter a protest.

There are, it may almost be said, three styles in Ruskin. The first and most popular is that of *Modern Painters*. There is his later and mature style; and Mr. Ruskin himself would distinguish a third, which he calls his last manner, and which consists in writing just as the fit comes to him. It may be admitted, in effect, that there is the hasty Ruskin of *Fors Clavigera* and the letters to newspapers, as distinguished from the Ruskin of the lectures; but for our purpose the division we have made is sufficient.

Everyone knows the Ruskin of the early volumes: it is the Ruskin that men love — and women; the style which secured him celebrity, and still makes *Modern Painters* the best read of his books. It is a style of full and copious eloquence, based on the great seventeenth century writers, the masters of rhythmic prose. The sentences are stately and involved, holding in suspension a multitude of clauses, and are sometimes of a length at which Mr. Ruskin himself, in later days, held up hands of playful protest. What he had to say was said with abounding words, with small attempt at succinctness. But what doubtless contributed, and contributes, to secure its paramount popularity was the numerous descriptions of nature in which it abounds, offering full scope for his fancy, his imagination, and his brilliant redundance of diction. These were things which could be followed and enjoyed by any fairly cultivated reader. They appealed also, and still appeal, to women— no bad barometer of popular taste. In the *Frondes Agrestes* (a collection made by a woman) passages of sentiment and natural description largely predominate — as Mr. Ruskin himself gently deprecates in the preface to that selection from *Modern Painters*. This, we suspect, rather than any abstract preferences as to style, or for his earlier art-views rather than his later, explains the greater vogue of the early book. It seems useless to quote specimens from a work so well known. All have seen, for example, at least in quotation, the splendid passage on cloud. But we have the sweep, exuberance, and splendour in this example:

Green field, and glowing rock, and glancing streamlet, all slope together in the sunshine towards the brows of ravines, where the pines take up their own dominion of saddened shade; and with everlasting roar in the twilight the stronger currents thunder down, pale from the glaciers, filling all their chasms with enchanted cold, beating themselves to pieces against the great rocks that they have themselves cast down, and forcing fierce way beneath their ghastly poise.

As the power of this is obvious — its command of pictorial phrase, such as the lovely "enchanted cold," its ardour and swell of sound — so also are the defects to which it is exposed, and which Mr. Ruskin does not always escape. Sometimes he is betrayed into a touch of slightly obvious sentiment, of somewhat weak fancy — as when he speaks of foam "like the veil of some sea spirit." It is the defect and the strength of youth.

Mr. Ruskin's less regarded later style, if without the redundant splendour, is to our thinking more exquisite, as it is certainly more mature. It appeals, one can understand, less to the many. The flash and spray of many-tinted language he forsakes. But there is a quieter, closer, more intimate beauty of diction, a research of simplicity and directness. Not that he confines himself to Anglo-Saxon; he will use such a word as "accipitrine" unhesitatingly, when it is in the right place. The simplicity is in the fewness of words, as compared with the early copiousness, the endeavour after conciseness and pregnancy, the closeness between word and idea. The sentence-structure correspondingly alters; the torrentuous sentence disappears, with its multitudinous members, and instead we have sentences mostly short, direct, of limpid flow. Yet when he uses a longer sentence, nothing can exceed its skill; the charm of the diction, the sweet grace of movement, the lovely shepherding of ordered clauses. Take this quite average example — there are many much finer:

As this ghastly phantasy of death is to the mighty clouds of which it is written, "The chariots of God are twenty thousand, even thousands of angels," are the fates to which your passion may condemn you — or your resolution raise. You may drift with the phrenzy of the whirlwind — or be fastened for your part in the pacified effulgence of the sky. Will you not let your lives be lifted up, in fruitful rain for the earth, in scatheless snow to the sunshine — so blessing the years to come, when the surest knowledge of England shall be of the will of her Heavenly Father, and the purest heart of England be the inheritance of her simplest children?

The difference between the tranquil, pellucid beauty of this and the tumult of our previously quoted passage must be evident at once. But another charm in the later Ruskin is the greater variety of range and mood. There are passages in which he displays a delightful playfulness; others, again, of an exquisite Socratic irony. Indeed, Plato seems to us largely to have influenced the style of his lectures. A quite Greek mingling of elegance, simplicity, austerity and winning grace, presides over many a page of these Oxford or other addresses. Often they give the best English idea we know of a page from Plato.

When all these qualities are made the medium of high thinking, fine and saddened feeling, noble exhortation, rare, if rather capricious taste, and wide knowledge, the result is work captivating and authoritative for all time. Wise, inconsistent, polished, spontaneous, freakish, exasperating, irresistible, Ruskin is a treasure for the man of understanding — and perdition for the fool. He should be in all hands, except those that would burn their fingers with him. For Ruskin is decidedly of private interpretation, and they who follow him blindly will fall into the pit.

A. C. S.*

[*Academy*, September 17, 1904]

There are vestiges here of Thompson's early admiration of Swinburne, but it is clearly in eclipse.

A NEW volume from the one living poet who survives to us out of the great Victorian choir which began with Browning and Tennyson; the one survivor, too, of the poetic movement which centred in Rossetti, and (with Rossetti himself) its greatest figure:

---

* *A Channel Passage, and Other Poems.* By Algernon Charles Swinburne.

this must always be an event of more than common interest. For the sake of the sumptuous music he has long since given us we must needs listen with hushed attention when Mr. Swinburne again breaks silence. This new book is of very respectable size, and contains very various lyrics in many of Mr. Swinburne's well-known modes. There are sea rhapsodies and Nature rhapsodies, political poems and child poems, rondels and sonnets and pro-logues; there is a dedication, characteristically, at the end instead of the beginning. One prominent feature of the younger and typical Swinburne is absent: we hear no more the voice of passion: the roses and raptures of love are with the snows of yester-year. Nor yet do classical themes engage him now as once they did: he confines himself almost exclusively, indeed, to themes which are the direct suggestion of actuality. Even his sea rhapsodies are labelled with a place. The poems, one might say, are more purely personal and less motived by the sheer desire of artistic beauty.

It is in the rhapsodies already mentioned, especially those on sea or lake, that we find most of the Swinburne we knew of old. Here we meet again the pulse, the rush, the abandonment, the long, leaping line, the lavish profusion of cunning vocabulary. Here, too, there is much of the old ardour, something of the old beauty. "A Channel Passage," for instance, is amazing work, with Mr. Swinburne's stamp throughout. But yet we seem to feel a difference. He has given us such lyrics of oceanic storm before; one remembers "Les Casquettes." And we prefer that older work. "Rhapsodies" we have called these poems: and it is the only word. In Mr. Swinburne's handling of such themes there has always been something rhapsodic — an unrestraint, a vehement overflow-ing of all bounds, an unleashed fury of words, a piling-up of phrase and epithet, an endeavour to get by accumulation of sound, dic-tion, and imagery an effect wild, wasteful, and multitudinous as Nature's own. But in this poem the effect seems overpiled, the excess excessive, the redundance strained till impressiveness is lost through incessant threshing on the wearied nerves. There is, in-deed, more than a suggestion of effort, of the poet lashing himself into the desired tempest of emotion. The imagery, too, is no longer always so fresh or various as it used to be: sometimes the splendour is somewhat factitious, while there is no little repetition of what grows to seem stock-imagery. Nevertheless, this and its brethern are the most satisfying poems in the book, despite a tendency to rhetoric; and the metre has all the music and accomplishment of old.

That metric faculty and variety are what never desert Mr. Swinburne throughout the book. He keeps it in the political poems, where, to our mind, rhetoric and invective, reinless and redundant, quite usurp the place of poetry. It is singular to see the vehement republican appearing as a no less vehement Unionist, with measureless vituperation of Mr. Gladstone. But is there any poetic strength, or even rhetorical strength, in saying that Dante, "down the deepest and the loathliest ways of hell," saw not "depths whose fiends could match the Muscovite"? The patriotic poems, again, are rhetoric — not, we think, of Mr. Swinburne's best. Nor, save in some poems on children, touched with his lighter grace, do the miscellaneous pieces appear to us to reach his true quality. On the whole, despite those still striking echoes of the old impetuous lyric music, this is a volume which will send the reader back to the splendid poetry which Mr. Swinburne has written. We can find in it nothing, for instance, equal to the beautiful "Nympholept" of his last miscellaneous volume.

STUDIES IN PROSE AND VERSE *
[*Academy*, January 7, 1905]

Thompson's remarks on the advisability of reprinting reviews comprise the best that can be said *pro* and *con* such a project. His allusions to the decadents are, in germ, what he elsewhere develops concerning the men of a period that cultivated its nerves "at the expense of its brain."

THE advisability of reprints from reviews is always questionable, and especially so when these make no pretence to a complete treatment of their respective subjects. Most of Mr. Symons' essays aim

* *Studies in Prose and Verse.* By Arthur Symons.

at the mere rendering of some particular feature of the person under consideration, and make no attempt to depict the entire man. If, however, there is place in art for the sketches of an impressionist, so there may be in literature for the like brief and fugitive, but often picturesque and incisive, memoranda on really notable aspects of things. We can scarcely expect this volume to add to Mr. Symons' reputation, or to occupy any considerable place among his writings, but we are certainly glad that so many excellent remarks have been rescued from the oblivion of the periodical press and preserved in a form admitting of easy reference. Some of the writers he discusses are barely worth the pains taken with them; yet even when treating of a Zola or a Maupassant Mr. Symons frequently enunciates views of far wider interest than themes so unpromising would have appeared capable of affording; while such remarks as the following on the poetry of Robert Bridges show how well he can appreciate the unobstrusive beauty of a really noble writer: "He has left, by the way, all the fine and coloured and fantastic and splendid things which others have done their utmost to attain, and he has put into his poetry the peace and not the energies of life, the wisdom and not the fever of love, the silences rather than the voices of nature. His whole work is a telling of secrets, and they are told so subtly that you, too, must listen to overhear them." The excellent essays on Hawthorne and Yeats, more elaborate in treatment than usual with Mr. Symons in this volume, teem with similar felicities of criticism. Sometimes he may seem to refine overmuch, as when he propounds a sort of apology for the imbecilities of Tolstoy's art criticisms on the ground that Tolstoy is not, as he imagines, writing out of his own mind, but, as in his fictions, expressing the mind of his peasant public. "The fatal difference is that in the stories he knew that he was speaking dramatically, while, in the doctrines and theories, he imagines that he is speaking in his own person." We are confident that Tolstoy is didactic in his own person, and that, in this department, he is as much of a boor as any peasant in Russia.

It will be seen that Mr. Symons' book is rather one for the literary critic than for the general reader. The latter important personage will find little to attract him either in the matter or the manner, but the student, whether of literary psychology or of literary expression, will find it not only a book to be read, but one to be preserved for reference. Taken by itself, it would convey an unfavourable notion of the sanity of nineteenth-century literature. Mr. Symons' business is mainly with the decadents, and even when he deals with really great authors like Tolstoy, Meredith, or Stevenson, he is led by his momentary point of view to regard them on their weakest sides. We should certainly derive from him the impression that the nerves of the period had been cultivated at the expense of its brains. He knows well, however, that this corner of the vineyard is a very small one, and we are glad to find him pledged to a general history of English nineteenth-century poetry, a work demanding the most catholic sympathies. Even in this volume he has in one instance gone far afield with excellent effect, in the case of the Spanish poet Campoamor, whose shrewd and terse epigrams, excellently rendered by Mr. Symons, indicate that the mantle of his countryman Martial has fallen upon him.

THE LIFE OF TENNYSON *
[*New Review*, November, 1897]

Although sympathetic with the filial devotion that prompted the work, this review shows the limitations of the result — not a biography, but a too abundant mass of material from which, "by compression and selection," a biography might have been made. The improvement of the original in Thompson's résumé resembles the transmutation of Juvenilia, when a mature poet has refashioned them. The *Weekly Register* (November 6, 1897) in reprinting part of this review remarked: "Let it be said at once that this is by far the best review that has distinguished itself from the chorus of the daily, weekly, monthly, and quarterly press."

WE ALL know the character of things official, and among things official belongs the much-awaited life of Tennyson by his son. It is official biography. So it must have been in any case: a man's very

* *Alfred Lord Tennyson.* By his Son.

near relations are not they from whom one can expect the ideal portraiture which Tacitus sketched, but was too much Tacitus to execute; poised between the saturnine presentment and the good man with a *nimbus*. But special circumstances make this biography even officially official. The very bugbear of Tennyson's life was the dread that after death he would be "ripped up like a pig." So he conceived and made provision for an official autopsy, which should report authoritatively to the public, and thus shut out any unofficial exhumation and indecently plain *post-mortem*. Here we have the authorised autopsy, and we must even make the best of it. His son does not disguise its nature: he tells us that it is designed to exclude a fuller and more searching memoir: that we should not have had it at all but for the fear lest hands less filial should take up the omitted task, and that it was in this spirit his father desired him to prepare a biography. Such, and no other, is the meaning of his prefatory words. We must sympathise with the motive; we must recognise his necessity to produce nothing other than he has produced; yet we must be allowed to regret the necessity and the result. Hands other than a son's might have given a portrait no less homageful in all essentials, but bolder — not shrinking from the shade without which there can be no modelling in a world where day and night, even in the highest noon, are ever at grips, and without which light itself loses the value of light. As it is, two bulky volumes have been spent to tell us nothing new — or, at least, little essentially new. To his own biographical work the present Lord Tennyson has appended recollections of his father by various eminent hands. Yet well-nigh all singularly fail to give us the presence of a living man: they present to us an unindividualised catalogue of amiabilities, accompanied with some partially-recollected and not always discriminated, talk. Indeed, they succeed chiefly in suggesting the characters of their authors: from Jowett we get Jowett, from Myers Myers, from Palgrave Palgrave; but Tennyson -- —? Tyndall I would make some exception; not because his sketch notably individualises the poet's personality, but because he records some really characteristic jets of talk. In the body of the book there is, however, one real exception. Mr. Aubrey de Vere, wherever his recollections crop up, does convey some notable suggestion of the man; hints to us a personality of unshorn power, a tree rough of bark, rugged of limb no less than golden of fruit. These are the realising touches we need, and hardly anywhere else get. A letter or two of FitzGerald's adds some welcome strokes in the same direction; but I seem to recollect letters of "old Fitz.," not here given, which would have further helped the portraiture of the *man* — no mere schoolgirl's impeccable vision of a poet, but faulty often, melancholy often, morose often; enveloped in moods, blue cloak, and tobacco-smoke; full of imagination, and gruffness, and kindliness, and strength.

Yet, if the book has not all the interest we could desire, it must be read — yea, and with interest. If it do not tell us all we would fain be told, yet we are all hungry for what it tells us. If it tell us, even, things we could well have away — giving us diaries of travel, chopped and pedestrian, redolent of portmanteaus and Baedeker, which might plausibly be signed "Smith"; snippets of letters about vacuous snippets of things — yet we compound with all these for the sake of the residue. For that residue is the story, however clipped and gapped, of a great achievement which has left neither England nor England's speech as it found them; which is for all time a seal on these latter days of England, and has taught her many-flowering tongue to blossom after new, unwithering ways. The most prosaic nation that ever abounded in poets as the grass of the Savannah, it is good for us to glory over a life such as this, given with so single a devotion to literature. Every one knows that Tennyson was the son of a Lincolnshire rector, and was born at his father's rectory of Somersby in August, 1809. I like to trace in his parentage, more clearly than is often possible, the sources of that constitution which made him a poet. Those who knew him in later years marvelled at the union in one man of an imposing physique, a virile ruggedness, with a feminine sensibility which made him the most thin-skinned of men. He was literally, as well as metaphorically, thin-skinned. "Just feel my skin," he said to Tyndall. "A flea-bite will spread a square inch over its surface." From his father came his grand physical stature; and also, it is clear, his masterful masculinity. The "old Doctor" was known among the country-folk for his stern and dominating personality no less than for his kindness; and is recorded, like his son, to have been a brilliant talker and a great reader. No less evidently, Tennyson derived his sensibility from his mother. In after years, we are told how her tears would overflow at the most trifling appeal to her feelings. "Now then, mother, dam your eyes!" Tennyson would say; and with a smiling shake of the head at him, she wiped away her tears with her handkerchief. The equally-combined inheritance of two such natures could produce nothing less than a poet, according to all theory; and for once Theory was justified of her children. All the three Tennyson brothers were poets, the diapason closing full in Alfred. But how true, if lesser, a poet was Charles, is known to every reader of "Letty's Globe" — that lovely sonnet. Not much that is novel do we get regarding Alfred's boyhood. He had the run of his father's large library — the best training for an imaginative child, and it is long ago known how early he began to scribble verse. We have had the stories before: — of the half-guinea bestowed by his grandfather for a poem on his grandmother's death, with the assurance that it was the first and last money he would ever earn by poetry; and the old gentleman's declaration that, "If Alfred die, one of our greatest poets will have gone"; of the "Byron is dead!" which he carved on a stone when the news came of Childe Harold's closing pilgrimage; and so forth. The stories are not specially striking; the verses preserved not, perhaps, notably cleverer than have been written by other callow poets. Some extracts from plays written at fourteen show very fluent command of a blank verse more rhythmic than is usual in a boy's heroics. When, however, we are told that he "would reel off hundreds of lines" such as those I shall presently cite, are we to believe it? Did the poet's memory play no pranks of unconscious improvement in recalling his old-time verse? Mr. Dykes Campbell averred that poets lied fearfully about the dates of their early poems; but without using such vigorous language, it may be doubted that a poet's mind is a chemical atmosphere in passing through which juvenile lines suffer a change into something more "rich and strange" than they were in their season of first making. There is an observed difference between the style of the plays preserved in MS. (mentioned above) and these lines preserved in

Tennyson's memory: the former have no ring of the adult Tennyson, the latter partially anticipate the well-known Laureate cadence — though they are supposed to be of earlier date than the former. For instance:

> The quick-wing'd gnat doth make a boat
> Of his old husk wherewith to float
> To a new life! all low things range
> To higher! but I cannot change.

And yet more, hear this:

> When winds are east, and violets blow,
> And slowly stalks the parson crow.

Striking enough, if we can trust the poet's memory!

More interesting than any remainders of childish anecdote, with their supposed prophecy of future genius, is Tennyson's young attachment to the desolate Lincolnshire coast. Mablethorpe was the bourne to which his feet turned whenever there was question of a holiday; and it became so idealised in his mind that for ever after it was a standard of grandeur by which he tried all seas.

> The hollow ocean ridges roaring into cataracts

was one of the many lines in which he pictured that sea of Mablethorpe; and one cannot resist a doubt that those "cataracts" roared always in his mind with the added reverberation of boyish impressions, that no eye will ever see the Mablethorpe which Tennyson saw. His first education was received at Louth Grammar School (though he always said that his real education was given him by his father, whose learning made him a better teacher than any master of a country grammar school), and it was a Louth bookseller that published the famous *Poems by Two Brothers* — talked of, more than known. It was really the work of three: Frederick, as well as Charles, collaborating with Alfred. They got twenty pounds for it, though half was paid in books; and Alfred and Charles celebrated the event by hiring a carriage and driving to the well-beloved Mablethorpe. The book is not a *Lyrical Ballads*;

nevertheless, let Jackson of Louth be remembered with Cottle of Bristol.

Of Tennyson at Cambridge we get no further knowledge from this biography. We hear again about his membership of the "Apostles," that brilliant young society which included so many famous names; but of his doings in it little is recorded but silence and tobacco-smoke. We hear of the "Timbuctoo" prize-poem, dished up from a set of verses on the battle of Armageddon. We hear of his friends, Arthur Hallam, Spedding, Brookfield, Monckton Milnes, Trench, &c.; but we get little detail of him or them. It remains chiefly that he was drawing about him the little band which was afterwards to be his prætorian cohort, and make straight the ways before him wherever they got a chance, in the Press or in private; and that from Cambridge he issued *Poems, Chiefly Lyrical*. Of the work which bridged the interval between *Poems by Two Brothers* and this, the emergence of the authentic Tennyson, his son gives some specimens. They show that Tennyson was an artist in silence, as well as in speech. One, the "Coach of Death," is most noticeable as containing the theme of the "Vision of Sin," in a very boyish form. And in a fragment on "The Moon" there is one real Tennysonian stanza. The traveller sees from within the moon:

> Large as a human eye, the sun
>   Drew down the west his feeble lights;
> And then a night, all moons, confused
>   The shadows from the icy heights.

That is the old large utterance; the sure, instantaneous touch!

With a brief interlude, in which the poet and young Hallam started off for Spain to do a little rebellion with the insurgent chief, Torrijos, the book passes to the close of the Cambridge epoch. (Nothing much happened, we may add, in the Spanish business, save that Tennyson learned how a Spanish patriot may be a very pretty rascal.) Therewith comes the most interesting portion of his career. He enters on the long engagement with Emily Sellwood, deferred for over ten years by poverty and the intervention of her family — much mistrusting so ineligible a lover. It makes not much figure here, on the principle by which the intimate life of the poet is sealed against the public. He is in the full tide of young poetry, young friendship, and young struggle, ending with the crash of his affairs. A Dr. Allen lured him into a project for wood-carving by machinery. Tennyson embarked his little all in the speculation, which failed, leaving the poet almost destitute; and he was only saved by Milnes (at Carlyle's earnest entreaty) persuading Sir Robert Peel to bestow on him a pension. I suspect this Dr. Allen sat for the bitter portrait of the swindler in "Sea Dreams":

> With half his conscience and one eye askew.

During this period he added to his friends Edward FitzGerald, Carlyle, Aubrey de Vere, and old Samuel Rogers; and the letters to and from him at this date are full of gay spirits, character, and literary interest. One sees his poems being handed round in MS., discussed, praised, amended: we are allowed, as it were, to watch over his shoulder the two exquisite volumes of 1832 and 1842 in the making, to hear the enthusiasm of the staunch little band which hallooes him on. It is from his impression on them that we have to surmise the man in daily life; for conversation evaporates in the reporting of it, and to read the reminiscences of Tennyson's talk is to have a new admiration for Boswell. The pity is that we know geniuses only in the days when they are settled and celebrated; in their young fighting days they rest unportrayed, or but meagrely portrayed. Who ever thinks of the thin little Napoleon, with face and eyes of ascetic energy, terrible mouth, and revolutionary locks denouncing the fall of kings? Or who surmises a shaven Tennyson? To me it is a necessity of imagination to make some clean-conceived picture of the young poet who godded it over FitzGerald and the rest; and I seem to get some hints for it, in spite of the biographical reticence which denies me entire material. The Carlyles' are the most luminous vignettes, so far as they go. Here is Mrs. Carlyle's: — "A very handsome man, and a noble-hearted one, with something of the gipsy in his appearance, which for me is perfectly charming. Babbie never saw him, unfortunately, or perhaps I should say fortunately, for she must have fallen in love with him on the spot, unless she be made absolutely of ice; and then men of genius never have anything to keep wives upon."

This to many feminine fancies might suggest a lovely young Apollo, fascinating of manner. But the femininity that was in him by no means showed on the surface, which was virile completely, rather of Jove than Apollo. Hear Carlyle: — "A great shock of rough, dusky, dark hair; bright, laughing, hazel eyes; massive aquiline face, most massive yet most delicate; of sallow brown complexion, almost Indian-looking, clothes cynically loose, free-and-easy, smokes infinite tobacco. His voice is musical, metallic, fit for loud laughter and piercing wail, and all that may lie between; speech and speculation free and plenteous; I do not meet in these late decades such company over a pipe!"

Yet another draught of him has Carlyle tried: "A fine, large-featured, dim-eyed, bronze-coloured, shaggy-headed man is Alfred, dusty, smoky, free-and-easy; who swims, outwardly and inwardly, with great composure in an articulate element as of tranquil chaos and tobacco-smoke; great now and then when he does emerge; a most restful, brotherly, solid-hearted man."

Those "bright, laughing" eyes of the first sketch have, you note, become "dim" in this; the inner congruity not well perceptible, except haply to the inner Carlyle. He pictures him, moreover, "a man solitary and sad, dwelling in an element of gloom, carrying a bit of chaos about him, in short, which he is manufacturing into Cosmos" — carrying overmuch tobacco about him (say others), manufacturing thereby his blood into a saturated solution of melancholy. Broad-hatted, blue-mantled, of girth and stature more than meaner men, a pipe in the fine and sensitive mouth unambushed by beard, so he sat in Spedding's room at Mirehouse, pervading it with smoke and personality. Not his glooms and changes, but the oppression of sheer personality often, indeed, weighed somewhat on these other men; for he was of those whose very silence is dominant, who cannot take their seat without mastery. That splendid head, as of a supernal mastiff, is not without its virile hint of *cave canem*. The large figure voluming tobacco-smoke can also emit growls — "deep-chested music," and

brusque sayings, which have dismay for those unused to the ways
of the Olympian mastiff-kind; at which his friends smile, knowing his inward placability. Something self-wrapt and imperial of
mood, he is yet kindly, loyal to friends, loving children, much
loved by many women. Not only bursts of fascinating talk, but
wit and humour break through his moods of silence; yea, and fits
also of leonine play. A man that commands devotion as by right of
birth.

His friends' letters would be pleasant for this quality of devotion
alone. Here is FitzGerald's early testimony, for example: — "Alfred
Tennyson stayed with me at Ambleside. I will say no more than
that the more I see of him the more cause I have to think him great.
His little humours and grumpinesses were so droll that I was
always laughing. I must, however, say further that I felt what
Charles Lamb describes, a sense of depression at times from the
overshadowing of a so much more lofty intellect than my own."
Then he describes a row on Windermere, the two friends resting
on their oars while the poet quoted from the *Morte d'Arthur:*

> Nine years she wrought it, sitting in the deeps
> Upon the hidden bases of the hills.

"Not bad that, Fitz., is it?" he asked. And one feels a thrill of envy.

> What more felicity can fall to creature,
> Than to enjoy delight with liberty?

and here was one creature floating between sky and water while
he listened, from the lips of their creator, to those golden numbers
of which the world had yet no dream: the early Tennyson and his
poetry was all for him. Not the boat which carried Caesar and his
fortunes bore so rich a load! For the glorious volume of 1842 was
then beginning to be; a volume, in Tennyson's career, comparable
only to the *Lamia* volume in Keats': he was in full fertility of song,
pouring forth poem after poem; and these treasurable dainties were
passing from hand to hand among his friends. That thrill of envy
comes again when we read this letter from Spedding: — "I received
by Douglas and John Heath divers of your compositions, albeit

too few for my appetite: to wit, 'Sir Galahad,' which enjoys my unlimited admiration. The virgin-knight is as beautiful a spirit as Don Quixote in a more beautiful kind, if that could be. Also 'Nature, So Far As In Her Lies,' one of those pieces which nobody except yourself can write, and I think the most exquisite of an exquisite race. Of the rest I cannot find words to express what and how great is the glory. I have also the alterations of 'Oh, That 'Twere Possible' — improvements, I must admit, tho' I own I did not think that could have been . . . and

> Fair is her cottage in its place,
>> Where yon broad water sweetly, slowly glides:
> It *sees itself* from thatch to base
>> *Dream* in the sliding tides —

It is perfectly true; how on earth did you find it out?" In answer, Tennyson sends him "Love Thou Thy Land" and a fragment of what later became "Of Old Sat Freedom on the Heights." Enviable Fitz., enviable Spedding, *fortunatos nimium!* Arthur Hallam, in an earlier day, had similarly been the recipient of a charming sonnet on the nightingale; notable because its octave, with little but most felicitous change, has become the lovely passage in the "Lotos-Eaters":

> How sweet, while warm airs lull us, blowing lowly.

In spite of moods, the poet's letters at this time show a happy spirit. One or two are notably playful, but too long to quote. It is after Arthur Hallam's death, and still more after his reverse of fortune, that the grave mood gains on him almost wholly. In the year of his third volume he met another life-long friend, Aubrey de Vere, who brought about Wordsworth's introduction to his poetry. The old poet was content to judge the younger by hearsay— as is the way with old poets, more or less — until Mr. de Vere repeated to him "Of Old Sat Freedom" and "You Ask Me Why, Tho' Ill at Ease"; an admirable selection for a man of Wordsworth's austere tastes. "I must acknowledge that these two poems are very solid and noble in thought," said the Laureate; "their diction also seems singularly stately." Mr. de Vere likewise tells us of the final meeting between the two singers so little in contact. It was at a dinner given by Moxon, the publisher. Tennyson waited till the ladies had retired, and when Wordsworth, who had followed them, returned to the room, he went up to him, and "in a low voice, and with perceptible emotion," thanked him for the obligations his poetry had conferred on the world in general and the younger writer in particular. Wordsworth returned him thanks with manifest pleasure, and shook hands with him affectionately. In a letter to an American friend he afterwards mentioned the incident with evident delight, declaring Tennyson to be "decidedly the first of our living poets." So the setting sun hailed the rising, who was soon to wear his laurel.

Another and minor light of the past also hailed him, in the person of Leigh Hunt, who certainly has the rare distinction that to the last he never failed to recognise new genius. He had hailed Keats and Shelley, and he was to live to recognise Coventry Patmore and Rossetti. With the publication of the 1842 volume Tennyson had taken up his residence at Boxley, whence he could make easy visits to London; and in these London days, down to 1845, he made or consummated a host of friendships, including Coventry Patmore, Macready, Dickens, Forster, Maclise, and Lord Kelvin; but his two greatest intimates seem to have been Carlyle and Thackeray. Carlyle took to him from the first, and was loyal to the last. That they should coalesce at the outset is not surprising, but one would hardly have prophesied that the alliance could endure. They agreed so well in masterfulness, dyspepsia, and pipe-smoking, that an ultimate quarrel might have seemed certain. Perhaps the necessary element of unlikeness was found in the fact that they did not agree in poetry, of which Carlyle, as Tennyson afterwards said, knew nothing. In spite of the famous description of Tennyson sitting on a dunghill, with all his dead dogs about him, Carlyle shared the general admiration of literary London for the 1842 poems; but, according to Fitz-Gerald, Carlyle and he gave up all hopes of Tennyson's poetry after "The Princess." Thackeray was also a lifelong friend, whose poetic admiration did not cease with the others. There is a delicious story in these volumes of how the great novelist, in an after-dinner argument, refused to share the poet's admiration for Catullus, and roundly declared — "I could do better myself!" Next morning came a note, which Tennyson justly treasured for its fine character: — "I woke at 2 o'clock, and in a sort of terror at a certain speech I had made about Catullus. When I have dined sometimes I believe myself to be equal to the greatest painters and poets. That delusion goes off; and then I know what a small fiddle mine is, and what small tunes I play upon it. It was very generous of you to give me an opportunity of recalling a silly speech: but at the time I thought I was making a perfectly simple and satisfactory observation. Thus far I must *unbus'm* myself: though why should I be so uneasy at having made a conceited speech? It is conceited not to wish to seem conceited."

Do we not all know those after-dinner moments, and those "perfectly simple and satisfactory" conceits, which — luckily — most of us refrain from communicating? Another letter, *naïf* in another way, is that from a Lancashire mechanic, to whom, through the intercession of Mrs. Gaskell, the novelist, Tennyson sent an autograph copy of his poems. It is *naïf* in its primitive excess, the excess of a man of few books. "But your English! why it is almost unlimitedly expressive. This language of ours, what can it not be made to say?" It is interesting and good to read, because it recalls to us, with fresh impression and untutored speech, that true sense of miracle in poetry which in us is overlaid by too-repeated familiarity. It is like the delight of a blind man in his first moment of recovered sight.

One of the best things in the book is Mr. de Vere's description of Tennyson's visit to Curragh Chase in 1848. He does not shrink from giving us, in one or two touches, that brusquer side of the poet which these volumes in general withhold. One night there was a dance, which the poet declared "stupid." Lady G., "a brilliant and amusing person," took him to task: — "How would the world get on if others went about it growling at its amusements in a voice as deep as a lion's? I request that you will go upstairs, put on an evening coat, and ask my daughter Sophia to dance." He obeyed, and thoroughly enjoyed himself. A young lady spoke of a marriage as a very penniless one. Tennyson felt in his pockets, and slapped a penny down by her plate: — "There, I give you that, for that is the god you worship!" She took it in good part, and he sent her a beautifully bound Milton after his return to England. He read poetry to the family, was reproachful if no one wept over the pathetic pieces, joined in a charade, and altogether made his five weeks' stay delightful to them, in spite of such characteristic little episodes as those described.

Two years later came the publication of "In Memoriam," which was the turning point of his life. The pension in 1845 (already alluded to) had left him still a poor man, nor had the 1842 volume spread his fame beyond the inner circle of those who follow poetry for its own sake. "In Memoriam" was his steppingstone to wider fame. His long-deferred marriage followed; and, in quick succession, his appointment to the Laureateship — largely owing to Prince Albert's admiration for his just-published poem. But let it be always remembered that the laurel was offered first to Rogers — on the principle, we should conceive, that promotion in poetry, as in the army, must go by seniority! With this, and his removal to Farringford, begins his official career, and after the universally abused "Maud" (was the howl of attack in any way connected with his new appointment?), the "Idylls of the King." There begins, too, a change in the character of the correspondence. The letters are no longer chiefly from literary men, but from men of science, statesmen, &c. They are from very much greater people; very much longer, very much less interesting, and very much less quotable. The long letters from Jowett, for instance, with all their amiability, show the Master of Balliol to have very meandering ideas about poetry and literature; and so with correspondents more eminent. And this biography is chiefly, nay, avowedly, composed of letters with a thin connecting thread. The result is that the second volume moves very slowly, contains abundant repetition, and is — must I say it? — not a little dull. One brief, *living* letter of "old Fitz.," or James Spedding, or Milnes, has more matter and interest than a dozen of these long-winded productions. The descriptions of visitors tell the same story over and over again: laurels, cedars, fine old house, the grand figure of the Laureate in his blue cloak and wide-awake;

amiability, splendid courtesy, unceasing flow of anecdote, powerful talk covering widest range (of which the visitor seems by
instinct to remember the most obvious morsels), smoking-den,
pipe, abuses critics; garden, reads "Guinevere," "Boadicea," &c.;
good-bye, grand old poet, cloak, &c., again; never-to-be-forgotten
visit; visitor goes away hallelujahing and singing of anthems. Let
this brief abstract serve for all.

Nor need I comment on the section devoted to the Royal
letters, except to say that they are very kind Royal letters, and
the poet's replies very good loyal letters. Let me rather note, in my
remaining space, his relations with his own brethren. With most
of these he was more or less connected. In Volume I there is a
kind and encouraging letter to Jean Ingelow, warning her by the
way against Cockney rhymes, and confessing some early sins
of his own in that kind. Swinburne he seems to have seen once,
and speaks highly of his intelligence and modesty. When "Atalanta
in Calydon" appeared he wrote to congratulate the young poet
on that brilliant poem. "Altogether," he says, "it is many a long
day since I have read anything so fine; for it is not only carefully
written, but it has both strength and splendour, and shows, moreover, that you have a fine metrical invention which I envy you."
Praise indeed, that last sentence! Matthew Arnold too he writes
of with warm admiration. But it is with Browning that his relations are closest and most interesting. His own letters, indeed, are
few and contain little very quotable; even in his early days with
FitzGerald and Spedding it is notable how few and short his
letters are, how little they contain. He hated letter writing, clearly.
But the Brownings' letters to him are frequent and of the warmest
kind — FitzGerald's not more affectionate. The first is from Mrs.
Browning to Mrs. Tennyson, and is written after that famous
reading of "Maud" at Browning's house when Rosetti also was
present, and sketched Tennyson in the act of reading. It is impulsive, womanly, and characteristic in the highest degree. "He
did so much, and left such a voice crying out 'Maud' to us, and
helping the effect of the poem by the personality, that it's an
increase of joy and life to us ever. Then may we not venture to
think now of Alfred Tennyson, *our friend?*" And Browning adds

a postscript: — "God bless you, dear and admirable friends. My wife feels what she says, and I feel with her." All the world knows the friendship thus begun lasted till Browning's death, and of its closeness there are many indications in the second volume of this *Life*. Finally, amongst the younger poets of the day which now is, he hailed Mr. William Watson as patriot and poet; while the poet in whom that combination is finest and strongest he wrote to congratulate on his "English Flag." Mr. Kipling's answer pleased (as well it might) the old Laureate: "When the private in the ranks is praised by the general, he cannot presume to thank him, but he fights the better next day."

If I feel, in concluding, that I have merely "splashed about" in my subject, something of this (in spite of a certain proverb about tools and bad workmen) must be set down to the book. It is voluminous, partly unnecessary, and hardly attempts perspective. It is not the definitive biography of Tennyson which some of us — did *not* hope for. More, it is not a biography at all, and the author knows it. We have a mass of material which, by careful compression and selection, would excellently illustrate a biography. But the biography we have not: the illustrations are substituted for it. They attempt, by their much bulk, to appear a biography, and fail. The method of memoir-writing by the aid of letters (started, I think, by Lockhart) is pushed to a nullifying extreme. We have a selection of letters to or about Tennyson, with a few of Tennyson's letters thrown in. It could not be helped under the rules he appointed for his son. He wrote, apparently, too little to illustrate himself, and the more intimate portions of what he wrote were prohibited from use. The testimonies of others had to be called in. "Pity 'tis, 'tis true." They do not, they cannot, supply the place of a real memoir; and in some things the method tells as much against the poet as the intimate writing he dreaded could possibly do. For we hear much *about* his strong love and fascinating qualities, but we are not suffered to see them in action, and the impression is therefore remote, almost negative. Yet, since better might not be, we are thankful for this. We do get a picture, if we will take some pains to realise it, of a great man: strong and steady of purpose, in spite of surface fluctuation; self-withdrawn, yet social and benevolent; noble and rugged and human; a figure so veritably fine that the frankest detail of its human frailties could have injured it only for sentimentalists. But the present Lord Tennyson cannot justly bear blame for what we have not.

ACADEMY PORTRAIT XXIII

[*Academy*, April 17, 1897]

TENNYSON

The following article, published as one of the Academy Portraits, is not a formal book review, but it is here included as a general critique of Tennyson's achievement as a poet. Its compactness and inclusiveness are not easily matched. The slight but significant remark about Tennyson's failure to "recognise when the hour had come for silence," recalls, by way of contrast, Thompson's agonized but silent fidelity to Urania during the tragic and melancholy years when he realized that his inspiration was gone.

THERE was a time — in the Early Victorian period — when to admire Tennyson was to be advanced, when it was the test of a *recherché* and innovating taste. There was a time when this supremacy had become unquestioned matter of course; and, finally, when he was buried in the Abbey amid the mourning of a nation, the taste for Tennyson was regarded among *les jeunes* — or the more advanced of them — as *bourgeois* and outworn. The late Laureate himself lived to see the laurel a little faded on his brow, and to be extremely sensitive about the change. Reaction had much to do with it, but his own ill judgment more. Like Wordsworth before him, he did not recognise when the hour had come for silence; and he had to deal with an England more irreverent towards its great men, less patient with the infirmities of their age.

> The painful warrior, famousèd for fight,
> After a thousand victories once foiled,
> Is from the book of honour razèd quite,
> And all the rest forgot for which he toiled.

In the treatment of Tennyson there was too much of this spirit. "Œnone" and "The Lotos-Eaters" should have secured toleration for those latest poems which we will willingly let die.

Tennyson's early friends and admirers were most of them disappointed in their expectations of him. Not unreasonably, for to his early period belong the lines afterwards inserted in "Maud" — "I have led her home," &c. — lines unmatched and matchless. Leaving these out of account, the very marrow of his quality is found in those earlier poems. From the time he began to write long and important poems, the glamour (the word will not be refused) ceased from him. "The Princess," first of these experiments, is an avowed *capriccio*, showing the narrative skill in which he never failed, full of those jewelled lines and passages which were always in his power if nothing else was, but appealing solely to picturesque fancy, and more wrought than inspired. It depends for its vitality on the exquisite lyrics, and on that lovely episodical pastoral in miniature, "Come down, O maid, from yonder mountain height," where he returns to his finest early manner. "Maud" is singularly original in scheme and skilful in execution; but the bulk of it is too obviously executed, though there are lovely "bits," including the famous song. Its two finest things have lesser fame. One is that most pathetic and exquisite section: "Oh, that 'twere possible," &c. The other is the passage already referred to as having been written in youth: "I have led her home." It is in reality a perfectly detachable little poem; and nothing so wonderful in beauty, in music, in passionate intuition, did Tennyson ever write— or, it might almost be said, any other man. It is "of a higher mood" than the rest of his work; and both in style and for its insight into the very heart of love recalls some of the odes of Mr. Coventry Patmore, without losing anything of Tennyson's softer and more sensuous charm. Of "In Memoriam," the weakness is that small and shallow, if admirably expressed, philosophy which did much to make it popular; nor is the pose of perpetual intensity without a feeling of unreality and affectation. If he were mourning a woman, it would almost be suspect; in the case of a male friend, it is impossible to resist the sensation that the poet is laying out his capital of grief to the very best interest. On the other hand, that Tennysonian faculty for which "description" is too dull a phrase, and "word-painting" too vile, is here carried to the highest point of skill. The poem contains a marvellous series of miniatures in this kind. Lastly come the "Idylls." Their finish and brilliancy are undeniable. Their narrative power is not matched in modern poetry; such a poem as "Gareth and Lynette," for example, is a supreme example of a picturesque romance told with a pictorial beauty which holds the reader to the end. The pathos of some is not destroyed by the fact that there are details in which the pathos leans a little towards stage-effect. Diction and imagery retain their power, though with more evidence of labour. But the best critics are unanimous in refusing to consider the "Idylls" a great and unified work. Beyond the "Idylls" we, at any rate, will not go. The rest is dying embers.

To the earlier poems, then, we return. There Tennyson was content to be lyric and idyllic, and to be brief; his genius lay in miniature, and he kept to miniature. There is no attempt to make a long poem out of a sheaf of small poems. There he is magic and wonderful; his inspiration spontaneous enough not to be sicklied over by the careful choice of diction. There we have the series of classic idylls, the noble "Ulysses," "Œnone" with its glorious descriptive opening, the magical beauty and soft music of "Tithonus," "The Lotos-Eaters," that Tennysonian "Kubla Khan"; the "Palace of Art" and the "Dream of Fair Women" — which carry richly imaginative picture-making to its acme; the "Vision of Sin," with its strange melodiousness; all those smaller pieces, too numerous to name, which are filled with the very breath of young romance, and numbers of exquisite songs and lyrics; these belong to the early Tennyson. Those smaller pieces, indeed, we think the most quintessential of all Tennyson's work. The attempt to enumerate is an injustice, for the things we leave out are the very things we would have mentioned; and this shows the fertile richness of his genius at that youthful epoch. Here is the haunting Tennyson — the Tennyson, we believe, who will hold the ear of the ages.

That he is immortal let no reaction, no wish to be elect and distinguished from the multitude, make us dispute. Whether he or another was the greatest poet of his day is a thing of no moment to inquire. There is no such master of external finish in our tongue; his genius was like his style; he was not a prophet, save as every true poet has his measure of prophecy, greatest when he least dreams of it; he had little of the inward sight, but he saw outer things perfectly, and painted them unsurpassably. What remained constant in him throughout his career was the power of concentrating external images in a line or a phrase, so that they are veritably thrown and focussed on the retina of him who reads. The greatest masters, even Milton, did not surpass him in this; he cultivated it all his life, and it is the appropriate gift of a master of miniature. Examples can be taken by handfuls, even from those later poems which we have declined to think his greatest: we need go no further than the "Idylls."

> He bore
> What dazzled all, and shone far off as shines
> A field of charlock in the sudden sun
> Between two showers, a cloth of palest gold.

That "leaps on the eyes," as the French say. Here is another vivid picture, vitalised by his exact observation of natural things:

> Bowl-shaped, thro' tops of many thousand pines
> A gloomy-gladed hollow slowly sank
> To westward—in the deeps whereof a mere,
> Round as the red eye of an Eagle-owl,
> Under the half-dead sunset glared.

The same minute observation could furnish him with felicitously imaginative images for internal things:

> Some, whose souls the old serpent long had drawn
> Down, as the worm draws in the wither'd leaf
> And makes it earth.

Not less could he draw from it images Homeric in their homely but beautiful aptness:

> Slowly falling as a scale that falls,
> When weight is added only grain by grain,
> Sank her sweet head upon her gentle breast.

His style, in the Greek idylls and the finest parts of "In Memoriam," had the classic calm, dignity, and order, combined at will with modern richness. No man was more capable of *gnomic* utterance, couched in language of memorable justness and restraint: witness "Of Old Sat Freedom on the Heights," and many another piece. The truths were not subtle or original; but you felt that they were delivered straight to the target, and they were barbed to quiver in your mind. But the early poems had all these things and more. They had the air of the "golden clime" and the fields of dream, the "something afar," which is at the heart of all romance; and they conveyed it with a richness, as of spices and incense, which was like nothing else in our poetry. "Sir Galahad," "The Lady of Shalott," "Recollections of the Arabian Nights," the verses on "The Poet," all breathe it in different ways, as do the poems already enumerated. Then, too, Tennyson has passion, golden and wonderful. "Love and Duty" ranks with the Elizabethan love-poetry, with that great poem we have spoken of in "Maud," and with certain of Coventry Patmore's love-poems, for ardour and beauty, sublimated by imagination and the pathos of the "tears that are in human things." Grandeur and stateliness as a rule he did not reach. But that little fragment, "The Eagle," is so splendidly fine as to be not far from sublimity. And in one of the poems of his middle period, "Lucretius," it is impossible to deny grandeur. There the melodiousness of his own blank verse reaches at times something of a Miltonic involution and majesty. It is a masterly mingling of stateliness and beauty; his very greatest poem in the kind to which it belongs.

As a song-writer, looking to the number and the perfect beauty of his songs, we question whether he be not the greatest in the language. Wherever else he fails, in them he is never less than Tennyson. The *tours de force* of this versatile poet in experiments less purely or strictly poetical we do not care to discuss: it is not "The Northern Farmer" and its kind that will decide his place in song. At his best, he expressed external loveliness, whether of nature or romance, with beautiful perfection. It may not be the greatest thing a poet can do, but to the poet who can do it greatly I see not how we can deny greatness. What should be his place among other greatnesses — does it matter very much? Unhappy the man who, in the presence of a beautiful woman, must vex his soul regarding her place among other beauties!

EXCURSIONS IN CRITICISM
[*Academy*, October 23, 1897]

THE WITHHELD POEMS OF TENNYSON

Thompson, who omitted many poems from his published volumes, here gives his ideas on the posthumous publication of poems excluded and passages excised by Tennyson. This article supplements the formal review of Tennyson's *Life* by his son, printed in the *New Review*.

"THE artist is known by his self-limitation," said Tennyson; and he righteously condemned the publication of "chips from the workshop" of poets. Yet his son, in the recent biography of his father, has published a number of poems and lines which Tennyson withheld from the public. They prove, by Tennyson's own rule, that Tennyson was an artist. The only value of their publication is to show how little we lose, how much we gain, by such self-limitation; and to impress upon young poets the necessity of using like self-denial. The first thing needful to notice is the very early "Coach of Death." It has not a foreshadowing of the coming Tennyson in style, yet it contains the argument of "The Vision of Sin." The gaunt traveller, the thin-shanked host, are all there; but in style it is a youthfully wanton following of Burger and his German kin. His early University residence yields two fragments, both of which anticipate his maturer style: the one in description, the other in political utterance. But the earliest complete poem of importance is "Anacaona" His characteristic love of new and musical metrical combinations first shows itself in this. I referred but lately, in one of these essays, to the resemblance between Mangan and Edgar Poe in their treatment of the iterative refrain.

Clearly, however, the thing was in the air, for here we find the same device in a minor degree.

> Bathing in the slumbrous coves,
> In the cocoa-shadowed coves
> Of sun-bright Xaraguay,

quite hints the method of Edgar Poe; and not only Poe, but Mangan, excels Tennyson in this kind. "Anacaona" is as deficient in striking substance as Mangan; while its metre, for all its elaboration, falls short of the Irish poet's felicity. The rhymes did not satisfy Tennyson, we are told, which probably means the arrangement of rhymes — the metrical form. And he was right; it does not achieve its intention. The long "Hesperides," we are told, he was sorry for having omitted from his "Juvenilia." But we may thank his better and earlier judgment. In its form (and it depends on form rather than on substance) it is somewhere between the "Lotos-Eaters" and such poems as "The Merman." Coleridge, who rightly blamed him because in his first volume he had adventured novel combinations before he was securely grounded in regular metre, would have found yet more fault with the "Hesperides." Its unfulfilled intention came (metrically) to golden fruit in the "Lotos-Eaters"; and we lose nothing by its absence from his poems. A following sonnet — "Lasting Sorrow" — has an excellent final couplet:

> I am so dark, alas! and thou so bright,
> When we two meet there's never perfect light.

A sonnet on Cambridge, also, written in 1830, is good in a minor kind. And, finally, a sonnet on the "Nightingale" has an octave charming in itself, and notable as the basis of a lovely passage in the "Lotos-Eaters":

> Check every outflash, every ruder sally
> Of thought and speech, speak low, and give up wholly
> Thy spirit to mild-minded Melancholy:
> This is the place. Thro' yonder poplar alley,
> Below, the blue green river windeth slowly,
> But in the middle of the sombre valley
> The crisped waters murmur musically,
> And all the haunted place is dark and holy.

But so much — by far the greater part — of these poems reads like Tennyson imitating himself. "The Statesman" and "Truth" are of this kind; "The Mother's Ghost" is not even Tennyson's ghost; it is nothing. And of the patriotic songs what shall be said? "Britons, guard your own," is painfully poor; "Hands all round," in spite of lines which have the dignified Tennysonian manner, is quite below the high poetic mark. "The Philosopher" is a perfect example of workmanship without inspiration. But why go on? Tennyson thought none of these things worthy a place in his published work; and their publication shows that he had admirable self-judgment. It is the same with the omitted stanzas from his various poems; they deserved omission, and not posthumous publication. The best of them are some of those excluded from the "Dream of Fair Women." This astronomical stanza, for instance:

> Regions of lucid matter taking forms,
> Brushes of fire, hazy gleams,
> Clusters and beds of worlds, and bee-like swarms
> Of suns and starry streams.

This is fine and vivid: it and its companion stanzas were doubtless left out to gain compactness. He had intended (so we are told) to insert sculptures in that rich poem, but only finished two. The first, of Elijah, is good, but not magical like the pictures we possess:

> Tall, eager, lean and strong, his cloak wind-borne
> Behind, his forehead heavenly bright
> From the clear marble pouring glorious scorn,
> Lit as with inner light.

The second, of Olympias, I think better, and not unworthy of a place in the poem. The omitted prologue, on the other hand, to "The Gardner's Daughter" is all workmanship, workmanship, and decidedly is better away. Nevertheless, in that poem occurs the single omission which I find it possible to regret:

> Her beauty grew: till drawn in narrowing arcs,
> The southing Autumn touch'd with sallowed gleams
> The granges on the fallows.

That is magical, in Tennyson's finest style of pictorial suggestion. It is said to have been excised because FitzGerald said it was taken from a landscape — background in a picture by Titian — surely the very strangest reason ever assigned for an omission! Let us thank and admire the great poet's judgment, that it is the sole ill-advised excision which his son's Memoir has been able to bring to light.

MISCELLANY OF ENGLISH POETS AND POETRY

ENGLISH SATIRISTS *
[*Academy*, October 28, 1899]

When one has read Thompson's criticism of satirists included in this collection, one must regret that Thompson did not publish his own anthology of English satires. One wonders, had he lived to read Chesterton's later work, if he would still have written: "for a first-rate light satirist the age waits."

THIS volume of the "Warwick Library" is, let it be said frankly, a good idea indifferently executed. It was a good idea to compile a specimen-volume illustrating the main progress of English satire. But the editor has by no means shown the judgment which could be wished. His introduction, indeed, will serve; though in many respects it has a curiously old-fashioned air. We have, for instance, the ancient heresy revived that Pope "improved and polished" the versification of Dryden. Most modern critics have agreed with Leigh Hunt that Pope simply narrowed and mechanised it; and that his metre was (as has been said) "like a rocking-horse — long end up, short end down." What is more, the great modern poets (who ought to know), with Keats at their head, have gone to Dryden as their teacher in rhyming heroics, not to Pope. Mr. Smeaton relies on Prof. Courthope for the statement. The reader can choose between the poets and the Professor. We might produce more examples of what we mean; but Mr. Smeaton becomes exasperating when we follow him into detail. Nor does our quarrel lie with the preface, nor yet with the choice of authors, but with the choice of selections. Marvel is poorly represented by *Nostradamus' Prophecy*, when the far wittier

* *English Satires*. Edited by Oliphant Smeaton.

satire on the Dutch, or that on Flecknoe, lay to hand. Dryden again, apart from *Mac Flecknoe,* is represented by quite minor work. Pope is adequate; but from Swift only one extract is given which shows him at the height of his powers — the dedication of the *Tale of a Tub.* Addison appears in but one piece, and so does Moore, whose brilliant light satire might surely have been represented. Canning's *Epistle from Lord Boringdon to Earl Granville* and *Reformation of the Knave of Hearts* (but inferior work) might have given place to more specimens from the *Anti-Jacobin;* and of Byron only the excerpt from the "Vision of Judgment" can be considered a satisfactory example. Praed at Praed's best is really not represented; Calverley has but a single piece. And (though this is a lesser matter) should Browning's "Cristina" and "Lost Leader" come under the head of satire proper?

Satire (though Mr. Smeaton seems to think otherwise) in these latter times has fallen on evil days. That it has lost its personal virulence is true; but in doing so it has lost its very character as satire. We do not say the consequence was necessary; but so it is. It is impossible to rank with the literary satire of old the swarms of ephemeral "skits" which fill the daily and periodical press. The increased stringency and severe interpretation of the libel laws has killed personal satire. These laws are administered by men for the most part ignorant of, and indifferent to, the question of literary justification — men who would cast Byron in heavy damages, and comment severely on the scurrility of Pope. And this has tended to encourage a general thinness of skin in society. The old tradition of literary give-and-take is no more. We have lost our robustness. The change is ill for satire, and not good for society. In old days the man who was satirised hit back— publicly or privately. Though the assailant were a Pope, and he the veriest among the aborigines of Grub-street — a Dennis or less than Dennis (who was really a sturdy specimen of what stood for journalism in the eighteenth century) — it mattered not: he drew his quill and wrote back at his redoubtable adversary. And we know that in his own day he often held his ground much more stoutly than appears to posterity. Nowadays Dennis would yelp like a dog under a cart-wheel; call heaven, earth, and the Law Courts to witness his scandalous indignities; vow he would have damages if there was a Libel Act in England, and get them — from a judge who would talk scathingly about the necessity of protecting honest citizens against such unjustifiable allusions as those of this Mr. Pope, who seemed to be a writer of some reputation, and, therefore, all the more necessary to be taught that the good name of private citizens was sacred in the eyes of the law. When you can hardly use the name of Smith in a novel, lest some owner of that exclusive patronymic should object to its employment, things are getting crowded for the luckless satirist. The success of one angry man with a grievance encourages others. When you can make the satirist pay in pocket, only the man of sense will submit to satire without advertising it in an action. And satire does not thrive on men of sense, while all the absurdities are under the protection of the law. It is not good for private manliness that public opinion should encourage this excitable and weak sensibility.

What a forest of flourishing trees would be thinned out from English literature had the Parliamentary Vulcan earlier furnished the Law with its awful libel thunderbolts! Chaucer and Langland might stand; so might Hall (no very biting satirist), and Donne (pungent, clever, with metre like a rope all hanks and knots); but from Butler downwards they are all inveterate libellists. Who has done justice to old Sam Butler, most singular and unpatterned of satirists? Not Charles II, who neglected him, so that no wonder the saturnine wit needed to be wound up by wine and lost its brilliance again after a bottle or two. Not Mr. Smeaton, who contributes little to the criticism of *Hudibras* beyond the observation that it would have been better had it been shorter. Not M. Taine, whose Gallic mind sees only a coarse burlesque — bears and trulls, and boors and bone-thumpings. Not average English opinion, which sees only a curious and now highly unreadable specimen of obsolete satire, containing some stock-extracts, and, like *Hamlet*, very full of quotations. *Hudibras* has paid the penalty for the poor and clumsy scheme which doubtless helped its immediate popularity. As a narrative, no words of M. Taine can be too bad for it. The burlesque incidents are dull and coarse and stupid; the Skimmington and the bear and Trulla and the stocks and the whackings, all are in the most clownish vein of Anglo-Saxon humour. Butler is the dreariest Jack-Pudding that ever grinned at a fair; but when he forgets his framework, halts in the action, candidly confesses — "Story, God bless you! I have none to tell, sir!" and pours forth his personal reflections on men, affairs, and life; then what a difference! Then you have not merely satire, but the quintessence of a quite peculiar wit. Flash follows flash — brief, pregnant, admirably turned; illustrated by imagery the most comically apposite in its sudden juxtaposition of unexpected ideas, pointed by allusions drawn from the widest range of curious reading; and it is always Butler who reflects, whether the passage be put in the mouth of Hudibras, Whackum, Sidrophel, the Widow, or whom you please. Written frankly in the form of satiric monologues, these witty masterpieces would have been better and more enduring. Not all can relish them: they are apt to be too subtle for the average palate; though he mocks at metaphysics, there was much of Donne's metaphysical turn in Butler; his wit, too, almost demands a poet to relish it — it turns so much on analogy which, though comic, is really fanciful. You find the same thing in Congreve. When he describes two angry and breathless fools, "spluttering at one another like two roasting apples," the exquisitely ludicrous image is as much a stroke of fancy as if it had been serious. Once Congreve turns this power to serious use, and the result is charming. "You are a woman," his hero says, "one to whom heaven gave beauty when it grafted roses on a briar. You are the reflection of heaven in a pond, and he that leaps at you is sunk." A most graceful image! So Butler also trips into poetry when he writes of the moon's

> Mysterious veil, of brightness made,
> That's both her lustre and her shade.

Yet by the same exertion of fancy he can produce the satiric epigram,

> Like the world, men's jobbernoles
> Turn round upon their ears, the poles.

Or he can say:

> Some have been cudgelled, till they know
> What wood a cudgel's of by th' blow;
> Some kicked, until they can tell whether
> A shoe be Spanish or neat's leather.

For the lover of phantastic and subtly ingenious wit, *Hudibras* is still a treasury; to be dipped into like an anthology, not to be read through or continuously.

Only less read, if more talked about, is Dryden, Scott's (or Claud Halcro's) "Glorious John," who passed his life in cudgelling others, and was once literally cudgelled himself. Buckingham, who could, and did, revenge himself by a clever satire, might have spared that meaner vengeance. Yet, for the few who still love unfashionable letters, what a writer! What a careless bravery of strength, what a dexterity of touch, like the swashing brush of a Rubens! He just pats a verse, and leaves on it the dent of his leonine paw. Material seems immaterial to this wonderful gift of technique. He could have made a decent poem of *Bradshaw's Guide;* and what a satire he would have made of Kruger, on whom modern writers are puffing in the effort to be "smart"! Pope we know: his epigram is more akin to modern methods. But who reads Swift? It is the strangest irony of fate, more sardonic than Swift's own, that the grimmest satire of this gloomy and terrible master of irony should be chiefly known as a fairy tale for children! He had every gift of satire save mirth; he was an amazing master of English: but modern man finds life too sad that he should add to it the reading of Swift. You must take him with antidotes, as his own age did: the delightful archness of Addison's finished raillery, the sweet-tempered laughter of Steele.

Must not one take Byron also with some antidote? A magnificent satirist, who wasted an unfortunate amount of time in writing poetry, with him the great line ends. Nowise inferior, at his strongest, to the powerful satirists of the eighteenth century, he added a peculiarly personal quality of reckless dash and mordant mockery. "The Vision of Judgment" is well-nigh Satanic in the scathing and blasting force of its derision. There is something in it, perhaps, caught from Voltaire. It is this heartless quality which asks an antidote. He was the first to take a delight in persistently satirising the school-girl, the "bread-and-butter miss." Only Byron would have broken this butterfly on so cruel a wheel. You may find his antidote in Moore, whose serious verse has suffered more eclipse than Byron's own. But his light satiric pieces are brilliantly deft in workmanship, with the adroitest natural air of artifice; gay and stinging as dragon-flies. Why should not satire find a possibility of resurrection in the method of these? Formal satire, in all its plenitude of rhetorical art, is grown impossible. We will scarce give attention to an ode, much less to a lengthy piece of didactic ridicule. Nor will modern conditions permit Moore's personality. But surely the field of social and political satire is still open? And such glittering arrow-flights of polished, easy, daintily-edged and finished banter as his were the very thing to take modern taste. Any way, for a first-rate light satirist the age waits — with more cutting-power, more weight behind the fine edge, than is in Praed, or his many successors.

. PATRIOTISM AND POETRY *
[*Academy*, December 7, 1901]

Even in the face of the sorry poetry of national anthems, generally, Thompson holds that patriotism is and always has been "one of the prime motives of song" — a principle implicitly denied by Yeats and his com-peers in their zeal to "de-Davisize" Irish poetry. This review shows that Thompson was no less exacting with editors than with poets.

FROM the time of the legendary Tyrtæus down to the present day patriotism has been accounted one of the prime motives of song. Assuredly England has never been lacking in patriotism, even to a somewhat blatant degree, while in poetry she is foremost among the nations. One would expect, therefore, a collection of English patriotic verse to be very rich in poetry. Yet we must own to some

* *Patriotic Song.* Edited by Arthur Stanley.

feeling of disappointment in turning over the leaves of this collection, *Patriotic Song,* which Mr. Arthur Stanley has evidently
striven hard to make representative. Perhaps the patriotism of the
poets in general finds vent rather indirectly and in passages than in
poems devoted directly and exclusively to the love of country.
Certainly this collection is far from impressing us as the fine flower
of poetry, though inevitably it contains much fine poetry. Nor has
Mr. Stanley spared to fling the net wide. Not satisfied to include
merely English patriotic verse, he has embraced that of Ireland,
Wales, Scotland (including Jacobite songs, which hardly come
under the strict head of patriotism), and the British dependencies —
India, Australia, New Zealand, and even South Africa. Nay,
apparently it matters not to him what country is celebrated, provided it be by an English-speaking poet. Perhaps this very width
of the net impoverishes the impression produced by the collection.

Canada and South Africa, for example, yield not one true poem
of the patriotic order. It is sweeping, but true. The patriotism is
unimpeachable, but not so the poetry. New Zealand is little better,
and Australia not fertile. Wales, again, draws blank, or nearly so.
Coming to individual poems, our objections are many. What claim
has Adam Lindsay Gordon's hunting-song to a place in patriotic
verse? How does Marvell's "Bermudas" come under that heading?
Why is T. E. Brown's "Land-Ho!"—a religious poem — in the collection? And why include poems the patriotism of which is nowise
British — such as Byron's "Isles of Greece," or Mrs. Browning's
"The Forced Recruit" — yet omit others of a like kind? Once open
the door in this direction, it seems arbitrary to stop at a couple of
poems.

Taking, then, objections on other grounds, why are Dibdin's
poems arranged in two batches, separated by those of other writers,
whereas the rule of the book is to keep each author's poems
together? It is clear that Mr. Stanley has been lenient with regard
to poetic quality, in order to represent as many recent writers as
possible. But there can be no such excuse for the inclusion of early
work, or inferior work of great poets, where it was quite possible
to secure only poems of good quality. Why, then, include such a
snatch as "Here's a Health Unto His Majesty" — a Cavalier lyric,

alike contemptible in quality and quantity, a single witless stanza? Is "Down Among the Dead Men" a patriotic poem worth reading, divorced from its music? Dryden's "Song of King Arthur" is one of the most vilely bad songs that even Dryden ever wrote — and Glorious John was never lucky in his songs. The National Anthem is fiddler's poetry. Wordsworth is represented by several sonnets, but not, surely, by all that might and should have been included. "Milton, thou should'st be living at this hour," for example, should surely have found a place: we doubt, indeed, whether search would not discover almost as many deserving of quotation which have been omitted as those which have found a place. "Fair Star of Evening" is another that immediately leaps to mind. In "Men of Kent," by-the-way, "her haughty bow" is misprinted for "her haughty brow." Campbell, on the other hand, is represented not only by his fine and few patriotic lyrics, but by "Men of England" — a quite unworthy specimen. We fear, indeed, that poems have too often been admitted merely on the authority of a name. But last, and most surprising, why is Gerald Massey's poem on "The Revenge" inserted, yet Tennyson's "Ballad of the Revenge" omitted? We do by no means hold Tennyson's poem so high as it is customary to hold it. To our thinking, it is far from being among his best work, or inspired throughout. But it puts Gerald Massey's poem completely out of court — and that without denying to Massey a certain merit, of no very high kind.

Mr. Stanley's collection is none the less interesting, if far from impeccable. To quote the many poems in it which are known to every average reader of English verse would be idle. More profitable is it to notice some that are less, if at all, known. Drayton's fine "Ballad of Agincourt" we have all read. But how many know the anonymous poem which Mr. Stanley gives, and which has a spirit of its own, though greatly inferior? If it be the earlier of the two, it would certainly seem as though Drayton had taken his inspiration from it, as regards form:

> Agincourt, Agincourt!
> Know ye not Agincourt,
> Where English slew and hurt
>   All their French foemen?

> With their pikes and bills brown,
> How the French were beat down,
>   Shot by our Bowmen?
>
> Agincourt, Agincourt!
> Know ye not Agincourt?
> Never to be forgot,
>   Or known to no man?
> Where English cloth-yard arrows
> Killed the French like tame sparrows,
>   Slain by our Bowmen?
>
> Agincourt, Agincourt!
> Know ye not Agincourt?
> Dear was the victory bought
>   By fifty yeomen.
> Ask any English wench,
> They were worth all the French:
>   Rare English Bowmen!

The number of archers, by-the-way, seems slightly unhistorical. Passing over Marvell's great Cromwellian Ode, and much else, Dryden's verses on London in 1666, very characteristic of his early style, have one stanza curiously and strikingly appropriate to the present posture of England's affairs:

> Already we have conquered half the war,
>   And the less dangerous part is left behind;
> Our trouble now is but to make them dare
>   And not so great to vanquish as to find.

Save for the style, it might have come from a present-day poet, writing on the most recent aspect of the Boer War. Dibdin makes an excellent figure in this collection. At his best when he least strove to be "poetical" in the manner of his day, his thoroughly vernacular songs have much which enables us to understand that he must have been the sailors' Kipling of his time. In "Tom Tough" even the metre suggests that of Kipling's fine "Last Chanty," which begins:

> Thus spake the Lord to the jolly, jolly mariners.

This is Dibdin's poem:

> My name, d'ye see's Tom Touch, I've seed a little sarvice,
>   Where mighty billows roll and loud tempests blow;
> I've sailed with valiant Howe, I've sailed with noble Jarvis,
>   And in gallant Duncan's fleet I've sung out "Yo heave ho!"
>   Yet more shall ye be knowing —
>   I was coxswain to Boscawen,
> And even with brave Hawke have I nobly faced the foe.
>   Then put round the grog —
>   So we've that and our prog,
> We'll laugh in Care's face, and sing "Yo heave ho!"
>
> But the worst on't was that time when the little ones were sickly,
>   And if they'd live or die the doctor did not know;
> The word was gov'd to weigh so sudden and so quickly,
>   I thought my heart would break as I sung "Yo heave ho!"
>   For Poll's so like her mother,
>   And as for Jack, her brother,
> The boy, when he grows up, will nobly fight the foe;
>   But in Providence I trust,
>   For you see what must be must,
> So my sighs I gave the winds and sung out "Yo heave ho!"
>
> And now at last laid up in a decentish condition,
>   For I've only lost an eye, and got a timber toe;
> But old ships must expect in time to be out of commission,
>   Nor again the anchor weigh with "Yo heave ho!"
>   So I smoke my pipe and sing old songs —
>   For my boy shall well revenge my wrongs,
> And my girl shall breed young soldiers, nobly for to face the foe;
>   Then to Country and King
>   Fate no danger can bring,
> While the tars of Old England sing out "Yo heave ho!"

It is somewhat marred by the conventional ending; but it shows the true test of art — if it be translated into literary English the force disappears, as from a song of Burns. Not a few, however, may know Dibdin; but we doubt if many know Sydney Dobell's "Sea Adventure." Yet it has the true ring.

A greater contrast could not be than between verse such as "Tom Tough" and "Sea Adventure" and the strange muse of

Blake. Yet from his "Jerusalem" we may take our final quotation. It is patriotic in another sense than that understanded of "Maffickers":

> England, awake! awake! awake!
>   Jerusalem thy sister calls!
> Why wilt thou sleep the sleep of death,
>   And close her from thy ancient walls?
>
> Thy hills and valleys felt her feet
>   Gently upon their bosoms move:
> Thy gates beheld sweet Zion's ways;
>   Then was a time of joy and love.
>
> And now the time returns again:
>   Our souls exult; and London's towers
> Receive the Lamb of God to dwell
>   In England's green and pleasant bowers.
>
> And did those feet in ancient time
>   Walk upon England's mountain green?
> And was the holy Lamb of God
>   On England's pleasant pastures seen?
>
> And did the Countenance Divine
>   Shine forth upon our clouded hills?
> And was Jerusalem builded here
>   Among these dark Satanic mills?
>
> Bring me my bow of burning gold!
>   Bring me my arrows of desire!
> Bring me my spear: O clouds, unfold!
>   Bring me my chariot of fire!
>
> I will not cease from mental fight,
>   Nor shall my sword sleep in my hand,
> Till we have built Jerusalem
>   In England's green and pleasant land.

It will be seen there is various pasture enough in Mr. Stanley's book. Its error, on the whole, is to embrace too much rather than too little.

THE SONNET *

[*Academy*, February 21, 1903]

The explanation with which this review opens is pedantic only if it is taken as an instruction rather than a mere refresher. Criticism of the anthology is brief but adequate, and the comparatively long disquisition on the sonnet as a medium of poetic expression is in agreement with Thompson's practice. The sonnet—Shakespearean, however, not Italian—was his chosen medium in the "Ad Amicam" sequence inspired by Katie King. But it was inadequate for "Love in Dian's Lap" and its sequel, "Ultima," inspired by Mrs. Meynell.

THE sonnet is always with us. This is an age when the hurried reader, impatient of the effort required for prolonged attention, demands short poems, which he can read and master in their integrity during a casual hour of leisure. The much less capacity of most modern poets for prolonged and sustained effort (which is an observable fact, explain it how you will), together with their tendency towards lyric rather than narrative or dramatic poetry, renders them very willing to meet this taste of modern readers. Now the sonnet is a ready-made form of brief poem, consecrated by tradition and great example. It is not surprising, therefore, that it should have an unexampled vogue. Collections of sonnets have been beyond number these late years; and Mr. Bowyer Nichol's *Little Book of English Sonnets*, which belongs to the "Little Library," adds yet another. Though on the whole well selected, it has nothing to distinguish it from other collections but the skilful adaptation to its miniature size, which the editor has secured by limiting it to the poets before Tennyson; about whose time begins the extensive cultivation of the English sonnet. It interests us, nevertheless, by its preface, which is not only well written and judicious, but puts forward at least one view we have long entertained.

The sonnet is, of course, an essentially artificial form, and (so far as we can trace it with certainty) of Italian origin. It is not

* *Little Book of English Sonnets*. By Bowyer Nichol.

only artificial, but complexly artificial. Limited to fourteen lines, in its Italian or Petrarchan form (the recognised classical form), those fourteen lines are divided by an intricate arrangement of rhymes. The first eight lines (the octave) are divided into two portions of four lines each; the first and last lines of each quatrain (or four lines) rhyming together, while the middle two lines rhyme with each other. Moreover, there are but two rhymes throughout the octave (or first portion of eight lines); the first and last lines of the two quatrains being all on the one rhyme, while the middle couplets of the two quatrains are all on the same secondary rhyme. Represented by letters, the rhyme-scheme is: a b b a; a b b a. To correspond with this rhyme-construction, there should be a certain pause or division in the sense between the two quatrains (not necessarily a complete pause, that is, a full stop); and a complete pause at the end of the octave. Indeed, the octave should exhaust and bring to a close one aspect of the single idea or feeling which forms the subject-matter of every sonnet. A second and closing aspect is taken up in the last six lines (the sestet). This sestet, or last six lines, the poet can rhyme as he pleases; save that the Italians (who should be the best judges) object to their closing with a couplet. It gives too epigrammatic a character to the sonnet; which should rather die gravely and collectedly away, after reaching its climax in the close of the octave.

At the risk of pedantry we make this explanation, because no discussion of the sonnet is possible without understanding its strict Italian form. The English form to which Shakespeare has given his name (though the Earl of Surrey seems to have invented it) is far simpler. It consists of three quatrains (or sets of four lines each) rhyming alternately — a fresh set of rhymes for each quatrain; with a rhyming couplet to conclude the whole (a couplet, need we say, being two lines rhyming together?). Such, in the clearest explanation we can give, are the chief rival forms, the Petrarchan and the Shakespearean. And Mr. Nichol contends that the Shakespearean is the more satisfactory for English use.

Coventry Patmore (the passage is quoted in his *Life*) contemned the Petrarchan or Italian sonnet altogether, largely for

reasons connected with its metrical structure. Without entering
into questions so subtle, we are disposed to think it over-valued for
English purposes — whatever may be said of it for Italian purposes. It is consecrated in men's eyes by Milton and Wordsworth,
who employed it exclusively; since when (in the language of
Pear's soap) poets have used no other — or seldom any other form.
The Miltonic sonnet (as Mr. Nichol remarks, following Mr.
Bridges) is an Horatian ode in little, so to speak. Milton attained
this majestic and unified quality by neglecting the prescribed
pauses, not only between the quatrains, but even between octave
and sestet, and making the sense continuous, at pleasure, throughout the sonnet. Wordsworth imitated his licence with greater
licence; sometimes adding besides a third rhyme in the middle
couplet of the second quatrain. They attained noble effect. But
why adopt a structure in form, merely to violate it in essence?
Why not adopt a form which shall frankly accord with your
design, instead of one you must wrest to your design? The reason
of the form being gone, it becomes meaningless; nay, the form
means one thing, the internal structure another — they are con-
tradictory. It is like the violation of the pause prescribed by the
heroic couplet, so painful in "Endymion." The defiance of the
sonnet-form is no whit more reputable because the intricacy of
that form prevents the ear's swift recognition of the defiance.

But, say you, that is past; we can now write true Italian sonnets;
there is Rossetti. There is Rossetti. At his best he triumphs, this
beef-fed Italian. But at other times, even with him, the rhyme is
apt to be unpleasantly prominent. With native-born poets it is
often prominent, and one has a general sense of difficulty overcome which one should not have. The English muse does not
breathe freely in the form. It has too much whalebone for her
large movements. The Shakespearean form, without the Italian's
crafty completion for its chosen aims, is simpler, native, capable
both of sweetness and majesty; a better instrument, we think, for
our English muse. As Mr. Nichol observes, Keats ended by using
it, though he began with the Petrarchan model; and Keats had
instinct.

Throughout the greater portion of her career, indeed (until, that is, the Victorian period), the English muse has not taken kindly to the sonnet. That is the reflection which comes to one in glancing through this little book. There is a disappointingly small proportion of first-rate merit, apart from its interest as experiment in an originally foreign form. A selection of lyric, or narrative, or any other manner of poems, during the like period would pan out far richer in pure gold. Wyatt (speaking always from the austere poetic standpoint) Wyatt is nothing, and Surrey not much; Raleigh's sonnet is somewhat overrated; Spenser never so little found himself as in this medium; we cannot share Mr. Nichol's admiration for most of Henry Constable's sacred sonnets; Daniel is surely an ambler with fine lines (though it be treason to say so); vigorous Drayton has yet (like Daniel) but one quite fine sonnet, though others have partial power; Jonson, and Herrick, and Herbert fail in this who do not fail in other things; Habington is naught; the eighteenth century all but barren: and so we reach Wordsworth. The great names (apart from writers of an odd good sonnet or so) can be reckoned on the fingers: Sidney (we do not admire Mr. Nichol's selection from him), Shakespeare, Drummond of Hawthornden, Milton, Wordsworth, Keats. Add to these Mrs. Browning and Rossetti in our day, and you exhaust the list — not a long one for our opulently poetical England. One of the surprises of the book to the average reader, by the way, will be two excellent sonnets by Thomas Russell. Individual sonnets are not wanting. Two of Constable's are good; there are fine ones by Sylvester and William Browne; others of his and one of Campion's are like dainty lyrics more than sonnets. Donne's are well known and ruggedly strong. Gray and Egerton Brydges have each a fine and known sonnet. At least one of Lamb's, Blanco White's, one of Shelley's, and one or two of Hood's outstand from the book. And that, if we have any judgment, is all. Surely, we are driven to repeat, the sonnet is ill-suited to English genius. The present day tells a different tale, to some extent. Yet we question whether a simpler form be not needed; and we ask, with Mr. Nichol, why not the Shakespearean?

CALVERLEY *

[*Academy*, July 13, 1901]

The essence of this review is Thompson's sense of humor — very different from a sense of the ridiculous. He makes out a strong case for the necessity of a classical education for perfection in writing humorous verse. And he establishes a very close relationship between "accomplished comic verse" and "her laurelled sister." The basis of this relationship is the restraint achieved by the skillful use of "classical" technique. It transforms buffoonery into fun, and gives us parodies instead of travesties.

CALVERLEY in one handy volume, at a moderate price. It should soon be in the hands of all who love wit and scholarship, freshened with never-failing humour. Calverley's life-work sums up to a greater bulk than one would have surmised. But the greater part of it is comprised in the translations — the *Virgil's Eclogues*, the *Odes* of Horace, and the *Theocritus* — which are, of course, sterling work. Besides these, a few Latin poems, original and translated, and a handful of *vers de société*, are all that he has done. It is upon these light poems that his ultimate fame must rest; and in going through them one is struck by the fact how seldom the *lyra elegantiarum*, the tricksy lighter Muse, reaches its true mark. With most poets it is only a certain core of their work which satisfies the finer palate. But this seems specially the case when Puck's wings brush the lyre. But a handful of Hood is Hood's best; though a fairly large handful, it may be. Hood, however, jested for a living, and much must be laid to the score of that. Not so Moore, and Moore's lighter verse needs only less sifting than Hood's. Not so Calverley, and Calverley, unlike the other two, did not labour his powers by over-production. His verse, as we have said, is itself but a handful; yet even that handful needs to be sifted, and out of the sifting comes a small posy, merely, of pieces which show his gift perfect. But this attar of

* *The Complete Works of Charles Stuart Calverley*. With a Biographical Notice by Sir Walter J. Sendall.

Calverley is attar of light verse, quite among the best of its kind in the language. This (we say unhesitatingly) comes of his scholarship. "What! Scholarship needed to write a skit or a copy of humorous verses?" guffaws the contemner of "useless classics" in education. Why, not absolutely needed, but exceedingly helpful. Has it ever struck you what a gallant proportion of the men who have won repute in this kind hail from our Universities? Praed, Calverley, Locker-Lampson, Traill, Owen Seaman — nay, Moore himself was a classical scholar, and one of his early exploits was a very Moore-ish version of Anacreon. Most accomplished classic of them all was Calverley, and his best comic verse is an advertisement of the fact. With all his overflowing wit and the metrical mastery he possessed as a poet, Hood lacked something which Calverley had (apart from native interior gift). That is the trained sense of form and finish; the dexterity which flings the verse into just the right form for suggesting and aiding the airy effect of the humour, which fledges and tips the line to carry the point of wit like an arrow-shaft; the felicitous turn which brings diction and metre pat on the quick of the jest, and tickles you to instant laughter. Of these qualities all feel the effect, but only a student of technique will realise the cunning art of them. Add to these the sense of clearness, of sparingness, the avoidance of the too-much; and you will realise what Calverley's light verse owed to his classical scholarship. Some of them he might have learned from earlier English serious poets; but the treasury of them in their unison is the classics. The craft he so dearly loved and so thoroughly knew in a Greek poem or an Horatian Ode gave Calverley his mastery of measured laughter in English rhyme. Mastery — mastery of form and technique — is the thing which obviously differentiates him from most before him and many after him. Not from a popular education could you get a Calverley, though the aspirant had the wit of Butler and the humour of Rabelais. He might make you laugh consumedly, but never with the feathered dexterity and elegance which make epicurean laughter.

Take some concrete example of what we have said. "Forever" is a little gem as perfectly, lucidly, and compactly formed for its playful purpose as anything of Horace for its graver intent. The mould of the stanza delicately enhances the fun:

> Forever! What abysms of woe
>   The word reveals, what frenzy, what
> Despair! For ever (printed so)
>   Did not.

How the antithetic and wilful bathos of the close is clenched by the capricious brevity of the last line! Even more dainty in its effect of whimsied humour is the semi-final stanza:

> Forever! Passion-fraught, it throws
>   O'er the dim page a gloom, a glamour;
> It's sweet, it's strange; and I suppose
>   It's grammar.

There is a like effect in a poem otherwise not so perfect and rounded, "On the Brink":

> I watch'd her as she stoop'd to pluck
>   A wildflower in her hair to twine;
> And wish'd that it had been my luck
>   To call her mine.
>
> Anon I heard her rate with mad,
>   Mad words her babe within its cot;
> And felt particularly glad
>   That it had not.

Mr. Owen Seaman and others have learned and copied with success this particular art which Calverley was first to invent — surprising it, perhaps, from the effect of the curt final line in Horatian Sapphics. That is a surmise; but that he gained it from his classic studies, we have no doubt. So close is the accomplished comic Muse to her laurelled sister. Congreve himself, while he is pouring forth his brilliant comic wit, stumbles (in "Love for Love"), apparently by sheer haphazard, upon a charming poetic image. "Thin partitions do the bounds divide," at times, of fine comic and fine serious verse. It is but a veering of mood, a turn of the wrist. Nay, Calverley once deliberately writes a humorous poem, "Contentment," "after the manner of Horace." He has done better when he was not avowedly imitating his master. But there is one stanza at his best, when he is describing the imperturbably contented:

> And when they wax a little gay,
>   And chaff the public after luncheon,
> If they're confronted with a stray
>   Policeman's truncheon
>
> They gaze thereat with outstretched necks,
>   And laughter which no threats can smother,
> And tell the horror-stricken X
>   That he's another.

Alas! that the too successful crusade against musty Greek and Latin forbids us more than lightly to touch upon Calverley's actual inroad into the stately classic domain. Call "dead," forsooth, the language of "Carmen Sæculare"! How grandly classic the picture of the youthful undergraduate invading the tobacco-store of Bacon!

> Pervigil ecce Baco furvâ depromit ab arcâ
> Splendidius quiddam solito, plenumque saporem
> Laudat, et antiquâ jurat de stirpe Jamaicæ.
> O fumose puer, nimium ne crede Baconi:
> Manillas vocat; hoc prætexit nomine caules.

The delightful parody of the last two lines must thrill chucklingly the midriff of every scholar. Nor less accomplished in its way is the description of the billiard-votaries:

> Ille petit virides (sed non e gramine) mensas,
> Pollicitus meliora patri, tormentaque flexus
> Per labyrintheos plus quam mortalia tentat,
> Acre tuens, loculisque pilas immittit et aufert.

This reads augustly poetic, but a crux indeed. The author comes to our help with a note no less beautiful in its mock-gravity than the text itself. With all the lumbering solemnity of the dear, pedantic scholiastic Latinity, he comments on *tormenta plus quam mortalia:*

> Eleganter, ut solet, Peile, "unearthly cannons." Perrecondita autem est quæstio de lusibus illorum temporum, neque in Smithii Dict. Class. satis clucidata. Consule omnino Kentf. de Bill.

And on *loculis* he comments: "Bene vertas 'pockets.' " So throughout the most dignified seeming of poetic diction disguises the most base and mechanical of modern ideas, or masks the most clamorous "howlers." Only such a scholarly humourist as Calverley could have done it; and to any man of classic training the result is a Roman banquet of fun.

Fun he has always at command: apart from that accomplished cunning of technique, that artful caprice, at which we have glanced, he can capture a sure laugh by sheer unexpectedness of humour, as throughout the delightful verses on the organ-grinder:

> Half-a-bar sets several couples
> Waltzing in convenient spots;

> Not with clumsy Jacks or Georges:
> Unprofaned by grasp of man
> Maidens speed those simple orgies,
> Betsey Jane with Betsey Ann.

This, with the gift which made him an admirable Latin versifier, made him a parodist. For Latin versifying is essentially an imitative art. Calverley is surely the first of parodists. He may almost be called the founder of a new dynasty in parody. To an extent not previously approached, his parodies are likewise criticisms, and very keen criticisms, of a poet's weaker side. One grudges to call them parodies, so close and refined is the imitation, so inclusively does he catch and reflect all the elements of a writer's style. Only the one or two best of the *Rejected Addresses* come near his work in this kind — surely the most stupid of all forms of humour as it is usually practised, a coarse exaggeration of some obvious feature, unharmonised by the subtler traits of style which really constitute the poet so belied. In that wonderful imitation of Browning, "The Cock and the Bull," no single peculiarity of "The Ring and the Book" is suffered to get obviously tyrannic and out of focus. The clipping of "the smaller parts of speech" is a trifle — very slightly — forced for effect of caricature; but the other mannerisms (tempting as they are for violent burlesque) maintain their due perspective until the close of the parody, where they are all purposely allowed to cumulate for a final climactic *reductio ad absurdum*. The less notable features receive their due place, and those which a common parodist would ignore, such as the burly use of strong, cudgel-like Anglo-Saxon words: the movement of the metre is accurately given, though the Browning blank verse has no readily-caught rhythm like the Tennysonian, and it is just here that an ordinary travesty would come to grief. Calverley, in fact, does not travesty. His art is far too delicate for that. So in the parody of "The Brook," the finest stroke is not in the obvious burlesque, but the acute banter of a true Tennysonian mannerism, in the abrupt turn at the last:

> It was noised next noon
> That chickens had been miss'd at Syllabub Farm.

Yet the delicious skit on the Pre-Raphaelite ballad is perhaps a travesty, but a travesty which hits the mark, and is irresistibly suggestive of the model, for all its wild fun. When one remembers William Morris' early ballad, with the absolutely unconnected and cryptic refrain, "Three red roses across the moon," one can but laugh approvingly at stanzas like these:

> The farmer's daughter hath ripe red lips;
> (*Butter and eggs and a pound of cheese*)
> If you try to approach her, away she skips
> Over tables and chairs with apparent ease.
>
> The farmer's daughter hath soft brown hair
> (*Butter and eggs and a pound of cheese*)
> And I met with a ballad, I can't say where,
> Which wholly consisted of lines like these.

As for "Lovers: and a Reflection," quotation is a vanity, and praise a superfluity. In parody, Calverley (in fine) is Calverley, and Mr. Owen Seaman is his prophet.

With regard to the translations, we have one thing to say in mitigation of their conceded excellence; and it chiefly applies to the Virgilian *Eclogues*. Partly in the endeavour to render the Latin (as near as may be) line for line — and you can get more mono-syllabic or dissyllabic words in a line than you can polysyllabic, partly, no doubt, from his sturdy Yorkshire character, Calverley runs fatally to monosyllables and dissyllables. He has whole layers of these short words (no poet can call them lines) packed like sardines in a tin; till the line is choked and loses motion, it has never an open pore for breath. The danger of our strong, expressive, homespun English will ever be that it is overemphatic and curt — a procession of brief syllables hedged and impaled by thick consonants; even as our English landscape is intersected into a green chess-board by uncompromising rectangles of thorny fence. Calverley's Virgilian versions are heavy with chains of such clod-hopping syllables. One sighs for the long trample of a few Latin-born words, shattering the Saxon ice, and restoring movement to the curdled line. But that protest uttered, we accept these also as treasurable things.

THE TECHNIQUE AND HISTORY
OF ENGLISH POETRY

THE RELIGIOUS RONDELEER *
[*Merry England*, October, 1894]

This brief consideration of a relatively unimportant mould of English
poetry, is not without significance as an example of Thompson's wide
interest in the technique of his art.

THE sonnet, though a form imported from Italy, has a classic
place in English poetry:

> With this key
> Shakspere unlocked his heart . . .
> A glowworm lamp,
> It cheered mild Spenser, called from Faery-land
> To struggle through dark ways; and when a damp
> Fell round the path of Milton, in his hand
> The thing became a trumpet, whence he blew
> Soul-animating strains, alas, too few!

And Wordsworth himself added to that glorious volume of sound,
since enriched by the magic of Rossetti. The rondel has not had
quite so glorious a fate. It has proved itself to be a foreign form,
not only in lineage, but also in a certain fantasy which the gravi-
ties of the English tongue refused at first to humour. But the
modern minor poets have been at work to make English surprisingly pliant. The rondel must be light before everything; and,
light in form, it has also been usually light in theme. But so long
as fifty years ago an Englishman was at work with rondels, and
with rondels that had the gravest of motives. We allude to Mr. J.

---

* *Rondeaulx: Translated from the Black Letter French Edition of 1527.*
By John Richard Best.

271

R. Best, the son of Mr. Henry Best, an eminent Oxford convert to the Catholic Church some forty years before the Oxford Movement began. His son, the rondeleer — to use a phrase Mr. J. R. Best himself coined after the analogy of the sonneteer — went for his inspiration direct to some rondeaulx in a black letter French edition of 1527. The translations he made have a double interest therefore; for they represent to us the religious feeling of France during the sixteenth century, and the work of a pioneer among modern poets to mould the English language to rondel form.

In these rondeaulx there is, of course, little display of real fancy or poetical imagery; though on the whole they are not at all so extravagant as we might have expected from the chivalric era of Francis I. When love is not the subject, the rondeaulx are in general of a grave moralising character, sometimes treating us to a series of wise saws, formerly perhaps not so trite as they have now become. As the rondeau goes, the following specimen is remarkable at least for its earnestness of tone:

PAR TROP DE JOURS

Too long, alas! repentant now I know,
I wandered on in vice and tried to bow
  My mind to earth while leaving reason's way.
  But this the time, be this the happy day,
Whence o'er far different track my steps may go!
Each foolish joy, with which young bosoms glow,
Would still allure and still its promise show,
  While lingering on in unknown chains I lay
        Too long, alas!

Still did I follow, hope still beckon so,
Till thirty years were stamped upon my brow;
  Then did that blessed one all soothing say,
  "Repent, dear friend, repent! no more delay;
For thou hast led this life of sin and woe,
        Too long, alas!"

A series of equally serious rondeaulx, dealing with the seven deadly sins, is introduced to us by the following curious note of the translator:

To the English Protestant reader some explanation of the heading of this and the following pages may be acceptable. The Catholic Church has never, as such, and *ex cathedra,* described and defined its general and undisputed doctrines, either in any code of laws and belief, like the Thirty-nine Articles, for the guidance of men (and, at College, of infants,) or in shorter catechisms more peculiarly intended for the instruction of neophytes. Such catechisms have, however, always circulated with the sanction and approbation of its pastors. Thus it appears that, three or four hundred years ago, when these rondeaulx were printed — and before our Parliment had, by law, established the present Anglican liturgy — certain catechisms were in use in the Christian and then unreformed world, which denounced certain vices under the epithet "deadly." These little documents—unenrolled in any statute-book, unprotected even against alteration by any "Declaration" of the "Supreme Governour of the Church" — have yet maintained themselves in unchanged and unforgotten simplicity, notwithstanding the successive origin, improvement, and establishment of the varying faiths around them: and, in the little catechism circulated at the present day in England with the approbation of the Catholic clergy, the same vices are held up to execration by the very same title as that under which the ancient rondeleer marshalls them; and the same virtues are recorded as being peculiarly contrary to those vices which the rondeleer has portrayed under that identical title. Thus does a power exist independently of the aid of legislation.

We select for quotation the rondeau on Gluttony, in which, though we shall not say it is written against the grain, we observe how slyly the complacency of the *bon vivant* peeps out from behind the solemn veil of the moralist:

> The days speed on. Soon ev'ry pomp and boast
> Of ye whose hearts and souls in food are lost —
>   Who on yourselves delicious care bestow —
>   Soon will your boastful pomp be changed to woe.
> In your dear stomachs death will soon be host! —
> Those stomachs full of daintiest foods, of most
> Choice wines and fruits in luscious medley tost.
>   But though you think not why 'tis so, nor how —
>   The days speed on.

> The poor takes 'neath your cloth his wonted post:
> You, fat and dull, disdain him — all engrost
> By self, and let him die while meats o'erflow.
> Oh! quickly hither turn your eyes, and know
> That, while you feast and love and drink and toast,
> The days speed on.

Having despatched the seven deadly sins, the rondeleer could do no less than devote an equal number of his verses to the contrary virtues. In these he shows himself of a right courtly and gallant nature, and contrives with matchless ingenuity to make his muse do double duty. The name "Loise de Savoie," luckily containing neither more nor less than the precise number of thirteen letters, suggested to him the basis of an acrostic on each of the virtues in question, on the possession of all of which he compliments the fortunate bearer of the name aforesaid. Could flattery during life secure for its object reputation after death, how brightly would some great names shine which are now dimmed and dishonoured; but alas! the tinsel of adulation is soon tarnished in the breath of time. Thus it has fared with Louisa of Savoy.

This lady, the mother of Francis I, was one of those women who spring up at intervals to make the world stare. Many wise philosophers have been puzzled in attempting to account for the super-*male* energy often exhibited by heroines of this class; but they have overlooked a truth that "sweet woman loves her will," and gives effect to it with an engrossing singleness. We take the rondeau on Temperance, because while it is at least as good as any of the others, it is also the proper companion to that on Gluttony, and, above all, it celebrates perhaps the only virtue of the seven to which Louisa's claim seems to have been just:

> Like some fair mirror where thy sex might see
> Of every virtue the clear harmony,
>   I gaze on thee in whom I find no blame.
>   Sober — retiring — and most virtuous dame.
> Esteemed — in whose high praises all agree,
> Divine perfection God did blend in thee,
> Exquisite morals, sense, calm dignity.
>   So mark I thy staid soul and beaming frame
>   Like some fair mirror.

All rash excess will modest Temperance flee.
Vainly would bloated envious Gluttony
  Of aught unworthy taint thy honoured name.
  Invincible the heart where reason's flame
Exists: 'twill image truth's fair tracery
             Like some fair mirror.

Since the translator has humoured the rondeleer so far as to present us with his acrostics, he might have gone a little farther in his pains and used the English name of the lady, which contains just the proper number of letters.

COURTHOPE'S HISTORY OF POETRY *
[*Academy*, August 14, 1897]

A broad knowledge of the history of English literature, and a comprehending grasp of its technique, combine to place these reviews among Thompson's most characteristic criticisms. They exemplify that in literary criticism, as in life, *in medio stat virtus*. This, Thompson achieves by a reasoned rejection of extremes, not by an emotional recoil from them. Consequently, the full significance of what he has to say requires more than a cursory reading, whether he is in agreement with Courthope, or strongly opposed to his too academic theories.

THE second volume of Prof. Courthope's *History of English Poetry*, let it be said at once, is very valuable. At the same time, a distinction may be made as to the nature of its value. Prof. Courthope has the professorial mind in an absolute degree; and his history is valuable in the peculiar qualities of the professorial mind. It is deficient in the qualities which are outside the professorial mind. In criticism he is for the most part sound and reliable, where he has a defined and traditional body of taste to guide himself by. At the same time, and by a necessary result of the academic habit, there is little original and illuminative about his criticism. Where precedent in judgment fails him, and he has to depend upon native

* *A History of English Poetry*. By W. J. Courthope. Vol. II.

insight, he is as liable to be wrong as right. In the main, the value of his *History* is historical (which may seem a truism, but is not), and its peculiar historical value is evolutionary. He has worked out, as no previous historian has done, the origins of various literary forces in different countries, and the differing ways in which their momentum has communicated itself to English literature, and been responsible for the various streams of tendency in that literature. In this respect we reckon his work most thorough and authoritative. If anything, he lays too much stress upon the evolutionary derivations of the various English writers, and groups of writers, from foreign literatures, and too little stress upon the original elements superadded by those writers, which make their work very different from, and often transcending, the work of the foreign writers from whom they derived their suggestions. We do not mean that he gives no notification of this; but that he gives too little proportionate importance to it. To pursue all the intricate ramifications of his evolutionary analysis in a review would be impossible. Let us take a single instance, which involves broad and general principles. We mean the evolution of the literary tongue in England from the vulgar tongue. He goes back to the *Cortegiano* (the *Courtier*) of the Italian Castiglione. There Castiglione, as the basis of an elegant style in writing, lays down the following principles:

> Whatever is allowable in writing ought also to be allowable in speaking, and the most beautiful kind of speech is that which resembles elegant writing. . . . I would accordingly recommend (the courtier) not only to avoid all old and obsolete Tuscan words, but both in writing and speaking to make use of such words as are in vogue in Tuscany and other parts of Italy to-day, and which have some grace and charm in themselves.

It will at once be perceived that this is the exploded Wordsworthian theory — with an important difference. Both would have the writer to use only the words of conversation. But whereas Wordsworth would have him to use the speech of "simple livers," Castiglione would have him to use elegant speech. Each, of course, was wrong; but each was a most excellent influence in his time. When it was a case of forming a language out of rude elements, nothing better could be recommended as a standard than the speech of the Court. When it was a question of putting fresh blood into a language over-refined, nothing better could be recommended than the speech of simple men. In literature two wrongs do sometimes make a right.

The adoption of the Court language in England did furnish a much-needed standard. It settled the main lines of the language. At the same time, that standard being once fixed, the influence of great writers such as Spenser, who revived archaisms, and Shakespeare, who introduced Latinisms, while he kept in the main to the vernacular formed by previous writers from the standard of the Court, prevented the language of poetry from being stereotyped by the diction prevalent in conversation. And, finally, the influence of Milton, who revived many of the archaisms which Spenser had previously revived from Chaucer and his contemporaries, while at the same time he introduced new Latinisms of his own, created for poetry its present omnigenous diction, distinct from that of prose, and enabling a poet to express with ease what prose can only express with difficulty. This is but a partial sample of the evolutionary process which Prof. Courthope's book enables the student to trace on every hand. In this particular instance he has not altogether traced it himself. He sees that literary language became fixed, as to its basis, by the prevalence of the living language of the Court as a standard. He does not perceive — or, at any rate, does not state — that the language of poetry, if not of prose, was built up by a process more intricate.

Once the staple of the tongue had been fixed by the adoption of the language actually spoken in that most refined and brilliant Court of Elizabeth, the great poets enriched and enlarged it by interweaving with that staple, words adapted from the Latin, revived from earlier speech, or borrowed from the homely tongue of the people. The speech of the Court furnished the nucleus round which all these other elements crystallised. The first thing was to get a settled tissue. This was obtained by adopting the living diction used at Court. But once the earlier writers had supplied, by their practice, this accepted tissue, the way was open for Shakespeare (and, later, Milton) to embroider upon this tissue words of vulgar or Latin derivation, or even revived from archaic language. Shakespeare enriched the received tissue of the language by abundance of Latinisms and vulgarisms. Spenser added archaisms, but, owing to his too free use of them, they did not at the time find acceptance, or not to any material degree. The tongue was still too young, too much in process of formation; the experiment was premature. But Milton, succeeding to a poetic tongue by that time fairly settled (thanks to Shakespeare, whom Milton followed in his earlier work), was able to make a judicious selection from Spenser's archaisms, and — by means of his overpowering genius — add them to the recognised resources of poetic diction. Accordingly, most of Spenser's archaisms have become current poetic paper-money only where they were endorsed by Milton. Other and more modern poets, following Milton's example, have endorsed more and more of Spenser's at first unsuccessful archaisms; Shelley, for example, and Keats, and Coventry Patmore: till at last most of Spenser's daring revivals have passed into poetic currency, so far as they were worthy of such a fate. So has been built up that great body of poetic diction which makes England transcendently superior in poetic resource to all modern countries. France has gone but a little way from the starting-point of Castiglione. Its literary speech may indeed be richer than its conversational speech — no country has been insensate enough to adopt finally the dictum of Castiglione or Wordsworth, which would make literary speech one with the spoken speech of a given generation — but its poetic diction is one with its prose diction; the poet has no resource of language which is not shared by the prose-writer. Other nations diverge from France in this respect, till the climax is reached in England, which possesses an enormous range of poetic speech altogether denied to the prose-writer. The poet has a vocabulary which enables him to express all manner of things which the *prosateur* can either not express at all, or can express but feebly; while at the same time the whole range of the prose writer is his to command. Hence, chiefly, it is that the English vocabulary perhaps transcends that of ancient Greece in tropical fertility.

This point illustrates one great merit of Professor Courthope's work. He is uniformly fair. Even where his own conclusions are (to our mind) mistaken, he gives us, by his careful and representative citations, the means of deciding for ourselves on those conclusions; and arriving, if we please, at a different result. If the academic mind sometimes (we think) leads him astray in his judgments, he is singularly just in adducing the grounds of his judgments, so that we may reverse his results if we like. This is the favourable (and a very favourable) side of the professorial method. We know no fairer and more judicial history of his subject. No one, we should think, will dispute his valuable analysis of the evolution of English poetry. And on a most enlightened principle, he sees that the evolution of poetry cannot be kept separate from the evolution of literature at large. Accordingly we have a thorough analysis of the progress of prose as well as poetry. Indeed, but for Professor Courthope's modesty, this might have been called a history of English literature.

On one point, chiefly, we have to find fault with the author. He does not shrink from entering into an analysis of the progress of English metre. And here his conclusions are vitiated by the professorial mind. Nothing is more subtle and less understood; and Professor Courthope's ideas are such as no poet who had studied metre could accept. He follows, without an intrusion of doubt, the ordinary metrical principles of the grammarians (vitiated as they are by an attempt to conform the principles of English to those of classic metre), and his judgments are often mistaken in the extremest degree. But this is not the place to enter on a matter so intricate. We can only assure the student that he could not do better than accept the exact contrary of Professor Courthope's conclusions on this point.

There are, of course, points in which we differ from the author. We cannot agree with his general high estimate of George Peele, though we are glad to see that he recognises the value of Peele's one really fanciful (and neglected) play, *The Arraignment of Paris*. Still more, we disagree with his comparative disparagement of Greene. As a lyrist, Greene was worth three thousand Peeles. We could make this good were there space for it. Other such dubious points there are, but on the whole this is an invaluable book for the enlightened student. For the unenlightened student its value is much less. The value of it consists in the careful tracing of evolution in English poetry, and in the copious material Professor Courthope affords the student for arriving at his own conclusions. No matter how strong his bias, he never garbles or abbreviates quotations in order to support his own view — a thing how rare; how very, very rare!

But if the student have no power of judging for himself, if he take Professor Courthope's conclusions blindly, then he will remain fixed for life in some most grievous and damning errors with regard to poetry. Wherefore, the value of this book emphatically depends upon the reader. But yet it must, we think, endure — as a review of the development of English poetry. It supersedes anything previously in the field. And the learning, the labour, the accuracy, the painful fair-mindedness which have gone to the making of it only life-long students of English literature can estimate.

ENGLISH POETRY *
[*Academy*, October 31, 1903]

IN THESE two volumes of his valuable and elaborately thought-out *History of English Poetry*, Mr. Courthope deals with our poetry from the post-Spenserian period to the end of the seventeenth century. We have already expressed our opinion with regard to his general qualities as an historian of poetry. He is emphatically an academic writer, with the virtues and defects of the academic writer. Method, clearness, sanity, a safe pursuit of the *via media*, secure that his history shall embody the best results of modern scholarship in general. But for delicate originality of individual criticism one cannot look to it. He is not a Coleridge.

This does not prevent him from having a scheme or ideas of his own. While the fourth volume deals with the poetic drama,

* *A History of English Poetry*. By W. J. Courthope. Vols. III and IV.

from Shakespeare onwards, the third treats rather of poetry in general. His main idea is to trace in poetry the growth of the national genius: he pushes to its completest issue the principle inaugurated by Taine, of considering poetry in relation to the environment which brought it forth. After the defeat of the Spanish Armada, he holds the previous acquiescence in Constitutional Absolutism — in the Monarch and her counsellers informed by the national representatives — was replaced by conflicting currents, conflicting views as to the necessary means of securing the national unity on which all were bent: and this distintegration is represented in the national poetry. On the one hand is a certain continuous movement under the leadership of the Court, "showing itself partly in the simplification of ideas, and partly in the harmonious mode of expressing them. This line of poetical descent may be said to run through Daniel, Hall, Sir John Davies, Drummond of Hawthornden, Sir John Beaumont, Denham, and Waller, till it reaches its highest point of perfection in the poems of Dryden." On the other hand are poets stimulated to "novelties of fancy and diction" by "sectional and disintegrating forces" which are apart from the "onward stream of life" in the nation itself. These are Drayton, Browne, the "Wits," such as the two Fletchers, Donne, Ben Jonson, Herbert, and Cowley. While Milton stands apart from all.

This is very neat and convenient, as theories are apt to be. But like many academic theories, one doubts its truth, or at least its complete truth. Mr. Courthope seems to allow that disintegrating forces were at work in the nation itself. Why, then, are these individualising poets or schools of poetry apart from the national life? We should rather say that (as mostly happens in England when a great poetic impetus exhausts itself) some poets, throughout the period, academically clung to the preceding tradition (with, perhaps, insensible modifications), while others initiated or adopted new methods, following new impulses. Denham, Waller, and Dryden surely have only an artificial place in the list. They followed the Court, but it was the fresh influence of France, coming through the Court, rather than anything in the national life, which dictated their quite novel and un-Saxon clarity. While what was racy and poetic in Dryden owed far more to Cowley and the modified tradition of the "Metaphysical School" than to the Gallicism of the Court.

It seems to us, in fact, a somewhat vague and baseless theory, despite its outward precision. And it is, we think, partly connected with an erroneous view of the so-called "Metaphysical School," or the "School of Wit," as Mr. Courthope prefers to call it. He perceives that it was no isolated apparition; that a like poetic movement to that which began in Donne and culminated in Cowley spread throughout seventeenth-century Europe. He endeavours to account for it by a variety of subtle causes. Generally speaking, he assigns as its causes the decay of scholasticism and feudalism, with the revival of the civic standards of antiquity. It is "the efflorescence of decay."

Now, as we think, it is only in its superficial characteristics that this poetry can be regarded as the product of decay. It was really a partly thwarted development. The great poetry built on elements of universal appeal had reached its height; had done all which, for the time at least, could be expected from it. If anything vital, with the soul of permanence, was still to be achieved, it became necessary to exalt and specialise the poetic element in poetry, as distinguished from the elements of general appeal. This movement was, in fact, an attempt to *quintessentialise* poetry. It was an attempt to do what was done with success by Shelley, Keats, Tennyson, Rossetti — nay, by Wordsworth and Coleridge in their greatest work. It was experimental, and largely failed through misdirection. But despite that misdirection, it brought forth treasurable poetry in which we can all now recognise the foreshadowing of much modern poetry. In Vaughan we have beautiful strivings towards Wordsworth; in Crashaw towards Shelley and Coleridge. In many we discern a spirit which has been fulfilled (though it may often be after another fashion) in our finest modern work. Is it not, then, an imperception to call this the poetry of decay? Was it not rather a development partially *manqué*, an unfulfilled but fruitful experiment which showed the direction that English poetry would ultimately take to its triumphant gain?

But whatever we may think of the particular theory on which these volumes are based, they are worked out with excellent thoroughness, a cultivated taste, and in an attractive style. Nothing, for instance, could be at once more succinct and picturesque than the account of the peculiar atmosphere of the Restoration Court, with its mock Gallicism and the influence it exerted on literature. The volumes combine the qualities of solidity and interest, which seldom meet, and deserve to remain a standard work.

THE SCANSION CASE: VERDICT AND SENTENCE
[*Academy*, September 24, 1898]

Despite its rather tiresome and bewildering details, this article exemplifies Thompson's facility in passing from the realm of theory to the *minutiæ* of application. Only one who has read the original dispute in the files of the *Academy*, can fully appreciate Thompson's clarification of the issue, in his résumé, and the value of his suggestions concerning the subject-matter of the discussion, as well as the manner of its presentation.

A week or two ago the great Scansion Case was before the British public, or a certain section of the public. It was not in the Divorce Court, nor in the Court of Common Pleas, nor yet before Her Majesty's Judges in Chancery; it turned not on racing, nor swindling, nor burglary, nor libel — though it had a certain affinity with the latter. It was a case for a Court of Minnesingers, did we possess such an institution. It turned on the laws of verse, and ran through the court of the evening *Star*. The court pronounced no decision. Naturally, therefore, the matter comes up for review before the High Court of the *Academy*. Equally naturally, the affair has been held over, that we might have time to go into the *dossier* of the case — following the precedent established in the *affaire Dreyfus*. The contending parties are "J. D." and Mr. Stephen Phillips. Who is "J. D."? It cannot be Dreyfus — that supposition

is forbidden by the first initial and the French authorities. A mere
poet might possibly contend for John Davidson. Our own theory
is one that will commend itself to all legal persons. We hold that
"J. D." is none other than the celebrated and litigious individual
who from time immemorial has carried on law proceedings against
the no less celebrated and indomitable Richard Roe. Need we say
that we mean John Doe? As to Mr. Stephen Phillips, the case is
clearer, though the testimony is mixed. "J. D." himself (or provi-
sionally John Doe), in the outset of the case, declared him to be
a "new poet," author of "masterpieces" for which it was too
late in the day to "coin adulatory epithets"; a "great blank-verse
writer," a poet who "is so great that I would have him greater."
But "long or a' the play was played," "J. D." surmised he had
been "too adulatory," begged to "remind Mr. Phillips that he
lives in an age of poeticules" (there is no more fearful wild fowl
living than your poeticule), and that "there is only one great
poet in our midst"; he told Mr. Phillips that it would take many
minor bards such as he to make a Swinburne, and accused him
of being a bardling who had soared to the peak of Parnassus on
an inflated balloon of egoism. It is very rash and reprehensible for
a man to have anything to do with such ticklish craft as inflated
balloons of egoism, and we hope Mr. Phillips has not been so
incautious. For the rest, you have "J. D.'s" views, and you can take
your choice — there is plenty of it.

The case, briefly, is, that "J. D." accused Mr. Stephen Phillips
of passing upon the public bad metrical coin; and incidentally
called him (in a strictly metrical sense) a babe and suckling. Mr.
Phillips denied the charge, and considered "babe and suckling"
a false and defamatory expression. The difficulty of summing-up
the proceedings clearly is, that besides the original plaintiff and
defendant there are no fewer than three others intervening by
letter in the case, and introducing into it fresh matter. Setting
aside these as unnecessary to the original pleadings, we will adhere
as far as possible to the two protagonists.

The plaintiff, then, set forth that in his volume of *Poems* Mr.
Phillips did wilfully issue to the public no less than four illegal
and unscannable lines, to the auricular distress and hurt of Her

Majesty's lieges, the readers of the said book; among whom he
(the said plaintiff, "J. D.") had especially suffered grievous pain
of ear, and had further been put to the loss of a certain amount
of time and ink in protesting against this illegal act. The lines
were:

(*a*)   "Above my head the fields murmur and wave."

(*b*)   "Realises all the uncoloured dawn."

(*c*)   "O but I gloried and drank and wept and laughed."

(*d*)   "The Titan bowed, coming upon them, and seemed."

Line (*a*) was wrong, said plaintiff, because you have to accent
"murmur" on the second syllable. Line (*b*) was wrong, because
you have to read it thus:

> "Realíses áll the uncóloured dáwn,"

which gives only four accents to the line instead of five. Line
(*c*) was wrong, because "gloried and" was an inadmissible elision.
Line (*d*) was wrong, because "upon them and" was an impossible
elision. From all which it was clear that Mr. Phillips had an uncer-
tain ear, and was a metrical babe and suckling. At the same time,
he bears that high testimony to the general excellence of Mr.
Phillips's poetical character which we have already quoted.

Defendant answers categorically. In line (*a*) the accent is *not*
on the second syllable of "murmur." "Murmur" is read as a
trochee. In line (*b*) the accentuation is thus:

> "Réalíses áll the uncóloured dáwn."

So there are five accents after all. The unusual system of accents
expresses a special emotion. As for the line (*c*), the elision (or
"slur," as Mr. Phillips better calls it) in "gloried and" is so common
as to need no defence, and gives the line the right lilt. He over-
looks line (*d*), and introduces another line which we shall neglect,
because the dispute on it ends unsatisfactorily. Defendant gets
angry, and not only says that he is weaving harmonies of his

own on metrical law which he understands, but makes remarks less judicious, and sweeping. He knew years ago far more about metre than his critics have yet learned. Which, though we profoundly believe, yet we hold it not wisdom to have thus set down.

Plaintiff returns to the charge, and amends his pleading. If "murmur" is to be a trochee in line (*a*), then defendant has no business with a trochee in the fourth foot. Why? Because Milton never has a trochee in the fourth foot, unless to mark a pause after the third foot. As for line (*b*), defendant must not use three trochees running, as he does in the opening of the line. Again, because Milton never does it. Nor does he see that the accentuation expresses the emotion of the line. Trochees express only mirth. So in line (*c*) he cannot perceive the advantage of the "lilt." Moreover, you cannot elide "ied." Milton never does it. And he again calls defendant's attention to the unnoticed line (*d*), where he has elided the letter "m" — an awful act. Plaintiff also loses his temper, and makes the remarks about that weird aeronautic voyage to Parnassus on inflated balloons of egoism. End of Second Day.

Mr. Phillips opens his closing speech with spirit. On the point of line (*a*), he gives a string of examples where Milton uses a trochee in the fourth foot, and not after a stop. One example will suffice:

"Which now the rising sun gilds with his beams."

In defence of line (*b*) he tries to quote lines from Milton starting with three trochees; but they are hardly parallel to his own, and his success is indifferent. He shows "J. D." to be wrong about the trochee always making for mirth — the point hardly needed an answer. For the elision of "gloried and drank" in line (*c*) he attempts to quote parallels from Milton. Lastly, as to line (*d*), he declares that Milton elides the "m," and quotes examples. He perorates with something very like a cock-crow.

"J. D." answers for the prosecution. As to line (*a*), all the examples of a trochee in the fourth foot which defendant quotes from Milton he asserts are failures. Either the fourth foot is not a trochee or it does not follow an iambic foot, or (and this is "J. D.'s" point) there is a pause before it, though the pause is not

indicated by a stop. We shall return to this in our summing-up.
The Miltonic precedents brought by Mr. Phillips for his string
of trochees in line (*b*) he easily disposes of, showing that they
are wrongly scanned, or otherwise ineffectual. As to the emotional effects to be got from trochees, he has no case, and abuses
defendant's ear. He pooh-pooh's the precedents cited from Milton
for the elision of "gloried and drank" in line (*c*), but does not
deal with them. Instead, he pours exultant invective on defendant
for a mere slip of expression in speaking of the elision. Finally, he
takes triumphant revenge over line (*d*), where Mr. Phillips is
certainly mistaken in attributing to Milton the elision of the letter
"m," and has scanned the lines falsely. He perorates with a whoop
of derisive triumph, and the case is ended — to our, and probably
the editor's, gratification.

It is a very pretty little quarrel, the *Academy* must pronounce
in summing-up, but it has hardly enlightened the public on metre.
Even in our carefully succinct summary, it is technical and not
easy to follow. But the original quadrangular duel was a strange
tangle of swordpoints indeed. Both sides strayed from the real
question at issue. In regard to the first line about which he was
attacked, Mr. Phillips fairly carried his point. That Milton used
a trochee in the fourth foot, with or without pause, is clearly
shown by the one line we quoted from Mr. Phillips's letter:

> "Which now the rising sun gilds with his beams."

"Gilds with" is a trochee, it is in the fourth foot, and follows
an iambic foot. And it is absurd to say there is a pause between
"sun" and "gilds." What, indeed, can be more continuous in
sense than a verb immediately following its subject? But we see
no necessity to prove that Milton used it. Granted the general
licence to use a trochee occasionally in the course of an iambic line,
the place in which it is used must depend on the effect required.
It is pedantry to say that you must use it in no place where it
has not been used by some great poet before you; that, in fact,
you must use no effect unless you can cite a precedent for it.
Mr. Phillips, seeking his own effects of harmony, uses the means

conducive to them. What understander of metre will search the records to see whether the like has been done before, and not rather ask, "Is the effect appropriate or beautiful?"

But the whole point of this quarrel turns on elision. Mr. Phillips has missed his real defence and point of vantage, which sets on one side all the petty details raised by "J. D." The plaintiff, like the mass of critics, is mistaken as to the very meaning of elision. He actually thinks, for instance, that "murmur and wave" should be read "murm'rand wave." He says so. Now elision, in the practice of the great Elizabethans and their successors, meant not the missing out of a syllable, but the rapid gliding over it. The two syllables were pronounced in the time of one, that was all. It was the dull eighteenth century which began to write such passages with the vowel actually omitted, and so started a false tradition. The question is simply, therefore, whether two syllables are light enough to be pronounced in the time of one, not whether one of them can be eliminated before the other. Again, in modern blank verse actual anapæsts are not infrequently used for special effects. For instance, Tennyson ends the line describing the flight of Excalibur with the words, "And whirled in an arch." You cannot even glide over the syllables, "in an arch." It is a pure anapæst. On this ground alone Mr. Phillips's "gloried and drank" could be defended. As a matter of fact, the liquid "r" followed by the vowel-sound "ie" makes the final syllable of "gloried" so rapid in pronunciation that we think the case midway between elision proper and the use of the anapæst. Let this true meaning of elision be better understood, and there will be less mechanical criticism of metre. At the same time, we admit the line, "Realises all the uncoloured dawn," to be a quite unusual bit of daring handling, not covered by our remarks about elision, and only to be justified by its expressiveness — on which tastes may differ. Lastly, might we suggest that both parties to this case might be "cast" in apologies? The defendant to recant the somewhat self-conscious assertion of his metrical profundity — with all the more grace because he must be adjudged mainly the successful party! The defendant — well, the defendant might withdraw that imputed journey to Parnassus on "inflated balloons of egoism."

MR. BRIDGES AND METRE *

[*Academy*, January 25, 1902]

Because of Thompson's largely instinctive use of accent and quantity, and Patmore's more deliberate treatment of them as "lovers, but not wedded," these are particularly interesting reviews. Patmore's ideas on the technique of poetry, expressed in his "Essay on English Metrical Law" — one of the most valuable and least-known treatises on the subject — find their completest vindication in his odes, which were, in turn, the inspiration of Thompson's most successful odic performances. These ideas, propounded by Patmore and adopted by Thompson, form the basis of the criticism in these reviews.

Mr. Robert Bridges' essay on Milton's prosody has long been recognised by metrical students as a work of standing value. It is here reprinted, with the addition of an appendix on the lighter triple metres, or *stress-rhythms*, as Mr. Bridges calls them, and the "English accentual hexameter." Any attempt to examine essays so complex and dependent on *minutiæ* would be impossible within our limits. Regarded as an analysis of the chief licences, or departures from typical verse-structure, in Milton, Mr. Bridges' work is excellent for the poetical student, though whether it will be of use to the general reader of poetry is another question. "There are very few persons indeed," he truly says, "who take such a delight in rhythm for its own sake, that they can follow with pleasure a learned rhythm which is very rich in variety, and the beauty of which is its perpetual freedom to obey the sense and diction. And . . . some knowledge of the structure . . . is necessary to most persons before they will receive them as melodious; and they will accept or reject a rhythm to which they are unaccustomed, according as they can or cannot perceive, or think they perceive, its structure." But can persons destitute of this native sense for numerous metre really be taught to enjoy it, by any amount of explanation? And do they much matter? From the poet's own standpoint, at least, we fancy not.

* *Milton's Prosody*. By Robert Bridges. *Classical Metres in English Verse*. By William J. Stone.

Mr. Bridges' ambition, however, goes further than the analysis of Miltonic prosody. He designs this essay, with its appendices, to be at least a basis for a scientific scheme of English prosody at large. Even from this standpoint it has value: but (in our opinion) it is vitiated by the tendency (all but universal with writers on this theme) to conform English metre with analogies of classical prosody. Hence an immense intricacy of minute laws and rules. If one recognised English prosody as a distinct thing, and made a valiant effort (it needs valour) to get down to its native bed-rock, much of all this would be rendered needless. We know but two writers who have done this, the later (though not the profounder) of them being Mr. T. C. Oman, in his valuable pamphlet on English metre.

Mr. Stone's essay, appended to Mr. Bridges' book, is an uncompromising attempt to apply classic metres to the English tongue. Both he and Mr. Bridges do good service by pointing out the subtle and various nature of English quantity, and the futility of applying to it the laws of classic quantity. Since they did not use quantity as their metrical basis, English poets were free to recognise its numerous shades of weight or lightness; while the classic poets were under the necessity of adopting a general and partly artificial law (as our own classical verse does with regard to accent). But the adoption of classical metre is an illusion, which no poet has compassed or can compass. Were it possible, one may admit Mr. Stone's would be the way. It is not possible. There are two chief ways. Mr. Stone's, apparently, is frankly to make quantity, not accent, the metrical basis, leaving accent independent, as in Latin. This is going the whole length. It is impossible, because verse based on quantity, uncoupled with accent, the English ear will never recognise as metre at all. It is not the method of English speech; and our metre is simply speech systematised. The other way is to unite accent and quantity; to make the accent coincide with the long syllable. Setting other considerations aside, this is bad verse, from a classic or accentual standpoint. The Latins took care that accent should not coincide with quantity. And the great English poets take equal care that quantity shall not coincide with accent. Their aim is to maintain a lovely interplay between accent and quantity, approaching and receding from each other in a harmonious dance-measure. Never long apart, they are never constantly together; but even in their departure they regard each other, and circle back towards their desired union. The law of good English verse is, that accent and quantity should be lovers, but not wedded. The Latins observed a like principle, with the difference that quantity gave the law to the metre; while in English, accent takes that masculine place, and quantity the female. But that difference marks two opposite systems. You cannot make accentual verse quantitative by uniting accent with quantity. Nor can you make quantitative verse English by uniting quantity with accent. The commonest result of these attempts is just bad accentual verse. For it is bad verse — from either aspect — when the two elements immovably coalesce.

AMERICANA

A PARTNERSHIP IN SONG *
[*Merry England*, December, 1894]

Brief as this criticism is, it exemplifies Thompson's critical acumen and the flawless prose in which it so often found expression. It illustrates, too, Thompson's broad sympathy for the rough-hewn manner of poetry so alien to his own.

I N SPITE of Boston and culture, we have ceased to look much towards the West for poetry, since Longfellow was joined to Poe and Emerson among "the famous nations of the dead." But the authors of the small joint volume called *Songs from Vagabondia* have an unmistakable right to the name of poet. These little snatches have the spirit of a gipsy Omar Khayyám. They have always careless verve, and often careless felicity; they are masculine and rough, as roving songs should be; sometimes also unfinished, as no songs should be. For finish is not polish, though it is frequently confounded with polish; and a thing as rough as Esau's hand may have had the last touch which an understanding art exacts. But here, certainly, is the poet's soul; and how sick we all are of pratings about the poet's art! It is become as odious as "the word 'occupy,' which was an excellent good word before it was ill-sorted." Of the two auothors, Mr. Bliss Carman's previous work has not gone without favourable notice in the English press; but Mr. Hovey's is a new, or almost new name. You have the whole spirit of the book in such an unforgettable little lyric as "In the House of Idiedaily." Here is the opening:

> Oh, but life went gayly, gayly,
> In the house of Idiedaily!
>
> There were always throats to sing
> Down the river-banks with spring,

* *Songs from Vagabondia.* By Bliss Carman and Richard Hovey.

When the stir of heart's desire
Set the sapling's heart on fire.

Bobolincolns in the meadows,
Leisure in the purple shadows,

Till the poppies without number
Bowed their heads in crimson slumber.

And the twilight came to cover
Every unreluctant lover.

Not a night but some brown maiden
Bettered all the dusk she strayed in,

While the roses in her hair
Bankrupted oblivion there.

This Vagabond is something Elizabethan when it pleases him, as those last two beautiful stanzas show. And throughout the book, in addition to the more omnipresent qualities we have before noted, start up touches of a higher mood; as when, for example, in the admirable "Joys of the Road," lilting, vagrant, irreflective, as a road-song should be, we are suddenly startled by such a Wordsworthian subtlety of expression as this:

The outward eye, the quiet will,
And the striding heart from hill to hill.

Wordsworth has taught us the divinity of the "inward eye"; but it was left, appropriately, for this roaming singer to discern, that the outward eye is in its season a gift of the gods, seldom truly possessed but by the child and the poet. A shorter snatch, "In the Workshop," strikes a veritably individual thought and manner; though this, we incline to think, is one of the examples where the form might have been a trifle less rude without destroying its proper air of unstudiedness.

Once in the Workshop, ages ago,
The clay was wet and the fire was low.

And He Who was bent on fashioning man
Moulded a shape from a clod,
And put the loyal heart therein,
And another stood watching by.

"What's that?" said Beelzebub.
"A lover," said God.
And Beelzebub frowned, for he
        knew that kind.

And then God fashioned a fellow shape,
As lithe as a willow-rod,
And gave it the merry roving eye,
And the range of the open road.

"What's that?" said Beelzebub.
"A vagrant," said God.
And Beelzebub smiled, for he
        knew that kind.

And last of all God fashioned a form,
And gave it, what was odd,
The loyal heart and the roving eye;
And he whistled, light of care.

"What's that?" said Beelzebub.
"A poet," said God.
And Beelzebub frowned, for he did
        not know.

We may finally quote a few stanzas from the "War-Song of Gamelbar," to show how fierily these authors can handle the old martial ballad. The names have a pleasant ring of the old country, pleasant for kindred's sake in the mouth of an American.

Bowmen, shout for Gamelbar!
Winds, unthrottle the wolves of war!
    Heave a breath
    And dare a death
For the doom of Gamelbar!
    Wealth for Gamel,
    Wine for Gamel,
Crimson wine for Gamelbar!

Armourers for Gamelbar
Rivet and forge and fear no scar!
  Heave a hammer
  With anvil clamour
To weld and brace for Gamelbar!
  Ring for Gamel!
  Rung for Gamel!
Ring-rung-ring for Gamelbar!

Roncliffe, shout for Gamelbar!
Menthorpe, Bryan, Castelfar!
  Heave, Thorparch
  Of the Waving Larch,
And Spofford's thane, for Gamelbar!
  Blaise for Gamel!
  Brame for Gamel!
Rougharlington for Gamelbar!

Trumpets, speak for Gamelbar!
Blare as ye never blared before!
  Heave a bray
  In the horns to-day,
The red war-horns of Gamelbar!
  To-night for Gamel!
  The North for Gamel!
With fires on the hills for Gamelbar!

Shout for Gamel, Gamelbar,
Till your throats can shout no more!
  Heave a cry
  As he rideth by,
Sons of Orm, for Gamelbar!
  Folk for Gamel,
  Fame for Gamel,
Years and fame for Gamelbar!

Good is here, but no less good remains behind; for which we refer the reader to the delightful little volume itself, which comes as a welcome interlude amidst the highly-wrought introspective poetry of the day.

THE KINSHIP OF NATURE *
[*Academy*, February 27, 1904]

This slight review of Carman as an essayist shows Thompson's facility in grasping and synthesizing a writer's ideas, and the dispassion of his judgment in appraising the literary merits of one with whose philosophy he is in almost complete disagreement.

FROM the days of Dryden — nay, from the days of Ben Jonson and Cowley — poets have had a tendency to fall into essay-writing. In modern times the tendency has increased rather than diminished; and it has throughout been of such advantage to the essay that the reviewer must needs look kindly on it. Ben Jonson, Cowley, Dryden, Leigh Hunt (to stop short of the present day) form a lineage illustrious enough amply to justify the practice. The poet's prose is usually excellent prose; sometimes rich, and seldom other than idiomatic and pure. The latest recruit to the growing band is Mr. Bliss Carman, a Canadian poet of deserved repute this side the water, with a lusty and individualised joy in nature. It is the outward eye, rather than the "inward eye" of Wordsworth, which inspires the nature-poetry of Mr. Carman, on whom is the roving impulse of the New World. Does a like inspiration show itself in his prose?

Well, these essays are not altogether as his verse. The essential man of the poetry is discoverable also in the prose, if you understandingly look for him. But Mr. Carman's philosophy is very much more to the front, more predominant, one might almost say more exclusively evident, in these essays. We say "philosophy," because such is the term loosely applied nowadays to all theorising upon problems of life or nature. But in the stricter and older sense of the term, Mr. Carman, like most poets, is too in love with the concrete for his speculations to be classed as philosophy. But a poet's thought by any other name will smell as sweet. Briefly, these essays are dominated by a conviction that the

* *The Kinship of Nature.* By Bliss Carman.

faculties of men at large are oppressed, confined, in part atrophied; and that in giving them free play lies the salvation of society. Commercialism, there is the enemy. It is commercialism which suppresses some of the noblest and most necessary faculties in the masses of men.

Body, mind, and soul, cries the author, are all equal; he can make no distinction of nobility between them. So, likewise, taste, reason, and conscience are to him equal faculties, and to be cultivated equally. Human happiness lies in the equal cultivation of all human faculties "to a normal degree in a normal way." No one faculty should be thought inferior to another faculty, or depressed in favour of another faculty. Let the bit be taken off all these powers of humanity, and let them race neck-for-neck. Freedom for every faculty of man. To distrust the result is to "believe in the ultimate evil of the spirit"; for if the good be stronger than the bad, the less repression the better. Release all human powers, and full steam ahead.

Such is Mr. Carman's theory. He is, in effect, a democrat — if we might not say an anarchist, or at least a socialist — carrying his democracy into the region of thought. The native righteousness of human nature, therefore liberty and equality for all the faculties of humanity — such is the logical outcome of the poet's democracy applied to speculative principle. We are not concerned to dispute or agree with, but merely to emphasise it. What really and chiefly concerns him, however, is the suppression of one human faculty — the faculty of taste, the native perception of beauty. All work should be art, should be the expression of the workman's self, and therefore a joy in the doing of it. Modern conditions make this impossible, brutalise the workman by stamping out individuality or the chance of individuality in his work. There is in his work no outlet for himself, therefore he has in his work no joy. Art is divorced from life, and becomes etiolated; life, divorced from art, becomes base. There must be freedom for the common workman as there is freedom for the thinker and artist; that is the radical, only cure. We are minded to ask, is there freedom for thinker and artist in the modern Western state, gripped by the dollar and the driving-wheel? But, however we may view the all-sufficiency of Mr. Carman's cure and theories, there can be no question that commercialism is, as he declares, the enemy, the crushing and throttling influence upon modern life. Nor are these essays without abundance of other things: happy natural observation which recalls the writer's poetry, suggestive artistic theory. One essay, "Rhythm," reads like a variation on the subtle essay of an English poet and prose writer, but has its own observation and personality. Always the style is pure, clear, direct, with that undenotable quality which comes from the habit and exercise of poetry. "Trees" is Mr. Carman the poet, pure and simple; and very delightful it is. It is a gain to know Carman the essayist; though he does not weaken our preference for Carman the poet. Which, probably, is as he would have it be.

THE GOLDEN BOWL *
[*Academy*, February 11, 1905]

Here we have psychoanalysis — the reality, before the name was commonly known — James' psychoanalysis at work, and Thompson's keen sense detecting it on every page. Particularly in his novels, Thompson finds James a fastidious prober. What his probing discovers is, in Thompson's opinion, of no great significance. But he has praise for its masterful expression, excepting the startling lapses quoted from *The American Scene*.

MR. HENRY JAMES has here put forward the most important work, in point of bulk and complexity, which he has issued for some time. It is, indeed, the longest novel we have of late years read; close-packed, full of matter, elaborated with remarkable and meticulous precision of labour. It is no novel which he who runs may read. Its every page exacts of the reader concentration; it must be followed with care and patience; nor can the critic without much diffidence judge on a first reading, work of such a scale and prepared with so manifest, so conscientious a deliberation. For it is pre-eminently Henry James, and Henry James of the latest, the

* *The Golden Bowl*. By Henry James.

most difficult refinement. The plot is cunningly contrived, artfully interwoven. Perhaps for "plot" we should say "situation," since (as in all James novels) it is the evolution of character under the development of a situation rather than plot in the usual sense, which is the groundwork of the story. A James situation is always subtle; but this is intricately subtle — so intricate in its subtlety as to intimidate any attempt at brief description or analysis. It is the case of a couple (an Italian Prince and an Anglo-American girl) forced into a false position by a love affair preceding the Prince's marriage to an American heiress; a love affair concealed from the bride, who is the Anglo-American girl's bosom friend. Conceive that the latter girl afterwards marries the bride's millionaire father, is thus brought into permanent relation with the Prince and his bride, and that circumstances drift her into renewing her former connection with the Italian — you then have but a part, the most obvious part, of the tangled web woven by Mr. James. The interest is heightened by the fact that all the four people thus netted in domestic tragedy — indeed, all the chief people of the story — are in their varying measure sympathetic to the reader. The issue (as one foreknows in a James novel) is partial and unsatisfying as life itself. The emotion, the tragedy, though keen, is never violent, never full-blooded. Mr. James knows that modern domesticity is a thing of half-tints, even in its suffering: it bleeds, but it does not bleed red. The Golden Bowl is a crystal vessel cased in gold, which plays a part in the tale with somewhat Ibsen-like symbolism; a crystal vessel with a secret flaw, which finally shatters — allegorising the character and fate of the Italian Prince. Not only in length and elaboration is this a novel which claims attention, even among Mr. Henry James' work. As the plot, so is the execution, subtly intricate. Often, alas! but too much so! Mr. James' later work has frequently carried his peculiar qualities to a baffling extreme, and much of this book has the defects of those qualities harassingly in evidence. The intellectuality overpowers the sensuous and objective traits proper to a novel, until one has the impression of reading an abstruse treatise of psychology rather than a tale. The reader is never for a moment allowed to "take it easy." He is required to be alert always and at all points. Even the inverted commas, to which the schoolgirl looks as marking the green oases in the sands of narration, betoken for him no relaxation of vigilance. We know that in life people often answer to each other's meaning rather than to the thing actually spoken; that you may have passages of dialogue wherein the actual words are but signposts pointing to the intended significance. Especially is this the case with very cultivated intelligence or very uncultivated intelligence, where the sense and habit of language is very trained or very untrained. In the one case it is an art of delicate suggestion, in the other a groping for expression. Mr. Meredith, at his best, handles this manner of dialogue admirably; so, in his separate way, can Mr. James. But in this book it is at times pushed to a nebulousness, a tenuity, which gives one the feeling of walking on tight-ropes. Moreover, people, after all, talk in this way but at moments, under stress of some withheld emotion, impelled by some particular motive. But here people often propound enigmas to each other for page after page, till the wearied reader rebels. Then, too, Mr. James' extraordinary gift in detecting and expressing the most evanescent complexities of psychological feeling, subconscious or unconscious thought, has seemingly become such a passion that he cannot for an instant disembarrass himself of it. It overpowers his instinct of proportion: he must analyse everything, important or trivial, with like minuteness and like prolixity. Thus you have page upon page in which the game is beautifully played, but the game was really not worth the candle. Nay, at one point there is the (we should think) unparalleled exhibition of three successive chapters almost wholly engrossed by analysis and unbroken by a single conversation. It is magnificent, but it is scarcely novel-writing. Also, Mr. James' faculty of finessing with and reducing to psychological abstractions what with any other would be the most pedestrian commonplaces of statement, in association with these other things grows rather appalling to the jaded attention of the much-tried reader. But his analysis, in the proper place, triumphs. A father marries his daughter's young friend mainly to satisfy his daughter; and we believe it, for Mr. James persuades us of its truth. When he does concentrate on his story there is the old power and art. He is admirable in sureness and cumulative convincingness:

through all the intricate evolutions and changes of emotional situation, which from another hand would seem artificial as a Congreve comedy, he guides us with perfect persuasion of natural truth. Despite exasperations of detail, the novel in the main is masterly. The three leading women are differentiated with the nicest skill: each is living and persuasive. The Prince, in a position somewhat recalling that of Tito Melema, never forfeits the reader's sympathy, or appears less than a natively high-minded man — a Southern man. But the women are the success of the novel. To analyse its charm, its power, is far less easy than to note its defects. But it fairly ranks as a master-work — if a master-work flawed by some of his obscurest later mannerisms. It is not built for popularity; but no lover of Mr. Henry James can neglect it without loss. It is a last word of subtlety, marred at times by subtlety out of place.

THE AMERICAN SCENE *

[*Athenæum*, March 9, 1907]

To READ this latest book of Mr. Henry James is like tackling one of those exasperating puzzles called "mazes," with a little arbour in the middle, and a tangle of ways which all run up against something — unless you hit on "the only way." The things you run up against are of course connected with Mr. James' style and (what is largely the same thing) his way of thinking. Readers may conceive that, having mastered his novels, they can be daunted by nothing more. But in the novels the necessity of narration does sometimes oblige Mr. James to write almost like the kindly race of men. Here, "story, God bless you! he has none to tell, sir"; and throughout four hundred and sixty-five broad pages there is no oasis in the level, unbroken expanse of Jacobean style. He has seized so rare an opportunity relentlessly, and holds his audience in the toils like the Wedding-Guest; "the Mariner hath his will." Nor

* *The American Scene.* By Henry James.

has his style improved with years. In this latest example it has an irritation once absent; for to the defects of his own qualities he has added carelessness. "There's no step," he writes, "at which you shall rest, no form, as I'm constantly showing you, to which, consistently with my interests, you *can*." Which seemingly means that there is no form *to* which we can rest — a construction scarcely to be dismissed as a grammatical licence. Later we read, "The great thing is not to suffer it to so much as begin," and meet sentences like this: "The present Public Library, however remarkable in its pomp and circumstance, *and of which* I had at that hour received my severe impression." Extremes meet. By the road of fastidious and defiant individuality Mr. James has, in fact, arrived at some of the results which the callow novelist achieves as a child of nature. With this he has the curiously contrasting vice of the Gallic use of the word "so": "From his so interesting point of view"; or again, "New York, with the so ambiguous element in the launched foreign personality," &c. This manner of idiom is sometimes harassingly frequent. Against the appearance of such symptoms in Mr. James' writing his admirers (among whom we are not the least sincere) have a right to protest; for these are not vices of style, but result from the want of it.

Though, however, they fret and exaggerate (by their needless slovenliness) one's sense of the difficulty, they are not the difficulty. That is in Mr. James' manner of thought. If you expect from him a guide-book to America, or a record of sight-seeing as people in general understand sight-seeing, you may close the book. It is an elaborated impression of America as it vibrates on the very conscious consciousness of Mr. Henry James — an impression on a minutely large scale. Yet it is not even impressionism as usually understood — the immediate sensitive impression of eye and emotion, stripped of afterthought and analysis. That would not be Mr. James, who is nothing if not analytic. Rather, it is the application to sight-seeing of the methods of Mr. James the novelist — an endeavour first to capture, then to tease out and analyse the elusive subtleties of human atmosphere and suggestion in scenes and localities. We say "human atmosphere and suggestion," since for nature, apart from its connexion and reciprocal interaction with man, the novelist can spare little interest. And the novelist in Mr. James is always hankering after elusive subtleties, always aiming at them, even when he fails to get them. The result, whether one thinks it successful or not, is something curious — and very tough reading. For, despite this inveterate quest of the elusive, gendered in him by the calling of a lifetime, the ideas suggested to Mr. James by a revisited "American scene" are inevitably, at bottom, often much what might occur to any other reflective observer. But the expression does not accommodate itself to the relative obviousness of idea. That must still preserve all the paraphernalia of elusiveness, though there is nothing which eludes. He must still write about and around it, and every way but *of* it — must approach it by stealth and tortuous indirectness, and deck it with the most elaborated precisions of impreciseness, as if it required hinting afar off. He must (habitual microscopist!) still use his delicate microtome, though only to make sections of butter. The language invented, and the manner of thought developed, for his psychological subtleties he uses for matters the most familiar, and so reduces them to a strange, phantasmal abstraction of their workaday selves, bafflingly implying subtlety which is not in them. It is more difficult to follow than really inherent subtlety. For through the swathings you laboriously arrive at relative commonplace, and strenuous attention exerted to such a result exhausts one more than if the evasive expression had been compelled by a true evasiveness of idea.

Mr. James, for example, staggered by the huge alien masses of the United States, and especially of New York, wonders, like other thinkers, what will issue from the Americanisation of them which is furiously going forward, and recoils from answer. He tells you that, among the vast numbers newly cast into the machine (so to speak), the most striking feature is their featurelessness, the dead blank of monotonous uniformity which has resulted. He regrets, in particular (and with a special eye on the Italians), the loss of those racial amenities which make various nations engaging to the traveller's observation in their own land. The Italian has no longer the soft and amiable address universal in Italy. And these traits of national charm go with instant swiftness and absolute completeness; they are cast off on contact with the soil, as if they were contraband, and confiscated at the custom-house. This, in effect, Mr. James has to say. It is interesting, but not very difficult to say, one would think. Mr. James contrives to say it at great length, with an accumulation of every Jacobean resource for uttering the unutterable; so that when you exhaustedly look back and note what he *has* said, you can scarce credit your memory that this, essentially, is all.

To render any account, any description, of a book so written is manifestly impossible. It is not to be read through like other books, but should be taken up and read slowly by portions, when one is in a mood for the effort. So doing, you will find suggestion enough and to spare. For it is, after all, Mr. James; and what counts in it is less the subject than the author. The point is that such is the way things affected Mr. James. It happens to be America — it might have been Astrachan or the Samoyedes; the main interest would have been the same, so long as there were men, and Mr. James, insatiably curious, watching them. He does not describe, he gives no information; he exposes himself to impressions, and discusses and analyses the result. Very characteristically, he mostly ends by leaving the result an open question; he is indisposed to commit himself even as to what his impression is after all. His attitude is curiously dispassionate, critical, and a-patriotic rather than un-patriotic. The colossal utilitarianism and restless mutability of the American atmosphere stir him to perpetual hostility. Everywhere he finds the America of his own day "coming down," and declares "coming down" to be the law of American life, fatal to all asso-ciation. America is a top, which stands only on condition that it perpetually "hums" — in the most American sense of that word. Yet it interests him, even the modern city with its "sky-scrapers" that provoke him to blasphemy against the American idea; for it is human, and the novelist in him perpetually speculates on the possibilities of its evolving charm. It is a gigantic note of inter-rogation; he can neither answer it, nor cease from subtilising on what answer the future may give. A good example of his manner is the chapter on the Bowery, with the contrast between the alien audience of its theatre, munching sausages as in their German homes, and the conventionally American play at which they stare; or the account of the immense impression made on him by the Ghetto of New York, prosperous, a New Jerusalem, the strong Judaic features dominating its streets with aggressive vitality. These things are impressions, singularly communicated, of a singular commixture, yet only possible from a unique personality.

Never can one forget the novelist. The book has an effect as of a man who in a dream makes struggling motions of running. We have the feeling that we should know better Mr. James' revised perceptions of New York or Boston if he made those cities the scene even of a short story, than we do from this minutely complex *compte rendu* of them. Further, he seems (to us) always wanting to write that story. He says of himself that he was always wanting to *get inside* the picture. When he quits the city for the country, where poet or painter would be content with the solitary charm of nature, he is restless to penetrate its human meaning, to discover in it the soul of its inhabitants: lonely loveliness which will surrender no such message leaves him but half-pleased. Were he not busy with other matters, no man could give you the impression of it in fewer touches. Read, for instance, this of Cape Cod:

A broad band of deep and clear blue sea . . . limited in one quarter by its far and sharp horizon of sky, on the other by its near and sharp horizon of yellow sand overfringed with a low woody shore; the whole seen through the contorted crosspieces of stunted, wind-twisted, far-spreading, quite fantastic old pines and cedars, whose bunched bristles at the end of long limbs, produced against the light the most vivid of all reminders. Cape Cod, on this showing, was exactly a pictured Japanese screen or banner.

He throws off Cotuit with a pen-scratch or two:

The little white houses, the feathery elms, the band of ocean blue, the stripe of sandy yellow, the tufted pines in angular silhouette, the cranberry-swamps stringed across, for the picking, like the ruled pages of ledgers.

You retain a distinct impression of the New Hampshire villages: the long straight road, the double file of verdurous branching elms, the white-painted wooden walls splashing the shadow with bright coolness, the far horizons that "recall the Umbrian note." But from all this, and through all this, he zigzags and feels his verbose way to the hesitant conclusion that these are the paradise and sphere of the "common man" and woman, the passive and negative people who "simply invest themselves for you in the grey truth that they don't go to the public house." That description of them is in turn debated into dubiety, with as meticulous an earnestness. The rest is a felicitous incident: this it is that interests him. He is throughout instinctively seeking psychological problems as a dislodged limpet seeks a rock or stone to fasten on. You will be gratified with all manner of incidental felicities by the way, such as the half-revealed glimpses of the delicate shyness of Newport; but you must go problem-seeking to get them. Nor must you care overmuch about the results reached. We doubt whether the tabulated conclusions of the whole book (but who shall formulate them?) would yield much new light on the States or even their possibilities. The pleasure of the chase must content. Distinctly it is the process rather than the result that fascinates Mr. James, and you must let it fascinate you. That is how we are reduced to take this tantalising, endlessly clever, engaging, perverse, compelling and repelling by-product of the most fastidiously probing mind in present literature. As the peculiar and specialised methods of a novelist applied to a purpose outside fiction, it may or may not be successful. Interesting it must be — with the interest Browning felt in Dante's drawing of the angel, and we all feel in the essay of a great specialist in an art outside his own. Not even slipshod blemishes can make Mr. James' style other than distinguished, as Mayfair may drop its *g*'s, which Bayswater neglects at its peril.

THE OFFICIAL "LOWELL" *

[*Academy*, January 11, 1902]

Thompson here reflects a broad understanding of America and Americans, with no trace of the "certain condescension in foreigners," satirized by Lowell in his essay of that name. What is said in admiration of the harmonious blend of environment and training, issuing in Lowell's singularly happy life, reminds us, by contrast, of the reviewer's life and the self-revealing lines in "The Sere of the Leaf":

> I know not equipoise, only purgatorial joys,
> Grief's singing to the soul's instrument.

The comments on Lowell's unsympathetic reactions to Rome are a model for all future writers who may comment upon the lack of understanding of things Catholic, still a characteristic of the vanishing Puritans of New England.

THIS is what must, we suppose, be considered the official or standard biography of Lowell. Mr. Scudder's object, he explains, has been to supplement Mr. Eliot Norton's edition of the *Letters* (which we reviewed at the time) by a formal biography, printing only such letters, or parts of letters, as might serve to illustrate his subject. Contrary, in fact, to the fashionable method, he has produced a narrative of Lowell's life, rather than followed the semi-Boswellian plan of leaving Lowell to reveal himself, with a connective setting of narration. This, in spite of the fact that he had supplementary letters of Lowell in his possession. He has relied largely on Lowell's literary writings, collected and uncollected. We are disposed to complain that he has used the letters but too sparingly, and in general has not been too successful in the art of making us feel personal members (so to speak) of Lowell's *entourage*, which is a main element in successful biography. We know, for example, that Lowell, throughout his life, and especially during those brilliant early Boston days, was part of an electric chain of brilliant American mentality. Yet we get no impression,

* *James Russell Lowell: A Biography*. By Horace Elisha Scudder. 2 Vols.

no intimate and realised impression of all that fascinating circle. Lowell remains detached, so far as our personal realisation is concerned. It is only when his own pen is suffered to speak that we get this living sense of environment: we do not, as it seems to us, get it from the biographer. The remedy for this would have been a freer use of letters and impressions — Lowell's or others. But the biography is none the less good, well arranged, sympathetic, and free from any exaggerated partiality. And if it err at all, it errs on the commendable side of avoiding tedious expansion, the prolix elaboration of *minutiæ* which mars so many modern biographies.

Lowell's was, in almost every respect, a fortunate life. He had no more than such amount of early struggle as is good for a healthy and energetic man; he was able to develop himself without impediment through the whole gamut of his faculties; and his abilities obtained complete recognition with no excessive or disheartening delay. For the gods (or, rather, men) to be thus favourable there needs steadiness, social faculty, and not too much originality, but just originality enough. All which happy gifts of the *via media* were Lowell's. He was born and bred under the right conditions for a fine and lettered, yet physically sane and equipoised bookman, in a *Toryfied* old country seat at Elmwood, Cambridge, New England. His parents combined conservative instincts with democratic principles in just the right proportions to promote that "all-round" mind afterwards so characteristic of their son. Of Charles Lowell, the father, we are told that he was "minister of the West Church in Boston"; but though this may be very clear indication to an American, it leaves an Englishman very vague about his religious sect — nor does Mr. Scudder give us any subsequent enlightenment, except that the father is antithesised with the Episcopalian mother. Charles Lowell is described by his own son as a Dr. Primrose. A preacher of remarkable personal gifts, a zealous parish-worker, mild and disliking violent reforms, above all (from the standpoint of his son's future) a trained lover of literature. A female parishioner, who had decided for reform and public speaking, describes his benign horror at her defection from the feminine domesticities. "In a long white flannel dressing-gown, with a short shoulder-cape hardly reaching to his belt," he rose to receive her from the old easy-chair, and, "standing erect, cried out: 'Child, my child! what is this I hear? Why are you talking to the whole world?' " One likes the picture, and is not without sympathy for the old man's distress at women who talk "to the whole world." Lowell's mother was said to have second-sight, and, anyway, was an imaginative creature, who (to our thankfulness) filled "Baby Jammie's" head with Scotch songs and Scotch ballads, like "Annie of Lochroyan," and its splendid kindred. The work of education (far truer than the learned fowl-cramming of any 'Varsity) was well continued by his eight-year-elder sister Mary, the little nurse who early loved poetry, and read him to sleep — or kept him awake — from Spenser. No wonder that (as it has chanced with so many a poet) the *Faerie Queene* was the first poem he ever read. No wonder, either, that the child was subject to visions, day-dreams, and night-dreams; that he often saw the earth put into his hand like an orange, or of evenings had by his side "a figure in mediæval costume." To these was added the stimulus of nature, and the healthy visions of the outward eye: "the balancing of a yellow butterfly over a thistle-broom was spiritual food and lodging for a whole forenoon."

Lowell's schooldays were no wise different from the school-days of the average clever boy and youth. The most noteworthy thing is really that merciless training in Latin — at the rod's point, though to him it was never applied — which he received at the boarding school of Mr. William Wells. How many a masterly turn of diction in his prose may we not owe to that? for Lowell was the most scholarly of writers. The other notable feature is his early acquaintance with Emerson, his intimacy with whom largely derived from the "happy fault" which rusticated him temporarily from Harvard to Concord. He attacked Emerson, in those days, for his heterodoxy, though the college verses in which he did so were afterwards regarded as "baby arrows" directed at the "woundless Truth." But despite contributions to the Harvard periodical, clever enough as such things go, he only began to "train on" after he had left college. An unfortunate love affair, and much difficulty in finding a profession, belonged to that period of "thick-sightedness" which Keats deplored as incident to youth.

He finally got harnessed to law, but Fate denied him clients and
sent him editors. Moreover, he met Mary White, by all accounts
a brilliant girl, and she stimulated his own tendency to literature,
both before and after their marriage. The natural result was a
crop of poems, which, as *A Year's Life,* introduced him to the
American public. It was no less just than romantic, for she was
his inspiration in all things, even in that anti-slavery crusade of
which he was to become so prominent a champion. The centre
of a band of young people, the love-letters of Lowell to Mary
White were actually passed about among them — an amorous
publicity surely without parallel, and which few hero-worships
could survive!

A Year's Life brought Lowell immediate reputation, if not
money: even Hawthorne thought him the poet of the generation
entering on the arena. Strange judgments which could give him
such leadership; though Poe, Emerson, Longfellow, and Whittier
were in full fecundity, and of that band he was nearly the weakest — in verse. At this time he started the *Pioneer*, short-lived as
our own *Germ*, which first brought forward his finest gift, criticism. Young though he was, he was then the recognised brother-
in-arms of the brilliant writers whom America has not since
rivalled. Poe, Hawthorne, Story, and Dr. Parsons (famous for
those two noble stanzas on Dante), contributed to the three numbers which appeared, before Lowell's eyes — and the funds — gave
out. But editors became increasingly ready to accept his wares:
he was able to marry —somewhat at a venture — and entered on
a hot campaign in the *Anti-Slavery Standard*, which is memorable
in that it led up to the *Biglow Papers*, with a popular success and
a secured fame. Almost simultaneously appeared the *Fable for
Critics*, with its sometimes dexterous sketches of American writers
and its rather lumbering anapæsts. Mr. Scudder thinks it was
suggested by Leigh Hunt's "Feast of the Poets," and that in its
turn by Byron's *English Bards and Scotch Reviewers*. But however this be as concerns Lowell (who may then have known more
of the sixteenth than the seventeenth century), Leigh Hunt's
poem is surely derived — metre and all — from Suckling's happy-
go-lucky and sufficiently untrimmed satire on the courtly poets of

his day. The device of making Apollo assessor there crops up; and for the metre take a stanza:

> Wat Montague first stood forth to his trial,
> And did not so much as suspect a denial:
> But wiser Apollo asked him first of all
> If he understood his own Pastoral?
> For if he did, it would plainly appear
> That he understood more than any man there.

This is clearly the ancestor of both poems. Thenceforth begins Lowell's triumphant period. For, besides his serious poems, it was crowned by his editorship of the *Atlantic Monthly*, and those contributions to the *North American Review*, afterwards republished in *My Study Windows*. It is by such admirable prose, critical or reflective as this, that Lowell holds his secure pride of place.

It was in the maturity of his life and genius that he was offered the ambassadorship to Spain, which began his diplomatic career, and added the laurels of a publicist to his full and rich life. Mary White he had already buried, and his second wife — the governess of his children, Frances Dunlap — whose beautiful face looks forth from Mr. Scudder's second volume, died after his transference to the English ambassadorship. These were the two great sorrows of his life, which marred its otherwise serene prosperity. It is here that one would most wish for more letters. Lowell's eminence in the peculiarly American art of after-dinner oratory can only be recorded in a life, though it was the great triumph of these latter years. But he was a letter-writer with excellently observant powers, and his shrewdly genial surveys of new men and things were delightful. During his first European journey, before the *Atlantic Monthly* days, he had shown this gift; and Lowell in Rome is a pleasantly characteristic picture as drawn by himself. Cosmopolitan by nature and reading, there are yet grains of the New England Puritan in him, and sometimes he is quite John Bull in his *noli me tangere* attitude towards the foreigner and the Scarlet Woman. The Church ceremonies, which he did not understand, naturally bored him: and Gregorian, for which he had no taste, bored him still more:

The chief quality of the music is its interminableness, made up of rises and falls, and of the ceremonies generally you may take a yard anywhere as of printed cotton, certain that in figure and quality it will be precisely like what has gone before, and what will follow after. . . . I stood wedged between some very strong devotees (who must have squandered the savings of a year in a garlic debauch) in abject terror lest my head should be colonised from some of the over-populated districts around me.

He meets a Cardinal — evident emissary of Her of Babylon (did not his very scarlet bewray him?) — and True Blue scruples are militant within him, as in the John Bull aforesaid. However:

He was old enough to deserve it, cardinal or not, so we bowed. Never did man get such percentage for an investment. First came off His Eminence's hat. At a respectful interval came that of the confessor, at another respectful interval those of the coachman and footmen.

The amusing thing is the Anglo-Saxon pother and surprise over a very simple piece of Latin courtesy. He sketches brightly the Pincio:

Here one may see all the Fashion and the Title of Rome. Here one may meet magnificent wet-nurses, bareheaded and red-bodiced, and insignificant princesses Paris-bonneted and corseted. Here one may see the neat, clean-shirted, short-whiskered, always-conceited Englishman, feeling himself quite a Luther if he have struggled into a wide-awake hat; or the other Englishman with years of careful shaving showing unconquerably through the newly-assumed beard.... Here you may see the American, every inch of him, from his hat to his boots, looking careful not to commit himself.... Here you may see the worst riding you can possibly imagine: Italians emulating the English style of rising in the stirrups and bumping forlornly in every direction; French officers reminding one of the proverb of setting a beggar on horseback, and John Bulls, with superfluous eye-glass wedged in the left eye, chins run out over white chokers, and a general upward tendency of all the features as who should say, "Regard me attentively but awfully; I am on intimate terms with Lord Fitzpollywog."

The Spanish letters are still better, for the visitor becomes merged in a cordial understanding of the people, while the eye for weaknesses remains. The glimpses of his own domestic life are charming in all his letters. When at length the brave, bright, gentle, wide-sympathised life sets peacefully in that house of Elmwood where it rose, one is left with a warm respect and admiration for the man who lived it out. Except for the latter phase of diplomacy, it is a life devoid of all but literary incident, and possibly one gets a fuller idea of Lowell from his books than from any biography. At once shrewd and expansive, Johnson would have called him a *clubbable* man. His kindness, even to men like Poe, who spoke ill of him, appears strongly in his life. A clever satirist, a poet with dignity and thought, but without impulse, he was a fine critic and a writer of veritably classic prose, having the finest resources of the English tongue at his command. And his name must rank in that select band of American writers who belong not to a country, but to a language.

SHELBURNE ESSAYS *
[*Academy*, August 19, 1905]

In this severe but dispassionate review, Thompson gives a rather complete sketch of himself as a reviewer, in his description of More's limitations as a critic. He was as austere as More in his adherence to truth. But his austerity was joined with a wholesome sympathy with man and human interests.

WE were much taken with Mr. More's first volume of Shelburne Essays. He used a plain philosophic style with careful ease and fair precision. He wrote on Thoreau, Hawthorne, Carlyle, Tolstoy, Mr. Arthur Symons; and showed training, reading, and a grave interest in literature, which were remarkable in what we believed to be a first book. The essays in the second volume are of the same order. He writes of Lafcadio Hearn, Lamb, FitzGerald, Crabbe, Mr. Meredith, and Mr. Kipling, Hawthorne again, and always with the same lofty reasonableness, yet with a monotonous severity and respectability that have in the end the same effect as a

* *Shelburne Essays*. Second Series. By Paul Elmer More.

nasal unctuousness in the voice — that is, laughter. If the whitened statue of Cobden, which looks seriously upon the Hampstead trams, were to speak, even thus would he comment upon books and life, after so many days and nights of elevated and solitary immobility.

Mr. More would not deny this; for in his title-page he has put some words from *The Republic* which insist that a man must not be considered in preference to the truth. Also, in his essay on Mr. Meredith, he has pointed out with disgust, which is as near animation as dignity would allow, that Stevenson and Mr. William Watson and others have expressed diverse views of the novelist, without giving "a rational explanation of their opinions"; and has asked "in amazement" whether this "irresponsible impressionism" is to oust the judgment from criticism. Many other passages in Mr. More's two volumes would lead us to attribute this attitude to a belief in Matthew Arnold and the dignity of criticism, as much as to a regard for the truth. Arguing in an abstract way, we should not care to urge that "irresponsible impressionism" is to supersede reasonable judgments; but we think that reasonable judgments have caused more waste of paper and more of that tedium which is sapping the vitality of the old races, than all the irresponsible impressionism. Reasonable judgments are so often related to obesity of mind, to unconscious hypocrisy and a retarding respect for authority, whether conventional or not, that we are disposed to pass them over eagerly in search of the voice of a human being. We are weary of hearing a man saying, without a smile or even a vigorous frown, that "Ibsen has violated the law of tragedy by descending to trivialities and by using prosaic language"; that *Macbeth* "purges the passions"; that ours is a "prosaic civilisation."

But leaving these little matters, it is useful to see to what discoveries Mr. More's judgment leads him in the study of Mr. Meredith. He reminds us that "an eminent critic" has said that the novelist cannot tell a story, has distorted language "in order to surcharge it with thought and sensation." But let that pass. Then he compares *Henry Esmond* (which, like Pater, he calls "the most perfect specimen among English novels," &c.) with *The Egoist*, and concludes that "in any true sense of the word there is as much depth of reflection" in the new book as in the old — a remark which is unsupported. Of Mr. Meredith's style he says:

There is after all a note of sincerity in it, something so naturally artificial, if the paradox may be pardoned, that we are prone to overlook its extravagances, and can even appreciate its fascination for certain minds. It may be pretty well characterised in his own words as "the puffing of a giant; a strong wind rather than speech."

His authority, the ground for his reasonable judgment against Mr. Meredith, is a careful study of two books, *Henry Esmond* and Castiglione's *Il Cortegiano*. It follows, then, that he finds Mr. Meredith "uncomfortable," and full of "dreary affectation," and guilty of showing "unusual genius in a wrong direction." The problem in *Richard Feverel* is to him "a fairly disagreeable one": the book "remains perfectly decent throughout," he remarks with approval. Later, he goes to the trouble of quoting, in order to show that the novelist has observed the movements of the eyelids in women; and, instead of admitting the observation, he is disturbed, probably because it is not in the *Psalms*, laughs and passes on, leaving us pleased by this fall into half-hearted impressionism. In the end he takes leave of the "perilous subject" of Clara Middleton and Diana, having given us something to ponder on, in the remark that "the infinite variety of human activity is unrolled before us" in *Pendennis* and *Tom Jones*.

All this seems to us, whether it is reasonable judgment or not, to be really timid impressionism. Mr. More has received some impressions from Mr. Meredith's work. It is not like Penn or Washington Irving or Confucius. Therefore, he has run to his old books and set them to the ungracious labour of abusing the new. Our own feeling is that a reasonable critic would have refused to say a word on one so antipathetic.

It is a truism that a critic, as distinguished from a reviewer, should praise. The truth seems to us to be that he should be enthusiastic — should see a book, as a man who is not a critic sees a landscape or a character — should, in short, be inspired by it. Arnold was, in a measure, inspired in his *Maurice de Guérin*, which is good; but not in his *Shelley*, which is indifferent. Pater was inspired in his *Æsthetic School,* which is good; Stevenson was not, in his *Thoreau,* which is indifferent. But Mr. More does not see that the pure intelligence can never exhaust a subject or produce a perfect impression, while the enthusiasm, of which we have spoken, means to us a power which, perhaps wilfully, but divinely too, makes one aspect of a thing entirely its own. The difference is as the difference between a man going about with a lantern in a dark wood, and a man sitting afar off and seeing it in the glimpses of the moon. In Mr. More, this fatal ignorance of the true value of impressionism is everywhere illustrated. Would he, otherwise, have wished that Lamb could more often have "laid aside his pose" and have found confidence "to lose his wit in the tragic emotions that must have waked with him by day and slept with him at night"? We think not, and in his strange willingness to record in print his laboriously but incompletely considered antipathies, we see a grave fault. In criticism it is so grave as often to refuse admittance to any of the virtues or the graces. Anger is bad enough, but at least it is a passion; contempt is worse, but at least it may be allied to irony; but reasonable judgment is barren, like the critical exercises of schoolboys and professors. For it is in reading such criticism that we see the grain of truth in the vulgar remark that many critics have less knowledge than the men criticised.

It is, then, the duty of a critic to be open, passionately open, to impressions, to have a personality, just as it is his duty to detect the same openness, the same personality in writers of books. When Mr. More not only fails very often to have the rich and joyous perceptions of an enthusiast, to have a personality, but fails also to detect the personality in his author, he seems to us condemned. He sees that Mr. Meredith is extraordinary, and he merely complains. Our critic is thus one of the immense number of men who do not know what they like, or if they like a thing cannot like it heartily, and go about the world trying to be interested. He likes Hawthorne and Lafcadio Hearn; he can write of them like an educated man; but he has so wasted his abilities in pondering his dislikes that he is very nearly dull. The result is that he — a man of many remarkable and rare abilities — has become little more than a "cultured" talker about books to persons who like a "cultured" man. Such readers will find much to enjoy in his essays. They are full of educated, shrewd comment, gracefully expressed, on interesting subjects. In "Lafcadio Hearn" he shows a knowledge of East and West so great, that we reflect sadly that, had it been a little less professorial, it might have pleased lovers of Hearn by other means than mere critical explanation, *i.e.,* by original composition. Then his essays on "Delphic and Greek Literature" and "Nemesis, or the Divine Envy" are grave and learned enough to accuse us fairly of violating our own laws of good criticism, by refusing to see the full and peculiar value of Mr. More's work. But then we are only reviewing.

A DREAMER OF THINGS IMPOSSIBLE
[*Academy*, September 28, 1901]

EDGAR ALLAN POE

Thompson's power of critical analysis is here particularly shown, in discovering the nature and secret of Poe's skill in presenting terror inseparable from beauty.

IT IS a singular and not very creditable fact that (as we have recently experienced) the tales of Edgar Allan Poe should be difficult to procure in their entirety — apart from complete editions of his works. It is the more regrettable and singular because these creations of genius touch on two sides of the most popular modern schools of British fiction. Perhaps, indeed, this is the explanation of it: that the derivative has ousted the original. On the one side they have relation to the "detective" fiction of Dr. Conan Doyle, on the other they are in contact with the fantastic fiction of Mr. Wells. And between these two extremes is enthroned the very Poe — single, singular, with no predecessor and no authentic successor — unless it be the Stevenson of *Dr. Jekyll and Mr. Hyde.* That central and — artistically — supreme class of his tales is difficult to describe, for, indeed, to describe it is to describe Poe himself. It has been the tendency of the modern romantic school, and of modern poets in general, to make themselves the heroes of their own work. Chateaubriand, Byron, Shelley, are instances that come at once to one's mind, and Byron had strong influence on the early Poe. But not Byron, not even the author of "Epipsychidion" and "Alastor," hardly the author of *Atala*, had such a peculiar gift for arabesquing their own lives, for transcendentalising themselves, their happenings, and environment. In nearly all these tales of idealistic terror or beauty, of which the "House of Usher" is an example, the hero is Poe himself; while they constantly revolve round situations suggested by his own history. To consider Poe is to consider these tales, to consider the tales is to consider Poe.

It is significant that his family was alleged to be descended from the Irish family of Le Poer — one of the English Pale, it is true, but thoroughly Irished by long residence and intermixture. The spirit of his work is Celtic, if the form of his poetry be not, indeed, of direct Celtic origin. It is at least possible that he should have seen some of Mangan's poems, and that unfortunate Irish poet anticipates Poe's peculiar form so strikingly that it is difficult to believe the resemblance can be accident alone. Yet, hardly less singular than such a coincidence would be, is the coincidence between the lives of the two men — identical in drudgery, misery, poverty, bondage to stimulants, and not far from identical in their deaths. It is the visionary and ethereal spirit of Celtic romance which informs the central group of tales no less than the poems. The Celtic temperament would go far to explain Poe's weakness and strength; his brilliant caprice, his pride and passion, his literary quarrels, his lack of robust moral stamina, his ready enslavement to alcohol. The Celtic visionariness, with its lack of hold on earth, is further accentuated in him by the love of strange ways in reading which he shared with Shelley. The trait is constantly appearing — implicit or explicit — in his heroes. The hero of the scarcely-sane "Ligeia" relates:

With how vast a triumph, with how vivid a delight, with how much of all that is ethereal in hope did I feel — as she bent over me in studies but little sought, but less known — that delicious vista by slow degrees expanding before me, down whose long, gorgeous, and all untrodden path I might at length pass onward to the goal of a wisdom too divinely precious not to be forbidden?

His quotations testify to the same thing. Glanville, Raymond Lully, Platonists like Henry King; by his citation of them he indicates the shadowy and mysterious authors whom he found congenial to his mind. But not to penetrate them, so far as we can see, with the zeal of the thinker. He loved, as he says himself, "those who feel rather than those who think." They give him dreams, suggest the stuff of tales or poetry; they are, indeed, to him, in no disparaging sense, "such stuff as dreams are made on." When a mind thus exalted, and of such natural development in one supermundane direction, applies itself to fiction, the result must needs be strange, almost monstrous. The pearl is an abnormality, the result of external irritation which provokes the precious excretion. These tales are no less precious and abnormal. One feels the reading of them as it were an unlawful pleasure, wrung from pain, disease, calamity, and the fruitage of delirium. The cost is too great, and the pleasure itself scarcely human. We said of "Ligeia" that it was hardly sane; we might have said thus of all the group to which we refer. Poe was conscious of this, and absolutely suggested – before Lombroso — a relation between madness and genius. For the hero of "Eleonora" surely speaks in the name of Poe:

Men [he says] have called me mad, but the question is not yet settled whether madness is or is not the loftiest intelligence, whether much that is glorious, whether all that is profound, does not spring from disease of thought, from *moods* of mind exalted at the expense of the general intellect. They who dream by day are cognisant of many things which escape those who dream only by night. In their grey visions they obtain glimpses of eternity, and thrill, in waking, to find that they have been upon the verge of the great secret. In snatches they learn something of the wisdom which is of good and more of the mere knowledge which is of evil. They penetrate, however rudderless or compassless, into the vast ocean of the "light ineffable."

This perilous doctrine is at least not far from descriptive of Poe's own genius. There was something uncanny about the man which forbade intimacy, almost approach. Of the hero (there is virtually but one) who paces through these tales in Poe's image you feel that no woman could live with him without going mad — or dying. And death, accordingly, is Poe's gift to all his women. The tales are vital with a wrongful vitality. They are told by heroes whose sensitive nerves have the preternatural acuteness of initial insanity; colour, sound, scent — every detail of description in their rendering becomes morbidly distinct to us, like the ticking of a clock in the dark. In the "House of Usher" this feature becomes conscious of itself; the hero hears the beating of a woman's heart while she stands without the closed door. Beauty and terror are alike portentous, "larger than human," like figures in a mist. The landscapes are preterhuman, painted as with fire, and blinded with a light such as only streams from the fountains of the dreaming brain. The heroes live by choice in chambers out of nightmare, where curtains like molten silver fall in cataracts on carpets of burning gold, lighted by coloured flames which writhe from antique lamps, and perfumed from carven censers; on golden tapestries phantasmal figures waver in the rushing of a continuous wind. Amid such surroundings women of unearthly beauty, or the shadow of Poe's own child-wife, pass and die, and dying, give rise to tragedies of impermissible terror; the Red Death incarnates itself among the fated revellers; or a man flies through life pursued by the visible presence of himself. Beauty which cannot separate itself from terror, terror haunted by beauty, are the powers which rule this world of an opium-dream.

It is the deliberate turning away of a man from the normal; it is the obsession by the desire for better bread than is made from wheat. When Poe theorises on landscape-gardening, he avows his preference for the artificial style, but must have a "spiritualised" artificiality, an artifice which suggests the more than mortal. Yet this world at which the human heart aches becomes real while we read — there is the genius. The art is admirable in its sureness and delicacy. The imagination has seized these things of beauty and terror with more than the closeness of a poet — with the closeness of a dream; and there is no closeness, either to terror or beauty, so appalling as that of a dream. The scope is strange and narrow, but the mastership is absolute.

Yet the same man who can thus handle ideal horror and loveliness with the touch and arts of a poet is also, on another side, and within the limits of romance, one of the most convincing of realists. The man who wrote "The Fall of the House of Usher" and "The Masque of the Red Death" wrote also "The Narrative of Arthur Gordon Pym" and "The Descent into the Maelström." For the dreamer was also a keen analyst and an amateur of science; and had his active days in youth. Mr. Wells himself has not combined romance and realism more startlingly than that feat is achieved in "Arthur Gordon Pym." The seizure of the ship, and, above all, the whole episode of the storm and subsequent starvation, are done with amazing wealth and verisimilitude of imaginative detail. In reading the description of the escape from the Maelström, in the other tale we have mentioned, it is hard to realise that Poe, in all probability, never was in the neighbourhood of the Scandinavian seas. The little vivid touches seem the result of experience. For instance:

The boat made a sharp half-turn to larboard and shot off in its new direction like a thunderbolt. At the same moment the roaring noise of the water was completely drowned in a kind of shrill shriek — such a sound as you might imagine given out by the waste-pipes of many thousand steam-vessels letting off their steam all together.

Or again:

The rays of the moon seemed to search the very bottom of the profound gulf; but still I could make out nothing distinctly on account of a thick mist in which everything there was enveloped, and over which there hung a magnificent rainbow, like that narrow and tottering bridge which Mussulmen say is the only pathway between time and eternity. This mist or spray was no doubt occasioned by the clashing of the great waters of the funnel as they all met together at the bottom; but the yell that went up to the heavens from out of that mist I dare not attempt to describe.

The hackneyed comparison is doubly intrusive in the mouth of a Scandinavian fisherman; but otherwise the passage has an admirable air of eye-witness. The effect of the story, however, is not in single passages, in any cataract of "description," such as an inferior artist would have attempted, but is gradually built up from the accumulation of small matter-of-fact details. It is the very opposite pole of style and art from that in the first-mentioned group of tales; yet both are handled with equal power and effect. Perhaps in this group of tales the "MS. Found in a Bottle" most directly anticipates the wonder-tales of Jules Verne and Mr. Wells. The material is not, like theirs, scientific; but the method strikes the note which all have since followed, according to their ability.

Finally, this wonderfully original artist has struck out and set the method for yet another class of tale — the "detective story" now represented by Dr. Conan Doyle. For, with Mr. Blatchford, we refuse to concede that the deductive method is undeveloped in Poe's tales of this class.

Certain applications of the deductive method Dr. Doyle has developed from his medical experience which are not to be found in Edgar Poe. But the deductive method itself is used by Poe with consummate skill. Dr. Doyle may also pride himself that in many cases he has trusted his mystery entirely to the ingenuity of the problem: whereas Poe holds back the essential clues the better to effect his surprise. But the merit of the tales lies deeper than their display of analysis. It is the finished art of construction and narrative, bringing out the ghastly element or the thrill of excitement with exact *crescendo* of effect; the beauty of the exposition; and, over all, the style of a master, which can endow with immortality a thing in its essence so ephemeral as this species has shown itself in other hands. Let it be, if you will, that the great Dupin was the bungling pretender which the great Holmes, we know, once declared him to be. Yet Poe makes us believe in his greatness — and that is *the* thing which matters in art. Perhaps the truth is that Dr. Doyle, too, is an artist, and knows the artistic value of "bounce" in the right place. From the artistic standpoint, however, these latter tales — "The Murders in the Rue Morgue" and their kind — though they were the first to make Poe's fame as a tale-writer, will be the last to keep it. It is on the two former classes that his fame must chiefly rest — and rest securely.

AMERICAN CULTURE *
[*Academy*, October 20, 1906]

Particularly when referred to the caption given it, this review is not flattering to the cultural life of America at the dawn of the present century. But few, nearer the scene, will have the hardihood to say that Thompson's strictures are unfounded.

FIFTY YEARS ago the American mind promised to become one of the grand intellectual forces of modern civilisation. In the period of intellectual stagnation in Europe, between the decline of romanticism and the rise of evolutionism, a new school of thought was formed in America in which the ideas of the Orient were combined with those of the Western world. Emerson framed a Buddhistic view of life in which there was retained an exhilarating sense of the worth and poetry of the material universe. Whitman found in the mystic idea of the soul something that clothed flesh and matter with a fresh beauty and a fresh significance, and in the philosophic idea of evolution something that gave to individual existence a new purpose and a new grandeur. Whistler, some years later, discovered in the decorative style of Buddhistic art the principle of a new manner of painting, and Peirce recognised in the connection between thought and purpose the ground of a new system of philosophy. None of these pioneers, however, has found among his countrymen another man of genius to resume and consummate his work. This sudden decline of American thought is the strangest of all the events of the Civil War. And in view of its effect upon the spiritual life of the nation we are sometimes inclined to doubt whether the victory of the Northern States was a just one. A race of sincere and generous liberators does not, on turning home from a glorious battlefield, dedicate its mind entirely to low and material ends. Yet this is what the Americans seem to have done. Their culture is now a borrowed thing animated by no life of its own. Their art is become a reflection

* *The Secret Life*. Being the Book of a Heretic.

of French art, their literature a reflection of English literature, their learning a reflection of German learning. A velleity of taste in their women of the richer class seems to be all that maintains in their country the semblance of a high, serious and disinterested passion for the things of the mind. And, to judge by the works commonly produced by these women, it is indeed only a semblance:

> I am just home from a meeting of one of those literary clubs we American women affect in the absence of any masculine society, and we have been talking about Stevenson as the poet most typical of the mind of the nineteenth century.

The anonymous book, *The Secret Life*, from which this illuminating passage is taken, is a thing of melancholy interest. Ostensibly it is a diary in which a married woman, of middle age, moving in a cultivated circle of American society, sets down the wild, original and heretical ideas which she has elaborated during her travels in Europe. Actually it is a story of the spiritual adventures of a commonplace mind of a chameleon nature vagrant among unrealised worlds of thought.

From it we do indeed learn the secret of the author's life and of the lives of many women of her order, but it is not the secret that she wishes to disclose. She labours to prove that she is a remarkable person with two modes of existence, in one of which she lives according to the gospel of comfort, and in the other, according to the gospel of culture. But she unwittingly reveals the fact that her interest in art and literature is as material a thing as her interest in dress or jewelry. She collects ideas not for use and delight but for effect and parade. They are part of the apparel by means of which she endeavours to acquire an air of distinction. This is the explanation of the note of artificiality of her book, of the insincerity that shows beneath its restless effusiveness. The writer has taken the most glittering things she could discover in the authors now fashionable in America — Nietzsche, Lafcadio Hearn, Pater, and Stevenson — and has strung them loosely together as the latest novelties in the wares of conversation. They are not thoughts which have sunk into her mind and have there grown and harmonised into a philosophy of life, but motley shreds of knowledge gathered for the purpose of display. The Nietzschean view of Christianity and its Founder, which she adopts on one page, conflicts with the humanitarian view which she assumes on another; the love and admiration of Apollo, which she affects in the early part of her diary, is incompatible with the love and admiration of the ordinary Philistine which she avows in the latter part. These inconsistencies, however, do not trouble her; such slight defects she regards perhaps as things incidental to the most brilliant forms of heresy.

The title of heretic is one that the author of *The Secret Life* strangely covets. She seems to regard it as a mark of supreme intellectual distinction. Unfortunately for her ambition, her heresies in matters of religion resemble the heresies in matters of taste of those friends of hers for whom Stevenson is the typical poet of the nineteenth century. They are founded on ignorance. She can scarcely be allowed the title of infidel. She is merely a heathen of that bourgeois type of soul which in the order, routine, and security of modern life loses the primitive sense of awe and terror and environing mystery, and remains incapable of acquiring the finer emotions of reverence, worship, and infinite wonder. Her paganism is, in fine, a matter of shallowness of thought and vapidity of feeling; and neither the ideas which she takes from Nietzsche nor the sentiments which she borrows from Pater serve to disguise the native poverty of her nature. It is not given to the daughters of the new Philistines, who masquerade in bacchanalia of nonsense as the children of light, to feel either the maddening spell of Dionysus or the benign influence of Apollo. Over them Momus alone condescends to exercise his power. Were their race now to perish from the earth as completely as did the Phœnicians, there would perhaps be just as slight a diminution of the spiritual and intellectual wealth of mankind.

THE IRISH LITERARY REVIVAL

A SCHISM IN THE CELTIC MOVEMENT *
[*Academy*, July 1, 1899]

In his treatment of the dispute between Larminie and Yeats, Thompson characterizes as sheer literary cant their affected condemnations of Shakespeare, Wordsworth, and Dante. His critical common sense is a Prospero's wand that dispels the mist of Yeatsian verbiage, and exposes Yeatsian "Externality" as a commonplace, restricted Realism. Yeats' "Symbolism" he identifies as extreme, narrow Idealism.

In those early days of the Irish Literary Revival, Thompson seems to have taken for granted that Eglinton, Yeats, AE, and Larminie were genuine and complete Irishmen. Had he been aware of all that followed from the fact that they were of the Ascendency he would not have attributed their views, their quarrels, and their conclusions to the "Irish." For, despite loud protestations to the contrary, these men were not completely Irish. They were English in blood, Protestant in religion, and in all else a strange anomaly — more Irish than the English and more English than the Irish. However, they builded better than they knew. They laid the foundation of a literature that we have lived to see, authentically and completely Irish, although still in the early stages of development. Thompson would have loved its truth, its compactness, its power born of restraint, and its versatility. He would not have failed to recognize and laud in the flower the qualities he missed in root and stem. Had he lived to know the nature of authentic Irish poetry as it is now being revealed, he would have been confirmed in his opinion that the chief defects of poetry written in English by Irishmen in his day, were the consequence of adopting the inspiration and technique of English poetry, instead of their native Irish mode and inspiration. But these were lost when Irish culture was destroyed. The volumes which Thompson reviews reveal the first faint stirrings, only, of its renascence.

In view of Thompson's criticism of contemporary Irish poets who wrote in English, it is interesting to note the marked influence his own poetry exerted upon Irish poets of a later day. Prominent among the books in

---

* *Literary Ideals in Ireland.* By John Eglinton, W. B. Yeats, AE, and W. Larminie.

Joseph Mary Plunkett's library, which I was once permitted to examine through the graciousness of his widow, are volumes of Thompson's poetry which so greatly influenced the early work of the poet-patriot of 1916. In our own day, the most authentic poet of Ireland, Roibeard O Faracháin, whose glorious Irish name an English publisher has flattened into "Robert Farren," chose as title of his first book of poems, *Thronging Feet,* an expression from one of Thompson's profoundest poetic utterances, "Contemplation," and several poems in the volume are frankly imitative of Thompson. Both of these Irish poets, as they matured, followed the recommendation Thompson makes in his reviews. They sought inspiration in Irish themes, and expression in the Irish mode. In the end, they no longer produced "academical exercises after English models," even though one of the English models was the poetry of Thompson himself.

W E HAVE long heard of the Irish Literary Movement — a principal branch of the great Celtic Movement, or even the centre of it. It was vaguely supposed by the outsider that it had common aims and ideals. But now two principal writers of the Movement have come wholly to loggerheads as to what should be its aims, in the columns of the *Dublin Daily Express;* and their controversy, assisted by two subordinate writers (one of whom is content with the modest initials of "AE"), is republished, plain for all folk to see, by Mr. Fisher Unwin. But the two protagonists are Mr. John Eglinton and Mr. W. B. Yeats. It is a very pretty controversy, and starts from the proper line to be taken by a (wholly conjectural) future Irish drama. It opens with mutual compliment and a considerable fundamental agreement, hidden from the disputants under a cloud of words. (For do not most disputants wrangle as to black or white, when in truth they both mean grey?) Finally they both become heated, fly asunder into irreconcilable difference; and, their blood being up, spare neither ink, nor each other, nor established reputations. Both speak blasphemies against the gods of literature. Probably not much harm is done, and Olympus may sit safe, in spite of the splinters which fly from this quarrel of the Irish Titans. Coleridge and Rossetti will persistently be Coleridge and Rossetti, though they please not Mr. John Eglinton; Shakespeare and Wordsworth, nay Dante, will not be materially, at least, affected, though Mr. Yeats condoles with them on their subjection to narrowing conditions. Wordsworth, indeed, moves our commiseration, since he suffers incidentally from both champion Eglinton and assailant Yeats. He reminds us of Mr. Pickwick in the immortal combat between the two Eatanswill editors, upon whose intervening person fell the blows destined for each other. It is a very pretty controversy.

Yet at bottom, into what does it resolve itself? Nothing else than the old, old quarrel between Realists and Idealists. To think that an Irish Literary Movement, at its very outset, should come to blows upon this familiar dispute! For this it is, disguise it under what new-fangled names they will. Nor is anything more natural. These are the two tendencies which divide all art, and all life. And it is true, as Mr. Yeats says, that the struggle between them is now acute and observable throughout Europe, though he cloaks it under the names of externality and symbolism. Title it how you will, it is just old Real and Ideal writ large. True, also, that idealism, under the name of symbolism, has prevailed in France, and (happily under no narrow label) is beginning to prevail in England. But there our agreement with Mr. Yeats ends. In truth, we can agree with neither combatant.

Both are extremists. Never had idealism (to give it the old name) a more extreme and narrow defender than Mr. Yeats. He concedes Wordsworth to his adversary as a realist; while that adversary actually describes Wordsworth as a man "certainly without great poetic talent or artistic faculty"! We ironically commiserated Wordsworth. We seriously commiserate the Irish Movement. If it had one poet with the genius ("talent," good heavens!) of Wordsworth, it might make itself a national power. But Wordsworth a mere realist! This is the penalty he pays for his famous theory, laughed at by his warmest sympathisers, notoriously defied in his own finest practice! Few poets are more symbolic than Wordsworth; everywhere he finds in Nature the shadow and image of things beyond Nature:

> 'Tis my faith that there are powers
> Which of themselves our minds impress;
> That we may feed this mind of ours
> In a wise idleness.

That might satisfy even Mr. Yeats. And when he is older and wiser he will find this great poet brimful of the subtlest "intimations of immortality." The fact is, that Wordsworth, even now, is truly understood by very few. Several years ago one poet, now dead, said to another, still living, but old: "It will be a hundred years before Wordsworth is really understood."

It was with regard to the subtler meanings of the great poet that the words were uttered; but the conjoined utterances of these two Irish disputants, both men of undoubted ability, one a poet of very genuine, if lesser, gift, show that they are partly true in a grosser sense.

Think, too, of Mr. John Eglinton, who classes among "the poets of art and artifice" — whom does the reader think? Even Coleridge, most authentically inspired and direct of modern poets, in whose best work the word is so vitally close to and one with the thing that not even Wordsworth has equalled it for so sustained a length; and all, to any poet, obviously the birth of the immediate dictating spirit! But let us track no further these headlong errors of criticism, which should never have been perpetuated. What is the contention of Mr. Eglinton? That the incarnate poetry of the present day is "the steam-engine and the dynamo, . . . the kinematograph, phonograph," &c. There you have it in one word, the vital heresy of the present day, except by denial and direct defiance, of which no lofty poetry is possible. (We do not say absolutely no poetry.) Show a blockhead in England (as will one day be done) the face of another blockhead in India, and you shall be cried up for great, your pockets bulged with gold. Show him the face of the living God, and he will not pay five shillings to look at it. That is the attitude which Mr. Eglinton would have literature take. Mr. Yeats is at the very opposite swing of the pendulum. Idealism is not enough for him: poetry must be nothing less than mystic. It is to be suggestive — nay, super-suggestive, so that Mr. Yeats himself can only describe it in metaphors borrowed from French poets, the very meaning of which is doubtful and matter for discussion to him. Dante is tainted with a too material system of diction; Shakespeare "shattered the symmetry of verse and of drama that he might fill them with things and their accidental relations." Why, this is a more excellent song than the other! as Cassio says. Here is an extremist with a vengeance. And the models of this new Irish national poetry are to be Villiers de l'Isle-Adam and Mallarmé — Frenchmen!

Between these two fierce extremes there is a medium. The Muse is not so narrow as partisans would have her. There is room in a nation's poetry for very diverse singers. The poetry which is occupied with daily life and the poetry of transcendental things need not exterminate each other; there is room for both; there are readers for both; both have their legitimate place. To fetter the entire poetry of an Irish people down to mysticism, France, and Mallarmé, is suicidal, but happily impossible. Does Mr. Yeats think, because he is mystical, there shall be no more cakes and ale? Yes, by St. Anne, and ginger shall be hot i' the mouth! A whole tribe of young men rushing with one accord to be "mystical poets" is a dismal forecast. It means bad poetry and bad mysticism. One in a hundred poets has such a vocation, and a man must labour in his vocation, Hal! Most poetry should treat divine truths indirectly, through its handling of life. The law which is behind life comes out in the poet's attitude towards life. It is the way of the dramatist, of Shakespeare, who knew better what he was about than to make his plays "mystical," as Mr. Yeats would have had him do. Mystical drama, like Maeterlinck's, is only for the closet. And it was from the subject of the future Irish drama that this controversy began.

It has, in truth, its melancholy, half-humorous side. Other writers step forth to staunch this literary feud, which, says one, "is bewildering to a country which has hesitated so long before adopting a literary ideal." Alas, yes! Our Celtic Movement, with fervent pushing and hauling, was got verily to move. Our Irish literature was really about to be made; and now, behold! a large rift within the Celtic lute which emits flat discord for tuneful music; and it appears we have *not* got our "literary ideal." The movement threatens to cleave along the old lines of Real and Ideal, pushed to modern extremes, with modern names and terminology. One section wishes to use the old Irish legends in the interests of a mystical and symbolic poetry, founded on quite modern Parisian modes. The other, kicking against mysticism and Mallarmé, would go directly to the life of the people, and calls (seemingly) for an Irish Wordsworth. Well and good — if they can get him. Provided it be a true Wordsworth, not an unspiritualised Wordsworth, or perchance an Irish Whitman — for let our Celtic movement *be* literary. And what harm if the movement do thus divide? Is there not room for both? Would it not even be stronger for comprising both?

But a much more serious consideration is the fact that there should be all this palaver and discussion. A knot of men getting together solemnly to constitute a movement and commence a National Literature by writing

> About it, goddess, and about it,

as the French Convention tried to make a National Constitution by oration and on paper. Not so has any great movement arisen in English literature; not so was Elizabethan literature made. The one movement in that age which was thus conscious of itself was the classical movement for reconstituting our metres on classical models. It had a Spenser and a Sidney in its ranks; it pamphleteered and was counter-pamphleteered, and it failed utterly. The truly national movement was too great and manifold to be self-conscious; it did not stew theories and write about itself; but each man looked in his heart and wrote literature, influenced by his time without stopping to consider how, and individual without taking thought to himself how he should be individual. It triumphed, drew to itself repentant Spenser and repentant Sidney, for final result producing a Shakespeare, who never wrote a pamphlet. "Which of you by taking thought can add to his stature one cubit?" or produce a lily of the field or a national literature? Wordsworth indeed theorised — too much, and spoiled some of his poetry by it. But ultimately the poetry swallowed the theories, and grew fat on its meal, to the satisfaction of Wordsworth's own friends and disciples. A little less theory, may we recommend our Irish friends, a little more literature — literature which does not pause to consider the anatomy and physics of its flight before unfurling its wings? For they have able writers, who have done no little, or we should not deem it necessary to advise them.

IRISH MINSTRELSY *
[*Dublin Review*, April, 1889]

When Thompson wrote the reviews here grouped together, the Irish Literary Revival was in its infancy. But he was quick to recognize the virtues and defects of the movement which less skilled critics failed to detect until these characteristics were more fully developed. For instance, in a review of Dora Sigerson Shorter's work, too slight for inclusion here, Thompson calls attention to a "strange Celtic note of retrospective melancholy," and a strain of pessimism "neither wailing nor weak." He remarked the bad state of poetry that, in his day, had been written by the Irish in an alien tongue. Long before they were discovered, he sensed the existence of ancient, hidden treasures, since unearthed beneath the ruins of "a shattered language." He condemned without reservation the strange national injustice done Ireland when England destroyed her native tongue, and he drew an appalling picture of the fate that England would prefer to this crowning sorrow of "a dethroned race." The criticism of Thomas Davis as a poet is severe but just. There is tolerance of Rosa Mulholland's limited inspiration. There is generous but qualified praise of Katharine Tynan, with unmistakable intimations of Thompson's envy of her warmth and content which he later expressed with such melodious pathos in "The Sere of the Leaf."

THE little volume which bears the title that we have borrowed for the present article, is one in the series of "Canterbury Poets"; and let us say at once that it appears to us excellent in its kind. The Irish are generally accounted a poetical race — far more so than their cool, matter-of-fact English neighbours: and as regards certain poetical qualities, notably quick and lively fancy, their gifts are unquestionable. Yet we cannot but think that the Irish, like the Celtic race in general, are deficient in those deeper and

* *Irish Minstrelsy. A Selection of Irish Songs, Lyrics and Ballads*. Edited by H. Halliday Sparling. *Vagrant Verses*. By Rosa Mulholland. *Louise de la Vallière, and Other Poems* and *Shamrocks*. By Katharine Tynan.

loftier qualities of imagination which are the heritage of their Teutonic brethren. Men estimate, after all, a nation's poetical capacity by the poets and poems which it produces. Now what are the facts with respect to Ireland? We must set aside, as practically a sealed book to English critics, the old poets who wrote in the native language: and since English has long been virtually the mother-tongue of most educated Irishmen, we can set them aside with the less injustice. In most departments of literature England has little, if any, advantage over the sister isle. In oratory, if Grattan and O'Connell were forgotten, Burke would still bear the cause of Irish supremacy on his Atlantean shoulders. In prose, the same brilliant genius is but one of a numerous band. In poetry, however, it is otherwise. We look in vain for Irish singers to companion Wordsworth, Coleridge, Shelley, and Keats; although by restricting the comparison to modern times, when the use of English has become general in Ireland, that comparison is rendered entirely fair. A fact so patent would seem to argue a racial defect; and on the whole the present volume, we reluctantly confess, impresses us as bearing out such a conclusion.

When we compare this collection of Irish with a collection — for instance — of Scottish minstrelsy (perhaps the richest in fine ballads and lyrics of any in the three kingdoms), we are struck, more particularly in referring to the popular and traditional element, with the absence of ballads or songs distinguished by those subtle imaginative touches which illumine like lightning-flashes the best old Scotch work. There is nothing to equal, *e. g.*, the Scotch ballad on the subject of Chevy Chase, with its stanza in which the doomed Douglas relates his dream:

> For I have dreamed a fearful dream
>   Beyond the Isle of Skye;
> I saw a dead man win a fight,
>   *And I think that man was I;*

nothing to equal the "Demon Lover," lately made familiar to the public by the musical setting of a Scotch composer; or the pathetic, restrained simplicity of such a lyric as that which laments the fate of "bonnie John Campbell";

> Saddled and bridled,
>   And gallant rade he;
> Hame cam his gude horse,
>   But never cam he!

Still less is there anything of the simple directness without high imagination which characterises the old English ballads; indeed, racial differences make this a thing hardly to be expected. The absence of restrained simplicity, of a knowledge when to stop, appears to us a frequent defect in many of the poems which make up the bulk of this volume; the true Celtic effusion broadens only too often into diffuseness; nor is the diffuseness compensated for by richness of diction or wealth of striking imagery. On the whole, when compared with such national collections as we have referred to, this collection affects us as being, in its main pretensions, distinctly on a lower level. Too many of the average poems express undistinguished ideas in undistinguished language. This is not simplicity of the genuine poetical kind. The simplicity of diction which tells in poetry is a choice simplicity, unconscious perhaps of its own choiceness, but none the less, whether strong and virile, tender or mournful, choice. And these defects counteract the redeeming qualities of genuine emotion or heartfelt passion, which few of the poems are entirely without.

While, however, we feel bound to record this general impression, far be it from us to deny that there *is* excellence in the volume, though perhaps it requires a little search. For this, perhaps, must be blamed the very comprehensiveness which is one of the book's chief merits; a smaller, more confined selection might have produced a higher effect. It is entirely catholic in its range; embracing translations from the Erse, popular songs and ballads (whether traditional or by writers more or less modern), street-songs, and a few poems by modern Irish authors, which (though scarcely of a popular kind) are national in subject. Nor does it limit itself to the popular side; it comprises also some of the best known Orange effusions. It would be strange indeed if, amidst

so wide and various a body of verse, there were nothing noteworthy; and in a brief review of these more noteworthy things,
we shall follow, as far as convenience will permit, the rough
classification given above.

Coming to consider the translations from ancient Irish poetry,
we are confronted at once with *the* disability under which Irish
minstrelsy halts as compared with her Scottish sister.* That sister
has sung from time long remote in what is virtually a dialect of
English; so that Englishmen have little more difficulty in understanding her than in reading their own more archaic poets. But
Ireland, in her bygone ages of literary cultivation, complained,
loved, exulted, in a language which is now as dark to the majority
of educated Irishmen as to educated Englishmen. Upon her has
fallen that strangest, saddest calamity which can fall upon the
bowed head of a nation, when in the ears of her own children her
speech sounds faint and alien, when to all but a surely-narrowing
few of her own chosen sons she must voice through interpreters
her ancient woes. Englishmen who speak an imperial and imperious
tongue, whose rule is wider and mightier than their empire itself,
can scarcely realise this crowning sorrow of a dethroned race.
Better, they may well think, that England should go down to
the oblivious tomb of Babylon or Rome, her ear deaf, her hair
blanched in the unrelenting dust, than survive, a ghostly nationality, haunting disconsolate a ruined throne, to hear her offspring
imitate the accents of a rival and a foe. But because this thing has
befallen Ireland it is impossible to judge what may, or may not,
be the poetical treasures buried underneath her shattered language.

This book throws little light upon the question. Poetical translation in its true sense is one of the rarest, most difficult achievements
in literature: in English literature the masterpieces of this kind
may almost be counted on the fingers. And the translations in this
volume but confirm an impression derived from preceding specimens which we have seen of the sort — that either there is something in Irish, perhaps in Celtic poetry as a whole, essentially

---

* *Her Scottish sister:* for the Lowland Scots, in whose tongue the minstrelsy
referred to is written, though doubtless a mixed race, must have some Celtic,
if not Gaelic, blood in their veins.

untranslatable (at least into our Teutonic tongue); or else that Irish
poetry has been singularly unfortunate in its translators. Both
reasons, perhaps, are accountable for what is, we think, an undeniable fact — the slightness of the effect which any translation
from the old Irish produces upon an English reader. The only
really impressive poem ranging under this head in the collection
is Clarence Mangan's "Dark Rosaleen." And as if to prove the
rule which we have ventured to assert, it has just a little more claim
to the title of a translation than have the beautiful lines on the Hel-
lenic gods in Coleridge's "Wallenstein" to be a translation of the
two slight lines in the German original. If the reader turn to page
116 of the *Minstrelsy*, he will find a rendering by Furlong of the
same poem, a rendering which the editor (nor do we doubt his
word) declares to be far more literal than Mangan's. The reader
can thus judge for himself what liberties Mangan must have taken
with the Irish poem. They are outrageous, or would be outrageous
were the success not so complete. If attention had not been called
to the fact, the two poems might conceivably be read without
suspicion of their common origin. But poetry is a rootedly im-
moral art, in which success excuses wellnigh everything. That in
the soldier is flat blasphemy which in the captain, the master of his
craft, is but commendable daring. Exactly as a great poet may
plagiarise to his heart's content, because he plagiarises well (since
Spartan law holds good in literature, where stealing is honourable,
provided it be done with neatness and dexterity), so the truly
poetical translator may rewrite a foreign poem and call it a translation, nor will any one seriously object except the excellent persons who understand something of translation and nothing of
poetry. Who cares one doit what was the measure of FitzGerald's
fidelity to Omar Khayyám, or would be gravely disturbed could
it be discovered tomorrow that Omar was as utter a myth as
Rowley himself? A few oriental students perhaps: that is all. One
of these self-justifying pieces of poetical immorality is "Dark
Rosaleen." Poet as Mangan was, we have seen nothing of his so
poetical. It is a beautiful, impassioned song, passionate indeed to
the heart's core. The truest lyric melody chimes throughout its
fervour; in which respect again it differs from Mangan's usual

style. It is addressed to Ireland under her mystical title of "The Little Dark Rose"; and though long for quotation, it is at once so unique of its kind in this volume, and so practically unknown to the general public, that we cannot deny ourselves the pleasure of quoting it.

> O my Dark Rosaleen,
>   Do not sigh, do not weep!
> The priests are on the ocean green,
>   They march along the deep.
> There's wine from the royal Pope
>   Upon the ocean green;
> And Spanish ale shall give you hope,
>   My Dark Rosaleen!
>   My own Rosaleen!
> Shall glad your heart, shall give you hope,
> Shall give you health, and help, and hope,
>   My Dark Rosaleen!
>
> Over hills, and through dales,
>   Have I roamed for your sake;
> All yesterday I sailed with sails
>   On river and on lake.
> The Erne, at its highest flood,
>   I dashed across unseen,
> For there was lightning in my blood,
>   My Dark Rosaleen!
>   My own Rosaleen!
> Oh! there was lightning in my blood,
> Red lightning lightened through my blood,
>   My Dark Rosaleen!
>
> All day long in unrest,
>   To and fro, do I move,
> The very soul within my breast
>   Is wasted for you, love!
> The heart in my bosom faints
>   To think of you, my queen,
> My life of life, my saint of saints,
>   My Dark Rosaleen!
>   My own Rosaleen!
> To hear your sweet and sad complaints,
> My life, my love, my saint of saints,
>   My Dark Rosaleen!

Woe and pain, pain and woe,
　　Are my lot, night and noon,
To see your bright face clouded so,
　　Like to the mournful moon.
But yet will I rear your throne
　　Again in golden sheen;
'Tis you shall reign, shall reign alone,
　　My Dark Rosaleen!
　　My own Rosaleen!
'Tis you shall have the golden throne,
'Tis you shall reign, and reign alone,
　　My Dark Rosaleen!

Over dews, over sands,
　　Will I fly for your weal:
Your holy, delicate white hands
　　Shall girdle me with steel.
At home, in your emerald bowers,
　　From morning's dawn till e'en,
You'll pray for me, my flower of flowers,
　　My Dark Rosaleen!
　　My fond Rosaleen!
You'll think of me through daylight's hours,
My virgin flower, my flower of flowers,
　　My Dark Rosaleen!

I could scale the blue air,
　　I could plough the high hills,
Oh, I could kneel all night in prayer,
　　To heal your many ills!
And one beamy smile from you
　　Would float like light between
My toils and me, my own, my true,
　　My Dark Rosaleen!
　　My fond Rosaleen!
Would give me life and soul anew,
A second life, a soul anew,
　　My Dark Rosaleen!

Oh! the Erne shall run red
　　With redundance of blood,
The earth shall rock beneath our tread,
　　And flames warp hill and wood,

And gun-peal and slogan cry
  Wake many a glen serene,
Ere you shall fade, ere you shall die,
    My Dark Rosaleen!
    My own Rosaleen!
The Judgment Hour must first be nigh,
Ere you can fade, ere you can die,
    My Dark Rosaleen!

There are other translations by Mangan in the volume, but none at all equal to this. Of these others, "Kathleen Ny Houlahan" is, we think, the best; but though it contains graceful stanzas, it is not a very striking poem. "Kincora" adequately represents the level of his remaining versions, and exemplifies at the same time some of the difficulties which beset the Celtic translator. It is little more than an enumeration of vanished glories, something after the mode of Villon's famous "Ballade des Dames du Temps Jadis"; but, unlike that poem, its lengthy catalogue of names stirs no ripple of associations in the mind of the cultivated Englishman; nor is there any magical refrain such as

Où sont les neiges d'antan?

to point with pathos the melancholy moral. To the Irishman it may possess interest, to the English reader it becomes simply tedious. Among the versions by other hands we notice especially two — a graceful little love-song by Edward Walsh, "Mo Craoibhin Cno"; and a spirited boat-song by Samuel Ferguson, so virile in its lilt as to be worth quotation.

Bark that bears me through foam and squall,
You in the storm are my castle wall;
Though the sea should redden from bottom to top,
From tiller to mast she takes no drop.
    On the tide-top, the tide-top,
    Wherry aroon, my land and store!
    On the tide-top, the tide-top,
    She is the boat can sail *go-leor!*

She dresses herself and goes gliding on,
Like a dame in her robes of the Indian lawn;
For God has blessed her, gunnel and wale —
And oh! if you saw her stretch out to the gale!
    On the tide-top, &c.

Whillan* ahoy, old heart of stone!
Stooping so black o'er the beach alone,
Answer me well — on the bursting brine
Saw you ever a bark like mine?
    On the tide-top, &c.

Says Whillan, since first I was made of stone,
I have looked o'er the beach alone;
But till today on the bursting brine
Saw I never a bark like thine!
    On the tide-top, &c.

God of the air! the seamen shout,
When they see us tossing the brine about;
Give us the shelter of strand or rock,
Or through and through us she goes with a shock!
    On the tide-top, the tide-top,
    Wherry aroon, my land and store!
    On the tide-top, the tide-top,
    She is the boat can sail *go-leor!*

In the department of popular songs and ballads we propose first to deal with those by modern writers, and this for the reason that they are in an overwhelming majority. Here the name of Thomas Davis overshadows all competitors. There are three of his ballads for every one of other authors. And since his reputation is so established that it can receive no injury from our weak dissent, we have the less hesitation in liberating our artistic conscience by a considered protest. We cannot regard Davis as in any way a fine poet. The selection from his writings in this volume includes the famous "Fontenoy," darling of schoolboys and public reciters, which is certainly one of the best of his ballads in the *Minstrelsy*. Yet for all its undeniable spirit, the genuine glow of patriotic

---

* A rock off Blacksod Bay.

feeling which informs it throughout, it is nothing more than a favourable specimen of the Macaulay-*cum*-Scott ballad; and the Macaulay-*cum*-Scott ballad does not belong to a high order of poetry. We had Davis especially in our mind when we spoke of the Celtic effusion which readily broadens into diffuseness. The other ballads given as specimens of him display, far more than "Fontenoy," in painful measure his characteristic weaknesses. They differ from the best of Scott's martial ballads where they resemble Macaulay's, in being declamatory and rhetorical. But Macaulay's rhetoric was at least a concentrated and pointed rhetoric; the rhetoric of Davis sacrifices concentration, and in sacrificing concentration sacrifices effect. His diction is in its general character too much of the conventional type, undistinguished by originality or freshness; his ardour too liable to evaporate in profuse and exclamatory "gush." The undoubted presence, amid all these defects, of the ardour to which we have alluded, is the one thing which saves his average ballads from being the mere clever work of a facile writer. But we cannot concur in assigning him the high position among Irish poets to which he has been elevated by the general voice of his own countrymen. Yet that he should be a popular and influential poet is quite comprehensible. His writings are framed for popularity; their merits readily appeal to the uncultivated, their defects alienate only the cultivated lover of poetry. The two best of his ballads here given, "The Sack of Baltimore" and "Fontenoy," are hackneyed beyond quotation. We select, therefore, instead, a little love-song marked, we think, by a certain simplicity and tenderness, if not very strikingly original.

> Come in the evening, or come in the morning,
> Come when you're looked for, or come without warning,
> Kisses and welcome you'll find here before you,
> And the oftener you come here the more I'll adore you.
>   Light is my heart since the day we were plighted,
>   Red is my cheek that they told me was blighted,
>   The green of the trees looks far greener than ever,
>   And the linnets are singing, "True lovers, don't sever!"

I'll pull you sweet flowers, to wear, if you choose them;
Or, after you've kissed them, they'll lie on my bosom.
I'll fetch from the mountain its breeze to inspire you;
I'll fetch from my fancy a tale that won't tire you.
    Oh! your step's like the rain to the summer-vexed farmer,
    Or sabre and shield to a knight without armour;
    I'll sing you sweet songs till the stars rise above me,
    Then, wandering, I'll wish you, in silence, to love me.

We'll look through the trees at the cliff and the eyrie;
We'll tread round the rath on the track of the fairy;
We'll look on the stars, and we'll list to the river,
Till you'll ask of your darling what gift you can give her.
    Oh! she'll whisper you, "Love as unchangeably beaming
    And trust, when in secret, most tunefully streaming,
    Till the starlight of heaven above us shall quiver
    As our souls flow in one down eternity's river."

So come in the evening, or come in the morning,
Come when you're looked for, or come without warning,
Kisses and welcome you'll find here before you,
And the oftener you come here the more I'll adore you.
    Light is my heart since the day we were plighted,
    Red is my cheek that they told me was blighted,
    The green of the trees looks far greener than ever,
    And the linnets are singing, "True lovers, don't sever!"

Yet even here there is visible a tendency to cheap imagery, facile imagery devoid of selectness, in such lines as —

    Oh! your step's like the rain to the summer-vexed farmer,
    Or sabre and shield to a knight without armour.

We do not deny that the step of the lover is welcome gladness to the maiden; and so likewise, we admit, is rain after drought to the farmer, or arms to an unarmed knight, or a pipe to the hardened smoker, or a loose ball to a batsman on a soft wicket, or two-penn'orth of rum to the irreclaimable drunkard, or a whole holiday to the lesson-vexed schoolboy, or — "various dings," as Hans Breitmann has it. And this is exactly the kind of imagery which can be turned out by the yard. *Fiat justitia;* there is precedent for it, we regretfully confess; an apologist could swim in precedent. Virgil, to go back only an odd two thousand years or so, has an amiable little partiality for this brand of imagery: "Sweet" (we apologise for forgetfulness of the original and a prosaic version), "Sweet is moisture to the standing corn, to weanling kids the arbutus, to teeming flocks the limber willow, Amyntas only is sweet to me." There is much more of the same kind throughout the Eclogues; and we candidly avow our opinion that were it not for the superstitious homage accorded everything classical, it would be recognised as weak imagery, futile and primitive in kind. Indeed it is not in imagery that the power of Virgil, or of most Latin poets, resides: one page from "The Eve of St. Agnes" would outweigh in sheer loveliness of this description the whole *Æneid*. But there are other examples, and more modern examples, of the device: amongst them one which is almost sufficient in itself to glorify the thing and stagger our judgment, since to this class of imagery must be referred those lines from Marlowe which every literary student knows.

> Oh, thou art fairer than the evening air
> Clad in the beauty of a thousand stars!

For one moment censure droops its head rebuked: the comparison so indubitably falls within the proscribed species, yet the lines are so indubitably beautiful. But a little consideration will show that the exception is only a seeming exception: the image is beautiful, not *as* an image, but as a poetical picture; the charm is latent, not in the aptness of the simile, but in the isolated enchantment of the diction which sets before us the star-sown evening firmament. Were it not for this, we should cast aside as valueless a comparison which rested its sole ground of analogy on the fact that both the objects brought into relation were beautiful. We fear, therefore, that in default of similar compensation this precedent will not serve Davis' turn; and if it will not, we are ignorant what will. The mere defence that such similes have been used by great poets before him will not suffice; otherwise almost every vice in poetry might be sheltered under the great name of Shakespeare. For Ben Jonson was right: Shakespeare's lines would have been none the worse for an occasional blot; only thank heaven that Ben Jonson had not the blotting of them!

Something too much of Davis: if we have devoted rather an undue space to him, it is because of the great prominence given to his name in this collection, and the not undeserved influence exercised by him as a popular poet in Ireland.

Among the remaining ballads, one of the best, we think, is "Shaun's Head," by John Savage; the supposed address of an Ulster clansman to the head of Shaun O'Neill, which the faithful follower discovers at night upon the battlements of Dublin Castle. It is full of the passion which animates nearly all — even those otherwise least notable — of these poems; while it possesses a dramatic force and point not so often present in them. Though it is too long to be extracted, we may quote the second stanza as a specimen:

> Is it thus, O Shaun the haughty! Shaun the valiant! that we meet —
> Have my eyes been lit by Heaven but to guide me to defeat?
> Have *I* no chief, or *you* no clan, to give us both defence,
> Or must I, too, be statued here with thy cold eloquence?
> Thy ghastly head grins scorn upon old Dublin's Castle-tower,
> Thy shaggy hair is wind-tossed, and thy brow seems rough with power;
> Thy wrathful lips, like sentinels, by foulest treachery stung,
> Look rage upon the world of wrong, but chain thy fiery tongue.

Finally, we may quote two songs. Banim's "Soggarth Aroon" is well known, but is so full of true, homely peasant simplicity (though not destitute of warm Irish tenderness), so free from what Mr. William Morris once called his "cursed Celtic love for fine language," that it cannot be omitted.

> Am I the slave they say,
>   Soggarth aroon?
> Since you did show the way,
>   Soggarth aroon,
> *Their* slave no more to be,
> While they would work with me
> Old Ireland's slavery,
>   Soggarth aroon.

Why not her poorest man,
    Soggarth aroon,
Try and do all he can,
    Soggarth aroon,
Her commands to fulfil
Of his own heart and will,
Side by side with you still,
    Soggarth aroon?

Loyal and brave to you,
    Soggarth aroon,
Yet be not slave to you,
    Soggarth aroon,
Nor, out of fear to you, —
Stand up so near to you —
Och! out of fear to *you*,
    Soggarth aroon!

Who, in the winter's night,
    Soggarth aroon,
When the cold blast did bite,
    Soggarth aroon,
Came to my cabin-door,
And, on my earthern-floor,
Knelt by me, sick and poor,
    Soggarth aroon?

Who, on the marriage day,
    Soggarth aroon,
Made the poor cabin gay,
    Soggarth aroon? —
And did both laugh and sing,
Making our hearts to ring,
At the poor christening,
    Soggarth aroon?

Who, as friend only met,
    Soggarth aroon,
Never did flout me yet,
    Soggarth aroon?
And when my heart was dim,
Gave, while his eye did brim,
What I should give to him,
    Soggarth aroon?

Och! you, and only you,
    Soggarth aroon!
And for this I was true to you,
    Soggarth aroon;
In love they'll never shake,
When for ould Ireland's sake,
We a true part did take,
    Soggarth aroon!

The next is an even simpler and very quiet little song, by a well-known dramatic author — Dion Boucicault — the song of an Irish peasant woman in the backwoods of Ohio.

I'm very happy where I am,
    Far across the say,
I'm very happy far from home
    In North Amerikay.

It's lonely in the night, when Pat
    Is sleeping by my side,
I lie awake, and no one knows
    The big tears that I've cried;

For a little voice still calls me back
    To my far, far counthrie,
And nobody can hear it spake
    O! nobody but me.

There is a little spot of ground
    Behind the chapel wall,
It's nothing but a tiny mound,
    Without a stone at all;

It rises like my heart just now,
    It makes a dawny hill;
It's from below the voice comes out,
    I cannot keep it still.

O! little Voice; ye call me back
    To my far, far counthrie,
And nobody can hear ye spake,
    O! nobody but me.

Banim's poem is an example of a poetic species unaccountably neglected (if we may judge from this collection) by modern Irish singers; yet in which there surely sleep rare opportunities for breaking new ground. We mean poems interpreting the mind of the Irish peasant in his own picturesque brogue. Why has none ever attempted the *rôle* of an Irish Burns? When it is reflected what jewels of original fancy, warm and tender, or bright and vivacious, are rough-set in the speech of the humble Irishman, it is almost heartrending to read the series of academical exercises after English models (few of them attaining a really high level) which form so large a portion of this book, and to which a few of those jewels would have given a distinct value. There is one such piece of academical prettiness in the collection, which at the close is lighted with a sudden scintillation by a genuine Irish fancy.

> Young Pat feels his heart, as he gazes, depart,
> Subdued by the smart of such painful, yet sweet love;
> The sight leaves his eye, as he cries with a sigh,
> *"Dance light, for my heart it lies under your feet, love!"*

O si sic omnia! Banim's lyric, no less than a line like this, indicates what a mine remains well-nigh unworked. And Banim's poem is thoroughly Irish: despite its simplicity, it has the true Celtic effusion, showing that the two qualities are not incompatible. It is otherwise in the case of the little song with which we have companioned it. That also is simple; but it possesses in addition the un-Irish characteristic, almost essential to the deepest and tenderest pathos — the characteristic of restraint. This quality, valuable in all art, invaluable in pathos, this lurking power, the simple words conveying by some subtlest inexpressible magic those things which find no words — the tears in the eyes which do not fall, the pang in the voice which cannot break in sobs, the dumb passion looking piteously out through the voiceful passion — this is here present, and is present in few Irish poems. It is not unattainable by an Irishman, for Goldsmith possessed it in perfection. But it is found chiefly among English and Scotch writers, and not amongst all of them. It differentiates the pathos of Dickens from the pathos of Thackeray, the lachrymose pathos in the death of "Little Nell," from the still, deep pathos which characterises the finding of Colonel Newcome in the Charterhouse. Misery may be multitudinous in words; sadness may clothe herself with pomps of lamentation; despair may diadem herself with clamorous griefs, may lift her head to the clouds, may beat vain hands against the sky; but pathos, in her most touching utterance, is ever half-articulate.

Yet here the whispering demon whose mission it is to perplex all conclusions by the suggestion of an alternative aspect, breathes a chill, a doubt. Is the principle which we have enunciated indeed an eternal and immutable canon of art; or is it a narrow, partial view, founded on racial idiosyncracy? As on the one hand it may be argued that pathetic restraint is rooted in the irreversible verities of Nature, where profound sorrow so infinitely transcends the potentialities of speech that language withers at the root; so, on the contrary, it may be considered a mere emanation from the invincible reticence of Teutonic character. To the perception of the more free-tongued Celt, what we account diffuse or artificial may appear the inevitable expression of feeling; what we account the essential expression of profoundest feeling may appear coldly inadequate. It is an interesting question in what we may christen comparative psychology; and a satisfactory answer might conduce to the serenity of criticism.

We need not linger long over the more or less traditional poems. One of the oldest is a Jacobite relic — "The Blackbird." It has much of that attractive quaintness which characterises the Scotch Jacobite songs; but apart from this attraction — largely resident in the obsolete form — it does not seem to us of high poetical merit, and is in any case too long for quotation. Many of the others are well known as songs, and are indeed (if we may invent a verbal distinction for the nonce) excellent *songs*, but not *lyrics* of great mark. In other words, while really spirited verses, they lack the poetical infusion which makes a song of literary value. Take, for instance, the well-known "Rakes of Mallow," which is so well known as not to require quotation. Its spirit is undeniable; but where is that breath of poetic fancy which gives a distinct merit to the best bacchanalian lyrics — to those, for instance, of Horace? Nay, we need not go back to lyrics so perfect in form as these.

Take a mediæval effusion like the one ascribed to Walter de Mapes, beginning —

> Mihi est propositum
> In taberna mori;
> Vinum sit appositum
> Morientis ori;
> Ut dicant quum venerint
> Angelorum chori,
> "Deus sit propitius
> Huic potatori!"

and containing such lines as —

> Cor imbutum nectare
> Volat ad superna;

and such stanzas as the following one —

> Mihi nunquam spiritus
> Prophetiæ datur,
> Nonnisi quum fuerit
> Venter plene satur:
> Quum in arce cerebri
> Bacchus dominatur,
> In me Phœbus irruit,
> Ac miranda fatur!

the first four lines of which have been excellently paraphrased by a writer whom Leigh Hunt quotes:

> Mysterious and prophetic truths
> I never could unfold 'em,
> Without a glass of Burgundy
> And a slice of cold ham.

Compare with this what is perhaps the cleverest of the convivial songs included in the present collection. We think the mediæval writer carries off the palm, although the traditional Irishman should be at his best in a convivial effusion. The production in question was written by Curran for those "Monks of the Screw" whom one of Lever's novels has rendered familiar to the English reader.

When St. Patrick this order established,
    He called us the "Monks of the Screw!"
Good rules he revealed to our abbot,
    To guide us in what we should do.
But first he replenished our fountain
    With liquor the best from on high;
And he said, on the word of a saint,
    That the fountain should never run dry.

"Each year, when your octaves approach,
    In full chapter convened let me find you:
And when to the convent you come,
    Leave your favourite temptation behind you.
And be not a glass in your convent —
    Unless on a festival — found;
And, this rule to enforce, I ordain it
    One festival all the year round.

"My brethren, be chaste — till you're tempted;
    While sober, be grave and discreet;
And humble your bodies with fasting —
    As oft as you've nothing to eat.
Yet in honour of fasting, one lean face
    Among you I'd always require;
If the abbot should please, he may wear it,
    If not, let it come to the prior."

Come, let each take his chalice, my brethren,
    And with due devotion prepare,
With hands and with voices uplifted,
    Our hymn to conclude with a prayer.
May this chapter oft joyously meet,
    And this gladsome libation renew,
To the saint, and the founder, and abbot,
    And prior, and monks of the Screw!

Two daring spirits, and two only, have awakened their lyres in
praise of the national beverage. Here is a strain from one effusion:

Greek and Roman sung
    Chian and Falernian —
Shall no harp be strung
    To thy praise, Hibernian?

Yes, let Erin's sons —
  Generous, brave, and frisky —
Tell the world at once
  They owe it to their whisky.

He commiserates Anacreon:

As the best then known,
  He to wine was civil;
Had he *Inishowen*,
  He'd pitch wine to the divil!

Over the street-songs, also, we shall not linger long. They have, doubtless, a peculiar and curious value of their own. They are the spontaneous, uncultivated revelation of the lower Irish mind; the only such revelation which we possess, for a writer in a comparatively recent number of *Macmillan's Magazine* declares that even the ballads of Davis are unknown among the peasantry. This is only what — under modern conditions of existence — we might expect. What constitutes the true expression of the low-class English urban mind? — street broadsides and the songs of the music-hall, by the perusal of which alone can the student estimate, in all its sad reality, the spirit of those dingy multitudes which throng our London pavements: not by the semi-literary productions of Mr. G. R. Sims and kindred writers, popular though they are amongst a half-cultivated section of our countrymen. From this point of view, it is a matter for congratulation that there is so little in Irish street-songs absolutely vulgar, so entire an absence of everything objectionable, so much which is veritably racy — indigenous to the soil. But how much *literary* value is there in "The Night before Larry was Stretched," or "Castle Hyde" (the original of the famous parody, "The Groves of Blarney")? We may quote, as a very favourable specimen of its class, a single stanza from the popular "Wearing of the Green":

Then since the colour we must wear is England's cruel red,
Sure Ireland's sons will ne'er forget the blood that they have shed.
You may take the shamrock from your hat and cast it on the sod,
But 'twill take root and flourish there, though under foot 'tis trod.

When law can stop the blades of grass from growing as they grow,
And when the leaves in summer-time their verdure dare not show,
Then I will change the colour that I wear in my caubeen,
But till that day, please God, I'll stick to wearing of the green.

There is both feeling and fancy here; but it is the exception, not the rule.

Turn we to poems with regard to which no such objection can be taken. There are included in the *Minstrelsy* some compositions which — whatever may be their animating sentiment, in virtue of which they here find admission — are of too altogether literary and English a cast in their execution to be, in any sense, really popular. Amongst them is one by a name with which English readers used to be familiar — the now dead laureate of the Land League, Miss Fanny Parnell. It is somewhat lacking, we think, in art. The metre is unwieldy, centipede-like; nor is the execution of the highest kind. But it contains an unhackneyed idea, and that is a mercy to be thankful for in these latter days.

Shall mine eyes behold thy glory, O my country?
　　Shall mine eyes behold thy glory?
Or shall the darkness close around them, ere the sun-
　　blaze break at last upon thy story?

When the nations ope for thee their queenly circle, as a
　　sweet new sister hail thee,
Shall these lips be sealed in callous death and silence,
　　that have known but to bewail thee?

Shall the ear be deaf that only loved thy praises, when
　　all men their tribute bring thee?
Shall the mouth be clay that sang thee in thy squalor,
　　when all poets' mouths shall sing thee?

Ah! the harpings and the salvos and the shoutings of
　·　thy exiled sons returning!
I should hear, tho' dead and mouldered, and the grave-
　　damps should not chill my bosom's burning.

Ah! the tramp of feet victorious! I should hear them
　　'mid the shamrocks and the mosses,
And my heart should toss within the shroud and quiver as
　　a captive dreamer tosses.

I should turn and rend the cere-clothes round me, giant
    sinews I should borrow —
Crying, "O, my brothers, I have also loved her in her
    loneliness and sorrow.

"Let me join with you the jubilant procession; let me
    chant with you her story;
Then contented I shall go back to the shamrocks, now
    mine eyes have seen her glory!"

When we arrive at the name of Mr. Aubrey de Vere, criticism becomes unnecessary, and the cessation of a popular element marked. No one will imagine that Irish car-men sing "The Wedding of the Clans," as they rattle their fares along the road. There are three poems of his given, of which the longest — too long for quotation — is the "Wedding of the Clans," excellent in its dramatic simplicity.

I go to knit two clans together;
    Our clan and this clan unseen of yore: —
Our clan fears nought! but I go, O whither?
    This day I go from my mother's door.

Thou, red-breast, singest the old song over,
    Though many a time thou hast sung it before;
They never sent thee to some strange new lover: —
    I sing a new song, by my mother's door.

But let us give ourselves the pleasure of quoting a little lyric in which feeling and execution are on a level. "The Little Black Rose" is said to be one of the mystical names of Ireland, as is also "The Silk of the Kine":

The Little Black Rose shall be red at last;
    What made it black but the March wind dry,
And the tear of the widow that fell on it fast?
    It shall redden the hills when June is nigh!

The Silk of the Kine shall rest at last;
    What drove her forth but the dragon fly?
In the golden vale she shall feed full fast,
    With her mild gold horn and her slow, dark eye.

The wounded wood-dove lies dead at last!
The pine long bleeding, it shall not die!
This song is secret. Mine ear it passed
In a wind o'er the plains at Athenry.

The compiler of the *Minstrelsy* has given place to two poems
by Miss Rosa Mulholland, both of them taken from her volume
of *Vagrant Verses*, which we have named at the head of this article,
and we cannot do better than quote one of them, the graceful little
"Shamrocks":

I wear a shamrock in my heart.
Three in one, one in three —
Truth and love and faith,
Tears and pain and death:
O sweet my shamrock is to me!

Lay me in my hollow bed,
Grow the shamrocks over me.
Three in one, one in three,
Faith and hope and charity,
Peace and rest and silence be
With me where you lay my head:
O dear the shamrocks are to me!

These verses excellently represent the prevalent note of Miss
Mulholland's poetry. Her muse could hardly be better described
than in the well-known words of Milton; it is indeed a

Pensive nun, devout and pure,
Sober, steadfast, and demure.

Or her poetry might be characterised in a verse of her own: —

Gray and chill, yet safe and sure,
Fringed with snowdrops pale and pure
Underneath a sky that grieves
O'er barren boughs and fallen leaves.

A tender simplicity of subdued tincture, a pensiveness often religious mark her work. No reader who can appreciate thoughtfulness and quiet charm will read *Vagrant Verses* without pleasure.

The verses we have quoted illustrate, as we have said, her general mood, but there is one poem, not quoted in the *Minstrelsy*, which shows all her best qualities at their highest, combined with a closeness of imaginative realisation and a felicity of diction less conspicuous elsewhere. We may exemplify this by a few stanzas from the poem in question, "Saint Barbara" (the saint, as the reader may remember, who was enclosed in a tower).

> Girl, they have cut from 'neath thy dancing feet
>   Earth with her rose and lily,
>   Her violet and her light-winged daffodily —
> Stole from thine ear the sound of children singing;
> The low of kine and pleasant sheep-bells ringing
>   Are silent to thee, sweet!

> No tender human fingers touch thine own;
>   The cold winds round thy bed
>   Caress thy motherless young golden head.
> The silence widens not when thou art sleeping,
> Save by the absence of thy hopeless weeping,
>   Echoed by walls of stone.

> Yet thou hast company the clouds among,
>   The birds' loud songs surround thee,
>   The legions of the storm whirl round and round thee;
> The tranquil saints, from their eternal places,
> Look out and show thee their enraptured faces —
>   The stars shine clear and long.

> To such high company thy soul doth leap,
>   The lark's wild hymn repeating,
>   Flinging the tempest thine impassioned greeting,
> Watching the stars until thine eyes become
> A fire amidst them in the midnight gloom,
>   No longer doomed to weep.

To pass from Miss Mulholland's verse to Miss Tynan's is as if we passed from a sober evening heath to the sunrise which beats its sanguined wings like a flamingo across a southern water. The compiler of the *Minstrelsy* quotes her "Shamrock Song," a finished and artistic work, and we shall be excused, in the case of a living writer of such ability and even further promise, for naming two of her volumes at the head of our article, and now illustrating our remarks by some quotations from them at greater length.

It was long a conviction in the mind of the average English Protestant that Catholicity exerted a stunting influence on literary development, a belief which the educational disabilities incidental to English Catholicity for some time tended to confirm. The idea in the Protestant mind was something after this fashion — that from Martin Luther came the Reformation, from the Reformation came those twin gifts of Heaven, Good Queen Bess and William Shakespeare, from Good Queen Bess came our greatness, and from William Shakespeare came our literature. Q. E. D. The present century has dispelled the illusion in regard to general literature, and the present generation has done something to dispel it in regard to poetry. It would be unfortunate were it otherwise. With perhaps one exception, the poets of to-day lie under a general reproach — the lack of sustained power. Living poetry is too like a dwarf tree, such as those of which China and Japan monopolise the secret, perfect in form and proportion, but so diminutive that it might be used for a table ornament, a forest giant in miniature. The age prefers short poems, and it gets them. But within these limits the present day is singularly fertile in highly finished and often very subtle poetry. It is very fit that Catholicity should contribute its share to this luxuriant poetical garden, and in the ranks of Catholic poets Miss Tynan is the latest recruit, and a recruit of high promise.

The first impression which her poetry makes on the reader is that of buoyant youthful impulse, lavish prodigality of colour, and true lyrical melody. It is, indeed, strikingly youthful, not merely in tone but in quality, so that in time riper and completer work may be justly anticipated from a poet who, while not destitute of performance, is still more distinguished by her abundant evidence of promise. This youthful quality is at once a main source of much of her defect and at the same time a piquant attraction. While a little less copious measure, a little of that selecting faculty which will doubtless come with practice, would often strengthen her verse without diminishing the unlaboured fervour, nevertheless its generous spontaneity imparts to it a charmingly true lyric element. The wealth of colour above mentioned is everywhere visible throughout her work. It is true painter's work. Many of her lines and stanzas flash before the eye like humming-birds, though, unlike the humming-bird, they combine music with colour. We may take examples at random. Here is one from the "Angel of the Annunciation":

> Down through the village street,
> Where the slanting sunlight was sweet,
>   Swiftly the angel came;
> His face like the star of even,
> When night is grey in the heaven;
>   His hair was a blown gold flame.
>
> His wings were purple of bloom,
> And eyed as the peacock's plume;
>   They trailed and flamed in the air;
> Clear brows with an aureole rimmed,
> The gold ring brightened and dimmed,
>   Now rose, now fell on his hair.
>
> Oh, the marvellous eyes!
> All strange with a rapt surprise
>   They mused and dreamed as he went;
> The great lids, drooping and white,
> Screenèd the glory from sight;
>   His lips were most innocent.
>
> His clear hands, shining withal,
> Bore lilies, silver and tall,
>   That had grown in the pleasaunce of God;
> His robe was fashioned and spun
> Of threads from the heart of the sun;
>   His feet with white fire were shod.
>
> *   *   *   *   *
>
> All in the stillness and heat,
> The Angel passed through the street,
>   Nor pausing nor looking behind:
> God's finger-touch on his lips;
> His great wings fire at the tips;
>   His gold hair flame in the wind.

One thing is noticeable about Miss Tynan's colour-pictures. They are all thoroughly realisable. Did the reader ever try to realise within himself that gorgeous description of the snake in "Lamia"? We have; and the result is a thorough conviction that (quite apart from the material limitation of his pigments) no painter could put on canvas the description as it stands in the text. There is not room on a serpent's back for all the confusion of hues and devices which Keats has poured out till he must have exhausted his fancy and vocabulary. It is chaotic. The mind cannot resolve it into a coherent vision. But Miss Tynan's dreams could be transferred directly to canvas. Setting colour aside, indeed, her conceptions have often a noticeable pictorial quality. They read almost like the poetical description of a picture, a characteristic due, perhaps, in some degree to the diffusion of artistic taste among the cultivated classes which has certainly taken place in the present time.

As an instance of this pictorial quality let us extract the first two stanzas of "The Dead Spring":

> Like Elaine, with small dead hands
>   On her resting heart,
> Cowslip hair in silken bands,
>   Dreaming lips apart,
> Lieth Spring; in her wan face
> Only white wild-rose hath place;
> Eyes of dewy violet,
> 'Neath their snowdrop lids, forget.
> Stilled is her sweet hawthorn breath,
> And her kiss is cold in death;
> She hath spilled her life-blood sweet
> At her cruel lover's feet.
>
> Ah! the morning when he came
>   Down the golden skies,
> Flushed her flower-face, all aflame
>   For his passionate eyes;
> But he turned, nor saw her there;
> For the Summer, brown and fair,
> Stood, with eyes of misty grey,
> Cheeks like dawning of the day,

Lips like poppies wet with dew,
Sheeny hair of rust-gold hue —
Went to her, with arms outspread,
And the gentle Spring lay dead.

The "poppies wet with dew" is a refreshing change from the eternal rose-buds which the reader has grown haplessly to acquiesce in whenever a poet has occasion to describe lips.

Nor is her sketching of nature inferior. Here is a dreary scene (from the "Story of Aibhrich") very faithfully rendered, with touches of genuine weirdness:

The stag had vanished; — a long, gold gleam in the west
    The grey pools mirrored all chill,
And the shrieking water-fowl flew up from the nest,
    The wind in the reeds sobbed shrill.

Dreary, dreary seemed the place and strange,
    The moon was barred with the drifts,
And great cloud-mountains rose stormily, range after range,
    And broke into rifts;
An eagle sailed overhead with a flapping wing
    And a wild, long cry.
I stayed my horse, and I mused with much questioning,
    In what strange country was I.

The hounds looked up in my face and shivered with dread,
    Then cowered and were still;
Only the moon's wild face, like the face of the dead,
    Looked up from each marsh-pool chill;
And the reeds and the rushes shook, and the wind wailed by,
    The flat land stretched on each side,
Down to the grey, sad line of the boding sky,
    The gold gleam flickered and died.

With all the plentiful promise, however, of which these few extracts give but a faint idea, and with a vein of sincere tenderness which she possesses, Miss Tynan has as yet written only two or three poems which we regard as complete performances. The two that we would specially note are "Poppies" and "The Dreamers." These are truly fine lyrics, of full achievement in themselves; and represent the excellence which the bulk of her verse ought ultimately to attain. Were we a poet, and had produced "Poppies" and

"The Dreamers," we would never rest until we had written our general verse up to the same level, and had written a few poems to surpass them. "The Dreamers" is too long to extract, but we must quote a few stanzas from the first and finer portion:

> Lieth outside in the perfect night
>   The land at rest,
> In the stainless snow of the May moon's light;
>   And the bird i' the nest,
> And the hawthorn sleep in a world of white.
>
> *   *   *   *   *   *
>
> O dreamer! turn from thy grieving now,
>   Hark! in the hush
> A small wind ruffles with fingers slow
>   The grasses long and lush,
> And O the choir in the elm-tree bough!
>
> The brown bright shapes that swaying sit
>   I' the heart of shade,
> Their throats are amber and chrysolite.
>   *Frail each body was made,*
> *But the gold voice poured into it.*
>
> *   *   *   *   *   *
>
> My tardy dreamer wakes, to behold
>   A pageant wide,
> Rose-hued banners waved fold on fold,
>   The sun and his good knights ride
> Up the eastern Field of the Cloth of Gold!

The lines which we have italicised are in the very vein of the old Elizabethan poets.

The faults of Miss Tynan's poetry have been, perhaps, sufficiently indicated by implication in the remarks already made. We may add that she adopts enthusiastically the diction of Rossetti and his school. She must be on her guard against carrying it to an excess which might interfere with individuality. Such is not the case at present, but it is a diction easily abused, and she does not, even now, always escape its snares. We may suggest, too, that she should not rhyme "winter" and "stir." In spite of Rossetti's example, it is certainly an affectation.

Turning back from Miss Tynan to the volume with which we started, and the gathering of writers from whose works it is selected, we would like, in conclusion, to correct a possible misapprehension. We are not insensible to the difficulties, militating against literary perfection, under which many of the poets included in this volume wrote, and under which Irish poetry has grown up: still less are we insensible to the burning love of country which all these poems display, and before which we can only bow in respect. But a volume put forth in the fashion of this volume, by an English publisher, appeals to the English public solely on its literary merits; and from such a point of view we have judged it. It would be a poor compliment to test an Irish poet by a standard other than that which we apply to our own countrymen.

One other misapprehension we would guard against. We have spoken somewhat contemptuously of "fine language." Let no one suppose from this that we have any antipathy to literary splendour in itself, apart from the subject on which it is exercised. Quite the contrary. To write plainly on a fine subject is to set a jewel in wood. Did our givers of literary advice only realise this, we should hear less of the preposterous maxim, "Aim always at writing simply." Conceive merely Raleigh, Sir Thomas Browne, Jeremy Taylor, Milton, and De Quincey rendered into "simple English." Their only fit place would be the fire! The true abuse of "fine language" is rich diction applied to a plain subject, or lofty words to weak ideas: like most devices in writing, this one also is excellent when employed as a means, evil when sought as an end.

JAMES CLARENCE MANGAN *
[*Academy*, September 25, 1897]

There is poignancy in Thompson's remarks about Mangan and his centenary. And it is a manifestation of his power as a critic that his kinship
with Mangan and his sympathy for him did not darken his understanding
in appraising the Irish poet's rare but limited gift. In attacking Louise
Imogen Guiney's conclusion that it was pathologically impossible for
Mangan to be a drunkard because she thought that he must have been an
opium-eater, Thompson's rapier thrusts are a delight—playful but deadly, as
always when he discusses feminine logic. It is not difficult to understand his
digression on the possibility of a man being both a drunkard and an opium-
eater. And his unduly long comparison between Mangan and Edgar Allan
Poe is best explained by the obvious parallel between his own life and theirs.

WHEN the editor of a "popularised" edition of Chaucer requested
by letter from a well-known author his support for the project
in question, the author sublimely answered, that "he did not want
Chaucer popularised, he wanted to keep Chaucer for himself and
a few friends." I never ascertained the author's name, the editor
said he was "well-known" or "distinguished," or something of the
kind, and I took it on faith; since his answer revealed that he must
have been a man of very great mind. It was Sultanic. What has this
to do with Mangan? What is he to Chaucer, or Chaucer to him?
Simply this, that I and a few friends have for a number of years
felt a kind of private proprietorship in Clarence Mangan. We cannot all appropriate Chaucers; so we were humbly content with
our Mangan. Even we did not know much about him. We only
knew him as the author of three or four poems, not all of which
we greatly admired. One was an imperfect, but deeply felt and
moving poem on his own misfortunes, ending with a noble stanza:

> Him grant a grave to, ye pitying noble,
>   Deep in your bosoms; there let him dwell.
> He, too, had tears for all souls in trouble
>   Here — and in hell.

* *Selected Poems.* Edited with an Introductory Study by Louise Imogen Guiney.

There could be no suspicion of pose, for the poet had lived and died in the deepest misery. The other, "Dark Rosaleen," was a splendid and impassioned love-song, a fantasia on an old Irish poem addressed to Ireland under the allegory of a woman. A fantasia, I call it, for it was expanded with a freedom and originality which left translation panting behind. It is too long to quote, and single stanzas would only scandal the torrent vehemence of the whole. This was all we knew of him; but outside his own countrymen we met none who knew as much. Therefore we possessed him, and imparted him to those poorer than ourselves. Of late years I dreaded that our monopoly was coming to an end. I surmised that he would presently go forth to the English public in a volume, and the critics would find he had the Gaelic glamour, or some other infectious complaint. And I did not think Mangan would at all like it. Now here is the volume, issued by Mr. John Lane, with a preface by Miss Louise Imogen Guiney, an American essayist and poetess. When I had timidly glanced through her pages, and satisfied myself that there was no Gaelic glamour, even in a suppressed form, I was able to read the preface with a heart at ease. And now I am reconciled to the failure of my monopoly.

The story told in that preface should alone be sufficient to give the volume something of a "send-off." The public loves "sad stories of the deaths of kings" — and poets. And here is tragedy enough, in all conscience. Mangan was the son of a small shopkeeper in Ireland, grew up under harsh and capricious paternal rule, received but a poor education, and was straightway put to copying to support his family, in which he slaved from morning till night. Thence he was transferred to an attorney's office, where he slaved yet harder amid coarse companionship which was to him brutal and hideous. He contrived somehow to supply the defects of his education by self-teaching, in spite of work, poverty, and friendlessness, and became known to a number of young men with literary tastes. He became an occasional contributor to various obscure papers, and also to the *Dublin University Magazine;* was finally enrolled among the band of brilliant men who contributed to the *Nation,* but nowhere found firm rest for the sole of his foot. Why is not quite clear. His work was of an unpopular cast, he was crippled by having to support his family, who preyed on his earnings; he had no push or energy, no doubt. But there was something behind, which has been very plainly asserted to have been drink. Anyway, his habits were appallingly irregular, and through them he lost a post which had been procured for him in the library of Trinity College, and went steadily down and down. In his latter years, when misery and prematurely broken health had completely sapped the last remains of will, there is no question that he was a drunkard — with spasmodic attempts at reformation. At last he was discovered destitute and ill in his room, taken to hospital, and there died of starvation.

That is about all, except circumstances connected with his writings, and his friends' descriptions of his oddity, his sweet nature, and the charm of his talk. Half of his life is hidden. He disappeared from view for long periods, during which he is surmised to have sought refuge in the depths of outcast society. Then he would reappear, the same as ever, in his brown cloak of prehistoric ages, with a no less marvellous hat surmounting his early whitened hair. The rest is conjecture — conjecture of a love-disappointment, of which nothing seems really known beyond his own bare reference, and conjecture as to what was his besetting vice. Miss Guiney will not listen to the tradition that he drank before those later years when his liability to couch in the gutter puts the matter past dispute. He was an opium-eater, she says. Carleton declared that he took opium, and Mangan denied it. That is all. The rest is, as usual, conjecture. We have descriptions of his personal appearance, and they remind Miss Quiney of the descriptions of De Quincey. Also a medical acquaintance of hers was struck by the same fact, and said that opium would account for Mangan's queer habits, while drink would not. All which establishes a bare "perhaps" — particularly since the medical friend avowed his candid anxiety to saddle Mangan with opium rather than with alcohol. Opium, you see, is rather poetic, while whiskey is decidedly vulgar. But he drank at last, it is plain, you may say. Ah, yes, says Miss Guiney, but he drank in order to get rid of the opium. He cast out the devil opium by alcohol, the prince of devils. Proofs — none. That is the way she is sure it *must* have been. On second thoughts, there *is* a proof. A man cannot be a drunkard and an opium-eater at the same time. Therefore, since Mangan was a drunkard at the last, he must have got rid of the opium before he took to the alcohol. Therefore he took to the alcohol in order to get rid of the (hypothetical) opium. It is a pretty piece of tangled reasoning on which we need not comment. Because, *why* cannot a man be a drunkard and an opium-eater together? It is "pathologically impossible," says Miss Guiney. When a lady takes a large scientific word in her mouth at the crisis of an argument you know pretty well that you are having a particularly unsupported assertion thrust down your throat. Unfortunately, it is but too "pathologically possible" to combine the two habits, and in the alcohol-drinking West the combination too often results. A man happens to take a glass of wine, for example, while he is under the influence of opium, and discovers that a powerful and Bacchic exaltation results, very different from the serene and luminous exaltation of opium alone. He pursues the discovery, unknowing his danger, to find too late that he is in the hands of the most fearfully destructive power conceivable — infinitely swifter and more deadly than either habit singly. A man may escape from the one; it is no common grace of Heaven if he escape from the two. *If* Mangan began by taking opium, then I have little doubt this is what ultimately happened to him.

But I am keeping the poems waiting. In some respects I confess to a disappointment. There is no other outburst of swiftness and passion like the "Dark Rosaleen." The best of them are dreamy, deficient in substance, passion, or imagery, depending for their effect almost solely on metrical melody. Yet some of them are undoubtedly noticeable. They would be remarkable for one thing alone — the discovery (pointed out by Miss Guiney) that Mangan had elaborated the artifice of the reiterated refrain exactly in the manner of Edgar Poe, *before the date* when Edgar Poe first began to use it. In fact, the whole manner of the best poems is so startlingly like that of Edgar Poe that it is difficult to resist the suspicion that Poe somehow came across specimens of them, and turned the discovery to account with his usual unscrupulousness and power. Take an example cited by Miss Guiney:

The pall of the sunset fell
Vermillioning earth and water;
The bulbul's melody broke from the dell,
A song to the rose, the summer's daughter!
The lulling music of Tigris' flow
Was blended with echoes from many a mosque
As the muezzin chanted the *Allah-el-illah*:
Yet my heart in that hour was low,
For I stood in a ruined Kiosk:
O my heart in that hour was low,
For I stood in the ruined Kiosk
Of the Caliph Moostanzar-Billah;
I mused alone in the ruined Kiosk
Of the mighty Moostanzar-Billah.

Again, take this from the song of a dying Arab, "The Last Words of Al-Hassan":

The wasted moon has a marvellous look
Amiddle of the starry hordes;
The heavens, too, shine like a mystic book
All bright with burning words.
The mists of the dawn begin to dislimn
Zahara's castles of sand.
Farewell! farewell! mine eyes feel dim:
They turn to the lampless land.
'Llah Hu!
My heart is weary, mine eyes are dim,
I would rest in the dark, dark land!

The "Karamanian Exile" has the same note, in yet another arrangement, as a stanza will show:

O none of all my sisters ten,
Karaman!
Loved like me my fellow-men,
Karaman, O Karaman!
I was mild as milk till then,
I was soft as silk till then;
Now my breast is as a den,
Karaman!
Foul with blood and bones of men,
Karaman!
With blood and bones of slaughtered men,
Karaman, O Karaman!

Let me quote one more stanza from another poem, for the sake of its pictorial expression, and I have done:

> The silks that swathe my hall divan
> Are damascened with moons of gold;
> (Allah, Allah hu!)
> Musk-roses from my gulistan
> Fill vases of Egyptian mould.
> (Allah, Allah hu!)
> The Koran's treasures lie unrolled
> Near where my radiant night-lamp burns;
> (Allah, Allah hu!)
> Around me rows of silver urns
> Perfume the air with odours old.
> (Allah, Allah hu!)
> But what avail these luxuries?
> The blood of him I slew
> Burns red on all; I cry therefore,
> All night long, on my knees,
> Evermore:
> Allah, Allah hu!

It will be clear from these extracts that the man who could thus anticipate Poe's metrical feats, though chiefly self-educated, in a country where literary culture could hardly be said to exist, and where there was nothing which we should call literary society; and who yet showed in conception and expression so trained and literary a sense, was of no common gifts. He has, too, something of Poe's atmosphere, if his imagination is weaker. As to that, it is clear his imagination must have been literally starved. To complete the coincidence, Miss Guiney calls attention to the fact that both men died in the same year, and both in a hospital.

A BEWILDERED POET
[*Academy*, May 16, 1903]

LITERATURE has had many spectres, and by this we mean not men who had outlived the common meed of their fame, but rather men who had exhausted their own emotions. Of these spectres

Alfred de Musset was perhaps the most significant, because he was the most pitied and the most loved. But De Musset lived his hour, and could always remember that once the wine of life had tasted sweet, that once the rhythm of hope and youth had rung true, that once a woman's smile had reflected destiny. But there are other spectres to whom there is no consolation, for whom there is no appeal from the stale verdict of the world. And of these condemned ones the most pathetic figure of all is James Clarence Mangan, the centenary of whose birth is being celebrated this month.

Others have turned consciously aside from the mental grooves of their generation, and sought from art not the healing consolation which should be common to all, but rather a personal enjoyment, exclusive, exotic, dangerous. Such were Charles Baudelaire and Edgar Allan Poe. But there is no just parallel between either of these and the unfortunate Irish poet. For each of these, after his manner, obtained the reward of his sacrifice. The Frenchman who had exchanged, as it were, his store of human life blood for strange artistic vibrations, fashioned from these poisoned dreams masterpieces of form, permanent manifestations of what he had purchased from art at the expense of life. The American, abandoning the main currents of the national life around him, none the less drew, from his very loneliness, his suffering, his despair, the joy of the artist. Neither of these could ever have regretted their strange barter. Such as they were, in spite of external circumstances, these men were masters of their destinies and did the thing they willed in the way they willed. But it was quite otherwise with Mangan.

The Irish poet was not at all a rebel in any sense of the word. He came into the world incongruous and alien, and he lived and died incongruous and alien. Sensitive, imaginative, beautiful, he was the son of a Dublin grocer. Then, after a few years of study under an erudite Irish priest, necessity turned him into a breadwinner for his family. He worked at a scrivener's for seven and at an attorney's for three years. They were long years for Mangan. They were long years and bitter years, for his fellow-clerks knew well that this strange figure was such as no other clerk had ever been or could ever be. And their subtle intelligences resented the incongruity, and for ten years it was driven home to Mangan that it is a hard world for those who do not fit into the settled niches. But Mangan never fitted in, could not fit in after any fashion. It was as though one were to initiate the Faun of Praxiteles into the mysteries of Wall Street, this moulding of a dreamer to the mental standpoint of a scrivener's office. It may have been discipline in realities, but Mangan was incapable of learning from realities — that was the secret of his temperament. But he was very sensitive, and between them all they knew well how to handle him: he was their butt for ten difficult years. Mangan came out of it all more confused by actuality than ever. It was still necessary, apparently, to remain in this odd world, and so, after trying two or three other phases of employment, he took definitely to journalism. His past, incidentally, had not driven him mad, but it had driven him to the hopeless relief of alcohol. Mangan the poet-dreamer, who sought vaguely from life the fleeting illusions of a lost poetry, had become a "case" for well-meaning philanthropists. It was certainly an odd world, but they never drove him mad — he died at forty-six.

Mangan was probably no more a journalist in the accepted sense than he had been an attorney's clerk. But even he had at one time some glimpses of the actual wonder of life. We need not recall the poor faded romance of the lady who had once the power to woo Mangan from his dreams. It is enough to say that the memory of this futile little tragedy blended easily with such sombre impressions as had been stamped upon the poet's heart.

As a man he seems to have been not so much miserable as dazed. He could not suffer from life quite as his companions intended that he should suffer, because he was bewildered. But sometimes the poet in him, so much greater than the man, burst out. Then he spoke as one who had peered into the depths of life. But these were only glimpses, for Mangan the poet, as well as the man, was baffled by reality.

He adhered always with curious tenacity to the two sources of his inspiration. Everybody knows that he "translated" foreign languages of which he was completely ignorant, but he did learn

German, and he did appreciate that detachment from actuality which is to be obtained from German philosophy. That, together with the legends of the past — Eastern and Celtic — was the woof out of which Mangan's fantasies were woven.

It is well that we should remember him, for he was a poet, and a poet, moreover, who, not consciously like Baudelaire and Poe, was yet true to the divine suffering within him. This was a suffering of which attorneys' clerks and well-meaning philanthropists never dreamed. And he gave it out in song, too bewildered to recognise that the artist's fire and the poet's rapture were really his. Pathetically noble in an ignoble setting, revealing the dreams of the centuries without interpreting his own, giving gold and having, as it were, alms thrust upon him, he stands forever a symbolic figure of his race.

WILLIAM BUTLER YEATS *
[*Academy*, May 1, 1897]

At first, Thompson characterized Yeats' Celtic Twilight as glamorous and delightful. But he soon recognized how inadequate a symbol of the Gael was twilight that comes before dawn and sunrise and high noon with their growing light and warmth. He made an interesting distinction between the clarity of Yeats' style and the haziness of half-truths in his "dream-heavy" utterance. He easily identified the supernatural elements of Yeats' poetry as pagan, and he foresaw the danger of his fondness for spiritism which ultimately arrested the full growth and maturity of his spirit and his art.

IT IS a hard case when the one right word for a critic to use is a word that has been so hackneyed, so bandied about in vague characterisation, that it has become rightly suspect and almost even tabooed. Yet hackneyed or not, there is only one word which describes the quality of Mr. Yeats' stories, and that is glamour — the glamour of the Celt. His tales have a good deal of talk about magic in them, more, in fact, than is to everybody's taste, for not

* *The Secret Rose.* By W. B. Yeats. With Illustrations by J. B. Yeats.

everybody can be brought to take spirit-raising seriously; but on every page in the book there is proof given of a magic to which all lovers of literature must be submissive — the natural magic of style. Here is no artifice of haziness, no mist of words; rather, the extraordinary thing about these stories is the distinctness with which they bring present to the senses whatever is related. Take, for instance, a few words from the first one, "The Binding of the Hair," which tells of Queen Dectira and the bard Aodh's (Hugh's) last song, upon whose prelude there broke in the alarm for battle.

Then he took down from a pillar his shield of wicker and hide, and his bronze helmet and sword, and passed among the crowd that went shouting through the wide door; and there was no one left in the room except the queen and her women and the foolish king, who slept on, with his head against a pillar.

How that conjures up the sense of desolation and vastness in the hall that a moment before had been crowded; one seems to feel the noise of feet dying away. It is all distinct, but with the distinctness of a dream; and Mr. Yeats' utterance is, like Aodh's, "dream-heavy." The thing is done partly by a singular felicity of comparison, as in this phrase: "A very old man, whose face was almost as fleshless as the foot of a bird"; but chiefly by the distinctness of the artist's own vision. Yet this constant appeal to the eye is never allowed to predominate or to mask the central thought which each study conveys, as, for instance, "The Heart of the Spring," which sets out the aspiration of the alchemist and life's ironic commentary upon it. Dreamy as the stories are, they are not fantastic; their characters act with human coherency. Mr. Yeats is fond of the supernatural: in "The Curse of the Fires and of the Shadows" he has introduced it for his own pleasure since in the tradition it was no one of the Shee who led the five Cromwellians to their fatal gallop over the precipice, but a simple peasant. Yet we like him best when he does not stir outside of the human pale. "The Crucifixion of the Outcast" is a grim tale of the way in which respectable folk dealt with the strolling gleeman when respectability had full power to make itself respected; we suspect an

apologue. Anyhow, this is one of the only two stories in the book
touched with the humour that made *Celtic Twilight* so delightful.
The other is by far the best of them all, the tale or series of tales
relating to the adventures of Owen Hanrahan the Red, last of
the Gaelic singers in Ireland. Here is a splendid touch. The poet
whose power over women had been not less than his passion for
them sees a girl crying, and offers help:

"My father and my mother and my brothers," she went on, "are marrying
me to old Paddy Doe because of the hundred acres he rents under the
mountain, and I would have you put him into a rhyme as you put old
Peter Kilmartin in the days when you were young, that sorrow may be
over him, rising up and lying down."
    "I will put him into a little song that shall bring shame and sorrow over
him; but how many years has he, for I would put them into a song?"
    "Oh, he has years upon years — he is as old as you are, Owen Hanrahan."
    "As old as me," said Hanrahan, in a broken voice. "There are twenty
years between him and me if there is a day. An evil hour has come for
Owen Hanrahan when a colleen with a cheek like the blossom of May
thinks him an old man. Colleen, colleen, an arrow is in my heart."

Beautiful as is the "Vision of Owen Hanrahan" with its fine
symbolism, there is nothing in it worth that. But beautiful it is,
a new and genuine inspiration from the old mythology of the
Gael. The old gods are no more dead for Mr. Yeats than were
Pan and Apollo for Milton. "When one looks into the darkness,"
he says in his preface, "there is always something there." Most
of us look very little into the dark; and we are inclined to retort
that those who look into the dark see nothing but fancies. Yet
such a book as this makes one ponder whether the light of common
day does not blind us to many starry presences. For all that we
have no patience with the last and longest story, "Rosa Alche-
mica," which is totally distinct from the rest and resembles the
recital of an opium-dream. Like everything else in the book, however, it is beautifully written — in long, slow, undulating sentences,
easy and sinuous in their progress as the motion of a serpent.
    The illustrations are admirable. There are not many points of
likeness between Mr. Yeats and Mr. Kipling; but each has a father
who draws beautiful pictures for his son's books. Print and paper

leave nothing to be desired; but it was a pity to use ridged not smooth material for the binding, as it impairs the effect of Miss Gyles' intricate symbolic design for the cover — a model of decorative work.

FIONA MACLEOD ON MR. W. B. YEATS
[*Academy*, October 25, 1902]

At the request of Hind, then editor of the *Academy*, Thompson wrote this article, prompted by Macleod's "The Later Work of Mr. Yeats," which appeared in the *North American Review*, October, 1902. Two years later it was reprinted as "The Shadowy Waters," in Macleod's *The Winged Destiny, Studies in the Spiritual History of the Gael.*

In 1902 Fiona Macleod had not been identified as William Sharp, and it is amusing to read Thompson's "she's" and "her's" referring to his male contemporary. An Irish writer — was it Lady Gregory? — said that the only reason for calling the Irish Literary Revival "Celtic" was to induce Scotsmen to buy Irish books. Whatever the reason, the result has proved most confusing, making little or no distinction between "Celtic" and "Gaelic" or "Irish." While the Celtic element with its Anglo-Irish exponents was left to develop as it would, the Gaelic strain was violently arrested but fortunately not destroyed by the execution of the poet-patriots of 1916 and the later activities of the Black and Tans.

AN interesting literary event. No one can have a greater claim to write understandingly concerning Mr. Yeats than the writer who has devoted herself to clothing in modern literary speech the legends and tales which haunt the wave-acquainted rocks of Gaelic Scotland: from no one, we may conceive, could appreciation be more valued by the poet himself. Fiona Macleod writes, of course, as an apostle of the "Anglo-Celtic" Movement, which we know under various names. It has given "ample room and verge enough" for the scoffer: there has, in truth, been not a little "flummery" about it, not a little tall talk; and it has been represented to the public mind largely by the weaker links of its chain, by those whose own work could least claim to stand for anything specially Celtic or large in literature. Even now it would be impossible to say that it had produced anything robust or of commanding significance. But robustness is scarce a Celtic quality, the movement is yet young; and it has indubitably produced a certain small but distinctive quality of delicate work having a common breath of life, which we may describe as a spirituality and aloofness from the tallow and lard, the greasy materiality of modern life. The English writer who "returns to Nature," nowadays, goes back to the soil, to the "good gigantic smile o' the brown old earth." But the return of these Celtic writers is to a spiritualised nature. Wordsworth, of course, did that long ago. But for these Celts, Nature is spiritual in a more direct, a more overt way. She not merely hints remote and mysterious influences; she is transfigured before their eyes, her "limbs are burning through the veil which seems to hide them." They have, indeed, more kinship with Shelley than with any other English poet.

That is a strange and remarkable new development in Ireland, particularly the Ireland whose first literary avatar was through such poets as Davis and his comrades, in patriotic ballads and the like, hopelessly "actual" and of no lofty order in literature. It is the neglected Mangan who has triumphed after all; for assuredly the spirit of "Dark Rosaleen" comes nearer to that of the present school than does the spirit of Davis. But the poetic standard-bearer of the movement is certainly Mr. W. B. Yeats. Fiona Macleod is not wrong when she says, in the *North American Review*, that even the contemners of the Anglo-Celtic school allow his position in literature. Her article is specially given to his later work, in which she recognises the "beginning of a new music and a new motive." It is a finely written article — here and there a thought too remote for perfectly-expressed criticism, but that is a trait inherent both in her subject and herself. There is one quite lovely phrase, where she says of a certain passage in "The Shadowy Waters" (comparing it with the preceding passage) that it is "the cold radiance of precious stones after the glow and flame of that little infinite trouble in the dark, the human heart." Mr. Yeats' latest poems do, as she says, display the dawning of a new motive; but of a new music we are not so sure. There are poems in the older volumes which seem to us to have all the quality of the latest ones. The new motive is the uncontrolled set of his poetry towards that mysticism to which it always, consciously or unconsciously, tended. It has its dangers, which Fiona Macleod clearly sees and indicates. The greatest lies in his research of symbolism. For it is more than a use of symbolism; we would go further than Fiona Macleod, and call it an actual abuse of symbolism. Symbolism is used (to our mind) where not only was its employment unneeded, but the meaning could more beautifully have been given without it. This, however, is a temporary phase, we believe, which will rectify itself. In Mr. Yeats' discovery of a novel power (since symbolism is no less) he has come to love and use it for the mere delight in using it; as a young artist revels in technique for the sake of technique. The painter presently learns to handle technique severely as a means to an end; and the like sobering will come about in Mr. Yeats' handling of symbolism. Yet we cannot quite sign to Fiona Macleod's dictum that "the things of beauty and mystery are best sung, so that the least may understand." If it were always possible, then it were indeed best so. But the highest "things of beauty and mystery" cannot be sung so that they may be understanded of the least. Where, else, were the mystery?

But in the bulk of Mr. Yeats' work, even of this latest work, there seems to us nothing beyond the proper and beautiful indefiniteness of remote suggestion. Such is that exquisite poem which Fiona Macleod quotes:

> Had I the heaven's embroidered cloths,
>   Enwrought with golden and silver light;
> The blue and the dim and the dark cloths
>   Of night and light and the half light;
> I would spread the cloths under your feet;
>   But I, being poor, have only my dreams;
> I have spread my dreams under your feet,
>   Tread softly because you tread on my dreams.

There is a poem by an older Irish writer, which ends with one fine line:

> Dance light, for my heart it lies under your feet, love!

If Mr. Yeats ever saw the poem, then with the skill of a consummate artist he has ennobled the line into a thing of perfect beauty, which is rightfully his own. His highest work, like this poem, stirs echoes in the imagination which reverberate to the dimmest verges of consciousness. It is this unique power of subtly remote suggestion which makes him typically the poet of what we understand by Celtic spirituality. The words seem to awaken a series of answering harmonics, which are lost at last on the other side this life. Whether Fiona Macleod's final conjecture be correct, that Mr. Yeats may yet work out a new and spiritual drama, ranging under no existing precedents, is another matter. To us, as to her, it seems impossible at present that his genius should fit the stage. He has declared his conviction that such a drama must revert to the Shakespearean stage, and shake off the trammels of scenery. Wagner's conception of a new drama went the other way, demanding the last perfection of scenery and mechanical device. Yet we strongly incline to it, that in this matter Mr. Yeats is right. Nothing would drag us to see *The Tempest* mounted with even Bayreuthian completion. But is spirituality possible short of a Greek or lyric drama? And after all, Mr. Yeats' ethereal gift seems to us to have no rightful connection with passion at all, save the clear passion of yearning for the infinitely far, and regret for the unknown, which is plaintive in all his verse.

FRENCH LITERATURE AND FRENCHMEN

THE EARLY DAYS OF CHATEAUBRIAND *
[*Academy*, September 13, 1902]

These two reviews of Chateaubriand's endless *Memoirs* reflect Thompson's scrupulous labor as a reviewer. He left nothing unread, even in volumes of such riotous irrelevancies as these. And in the end he gives a brief, adequate summation of it all, and a sober judgment of its worth.

To-DAY it is not necessary to apologise for writing about Chateaubriand. Yesterday (so to speak) we might have feared rebuke from the great young Frenchmen with whom alone is the way and the truth — their staunchest admirer would not add "life." For it is, we conceive, their boast that they are dull — but how hopelessly dull! All true art being decadent, ditchwater is its natural symbol, combining the two artistic qualities of deathly dulness and deathly odour, besides its third (and scarce less artistic) quality of dismaying the soap-loving *bourgeois*. This by the way. The point is that to-day Chateaubriand has become an orthodox — or rather unorthodox — immortal (since to be immortal and ortho-dox is not possible in the decadent calendar). He has received a patent from M. Pierre Louÿs. Here it is, in the "Note" which Mr. Teixeira de Mattos prefixes to his *Memoirs of Chateaubriand:*

Many years ago, M. Pierre Louÿs, who had not then achieved his aston-ishing successes, and I were talking literature in a Paris café. The future author of *Aphrodite* had praise for none save the moderns of whom he has now become a recognised type and leader. I turned to him suddenly and asked:

"Is there any nineteenth century French writer at all whom you others read nowadays and approve of?"

"Yes," said Louÿs, "Chateaubriand."

* *Memoirs of François René, Vicomte de Chateaubriand.* Translated by Teixeira de Mattos. Vols. I-IV.

"How do you mean?" said I. "The novels? *Atala?* The essays?"

"Ah, no," he answered: "but the *Mémoires d'outre-tombe*, yes. That — that is monumental; that will live for ever."

And so we have this translation of the *Mémoires*, under the title *Memoirs of François René, Vicomte de Chateaubriand*. That is very characteristic of the (Parisian) "moderns'" who recognise M. Louÿs as their type and leader. It is also eminently logical. For if the school of which M. Pierre Louÿs is "the recognised type and leader" make for righteousness, we must reconsider all our ideas of greatness in letters. But that it should seriously be advanced as a testimony to Chateaubriand is more than a little surprising. None the less, despite their sponsorship, these four stout volumes (there are two more to come) are very welcome. It is extraordinary that we should have waited so long for a complete version of the *Mémoires d'outre-tombe*. We should hesitate to call it a masterpiece. It defies proportion and symmetry, it riots in digressions and the most prolix *minutiæ* on every topic started; not a town nor a country, scarce an island, can the author visit but you must be told its history, its features, its topography; the narrative flags and is interrupted in shameless fashion: yet withal it is supremely interesting. For it is at once the relation of a very full life and of an imaginative temperament throughout its process of development. It is history, it is psychology. And it is told with fidelity, with charm, with the romancer's eye for romance. It is coloured with the writer's strong individuality. It is morbid (for Chateaubriand was morbid), particularly in the boyish details; and this, one conceives, was its claim to immortality in the eyes of M. Pierre Louÿs. But it is vastly more. It is the life of a great imaginative writer whose wanderings, vicissitudes, misfortunes, and glories make those of Byron pale. Thus he can boast, in the large rhetoric of his preface:

I have met nearly all the men who in my time have played a part, great or small, in my own country or abroad: from Washington to Napoleon, from Louis XVIII to Alexander, from Pius VII to Gregory XVI, from Fox, Burke, Pitt, Sheridan, Londonderry, Capo d'Istrias to Malesherbes, Mirabeau and the rest; from Nelson, Bolivar, Mehemet Pasha of Egypt to Suffren, Bougainville, La Pérouse, Moreau and so forth. . . .

I have explored the seas of the Old World and the New, and trod the soil of the four quarters of the globe. After camping in Iroquois shelters and Arab tents, in the wigwams of the Hurons, amid the remains of Athens, Jerusalem, Memphis, Carthage, Grenada, among Greeks, Turks, and Moors, in forests and among ruins; after wearing the bearskin of the savage and the silken caftan of the mameluke; after enduring poverty, hunger, thirst, and exile, I have sat, as minister and ambassador, in a gold-laced coat, my breast motley with stars and ribbons, at the tables of kings, at the feasts of princes and princesses, only to relapse into indigence and to receive a taste of prison.

What an exordium! — and we have but quoted part of it. Yet this man moans that his life has been a disaster and a tragic search for happiness. All these things likewise are vanity.

Chateaubriand would have been unhappy in a serpentless Eden, where apples were licenced. He would have wept, and said the Snake was just the one thing missing: a superior person like himself could not taste the flavour of apples without it. He was born with the desire for fairyland, for better bread than is made of wheat. He desired virtue, but the paths of virtue were too humdrum; he desired sin, but the sins of men were too gross; he thirsted for love, but women were all-too-mortal. He desired a supersubtile virtue, a supersubtile sin, a supersubtile love, a woman created to his measure. He wished all the nobilities, beauties, and raptures of life without the vulgar sweat of attainment: he coveted an attar of existence. No length of years could teach him to cut his coat of living according to the cloth of actuality. Such a man should have been a great saint or a great sinner: he was only a great writer — and modern France makes question of that. He never seized the hour, for he was always dreaming of the hour to follow or the hour past. Proud of his lineage, proud of his aloofness from the rest of men, vain as most poets are vain, wilful at once and weak, his training nurtured all that was morbid in him and made for unhappiness.

His mother was timid and pious, his father aloof and severe. Pride and unwholesomeness ran in the family: his father had it, in his elder brother it ran to mania. That father he loved and held in terror. A silent, reserved, undemonstrative, gloomy, disappointed man, never showing affection, the paternal Chateaubriand was the very person to drive a sensitive lad in upon himself. His blue blood, his penury, his blue devils, were always in his thoughts. His study-table strewn with title-deeds, a family-tree over the mantel-piece, he worshipped his ancestors like the Chinese. After supper in the great hall of Combourg Castle, wife and children sat dumb by the fire — dumb, but for the wife's sighs.

> My father then began a tramp which lasted till he went to bed. He was dressed in a white ratteen gown, or rather a kind of cloak . . . his half bald head was covered with a big white cap which stood up on end. When he walked away to a distance from the fire-place, the huge hall was so badly lighted by its solitary candle that he was no longer visible; we could only hear him still walking in the darkness; then he would . . . gradually emerge from the dusk, like a ghost, with his white gown, his white cap, his long pale face. Lucile and I exchanged a few words in a low voice when he was at the other end . . . we hushed when he drew nearer to us. He asked, as he passed, "What were you talking about?" Terror-stricken, we made no reply; he continued his walk. For the rest of the evening, the ear heard nothing but the measured sound of his steps, my mother's sighs, and the murmuring of the wind.

Sometimes he would sit for a while, and talk of his travels and misfortunes. At ten, he took his candle, the children pressed an unreturned kiss on his cheek, he retired to bed, and a babble of suppressed talk broke out.

In this gloomy castle, tenanted by a few retainers besides the family, young Chateaubriand passed his early youth, after a childhood of rough play among the ships of St. Malo with all the ragamuffins of the town, and a boyhood at Rennes College. From the first, his pride and passions peeped out. He read certain sermons of Massillon for the descriptions of disordered passion which chanced to occur in them. He is always proclaiming his penitent devotion to religion; but he dwells on his "youthful errors" with a most suspicious lingering which does not smack of penitence. They were strange "errors." An accident turned his thoughts towards women; but his indulgences were morbidly ideal. He created for himself an imaginary woman, compounded of the few women he had seen and his conceptions of sylphs and goddesses. In his small room at the summit of a turrett, where the moonlight fell athwart his bed, the owls flitted by, the winds moaned through the castle and shook his door, he gave himself up to wild raptures with this "sylph."

In company with my witch I mounted the clouds; enveloped in her tresses and her veil, I was swept along by the tempest, shaking the forest-tops, hustling the mountain-summits, whirling upon the seas. . . . The breath of the north wind brought to me but the sighs of voluptuousness; the murmur of the rain summoned me to sleep upon a woman's breast. The words which I addressed to that woman would have revived the senses of old age, and softened the marble of the tombs. . . . The air exhaled from her moist mouth penetrated into the marrow of my bones, coursed through my veins instead of blood. . . . To this madness was added a moral idolatry . . . the Phryne who clasped me in her arms also represented glory to me, and, above all, honour. . . . I divested myself of my nature to become one with the maiden of my desires . . . to be at once passion given and received, love and the object of love. Suddenly, struck with my madness, I flung myself on my couch; I rolled myself in my grief; I watered my pillow with scalding tears which none saw, piteous tears which flowed for a non-existent thing.

In company with this dream-woman he roamed the country in solitary walks, from which he returned pale, with rain-dank hair. It is not surprising that this morbid exercise of the imagination preyed on his health, that he became wild-eyed and lank of cheek. The remarkable thing is, that it lasted well into early manhood. His one human companion was a sister, Lucile, a strange girl no less morbid than himself, though her mind took a religious turn. In her, the family taint (one can hardly call it otherwise) put forth symptoms which hint strongly at an overbalanced brain — in fact, a strain of latent insanity. She first urged him to composition, and played the part of Wordsworth's sister Dorothy, in a less wholesome fashion.

The death of his father drew him from solitude, and brought him to Court. Thereafter he began reluctantly to mix with men — none too soon. The youth who was so shamefaced that he fled the presence of women in his country solitude and the Parisian assemblies, had no lack of spirit or perception. He saw Mirabeau, and vignettes him:

Mirabeau's ugliness, laid on over the substratum of beauty peculiar to his race, produced a sort of powerful figure from the "Last Judgment" of Michelangelo. . . . The scars dug into the orator's face by the small-pox had rather the semblance of gaps left by the fire. Nature seemed to have moulded his head for empire or the gallows. . . . When he shook his mane as he looked at the mob, he stopped it; when he raised his paw and showed his claws, the plebs ran furiously. I have seen him in the tribune, amid the awful disorder of a sitting, sombre, ugly, and motionless: he reminded one of Milton's Chaos, shapeless and impassive in the centre of his own confusion.

He met Mirabeau twice at banquets, and was charmed by his fervid talk of love and the delights of retirement. At the end of dinner, talk turned on the Tribune's enemies. Turning to the silent youth by his side —

He looked me in the face with his eyes of pride, vice, and genius, and laying his hand on my shoulder, said: "They will never forgive me my superiority!" I still feel the pressure of that hand, as though Satan had touched me with his fiery claw.

Wherever Chateaubriand goes, he keeps the eye of the novelist. He joins the *émigrés*, and at once you have the Royalist camp and army, clear as the camp of Buller or Kitchener. But by then he had made his journey among the Iroquois, and was no longer the timid enthusiast, shrinking from a woman's skirt to court the arms of a dream. To that later Chateaubriand we shall return.

THE LATER YEARS OF CHATEAUBRIAND *
[*Academy*, October 11, 1902]

IN OUR former article we left Chateaubriand at the blood-stained lintel of the Revolution. Heads on pike-irons were dismally ominous to young aristocrats; he "liked not such grinning honour." It set his thoughts towards America, where they managed revolutions better: with the blessing of Malesherbes on his head and a

* *Memoirs of Chateaubriand*. Translated by Teixeira de Mattos. Vols. V and VI.

letter for Washington in his pocket, he sailed off on the wild emprise of discovering the North-West Passage.

Nothing could be less eventful than his youthful journey to Niagara, nor in other hands less interesting; but it all has the eventfulness that it befell François Chateaubriand, the interest that it was witnessed with his eyes. Here he began the list of his shadowy loves, less real than his dream-amour. The little Breton, lately dumb before the ladies of Paris, started with a dual affair — a brace of Cherokee half-breeds. Oval visage, shaded complexion "which one seemed to see through a light, orange-tinted smoke," hair black and soft, eyes long, "half-hidden beneath the veil of two satiny eyelids that opened indolently"; the one girl proud, the other sad, both tall, — such were the cousins who usurped the place of Chateaubriand's dream-sylph:

> They wore the petticoat and the wide, slashed sleeves of the Spanish women, the body and cloak of the Indian women. Their bare legs were cross-gartered with a lace-work of birch. They plaited their hair with posies or filaments of rushes; mailed themselves in chains and necklaces of glass beads. From their ears hung purple berries; they had a fine talking paroquet; they fastened it on their shoulder like an emerald, or carried it hooded on their hand. . . . They lived in an atmosphere of perfumes emanating from themselves.

Could you ask better from a dime novel? And it all happened just as in the correctest dime novels. The Indian hunters went a-hunting, and the young Pale-face stayed behind with the squaws. He placed an ornament on their heads; one prayed, the other sang "in a voice of velvet": they knew not the language of the Pale-face, nor he theirs. Then there was a fishing-party; he was left alone, and night fell on him among the trees, amidst azaleas and lilacs. Moonlight, fireflies, lapping of lake-water, splash of leaping goldfish: the white youth sleeps:

> When I emerged from this Lethe, I found myself between two women: the odalisks had returned; they did not wish to arouse me; they had sat down silently by my side; whether they had feigned sleep or had really slumbered, their heads had fallen on my shoulders. A breeze blew through the grove and deluged us in a shower of rose-leaves from the magnolia. Then the younger of the Seminoles began to sing. . . . No one knows the

strength of the passion that glides with melody into a man's breast. A rude and jealous voice replied: a half-breed was calling the two cousins; they started and rose; the dawn was beginning to break.

The interruption, it would seem, was somewhat timely. Of course, every boy knows that it came from the ill-favoured lover of one of the girls, and that he will plot with the stern brother of the other lady to carry them off from the noble young Pale-face. It is even so. Just when the white youth is separated from them for a space at noon, the beauteous Indian maidens are seized, thrown on the cruppers of two horses ridden by the half-breed lover and the Seminole brother, and carried off like a whirlwind in the midst of the band. There, alack, the dime novel comes very vilely to grief. The Pale-face does not vow to pursue them to death, though he avows himself disconsolate. Worse still, the unpoetic guide asserts that the fair Seminole maidens (who were not fair, by the way) were also not maidens. He does not stick to call them "painted girls" — which among the Indians means what it means. "Which," says Chateaubriand, "shocked my vanity." It is a fair specimen of his love affairs. Though he talks repentantly of his "passions," they never, on his own showing, seem to have gone further than in the matter of the painted ladies.

The next turn of fortune brought him into the emigrant ranks invading France under Brunswick, and sat him down to besiege Thionville. It gives opportunity for an admirable realisation of the Royalist army — regiments of nobles, grey fathers beside their smooth-cheeked boys, all making war at their own expense. One body, attacked by the republicans, have to charge with the bayonet because their muskets will kill nobody, except perhaps the owner. Take this vignette of the Royal troops recreating under arms. A brevet-captain was called "Dinarzade" (mistake for "Scheherazade") because of his yarning gifts. The description of this rude, primitive tale-teller and his blundering improvisations is lifelike:

As soon as we saw him, we ran up to him, fought for him: we vied with each other as to who should have him on his score. Short of body, long of leg, with sunk cheeks, drooping mustachios, eyebrows forming a comma at the outer angle, a hollow voice, a huge sword in a coffee-coloured scabbard, the carriage of a soldier-poet, something between the poet and the jolly dog, that solemn wag Dinarzade never laughed, and it was impossible to look at him without laughing. One night, when it was drizzling, we were seated round the tap of a wine-cask tilted towards us in a cart with its shafts in the air. A candle stuck on the cask lighted us; a piece of packing-cloth, stretched from the end of the shafts to two posts, served us for a roof. Dinarzade, with his sword awry after the manner of Frederic II, stood between one of the wheels and a horse's crupper, telling a story to our great content. The canteen-women who brought us our rations stayed with us to listen to our Arab. The attendant group of Bacchantes and Silenuses which formed the chorus accompanied the narrative with marks of its surprise, approval, or disapproval.

Brunswick rolled back from Valmy in ruinous retreat; and from Verdun to Brussels the strange young aristocrat-romancer struggled alone, a gangrened shell-wound in his thigh, and half-delirious with the horrors of confluent small-pox. After long illness in Jersey, he reached England seemingly doomed to death, and certainly to the pains of slow starvation. Literature barely saved him; and pacing Kensington Gardens he thought out the works which brought him fame. At Beccles, in the household of a country vicar, he had his next love affair. He had married in France — a *mariage de convenance* with a young girl whom he did not love, engineered by relations for money it did not bring. Yet he philandered with the vicar's daughter, to whom he acted as French tutor, and she fell in love with him. The poor mother, blushing and embarrassed, offered her child to the indigent emigrant:

Of all the sorrows that I had undegone, this was the sorest and greatest. I threw myself at Mrs. Ives' feet; I covered her hands with my kisses and my tears. She thought I was weeping with happiness, and herself began to sob for joy. She stretched out her arm to pull the bell-rope; she called her husband and daughter.

"Stop!" I cried. "I am a married man!"

She fell back fainting.

The sentimental egotist has the grace to be ashamed of himself. While he declares it the chief and purest love of his life, he owns it would not have satisfied him. Would anything? But the observations of English public men and affairs, above all the vignettes of his curious fellow-exiles, are vivid as ever. That of Peltier, whom he truly calls a Gil Blas, shady journalist, waiter on life, minister to the Black King of Hayti, is a gem. You see the uproarious, good-natured, go-as-you-please fellow before you. Back to France under Napoleon, after his hungry gazing into London cook-shop windows, and a celebrity with the publication of *Atala* and the *Genius of Christianity*, his perception is as keen, with an added vein of mockery, which he religiously deplores — and indulges. He meets the Abbé de Faria (celebrated by the idealisation of him in *Monte Cristo*) who boasts at dinner that he can kill a canary by mesmerising it:

> The canary was the stronger of the two, and the Abbé, beside himself, was obliged to leave the party for fear of being killed by the canary. The sole presence of myself, the Christian, had rendered the tripod powerless.

Atala, the *Genius of Christianity*, and *René* (which, like *Atala*, was conceived as an episode of the larger work), all published as the work of his exile, after his return to Napoleonic France, were the works which at once gave him European fame and influence. That *René* in particular, was the chief model for that Byronic pose which found expression in "Childe Harold," no one can doubt who carefully considers the matter. The pose of a gloomy and impassioned nature, solitary by native superiority to its fellows, which has wandered in many lands seeking happiness in vain, and cursed by a mysterious sorrow, a malady of the soul, was first thoroughly assumed in *René*, and became the fashion of French literature. It was Chateaubriand's own morbid character, "touched up" with the irrepressible Gallic research of rhetorical and melodramatic effect. A firm believer in Byron, he recognises, himself, Byron's indebtedness:

> One a peer of England, the other a peer of France, both Eastern travellers, . . . Lord Byron visited the ruins of Greece after me: in "Childe Harold" he seems to embellish with his own pigments the descriptions in the *Itinéraire*. At the commencement of my pilgrimage I gave the Sire de Joinville's farewell to his castle: Byron bids a similar farewell to his Gothic home.

Other resemblances are noted, but we need not pursue the theme. The latter volumes of the *Memoirs* progressively decline in attraction for the general reader. Chateaubriand the statesman is less interesting than Chateaubriand the writer and wanderer: stars and orders are less brilliant than young ardours. The *Memoirs* grow like other memoirs, the anecdotes like other anecdotes, the padding bursts through the pages. Much is sheer history of the July revolution and the like, in which the writer himself plays small part. And it is small history: the last Bourbons and the men of July are poor creatures, impermissibly dull. Here a touch and there a character shows the old keenness: but on the whole Chateaubriand old is the dregs of Chateaubriand young. Excellently Englished, these volumes impress by the man in his vigour; vaunting religion and ogling the world, vaunting indifference and vain to the point of embroidery, fascinating though one doubts whether one emotion be wholly unsophisticated, and displaying in his memoirs the gifts of a novelist which he never displayed in his novels.

DANTON *
[*Academy*, April 1, 1899]

The simultaneous publication of two studies of the same personage, drawn from the same sources and having the same aim, was, as Thompson remarks, unfortunate for readers and publishers. But it afforded him the opportunity of using the comparative method in his review — a method he adopted in similar circumstances, only. Even in judging poetry, he never condemned a thrush because it was not a skylark. The allusions to "criminal anthropology," though not profound, show that Thompson was not altogether a stranger in this interesting field. And Danton emerges from the brief description of him, as clearly sketched as a Holbein drawing.

THERE was a real need for an account of the great Revolutionary which should be based on the most modern investigations, and, therefore, neither of these books is in itself superfluous. But it must be said that their combination is unfortunate for the reader, as it certainly is for the authors and publishers concerned. The simultaneous appearance of two volumes, covering the same

* *Danton: A Study.* By Hilaire Belloc. *Life of Danton.* By A. H. Beesly.

ground, from the same standpoint, with the same aim, relying more or less on the same new investigations, affects us with the sense of too much Danton. Of the two biographers, Mr. Belloc (whom we take to be of French extraction) is the more pictorial, and gives us a clearer *coup d'oeil*. Mr. Beesly, on the other hand, affords us more detail, and, on the whole, more precision of narrative. Both are uncompromising admirers of Danton, and in full sympathy with the Revolution. They have done undoubted good work by clearing away the garbled view of Danton with which Englishmen are familiar. But we must needs say that their advocacy is liable to become special pleading. Mr. Beesly, in particular, indulges in an audacious latitude of hypothesis when he desires to turn the flank of a story adverse to his hero, which can only be paralleled by Macaulay's explaining away of the charge against Addison that he arrested Steele for debt. Nevertheless, in this respect we prefer Mr. Beesly to his rival; for he squarely faces the music, so that we can judge for ourselves the validity of his conclusions. Mr. Belloc is apt to keep the hostile evidence out of court, and state only his results. It must not be understood, however, that there are not numerous cases where he directly proves his defence. He does so in regard to the charge that Danton acquired houses and property in the names of others in order to disguise his unrepublican wealth. In this and other ways the two books do, for some part, usefully complement each other; however, from a publishing standpoint, their simultaneous explosion upon the public must be adjudged unlucky and ill-considered. And in their common endeavour to overset the traditional conception of Danton they must be pronounced largely successful. "White-washed," perhaps, he is not — except in the eyes of such as accept unshrinkingly the entire revolutionary formula. But no one can read these volumes without feeling it necessary to revise much in his previous ideas of the Samson who pulled down the walls of the French monarchy.

The strong man of the mid-Revolution was himself no *sans-culotte*. At this day you may take the odds that a French Republican leader is a lawyer or a journalist. Danton was a lawyer, and — what is more rare — he was a successful lawyer, making a good income. His father was *procureur* at Arcis-sur-Aube, so that it was in a legal nest the young bird saw the light on October 26, 1759. *Candide* was born that same year, which was also in labour with the *Encyclopædia*. *Candide*, the *Encyclopædia*, *Danton* — three portentous births. He was educated at a Jesuit college, and was actually destined for the priesthood. It is not surprising that he cried off. Can you fancy him *le Père Danton?* The Revolution found him a leader among the reforming young politicians of his district in Paris — the Section of the Cordeliers, whence sprung the famous club. His ascendancy of character, no less than his oratorical gifts, carried him to the front. You can figure him to yourself with the aid of the portrait which precedes both these volumes. The three representative men of the middle and later Revolution are well known by their portraits — Danton, Marat, and Robespierre. With every respect to Danton's admirers, we assert that all three faces belong to criminal anthropology. A student of that science would recognise the types at once. All three, to our thinking, are hideous. Marat shows strong traces of the criminal lunatic. Robespierre — narrow, callous, egotistic — belongs to the type from which one might expect an educated poisoner. Danton alone has the redeeming quality of power. It is a formidable head, in which the criminal streak is introduced by the abnormal brevity of the nose, the tip of which occupies the centre of the broad countenance, leaving a disfiguringly long upper lip. Such was the case with Titus Oates. Everyone remembers the Greek physiognomist who declared Socrates to have the visage of a criminal, and Socrates' defence of the man. That incriminating nose branded the famous Greek, and quite justified the physiognomist. Whether Danton also was saved by philosophy every man must judge for himself. To enhance this deformity his nose was crushed by an accident, and his lip torn by another accident. Add to this countenance of a disfigured bull a voice of immense power, deep and trumpeting; imagine this being, huge and lowering of form, pouring forth menacing invective with a terrible and truculent regard; and you have the Danton who moved the Cordeliers, dominated the Convention, and left a legend of terror not easy for calm analysis to dissipate.

The legend of terror, in truth, was right; but it is Danton's misfortune that it should be associated with a legend of bloodthirstiness. "Terrible Danton" he was; bloodthirsty he was not. The ferocity of the Revolution was incarnate in Marat, its cold cruelty in Robespierre, in Danton its volcanic energy. To understand this we need only note the circumstances in which he came to the front. At different crises the Revolution put forward different men. It put forward Danton only when there was need of swift daring and organisation. To energise and to organise — those were the two things he could do supremely well.

Consider the crises at which he emerged. During the beginnings of the Revolution, with leonine Mirabeau over all, none heard of this "Mirabeau of the *sans-culottes*." He was addressing the daily meetings of his section (that is, district), the Cordeliers; seeing to its drill, and that it was provided with pikes. He had no lead in the taking of the Bastille, which was indeed a rough affair, succeeding only through the complete unpreparedness of the Royalists. That event paved the way for his local power in the Cordeliers, for it taught the sections to organise and constitute themselves an armed force. Suppressed as a section, the Cordeliers revived as a club, and became the centre of the *Théâtre Français*, the new section in which the old one was merged. Meanwhile had occurred the first direct conflict between Crown and people. The Flanders regiment had sung *"O Richard, O mon roi,"* at Versailles. It was feared that the king would retreat to the provinces and unfurl the standard of civil war. On the walls of Paris appeared a proclamation demanding insurrection — a proclamation issued by the Cordeliers. The tocsin rang, the mob gathered, and filled the road to Versailles. The palace was forced, and the king brought in triumph to Paris. It was the first demonstration that the people would prevent by insurrection the king from opposing the Revolution. That call to insurrection was signed by Danton. Then first Paris learned that whenever swift and unquailing energy was needed by the Revolution it was to be found in a certain big-headed young man belonging to the district of the Cordeliers.

During the time when Lafayette was striving to put the Revolution in swaddling-clothes, Danton again recedes into the background; heard only as a thunder playing round Lafayette's head at the Jacobins. He starts into the streets to prevent the king's journey to St. Cloud, bearding Lafayette, and compelling the king to renounce his project. He attacks the hapless Lafayette again as an accomplice in the king's abortive flight; and has to fly before that General's brief triumph in the Champ-de-Mars. But when the Tenth of August found the allies advancing on Paris, and revolt threatening in the provinces, Danton comes to the front before Europe. He is insurrection incarnate. While the tocsin tolls through the night he is organising, exhorting, bringing the pikes of the sections to the muster. The fall of the Tuileries finds him Minister of Justice, and the inspirer of France against the foreigner. Again, when the fresh successes of the allies, the war in La Vendée, and the revolt of the Girondin Departments menace the republic with downfall, he thunders forth encouragement, establishes the Revolutionary Tribunal, and the Committee of Public Safety, begins the *levée en masse*, and a second time saves the Revolution. But there his labour ends. In the working of the terror he had no part. Blood for blood's sake he did not love. And he came back at last to combat the terror, and die in the effort to begin the reign of clemency before the passions of men were exhausted enough to suffer it.

For he was no truculent ruffian. His speeches were truculent, because so only could he keep his position with the fierce democracy. But at heart this formidable man hated blood. He would spill it for a purpose, but not for love of victims. He permitted the September massacres, for he dared not oppose them. But ever after he sought to guard against their recurrence by establishing a tribunal, to secure, at any rate, a fair trial before execution. That was his aim in the Revolutionary Tribunal, so terribly abused by his successors. He was the one man among the Revolutionists with an idea of government, an idea of diplomacy; the one man who perceived that the Revolution must end, if the Republic was to be saved. Among that crowd of theorists with their muzzles off, he alone was practical, and cared more for government than doctrines.

But he was not the man to end the Revolution. An immense

volcanic force, he lacked perseverance; he must rest and recuperate after his fits of vast exertion. He had no ambition, no desire for rule. So lesser men and weaker men were allowed to capture the powerful engines he created; and when he attempted to cross their sanguinary policy they turned those engines against himself. A man roughly and spontaneously eloquent, undignified and even foul of tongue in private; generous to his private, terrible to public enemies, with a burly magnanimity of nature; after being identified with the crimes of others, such as Marat, he perished in the effort to put an end to crime; and history has merely regarded him as a criminal caught in his own trap. But always he had tried to moderate between the fierce factions of the Convention. Let it be at length known and recorded of this fearless, vast volcano of a man, that he died in the deliberate attempt to end the terror. It was his misfortune that, powerful for destruction, he was impotent to save. But he dared the effort, and let him now have the honour for it. "To dare, and dare, and without end dare," was the advice by which he saved France from the allies. His life was one long daring; and the daring which brought him to the scaffold was the noblest of all.

A SIX-FOOT CHILD OF GENIUS *
[*Academy*, September 6, 1902]

Thompson here explains Dumas' limitations as he explains Shelley's. He was a child to the end. Thompson does not sentimentalize Dumas. But he judges him with kindly good nature and indulgence, as one judges a child — even a spoiled child. Anyone who reads this review will have a more kindly feeling for Dumas, and a kindlier one, still, for Thompson.

THE DUMAS centenary was an appropriate moment for an English study of Dumas' life and works, and Mr. Davidson has utilised the occasion very well. He has given us a compendious biography of Dumas the Elder, embodying a compendious account and

* *Alexandre Dumas* (*Père*): *His Life and Works*. By Arthur F. Davidson.

discussion of his principal writings; and his book, on both its sides, is excellently written, with taste, selection, discrimination, and narrative interest. Interest, indeed, is difficult to miss in dealing with Dumas; but dull writing has a surprising power of spoiling the best material. Mr. Davidson has not spoiled his.

Neither in literature nor life was Dumas subtle: he lies on the surface, and only a fool could mistake him — which is perhaps why so many have mistaken him. The riotous obviousness, the frank extremeness of the man in all his works and pomps (pomps is a good word with Dumas), tempt the obvious and one-sided, for whom two diverse extremes are irreconcilable. A jovial volcano, a wasteful revel of energies good and bad, untamed nature, unmoral and instinctive, that was Dumas. Though by his novels better known in England than is any other French author, his work outside the novel is not known, nor yet his personality — apart from a few characteristic anecdotes regarding him. But a more vital and distinctive personality is not to be found in literature.

Luck came to this Creole throughout. His first big play (or the first produced, for the previously written *Christine* was postponed, and afterwards brought out in an improved revision) succeeded brilliantly; it was *Henri III* — a subject he rehandled in his novels. Its success came just in time to compensate dismissal from his secretaryship, the result of neglecting business for literature; and doubtless helped his speedy reinstatement in another department. So it was: this reckless hawk flew at everything, and every quarry he struck at he brought down. He began with plays, and had but to touch a drama to succeed; for he was a playwright to the marrow. He was a romancer miraculous. He may be said to have invented the *causerie*, and his *causeries* were delightful. He wrote travels, and their *bonhommie* is taking still. Between the plays and the romances he had tried history; and if one cannot call him an historian, it would be difficult to say he failed. To the provincial big-wig who said his (Dumas') history of Cæsar was not spoken of among the learned, he answered: "Learned people never do speak of me." "Yet a history of Cæsar ought to have made some stir." "Mine made none: people read it — that was all," rejoined the *insouciant* Dumas. "It is the unreadable histories that make a stir: they are like the dinners which you can't digest: digestible dinners give you no cause to think about them on the next day." That was the secret: the materials might be begged, borrowed, or stolen; but the cookery was superb.

The apotheosis of Dumas — Dumas at his best, worst, and most magnificent — is after his Austerlitz or Worcester, the "crowning mercy" of *Monte Cristo*. Then he became a land-proprietor, and built the costly, never quite-finished house called after that most widely known of his novels. Then he lived there with royal prodigality, keeping open house for friends and a perpetually shifting train of hangers-on. Outside the famous house was a frieze of medallions, showing the illustrious authors from Homer to Victor Hugo. "I don't see you among them, M. Dumas," said a visitor. "Me? Oh! I shall be inside," replied the gay romancer. Every rascal had his money — every friend, everyone in distress or professing to be in distress. A man turned up with what Dumas thought an umbrella-case. "You are wrong, sir," cried the fellow; "this is the skin of a splendid boa-constrictor." "And what on earth do you suppose I want with the skin of a boa-constrictor?" asks Dumas. The cunning villain had his answer pat. "I am sure, M. Dumas, you will value it as a relic when you know that the creature to which this skin belonged was shot in Egypt long ago by your father, General Dumas." The exquisite absurdity of course sold the skin and kept the liar in free quarters at Monte Cristo; for Dumas' vanity was as credulous as his good-nature. Stray dogs found open house there, too, besides the novelist's own animals. Michel, the head-gardener, reported thirteen dogs in the place. The dogs, none the less, must stay; but thirteen was an unlucky number — they must not be thirteen. Then Michel would turn one away. "No, Michel, you had better let an extra one come in — that will make fourteen." Michel sighed, and went away. It was Dumas' method all over, in money no less than dogs. The house-lady for the time being wrote that the servants' wine was exhausted — there was nothing in the cellar but champagne. What *was* she to do? "Let them have the champagne," came the return-letter; "it will do them good."

Those house-ladies were the most prodigal feature of all — in every sense of the word "prodigal." Dumas, only once married, then to a lady for some time in need of it, and not for long — Dumas had an endless succession of provisional wives (so to speak), mostly actresses, and all of the harpy class. Women were his hopeless vice — perhaps the one thing we can find it in our heart to call a vice in the great six-foot child of genius. He said one day to a friend, "with a comical pride," that he did not wish to exaggerate, "*mais je crois bien que j'ai, de par le monde, plus de cinq cents enfants.*" It is perhaps better untranslated. His years grew venerable, but not his conduct. Those last years are melancholy reading. The adult child who had lived as if he should never grow old, saw age upon him and death. "Unfortified by philosophy and unconsoled by religion," he perceived the arrival of the end "with tears and lamentations." Then senility and gradual coma. Let us turn away, sad.

He was, as Mr. Davidson truly says, a perfect example of what theologians understand by nature without grace. All his natural virtues, his natural faults, he retained from childhood unmodified and without a notion of modifying them. Parisians jested at the contrast with his prudent son. A comic paper drew Dumas the younger as a man with his father as an infant, and the legend: "Here is a child who gives great anxiety to — his son." The son had his own jests on the subject; though the famous one about his father's vanity being enough to make him pose as his own coloured footman is said by the present biographer to be probably apocryphal. But the elder Dumas' vanity was all on the surface, was childlike: even as that of Goldsmith, and more than Goldsmith's, it was unaccompanied by conceit or pride. He was kind-hearted, generous, and magnanimous to a degree, ever ready with praise of his great contemporaries, who were not always generous to him. Balzac had a special venom against him. Alphonse Karr relates that Balzac, leaving a party, said as he passed Dumas: "When I can do nothing else I shall take to writing plays." "Begin at once then," swiftly retorted Dumas. But the great romancer candidly acknowledged that the great novelist was a rare genius, and warned his readers not to take over-seriously any hasty things he might say about Balzac. He had a vague sentiment of religion rather than any fixed beliefs. Nevertheless, when a general sneered at the idea of God, saying: "I cannot form the slightest conception of that mysterious being known traditionally as *le bon Dieu*"; Dumas rejoined, "General, I have in my house four dogs, two apes, and a parrot; and I can assure you that their opinions are absolutely and entirely identical with yours." Of the amazing fecundity and energy of his genius, especially of his dramatic genius, too neglected by Englishmen, we have left ourselves no space to speak. For that we must refer the reader to this singularly interesting book.

A PASTOR OF COURTLY SHEEP *
[*Academy*, November 2, 1901]

What might have been a monotonous introduction to the task of again reviewing two volumes of the same subject and scope is avoided by Thompson's rather adroit use of the metaphors of sailing. His description of John Bull's preference in things spiritual, and the British habit of lordly mishandling, are refreshingly frank. Adopting his own metaphor, he never trims sails in such matters. In commenting upon the various views of Fénelon presented in the volumes, he displays the same catholic sense in judging men as in judging literature. His summation of Mme. Guyon's pseudo-mysticism and the Fénelon-Bossuet controversy, is most forthright and understanding.

THERE is a theory, held by modern transcendentalists, which Mr. Clifford Harrison has recommended with some happy and persuasive rhetoric, that there are mental no less than electric currents, so that minds can act on minds from a distance, and ideas, without any figure of speech, may be "in the air."

If those who hold it wished for plausible confirmatory instances, they might well point to the recent course of the publishing world. The "trade" shows a marked tendency to give birth to twins, or even triplets; and this in cases where the lust of gain (one should

* *François de Fénelon.* By Viscount St. Cyres. *Fénelon, His Friends and Enemies.* By E. K. Saunders.

think) would hardly tempt a publisher to "blanket" his rival. (We thank thee, Lipton, for the word! So much more handy than "take the wind out of his sails.") That might explain the flight of books on Cromwell, when everyone was talking Cromwell. But it seems the rule now that biographies, however unforeseen their heroes, come out in pairs, crossing the line together in a most level start. (Again, our acknowledgments to Sir Thomas.) It is not very long since we had to judge two books entered, so to speak, for the Danton Cup; and now two are launched simultaneously bearing the name of Fénelon. Yet Fénelon is not precisely a burning subject.

Once in the clutches of this seductively popular metaphor, it seems irresistibly convenient to call them Fénelon I and Fénelon II — carrying respectively the flags of Viscount St. Cyres and Mr. E. K. Saunders. Of the two, Fénelon I seems to us the better — it certainly is the cleverer — book. Their construction is remarkably similar in their outward lines: they often follow each other chapter-heading for chapter-heading. But Fénelon II is the usual panegyrical biography, and Mr. Saunders the usual biographer, with a firm faith in his hero's all-righteousness. From this standpoint he tells the story of Fénelon's life clearly and straightforwardly, though with no special graces of style. In point of substance there is not much to choose between them: neither has any advantage of information. But Fénelon I is not merely a biography, it is a study — a clever study; and Viscount St. Cyres has a cultivated style, which keeps his book at a constant level of attractiveness. It has the disadvantage, perhaps, of seeming a little "down" on his hero: not because he has any real lack of admiration for him, but because he is continually holding level the scales between the violent partisans and violent assailants of Fénelon. For any faulting impression which this may cause, Mr. Saunders will be found an efficient corrective, never failing to put Fénelon's case as strongly as he can. Between them the reader can hardly fail to receive a full impression of the great Archbishop of Cambrai.

Viscount St. Cyres is of mind that Fénelon has suffered in his own land from the flux and reflux of extreme biography; and it was his aim to produce a judicial biography, clean alike of malice or extenuation. To our thought he has succeeded excellently well.

Few English biographers could have kept such steady way among the quicksands of the controversy with Bossuet. The whole Quietist business turns on matters which John Bull has gruffly made up his mind that no fellow can understand, and, therefore, they cannot be worth any fellow's understanding. The beef and pudding of spirituality are good enough for him, and should be good enough for everybody else. That on the Fénelon and Bossuet matter Viscount St. Cyres largely countersigns John Bull's view does not betray him into obtuse contempt and slovenly misunderstanding. It is treated with singular grasp and judiciality, so that we doubt if an account as steadily impartial has appeared. Mr. Saunders on these affairs is given to cutting the Gordian knot with an amusingly Britannic lordliness of mishandling. Yet Viscount St. Cyres is human; he has "a bee in his bonnet" on the subject of the Jesuits, who never fail to irritate him from his calm, apparently because he has a special cult of the Jansenists.

It was time that Fénelon should find such a biographer, for he was exactly the character to arouse warring judgments. Born of an impoverished aristocratic family in Périgord, he was eminently a Southerner — quick, mobile, intelligent, various, of sympathetic adaptability, a man of many characters, yet far from a man of no character, as is too often the result of such combinations. Bossuet saw and said that he had no simplicity. This heterogeneity always fares ill at the hands of an impatient world, which loves to clap a hasty label on its great men, and know that they are ready docketed for future use. Therefore it has seized now one, now another prominent aspect of him, transferring him from this little drawer to that, and unwilling to confess that he belongs outright to neither. He has descended to us as a writer, but, like Johnson, it was the tongue which gave him greatest influence in his lifetime. Not all at once did he realise his true power. He aspired to Bossuet's eloquent reputation, and his first public employment was as a missionary to the Huguenots, then in process of state-aided conversion. Here idealisation begins at once, representing him as an enlightened apostle of toleration. But Viscount St. Cyres has little trouble in showing that his toleration was of a modified kind. He acquiesced in the general methods of his employers, softening them only in detail. For mild and humane he always was: so much of the legendary Fénelon is undeniable. His true powers developed when his friends, the Duc de Beauvilliers and the Duc de Chevreuse, introduced him to Mme. de Maintenon, and Mme. de Maintenon to the King and to Court.

He seemed born for a pastor of courtly sheep. Sincerely religious he was even then, sincerely ambitious he perhaps scarce ceased to be even in later days. The Duchess of Orléans draws him: a man "with deep-set eyes and ugly face all skin and bone, who talked and laughed quite unaffectedly and easily." And St.-Simon, at the time of his appointment to Cambrai: "tall, thin, well-built, pale with the exceeding pallor that has been called *pulchrum virorum illustrium colorem* by a Father of the Church, with a great nose, eyes from which fire and genius poured in torrents, a face curious and unlike any other, yet so striking and attractive that, once seen, it could never again be forgotten." His manners were exactly calculated to fascinate these highbred men and women, among whom Madame de Maintenon had brought religion into fashion. He knew how to address them with a dexterous air of light and flattering raillery, and no man could better carry out St. Paul's counsel to be all things to all men in the service of religion. There was a woman in Fénelon. His ascendancy was of the feminine order, and he instinctively preferred the woman's road to rule — by subtle accommodation, persuasion, and adroit management; his love of power was almost a woman's love of power in its all-absorbingness, its lack of the magnanimity which can acknowledge an equal or a superior; his curious capacity for uniting the most inconsistent qualities in one undeniable personality, for surprising alternately by his greatness and his pettiness; his moods and subtleties — all these things were feminine, and so was his unaccountability to himself. "When I examine into my mind," he said, "I seem to dream; I am to my own conscience like a vision of the night." Woman-like, no less, was his instinctive resort in difficulty to indirect and evasive ways, of which doubtless he was but half-conscious.

Such a man was almost maternally in his place as educator of the Dauphin's son, the young Duke of Burgundy, to which position the De Maintenon influence procured his appointment. He had a difficult pupil — arrogant, passionate, with a keen, sarcastic tongue, quick of intellect, ready to argue with his master, curiously inaccessible to anything but reason, and not even to that in his rages. Yet withal the lad was affectionate. Fénelon has drawn him in his rebellions:

Nothing without, everything within. There was a wrinkle in his stocking this morning, and we shall all have to suffer for it. He cries, he roars, he alarms, he moves pity. Don't speak to him of what he likes best, for that very reason he won't hear a word in its favour. He contradicts others and tries to annoy them; he is furious that they will not be angry. Or else he turns on himself, is wretched, and will not be consoled. He wishes for solitude, but cannot bear to be alone; he comes back to us, and at once quarrels with us all. We must not be silent, we must not talk, we must not laugh, we must not be sad. There is nothing to do but wait until he recovers.

When he recovered, he was ready to jest at his own unreason — presently to give way to it again. This boy Fénelon treated with endless patience and tact, making his lessons a pleasure to him by skilfully humouring his intellectual propensities, and passing with an agreeable desultoriness from subject to subject. A child, he said, could not long fix his mind on a single theme. He appealed carefully to his dominant faculty of reason, attached the boy to him by his affections, and was ever at watch to preach the total regulation of life by principles of religion and humanity. Yet when banishment from Court interrupted the preceptorship, he left behind a one-sided pupil. He had trained him in religion and conduct; but he had deferred the training for royal duties as an after-matter. And there remained a painfully conscientious devotee, full of the most excellent maxims and ideas, but shy, morose, awkward, without decision or character. He had been broken to absolute obedience, but had never learned self-reliance, and the staff withdrawn, Burgundy had no power to walk alone. It was fatally proved when, in later years, he was sent, with Vendôme, to command against Marlborough and Eugene. Anxious and cautious, he originated nothing, opposed everything, would not fight unless sure to win, and prayed in his tent instead of mixing with his captains and soldiers. His return in disgrace cast obloquy on his old teacher:

> Acknowledge your pupil, my lord of Cambrai,
> When Lille is blockaded, he's far from the fray,
>   In action takes never a part.
> His face is so doleful, his mien is so sad,
> That — answer me — is not the sanctified lad
>   A Quietist after your heart?

Such was the contemporary epigram. Could Fénelon, indeed, have given his pupil those qualities of swift, masculine decision which, so far as we can see, he had not himself? At any rate, he never tried.

The Quietist controversy, to which this epigram alludes, was the turning-point of Fénelon's life. Coming just after his appointment to the Archbishopric of Cambrai, it banished him from Court, and showed his weakest side. It arose out of his acquaintance with that much-debated "mystic," Mme. Guyon. Viscount St. Cyres has the courage to question the praises which it is the fashion to heap upon her. Left a widow, she formed a peculiar "spiritual friendship" with a Barnabite priest, one Lacombe. Thereafter, her mysticism took strange forms. She virtually could not sin, for she was united with God: He gave her power to preach, and guided her pen from error:

She could perform miracles, knew what was passing in the minds of others, had absolute power over their minds and bodies. And at her first meeting with Lacombe she developed a new mastery over Graces physically bestowed — the Plenitudes and Spiritual Maternity and Fecundity that an indignant Bossuet was one day to declare unexampled in the Church — and later defined as an influence so pure that there was nothing of human sentiment in it, a mere flux and reflux, that went from her to Lacombe and back again, to lose itself in the Divine and Invisible Unity. And in her later career these Graces came upon her in such numbers that she must take to her bed till she could discharge them on someone; it was only after long practice that she learned how to bestow them in silence and from a distance.

She became acquainted with Fénelon through Mme. de Maintenon, and he fell under her religious spell. He was never very intimate with her, but, unhappily, he recommended and partly made himself responsible for her, while through her his own doctrine was called in question. Attacked by the Bishop of Chartres, she (by Fénelon's advice) appealed to the great Bossuet, Bishop of Meaux: and, after many troubles, a commission, headed by Bossuet, assembled at Issy, and condemned her writings in very guarded terms. Fénelon signed the articles reluctantly. But Bossuet proceeded to prepare a pamphlet, laying down the doctrine of the Church on the whole subject of mysticism, and the Quietist errors of which De Guyon was accused. Fénelon at first promised approval, but then withdrew his promise, and prepared a counter-statement of his own teachings on the matter, *The Maxims of the Saints*. He promised not to print it till Bossuet's pamphlet had appeared. But by giving it to his impetuous friend De Chevreuse for publication, without telling him that he had explicitly promised to delay it, he secured that De Chevreuse should issue it in his own absence, *before* Bossuet's pamphlet. Then, of course, he disavowed responsibility for the act. Bossuet was furious. He accused the *Maxims* of heresy; and a fierce conflict of pamphlet and tongue resulted in Fénelon's appeal to Rome. There the extravagances of Fénelon's system were formally condemned, together with the book; but his doctrine on the main issue was left cautiously alone, nor was he accounted heretical. He accepted the condemnation, and retired to his diocese, whither he was banished by the king.

It was a blessing in disguise, rebuking his ambition, deepening his religion, and educing his finest qualities. Thenceforward we see nothing but the great and wise Archbishop, energetically governing his diocese, winning all hearts by his sympathy, his adaptability, his humanity, his sagacious moderation, his charity; the great Director, guiding a flock of souls drawn from the *élite* of France, and to this day edifying men by the gentle wisdom of his letters to these many spiritual clients. The horrors of the war on the Flemish frontier filled Cambrai with sick and wounded soldiers, for whom his benevolence was untiring, lodging them in his palace, aiding them with food, medicines, clothes, money, and personal attendance. If with all his wisdom he still accustomed his clients to an over-reliance in himself, a too blind obedience; if he still had glancings towards the Court whence he was banished, these are human weaknesses. Of that *Télemaque*, which brought on him at first fresh obloquy, and finally lasting fame, as of his other writings, we cannot here speak in detail. The political and humanitarian wisdom of *Télemaque*, with its political and humanitarian extravagances; its beautiful, musical, and evenly-flowing prose; its anticipations of the eighteenth century and Rousseau — on all these things Viscount St. Cyres writes with admirable insight and judgment. But his chief praise is to have given a thinkable picture of a brilliant and bafflingly varied personality, and to have shown its greatness and wisdom, not excluding, but reconcilable with, its liability to error, tortuousness, and self-centredness. For there Fénelon recognised his own peril. Friendly and charitable to all, he took none to his inmost heart; and all his plans for the good of others he was under the necessity of centring round himself. "*L'église, c'est moi,*" he might have said.

HUGO IN ENGLISH *
[*Academy*, March 29, 1902]

In view of Thompson's translations from Hugo, his critique of another's effort is doubly interesting. His own translations clearly avoid the defects he here points out, and they excel in the good points.

Sir George Young is in some respects the most daring of Hugo's translators. Not content with a modest little sheaf of renderings, he has adventured widely on specimens from almost the whole range of Hugo's poetic work. It is a perilous enterprise, yet he is far from lacking justification for his attempt.

We conceive it no slight praise to say that Sir George Young makes good his title to translate Victor Hugo, and to translate him metrically. But, beyond this, our appreciation must be of very mingled yarn. Sir George Young, in fact, exasperates one into

* *Poems from Victor Hugo.* By Sir George Young.

antithesis. He shows the right poetic mettle, even to daring; and he startles you by the most traditional conventionality. He succeeds in difficult ventures, where a feeble spirit would fall headlong — succeeds in the teeth of wantonly unreasonable licence; and he is dull to futility where it needed no miracle to succeed. Displaying so much of the poetic sense as he does at times, and rising highest when there is peril in the attempt, he has yet made the mass of his selections with as deadly an instinct for mediocrity as the bitterest Philistine could parade. With a leaven of exceptions, on the whole he has skimmed the cream from Hugo — and presented us with the milk. Seeing what cream there is in the great French poet, that is a feat — of a kind. We never before realised how much mediocrity there was in Hugo. Whether this be timidity, which clung for safety, in general, to the *via media*, or sheer antithetic perversity of taste, we cannot guess. Certainly there is far too much in the book which, to our thinking, did not merit translation — rash though the assertion may seem of a great poet.

Coming to the manner of the translations, we are still faced by curious contradictions and inequalities. We do not object to licence where it has a poetic *raison d'être*, and as a rule Sir George Young's licence is conceived in the true poet's vein. But he has one trick which amazes us alike by its boldness and uselessness: a trick of wholesale inversion. The order of the original is turned upside down wherever it suits his convenience: sometimes persistently through stanza on stanza. Mere convenience cannot justify this, and there is no gain of poetic effect to carry it off.

We may at once exemplify this, and show Sir George Young at his best, by quotations from the "Ascent of Man" (in the *Chansons des Rues et des Bois*). For, as we say, he is never more given to this trick than when he is most successful in adventurous dexterity. Other characteristic inequalities are displayed in this translation, which is yet, in its entirety, bold and felicitous beyond the average even of good metrical versions:

> Quand il maintient d'âge en âge
> L'hiver, l'été, mai vermeil,
> Janvier triste, l'engrenage
> De l'astre autour du soleil,

Quand les zodiaques roulent,
Amarrés solidement,
Sans que jamais elles croulent,
Aux poutres du firmament,

Quand tournent, rentrent, et sortent
Ces effrayants cabestans
Dont les extremités portent
Le ciel, les saisons, le temps.

This is rendered with an admirable balance of directness and virile freedom by Sir George Young:

When from age to age He marshals rosy May, December dun,
When He implicates the cog-wheels of His planets round the sun,

When the zodiac signs go rolling, coupled fast in one intent,
Never crashing on the sleepers of the solid firmament,

When the cable-ropes that draw the stars, the seasons, and
    the weather,
On the windlasses of God come taut and slacken, all together.

That is English poetry, impressive even to grandeur, and we congratulate Sir George Young on the result. The inversion of the last stanza is not more than allowable. But afterwards, though the translation maintains an equal level, the inversion of Hugo's order becomes exasperatingly wanton. It is too complex, too wholesale, to be shown except by a considerable quotation:

Pour combiner ces rouages
Précis comme l'absolu,
Pour que l'urne des nuages
Bascule au moment voulu,

Pour que la planète passe
Tel jour, au point indiqué,
Pour que la mer ne s'amasse
Que jusqu'à l'ourlet du quai,

> Pour que jamais la comète
> Ne rencontre un univers,
> Pour que l'essaim sur l'Hymète
> Trouve en juin les lys ouverts.

Sir George Young simply throws these stanzas into a mortar and brays them together, so to speak. They come out in the following amazing mixture:

> To combine their mazy wheelwork in exactest synchrony,
> To prevent the tide from mounting past the kerbstones on the quay,
>
> To upset the cloud-filled vessel when the time is come for showers,
> For the bees upon Hymettus to unfold in June the flowers,
>
> So to order that the comet with a world encounter not,
> That the planet should attain, on such a day, its nodal spot.

It is a patchwork, a mosaic rearrangement of the original, too intricate for us to point out in detail: so causeless that even the rigour of the translation cannot persuade us to pardon.

But here, despite its licence, is (as we have said) a fine translation; of a poem, too, conspicuously demanding power. The more strange that in quieter and easier examples Sir George should so often fail. Take the "Inscription for a Crucifix," which demands only closeness and restraint. Sir George paraphrases it — a mistake at the outset:

> Come to this God, ye weepers, for He weeps;
> Come to Him, watchers, for He never sleeps;
> Come, ye who mourn, for He can soothe your grief;
> Come, heavy-laden, and obtain relief;
> Come, sufferers, for He hath suffered too;
> Come, all ye tremblers, for He smiles on you;
> Ye who are far, come to Him, He is near;
> Come, ye who pass, for He is waiting here.

He adds a closer version, but both conventionalise the simple and touching original. The last line, in particular, is quite missed by both versions. Let the reader judge:

> Vous qui pleurez, venez à ce Dieu, car il pleure.
> Vous qui souffrez, venez à lui, car il guérit.
> Vous qui tremblez, venez à lui, car il sourit.
> Vous qui passez, venez à lui, car il demeure.

"He is waiting here" misses the antithetic force of "demeure," which means, "He remains," He does *not* pass. But though we could quote numerous poems which display a similar commonplace fashion of translation, we prefer to dwell on the fact that there is a certain proportion of work which justifies the volume. Sir George Young is evidently at his best where strength, rather than grace or felicity, is demanded; and where, too, he can eschew what is called "scholarly" version, to trust his own poetic feeling of the original. The more pity his general selections are so timorous.

MONTAIGNE *
[*Academy*, July 2, 1898]

This review, perspicuous but not profound, illustrates Thompson's clarity of thought and his power to see the significance as well as the nature of men and things. Much that he says about Montaigne is literally true of himself. His analysis of Montaigne's character is Thompson at his best, and his suggestion that the essays inspired *Hamlet* is most intriguing.

MR. LOWNDES has given us a very excellent and compact book upon Montaigne, entirely worthy of the University stamp. It disclaims the title of a biography: yet, in effect, it furnishes as good a modern biography of the essayist as could be desired; collating all that latter-day research has discovered in regard to him with the material supplied by the essays themselves. Neither does it profess to be an appreciation of Montaigne as essayist. It aims,

* *Michel de Montaigne.* A Biographical Study. By M. E. Lowndes.

rather, at studying the man, as revealed through his work and life; and rather the inner than the outer man. To this task Mr. Lowndes brings a wide knowledge of Montaigne's epoch; in particular of the men of thought who formed the marrow of that epoch, and the writers upon whom Montaigne and his contemporaries fed — writers, in most cases, forgotten by, or obscure to, the present age. He brings, also, a balanced and judicial mind, peculiarly necessary in studying the singularly tolerant and dispassionate essayist. Some partialities he has, of course, and those naturally on the side of his author; but they are as few as one would hope to find.

Montaigne is a patriarch, the father of a great people. From him are descended all they upon the face of the earth that write essays; from him all they that combine a bold garrulity with the *cultus* of the first personal pronoun. He invented the essay, both name and thing. Nor have any talked about themselves with more applause to more crowded European houses. Rousseau, indeed, is more read; but the fame of the *Confessions* is marvellously allied to infamy. And, then, Montaigne had a century or two the start of him with readers. Montaigne's book founded no social revolution; but its intellectual influence throughout Europe, down to the eighteenth century, was immense. To name its mightiest disciple, Shakespeare drew on it frequently for his philosophy, and was evidently a profound student of it. Nay, in the close of this article we shall bring forward a still grander claim. It would be difficult to say by what great English writer of the sixteenth or seventeenth century he was not quoted, down to Butler in *Hudibras*. Mr. Lowndes says of him that, with all his popularity among his contemporaries, he did not interpret his age. But in every age there are two currents to be distinguished — the surface-current and the under-current. Montaigne belonged to the under-current. The greatest writers usually belong to the under-current; for the under-stream represents what an age produces, the surface-stream merely what it develops. The leaf does not fall from the bough till it has prepared the germ of the future leaf; an age does not end till it has prepared and enunciated the ideas which are to govern the succeeding age. This is its real contribution to the progress of thought, and this is the work of its writers who belong to the under-current. On the other hand, the ideas which govern it are the legacy of the preceding age, which it merely popularises. Montaigne's ideas are those with which his epoch was in travail; he was part of his age as truly as the child in the womb is part of the mother. In effect, Mr. Lowndes acknowledges this. He fails only to perceive that Montaigne was not exceptional in his position, and that every age has two classes of representative writers — "representative" in two distinct ways.

Montaigne was fortunate in his birth. He came of mercantile origin, but by the purchase of his fathers was a landed proprietor. He was therefore without the prejudices of the born aristocrat, and had sympathies with the people. His father was a great supporter of scholars, as well as mayor of his town, Bordeaux; and from these various causes Montaigne possessed a peculiarly "all-round" mind. Scholar and man of affairs, aristocrat and man of the people, sympathising with very various elements, partizan of none. One of the founders of the French language, he was brought up in childhood to speak nothing but Latin. His preceptor talked Latin to him; his father talked Latin to him; he prattled Latin as other children French. At college more Latin and Greek. Yet he obstinately refused to follow the example of other men of gifts in that age, and become a mere grammarian, a scanner of syllables and commentator on the classics. His defects fought for him. He was not a bright lad; he had a bad memory; and so he was saved to become a genius. He served his time as mayor of Bordeaux, he spent a period at Court, he corresponded with Henry of Navarre and other leaders of affairs, he was the friend of politicians such as L'Hôpital. And finally he deliberately retired to his estate, and took up the retired life.

Out of all this came the most delightful, shrewd, compact of rambling essayists; the most popular writer that ever professed the creed of systematic selfishness. He did not so much lack method — he was indifferent to it; he was, in truth, much too lazy, too self-indulgent, to trouble himself with system. An hour's reading, he declared, was a great stretch for him. The sagacious givers of advice to young men who warn them against vagrant reading would have found a frightful example in Montaigne. He wrote as he read, and he travelled as he wrote. When he was journeying through Germany and Italy to Rome, his chief end was not to reach his end. The longer he could delay on the way, the better he was pleased.

"When the complaint was made" (says his amanuensis) "that he often conducted the party by devious and contrary ways — often getting back close to the place he had started from — he replied that, for his part, he had no other destination than the place where he chanced to be; and that he could not go wrong, or out of his way, having no other end in view than to reside in new localities."

This might stand for an excellent description of the methodical absence of method in the essays. It is decidedly the right way to see countries, the Cook's tourist method being the way to overlook them. And every reader of the essays entirely agrees that when he most goes astray he "then does most go right."

But this writer, so sauntering and *insouciant* in method, is direct, quick, pregnant in style. Excursive in method means generally diffuse in style; but Montaigne is all point, vividness, picturesqueness. He loved directness in others — a good deal, we suspect, because of his constitutional aversion to taking trouble. He objected to Cicero, the eloquently diffuse, though Cicero was the idol of Montaigne's age; he admired Seneca the sententious, Plutarch the full of matter. "Meatiness" he loved in others, and "meaty" he was himself. If he wanders, he never leads you through dry places. This is the more remarkable because it is so total a breaking away from the spirit of his time. To write not only in the vernacular, but in the spirit of the vernacular, was a new departure for that age of imitative classicism: and it is one of Mr. Lowndes' merits that he brings this home to us. The memoirists are an exception; but the memoirists were as unconsidered in their day as journalists in ours.

Montaigne's chief reputation with us is that of a picturesque and gossiping observer of life; and upon this, indeed, he chiefly prided himself. But he was also a philosopher, and observed life with the *parti-pris* of a philosopher. He was the forerunner of the sceptical and *laisser-aller* philosophy which afterwards gained such power. Not of strong affections (he seems never really to have been in love), averse from practical affairs, cursed with irresolution, yet gifted with a keen analysis of human nature, sceptical philosophy was his natural refuge. He belonged to the cross-benches of the human mind. We cannot but agree with Pascal, against Mr. Lowndes, that Montaigne's philosophy was an ignoble thing in its application to practical life. It is a skilful blend of whatever is selfish in the Stoic with whatever is self-gratifying in the Epicurean. It enforces the Christian counsel of detachment, but deletes the one thing which makes that detachment noble. Detachment from the affections of the world becomes purest selfishness, unless it be to attach oneself to the affections of the other world. Yet this is Montaigne's rule of life:

> One must have wife, children, possessions, and above all health, if one can, but not hold to these things so that one's happiness depends upon them. . . . One must disavow these overstrong obligations, and love indeed this or that, *but espouse nothing save oneself.*

The italics are ours. This is the higher selfishness with a vengeance! Again:

> In household cares, in study, in the chase, and in all other exercise, one must indulge to the limits of pleasure and beware of pledging oneself more deeply where pain begins to intermingle.

We once heard a gentleman of the "bounder" persuasion expatiate on the perfect life of another gentleman of the "bounder" persuasion whose house ran with drink, but who never got drunk. This, he affirmed, was the true art of life — to manipulate your drinks so that you stopped short of intoxication. It seems to us that this gentleman was an unconscious, but rigidly logical disciple of Montaigne. If Montaigne had placed the *summum bonum* in whiskey and soda, to this complexion he must logically have come.

On the theoretical side he played with great effect the Pyrrhonic juggle of balancing *pros* and *cons* till they killed each other, and was an adept in sitting between two stools without coming to the ground. Of this Kilkenny cat philosophy he was the modern founder, and, did he live now, would be an agnostic. Yet his book is not odious, like the productions of most sceptical egotists; it is saved by the geniality of his scepticism. He is better than his creed; takes keen interest in humanity while professing to consider it a very poor affair; and shows himself a good and kindly neighbour, a warm friend. And so they last for ever, these shrewd, strolling, zig-zag, fascinating, personal essays; with their racy, original, pregnant style, like the architecture of an old French town; professing an inhuman creed in the most human and humane way; shaking the head over that sad dog Man, and finding nothing in the world so well worth writing or meditating about.

We said that we had one claim on behalf of Montaigne which we reserved to the last. This is it. We do in conscience believe not only that he furnished Shakespeare with philosophy, but that he actually suggested the whole conception of *Hamlet*. Hamlet, that is to say, was suggested to Shakespeare by Montaigne's description of himself. He found portrayed in the *Essays* a man who was an onlooker upon life, a constitutional speculator upon men and human affairs, addicted to an indecisive philosophising which examined everything, analysed everything, but decided nothing; a man averse to action, and unfit for affairs (for so Montaigne pictures himself); cursed, moreover, with a disabling *irresolution*.

He was incapable (so Mr. Lowndes summarises Montaigne's confession) of taking part in a dubious enterprise because he saw always the reasons on both sides — so that he reserved his judgment until occasion forced his hand, and then, he confesses candidly, he mostly flung reason to the wind, and followed the lead of circumstance and chance.

That is a perfect description of Hamlet. So he hesitates, "seeing the reasons on both sides"; so, when his hand is forced, following the lead of circumstance and chance, he kills Polonius, and, finally (by a mere sudden thought), kills the king. To take such a character as that sketched by Montaigne, to place it in a situation which clamoured for action, and then to work out the inevitably resulting tragedy — that was the idea which dawned on Shakespeare, if we are right. Viewed in this light, it becomes most natural that *Hamlet* is full of Montaigne philosophy, and that we should encounter a direct quotation from Montaigne: "For there is nothing either good or ill, but thinking makes it so." Montaigne has a whole essay on the theme, *That the taste of good things and ill depends in great measure upon the opinion we have of them* — a maxim which he in his turn borrowed from Epictetus. That Hamlet is younger than the Montaigne of the essays, that he differs in many subordinate details of character, does not defeat our thesis. Shakespeare was too good a dramatist not to make such divergences from his model for the sake of dramatic requirements. We think the theory has at any rate something to say for itself.

AN AGNOSTIC OF THE SIXTEENTH CENTURY *
[*Academy*, November 22, 1902]

Thompson seldom fails to see the forest for the trees. But he does not miss the trees while viewing the forest. His eye for details, while grasping the significance of the whole work, is notable. In this review there are many digressions but few irrelevancies, and the whole is expressed in Thompson's most delightful and raciest manner.

THIS is a re-issue of an edition published in 1877. But though that edition bore Mr. W. C. Hazlitt's name, he really contributed (as he tells us) only the introductory matter; the revision being the work of his father. Finding that Cotton's text remained full of errors, he has now brought out a new edition, based on the first issue of Cotton, in which Cotton's text is revised from comparison with the original and with Florio, his liberties corrected, and his interpolations transferred to footnotes. The work, on the whole, has been well done, the text much cleared and improved, so that it comes closer to Montaigne than any now on the market. Here and there we find a fault. Mr. Hazlitt says that he has taken pains with the text and translation of Montaigne's incessant quotations — a credit he deserves. But his translation of them is not always impeccable. Cicero's *Nulla ars in se versatur* looks strange as "No

* *Essays of Montaigne.* Translated by Charles Cotton. Edited by
William Carew Hazlitt. 4 Vols.

art ever reverts on itself." The meaning surely is: "No art is occupied with itself"; that is, "No art is exercised for its own sake." Neither Cicero nor Montaigne believed in "Art for Art's Sake." Sometimes, also, an awkwardness in the rendering of Montaigne himself, from the standpoint of elegance rather than meaning, might well have been remedied while the editor was at the task of revision. But these are details.

Much more important is Mr. Hazlitt's choice of a translation. Cotton is not lovely and beautiful: belonging to the late seventeenth century, his style is a foreboding of the century to follow, without the excellence of either period: diffuse and languid, it is more like poor eighteenth than vigorous seventeenth century. So bloodless a writer ill represents the racy Montaigne. Since severe revision was needful for a faithful version, had he not better have revised Florio? Not of the best sixteenth-century, Florio's is yet redder English than the lily-livered Cotton's. He is at times chuckle-headed and unintelligible: we could cite passages where Mr. Hazlitt's Cotton clears what in Florio is nonsense. He has used comparison with Florio to advantage; so that often the present version might not uneasily pass for a modernised Florio. Any passage will serve: as where Montaigne prefers rather to laugh with Democritus than weep with Heraclitus, at men's follies; because laughter means contempt:

And one thinks we can never be sufficiently despised according to our merit. Bewailing and commiseration are commixed with some estimation of the thing moaned and wailed. Things scorned and contemned are thought to be of no worth. I cannot be persuaded there should be so much ill luck in us as there is apparent vanity, nor so much malice as sottishness. We are not so full of evil, as of voidness and inanity. We are not so miserable, as base and abject.

That is Florio. This is the revised Cotton:

And I think we can never be despised according to our full desert. Compassion and bewailing seem to imply some esteem of and value for the thing bemoaned; whereas the things we laugh at are by that expressed to be of no moment. I do not think that we are so unhappy as we are vain, or have in us so much malice as folly; we are not so full of mischief as inanity; not so miserable as we are vile and mean.

The phrases are often identical in the two. Yet, though a favourable example of the new version, despite Florio's redundancies,
there is a marrowy flavour which gives him the advantage. There
had been better ground for Mr. Hazlitt's labour, we think, in a
revised Florio.

The modern essay is strictly thematic: Montaigne is a licenced
rover. He boasts his roving, and says his best things by way of
excursion. Yet he has that pleasant and wise worldliness which
gives Horace immortal modernity; and he has the special link with
our day, that he is a typical agnostic. For the man who likes
to read "about it, and about it," and to read exceeding shrewd
and sagacious discourse "about it," Montaigne is treasure-trove.
For the man wishing some issue of so much and various meditation,
he may be exasperating. "My mistress-form" (says he in Florio's
phrase) "is ignorance" — *i. e.*, the agnostic spirit. Do you list to
be told (after the manner of the connoisseur in the *Vicar of Wake-
field*) that "there is much to be said on both sides," Montaigne is
the man to tell you how much. But you "don't seem to get much
forrader," and if you are of a mind with Punch's farmer, this may
fatigue you. There was no pole-star in Montaigne's astronomy;
his planets were interesting complexities, which in their curious
evolutions had no ascertainable sun, — and the sun, to his mind,
did not really matter. There was quite enough fun in watching
the planets, and throwing out speculations concerning their law
of motion, any of which might be the true one — or might not be.
Did it matter? The game was the thing. The object of the chase
was the chase, not the fox. You enjoyed yourself quite as much
though the fox saved his brush. He had as lief Truth got away, as
nose her to her burrows and send in the ferrets. You could hunt
her another day. He had no zeal after Truth, but only after the
search of her. In a characteristic passage of the essay on Coaches,
he says:

It is very easy to verify, that great authors, when they write of causes,
not only make use of those they think to be the true causes, but also of those
they believe not to be so, provided they have in them some beauty and
invention: they speak true and usefully enough, if it be ingeniously. We
cannot make ourselves sure of the supreme cause, and therefore crowd a
great many together, to see if it may not accidentally be amongst them.

And he proceeds to quote from the sceptic poet, Lucretius, a passage to the like effect. It is all absolute Montaigne. His eye is always upon "invention," or as we should say, originality. That an opinion be established, is enough reason for him to examine it. His keenness for truth is negative — that he may dissect and refute what is false, rather than demonstrate what is true. Of the apostolic injunction to prove all things, and hold fast what is good, he obeys the first half. He proves — *i. e.*, tests — all things. His criticism is a dissolving acid. But when it comes to deciding what is finally true, he prefers to play with a number of possibilities, and leave the reader to decide. Only on practical matters, of conduct and the like, will he pronounce; and then it is mostly an "I myself prefer," "as I think," or the like: so temperamentally does he shrink from the responsibility of fundamental decision.

Such a temper could have no hates and no enthusiasms. For this sceptic turn is with him no mere mental attitude: it throws deep roots into his whole physical organism, and is indeed as much physical as intellectual. In the same characteristic essay he says:

I do not find myself strong enough to sustain the force and impetuosity of this passion of fear, nor of any other vehement passion whatever: if I was once conquered and beaten down by it, I should never rise again very sound. Whoever should once make my soul lose her footing, would never set her upright again: she retastes and researches herself too profoundly, and too much to the quick, and therefore would never let the wound she had received heal and cicatrise. . . . I have no after-game to play: on which side soever the inundation breaks my banks, I lie open, and am drowned without remedy. Epicurus says, that a wise man can never become a fool; I have an opinion, reverse to this sentence, which is, that he who has once been a very fool, will never after be very wise. God grants me cold according to my cloth, and passions proportionable to the means I have to withstand them: nature . . . having disarmed me of strength, she has armed me with insensibility and an apprehension that is regular or, if you will, dull.

There you have the temperamental soil of this shrewd but indecisive intellect; a nature constitutionally unable to support any vehemence of passion or affections, and always sedulously providing against their approach within striking-distance. A man not only without enthusiasms, but fearing and guarding himself from them; dreading nothing so much as to lose for a moment the even keel of his judgment. As himself records in this essay, with a nice sense of subtle connection, this temperamental aversion extended even to physical agitation; he was qualmish at the irregular motions of a small boat, the jolting of coaches (and coaches did jolt in those days) or the shaking of litters. He was a born Moderate in all things, esteeming nothing so much as quiet and the shunning of extremes in mind or action. His introspectiveness is both a source and a result of his indecisive temper. Very significant is that saying, that his soul "retastes and researches herself too profoundly and too much to the quick" for her to recover any shock to her self-esteem. There is so much of Hamlet in Montaigne, that one is not surprised there should be traces of Montaigne in *Hamlet*. We might well believe that it was Montaigne who suggested Hamlet to the great dramatist. Hamlet is Montaigne with an imagination, a Teutonic Montaigne, visited with that very inundation of passion and fear which Montaigne dreaded for himself, and breaking down under the visitation, with its call for violent action. His soul is, indeed, unable to right itself from the shock to its self-esteem. Montaigne sketched a possible tragedy in a nature like his own; and *Hamlet* is the working-out of it, on the stage of a like but more exalted soul. If Bacon had aught to do with Shakespeare, he might well have suggested this theme. For Montaigne was the very writer to commend himself to the opportunist and temporising Bacon, himself an essayist.

It is part of this ruling disposition that he delights to expatiate on the immensity of things men do not know, and the insecurity of the things they conceit themselves to know:

We do not go; we rather run up and down, and whirl this way and that; we turn back the way we came. I am afraid our knowledge is weak in all senses; we neither see far forward nor far backward; our understanding comprehends little and lives but a little while. . . . Though all that has arrived, by report, of our knowledge of times past should be true, and known by some one person, it would be less than nothing in comparison of what is unknown. And of this same image of the world, which glides away while we live upon it, how wretched and limited is the knowledge of the most curious; not only of particular events, . . . but of the state of great governments and nations, a hundred more escape us than ever come to our knowledge. . . . There is nothing single and rare in respect of nature, but in respect of our knowledge, which is a wretched foundation whereon to ground our rules, and that represents to us a very false image of things.

There have you a catholic profession of agnosticism, which is an excellent foundation for a man with an insatiable curiosity, and a constitutional dislike to deciding anything. No less did Montaigne's temperament favour his adoption of the rule that nature (by which he meant inclination) was a safe guide in life. A disposition which not only lacked but dreaded any strong passion might follow its bias without danger of betrayal into obvious and unseemly disorders. The worst peril of such a nature is egotism; and balanced by native horror of "giving oneself away," egotism is not an overt or offensive vice. Montaigne had it in heaped-up measure; but one may be sure he was too conscious of having it, and too little assertive, for it to jar upon the vanity of his fellows. You may be as egotistic as you please, provided you are alive to, and manage the vanity of others. Montaigne was too shrewd a contemner of human nature, not to practise the propitiation of it. He was for tolerating in others the weaknesses he knew in himself: which is the worldly substitute for theological charity.

There is his congeniality, his appeal, in a literary sense of the word, his greatness. He was the keenest, most cultivated, most alert, most sagacious man of the world who had found voice in literature since Horace. One is never tired of admiring his strong sense, his balance, his practical discernment, his perfect grip of that golden mean in all mundane matters, which every man of the world aims to have. And all this is recommended by a richly idiomatic and sap-fed style, by the flavour of a ripe and scholarly mind, turned to the sun of many literatures. Intensely curious concerning all life, and most of all his own, he talks of all things and interests us, but most when he talks of himself. That grew more and more his theme; and his interest grows with his egotism. He is one of the men who could talk immortally about themselves; and perhaps there is nothing so interesting on paper as this which disgusts in the chamber. He is loved by posterity because he loved himself — artistically.

ITALIAN LITERATURE

A HISTORY OF ITALIAN LITERATURE *
[*Academy*, May 14, 1898]

Here, as usual, Thompson is amused rather than angered by Garnett's prejudices bordering on bigotry, where things Catholic are concerned. He treats the matter seriously, but lightly, and passes on to an objective criticism of the volume. In the process, his clear thinking is expressed in language of acknowledged indebtedness to Mrs. Meynell, whose subtleties of thought and expression he so admired, and to Coventry Patmore, whom he found "rich enough to lend to the poor," in more than poetry.

THIS volume is the fourth in the series of *Short Histories of the Literatures of the World*. It is well arranged and perspicuous, written in lucid and cultivated style, with the scholarly refinement and wide knowledge of various literatures which we associate with Dr. Garnett. Only here and there are we disturbed in the full acceptance of his conclusions by a passing doubt as to the entire impeccability of his taste; when, for example, he classes Byron with Goethe and Shelley as modern masters of sublimity, or talks with most unnecessarily exalted respect of Bryant's respectable "Thanatopsis." The one real failing on which we are inclined to remonstrate with him is an insistent obtrusion of controversial matter, which might have been avoided or minimised in a history of literature, and a *naïf* partiality where such matter presents itself. A single instance is so unconsciously amusing that we may cite it. Cardinal Guido Bentivoglio, a Papal nuncio, wrote a history of the revolt of the Netherlands. It is, says Dr. Garnett, "necessarily defective as coming from the wrong side." Not, you observe, because it is the work of a partisan, but because it is the work of a partisan "on the wrong side" — the side, that is, opposed to Dr. Garnett's sympathies. If a book happen to be the work of a partisan on the "right

* *A History of Italian Literature*. By Richard Garnett.

419

side," Dr. Garnett figuratively backs it for all it is worth. Another drawback inevitable to all such work is the inefficiency of most poetical translations. In the early portion we have the invaluable aid of Rossetti's versions; but in the later part, except for the late Mr. Symonds and some very pleasing specimens by Miss Ellen Clarke, the translations mostly leave us in darkness, with an impression that the merit we are invited to see in the originals must be wholly a merit of diction and external form, which has evaporated in transmission.

The first sensation, when we have laid down the book, is a sensation of disappointment. Accustomed to our own opulent literature, Italian literature seems such an unexpectedly small thing. We expect that behind the world-wide names known by repute to every cultivated general reader we shall be introduced to a feast of lesser, yet distinguished glories. But expectation is foiled. When the trees are cleared whose spreading branches fill the foreground of literary history, there is revealed only a sparsely verdurous tract, which would pass unnoticed in any of the great spaces of English literature. The reason of this is indicated by Dr. Garnett in his preface. Italian literature, great though it be, is not the chief outcome of the Italian mind. Why this should be so Mrs. Meynell has shown in an unrepublished essay. The racial gift of the Latin nations, she says, is *intelligence*, of the Teutons *intellect*. The Latin has the outward eye, the quick, sympathetic receptivity of the child: he is intelligent. And this makes for art, for acting. The Teuton is not a born actor, a born artist (take him in general); he lacks the childlike intelligent receptivity, the quick telepathy between eye and hand, passion and word, impulse and gesture: he is too slow, inward, and reflective; he is too intellectual. But this, which is our loss in art and acting, is our gain in literature. It is our prerogative that we are an intellectual nation, that our greatness is insurpassably seated in literature. Our masterpieces do not fill the galleries of Europe, because our gallery of poets is the richest the world has seen. Our actors are hopelessly inferior to the actors of the South, because our drama is the greatest in Europe. From this distinction of national character it comes that Italian literature is after all a limited thing by the side of ours. Coventry Patmore, in what Dr. Garnett calls "a very just remark," though he does not quote it textually, observed that Italian poetry was marked by acuteness rather than breadth; that Dante was to Shakespeare as the Peak of Teneriffe to the Tableland of Thibet. And on Dante really rests the greatness of Italian literature — at least its main greatness. Besides Shakespeare, we have ourselves only one other poet of supreme rank. But our poetry does not drop plumb from Shakespeare as does the poetry of Italy from Dante tò Ariosto, Tasso, and Petrarch. It descends by equal steps through Milton, Chaucer, Spenser, to Wordsworth, Coleridge, and the rest — Wordsworth and Coleridge, if essence is to rank before length, being in our humble opinion greater than any of Dante's successors. But the stream of Italian energy which flowed into the mould of literature was a small portion of the nation's energies. The intelligent genius of Italy was mainly occupied in producing the most wonderful succession of artists in Europe. The marvel is that she had yet energy left over to create the second greatest literature in Europe.

It is a curious fact, disclosed by Dr. Garnett, that Italian literature can hardly be said to have had beginnings. A little ring of poets singing at Palermo, under the patronage of Frederick II of Germany, on Provençal models, but in Tuscan dialect — that is the first trace we get of it. And then we come immediately upon the forerunners of Dante. Here is a charming lyric by Frederick himself, who wrote better than his namesake the Great, if he did not fight better.

> "Each morn I hear his voice bid them
>   That watch me, to be faithful spies
>   Lest I go forth to see the skies;
> Each night to each he saith the same;
>   And in my soul and in mine eyes
>   There is a burning heat like flame."
>
> Thus grieves she now; but she shall wear
>   This love of mine whereof I spoke
>   About her body for a cloak,
> And for a garland in her hair,
>   Even yet; because I mean to prove,
>   Not to speak only, this my love.

By this Sicilian school the seed was sown, and it was from Provence that the inspiration came, as from Italy came the inspiration of the early Elizabethans. The seed sprang up with marvellous rapidity. Guittone d'Arezzo is the first conspicuous name of the indigenous Italian school which quickly followed these Provençalised Sicilians; conspicuous because he was the first who gave its permanent shape to that peculiarly Italian form, the sonnet. Then the Florentine school starts into being with Guido Guinicelli, and treading on his heels came Guido Cavalcanti, who eclipsed him, in turn to give place to Dante, the eclipser of all. Thus, in the very outset, with unparalleled swiftness, Italian poetry reached the greatest height it ever attained. The two forms which Dante's predecessors established in permanent use were the sonnet and the less-known *canzone* — less-known in England. The *canzone* has variations in form; but of the most typical Dr. Garnett gives a specimen in a fragment from Cavalcanti. Since the form is so unfamiliar to Englishmen, we may quote it.

> But when I looked on death, made visible
>> From my heart's sojourn brought before mine eyes,
>> And holding in his hand my grievous sin,
> I seemed to see my countenance, that fell,
>> Shake like a shadow: my heart uttered cries,
>> And my soul wept the curse that lay therein.
>> Then Death: "Thus much thine urgent prayer shall win:
> I grant thee the brief interval of youth
>> At natural pity's strong soliciting."
> And I (because I knew that moment's ruth
> But left my life to groan for a frail space)
> Fell in the dust upon my weeping face.

Over Dante himself we need not pause. Dr. Garnett himself recognises the necessity of taking the reader's Dantean knowledge largely for granted, so vast is the theme. Along with him was a band of other poets, who may be studied in Rossetti's *Dante and His Circle;* most conspicuous, perhaps, after Cavalcanti, at once his predecessor and contemporary, being Cino da Pistoia, in whom may be recognised echoes of Dante, as in Dante the influence of Cavalcanti is traceable enough. But one thing should be noted, which is generally overlooked, that in Dante we have also the beginnings of Italian prose, as well as the high-water mark of Italian poetry. The greater part of the *Vita Nuova* is, after all, prose, and very distinguished prose.

After the passing of Dante and the *trecentisti*, another flower-time of Italian literature bursts upon us in the latter fourteenth century, with the advent of Lorenzo de' Medici and the Renascence. Lorenzo was himself a poet, elegant if not powerful; and about him arose a race of poets. Politian, famous for his Latin writings, left us also vernacular poems of great grace and polish. His lyric tragedy, *Orfeo*, marks the beginnings of the Italian drama — never a very strong plant. The *Giostra* celebrates a tournament of which Giuliano de' Medici was the hero, and the prince's love for Simonetta. But Politian's minor poems are his best. Of this period, however, the ultimate outcomes are Petrarch and Boccaccio. What Boccaccio did for the prose of Italy needs no recounting. Italian became a prose language in his hands. But his poems are also among the permanent things of literature, though overshadowed by the glories of Petrarch. Petrarch's famous series of sonnets and *canzoni*, the zenith of Italian lyric poetry, is known to all men by name; but beyond the fact that his mistress was named Laura, and that he was crowned in the Capitol, few Englishmen have any practical knowledge of him. Truth is, he does not bear translation. Only a Rossetti would have had much chance with poems so dependent on their beauty of diction; and Rossetti's tastes did not lie in the Petrarchan line. From Surrey and his compeers downward, Petrarch has been sometimes translated, more often imitated, by Englishmen; but no poet and no versifier has succeeded in naturalising him, as Dante has been naturalised by Rossetti, or Tasso by Fairfax. We quote a specimen of his sonnets, which is perhaps as near the original as our language will allow:

> Exalted by my thought to regions where
> I find whom earthly quest hath never shown,
> Where Love hath rule 'twixt fourth and second zone;
> More beautiful I found her, less austere.
> Clasping my hand, she said, "Behold the sphere

> Where we shall dwell, if Wish hath truly known.
> I am, who wrung from thee such bitter moan;
> Whose sun went down ere evening did appear.
> My bliss, too high for men to understand,
> Yet needs thee, and the veil that so did please,
> Now unto dust for briefest season given."
> Why ceased she speaking? Why withdrew her hand?
> For, rapt to ecstasy by words like these,
> Little I wanted to have stayed in heaven.

Mr. Symonds' versions are good as anything we possess, short of Rossetti's poetic inspiration. Assuredly we get beauty here. Yet, in English, we feel the Dantean mysticism, without the arduous simplicity which compels belief in Dante. No, Petrarch must be read in the original.

This period also saw the flourishing of the Italian *novelisti*, on whom our dramatists drew so largely for their plots; masters of the "short story" as it presented itself to the *naïf* and leisurely mind of that age. Some of them were also poets; and from one of them (Sacchetti) we take a charming lyric of the pastoral order, which exemplifies the concluding phase of fourteenth century lyricism:

> I think your beauties might make fair complaint
>   Of being thus shown ever mount and dell;
> Because no city were so excellent
>   But that your stay therein were honourable.
>   In very truth, now does it like you well
> To live so poorly on the hillside here?

> "Better it liketh one of us, pardie,
>   Behind her flock to seek the pasture-stance,
> Far better than it liketh one of ye
>   To ride unto your curtained rooms and dance.
>   We seek no riches, neither golden chance
> Save wealth of flowers to weave into our hair."

> Behold, if I were now as once I was,
>   I'd make myself a shepherd on some hill,
> And without telling anyone, would pass,
>   Where these girls went, and follow at their will.
>   And "Mary," and "Martin," we would murmur still,
> And I would be for ever where they were.

With the fifteenth century, prose subsided, giving place to Latin, the learned tongue; and poetry developed in the direction of the romantic epic. Sannazaro also set the model of the pastoral romance, followed by Montemayor in Spain, and by Sidney's "Arcadia" in England. The cycle of the Charlemagne legends was exploited. Pulci wove it into the "Morgante Maggiore," whence ultimately came Byron's "Don Juan," through Pulci's more burlesque successor, Berni. Boiardo constructed from the same source the "Orlando Innamorato," only to be overshadowed by Ariosto's "Orlando Furioso." Yet how little it deserved such a fate may be seen from the lovely passage quoted by Dr. Garnett, in which Rinaldo is attacked by Love and his attendant ladies. They beat him with rose-garlands, pelt him with flowers, and Love strikes him down with a tall lily-stem; leaving him bruised and discomforted by the magical assault — a charming allegorical fancy.

The sixteenth century saw the restoration of prose by the great historian Guicciardini and the famous Machiavelli. It saw also the learned and artificial genius of Cardinal Bembo, the friend of Michelangelo's friend, Vittoria Colonna. Alas for romance! He seems to have possessed more authority with her than the great painter. But the poets of the age were a poor set. It was the day of the Petrarchists, who possessed nothing of Petrarch's genius — Molza, Bernardo Tasso, Annibale Caro. But the great Torquato Tasso came to redeem it with the "Jerusalem Delivered" and the "Aminta." Guarini followed with the "Pastor Fido" — the model of Fletcher's "Faithful Shepherdess." The seventeenth century saw the ascendency of Marini, whose "conceited" style did much to mar Crashaw and the other English poets of the same day. Chiabrera, Redi, Filicaja, struck a manlier lyric note; so did Campanella, the author of some very fine and noble sonnets. But it was the setting of the sun. The eighteenth century paralysed poetic poetry in Italy as in England; though it saw the culmination of the Italian drama in Metastasio, the virile Alfieri, and the comedies of Goldoni. But Italy's drama was a poor thing at its best compared with France or Germany, much less England or Spain. With the nineteenth century came revival. Monti, Ugo Foscolo, Manzoni, all introduced a fresh lyric fervour, leading up to the modern

Italian literature of Leopardi and his successors. It is a feature of Dr. Garnett's excellent little book that he brings it down to date, considering at length even so recent a writer as "D'Annunzio."

It is, you will see, a scanty succession of really great names compared with our own gloriously rich literary history. For that very reason Dr. Garnett has been able to do better justice to it within a brief compass than would have been possible in the case of our own literature. A similar review of English authors would become a mere dry skeleton of a book. That Dr. Garnett's emphatically is not. It is well-proportioned, interesting, and scholarly, from start to finish, and should become a useful and popular handbook for those who seek an introduction to the second greatest literature of Europe.

THE STUDY OF DANTE *
[*Outlook*, August 27, 1898]

Criticism of a commentary would seem to be too removed from the poem itself to add to its appreciation. But no one who has read Gardner's study and Thompson's review can fail thereafter to experience increased delight in the greatest of Catholic poems.

WHEN we survey the studies of Dante with which the Press now teems, it seems incredible that in the 'thirties Dante was but the shadow of a name in England. Perhaps the revival of interest in him dates chiefly from the advent of Rossetti and his Italianising disciples. We are making up leeway with enthusiasm; and where the supply of Dante literature is so full, we may hope it signifies a like demand. Both the books which head this article can be commended to readers. Miss Phillimore's is popular — a picture of Dante's last days at Ravenna, written in a style attractive to all. Mr. Gardner's work is a book for the Dantean student—a commentary, and incomparably the best commentary on the "Paradiso"

---

* *Dante at Ravenna*. By Catherine Phillimore. *The Ten Heavens of Dante*. By Edmund Gardner.

with which we are acquainted in English. He has not only studied the chief commentaries, ancient and modern, the range of modern Dantean literature, and the collateral Italian writers to whom Dante directly or indirectly refers; he has also gone to the trouble of making himself elaborately acquainted with the mediæval system of theology — and, still more, philosophy — upon which the "Paradiso" is based; with Aquinas, and St. Bernard, and Dionysius the Areopagite. Moreover, he has sought the direction of modern experts on these points. The result is a book which the serious reader and student will find invaluable. It is complete, it is interesting, it is cultivated and scholarly. No English writer has dealt with the elucidation of the "Paradiso" in a manner so full, learned, and sympathetic.

Such a book was needed. The "Paradiso" is the most neglected portion of the *Divine Comedy*. It is entangled with the subtleties of scholastic philosophy; and only of late years has that philosophy begun to find students in England. To take a course of scholastic philosophy in order to read Dante is too much to ask of readers. Mr. Gardner has now spared them the task, and they may thank him for smoothing the ways of what Carlyle considered the supreme portion of the "Divine Poem." Assuredly it was not the scholastic technicalities which won Carlyle — least exact of thinkers — or won any of the great English lovers of the "Paradiso." These things are there: they complete, from an intellectual standpoint, the beauty of the "Paradiso," when they are rightly understood; wherefore the necessity of such a rigid and perspicuous commentary as that of Mr. Gardner. But outside any commentary is that which makes the "Paradiso" an astonishing poem. What is it?

It is not to be delivered in flashing epigram and paradox. One may deal so with Byron, not with Wordsworth. One may deal so with Pope, not with Coleridge. And assuredly one cannot deal so with Dante, and, above all, the Dante of the "Paradiso." It is a certain marvellous austerity of enticement, the asceticism of loveliness, the white light of intellectuality; an exquisitely choice apparel through which one feels the hair-shirt. It is a macerated beauty. Take, for example, the way in which the successive apparitions of the blessed souls are managed. It is spiritual to a rare degree.

By imagery drawn from human experience, Dante yet contrives to suggest a realm beyond all human experience. The grandiose imagery of the Miltonic heaven seems earthly and concrete beside this subtle suggestion of unearthly effects, evanescent as the thinnest phenomena of sunset and the remotest stellar heavens. Consider that exquisite description of the spirits in the circle of the Moon; beautiful female forms like reflections in lucid glass or translucent tenuous water. As the poet mounts higher, the spirits appear to us as the taper-flames of the altar, exalted to heavenly brilliance; as stars and constellations, but stars and constellations such as the poet only sees, the poetical transfiguration conveyed to us by the most marvellous suggestiveness of seemingly simple language. The supreme joy of the transcendentalised spirits is signified to us through those celestial dances, described in the most Uranian imagery, which seem (singularly enough) to be a stumbling-block to Mr. Gardner. They are altogether in accordance with the mediæval mind, which inhernted this expression of religious joyousness from the pagan ritual, wherein the religious dance played a prominent part. Nay, in a certain place of Spain the dance before the altar was a part of the ritual of the Mass. In the ancient religions it was regarded as an image of that dance of the spheres whereby the heavens set forth the divine harmony, the joy of conformity to its law.

This brings us to a point more requiring comment than the spiritual beauty of the "Paradiso," which all really great Englishmen are agreed in praising. We mean that union of pagan mythology with Christian teaching which (both in Dante and Milton) has been a stumbling-block to otherwise sympathetic critics. "Incongruous!" they cry. But it was not incongruous to the early Christians, who freely adapted both pagan mythology and philosophy. Neither was it incongruous to Dante. He discerned (what the early Christians discerned) the immense body of truth in heathen mythology, waiting only for its final application. In the work of some modern mystical poets nothing is more conspicuous than their blending of revived heathen myths with Christianity. The Golden Bough of Virgil, the Mistletoe of the Druids, symbolise the grafting of the Divinity on the humanity. So also the rudest early myths. Such is the meaning of that unbeautiful legend which relates how Baal cut off his head, and blending the blood with clay, kneaded it into man. It signifies the creation of the Perfect Man by the mingling of the spirit of the Divinity with the clay of imperfect humanity. Such intuition into heathen symbolism, such profound sense of analogy, presides over Dante's scheme of intermixture, nowise incongruous to those who can follow the inner harmony.

And this, finally, this deep use of analogy, is the most wonderful thing in the "Paradiso"; more wonderful than those external poetic qualities which have ravished the greatest throughout all ages. Not merely analogy between Paganism and Christianity. Its whole system is one in which type calls to type through an infinite ascending series; and the notes he strikes wake a vast sequence of harmonic echoes, dying away in "the intense inane." It will never be popular like the "Inferno." But to the few it will always be the consummate revelation of Dantean power. And even to the general reader, can there be anything more ethereally beautiful than that final vision of the "Rose of Heaven," where the closing strain, with dizzied wings, dies away in celestial impotence?

> Here vigour failed the lofty fantasy:
> But now was turning my desire and will,
> Even as a wheel that equally is moved,
> The Love which moves the sun and the other stars.

AND YET — HE IS A MASTER *
[*Academy*, June 2, 1900]

This is the type of review that shows Thompson at his best. His reasoned condemnation of the theme is strong and uncompromising, but he has high praise for D'Annunzio's technique. In giving a criticism of D'Annunzio's novel, he gives, as well, an appraisal of the best and worst elements in all decadent literature.

D'ANNUNZIO is a master of unquestionable genius in a very questionable school. It is the school which makes parade of the fact

* *The Dead City*. By Gabriele d'Annunzio. Translated by Arthur Symons.

that it is the offspring of decay, which seeks its charm in decay, and has veritably "made a covenant with death." Exceedingly perfect in technique, vividly imaginative, his masterly novels are impregnated with corruption in a much deeper sense than that of mere sensuality — though this at times is present. To him and the writers of his school we are often tempted to cry with Macbeth: "Out on ye, owls! nothing but songs of death?" And yet — he is a master!

This latest play of D'Annunzio's is most typical of its author and of a moribund age and art. As a play it is over-soft, over-luxuriant. The copious stage directions of Maeterlinck are carried to an excess in which one sees the novelist. They become veritable descriptive passages. Withal, it is most powerful in its kind, its strictly limited kind, though that is not the power of strength nor yet of spiritual insight. Infinitely delicate razor-edge of sensation pervades the play: its people see with their finger-tips, feel at every pore; but it is yet a purely material sensitiveness, it is subtilised, one might almost say volatilised, materiality. Symbolic it is throughout; but the symbolism is of the tomb. Incidents are artfully introduced, Maeterlinck-wise, and emphasised, for their figurative and bodeful significance. The scene is laid in Argos, looking out on the ashes of Mycenæ — a sultry and thirsting soil, an expired and dismembered city. The atmosphere is laden with death, the characters are marked with death like decaying or over-ripe plants; and, unlike Shakespeare, there is no character to suggest, however tacitly, the sanity from which the others deflect. A luxuriant and most sensitive beauty overspreads this dramatic cemetery, peopled by the mad. The whole play palpitates with a deadly beauty, a mortal and ruinous loveliness, which shines as putrescence shines. Our phrase is not overstrained; delirium seems not far from all D'Annunzio's characters; we feel as if we were in an asylum for diseased minds, where the ideas of everyone are monstrous and distorted, like shadows cast by firelight. The blind girl, Anna, at the very outset recounts a dream of sudden age — a dream undreamed by the sane, just possible in its hideousness to dawning madness: "I felt furrowing wrinkles breaking out all over my body; I felt the hairs falling from my head in great locks on my lap, and my fingers tangled in them as in unwound skeins; my gums were emptied, and my lips stuck to them." She complains of the hurry of life in its morbid perception by her senses: "In the silence and darkness, sometimes, *I hear life hurrying with such a terrible noise*, Bianca Maria, that I would gladly die, only not to hear it any longer."

Much of the vividly imaginative speech in this drama, like the words we have italicised, oversteps the verge of sanity. The very skylarks are *fin-de-siècle*. "One," says Alessandro, "fell, all of a sudden, at the feet of my horse, heavy as a stone, and lay there, dead, struck by its own frenzy, by having sung with too much joy." It is only a decadent skylark that would do that.

This blind Anna is one of the principal personages. Beautiful, though blind, she is of a preternatural perceptiveness, not inconceivable in one so afflicted, and described with touches of exquisite passion and poetry. Her husband is Alessandro, a poet, and they are dwelling with his bosom friend Leonardo, who is wrapped in the search among the ruins of Mycenæ for the buried remains of the Atridæ and Cassandra — victims of the terrible tragedy renowned in Greek drama. With him is his lovely sister, Bianca Maria, glowing with the flame of youthful life, and magnetic to those about her. Leonardo's discovery of the buried Atridæ (magnificently described) takes place at the close of the first act, nor has his pursuit any obvious connexion with the plot; but it is continuously suggested that from the soil impregnated with ancient crime the buried spirit of dark Greek passions rises as an infection upon the living searchers, fevering them with the obsession of like sin. The working out of these morbid passions among the four constitutes the theme of the tragedy. Bianca Maria and Alessandro are violently drawn to each other; and the poet's blind wife, Anna, from the beginning divines their love. Leonardo is infected with a more sinister disease, obscure to the others, until he himself, half-way through the play, reveals it to the horrified Alessandro. For this latter reason we cannot here deal fully with the play. We can but indicate it as the theme of John Ford's well-known play, and (from a very different standpoint) the basis of "The Revolt of Islam," as Shelley originally wrote it. Lovers of contrast may compare Ford with D'Annunzio. The former is far the more healthy (so far as is possible with so morbid a theme) and dramatic; the latter more finished and levelly poetic — more an artist in all but dramatic power. When Leonardo realises that Bianca Maria is the source both of his own and Alessandro's obsession, and that Anna is preparing to drown herself in order to free her husband for the woman she loves as a sister, he comes to the delirious resolve to liberate them all by the death of Bianca Maria. The play closes as Anna stumbles upon the drowned body of Bianca Maria, tended by the poet that loved her and the brother that has murdered her.

This sombre plot, lavishly and resolvedly designed to play upon all the nerves of horror, is worked out with marvellous intimacy of execution. Dramatic character neither exists nor is attempted, save in the most generic way. Anna is other-worldly, outside life; Bianca Maria is intended for the embodiment of plenitudinous youth. Yet she is no less a creature of naked nerve than her avowedly neurotic friend. But if you can reconcile yourself to this universal super-exaltation of sensibility, there is tragic keenness and the bare edge of suffering beauty in the play. The Italian genius is visible, acute rather than wide, as a great writer has described it. "Pain is the exceedingly keen edge of bliss" in the most voluptuous passages. Written, for the most part, in a strain of eloquence shot with gleaming threads of poetry, it rises frequently into poetry absolute and unmingled. D'Annunzio is *fëy* of flowers. Their scent, their colour, their profusion fill his imagination and overflow continually into his imagery. They lend an exquisite metaphor to the lovely passage in which the blind Anna fingers the loosened tresses of Bianca Maria: "What hair! what hair! It is as soft to the fingers as tepid water flowing! . . . It is a torrent. It covers you all over. It covers me too. What floods! what floods! It has a perfume; it has a thousand perfumes. A torrent full of flowers!" Note that adjective "tepid," in its connexion with the living warmth of hair. The blind girl's exaltation of perception is most subtly described: "It is as if your fingers saw. . . . Each of your fingers is like an eyelid that presses upon one. Ah! it is as if your soul came down into the tips of your fingers, and the flesh lost its human nature." With the same beauty Bianca Maria is delineated: "The desire of life radiates from your body like the heat of a lighted hearth."

The first scene of the second act, in which Alessandro declares his love to Bianca Maria, is a marvellous piece of eloquent passion, with flashes of lyricism intensified by daring imagery. Too long, perhaps, for stage effect, and almost certainly too subtle for a popular audience, the speeches carry one away in the reading by their impassioned enchantment. Here are a few snatches:

Alessandro. I have met you in dreams as now I meet you in life. You belong to me as if you were my creation, formed by my hands, inspired by my breath. Your face is beautiful in me as a thought in me is beautiful. When your eyelids quiver it seems to me that they quiver like my blood, and that the shadow of your eyelashes touches the root of my heart.

Bianca Maria. Be silent! Be silent! I cannot breathe. Ah, I cannot live any longer, I cannot live any longer!

Alessandro. You cannot live if you do not live in me, for me, now that you are in my life as your voice is in your mouth. . . .

Bianca Maria. You exalt with your breath the humblest of creatures. I have been only a good sister. . . .

Alessandro. But was there not also another creature living beside the good sister? . . . Wherever there was a trace of the great myths or a fragment of the imaginings of beauty with which the chosen race transfigures the force of the world, she passed with her reviving grace, passing lightly over the distance of centuries as if she followed the song of the nightingale across a country strewn with ruins.

This is splendid writing. With Leonardo's communication to Alessandro of his dreadful secret, in the ensuing scene, begin the most darkly oppressive portions of the play, preluding to the final tragedy. It is not possible, nor perhaps desirable, to suggest by extracts the power of these repellent, yet subtle, scenes. But even this part is relieved — or perhaps intensified — by passages of contrasting beauty. Such is the wonderfully lovely imagery with which Anna describes the statues in fountains:

They enjoy, at the same time, rest and fluidity. In lonely gardens they sometimes seem in exile, but they are not; for their liquid soul never ceases to communicate with the far-off mountains, whence they come while yet asleep, and shut up in the mass of lifeless mineral. They listen astonished to the words that come into their mouth from the depths of the earth, but they are not deaf to the colloquies of poets and sages who love to repose there, as in a retreat, in the musical shade where marble perpetuates a calm gesture.

Of the final scene, powerful and intensely morbid, we can give no conception. The play, as a closet-drama, is, perhaps, near perfection in its decadent kind. Nor need we attempt more formal criticism. In this case, to describe is to criticise, to criticise is to describe. But we should add, in conclusion, that Mr. Arthur Symons' translation is admirable — nay, beautiful.

MYSTICISM:
GENUINE AND SPURIOUS

A PEOPLE "RELIGIOUS TO EXCESS" *
[*Academy*, May 29, 1897]

Thompson's remarks on the religious history of Egypt are pleasant but scarcely profound. However, they are adequate for the task at hand and reveal his reaction to purely man-made efforts that would bridge the gulf between the seen and the unseen.

A LAND divided into forty-two provinces, each possessing a god believed by his worshippers to be the creator and ruler of the universe; a people so obstinately conservative that they accepted new ideas only on condition that they did not abandon the old; and a history stretching over fifty centuries, during which the country was repeatedly conquered by foreign invaders, who brought their own gods with them when they came and left them behind them when they went away. If the reader can picture to himself the kaleidoscopic faith likely to result from these three causes, he will have some idea of the difficulty of producing a bird's-eye view of the religion of Ancient Egypt. Yet Dr. Wiedemann has performed this feat, and has performed it well. Wisely throwing aside any attempt to portray, as a whole, either the Egyptian Pantheon or the Egyptian creed, he has compressed into a volume of 300 pages an account which leaves little to be desired of the Egyptian religion as it affected the daily life of the people. Here, for instance, the uninstructed reader can learn in a pleasant and easy way the curious ideas of the Egyptians concerning the wanderings of the soul after death, their deification of the kings of the country, and the true reason of their worship of animals. If he chooses to go further, he will find in the same volume a sufficient

* *Religion of the Ancient Egyptians*. By Alfred Wiedemann.

description of their chief gods, of the gradual transformation of these last into solar deities, and of all the ceremonies of the Egyptian religion which have come down to us. Nor is this information imparted in the didactic or professorial manner. Everywhere Dr. Wiedemann gives us full translations of the texts on which his conclusions are based, and although he is, of course, obliged to take some things for granted, he most honestly warns us that "in the study of Egyptian religion, as in all other branches of Egyptology, our knowledge is as yet very imperfect." If any fault can be found with his work, it is that his translations do not always reach the high literary level of Prof. Maspero's.

The impression which the book will probably leave on the minds of most readers is that to the "plain man" of Ancient Egypt the worship of the gods was much less a religion than a sort of magic. Sublime and noble conceptions can, indeed, be found in many of the hymns here given; but there is no reason to suppose that they ever reached the ear of any Egyptian who was not either a king or a priest. For the rest of the nation the smallest action of daily life was presided over by some god or other, and the favour of this deity could be obtained with the certainty of a scientific experiment by the performance of the appropriate ceremony. Even in the next world the same theory held good. The path of the soul to perfect beatitude was supposed to be beset with terrible difficulties, but they could all be overcome by a knowledge of what may be irreverently called the rules of the game. At almost every step in the underworld the dead Egyptian found a well-guarded gate, which was only opened to him on the presentation of the proper amulet and the utterance of the proper password. Hence the best preparation for the world to come was thought to be, not good conduct in this life, but a map of the country and a good memory for its dangers as handed down by the priests. The power which this put into the hands of the priesthood can easily be seen, and the story of its abuse forms one of the saddest satires upon humanly invented religious institutions that can well be imagined. Well suited as the religion of Egypt was to a people who, as we are apt to forget, were, after all, Africans, in the outset, it rendered great services to civilisation, and remained tolerant and kindly to the end.

But the failure of Khuenaten's reform made it possible for the priests to grasp at political power, and from that moment it began to decay. At length it broke down under the intolerable weight of its own ceremonies and the idleness which it enforced on the greater part of the population, and when it finally vanished the backbone of the nation seems to have gone with it. Never since she abjured her old gods has Egypt been independent.

The volume before us is in every way an advance on the German edition with which scholars have hitherto had to content themselves. It contains some seventy well-chosen illustrations, has been brought up to date by the author, and has an excellent index. Dr. Wiedemann has also been lucky in his translator.

STUDIES OF ENGLISH MYSTICS *
[*Athenæum*, July 14, 1906]

Thompson recognized, thus early, the nature of Dean Inge's ideas that were destined, later, to such widespread notoriety when they were more boldly stated. Here, again, we see the result of Thompson's clear thinking on a subject so frequently treated with deliberate vagueness.

YET another book on mysticism! Of late years there has been a steady and continuous, if thin, supply of such books from the press; and it is not an insignificant sign of the times. With this smoke there must be some fire; the books (one conceives) presuppose some public. It is, we imagine, a reaction against the forces of materialism and agnosticism. But though this, in itself, may be a good sign, we have no love for popular mysticism. The terms "mystic" and "mysticism" are so loosely used, indeed, that one is never sure beforehand what may be meant by them. If a man turns a table or keeps a private "spook," he is a mystic; if he writes poems of a more or less spiritual order (and very little will do), he is a mystic;

* *Studies of English Mystics.* By William Ralph Inge.

if he writes about people who were considered mystics, he is himself a mystic; nay, if he writes about people who wrote about mysticism, he is a mystic. We should not be surprised if acquaintance with the differential calculus were held to constitute a man a mystic; for ordinary people do not understand it — and that is "mysticism." Nor do we think that amateur and undisciplined dalliance with what is called mysticism (even when such dalliance is not mainly curious rather than reverent) is likely to be a healthy influence on most lives. It must often mean mere religious wilfulness and whimsicality.

Apart from our distrust of all popularisation of "mysticism," however, we have no special quarrel with Dr. Inge's book, which is likely to be as little harmful as such books may be. Dr. Inge (we say it without offence) is something of a half-baked mystic. The ultimate end of all mystical writers is intimate personal union and intercourse with God; and a great part of the most eminent among these writers profess to deal with guidance towards such union. It is necessarily intimate, personal, and transcendental or (that dreaded word!) supernatural. That is the summit: there are many half-way houses, many chalets, the dwellers in which have not reached the summit. But they believe and are encouraged by the reports of those who have, no less than by their own experiences. Dr. Inge, however, is chiefly concerned with the occupants of the chalets and half-way houses, and with the dwellers on the summit only in so far as their experiences tally with those of the less advanced mystical writers. The vivid, but comparatively vague intuitions and apprehensions of the Divine presence and guidance which are the elementary stage in mystical treatises make to him all that is worth acceptance. The rest he calls imagination and subjective delusion — extravagance, word dear to the sober English mind!

For Dr. Inge is rootedly Britannic. He likes an airing among the heights, but always provides for his return to the safe domestic hearth. He will ramble appreciatively among the aerial utterances of the mystics, but when at the end of his pilgrimage he unloads his scrip, he offers you with a sigh of satisfaction some scraps of solid beef and mutton — most wholesome fare, but scarcely worth (one thinks) such laborious questing, when they might have been picked up nearer home. For this reason, however, Dr. Inge's mysticism is calculated to be more wholesome for those to whom this popular mysticism appeals. The average Englishman needs precisely religious beef and mutton; nor can he do himself much good by spasmodic, unguided attempts to fare "o' the chameleon's diet," for which he is wholly unfitted.

Dr. Inge's methods naturally issue in not a little vagueness. It is visible at the outset, when he discusses the nature of mysticism. There is nothing over which a true-bred Anglo-Saxon is more comfortably vague than a definition. Usually it proves to be a description — and loose enough even so. The simplest definition, in the present case, is for Dr. Inge as satisfactory as any — "Mysticism is the love of God." As well say that gastronomy is the love of food. It subserves the love of food, and so with mysticism. But neither is what it subserves.

The constitution of the book is significant, in view of what we have said concerning the author's limited acceptance of mystical writers and writings. He has a very catholic range of authors, and from each he quotes much that is interesting and illuminating. But they none of them go much beyond the more elementary stages of the mystical road: they are not "advanced" mystics. Perhaps John Law is an exception: by virtue not of his own experience, but on account of the ideas he borrowed from Boehme — and Dr. Inge shakes his head over the more transcendental of these. We hold no brief for any ideas, certainly not Boehme's; we merely note the fact as a symptom. It would be the same were they St. Teresa's (and, indeed, the author is still more emphatic about some of the advanced Catholic mystics).

Accepting his deliberate choice of limitations, we find much of interest in Dr. Inge's book. We have Julian (or Juliana) of Norwich, the recluse whose "revelation" has recently been reprinted and edited; a monastic countryman of hers from whom Dr. Inge cites some very fine things; William Law, whose *Serious Call* was once frequent in every serious household; and to conclude, studies of Wordsworth and Browning as mystics. Perhaps the most attractive of these is Julian, by reason of the tender simplicity and modesty which throw into relief some surprising flashes of deep intuition. But of most general interest will be the studies of the two poets, since most people think they know Wordsworth, and a considerable number would like to know Browning.

The "Wordsworth" is characteristic of the author's merits and limits. He reviews very sympathetically and intelligently the main features of the poet's teaching, nor does he neglect its more esoteric elements. He notes appreciatively those passages of "The Prelude," in particular, which (in Shelley's words) "waken a sort of soul in sense," so that the very rocks to the poet become vital and quick, and seem to impress themselves on his being. But when Dr. Inge sums up, to our surprise all these things, all the more esoteric features of Wordsworth are dismissed as something peculiar to the poet's own nature, not significant to other men. All Wordsworth's teaching which matters, we discover, is reducible to a practical aphorism or two of undeniable excellence and utility (so undeniable, indeed, that one thinks of Mrs. Gamp's illustrious remonstrance), but these things scarcely required a stout volume of very wordy poetry for their enunciation. "There needs no ghost, my lord, come from the grave To tell us this." But they are good, safe Anglo-Saxon truisms; moreover, they are undoubtedly taught by Wordsworth.

The "Browning" gives more result, for under Browning's obscurity there was concreteness; he himself had a decided relish for beef and mutton. But we arrive at the conviction that on Dr. Inge's premises all poets of any seriousness are mystics, and there is no particular reason why any other singer should not have figured in place of Browning. Any one who (in Browning's own words) "follows the inner light" is a mystic. A great many people may thank the writer after the manner of M. Jourdain: "For these many years I have been a mystic without knowing it; and I have all the obligation in the world to you for telling me of it!"

But whatever we may think of Dr. Inge's own conclusions, let us say distinctly that his analysis of these various writers is always lucid, tends to understanding and illumination; he knows how to treat interestingly what in many hands would be dry; he has done his work well, and will be read with interest even by those who dissent from his ideas and some of his judgments. Only why does

he say that Wordsworth was "afraid of passionate love"? He dis-
approved the "tumults of the soul"; but there is in him profound
passion (which is just the distinction between him and his imitators). How few understand that deep passion, like deep waters,
is strong and tranquil!

SOME MYSTICISMS AND A MYSTIC *
[*Academy*, April 14, 1900]

This review might well serve as a model for Catholic book reviewers. On
the one hand, Thompson does not praise the volume because it is an honest
effort by a Catholic writer. On the other, his condemnation is not prompted
by a cheap effort to appear broadminded. His conclusions are closely
reasoned and in nothing arbitrary. Of special significance are Thompson's
sage remarks on popularizing mysticism. What is said about Patmore's
mysticism is the best possible expression of what, in the work of the elder
and more philosophical poet, influenced and molded the life and thought
and later poetry of his disciple. It is natural that one so adroit in "suasive
exposition" should deprecate its lack in Thorold. In general, this review
exemplifies the fine, philosophical balance of Thompson's mind that was
the source of his reasoned opinions in literary matters.

WITH MR. THOROLD's aim I have every sympathy, if I rightly
understand it. He aspires to ingratiate Catholic mysticism with
the intelligent public; to divorce mysticism from its popular
association with Mr. John Wellington Wells and the saltatory
education of drawing-room tables. The motive is excellent, but it
comes to mean in practice the popularisation of mysticism, and I am
sure that popular mysticism is an evil thing. The precise aim of Mr.
Thorold's present book is to present "the constituents of mysticism," and (it must be assumed from the title-page) to illustrate
them from the writings of the Franciscan mystic, Angela da Foligno. I do not see that he has presented the constituents of mysticism. This is a pity, for he is a writer of considerable distinction as

* *An Essay in Aid of the Better Appreciation of Catholic Mysticism.* By Algar
Thorold. Illustrated from the Writings of Blessed Angela of Foligno.

regards style. His most profound and illuminatively original points are taken from Coventry Patmore, whom he has evidently studied. Not that I impeach the general originality of his treatise. I would he had taken more; above all, Mr. Patmore's perspicuous sense of order, his pregnant condensation and concentration upon his subject. Mr. Thorold divagates with exasperating fluency upon the slightest provocation. He cannot resist a controversial opening, however far it may lure him from the matter of his professed thesis. He thinks it necessary, "incidentally and by way of illustration," to describe "a hypothetical process of conversion, and also to suggest the sort of way in which the modern Catholic mystic may be disposed, for the sake of his own peace of mind, to meet some current objections to Catholic faith and practice." This incidental illustration ultimately occupies the greater part of the treatise. I presume that I am more or less a "mystic," in Mr. Thorold's loose sense of the term; but it is not for my peace of mind to pursue and criticise him through his "incidental" divagation, and divagations upon divagation. I cannot see that they are "necessary," nor why they should absorb needful space. A controversy on "Bible Christianity," for example — what is it doing in this galley, or will it conciliate the outsider's sympathies towards mysticism? Suasive exposition should surely be the means employed. He elaborately piles the arguments for scepticism drawn from physical science, merely to explain that the "natural mystic" will start from a quite other basis of thought. Why waste time in such elaborate entrenchments if you intend to pass them by and leave them *en l'air?* And again, what a far cry from the "constituents of mysticism"!

This controversial zeal leads him into rash statements. "To the man of mystical temperament, . . . and to him only, is the message of the [Catholic] Church addressed." A tremendous limitation for a body Catholic! Or would Mr. Thorold persuade a consensus of theologians to endorse "the fact that it was the fall of Lucifer, rather than that of Adam, which for the first time introduced moral evil, with all its possible consequences, into the Creation"? This "fact" (a bold word!) sweeps away the traditional innocuousness of Eden; for Mr. Thorold means the physical

Creation. *Mais enfin*, these constituents of mysticism? After this preparatory labour, there crawls forth (to my eyesight, at least) but one. Adopting Coventry Patmore's view, that the supreme justification of dogma is the psychological value of the truth it contains, he bases mysticism on the doctrine of the Creation. He shows (to state it briefly) that full acceptation of that doctrine implies the subjection of the whole man in his whole being to God. But this is the basis of all true Christian life, and only the basis of mysticism insomuch as mysticism is the furthest and logical outcome, the ultimate flower, of true Christian life. It is not a specific basis. Nor does it help the reader to understand what mysticism specifically is. Yet beyond this and an historical introduction (which has its own elements of disproportion) there seems to me nothing to prepare the unaccustomed reader for the highly mystical writings of Angela da Foligno which follow — abruptly and without comment. He steps into them as from a bathing-machine — and I can fancy may gasp. Valuable for the acquainted student, they do not appear a good choice as an intro- duction to mysticism. They contain many "hard sayings," and the earlier portions have much of the physical character so repel- lent to the outsider. Even on the average Catholic some things will come with a douche of surprise.

I am sorry to say these things, for Mr. Thorold writes well, and there is method in his long approach. But he has a crocodile unwieldiness in revolving on his own axis. Lack of proportion crowds out or attenuates the central matter — which is surely the nature of mysticism. If he does not actually leave the rails, he is yet too fond of loop-lines.

The mystic is not (as Mr. Thorold's use of the word would seem to countenance) a student of mysticism, any more than a scientist is one who studies books on science. Nor yet is he a *devotee*, a devout practiser of religion. Mysticism is an interior ladder, at the summit of which is God. The mystic endeavours, by a rigid practical virtue, combined with prayer, meditation, and mortification of the senses, to arrive at a closer union with the Creator. Union with God is proposed as the state of the future life, and therefore the ultimate end of the Christian. But mysticism holds that some degree of such union is possible in this life. It is the belief of Plato no less than St. John of the Cross. There is an indwelling of the Divinity in every Christian. "Know ye not that ye are a temple of God, and that the Spirit of God dwelleth in you?" But the gradual purification of body and soul, with the turning of the whole man towards God, permits the Deity to flow in with a greater closeness, until there is finally accomplished, if not the spousal union of the next life, at any rate a betrothal union, we may say.

> These are only your espousals; yes,
> More intimate and fruitfuller far
> Than aptest mortal nuptials are.

Such, in brief, is the theory of mysticism. Its principles are many and not in a few words to be laid down. For it is no *terra incognita;* from the recorded experience of mystics the whole process has been mapped out elaborately. This *mystical theology*, as it is called, serves, however, mainly for the instruction of directors who have to deal with such persons. The mystic himself can pursue no beaten track, no guide-book path. The way to God is through Himself, and is conditioned by His Own nature. It is alike for no two men. And it is the study of its adaptation to the personality which is so psychologically interesting in the writings of individual mystics.

The process varies indefinitely with the individual concerned. "The mystic is the religious genius," says Mr. Thorold, and there is profound truth of analogy in the saying. But that mysticism has no necessary connexion with natural genius there could not be a better proof than his chosen instance, Angela da Foligno. Her psychological interest resides largely in the fact that she was the reverse of a "genius." In the unconscious betrayal and characteristic savour of her writings, she appears obviously to be by nature a very little woman, a woman of bounded and self-conditioned mind, with all that incapacity of vital conception outside the personal environment which Ruskin grieved over in her sex. Not for her a large and impersonal outlook. A young married woman, of irregular life previous to her entering upon the mystical way, she seems (if one may trust her own violent self-accusations) to have combined actual laxity with a show of religiosity. Among her latest and most serious sacrifices to the new way of life she mentions head-tires and the like beloved feminine adornments. At a yet later stage of her spiritual preparation, she makes the *naïf* confession that she ceased to laugh at Petruccio. Clearly a light damsel, to whom this unindentified Peterkin was dear matter of merriment — even more difficult to forego than head-tires. Her one quality beyond the common is a strenuous emotionality; and this was nowise conspicuous in an Italian woman belonging to a century of vehement passions. Of weak nature, she found conversion a slow and painful process; she was not "saved" in a moment, after the manner of the Salvation bench. She has no literary art, no special gift of expression: her account of her spiritual experiences is of a girlish *naïveté*. One would expect the character of her spiritual relations to be adapted to the limitations of her mind, since mysticism follows the natural order, which is elevated into the supernatural without violent wrench. And it is even so: these relations have an intimate littleness nothing less than startling to the general reader, and arresting to the most experienced. A homely Bride of the Song of Songs (so to speak), one wishes, in listening to her, for the veil of poetry. This reason precludes us from quoting what is psychologically most interesting in its adjustment to the simple and personal feminine mind. No less interesting are the numerous suggested analogies between divine and natural love, and equally interdicted from quotation by consideration for the general reader. But psychology is baffled by another aspect of these writings. For this unlearned woman of small mind, whose earlier visions have all that literal and physical character which we should *à priori* expect, in her later visions, attains an altogether unexpected height of abstraction, and subtle philosophical conceptions which I have known to astonish at least one philosopher. The abrupt transition to these transcendental summits from the infantile simplicity of the writer's previously exhibited mental outlook, and the prattle of her narrative style, is a chief riddle of this extraordinary book. A riddle it will be to the ordinary reader, whether he admits or does not admit the supernatural element, and to many readers a profane riddle. To myself, with all its interest from the standpoints which I have indicated, it appears a book for which publicity, the indiscriminate publicity of the bookseller's window, was unmeant. I feel as if I had been eavesdropping at a convent confessional. I can hardly think it will make one convert to the value of mysticism. But I fear it may repel many.

A MODERN STUDY OF SANCTITY *
[*Academy*, August 13, 1898]

That the intuitive gift of the poet is in no way incompatible with a keen intellect is here illustrated in Thompson's detection of the weakness in Joly's theory that savored of Modernism.

HERE is a very ably-written little book from the French; a prefatory study of sanctity in general, designed to introduce a series of biographies of the Saints which shall correspond to modern needs and methods. However you may dissent from it as to this or that conclusion, this or that argument, it is a clever and valuable attempt to apply modern methods to ancient problems; from which men of goodwill may derive much profit, whether they agree with or contravene its author.

The regulation hagiography has been a compost of tedious moralities and platitudinous reflections, served up in miraculous jam to get it down the light and worldly reader's recalcitrant throat. Our ancestors, like children, enjoyed the miracles (as a kind of religious *Arabian Nights*), and, it is to be feared, skipped the moral reflections. Then came the reaction. The Saint was treated as a very great man, of most excellent moral attributes; with regard to whom there were certain legends not necessary

---

* *The Psychology of the Saints*. By Henri Joly. Translated by E. Holt. Preface and Notes by G. Tyrrell, S. J.

to be forced on the reader's attention — like the legends of Egeria, &c., in the history of the early Roman kings. It was a very useful reaction, unless the Saints were to be on a par with the Enchanter This and the Magician That. But hypnotism arose, and the Psychological Society, and that eminent mystic, William Thomas Stead. The other-worldly side of the Saints was revived by the world itself. M. Joly's book endeavours to steer between both these modern attitudes, and to utilise both. It does not burke the thaumaturgic side of the Saints. On the contrary, M. Joly examines this at length, using the latest modern experiments for the purpose. But he strives to make it clear that — in the view of the Church to which the Saints belonged — such phenomena were but accessories of the sanctity; that the essential matter was the Saints' virtue. Nay, mysticism itself was not the science of wonder-working, but the science of divine love.

M. Joly comes to his difficult task unusually well equipped. He has published previous books on the psychology of animals, geniuses, and criminals. It is this *rapport* with science that makes his book interesting. Not many writers on such a topic carry a like weight of metal; religion, like politics, is a field in which every man thinks himself competent, needing no arms but opinion. He is of the "cross-bench mind," and is therefore likely to displease many. He will have no hard and fast line between the animal and the man, or between the various grades of human minds. Neither will he allow that everything may be traced to the mere development of our lower instincts. Mr. Leslie Stephen, in his new book, *Studies of a Biographer*, records a saying of Hawkins (Johnson's Hawkins) to the effect that Fielding had invented a new virtue, "goodness of heart," which was little more than the virtue of a cow. It delights not Mr. Stephen, as he shows by his ironical gloss upon it. Yet we agree with Hawkins — perhaps the only point in which we agree with that eminently disagreeable person. He meant the pet virtue which Fielding ascribes to all his characters designed for sympathy, to Tom Jones no less than to Parson Adams; and which in Tom Jones and his kind is supposed to cover a multitude of sins. This "goodness of heart" it is which Hawkins insinuates to be a mere animal good-nature, such as may be found in any dog worth one's intimacy. He might have gone further. There are much finer virtues than this in any dog of really elevated character, the kind of dog with whom none but a man of truly superior nature can have under-standing companionship. One does sometimes see such a dog yoked in fellowship with a Tom Jones; but it is always a painful sight; there can be no real equality in such a friendship, and the dog must probably undergo a subtle, if unnoticed, deterioration. Against this animal view of virtue, the idea of sanctity, as put forth by M. Joly, is a protest. He will not have it that sanctity is evolved from protoplasm; nor yet that it is a "sport," a "freak," as the Americans say, a special variety of the angel. His object is to show that the saint, in his most personal developments, never parts company with man. His contact with man, his charity, his zeal for his fellow-creatures, his wisdom and prudence, are easily established. It is less easy to show that his extraordinary experiences are based upon qualities existing in that humanity which does not pretend to the peculiar gifts of the saint. Yet this M. Joly attempts. He is helped by science, he is helped, also, by his study of the psychology of genius. This latter is a peculiar advantage for his task, which he shares with no previous student of the subject that we can recollect. The psychology of the poet, above all (or of the musician, or, less strikingly, the artist), affords the closest natural parallel to the special psychology of the saint. If M. Joly does not make quite what he might of it, this is doubtless because he is a Frenchman. A nation whose greatest poet is Victor Hugo cannot supply for study the highest and austerest type of poetic psychology. A German with Goethe, a Spaniard with Calderon, would have better chance; still more the countrymen of Dante, the countrymen of Milton and Wordsworth. Nor can the mind of Dante, for example, readily be followed by a mind of uncongenial national type. Englishmen have a special advan-tage in this way; since, as a Spanish critic has said, the authority of England in poetry can only be paralleled by the authority of ancient Greece in sculpture. Especially valuable is the com-parison between the saint and the genius in regard to mysticism, and that contemplation which is one of the features of mysticism.

And here, also, M. Joly makes too little use — we might almost say no use — of the comparison. Let us use the advantage of our nationality to consider the point a little.

Mysticism, M. Joly defines, following a French Abbé, as being the love of God. So also an English writer (Coventry Patmore) has defined it as the science of Love. The difference is characteristic. The Frenchman is the more rigid, the Englishman the wider. The Englishman regards all love as a ladder leading to the Divine Love. But in respect to the Saints, we may fairly accept the Abbé's definition, and call mysticism the science of Divine Love. This wide definition at once does away with the notion that a mystic is a man shut up in a cave or a monastery. But then comes in the bugbear of contemplation. Does not contemplation strike at the root of all external energy, nay, of reason itself? Is not the mystic, therefore, as Victor Cousin would have him to be, a man withdrawn from all modes of activity; yea, a contemner of reason? The idea is, that contemplation is something non-natural, having no root in the natural faculties. The answer is, that the poet employs a mode of contemplation. Most contemplative of poets was Dante; yet was the sometime ruler of Florence unfitted for external activities? Was the subtle logician of the "Paradiso" maimed in his reason? It is the old quarrel between reason and intuition. The weapon of poet or saint is intuition, and contemplation is the state, the attitude, which disposes the mind to receive intuitions. The supposition is that intuition is contrary to reason. But this is narrowing the term "reason" to a single faculty — the discursive reason, the dialectic faculty; as we say, the faculty of putting two and two together. This is quite arbitrary. Intuition is reason. It is a higher, a subtler, a nimbler mode of reason; it flies where the discursive reason crawls. The average man will not away with this idea, because it would be an admission that his own reason was but elementary. He has the true democratic hatred of distinction: he would clip the hedges of the human mind lest one spray shoot beyond another. "To have all men like me" is his unconscious aim. *L'homme rational, c'est moi*, is his dogma. Yet the thing is true; and it is only in modern times that the word "reason" has acquired its contracted and degenerated meaning. The insight of the poet springs from intuition, which is the highest reason, and is acquired through contemplation, which is the highest effort. For contemplation implies a concentration far greater than is needed for ordinary thought. We need not quote Wordsworth to show that such was the method used by him. So far we have been fighting the battle of the poet. But it is also the battle of the saint. These faculties native in the poet are the natural basis of what is called contemplation in the saint. The foundation is the same, the edifice more marvellous. The gap which appears non-natural between the saint and ourselves becomes apprehensible when it is bridged over by the poet, the man of genius. And so far from this mystic contemplation being inert and irrational, it is perceived to be the culmination of energy and reason. Let it be added, in fairness, that the poet does sometimes show a defect of external activity; but no such result is perceptible in the saint. On the contrary, most of them have been monsters of energy.

This is a case in which M. Joly might have used the comparative method to more advantage than he has done; but, for the most part, he uses it with excellent results. It is impossible to follow at large his very curious and interesting examination. But to any reader with a taste for the subject we can recommend his book as stimulant and suggestive, whether you accept his conclusions or not.

VARIA

LITERARY COINCIDENCE
[*Merry England*, April, 1889]

Thompson's opinion that the apparently deliberate imitation of one author
by another is often the result of "unconscious cerebration" was exemplified later by his own appropriation, in the Proem of *Sister Songs*, of an image
from Patmore's "St. Valentine's Day."

THERE is no literary phenomenon more inevitable, or without
which literature would find it more difficult to exist, than the
imitation of one author by another. The majority of instances, no
doubt, which pass for deliberate imitation, are the mere result of
unconscious cerebration; but even when the imitation is conscious,
there is no necessary stigma attending it. For the precious metals
of the mind *are* capable of transmutation; and the silver of one
writer becomes the gold of another. None has been more exposed
to charges of plagiarism than Coleridge; and none can better afford
to have his sources of indebtedness investigated, so magical is his
transforming touch. There is one instance of probably unconscious adaptation which happily illustrates this, and which has not,
we think, before been noticed. There is a passage in the "Ancient
Mariner" distinctively Coleridgean, which yet appears to be
founded on a stanza by a little-known Elizabethan poet. How
admirably the original is sublimated into imagination by Coleridge
needs no pointing out.

> Still as a slave before his lord
>   The ocean hath no blast:
> *His great bright eye most silently*
>   *Up to the moon is cast,*

> If he may know which way to go,
>   For she guides him, smooth or grim:
> See, brother, see how graciously
>   She looketh down on him!

451

The parallel stanza occurs in the "Orchestra" of Sir John Davies, a poet certainly known to Coleridge, and to the best of our recollection rather a favourite with him. Note especially the corresponding lines which we have italicised in both extracts.

> Even so the sea ,which fleets about the land
>   And as a girdle clips her solid waist,
> Music and measure both doth understand;
> *For this great crystal eye is always cast*
>   *Up to the moon, and on her fixèd fast;*
> And as she danceth in her pallid sphere,
>   So danceth he about the centre here.

Gray is well-known as a wholesale plunderer, though chiefly from the classical poets. It may be remarked, however, that the famous saying —

> Where ignorance is bliss
>   ' Tis folly to be wise,

is a happy alteration of two lines in a poem addressed by Prior to Charles Montague, afterwards Lord Halifax.

> If we see right, we see our woes:
>   Then what avails it to have eyes?
> From ignorance our comfort flows,
>   The only wretched are the wise.

Merely to enumerate the poets who have borrowed from Spenser, still more to cite all they have borrowed, would be a heavy task. The passages for which Milton is his debtor are well known; but Shakespeare's obligations are less familiar. They are, indeed, not very considerable; but still we may notice a single instance. There is a passage in *Troilus and Cressida* which Keats passionately admired; but, though an ardent student of Spenser, Keats himself probably overlooked the fact that it was a bettering of some already beautiful lines in the *Faerie Queene:*

> Through long languor and heart-burning brame
> She shortly like a pinèd ghost became
> Which long hath waited by the Stygian strand.

Only Shakespeare or Milton would have dared to tamper with so felicitously-worded an image: but the great dramatist succeeded in gilding even this refined gold:

> No, Pandarus; I stalk about her door
> Like a strange soul upon the Stygian banks,
> Staying for waftage.

Pope has a somewhat unusual method in many of his plagiarisms, and does not always justify them by improving his original. Most people know that the couplet —

> Vice is a monster of so frightful mien
> As to be hated needs but to be seen,

is a variation on a couplet in the "Hind and Panther":

> Virtue has such a face and such a mien
> As to be loved needs only to be seen.

But possibly few besides students of literature know that the famous and very dubious sentiment —

> For modes of faith let graceless zealots fight,
> He can't be wrong whose life is in the right,

has not even the merit of originality. Cowley had said long before

> His faith, perhaps, in some nice tenets might
> Be wrong; his life, I'm sure, was in the right.

The words were uttered of Crashaw, that

> Poet and saint, to whom alone were given
> The two most sacred names of earth and heaven,

who inspired Cowley with his finest verses; verses which, but for some slight roughness of metre, might well have been written by Dryden at his best. Another of Pope's famous couplets —

> 'Tis with our judgments as our watches, none
> Go just alike, yet each believes his own,

we have always thought may perhaps have been suggested by (one cannot say taken from) Sir John Suckling in the epilogue to *Aglaura*.

> But as, when an authentic watch is shown,
> Each man winds up and rectifies his own,
> So in our very judgments.

The images are certainly not the same: Suckling's illustrating the tendency of the many to take their judgment from an authoritative few, Pope's the obstinate independence of private judgment. Yet the cast of expression in each has so much in common (the very rhyme-sound being preserved in Pope) that the one passage may not improbably have been derived from the other. This is especially possible because Suckling was then a popular poet: witness the quotation from him put into the mouth of Millamant in Congreve's most brilliant play, and followed by the exclamation, "O natural, easy Suckling!" It would be quite after Pope's peculiar manner of adaptation to which we have already referred, and which is well illustrated in the parallel with Dryden quoted above. This consists in substituting for the original idea a cognate idea, but retaining the form of expression with comparatively little change. The usual method when poets borrow is to take the idea, but transform the expression. Most poets, in fact, cast the old metal in new moulds, while Pope casts his new metal in the old moulds. But the new metal has often a strong similarity to the old.

There are cases where the ideas, though very alike, are yet not so identical as to establish imitation. There is such a case in the instance of that lovely Spenserian line when Una

> Made a sunshine in the shady place,

which has an exquisite earlier counterpart in the line of Greene,

> Her lovely beauty lightened all the place.

And there are some images which are almost poetical heirlooms, but which in certain poets have a deceptive appearance of originality, from their conformity with those poets' genius. A writer on Blake in *Macmillan's Magazine*, a few years ago, defended, from the proposed emendation of critics, the epithet "flaming" applied by Blake to the hair. It was characteristic of Blake, he said, and Rossetti had sanctioned it by imitating the image in one of his sonnets. It is not clear why it should have needed Rossetti's sanction, when it had received the hall-mark of Shelley:

> "Aloft her flowing hair like strings of flame did quiver,"

says Laon of Cythna. But though characteristic enough in both Blake and Shelley, it, or images practically identical with it, could be traced we should not like to say how far.

> Her beams (which some dull men call'd hair) divided;
> Part with her cheeks, part with her lips did sport,

says Suckling; and there is store of such passages in Spenser. But the very image itself occurs in Chapman:

> The downward burning flame of her rich hair,

is the one beautiful line in an utterly worthless poem. And a classical scholar like Chapman might easily have had it suggested to him by the converse image in that most Shelleian of Latin poets, Catullus; whose imagery often approaches nearer to modern imagery in fire and fancy than that of any among his brethren. We refer, of course, to the "Epithalamion":

> *Viden'ut faces*
> *Splendidas quatiunt comas?*

> Seest how the torches
> Shake their splendent tresses?

There is no end to multiplication of such resemblances. A review of them leads not merely to great charity towards apparent imitation, but to a conviction that really original imagery is a thing so rare as can hardly be too highly treasured.

THE MACBETH CONTROVERSY
[*Dublin Review*, July, 1889]

Here we see Thompson's clear thinking and logical reasoning applied to a highly controversial question. He begins playfully enough, but presently shows his ability as a Shakespearean exegete, convincing in the presentation of his views, and avoiding the excesses of a special pleader.

TIME was when originality was an undesirable quality (outside certain limits) in matters theatrical. In those days, if some too daring actor elevated his left eyebrow when Kemble used to elevate his right, the critics and *the* profession rose against him like the bacchanals against Orpheus. Was it not certain that Kemble, at this particular point of this particular passage in this particular part, used to elevate his right eyebrow? And had not the tradition been handed down to Kemble from Garrick, and to Garrick from Betterton, who received it from Will Davenant, that Burbage or Will Alleyn did so elevate his right eyebrow? And here — oh! sheet-iron thunder and patent lightning! O shade of Shakespeare (behind invisible gauze)! — here was a presumptuous young man who sacrilegiously and corruptly elevated his left! If tradition and prescription were to be thus ignored, farewell all that made the stage great; farewell the tragic frown and the big mouth that makes of "virtue" "vir-r-rtue"; the stage would go to the dogs, "To the dogs, sir, egad!" Far different is it with this Athenian age, which desires but to hear some new thing, and cares not that it be a true thing; an age whose younger generation has embraced as an article of faith the Darwinian theory. And it is touching to observe with what piety many of our youths model themselves upon their ancestors.

Nothing can now be too new for an audience. We no longer mouth out blank verse: the ideal, indeed, of both actors and public seems to be something very different. "What," you exclaim, "was that blank verse? Why, it sounded exactly like prose!" "Ah," replies your more knowing friend of superior taste, "that was the triumph of the actor's elocution." The prevalent idea, in fact, would appear to be that blank verse is a comminuted fracture of prose, and the actor is the surgeon who sets it. Similarly, novelty of interpretation is not only tolerated but invited by an audience which confounds it with originality of interpretation, and believes itself influenced by the love of originality, when it is influenced only by the love of sensation. The actor is of small account now-a-days who cannot put the new cloth of an unfamiliar reading upon the old garment of a familiar character. Accordingly, when it was known that the Lyceum was about to give us a fresh Lady Macbeth and a matured (and possibly revised) Macbeth, people prepared themselves for a new version, and the new view of the characters which would infallibly follow it in the Press. Let us say at once that we have no intention of criticising the perform- ance. *Quot homines tot sententiæ;* each spectator may have a dif- ferent idea of the actor's idea; nor can the actor himself know how far his performance may be the embodiment of his idea. But the views to which the performance has given rise, and which have taken shape in the Press, these are concrete things, and can be criticised with some sureness.

The year just passed may be distinguished as having brought forth two notable offerings at the shrine of Shakespeare — the new view of *Macbeth*, and the immortal cryptogram. Of the two, we think we prefer the cryptogram, for it was at least decidedly amusing. Shakespeare must have laughed till Hades resounded like the Mermaid Tavern. We are not so sure whether my Lord Veru- lam laughed. For there was, in the first place, the agreeable sur- prise of finding that the great cryptogram gave rise to the great conundrum — *viz.*, if Bacon wrote Shakespeare, who wrote Bacon? Not Bacon, clearly, on the evidence of the great cryptogram, the style of which would justify an action for libel against Bacon's ghost on the part of the seventeenth century, unless style, like port, deteriorates when too long bottled. Then, there was the further pleasure of discovering that Queen Elizabeth considered Shakespeare's plays "a lot of stuff." Possibly to admirers of the Virgin Queen this was a little saddening. They knew already that she swore like a horse-jockey, lied like a Ministry, had more dresses than a Society actress, and nearly as much retiring modesty; but it had hitherto been supposed that she at least talked decent Elizabethan English, and had a pretty taste for poetry and personable courtiers. It was now regretfully perceived that her poetical taste resembled her reputation, and that she talked like a modern young lady who borrows her vocabulary from her schoolboy brother. What further piquancies might not be anticipated from such a beginning? It is only the first step *qui coute;* and her Majesty's first step had been of such a nature as to warrant the most hopeful anticipations of her future proficiency in nineteenth-century slang. Might not the next instalment of the cryptogram reveal Queen Elizabeth describing the "Astrophel and Stella" as "awful rubbish"? nay, might we not even be privileged to behold her Majesty at some Elizabethan antitype of lawn tennis, to see her make a mis-stroke, and to hear her exclaim with her own virginal lips, "What a beastly fluke!" Enough; " 'twere to consider too curiously to consider so"; and the second instalment of the great cryptogram lags. Possibly Mr. Donnelly feels (and rightly) that he has already done enough for fame. His position is henceforth secure to all future ages in the foremost rank of American humorists.

Like Mr. Donnelly's theory, the new view of *Macbeth* appears to us untenable, and, unlike Mr. Donnelly's theory, it is decidedly dull. It would not, indeed, be worth while to discuss seriously so wrong-headed a thesis, if, in the first place, it were not a reaction from the extreme traditional view, no less untenable; and if, in the second place, it had not claimed in its support a critical essay worthy of better companionship. What then is this view? As we gather it from the language both of its defenders and impugners (who seem to agree with regard to its essential nature in a manner rare among controversialists) it is this. Macbeth, they say, is by nature a dark, scheming, unscrupulously ambitious man, the mainspring of the whole murder-plot; his wife, a gentle-natured, essentially *womanly* woman, devoting herself, out of sheer affection for her husband and blind worship of his will, to the furtherance of designs from which she would naturally have shrunk. The theory has only to be stated to repel, and only to be attacked to fall. But, as if conscious of its weakness, it has invoked the authority of the pamphlet lately published by Mr. Comyns Carr; and amusingly instructive is the contrast between the patron and his clients. That a piece of criticism so careful and minute should be made the pretext for so coarse a perversion, is a curious example of popular inability to perceive that stripes of red, yellow, green, blue, and violet do not make the rainbow. Mr. Carr's view is altogether worthy of the consideration which we mean to give it; and while in some respects it affords a groundwork for (though it does not, we think, authorise) the theory of the Lyceum partisans in the Press, it is in other respects quite at variance with that theory. It is, in fact, so largely true that we could wish it had been entirely true; and supported with such searching discrimination, such close adherence to the text, that we feel even our modified dissent a somewhat ungracious and by no means easy task. To put in one's own words another man's view, especially if the representation be at the same time an abstract, is always an unsafe attempt. Words are such coarse media for ideas. But so far as a careful reading of Mr. Carr's essay has enabled us to seize his meaning, we hope that the following brief sketch may not do it injustice. To begin with the character of Lady Macbeth, for in this is to a considerable extent involved his view of her husband. In the first place, he does not pretend to bring forward any new idea, but merely to enforce more completely what has been already put forward by others. His main object, like that of the Lyceum partisans, is to protest against the traditional stage-view handed down from Mrs. Siddons, which makes of Macbeth's wife a stately tragedy-figure, overpoweringly dominating a weak husband and destitute of every gentle or womanly trait — in fact, what Malcolm calls her at the close of the play, a "fiend-like queen." This protest undoubtedly is not new: it is some twenty odd years since we first read *Macbeth*, and it has never been anything but familiar to us. Mr. Carr sees in her a woman "of the highest nervous organisation," truly and typically a woman, devoted to her husband, and assisting him in his crime merely in the blindness of that devotion; girding up all her powers, with a concentration oblivious of after consequences, to the achievement of the project by him suggested; stimulating him when he needs stimulation, advising him when he needs advice, devising for him when his resource gives way under the pressure of irresolution; and when the deed is done collapsing under the reaction, the retributive scourge of unforeseen mental horrors, and the equally unforeseen crimes which are the inevitable offspring of the first fruitful one. He does not ascribe to her a soft and gentle nature, nor does he distinctly deny her unscrupulousness, her absence of principle. On the other hand, it must be confessed that he leaves his opinion on these points so vague that it is open to the advocates of the new view to place their own construction on his language. And his general tone does certainly in some way convey the impression that he does not regard her as by nature in any sort ruthless, or devoid of moral principle. On the latter point, indeed, he says that it is useless to consider the question of morality with regard to either husband or wife; since the period for moral scruples is past with both at the time the play opens. On the former point his most explicit utterance is the remark that if Jael and Judith were essentially women, still more may Lady Macbeth be regarded as essentially feminine. A remark which does not help us much. Mr. Carr might as well have cited Charlotte Corday to elucidate the character of the she-wolf of France, or Brutus to elucidate the character of Macbeth himself. With regard to that character, in spite of his protest against dealing at all with the question of virtue, he conveys pretty plainly his opinion that the usurper is an unprincipled man naturally. He considers him to be a man of strong imagination, but at the period when the play opens, devoid of conscience, if he ever had any. "Neither conscience nor cowardice" causes his irresolution before Duncan's murder, but an imagination which reveals to him the whole after-results of his meditated act, and paralyses him by threatening future insecurity. His influence over his wife has drawn her into the crime, and she only stimulates him when his resolution falters before the vision of consequences which she, womanlike, with her less vivid imagination, does not foresee. The murder is done, and with it his irresolution. For the imagination which before kept him inactive is now the cause of his activity. None of the bloody *sequelæ* of his first sin take him by surprise or paralyse him (as they surprise and overwhelm his wife), for they were all anticipated. In facing the murder he faced them; in resolving on the murder he resolved on them; and when they come he is a prepared man. He proceeds without hesitation and without remorse, "more than an executioner might feel," in a career of bloodshed whose necessity he had foreshadowed, to a doom whose probability he had foreseen.

This, as we understand it, is Mr. Carr's opinion; and he explains that Shakespeare, in thus delineating his central characters, deliberately intended them "to be the embodiment and expression of the contrasted characteristics of sex" in the presence of crime. "The ideal motive of the drama lies in its contrast of the distinctive qualities of sex as these are developed under the pressure of a combined purpose and a common experience." Our means of knowing Shakespeare's purpose are like Mr. Carr's — *nil;* yet we will venture to say that Shakespeare never intended anything of the kind. He intended to develop as powerfully as he could a subject which had possessed his imagination, and that was all. We do not believe that Shakespeare ever addled his brain about such things as ideal motives. He left them to the dramatists of the nineteenth century, few of whose ideal motives will keep their plays as well preserved as Otway's *Venice*, and that is but fly-blown. No doubt, in developing his subject he *has* exhibited the contrast in question. But to suppose this his motive is to suppose him born two centuries odd before his time. It is only this analytic, psychology-mongering, philosophising age which thinks it can clothe with flesh the dry rib of an "ideal motive."

Having thus disputed Mr. Carr's postulate, let us, after his own example, take the play *seriatim*, and see how far it supports his thesis. "At the first entrance of Macbeth" (as he says) "we are allowed to see that the thought of Duncan's death has already found a lodging in his heart." The indications are not, we think, by themselves conclusive; but, taken in conjunction with succeeding passages, they form a body of strong proof as to Shakespeare's intention. There are first the significant words of Banquo:

> Good sir, why do you start, and seem to fear
> Things that do sound so fair?

Why indeed, except that they echo Macbeth's own previous musings? Then follows the speech:

> This supernatural soliciting
> Cannot be ill, cannot be good: if ill,
> Why hath it given me earnest of success,
> Commencing in a truth? I am thane of Cawdor:
> If good, why do I yield to that suggestion
> Whose horrid image doth unfix my hair
> And make my seated heart knock at my ribs
> Against the use of nature? Present fears
> Are less than horrible imaginings:
> My thought, whose murder yet is but fantastical,
> Shakes so my single state of man that function
> Is smothered in surmise, and nothing is
> But what is not.

If this be interpreted as referring to a newly-suggested temptation, the rapidity, the absence of any real moral struggle with which Macbeth yields to it, would make him a far worse character than the opposite supposition that the idea is already familiar to him, and its moral horror thus abated. For, as Mr. Carr observes, "in the next scene, even while his grateful sovereign is loading him with honours, his dark purpose is seen to have taken still more defined shape":

> Stars, hide your fires;
> Let not light see my black and deep desires:
> The eye wink at the hand; yet let that be
> Which the eye fears, when it is done, to see.

But pass we on to the fifth and seventh scenes, where the points of contact and repulsion between Mr. Carr and ourselves develop simultaneously. With regard to the letter which Lady Macbeth enters reading, Mr. Carr says: "His written message to her contains no hint of murder." This is apparently true; and her words in the seventh scene apparently refer to a previous communication of his design:

> What beast was't then
> That made you break this enterprise to me?
> When you durst do it, then you were a man;
> And, to be more than what you were, you would
> Be so much more the man. Nor time nor place
> Did then adhere, and yet you would make both:
> They have made themselves, and that their fitness now
> Does unmake you.

For other reasons, noticed by Mr. Carr, we hold with him that it does so refer; but we would point out that the reference is not so intrinsically certain as it seems, nor is his observation regarding the "written message" such a self-evident fact as he thinks. What Lady Macbeth reads is manifestly only a portion of the letter, the beginning of which she is supposed to have read before her entry. It would therefore be quite feasible, and the theory would be quite in accordance with Shakespearean methods, to hold that Macbeth was meant to have communicated his project in the former part of the letter, not read before the audience. In any case, his wife's words clearly show that Macbeth first proposed the crime: it is utterly impossible to evade this consequence. But though these things may be inconclusive, not so the words with which she follows the reading of the letter. As Mr. Carr says, they "have no meaning unless we suppose that the violent death of Duncan had long been the subject of conjugal debate":

> Yet do I fear thy nature;
> It is too full o' the milk of human kindness
> To catch the nearest way: thou wouldst be great;
> Art not without ambition, but without
> The illness should attend it: what thou wouldst highly,
> That thou wouldst holily; wouldst not play false,
> And yet wouldst wrongly win: thou'dst have, great Glamis,
> That which cries, "Thus thou must do, if thou have it";

And that which rather thou dost fear to do
Than wishest should be undone. Hie thee hither,
That I may pour my spirits in thine ear,
And chastise with the valour of my tongue
All that impedes thee from the golden round,
Which fate and metaphysical aid doth seem
To have thee crowned withal.

This passage, and this passage alone, thoroughly decides us that Mr. Carr's view of the point in question is the only correct one. He proceeds: "She has watched the working of the poison in his breast, and has already anticipated the hesitation which he afterwards displays." And again, in a subsequent passage: "With the woman's finer instinct she has partly divined and anticipated his mood." It is most true; she shows in this passage an intimate marital knowledge of Macbeth's nature, which is confirmed by her conduct throughout the play; she knows precisely when to apply the goad, and when also to be silent; precisely what taunts will be most effectual with her soldierly husband, and when to use affection. Yet so seductive is the instinct of special pleading, that even an able critic like Mr. Carr, after paying this tribute to her intuitive knowledge of Macbeth in order to serve one purpose, can, in the very next sentence, affirm the defectiveness of that knowledge to serve another purpose. For, according to Mr. Carr, her "generous interpretation of his halting action" is a mistake; it is not in accordance with Macbeth's nature. That this able, quick-sighted, practical, and (according to Mr. Carr himself) not over-imaginative woman, should have been meant by Shakespeare to entertain a fond illusion with regard to her husband's nobility of nature is a surprising idea, and not, we think, very complimentary to Shakespeare. What might not be the case with an individual woman of this character it is impossible to say, so strange are the vagaries of individual character. But Shakespeare, like a true artist, in his best work is rigidly attentive to the *probabilities* of character. It is only an artist of the Dickens stamp who will ascribe to a personage some curiously improbable act or incongruous trait, and then defend himself by saying that he once knew some one who was or acted exactly like that. Such oddities are interesting enough *as* oddities; but they have no place in characters designed to embody the prevalent truths of nature.* Now Mr. Carr himself would hardly, we think, deny the aptness of the epithets which we have applied to Lady Macbeth. And it is most unlikely that such a woman should so delude herself. It is only the somewhat foolish or weak women who credit their husbands (we do not say their lovers) with non-existent perfections. A sharp-sighted, clever woman may love her husband (as Macbeth is unquestionably loved by his wife), may exaggerate his excellencies to others, may not whisper his faults even to herself; but she knows them, and when calculating his action will instinctively reckon with his defects, and not credit him with absent virtues. That Lady Macbeth, therefore, should not know whether her husband naturally had or had not the milk of human kindness, was or was not without the illness that should attend ambition, did or did not desire to have honourably what he could only have with dishonour, appears to us an untenable idea, which it is difficult to believe, without some express confirmation in the text, that Shakespeare could have intended.

Again: it is rare to find in *Macbeth* a purposeless passage, we might almost say (were we not timorous of hasty generalisations) there is no such thing; yet, on Mr. Carr's supposition, the passage has no special bearing on the play. If Lady Macbeth be allowed to know what she is saying, it has. For — and Mr. Carr himself points it out — when the action of the drama commences, Macbeth's broodings, stimulated by the witches, have ceased to be greatly (not, as Mr. Carr says, entirely, and this we shall show) affected by scruples. Lady Macbeth's words, therefore, serve to reveal Macbeth's original disposition, which otherwise we could not certainly know; and thereby invest his career with an element of regretful interest such as could not attach to a mere unscrupulous man palsied in crime by his own selfish fears. For this purpose they were probably inserted. The whole passage goes to show that she has already had trouble with his reluctance to bring to act the

---

* We do not say that a character of this sort should be *without* incongruities, should be as regular as a character in a Greek tragedy. But there are harmonious and non-harmonious incongruities.

murder that is yet but fantastical, and does not for the first time chastise that reluctance with the valour of her tongue. It does not follow from this view of her speech that she considers her husband to be naturally a man of strong morality. We quite hold with Mr. Carr that Shakespeare never intended his hero for a man of much, if any, religious principle. The word "holily" as here used, has nothing to do with holiness in the theological sense. It simply signifies "without criminality"; and Lady Macbeth merely means that her husband, though a soldier, is not given by his original disposition to bloody courses, but is capable of compunction; and would gain his ends openly and honestly, being by nature straightforward; that, in fact, he is, in Antony's phrase, "an honourable man." And over many an honourable man religion has little more than a theoretical influence. Lastly, note in this speech, for the side-light it throws on Lady Macbeth's own character, the words:

> Art not without ambition; but without
> The illness should attend it.

This opinion, casually dropped in self-communing, that ambition ought to be attended by unscrupulousness, is quite in harmony with her subsequent utterance to Macbeth, which might otherwise be considered a mere dramatic utterance for his stimulation:

> When you durst do it, then you were a man;
> And, to be more than what you were, you would
> Be so much more the man.

And both are the language of a naturally unscrupulous woman.

Macbeth's entrance at the close of the scene brings her character still further to light. Macbeth has suggested to her the idea of the murder; she suggests to him its actual accomplishment. When he wrote the letter he had no settled plan, for he knew not of Duncan's visit to his castle. In the interim between his first learning Duncan's intention, and the meeting with Lady Macbeth, it has occupied his mind: the brief, evasive replies which he makes to his wife, the replies of a troubled mind, show this; but they show also that he is unresolved. Not so Lady Macbeth.

To his information, "Duncan comes here to-night," she replies significantly, "And when goes hence?" "To-morrow, as he purposes," is Macbeth's answer, and she instantly rejoins:

> O, never
> Shall sun that morrow see!

She takes the initiative at once, and in spite of her husband's irresolute "We will speak further," insists that he shall leave the whole organisation of the plot in her hands, contenting himself with presenting a fair countenance to the guests:

> You shall put
> This night's great business into my dispatch;
> Which shall to all our nights and days to come
> Give solely sovereign sway and masterdom.

Observe the last two lines, with the expression, "to all *our* nights and days." Mr. Carr contends that she is moved to the crime solely by marital devotion. But conjoin with these lines her words after the coronation:

> Nought's had, all's spent
> When our desire is got without content:
> 'Tis safer to be that which we destroy
> Than by destruction dwell in doubtful joy.

and we think it will be suggested that she, too, had her ambitious hopes which turned to ashes. Marital affection, if you like, played its part; but ambition also. It is only natural that so able and energetic a woman should not be indifferent to the prospect of becoming queen.

Upon the opening of the seventh scene is almost founded Mr. Carr's conception of Macbeth. For here occurs the soliloquy on which he relies to show that Macbeth's imagination presents to him beforehand all the consequences of his act, and so prepares him for the necessary sequent crimes; to show also that it is the fears for his own future security which this imaginative vision awakens, and not any lingering scruples, which shake his purpose.

With this object Mr. Carr quotes two passages, nearly the whole soliloquy:

> If it were done when 'tis done, then 'twere well
> It were done quickly: if the assassination
> Could trammel up the consequence, and catch,
> With his surcease, success; that but this blow
> Might be the be-all and the end-all here,
> But here, upon this bank and shoal of time,
> We'd jump the life to come. But in these cases
> We still have judgment here; that we but teach
> Bloody instructions, which being taught, return
> To plague the inventor: this even-handed justice
> Commends the ingredients of our poisoned chalice
> To our own lips.

And again he quotes:

> His virtues
> Will plead like angels, trumpet-tongued, against
> The deep damnation of his taking-off:
> And pity, like a naked new-born babe,
> Striding the blast, or heaven's cherubim, horsed
> Upon the sightless couriers of the air,
> Shall blow the horrid deed in every eye,
> That tears shall drown the wind.

There is certainly no trace of scruple here, or of anything except such fears as Mr. Carr speaks of. And for a very excellent reason. Mr. Carr has taken order to the contrary:

> He's here in double trust;
> First, as I am his kinsman and his subject,
> Strong both against the deed; then, as his host,
> Who should against his murderer shut the door,
> Not bear the knife myself.

This inconvenient little passage, which shows that Macbeth is even yet accessible to scruples of honour, though not of morality, Mr. Carr has somehow omitted. Then, as to Macbeth's supposed full vision of consequences, what do the passages quoted by Mr. Carr show? What does Macbeth foresee in them? That he who takes the sword shall perish by the sword; that he who gains the throne by blood may lose it by blood, by assassination, or revolt; that the murder will arouse against him universal execration. No more. Not a word to show that he foresees the necessity for further murders on his part; for the murder of Banquo, or Macduff. He foresees that his throne will be insecure, but not the sanguinary measures by which he will be gradually drawn on to uphold it.

This power of anticipating consequences Mr. Carr ascribes to imagination. Surely, however, it is not imagination, as Mr. Carr calls it, but prevision — a faculty often possessed in a high degree by men without the imaginative faculty; a gift generally found associated with the governing mind, and dependent on the dry intellect. It is a faculty exercised by the First Lord of the Admiralty every time he calculates how many unmanœuvrable ships will restore the supremacy of Trafalgar; and we hope none will think of accusing a First Naval Lord of imagination. A First Naval Lord with an imagination would shoot himself a week after taking office. Macbeth *is* strongly imaginative, but we learn it rather from the general cast of his speeches, and the wild flights in which he indulges immediately after the assassination. But setting this aside, Mr. Carr is certainly right in ascribing to this prevision the major part of his hesitation. In the ensuing scene with Lady Macbeth he alleges as his first reason for refusing to proceed with their scheme the honours in which he has been invested, and the good opinion in which he is held. He will not sacrifice these things when he has just won them. And he is so far from resolving to face the consequences of his crime that he would apparently have remained firm in his refusal had not his wife opened to him the prospect of evading those consequences. It is not until she suggests that the murder can be made to appear the work of Duncan's grooms that he yields. This belief that he can commit the crime and yet escape its infamy, that he can gain the throne without sacrificing his security or the good will of his fellow-men, produces an instant revulsion in his mind:

> I am settled, and bend up
> Each corporal agent to this terrible feat,

and the deed is immediately decided on. This in itself shows how far he is from that complete prevision of consequences with which Mr. Carr endows him. He could not have foreseen the necessity for the murder of Banquo. Had he foreseen it, he would have known that although he escaped the imputation of his crime, and so retained his fellow-soldiers' friendship, the necessity would still remain. For the menace was not from Banquo, but from his offspring.

After the murder, as Mr. Carr truly says, the relative positions of Macbeth and his wife are altered. But we cannot altogether agree with him as to the causes of the alteration. "She, who had foreseen nothing, is thrown back upon the past, her dormant imagination now terribly alert, and picturing to her broken spirit all the horrors she had previously ignored." True; though as to that "dormant imagination" we shall have a word to say later. "As the penalty of his crime is unresting action, her heavier doom is isolated despair; and it is significant to observe that it is she who suffers most acutely all the moral torments he had only anticipated for himself." All true, though not all the truth. But Mr. Carr would have us believe that she quails before the prospect of further crime, and supports this opinion by what we cannot but think ingenious special pleading. "The change," he goes on, "is already well marked in the scene immediately following the murder, when . . . she sinks appalled at the dark vista of unending crime which his readiness in resource now first opens to her view." This interpretation of Lady Macbeth's fainting-fit is surely the most special of special pleading. For it appears more than doubtful whether her faint should not be spelled with an "e" instead of an "a." He is inaccessible to her remorse, says Mr. Carr, and she can take no part "in those darker projects with which he seeks to buttress the tottering fabric of his ambition." Let us see. But first note that in scene 1 of Act III Macbeth speaks of the necessity for Banquo's death. There is not an indication in the text that he perceived this necessity before Duncan's murder. Then comes, in scene 2, an interview with his queen. As Mr. Carr shows, she is ignorant that he has resolved to destroy Banquo, and attributes his moodiness solely to remorse. Yet, when he discloses to her his

dread of Banquo and Banquo's son, she instantly suggests their
murder, as she suggested the opportunity for Duncan's murder:

> O, full of scorpions is my mind, dear wife!
> Thou know'st that Banquo, and his Fleance, live.

And she rejoins quickly, significantly:

> But in them Nature's copy's not eterne.

To emphasise the significance of her words, Shakespeare makes
Macbeth at once catch her meaning, and reply:

> There's comfort yet; they are assailable;
> Then be thou jocund.

If she remain ignorant of the actual measure he has already taken
for the assassination, it is because he chooses to spare her the
knowledge where he does not need her advice. Throughout the
banquet scene, according to Mr. Carr, she believes that he is
haunted "as she is haunted" by the vision of Duncan. Nothing in
the text shows it, but, since she is ignorant that Banquo's death
has been accomplished, Shakespeare very probably meant her so
to think. But we knew already that he had kept her ignorant of
the murder; and ignorance is not inability to comprehend. Even
when after the banquet he declares the necessity of engaging
boldly in bloodshed, "she listens without understanding," says
Mr. Carr (doubtless, for he still refrains from mentioning the news
regarding Banquo), and "answers him from the sleepless anguish
of her own soul":

> You lack the season of all natures, sleep.

As if the *sleepless* wife did not know whether or not her husband
slept! Besides, Macbeth, in the previous scene but one, has mentioned "the affliction of these terrible dreams that shake us nightly"; and a man so afflicted has either broken sleep, or such sleep
as is indeed no sleep. But to the assertion that she can take no

part in his darker projects, the suggestion of Banquo's murder is surely in itself sufficient answer. It is not because she cannot share them that she does not share them; it is because Macbeth no longer needs her stimulation or counsel.

From this point to the drama's end there is little or no question of controversy: the action of the play becomes obvious. Let us, then, sum up the conclusions to which we are led from the study of the text with Mr. Carr's observations on it.

In his review of Lady Macbeth's character, Mr. Carr quotes (apparently with approbation) a curious commentary on her probable personal appearance by Mrs. Siddons, who thought of her as "fair, feminine, nay, perhaps even fragile." The description is possibly a little staggering, till we reflect that it would almost apply to Becky Sharp. Whether Shakespeare imagined her light or dark is the purest matter of fancy; but personally we have small doubt that he conceived her as a little woman. Most of the magnetic women who influence the world are so. Cleopatra, we feel sure, was a little woman, and not particularly good-looking. For wit and beauty, though man often joins together, heaven has for the most part kept asunder. We have thus an equitable adjustment of gifts. Some women are pleasant to look at, some pleasant to speak with, and some, it is said, even pleasant to live with. Pleasant to live with Lady Macbeth doubtless was — for Macbeth. She could clearly love those she loved, though no tender woman in the general relations of life. Little we have fancied her: Shakespeare has drawn her nervous, fiery, energetic, able, unscrupulous; yet with the natural affections of a woman, and those natural affections strong, though only for her own; not a gentle woman, yet no fiend. You may meet such women, so restlessly energetic, so able, so independent, yet capable of submitting to one strong nature; affectionate where they fix affection, though not at all of what we call an affectionate nature; and capable of scorn masculine in vigour, feminine in keenness, even towards their beloved ones, where those beloved ones' weaknesses rouse their contempt, or thwart their cherished schemes. They may be either scrupulous or unscrupulous, according to training and their own will. And Lady Macbeth Shakespeare has drawn without a single scruple, and with but one momentary visiting of womanly compunction at the sight of Duncan. A *womanly* woman she is not. That she should be essentially womanly is no logical complement of the truth that she is not essentially unwomanly. When we call a woman womanly, we imply a gentleness of nature absent in Lady Macbeth. That because man or woman has the natural instincts of affection for mate or child or parent, he or she is not ruthless by nature, that the lioness will not prey because she gambols with her cubs — against this doctrine we protest. Ruthless in the literal sense of the term perhaps they are not. But, in ordinary parlance, we mean by a ruthless individual, not one who is insensible to the emotion of pity, but one who in the pursuit of his or her ends can and does disregard it at will.

She embraces Macbeth's plan partly because she is ambitious for him, partly because it appeals to her own ambition, and altogether because she is unscrupulous. A man does not break a plan of murder to his wife unless he believes her to have no strong principle, and no weak pity. Let those who think her a gentle-natured woman compare her language to her husband with the language of a character to whom no such suspicion can attach — Dionyza in *Pericles*. The taunts which Dionyza addresses to her husband might have come straight from the mouth of Lady Macbeth. No gentle nature could forge such language. And Lady Macbeth's taunts, we think, are not meant to be merely dramatic stimulants. His weakness (for such it appears to a mind which thinks that "illness" should accompany ambition) really moves her impatience and contempt. The murder done, she sinks, as Mr. Carr says, under the remorse which she had not foreseen, the terrors of her insecure throne, and the constant accumulation of her husband's crimes. But why does she so sink? Why are these things more fatal to her than to Macbeth? Not merely because her woman's physical system was necessarily weaker than the man's. Not because she had not previsioned her guilty tortures; for there is not a line to show that Macbeth had previsioned his. They neither foresee their mental sufferings. We all know theoretically the retributive pangs which nature herself sets upon the heels of sin; but when we admit temptation to the mind, we either forget them, or dismiss them with a fatuous belief that we shall not suffer as others have suffered,

> All this the world well knows, yet none knows well
> To shun the heaven that leads men to this hell,

as Shakespeare says of other sin. Nor is it because, as Mr. Carr says, "the woman's nature surrenders itself more completely to the passion of remorse." It is because Macbeth, the man, the ruler, can find some distraction in acting, though the act be but fresh crime, in the planning of action, and the cares of state; while she, the woman, is left alone, without occupation sufficient to withdraw her for a moment from her awful broodings. This, and not a nature less hard in crime than his, explains and amply explains it all. Macbeth himself, so situated, must either have maddened or died.

We remarked upon Mr. Carr's expression, "her dormant imagination." It is a small matter, but as it completes character we may notice it. Lady Macbeth has no imagination. Shakespeare has marked this very clearly; and it is the one point on which he has made her unable to understand her husband. When Macbeth, fresh from Duncan's murder, is venting the wild strainings of his excited imagination, her amazed exclamation "What do you mean?" would be almost comic if the situation were less terrible. The fact is that Shakespeare had small belief in women's imagination; he has given us a few women who are really imaginative, though they may make poetic speeches. But even Octavius Cæsar sometimes thaws into poetry. And Shakespeare knew what he was doing: the Turk was only a little astray when he said that women had no souls, for most of them have no imaginations. As far as that goes, a good half of their brethren have no more imagination than they can safely carry without rupturing their brain-cells; and for three-quarters of the other half — if the lover be of imagination all compact, their ladies may confidently accuse them of perjury.

In regard to Macbeth's character, the points in which we differ from Mr. Carr have been largely noticed during our review of the text. His natural disposition is that of a soldier, bold, decided, instant in action, accustomed to go straight and openly to his object. Though he has an imagination, and a strong one, he is not originally what is generally called a man of imagination, a man given to reverie or cloudiness; but, on the contrary, essentially a man of action. It was to strike this essential warrior-note in his character, no less than to show the estimation in which he was held, that Shakespeare, as we think, probably wrote the opening description of his valour in the battle. As regards his moral character, we have already stated our conviction, founded largely on that speech of Lady Macbeth's which Mr. Carr slights. Of strongly religious nature, like Banquo, he never could have been; but he was what ordinarily passed for good, of a noble, though mundane disposition.

Moral scruples cannot restrain him; they must have given way before he broached Duncan's murder to his wife, and by the time the drama opens he has completely set them aside, has resolved to jump the life to come. But honourable scruples, as we have seen, still have their weight with him, and once had more, if Lady Macbeth may be believed. And, as is not unnatural in a man who once had much of the "milk of human kindness," he prizes highly the love and esteem of his fellows. It is this, even more than the dread of an insecure throne; it is the thought of the execration to which he will expose himself, the safe honours, the "golden opinions" which he must exchange for insecure obloquy, that most powerfully operates to make a vacillating ruminator of this naturally bold man; even as it is the loss of these things — "honour, love, obedience, troops of friends" — which moves him most at the close of his career. It is but the close of his mental struggle that we see in the play; but we can judge the severity of what has gone before by the severity of what remains. Such a struggle is enough to make a falterer of the hardiest man. Mr. Carr compares his hesitation with that of Hamlet, and remarks that the speculations of the one are confined to this world, while Hamlet's indecision is caused by his brooding on the mysteries of the other world. We do not agree with the remark in respect to Hamlet, and the difference lies deeper than is stated by Mr. Carr. The principal cause of Hamlet's irresolution is that he is irresolute. He is constitutionally dreamy and averse to action. Macbeth, on the other hand, is a man of action rendered temporarily vacillating by a terrible mental conflict. Hamlet seeks pretexts to avoid action; Macbeth seeks to break down the barriers which restrain him from action. Hamlet is introspective and self-analysing; Macbeth's calculations are nearly all with respect to external and practical consequences.

The murder is done, and he ceases to waver. Not because he has foreseen all the issue of his crime (we have shown that in the text he foresees only a few general results), but because the decisive mental conflict once over, *the* resolution once taken and executed, his nature rebounds like a slackened bow to its natural determined temper. He faces all the *sequelæ* of his crime as a commander, once having decided to give battle, accepts and meets all the chances of the battle. Thenceforward he sets his face towards crime as he was accustomed to set it towards fight; and the witches' counsel, as Mr. Carr excellently says, only serves to intensify a desperation already fixed. The splendid hardihood of the man, as Mr. Carr again truly observes, rises to absolute grandeur in the final scenes. It is impossible to withhold admiration from his fine scorn of "the Roman fool"; and admiration swells almost into sympathy when, at the very culmination of his ruin, though Birnam Wood is come to Dunsinane, though the doomsman of prophecy confronts him, he will not yield, nor die other than the warrior he has lived; though the summons to surrender come from the lips of armed Destiny, he will yet oppose to the last against her invisible arm his unquailing arm of flesh. Such a being had indeed that in him which might well dominate, as — except for that one interregnum of mental turmoil — dominate it did, even the fiery energy of his wife.

THE WAYS OF CRITICISM *

[*Academy*, June 27, 1903]

The task at hand in this review is a challenge that Thompson meets with success. A multiplicity of critical opinions on matters great and small he treats with humor, but not contempt. Then he weighs the merits of the more important, approves, reproves, and adds opinions of his own, with comprehension that we should not hesitate to say sees Shakespeare whole, had Thompson not considered the ability to do so, "only less rare than Shakespeare's creative gift."

THE appearance of the "New Variorum Edition" of *Macbeth*, by Horace Howard Furness, as revised by his son, Mr. H. H. Furness, Jr., affords a curious, not to say unique opportunity for surveying the results and ways of Shakespearean criticism. Quite apart from the rich collection of comments by various hands which garnish the foot of each page, in the Appendix (or one of the several appendices) we have presented a veritable bird's-eye view of Shakespearean commentary, both English and German – seen as it were in a weltering and conflicting sea. The *quot homines, tot sententiæ*, the perplexing divergency with which individual temperament and opinion responds to the appeal even of an acknowledged masterpiece, towards which its general attitude has been settled by the consent of that formidable personage, Posterity, is opulently illustrated. As one reads, as critic A gives the lie to critic B, and critic C gives the lie three feet down in the throat to both; one is forced to the perception that in poetry there is nothing so apparent as will look of one colour to two out of any three casual people. How, you marvel, does an actor's rendering ever give general satisfaction, when there is no point so seeming-plain, but A sees it one way and B another? Or is this pestilent diversity, mayhap, a critical disease, with which the "plain man" (the "plain average man," as he loves to call himself) is uncontaminated? We know that the "plain man" has always a mighty opinion of himself,

---

* *New Variorum Edition of* MACBETH. By Horace Howard Furness. Revised by H. H. Furness, Jr.

that he could settle things very well if the critics would only leave him alone. We suspect there is really something in this. The critics, experience shows, often split hairs over a performance about which the public are of a mind. Their profession breeds that habit of mind. Therewithal, in the case of the myriad-debated Shakespeare, it has grown a point of honour with your critic to firk up some view which shall single him from his fellows: let us be original, were it but on the fashion of Rosalind's hose!

Allow for all this, it is yet divergent temperament and perception which is mainly at work. On such a leading case as the character — the plain character — of Macbeth and his Lady, you shall find no view under heaven unadvocated. You need not go further, nor seek into subtleties. So that presently you begin to ask yourself whether old Sam Johnson must not after all be right, who starts roundly with the assertion that there is "no nice discrimination of character" in the play at all! The critics, at any rate, are quite ready to supply the alleged omission with any amount of "nice discrimination." Macbeth is a fine and loyal nature gone wrong, say these. Not at all, say those, and Sir Henry Irving, loudest. He is (says the famous actor) "one of the most bloody-minded, hypocritical villains in all his [Shakespeare's] long gallery of portraits of men instinct with the virtues and vices of their kind." He "even cultivated assiduously a keen sense of the horror of his crimes" — by way of true æsthetic enjoyment, we suppose. "Macbeth is the perfect type of the man of action," says Mr. Moulton. He is without intellect, the "inner cultivation." That is one point settled, you think; but turn the page, and Mr. Rose clearly shows you that this Macbeth is a striking example of a "double character, halfway between the mere man of thought, like Hamlet, and the ideal man of action, like Othello." So you may further gather from various commentators that he is a moral coward, quite inferior to his resolute wife; and yet a man of dauntless determination, with true masculine supremacy over her. We might ring the changes further on this "obvious" character (as Lord Acton has told us all Shakespeare's are); but *place aux dames*. Mrs. Siddons conceived Lady Macbeth "fair, feminine, nay, perhaps even fragile." Another critic (German, this time) is equally sure she was "royal," with "powerful features and majestic bearing," a countenance display-ing "noble and energetic outlines" and presaging "demoniac forces." In like fashion you may learn that her character is murder-ous, remorseless, powerful, and unsexed; or that she has full share of feminine qualities, and perishes under a remorse she was not strong enough to bear. Some critics are confident there is no love lost between the Macbeth couple — one German is clear it was a mere marriage of esteem, while Mrs. Siddons is shocked by the lady's lack of tender anxiety over her husband when he returns from the wars. Another set admire the impassioned affection be-tween the two, and plainly perceive that Lady Macbeth wor-shipped her spouse. On the play at large, opinions are more uni-form; yet even here one critic has distinguished himself by an un-doubted originality of view. *Macbeth* does not satisfy him. It has the air of a draft, needing expansion. "Like the *Tempest*, we feel that it would be better if it were longer." And this, not because you cannot have too much of a good thing, but because "we want more of the subdued and calm." *Macbeth*, in fact, is too exciting for Mr. Hunter. He would like it toned down. Moreover, his chaste (we might almost use some more forcible adjective, such as "maid-enly") taste finds in it a great many turgid and incomprehensible passages, or (as he puts it) passages which exceed the "just limits which part the true sublime from the inflated or the obscure." From these phrases alone you could discern that *Macbeth* was likely to be trying to Mr. Hunter, as Mr. Hunter and "the true sublime" would be trying to Shakespeare. Yet we like Mr. Hunter, in that, thinking these things, he said them. It is a document. There are so many who think these things and do not say them.

Yet for all this, Shakespearean criticism is not the mere chaos which might at first sight be thought. It merely exemplifies the universal human tendency to arrive at truth by zig-zag progres-sion, by the passage from extreme to extreme. The need is for the correlation of ideas. If, for convenience' sake, we narrow the issue to the English critics, amidst the divergent views we can extract a large body of agreement, a large number of points in which the critics overlap. In the remaining points, by striking a mean between the diverse contentions, we can co-ordinate and bring them into harmony. The chief *crux* between disputants is the evident contrast between Macbeth and his wife; their apparent interchange of sex before the murder, his seeming "moral cowardice" (as one critic calls it) contrasted with her unhesitating resolve; and the counter-reversal of their relations after the murder, when he becomes desperately determined and independent of his wife's prompting, while she collapses under the terrors of conscience. All the perplexities and complexities in this matter can be reconciled, once you get the true centre from which to regard them. The fact is that Shakespeare, even in characters commonly thought "obvious," and which are obvious in the sense that they are broad and representative, not specialised and dependent on minute differentiations, nevertheless has the complexity and subtlety of Nature herself. He has always a psychological problem before him, and that problem is worked out as Nature works it, with broad general definition, but subtle, subordinate detail. Hence critics who see only the bold definition miss the significance of the delicate and suggested detail. Mr. Comyns Carr has summed the present problem with a true grasp of its central key, but not quite a complete grasp. He discerns, quite truly, that all the seeming-capricious divergence between Macbeth and his wife, their apparent (temporary) interchange of sexual character, really arises from sex — it results from a marvellously subtle study of sexual nature in face of a given situation. Just so, and not otherwise, must the situation affect a man and woman like Macbeth and his wife. What he does not seem quite to grasp is that Lady Macbeth's lack of her husband's vivid imagination (a lack on which so much depends) is itself a sexual matter. Macbeth is no moral coward (he shows moral courage in abundance); he is an *imaginative* coward. Few seem to have noticed that here (as elsewhere) Shakespeare shows remarkable intuition of national character. As Juliet is the elementally passionate Italian girl, as his Romans are the very genius of old Rome, so Macbeth is the superstitious Celt, swayed by the imagination, by bodements and omens — the very stuff on which the witches may act. But his wife, as a woman, is sexually deficient in imagination, practical in her ideas, and unable to follow his flights of high-wrought fancy. This distinction between the sexes Shakespeare habitually marks, for good and for evil; as it is marked in the history of many an artist whose practical wife was impatient of his imaginative aims. We do not say that Celtic women are never superstitious (nothing is more superstitious than a superstitious woman); we say that the average woman is less imaginatively minded than the man. And Shakespeare has made Lady Macbeth such a woman; while her husband is imaginative to the core. Therefore, it follows that while Macbeth's vivid imagination anticipates all the consequences of his crime, and shrinks before them (as any sensible man well might do), his wife is sexually unable to share his intense pre-realisation. Woman-like, she is wholly dominated by the emotion of the moment (which in her case is ambition, less for herself than for him), and everything else grows dim before its engrossing pre-possession. That is why she is so resolute, while he is shaken by hesitation. Once the deed is done (and here we wholly join hands with Mr. Comyns Carr) he proceeds unhesitatingly in his career of crime, reverting to his native boldness of action, and no longer needing his wife's counsel or prompting. For in assenting to the deed, he accepted its foreseen consequences, and they take him by no surprise. To her, on the contrary, they are a dreadful surprise. In her lack of imagination, she foresaw nothing. Now all that she unimaginatively scorned in her husband's forebodings seizes her with frightful amaze. Slave to this instant emotion of guilty remorse, as she was before slave to the immediate emotion of ambition, she cannot evade its tyranny. The male refuge of action denied her, she broods concentratedly over agonies unprevisioned, hiding them from her husband lest she should increase his griefs; and dies under them. It is a contrasted tragedy of sex, as inevitable as it is subtle. On the genuine and even tender affection between the murderous pair, the bulk of commentary is in substantial agreement. Altogether, by such balancing and harmonising of extreme opinions as we have indicated, it becomes patent that through Shakespearean criticism, as through the ages, "one increasing purpose runs"; while in regard to Shakespeare the "thoughts of men" have certainly "widened" since the grovelling eighteenth century. On minor points it is more difficult to evolve an agreement; such a point, for example, as whether Banquo's ghost have an external existence or be a creation solely of Macbeth's mind, and whether, therefore, it should be visible to the audience or no. We should answer, both hypotheses are true: Shakespeare, we think, pretty surely intended it to be as much a reality as the ghost in *Hamlet;* yet its evocation is responsive to the nervous tension of the murderer's mind, his obsession by the thought of his victim conjures up the spiritual presence of the victim. The poet has wedded psychical manifestation with psychology. This duality, or rather multiplicity, of Shakespeare's comprehensive mind is the cause of half the disputes about him. He never uses the supernatural without basing it in cunningest fashion on the natural: hence the unapproached lifelikeness of the supernatural in the great dramatist. In fine, this study of the ways of criticism forces on us one paramount conclusion: that the perception inclusive enough to see Shakespeare whole is a gift only less rare than Shakespeare's creative gift.

HAMLET AND OPHELIA
[*Academy*, October 8, 1898]

This brief article from "The Contributors' Playground," is here reproduced because of the concluding sentence in which Thompson, seldom so ambitious, offers his interpretation as "the key" to *Hamlet.*

Dɪᴅ Hamlet treat Ophelia heartlessly? He has lain under an obstinate imputation that he did.The one adequate defence brought forward has been ignored, and commentators proceed on the ancient lines, serenely assured. There are two views. One is that Hamlet was mad — in which case he was irresponsible for his behaviour. With that view I have no concern. Others hold, as I do, that he only feigned madness; and they can see but one explanation of his conduct towards Polonius' daughter. They say that he deliberately cast off Ophelia, and treated her with harsh scorn, in order to encourage the belief that his madness was caused by her refusal to hold further communion with him (as her father had ordered her to refuse). In which case no special pleading can acquit him of cruel disregard for her feelings.

But there is another explanation — the true one, past a doubt. It is, that Hamlet was really bitter against Ophelia, that his cutting gibes were meant in most profound verity. Consider the situation. He had loved her, and made love to her, by word and by letter. She had admitted his vows, encouraged his letters — at least by the tacit encouragement of not discouraging them. He had every reason to conceive that she smiled on his suit, and loved him in return. Suddenly, without a word of explanation, she denies him her presence, rejects his letters. What could he think? The audience know that she is acting on her father's bidding, and against her heart. But Hamlet knows it not. What *could* he think, but that he had been jilted by an inconstant girl, who was not what she seemed; that he had been deceived by a being he had deemed all innocence and truth? Like many a man, he becomes disillusionised, rails against her and all the sex. At the same time he learns of his father's murder, and the two things together increase his native misanthropy, his feeling that the world is out of joint. He has resolved to feign madness; and his real grief and bitterness present him with an excellent pretext to which he can ascribe it. Accordingly he does so, all the more readily that it allows him to give vent to his soreness against the sex and against her in winged words, which otherwise would not be tolerated in him. There is no heart-lessness here, for he believes her to deserve it all.

Study, in this light, his famous interview with Ophelia, when the king and her father conceal themselves to listen. You will see that he begins quite naturally, in the tone of an aggrieved and wronged lover. "I did love you once." He follows it with bitter cynicism, the fruit of destroyed faith, affecting to include himself in his sarcasms on mankind's inconstancy, which are really inspired by her supposed fickleness. Then he discovers her father's lurking presence. He questions her; she denies it. Her father is at home. Worse and worse! She has not only jilted him, she has plotted with her father to betray him, and has lied to him. He at once reassumes his madness, with an added extravagance caused

by his pierced heart, and pours out wild invective on her sex —
through which you can see the pangs of his wounded soul. Follow
this clue through the play, and you will see that it is *right,* that it is
indeed the key.

A CENTURY OF REVOLUTION *

[*Weekly Register,* April 12, 1890]

Thompson's clear grasp of a definite philosophy of life is here the basis of
his discussion of the theories of Rousseau, Darwin, and Morley. It adds
much to his authority and prestige as critic of a volume that rests squarely
upon a philosophical foundation.

IT HAS been given to few Catholic writers of our day and place
to view sacred and political subjects with such a wide outlook
and scale of proportion as those employed by Mr. Lilly. Upon
whatever thing his mind's eye fixes, he sees it in such far-reaching
and many-sided relations as would seem to entail inevitable confusion, or at least obscurity of presentment. From this he is saved
by his habit of following in all things the evolutionary clue. This
is the thread by which he winds through the whole labyrinth
of human history, and this is one cause of the interest which
attaches to what he writes. For not only does it impart originality
to his views, but — whatever we may think of such an application —
it is impossible to deny the order which his extensive use of the
theory enables him to evolve out of disorder. His favourite method
has less play than usual, though it frequently makes its appearance, in the striking volume he has last published. The book is a
refutation of those principles which the Revolution borrowed
from Rousseau, and which Professor Huxley, too, lately set himself to refute. Of the two writers, Mr. Lilly is far the better
equipped for his task. Professor Huxley shares the common weakness of most scientists when confronted with principles that you

* *A Century of Revolution.* By W. S. Lilly.

cannot investigate with reagents, or tease out with needles. These men are incapable of placing in their mental cabinet any idea, unless they can thrust a fact through its body and pin it to their brain. With regard to Mr. Lilly no one can say this. For the rest, like Professor Huxley, he attacks Rousseau's principles as the world has understood them. It is only since his volume appeared that we have all been assured that Rousseau's principles are in truth a string of platitudes with which preachers have sent their auditors to sleep since pulpits were first invented, but which, nevertheless, it needed the profoundly original genius of Rousseau really to teach us, and the profoundly original genius of Mr. Robert Buchanan to discover that Rousseau meant to teach us!

These principles Mr. Lilly begins by defining, and we may quote his brief summary of them. That "complete freedom is the natural condition of man; that all men are born and continue equal in rights; that civil society is an artificial state resting upon a contract between these sovereign units, whereby the native independence of each is surrendered, and a power over each is vested in the body politic as absolute as that which Nature gives every man over his limbs; that human nature is good, and that the evil in the world is the result of bad education and bad institutions; that man, uncorrupted by civilisation, is essentially reasonable; and that the will of the sovereign units, dwelling in every territory under the social contract — that is, of the majority of them, expressed by their delegates — is the rightful and only source of justice and of law." He then proceeds to test the revolutionary dogmas by the practical method of examining their fruits during the century following the Revolution, in regard to liberty, society, art, science, and democracy.

In his chapter on the Revolution and Liberty he begins by laying down, in pages traversing large tracts of consideration, what he considers to be true liberty. Moral liberty, he points out, cannot be absolute; it is conditioned by law. Nor is law, he says, quoting a noble passage from Coleridge, an abstraction; "its power is the same with that of my own permanent self, and all the choice which is permitted me consists in having it for my guardian angel or my avenging fiend. This is the spirit of law, the lute of Amphion, the harp of Orpheus. This is the true necessity which compels men into the social state, by a still-beginning, never-ceasing force of moral cohesion." True liberty is the safeguarding to every individual of his right to develop his own worthiness, in both the social and the spiritual order. And since men's worthinesses differ, inequality is an essential consequence of liberty, equality fatal to liberty. He embodies this contention in the pregnant words of Aristotle: "The one part holds that justice is equality; and so it is, not indeed for all the world, but only for equals. The other maintains that inequality is just, as it is in truth for unequals, not for all the world." Then he turns to modern France, and asks how far the Revolution has realised for it such liberty? Personal liberty is there destroyed by the all-permeating tyranny of the State; the State alone is free, and the State means a congeries of political adventurers. Individual right of property is interfered with by testamentary restrictions, paternal liberty by State monopoly of private education. As a result, the agricultural classes are a mass of selfishly isolated units, sunk in degradation. The artisans are filled with anarchic envy of all above them. Large numbers of citizens are driven from the direction of the State, which is left in the hands of mediocrities. Here, he says, is the outcome of revolutionary, as contrasted with true, liberty. Of course, the defect of this is that his picture of modern France is liable to be challenged in its details, as we have seen it challenged — particularly with respect to the alleged degradation of the agricultural classes. The latter detail he apparently bases on *La Terre;* but a novel, and a novel by Zola, is scarcely an authority which a cool critic would care to accept on such a point.

Dealing with the Revolution and Society, Mr. Lilly has the advantage of fronting definite statements and a definite antagonist, in the shape of Mr. John Morley, whom he takes as the accredited English apologist of the Revolution. He shows by a damning series of extracts from this apologist that the Revolution aims at abolishing religion, as we now understand religion, and God (though Mr. Morley himself is agnostic rather than absolutely atheistic), in order to make way for an antitheistic religion of its own. "Those who agree with the present writer" (says Mr.

Morley) "positively, absolutely, and without reserve, reject as false the whole system of objective propositions which make up the popular belief of the day, in one and all of its theological expressions." "It is conceivable that the world may have been created by a being who is not good, not pitiful, not benevolent, not just; a being no more entitled to our homage or worship than Francesco Cenci was entitled to the filial piety of his unhappy children." "Rousseau urged that Voltaire robbed men of their only solace. What Voltaire really did urge was that the solace to be derived from the attribution of humanity and justice to the Supreme Being, and from the metaphysical account of evil, rests on too narrow a basis either to cover the facts or to be a true solace to any man who thinks and observes. He ought to have gone on to persuade his readers that there is no solace obtainable except that of an energetic fortitude." The revolutionary advocate, Mr. Lilly further demonstrates, preaches Naturalism both in art and in the science of men; holds that the spirit is annihilated by death, and advocates "the great primitive principle, that we can know only phenomena, and know them only experientially." The religion which he would substitute for Christianity seems to be some form of Positivism, though he confesses the revolutionary creed to be as yet more negative than affirmative. "The coming modification of religion will undoubtedly rest on the solidarity of mankind, as Comte said." Yet still the heart does need a worship, and this we are to find in contemplating the grand operations of Nature, and in "an imperial sense of participation in the common movement and equal destination of eternal forces."

With the existence of God, and the immortality of the soul, the old ethical foundations go. Free will was the necessary result of those dogmas, and the root of man's duty; while Necessarianism is the result of their abolition, and is strongly held by Mr. Morley. Now the foundations of modern society, says Mr. Lilly, are legislation penally supported, and the family. Penal legislation is destroyed by Necessarianism, since such legislation is based on the theory of human responsibility, and what right have you to punish *l'homme machine?* At most you can, in self-preservation, shut him up out of your way. For the family, it blossoms from the

Christian teaching in regard to marriage; that again springs from the Christian teaching in regard to purity; and the Christian teaching in regard to purity springs from asceticism. Mr. Lilly has no difficulty in showing how utterly opposed is Mr. Morley to this spirit; that he palliates while condemning the excesses of the revolutionary apostles, thinks Diderot "keenly alive to the beauty of order and domestic piety," and at the most urges "some continence and order in the relations of men and women as a good thing." He denounces "that mean and poor form of domesticity which has always been too apt to fascinate the English imagination," "domestic sentimentality of a greasy kind," and says that "Byron helped to clear the air of this." In fact it would almost seem that Mr. Morley claims Byron for the Revolution; he praises him because "the domestic sentiment almost disappears in those works which made Byron most popular, or else it only appears to be banished with reproach." Byron, however, was no infidel, but a deliberately wicked Christian, who believed in the things he mocked and outraged. This is regrettable; for our generosity would have liked to present 1789 with Byron. We could imagine no loftier spectacle than the Temple of the Revolution adorned at once and supported by its twin caryatids, Byron and Zola.

It is with Zola that Mr. Lilly deals in the section on the Revolution and Art, and so, though it is eloquent, able, and interesting, we may be excused for passing it over. Zolaism in England dares as yet but peep from a corner. In the section on the Revolution and Democracy he has (perhaps inevitably) tangled up so much contentious political matter as to render discussion difficult. He proves the vicious political unsoundness of Rousseau's principles, and exhibits the necessary instability of a democracy reared upon them. Then he draws an ideal of the true democracy. But, unfortunately, he proceeds to examples, and not only selects as his type of true democracy the German Empire, but ignores the great Transatlantic Republic, the most conspicuous democratic fact of the day.

The Revolution and Science is perhaps the most arresting portion of the book, for it smites the revolutionary school with their own most favourite weapon – Darwinism. The Darwinism on which the Revolution relies is really, says Mr. Lilly, Darwinism as developed by Haeckel — that Haeckel of Jena about whom Mr. Herman Merivale once wrote flippant verses:

> Down on your knees, superstition and flunkeydom!
> Can't you accept my plain doctrine instead?
> What is so simple as primitive monkeydom
> Born in the sea, with a cold in its head?

Evolution as taught by Darwin simply lays the axe to all Rousseau's principles. Mr. Lilly proves this, taking the revolutionary dogmas one by one. What, he asks, becomes, if you confront them with Darwinism, of "the natural, inalienable, and imprescriptible rights of the individual, derived from the natural man?" The natural man! The natural man is the natural monkey. What are the "natural, inalienable, and imprescriptible rights" of the monkey? Absolute reason is unknown to Darwinism: reason is to it a relative term, just as are justice and right — right to be means might to be. Liberty, the sovereignty of the individual? "The message of scientific evolution to the masses is to know their masters, for that will be best for them; to recognise the provision of Nature, which has made the few strong, wise, and able; the many, weak, foolish, and incompetent." Equality, Darwinism pronounces contrary to Nature. Fraternity? Yes: the fraternity of Cain and Abel. The social contract? The individual is valueless to Nature. Natural goodness of man? Ferocious passions are the very groundwork of the natural man, are at the base of that struggle for existence which evolution proclaims. To the panacea of education Darwinism replied with Herbert Spencer: "Crime is really connected with an inferior mode of life, itself usually dependent upon an original inferiority of nature." "Ignorance is no more to be held the cause of crime than various other concomitants." After thus demonstrating that Darwinism is fatal to the revolutionary theory, Mr. Lilly proceeds to demonstrate that it is undiscordant with Christianity, and this leads to a glorification of evolution which is one of the most eloquent, as it is one of the most characteristic, things in the book.

And we could have wished that he had stopped here. But he

passes into a vehement attack on those who reject his pet theory, which provokes us into thrusting an arm of something like cool reason between the extreme Darwinians and extreme anti-Darwinians. Darwinism at present is no more than a working hypothesis; probable if you will, fruitful if you will, but still only a working hypothesis. "What, with so many facts in its favour?" Yes. Though it had twenty-two facts on its side, and but twenty-three were needed for its proof; until it had that twenty-third fact likewise on its side, science (if it is to remain science, not speculation) must refuse to class it as more than a working hypothesis. Biologists have borrowed from the chemist his experimental method; let them borrow also the chemist's method of estimating results — a rigid, inflexible, passionless method which is a model to all physical sciences. Is the theory of Darwin more strongly probable than was at one time the theory of Dalton, the evolutionary theory than the atomic theory? Mr. Lilly himself, we think, would admit that it is not. Have the fruits of the former been greater than of the latter? Mr. Lilly himself, we think, will admit that they have not yet been as great. Yet the atomic theory was enunciated by Dalton only as a working hypothesis, and at the time when the stream of facts ran most unbrokenly in its favour, chemistry never taught it as more than a working hypothesis. Why? Because it was not absolutely proven. Chemistry may perhaps have to congratulate itself on its inexorable caution. Now what is sauce for the atomic goose is sauce for the evolutionary gander. It is yet unproven, by the confession of its advocates; therefore they must either cease to demand its acceptance as more than a theory, or cease to talk of their scientific impartiality. Evolution is open to anyone, it is open to anyone to hold the Darwinian theory, it is open to anyone to preach the Darwinian theory, it is open to no one to teach the Darwinian theory.

Even the slight and necessarily imperfect outline we have given of Mr. Lilly's book has left us no space to dwell on its literary merits; on the style which, dealing with frequently abstruse subjects and carrying a multifarious weight of knowledge, nevertheless permits none but a dull reader to find this volume dull.

THE IMAGE OF GOD
[*Franciscan Annals*, July, 1893]

This article, written the year before Thompson met Patmore, illustrates the similarity of their ideas that was the basis of their rare friendship. Although the idea here developed is chiefly philosophical and theological, it is of the very essence of Thompson's poetry. Some of the expressions, even, are to be found verbatim in "Any Saint."

"LET us make man to our image and likeness." In all the distinctions drawn by Catholic psychologists between the "image" and the "likeness" in man, one thing is conspicuous — the quiet exclusion of the body from share in either. Nay, "exclusion" is too positive a term. The body has simply been ignored. Now, while I leave the learned to settle the "likeness" as they will, I ask that in the "image" should be included the body. Let me first define in what sense I would have the body included in the "image." Here I am at one with St. Thomas, who says that there is in the human body a resemblance to God *per modum vestigii*. Now *vestigium* means literally a *garment-trace*, and is used derivatively to signify first a *footprint*, and secondly a trace of any kind, a *vestige*. It is in its meaning of a footprint that we get most directly at the sense in which I interpret St. Thomas. Let us consider the difference between — for example — a sculptured image of the foot and a footprint. The sculptured image accurately reproduces the form of the foot, though in another material. Not so the footprint. What in the foot are prominences, in the print appear as depressions; what in the foot depressions, in the print as prominences. Now from the print we can construct a reproduction of the foot, but only on condition that we know the *system of correspondence*. Namely, we must know that the hollows of the print stand for prominences in the original, the prominences of the print for depressions in the original. This, then, is what I understand St. Thomas to mean by a resemblance *per modum vestigii* — an image by *correspondence*. And its distinction from an express image lies in this — that though we should know both the image and the thing imaged, we cannot apply the one to the other unless we know the system of correspondence. It is only through correspondence—and necessarily imperfect correspondence — that matter can image spirit. Thus the triangle is an image of the Trinity by correspondence, though the correspondence is not only imperfect but rudimentary. I affirm, then, that man's body is an image of God by correspondence.

From *à priori* reasoning this must be so. The body is given to the soul as its material shape. What, then, is the excellence of a material shape? To express, by correspondence, the spirit. Thus language is a material shape, the excellence of which is its correspondent expression of immaterial thought; and its excellence is much or little, as the correspondence is perfect or imperfect. If it do not express the thought, it has no excellence; it is not a shape at all. Does the body not express the soul? Then it is not merely an imperfect material shape, it is no shape at all. God is not merely a worse artist than the Feejian savage, He is no artist at all. But He is artist, and more than artist. He is Art. For Art is nothing else than the symmetry of God. Whence the body may not be doubted to be the perfect material shape of the soul; which is to say, an image of the soul by correspondence, perfect to the full capacity of matter. But the soul is an image of God. Then what is the body? The inference is obvious. Again: God, assuming *for* eternity a material shape, could not assume such a one as nowise expressed Him. That would unite the Deity to an eternal ugliness; for inexpressive shape is an ugliness. Nor could He assume such a one as, in its kind, imperfectly expressed Him; for so He would exceed humiliation, and take upon Himself an eternal imperfection. Therefore He must choose such a one as is the most perfect expression of Him which create matter can furnish of increate Spirit. But He chose the human form. Conclude, that the human body is the most perfect correspondence of Himself which lay within the possibilities of matter.

I insist on this, I confess, because the prerogative of the body seems to me somewhat undervalued. If man, created below the angels, has been raised above the seraphim, it is because of that body which the angels lack. For through that he becomes to God the little beloved focus point and brief compendium of His two creations — matter and spirit; a swinging-wicket between the material and immaterial universes, opening by his soul upon the angels, by his body upon the stars. "No man hateth his own flesh"; and I cannot believe but that St. Francis, who loved all things, loved not least the hardly-used Brother Ass. Rather are we intended to use this "sweet enemy" as a child, which we love, chastise, thwart, cherish; refusing now, because our dearest wish is its future greatness. Teaching and prophecy show us the whole visible creation waiting on the advance of Brother Ass; travailing in pain, waiting for the redemption of the body. For the life of Man, the genus, repeats in large the life of man the unit, and its years are centuries. The generic body, too, awaits redemption; and the body of Nature waits with it. Of Nature, also, it is true that "this corruptible must put on incorruptibility." The human body, in the hour of her final glory, shall not stand without fit bridesmaids before Him to whom the Bride says, "Come." Heaven shall abide at her right hand, and earth at her left, clothed in new wedding-garments, which the moth Time may not consume.

SANCTITY AND SONG *
(A Second Paper)
[*Franciscan Annals*, January, 1894]

The opinions here set down concerning the writings of St. Francis of Assisi supplement Thompson's views expressed in his first paper on the subject. It was printed in the *Franciscan Annals*, December, 1893, and included by Mr. Meynell in his definitive edition of Thompson's works. More important than Thompson's ideas on the writings of St. Francis is his view of pain here set forth. It is the essence of his message as a poet, and was to have been the explicit theme of a poem he planned to write, contrasting the Christian idea of pain with Swinburne's. But death intervened — not, however, before he had written an outline of the proposed poem, one of the most valuable items in the Boston College Collection of Thompsoniana.

THE metrical Canticles, I said last month, are among the works doubtfully ascribed to St. Francis. The general view is that the Saint wrote a number of poetical pieces in a prose — and perhaps

* *The Three Metrical Canticles of St. Francis of Assisi.*

unliterary — form; that from this prose one of his followers, perhaps Fra Jacopone, put into metrical shape the Canticles I have commented on. I must now notice a piece published among the Assisian's admitted works — a piece which lends countenance to this opinion, styled a "Prayer of the Blessed Father to obtain Poverty"; it is really a Canticle of Poverty in prose, and exhibits the same features, the bold and quite personal cast of imagination, the veritably *sancta simplicitas,* which individualise the metrical Canticles. Both to shew these qualities, and for its own striking beauty, I quote the greater part of it.

O my most sweet Lord Jesus Christ, have pity on me, and on my Lady Poverty, for I burn with love of her, and without her I cannot rest. O my Lord, who didst cause me to be enamoured of her, Thou knowest that she is sitting in sadness, rejected by all; "the mistress of nations is become as a widow," vile and contemptible; the queen of all virtues, seated on a dunghill, complains that all her friends have despised her, and are become her enemies;— they have proved themselves deceivers and not spouses. Behold, O Lord Jesus! how truly Poverty is the queen of all virtues; for, leaving the abode of Angels, Thou didst come down to earth that Thou mightest espouse her to Thyself with constant love, and produce from her, in her, and by her, the children of all perfection. And she clung to Thee with such fidelity that she began her service even when Thou wert in Thy Mother's womb, for Thy Body was of all the smallest; at Thy birth she received Thee in a manger and a stable; and during Thy life she so stripped Thee of all things that she would not even allow Thee a stone whereon to rest Thy head. As a most faithful consort she accompanied Thee when Thou didst go forth to fight for our Redemption; and in the conflict of Thy Passion she alone stood by as Thy armour-bearer; when Thy disciples fled, and denied Thy Name, she did not leave Thee, but with the whole band of her princes she fearlessly adhered to Thee. On account of the height of Thy Cross, even Thy Mother could not reach Thee; but Thy Lady Poverty, with her companion Want, embraced Thee more closely than ever, and was more firmly united to Thee in Thy sufferings. And when Thou wast consumed with Thirst, she, Thy faithful spouse, was there, and did not allow Thee to have even a drop of water; but, by means of the impious executioners, she prepared for Thee a draught so bitter, that Thou couldst only taste, not drink it. In the strong embrace of this Thy spouse Thou didst breathe forth Thy Soul. Nor did she forsake Thee at Thy burial, but she took care that Thou shouldst have neither sepulchre nor ointments, nor winding-clothes, except what were lent Thee by others. This Thy most Holy Spouse was not absent from Thy Resurrection, for rising gloriously in her embrace Thou didst leave in the Sepulchre all these borrowed things. Thou didst bear her with Thee to Heaven, leaving all that is in the world. And now Thou hast given to Thy Lady Poverty the seal of Thy Kingdom, that she may sign the elect who walk in the way of perfection.

One sees that St. Francis left to the frescoed allegories of Giotto little beyond the elaboration of details. The central idea of those famous frescoes is here, traced by the Saint's own hand. *Facta est quasi vidua domina gentium.* It is the quotation made after the death of Beatrice by the Tertiary Dante; himself a son of that despised widow, and knowing in his later days another's bread. But kindred evidences that this singularly individual poetic spirit came from St. Francis himself, not from any of his followers, are to be found outside his writings. His sayings are full of it. A similar and most winning parable regarding Poverty was uttered by him to Pope Innocent III, and is well known to every reader of his life. Indeed, like his Master, he spoke often in parables. Take the anecdote which is related of the period before his conversion. His mother, Pica, was preparing the table for dinner, and Francis placed on it very many loaves. Pica inquired why he put so many loaves for so few guests. "They are for the poor," said her son. "But where are the poor?" asked Pica. Francis answered: "They are in my heart." Comment could only mar the beauty of the story.

When I survey the poems which have formed the subject of this article there is one lesson which strikes me as specially needed by the day in which we live — it is the lesson of Pain. Pain — the modern world pales before it. If man's cupboard *has* such a skeleton, let us shut the cupboard very close, let us suppress all whisper of it: we will not have our actors play us tragedies, for they remind us of pain; unpleasant poverty — look to it, policeman, keep it from our ways when we walk forth, for it says "Pain is"; take, messieurs the philanthropists, millions of money, so you will scavenge away this pain from our doors; and for ourselves, shall we not form a Mutual Cotton-wool Society, whereby every germ of pain shall be filtered from our sacred air? It is upon this cowardly day that the voice of St. Francis breaks, crying, in the words of a modern poet, —

Delight has taken Pain to her heart.

They sum St. Francis' teaching on this point, sum it in a line. Pain, which came to man as a penalty, remains with him as a consecration; his ignominy, by a Divine ingenuity, he is enabled to make his exaltation. Man, shrinking from laving pain, is a child shuddering on the verge of the water, and crying, "It is so cold!" How many among us, after repeated lessonings of experience, are never able to comprehend that there is no special love without special pain. To such St. Francis reveals that the Supreme Love is itself full of Supreme Pain. It is fire, it is torture; his human weakness accuses himself of rashness in provoking it, even while his soul demands more pain, if it be necessary for more Love. So he revealed to one of his companions that the pain of his stigmata was agonising, but was accompanied with a sweetness so intense as made it ecstatic to him. Such is the preaching of his words and example to an age which understands it not. Pain is. Pain is inevadible. Pain may be made the instrument of joy. It is the angel with the fiery sword, guarding the gates of the lost Eden. The flaming sword which pricked man forth from Paradise must wave him back; through that singeing portal, "with dreadful faces thronged and fiery arms," he must return or not at all. Such seems to be the lesson even of a poet who strayed from Catholicism — Victor Hugo, in his posthumous poem, "Dieu." I have not the original, so the reader must accept my own inadequate version.

> To find once more his Father, man has need but of a tear:
> "Believe," from out adversity, and "Hope," ascendeth from the bier.
> In penitence he holds the keys of comfortabler days;
> God, after proof and sorrowing, at length to him repays
> For the Eden of the blossomings' the Paradises starry,
> And Eve, unto thy nakedness her veils affordeth Mary.
> The fire-glaived angel summons back Adam ex-paradised;
> The soul regains its native soil bearing the Cross of Jesus Christ,
> And the Eternal seateth the immortal by His side.
>
> The value of the human soul so high is magnified,
> That in the deep of Heaven supreme, where the irradiance smiles,
> Where the blent Father and the Son the Spirit reconciles,
> It seemeth as the azure interfused, commixed, enfurled
> Jesus, the spirit of mankind, and God, the spirit of the world.

I need only recall, in conclusion, that the spirit of song which was in St. Francis did not expire with him. Poetry clung round the cowls of his Order; and it was a Franciscan, Thomas of Celano, who gave to the Church perhaps her two greatest hymns.

MR. HENLEY'S ANTHOLOGY *
[*Academy*, November 20, 1897]

The interest in this review attaches less to the criticism of the volume than to Thompson's ideas on what an anthology should be.

IN this book Mr. Henley has done what every other lover of poetry would fain do: he has gathered his favourite lyrical poems together. Most of us are able only to copy them, or possibly merely their titles, in MS. Mr. Henley, being a critical power, has been asked to print his choice, and has complied. Naturally no other person in the world can be expected to approve every selection in these three hundred and sixty-nine pages. Every reader will be able to suggest omissions, but there are few, we fancy, who, taking it as it stands, will not have plentiful praise for Mr. Henley's volume. That, at any rate, is our own position. We have several remarks to make concerning it; we take exception to some inclusions, to its general scheme of arrangement, and also to its form; yet we are glad, very glad, to have the book on a shelf contiguous to the armchair by the fire. That is our dominant feeling.

Primarily, let us thank Mr. Henley for his tremendous gift of lyrical passages from the Old Testament. He has arranged each extract anew in rhythmical lines, with here and there an excision for concentration's sake, and they appear in this book so unexpectedly as almost to constitute a fresh body of poetry. Their unexpectedness is, indeed, well nigh too startling; for the Biblical

* *English Lyrics.* By W. E. Henley.

section comes between a batch of old anonymous Scotch love-poems and Gascoigne's "Lover's Lullaby," and the contrast between these northern singers warbling their little personal affairs and the mighty Hebrew symbolists is strangely striking. Mr. Henley has placed the section where it is, at the risk of incongruity, in order to keep his chronological sequence intact, and we are too glad to have his treatment of the passages to complain. None the less, the effect is certainly odd, almost disconcerting. The section, without doing any serious violence to the chronological scheme of the book, might have come first. As a specimen of Mr. Henley's arrangement let us quote the hundred and thirty-seventh Psalm, as he prints it:

> By the rivers of Babylon,
> There we sat down, yea, we wept,
> When we remembered Zion.
> We hanged our harps
> Upon the willows in the midst thereof.
> For there they that carried us away captive
>   required of us a song;
> And they that wasted us required of us mirth,
>   saying:
> Sing us one of the songs of Zion.
> How shall we sing the Lord's song
> In a strange land?
> If I forget thee, O Jerusalem,
> Let my right hand forget her cunning.
> If I do not remember thee,
> Let my tongue cleave to the roof of my mouth;
> If I prefer not Jerusalem
> Above my chief joy.
> Remember, O Lord, the children of Edom
> In the day of Jerusalem; who said: — Rase it,
>   rase it,
> Even to the foundation thereof.
> O daughter of Babylon, who art to be destroyed,
> Happy shall he be, that rewardeth thee
> As thou hast served us!
> Happy shall he be, that taketh and dasheth
>   thy little ones
> Against the stones.

Does it not gain—is not its beauty emphasised—by the new arrangement? When we say that Mr. Henley gives fifty-three full pages in all, selecting from Exodus, Samuel, the Psalms, Job, the Proverbs, Ecclesiastes, the Song of Songs, Isaiah, Jeremiah, Ezekiel, Joel, Amos, and Habakkuk, an idea of the exceptional interest of his volume is communicated. For his other surprises, his new gems — new, that is to say, to the ordinary reader, although familiar enough to the student of English poetry — Mr. Henley has gone to the Bannantyne MS., *Tottel's Miscellany*, the Royal MS., and other old collections. The following beautiful poem, of a quality not common in English verse, is, for example, from *The Paradise of Dainty Devices*. To some it will be familiar, but others may be surprised to learn that so homely and tender a lyric was written in an age when homeliness was not the fashion. We quote the first two stanzas, as modernised by their new editor. The author is Richard Edwardes (1523-1566), "sometime of her Maiesties Chappell":

> In going to my naked bed as one that would
>   have slept,
> I heard a wife sing to her child, that long
>   before had wept.
> She sighèd sore and sang full sweet, to bring
>   the babe to rest,
> That would not cease but crièd still, in
>   sucking at her breast.
> She was full weary of her watch, and grievèd
>   with her child,
> She rockèd it and rated it, till that on her it
>   smiled;
> Then did she say: "Now have I found this
>   proverb true to prove,
> The falling out of faithful friends renewing
>   is of love!"
>
> Then took I paper, pen and ink, this proverb
>   for to write,
> In register for to remain of such a worthy
>   wight.

As she proceeded thus in song unto her little
   brat,
Much matter uttered she of weight, in place
   whereas she sat,
And provèd plain, there was no beast, nor
   creature bearing life,
Could well be known to live in love, without
   discord and strife:
Then kissèd she her little babe, and sware
   by God above,
The falling out of faithful friends renewing
   is of love.

Alexander Scott yields four lyrics, a little marred, perhaps, for the modern reader by their archaisms. An archaism alone is often disturbing enough; but an archaism that is also Scotch can be quite a deterrent. *Tottel's Miscellany* offers this delicate tissue of philosophic resignation: "Upon consideration of the state of this life," the title runs, "he wisheth death"—

The longer life, the more offence:
The more offence, the greater pain:
The greater pain, the less defence:
The less defence, the lesser gain.
The loss of gain long ill doth try:
Wherefore come death, and let me die!
   The shorter life, less count I find:
The less account, the sooner made:
The count soon made, the merrier mind:
The merry mind doth thought evade.
Short life, in truth, this thing doth try;
Wherefore come death, and let me die!
   Come gentle death, the ebb of care,
The ebb of care, the flood of life,
The flood of life, the joyful fare,
The joyful fare, the end of strife.
The end of strife, that thing wish I:
Wherefore come death, and let me die.

And here, from the Bannantyne MS., is a jocund song of the amorous spring, under the title "Lusty May":

> O lusty May, with Flora Queen!
> The balmy drops from Phœbus sheen
> Preluciand beams before the day:
> By that Diana growïs green,
> Through gladness of this lusty May.
>
> Then Esperus, that is so bright,
> Till woful heartës casts his light,
> With banks that blooms on every brae,
> And showers are shed forth of their sight,
> Through gladness of this lusty May.
>
> Birds on bewïs of every birth,
> Rejoicing notes makand their mirth
> Right pleasantly upon the spray,
> With flourishings o'er field and firth,
> Through gladness of this lusty May.
>
> All luvarïs that are in care
> To their ladies they do repair,
> In fresh mornings before the day,
> And are in mirth ay mair and mair,
> Through gladness of this lusty May.

These are all welcome.

Criticising an anthology amounts to saying how one would have done it oneself, and that is what we propose now to do. Had the invitation to compile a volume of English lyrics been tendered to us, we should have set to work differently. In the first place we should, for two reasons, have discarded chronological arrangement altogether. One reason is, that the chronological arrangement of a collection of English lyrics such as this has the disadvantage of making the first part of the book so much livelier and more interesting than the last. The lyrics that were written by Englishmen prior to Marvell and those that were written after are so different in kind that it is almost necessary to find a new name for the later poems. The old inspiration suddenly ceased. Suddenly a moment came when to the poets the world ceased to be new every morning.

The Elizabethans, we can believe, actually thought that it was so. They had the happiness of infancy, of young, fresh growth. When joyous, their songs bubbled out of them. Even when they were melancholy or pensive the words seem to have followed each other as naturally and spontaneously as the notes of a bird. Theirs was the genuine lyrism. And then, partly because of the blighting Puritan influence, partly because of the Restoration's influence in the opposite direction, and partly because a critical spirit was abroad tending to make poets self-conscious workmen in a degree they had not hitherto reached, spontaneity vanished, and for a while genuine lyrism was no more. Poems no longer sprang into being as they once had done (or had seemed to do): they were now deliberately built up. A new type of mind was developed: cynicism for the first time turned to verse; architecture, in short, took the place of poetry. If Mr. Henley had not been more or less bound by his chronological scheme to take some note of the hundred and odd years between Marvell and Blake, maybe he would have neglected them altogether. In a general collection of English lyrics such as this we who write should have done so. It would be impossible, it is true, to part with "Sally in Our Alley"; but neither for the temperament nor the poetical achievement of the Earl of Rochester, who is one of Mr. Henley's principal intervening poets, can we share his enthusiasm. In a volume including the perfect stanzas of Lovelace we should not admit Rochester at all.

One other objection to chronological order is the applicability of the term lyric to poems springing from so many and diverse emotions—the result being a departure from homogeneity. An editor's duties do not consist merely in bringing poems together; he should also arrange them in order to prevent both dissonant juxtapositions and the effect of patchiness in his book. As it is, although on almost every page of this volume there are lines of beauty, there are yet portions of the book of far less distinction and worth than others. One patch to which we refer is the group of eleven poems by Blake coming after a very arid stretch, containing such artificial numbers as Pope's "Dying Christian" and Goldsmith's "When Lovely Woman." This objection, however, brings us to the statement that whatever the inducement, we should never attempt to make a general collection of English lyrics at all. The result is bound to be too heterogeneous. But discarding the idea of a general collection, we would willingly undertake to make some special collection, such as lyrics of love, or lyrics in praise of life, or lyrics distinguished by extraordinary beauty. And we should stipulate that the form given to the book was compact and slim, so that it might be a companion both out of the house and in it. Mr. Henley's book is far too large. He has been too generous. English lyrics are our bosom friends or nothing: and bosom friends should be empowered to nestle close. In other words, a smaller volume should have been made, one that would slip into the pocket. There is too much here. Few persons that want Wordsworth's "Ode on the Intimations of Immortality" want also Moore's facile fluencies; few that want the matchless music of Shelley's "Song of Pan" want also Jordan's "Careless Gallant," while few, again, that want the "Careless Gallant" will greatly prize the splendid contributions from the Authorised Version. It is possible to be too catholic. Mr. Henley, it seems to us, would have been wiser to have made a congruous collection, with, say, the joy of living as its motive. Mr. Henley is all for full-blooded life himself, and no one could make a book in praise of it better than he. To a large extent this book does perform such an office. The Elizabethan section, which, coming first, gives the note, is rich in enthusiasm for life; but it does not persist. Love poems, however, so predominate that we come to resent all else, especially such grave singers as Henry Vaughan and Pope and Ebenezer Elliott. The earlier part of the book, indeed, tends to transform several of the later poets into interlopers — Lamb and Wordsworth particularly. Poe's ecstasies seem quite unreasonably modern, and Byron's "Isles of Greece," Campbell's two naval ballads, Coleridge's "Kubla Khan," and much of Scott, strike one as clean out of place. Had Mr. Henley excluded some of these more modern pieces, he might have drawn from the golden age of English lyrical poetry more examples than he does offer of the kind which, so far as we gather, he likes best. There is, for example, an amatory song of Cartwright's, from his play, *The Ordinary*, beginning, "Come, O come! I brook no stay," which is quite good. Dr. Strode also, we think, deserves representation. But to complain of omissions is idle, and we have, perhaps, cavilled too much already.

The book might have been thought out more carefully by the publishers. The type of the introduction and notes — both of the highest interest — is painfully small, and that of the poems themselves might well be larger; while the title-page contains the odd contradiction, "Chaucer to Poe, 1340-1809." On the cover the error is not repeated: there we read, "1340-1849." We note also a misprint in Sedley's song, "Phyllis is my only joy." In the third line "coming" is given "cunning."

MAETERLINCK'S ESSAYS *
[*Outlook*, February 26, 1898]

Thompson's quiet but sure way of conceding that Maeterlinck was "individual" but not "new" is most characteristic. And it is interesting to see how diverse are the messages of speech tracked to its lair of silence by hunters such as Maeterlinck, Patmore, and Mrs. Meynell.

THE first act of justice in regard to this book is to say a word for that usually neglected personage, the translator, who, it must be confessed, usually deserves his neglect. Seldom is it possible to praise a translation so unreservedly as we can praise this. No one would suspect it for a translation. It is a daring affirmation, but we will affirm it — a young writer might do worse than take Mr. Sutro's version as a model of limpid and graceful English. Maeterlinck is fortunate. He has been rendered into English which it is a pleasure to read for its own beauty. What French-writing author of the century has had equal luck?

He is not quite so lucky in his introducer. Mr. Walkley is a very

* *The Treasure of the Humble*. By Maurice Maeterlinck. Translated by Alfred Sutro. With Introduction by A. B. Walkley.

able dramatic critic, and Maeterlinck is a dramatist; what more
natural than to ask Mr. Walkley to write an introduction? But,
unfortunately, this book touches the drama in but a single essay.
The rest is mystical, or what you will, but not dramatic; and it
needs not Mr. Walkley's implied disclaimer to perceive that he
is not by way of being a mystic, or anything within a mile of it.
The result is that his introductory essay, though clever and sympathetic, is not too well informed — which is ill — and takes a
hesitant, apologetic tone — which is worse. He is content to rest
his apology for Maeterlinck on the ground that Maeterlinck
sounds "a new and individual note" in his reaction against the
"positive" and "quasi-scientific" character of modern literature.
But this note has already been sounded in English literature with
far greater depth and definition by Coventry Patmore, and by
others after him. In France it has ceased to be a new note. The
originality of the Belgian writer is not in the thing said, but in the
way it is said. The "new note" in all these essays is — Maeterlinck.

It is an ill service to insist on his mysticism. There is so much in
this "mysticism" which any thoughtful reader might read, as M.
Jourdain spoke prose, without knowing it. The opening essay, for
example, is no more obviously mystic than Carlyle (whom it does
not at all resemble), or Mrs. Meynell (whom it does). Its title is
typical — "Silence." Maeterlinck is an apostle of silence — whence,
in part, the comparison we have just made with an essayist who
is the recognised devotee of reticence. To him, the beauty and
mystery of language lurk in its silent intervals, the interspace
where gathers (so to speak) the atmosphere exuded from the
words. To him every word is an organism, exhaling and enwrapped
by its own emanation, as the earth by its swathing air. Silence is
the lair of speech; and into silence you must track it, if you would
surprise its ultimate significance. This idea is pursued through its
relations to life and love and all things, with a beautiful subtlety
of idea and utterance which itself exemplifies his thesis, so uncapturable is its secret felicity. And this is really the burden of the
book. Maeterlinck is possessed by a passion for what we might call
(pardon the not too literary coinage) *interiority* — interior beauty,
interior goodness, interior love, interior morality, interior life —

yea, even interior drama; and in saying this we have summed the scope and purport of his essays. The something beyond, the elusive soul in the body of humanity, the unharkened thing, which we must hush the loud noises of life before we can hear: turn to what subject he will, it is for this he strives; it is this search which runs like a thread through all these essays. Therefore he wishes a drama in which what the critic condemns as "unessential to the action" shall be the only thing essential, and has endeavoured after it in his own practice; for do not these things pertain to the interior action, which alone really matters? Therefore he writes of women with rapturous reverence and exceeding beauty: for women are beset by intuitions, presentiments, irrational certainties — all which man calls weakness; but which Maeterlinck discerns as sensitive submission to the interior Inevitableness. "Women are indeed the veiled sisters of all the great things we do not see."

Maeterlinck is feminine, in fact — feminine, and therefore modern. He is feminine in his exclusive worship of beauty. The great masculine poets, with eyes quick for beauty, sought first truth, and beauty came to them as a rewarding accident. The reward, indeed, was plenitudinous. But Maeterlinck sees truth only in its mirror of beauty. He is feminine in his exclusively emotional perceptions. His mysticism, though it undoubtedly exists, does not go far. He is content to express what he feels; and, save through feeling, he cannot see. His most obscure sensations he interprets with singular felicity and fidelity; but he does not attempt to strike the root of his sensations, as a more masculine and philosophic poet would do. The whole power and originality of his book lies in the extraordinary gift of language by which the most vaporous and evanescing intimations of a sensitive soul are condensed into words. He does not escape the defects of this quality. Often the result is vague, unrealised, even extravagant. He attempts the scarcely accomplishable; and the result is, at times, the unaccomplished. But the style is the style of an exquisite artist, fluid, sweet, ingratiating, minutely expressive; the thought is the thought of a poet, subtle, unprevisioned, fragrant; and, over all, whatever else he fails to achieve, is the achievement of delectable beauty. His language, flower-like, is ever turning towards the light.

GUSTO *

[*Academy*, October 7, 1899]

This is a good example of Thompson's fidelity to his own precept that criticism should be in the style of the literary effort it criticizes. There is gusto in the review, as in Hewlett's little novels. But it is not without "that power of convincement" that the little novels lack.

WE HAVE before remarked on Mr. Hewlett's joy of living — his gusto; and here again, in his new book, it is his first characteristic. His gusto is immense, enough for himself and all his readers: a gusto that sweeps one into its course like a March wind, and carries one with it. At the beginning of his first story, "Madonna of the Peach-Trees," is a scene of laundry girls washing clothes by the Ponte Navi at Verona. With what an air Mr. Hewlett presents it; with what robust pleasure in the doing!

Having spat into the water many times, rubbed his hands, mopped his head, and cursed most things under heaven, and some in it, Master Baldassare found himself watching the laundresses on the shore. They were the usual shrill, shrewd, and laughing line — the trade seems to induce high mirth — and as such no bait for the old merchant by ordinary; but just now the sun and breeze together made a bright patch of them, set them at a provoking flutter. Baldassare, prickly with dust, found them like their own cool linen hung out to dance itself dry in the wind. Most of all, he noticed Vanna, whom he knew well enough, because when she knelt upright she was taller and more wayward than the rest, and because the wind made so plain the pretty figure she had. She was very industrious, but no less full of talk; there seemed so much to say! The pauses were frequent in which she straightened herself from the hips, and turned to thrust chin and voice into the debate. You saw then the sharp angle, the fine line of light along that raised chin, the charming turn of the neck, her free young shoulders and shapely head; also you marked her lively tones of *ci* and *si*, and how her slaking finger drove them home. The wind would catch her yellow hair, sometimes, and wind it across her bosom like a scarf; or it streamed sideways like a long pennon; or, being caught by a gust from below, sprayed out like a cloud of litten

* *Little Novels of Italy*. By Maurice Hewlett.

gold. Vanna always joined in the laugh at her mishap, tossed her tresses back, pinned them up (both hands at the business); and then, with square shoulders and elbows stiff as rods, set to working the dirt out of Don Urbano's surplice. Baldassare brooded, chewing straws. What a clear colour that girl had, to be sure! What a lissom rascal it was!

Throughout his work Mr. Hewlett is at this high pressure, as though he wrote at sunrise. Hence a vinous, exhilarating book; a book with the rush and merriment of a crisping wave.

Notable is it also for vivid pictorial effects. Italy is the land of colour, and little novels of Italy must have colour too. From beneath any illustrator Mr. Hewlett has cut away the ground, so living are these written pictures; even an illustration in colour would have little left to do. Here is Vanna, for instance, in the story from which we have quoted, "Madonna of the Peach-Trees":

Giovanna, flower in the face as she was, fit to be nosegay on any hearth, posy for any man's breast, sprang in a very lowly soil. Like a blossoming reed she shot up to her inches by Adage, and one forgot the muddy bed wondering at the slim grace of the shaft with its crown of yellow atop. Her hair waved about her like a flag; she should have been planted in a castle; instead, Giovanna the stately calm, with her billowing line, staid lips, and candid grey eyes, was to be seen on her knees by the green water most days of the week. Bare-armed, splashed to the neck, bare-headed, out-at-heels, she rinsed and pommelled, wrung and dipped again, laughed, chatted, flung her hair to the wind, her sweat to the water, in line with a dozen other women below the Ponte Navi.

And in landscape the same colouring hand is at work. Amilcare and Molly's journey to Rome, in "The Duchess of Nona," gives the example:

They made Rome a day or two after . . . ; trailed across the bleached marches (with the Sabine Hills like a blue hem beyond); caught the sun at Cervetri, and entered the dusty town by the Porta Cavallegieri on one of those beaten white noons when the shadows look to be cut out of ebony, and the wicked old walls forbidden to keep still. The very dust seems alive, quivering and restless under heel. St. Peter's Church, smothered in rush mats, was a-building, the marble blocks had the vivid force of lightning; two or three heretic friars were being haled by the Ponte Sant' Angelo to a burning in the Vatican.

But gusto and colour are, after all, only among the minor achievements of a novelist. We are glad to have them, but other qualities must come first. Knowledge of men and a power of convincement are in the van. Mr. Hewlett, in this book, is to seek in both. His stories move royally in that gay and forceful way of his, charming, amusing, stimulating; and there's an end. They do not persuade, they do not satisfy. They remain just entertainment, when we are hoping that the line will be over-passed and a new scene in the human drama displayed. We read them, delight in them, put them down — tales, tales! More, the suspicion creeps upon us that a whole book of such work is beneath Mr. Hewlett's genius: one story, "The Judgment of Borso" say, just to show that in this department of narration he is expert, were sufficient; after that he might bend his mind to some-thing really worthy. For these little novels are superficial at best, not all their author's array of resolute words, not all his gusto, not all his warm colouring, has altered that. Giovanna, madonna of the peach-trees, pursued from Verona by a hooting rabble, and returning mysteriously at night to be mistaken for the Blessed Virgin and to kindle in the town a blaze of pious fervour; Ippo-lita, beauty of Padua, so beset by lovers and their absurd cere-monies that she flies to the hills with the goatherds, and mates with the laziest of them; Molly Lovell, daughter of an English wharfinger, in those kissing times which so enraptured Erasmus, forced by an overweening husband to offer poison to Cæsar Borgia and dying of her humanity; Monna Selvaggia, beloved of Messer Cino da Pistoia, poet and friend of Dante, but loved only as a poetical idea, not as a reality; and lastly Bellaroba, slim Vene-tian and child of nature, wed most irregularly to the impudent Angioletto, and winning the favour of the wise Duke Borso — none of these wayward children (for they are little else) do more than please us. Neither they nor their lovers ever convince, ever touch us. Mr. Hewlett has yet to learn the art of so stating a thing that question seems impossible. At present he merely relates, he does not prove. Indeed, in all these narratives of real persons there is less persuasiveness and illusion of reality than in their author's confessedly improbable play of *Pan and the Young Shepherd*, which still represents his high-water mark.

But pleasing these bubbling stories remain, to a degree seldom if ever attained by any other living writer: even the one or two that end tragically, since, in the absence of the proof of which we have spoken, their gloomy issue hardly touches us. The impression, as a whole, is pleasure unalloyed. Both in variety, in charm, and in fun "The Judgment of Borso" comes first — a dainty, audacious piece of comedy in Mr. Hewlett's own vein. If Angioletto and his Bellaroba remind the reader over much of Prosper le Gai and Isoult la Desirous — well, it is no very serious matter. In adhering to a favourite type of puppet Mr. Hewlett indulges himself in good company.

To sum up, Mr. Hewlett is in no need to strive for tenderer humour or gayer fancy, for increase of gusto or the pictorial gift. These are his in brave profusion. But if he is to do the work which we hope to see from his hand, he must toil hard and continually for a deeper vision of the human heart, and that power of convincement without which the prettiest story in the world is only pretty.

A CRITICISM OF CRITICISM *

[*Academy*, September 1, 1900]

For revealing Thompson's principles and method of criticism this review is among the most important. When he deplores Worsfold's lack of perspicuity and precision of expression, and demonstrates how illogical are his conclusions, Thompson exercises a right pre-eminently his, possessing, as he does, the virtues that he misses in Worsfold. Despite the fact that this is a relatively long review, it is one of the best examples of Thompson's conciseness.

MR. WORSFOLD's book deserves commendation for its subject-matter, if it does not contain much that is absolutely new. It is a thorough and thoughtful attempt to trace the progress of criticism, and harmonise the results obtained by modern critics so as to obtain a unified teaching. Much labour has obviously been expended on the effort; and if Mr. Worsfold's conclusions do not always (as we think) go down to bed-rock, they are certainly worth examination. His greatest drawback (and it is an unfortunate one) is that he lacks the perspicuity, precision, and conciseness of expression so eminently desirable in treating subject-matter itself abstract and not easy to follow. His style is deplorably awkward, long-winded, verbose, and circumlocutory. It is less important, for his aims, that his literary taste does not always show itself of the finest order. There is, perhaps, somewhat too profuse a repetition, but this is a fault on the right side where the matter is not readily grasped.

We do not much love Mr. Worsfold's opening. He persistently uses the *real* as equivalent to the *phenomenal*, and such-like laxities of diction. The best done part of his book is, perhaps, the review of criticism from Plato to Victor Cousin, though its most important part is naturally that dealing with modern critical methods. From Plato, he shows, we derive the principle that art and morality are interdependent; also that truth (correspondence of the repre-

* *Judgment in Literature.* By W. Basil Worsfold.

sentation with the thing represented) is the chief merit of a work
of art. Aristotle gives us much, notably the view that creative
work presents universal rather than particular truth, the explanation and justification of tragedy; and those structural rules now
set aside, with the corollary that structural perfection is the test
of artistic excellence. For this Addison substituted the modern
test of imaginative appeal, which was worked out in detail by
Lessing and Victor Cousin. Particularly valuable is Cousin's principle that art is "the unconscious criticism of nature by the human
mind," which rejects and selects among nature's facts. This is
idealisation.

Many criticisms might be offered on portions of Mr. Worsfold's conclusions. Let us merely say that he is hasty in concluding
from Plato's principle (above mentioned) that "the great artist
must be a good man." The history of art refutes this. But he must
aspire after good, in his best nature (which finds vent in his work),
however his actual life may fall below his aspirations. And *habitual*
failure to correspond in life with his ideals will *ultimately* react
upon his power of noble work, though not at once. The flower
blossoms in water long after it is severed from its nutrient root.

Descending to contemporary criticism, Mr. Worsfold declares
that the judgment of literature by formal technical tests (after
the manner of the seventeenth and eighteenth centuries) is practically disused. "The practice of attempting verdicts upon new
works of literature is still maintained in the ordinary criticism
of the journals, but while there is much that is often both unbiased
and enlightened in these criticisms, it is well understood that the
writers of these reviews or notices do not claim to give a binding
verdict," anything but superficial criticism being prevented by the
conditions of such writing. He goes, therefore, to the deliberate
critics, and recalls certain principles at which they have arrived.

Wordsworth laid down the law that an original writer "creates
the taste by which he must be enjoyed," and that the giving of
pleasure by appeal to the imagination of the ordinary intelligent
man is the test of creative excellence — a test outside any technical
rule of judgment. Matthew Arnold enunciated the principle that
poetry is a "criticism of life," which is really involved in Cousin's

statement that it is a "criticism of nature." The test, therefore, of poetry, says Arnold, is its interpretative power, appealing to the *whole* man (his emotional no less than intellectual nature), in which it is superior to science, which appeals solely to the intellect. With this go the conditions that there should be the "high seriousness" of absolute sincerity, and that it should be in conformity with essential morality. It must satisfy "the general sense of mankind as embodied in the principles of morality." Ruskin emphasises this last principle with regard to all creative art. It is the finished expression "of the joy or grief of noble persons for right causes." Again: "The fineness of the possible art is an index of the moral purity and majesty of the emotion it expresses." Swinburne lays down the opposite principle of "Art for Art's Sake." Mr. Worsfold quotes Mrs. Browning as agreeing with him:

> Whosoever writes good poetry
> Looks just to art.

But from another passage he quotes, asserting that poets are

> The only speakers of essential truth,
> Opposed to relative, comparative,
> And temporal truths. . .
> The only teachers who instruct mankind
> From just a shadow on a channel-wall
> To find man's veritable stature out,
> Erect, sublime — the measure of a man;

it is clear that Mrs. Browning includes in "art" the element of moral nobility, and therefore is really at one with Ruskin. And when Mr. Worsfold opposes to Ruskin the maxim that moral worth cannot of itself endow a poet's work "with the characteristic charm of art," it must be answered that Ruskin never affirms so. He says that the nobility of art is determined by moral worth — "the fineness of the possible art," fineness here being manifestly equivalent to "nobility." "No vain or selfish person can possibly paint," he says again (somewhat too sweepingly), "in the *noble* sense of the word." And this is the true reconciliation of these opposing principles. Morality is not the principle of art; but, given the artistic spirit and adequacy of execution, the nobler the informing ethics the loftier the work of art. The "Epithalamion" of Spenser transcends the exquisite "Epithalamium" of Catullus largely by Spenser's beautiful austerity of ethical spirit. Mr. Worsfold's endeavour after reconciliation is not too definite or convincing, not easy to lay hold on. He takes his definition of morality from Matthew Arnold (a lax interpretation of Arnold, we think), and describes it as "the general sense of mankind." But it is more fundamentally true to say that poetical morality corresponds to the laws which underlie the unchanging government of the universe, laws of which there is constant tradition among the great poets — Homer, Virgil, Dante, Shakespeare, Milton. Ruskin's view is correct, says the author, applied to a work of art in its "external or objective aspect," regarded as "the interpretation of moral beauty by the assistance of physical beauty," but incorrect applied to a work of art in its "internal or subjective aspect" — regarded as "the expression of the artist's mind, as a 'conception converted into a creation.' " Which seems to us vague and unsatisfying. Will it be credited that, in grappling with this stubborn difficulty, Mr. Worsfold adventures lightly the casual statement that "Southey and Wordsworth" are "now regarded as our most spiritual poets"? *Southey* — immortal Poetry!

But Mr. Worsfold proceeds, having got his utterances from the critics, to apply them. The Aristotelian method of judging new work by reference to the various categories of composition based on the practice of previous writers is done away with, he says. We now take it for granted that a creative writer "will adopt the appropriate and necessary form of composition, and we look mainly . . . at the effect which he has produced by his composition as a whole; and if we find that his creation possesses the essential quality of appealing to the imagination, we do not trouble to consider whether . . . he has moulded his materials into the precise form of any previously existing model." This, we submit, is inadequate to explain the method of the best modern critics. They try sympathetically to identify themselves with the artist's mind, grasp his standpoint, think again his conception after him, divine and annex his *individual plan,* and *then* intelligently

criticise his work according to its proportion of success in developing that personal plan. According to their capacity of assimilating
his design, their criticism will be good or bad, complete or incomplete. And the measure in which a man possesses this sympathetic
intuition is the test of his critical gift. "Appreciation," the wise
it call, which we prefer to Mr. Worsfold's "interpretation" as a
name for the modern process of criticism.

Mr. Worsfold lays down three principles for applied criticism.
Firstly, truth — generalised truth. In essence, an agreement between the opinions and feelings of the writer and the general
sense of mankind. Hence the necessity for morality. From what
we have said it will be gathered that we would prefer to say an
agreement with the integral truth of nature, "a criticism of nature,"
as Cousin says. Secondly, symmetry: the adaptation of the external
qualities of a given work to the special purpose it is intended to
achieve. It is a very embracing definition. One would rather say,
a relation of ordered parts to produce an harmonious and organic
whole. But Mr. Worsfold evidently and deliberately joins symmetry with *selection*, which surely should be kept separate. He
quotes Meredith: "The art of the pen is to rouse the inward
vision, . . . because our flying minds cannot contain a protracted
description. The Shakespearian, the Dantesque pictures are in a
line or two at most." This is done by selection. But Mr. Worsfold
says: "So the test of symmetry is indirectly a means by which the
presence of this dominant artistic quality can be discovered and
measured in a work of literature." The selection of the fit earth
to make a jar is not part of the jar's symmetry, though it is an
indispensable preliminary to the making of a symmetrical jar.
Indeed, that species of selection to which the Meredith quotation
refers should rather come under Mr. Worsfold's third heading —
Idealisation.

This principle requires not merely that the mental aspect of reality should
be presented by the author, but that a selection from the mental aspect of
reality should first be made, and that the selection so made exclude such
matter as affects unpleasantly the æsthetic consciousness of the reader.

Here comes one of Mr. Worsfold's unpardonable imprecisions

of speech. He speaks of "that characteristic quality of a work of art which we call, from a subjective point of view, 'to give pleasure.'" How can "to give pleasure" be a quality; which is manifestly the outcome or effect of a quality? Under this head, Mr. Worsfold points out, comes the doctrine of "poetic justice," and he has many remarks on that doctrine — some good, some courting criticism. But what is the outcome of all this critical apparatus? How are we to apply it? By comparison, answers Mr. Worsfold; and it is practically the conclusion of his book.

Assume that we know not merely that we should look for truth in any given work, but also the sort of truth for which we should look — that is to say, the truth of logic, if the work be non-creative, the truth of art, if it be creative — if, then, we would ascertain the extent to which the work in question possesses this quality, we must compare it with a work of recognised merit. . . in the same department of literature. Gradually by the study of the best work. . . in the several departments of literature, our minds will become so familiarised with the several and characteristic excellences of each, that we shall almost instinctively welcome their presence, and resent their absence.

Now that last sentence is true, and understood in this general sense the principle of comparison is as right as it is obvious. But Mr. Worsfold does not leave it there. He lays down a detailed and mechanical comparison which can breed nothing but conventional judgment — where it is not impracticable. "If we wish to know how X has succeeded, we compare his work with the work of the same kind which A, B, and C have done, and admittedly done well." Thus, he says, to judge the detailed description of a love-declaration between two young people in *Richard Feverel*, we should compare it with the like scene in *Romeo and Juliet*. The critic who should do so would be lost — if he were trying to judge *Richard Feverel* as a new and unknown work! Even in Mr. Worsfold's comparison, with all its *parti-pris*, the differences are very much more conspicuous than the resemblances. The work of a great poet (let us say) is almost sure to be so novel and *sui generis* that such mechanical and detailed comparison with the work of any predecessor will be either impossible, or a snare for the feet of the critic so *banal* as to attempt it. It is precisely such rootedly mistaken efforts which are responsible for nearly half the conventional damnation meted out to poets at their literary birth. Arnold recommended readers to keep in their minds choice lines and passages of great poetry, as a standard of supreme poetic quality. But (though even this is liable to perverted application) Mr. Worsfold is not justified in citing it to countenance a method of criticism which would have prickled the roots of Arnold's hair! Such comparisons are sometimes interesting, when you have already captured and certified to yourself the excellence of a new writer, but they are pernicious as means of *a priori* appraisal.

And this is all that Mr. Worsfold has to tell us about the handling of the tools he has so painstakingly labeled for us. Let us confess that, as *Mr. Punch* says, "we don't seem to get no forrarder." The rest of the book is a brief synopsis of literary forms, with a jejune note on style. Decidedly, the book is not satisfactory, yet it has much which is satisfying. The evolution of criticism is traced with a system not before applied to it; and our modern critical gains are appraised, so that we can see where we stand in relation to our ancestors. This is good work, and we only wish it had been done with better command of style. Superfluous words should be thinned out of almost every sentence; for Mr. Worsfold has a fatal love of rotundity for its own ponderous sake. Were this done, it would save much labour to the reader of a book none the less worth reading.

THEOCRITUS *

[*Academy*, March 2, 1901]

Here Thompson gives scarcely less attention to Theocritus than to his translator. His appraisal of both is the work of an accomplished critic.

THIS is a revised and corrected edition of the book which Mr. Hallard published some six years ago. It well deserves a reissue, for,

---

* *The Idylls of Theocritus.* Translated into English Verse
by James Henry Hallard.

on the whole, we take it to be the best metrical version of Theocritus that there is. It is very good indeed from every point of view: above all, it has the prime merit in a verse translation that it reads like good English verse. Mr. Hallard lays special stress in his preface on the pains which he has taken with his metre, and it certainly justifies his care. The hexameters, in particular, are the best English hexameters we have seen; and this for the precise reason he assigns — the attention he has paid to quantity. There are none of those pebbly syllables which trouble the current of other English hexameters, even the best. If the hexameter is to be used in English (and it is always alien, neither Greek nor English, for it is absurd to think it represents the classic quantitative hexameter) then this is the best, doubtless, that can be done with it. Mr. Hallard's style is excellent, and recognises the thoroughly literary and artistic style of Theocritus himself, which (as he truly says) is not represented by the rusticities of Allan Ramsay. It is a translation which one can read with pleasure, as one reads an original; and the translations of which that can be said might be counted on the fingers.

Theocritus is not merely a great poet, he is a source, an ancestor; a whole species of poetry descends from him — the pastoral. His is a beloved figure — perhaps the sweetest name and fame in the stern literature of antiquity. To name him is to call up some such picture as Mrs. Browning's:

> Theocritus, with glittering locks
> Dropped sideways, as betwixt the rocks
> He watched the visionary flocks.

"Visionary" — yes, it is true, they were visionary; he was a poetic pretender after all, whose babble of shepherds and fields was written in polished Alexandria, as Thomson saw his sunrises in bed. Nothing could be falser than to regard him as a kind of Greek Wordsworth, whose songs breathe the rustic atmosphere he lived amidst and loved. It was a convention, this pastoral form: its author dwelt in the courts of kings, and had a right reverence for the broidered shoe of Ptolemy. Yet the convention was based on nature. Theocritus must have studied to some extent and with some intimacy the life he represents; perhaps like Virgil, in the earlier days before he became a courtly favourite. Virgil we know was a countryman, yet his pastorals never convince us of the country. Classicism, according to the eighteenth century conception, lay in generalising everything; and Virgil's pastorals are classic in this fashion. His shepherds have the air of belonging to a stage country, which might be set down anywhere. They would be just as probable — or improbable — in Windsor forest. But not so Theocritus. You look through his eyes, and see a landscape with figures which make you cry, "Ah! *this* I have not seen before!" It is individualised. Yet his object is not description; the individualising touches are only accessory, but they are the right ones. His eye for what vitalises a scene comes out in the smallest things. His shepherds, like Virgil's, call an arbiter to judge their singing-contest; the shepherd with the white-faced dog leaping among his flock. Virgil, if he thought of the dog, would have forgotten its bounds among the sheep, and above all would never have noticed that it was white-faced. It is that which gives you *the* dog, instead of *a* dog; and it is such touches which put life in Theocritus' background.

You know that country of his. It was "betwixt the rocks" that he watched his "visionary flocks"; for it was a rocky country, bordering the sea-shore, with pastures spreading inland, one fancies. The sound of the sea is seldom long absent from these pastorals, and he is as ready to sing of fishermen as of shepherds — nay, his fishermen have a whole pastoral to themselves. The frequent contrasts between the home of the field and the home of the rock show how contiguous were the two in the mind of the poet. His shepherds often live in caves, like Polyphemus, to whom two charming pastorals are devoted. One does not wonder he was a favourite with Theocritus; for by his love for the sea-nymph Galatea he seems to gather up in his own person the rocks, the pastures, and the sea.

The peasants of Theocritus, too, are thinkable beings, with passions single, primitive, and unrestrained. Love turns quickly to hatred or despair; and then the woman tries sorcery, and dreams of poison — for her lover, not herself. The girls are quite ready to make the first advances, by pelting the chosen shepherd with fruit, or other rustic hints. The formula of the poems varies little, but the fresh and sweet accessories keep monotony aloof. Sometimes, but not often, Theocritus indulges in set description. There is one famous instance, which Mr. Hallard has translated so well that we must quote it. It is the account of the *symposium* at the house of Phrasidemus:

> There we rejoicing
> Laid us deep on a couch of fragrant rushes and vine-
>   leaves.
> Poplars and rustling elms waved o'er us; a Sacred fountain
> Babbling and murmuring gushed from a grot of the
>   nymphs hard by us;
> Sunburnt merry cicalas aloft on the shadowy branches
> Shrilled their ceaseless song, and afar in the bushes of
>   bramble
> Softly the tree-frogs chirped, and the crested larks and the
>   finches
> Sang, and the turtle moaned, and around those plashing
>   waters
> Darted golden bees; all things smelt richly of Summer,
> Richly of Autumn; pears and apples in bountiful plenty
> Rolled at our feet and sides, and down on the meadow
>   around us
> Plum-trees bent their trailing boughs thick-laden with
>   damsons.
> Then from the wine-jar's mouth was a four-year-old seal
>   loosened.

This shows Mr. Hallard at his best, and also exhibits his skill in handling the English hexameter. But it is seldom Theocritus elaborates his touches in this way. He is a master of suggestion, and has never been excelled in the art of miniature; his dramatic sense, too, is admirable; but the poem which exhibits all these qualities in the most perfect way is not a pastoral at all, it is an idyll of the city. All Theocriteans know it, and many poets have attempted its translation. Of all these efforts Mr. Hallard's seems to us the best, and so very good that we cannot deny ourselves the pleasure of quoting from it at some length. It is simply the dialogue of two women who go to the Adonis festival in Alexandria, which

Ptolemy is celebrating with unusual splendour in his palace hall;
but it bridges the ages in the most vivid way, and that Alexandrian
festival becomes modern to us. It is a Greek Anstey, giving us a
poetic *Voces Populi*. Note the art with which the *milieu* is indicated.
As for the women, we know these good ladies; they are immortal
as sex, and may be seen and heard at every London gathering.

GORGO: How out of breath I am! I hardly got
To your house alive out of the dreadful crowd
Of carriages and people. Soldiers' boots
And cloaks here, there, and everywhere — I thought
The way would never end. Your house, my dear,
Is really much too far away from ours.

PRAXINOE: My madcap husband's fault. He came and took
At world's end here a beast's hole, not a house,
Merely to keep us apart, the jealous wretch!
And all for spite as usual.

GORGO: Hush, my dear!
Don't rail at Dinon so before the child.
Look, woman, how he eyes you. Never mind,
Zopyrion, dear, sweet boy, it's not papa
That mother talks of.

PRAXINOE: By our Lady Goddess,
The baby understands us!

*   *   *   *   *   *

GORGO: But come, put on your mantle and your gown,
And let's be off to Ptolemy's palace-hall
To see the "Adonis." It is said the queen
Is planning something splendid.

*   *   *   *   *   *

GORGO: Oh, Praxinoë, dear,
Look at that dreadful crush about the doors!

PRAXINOE: Oh, terrible! Gorgo, dear, give me your hand,
And, Eunoë, you take Eutychis', and mind her —
No straggling — let us all get in together!
Oh, Eunoë, Eunoë, do stick fast to us!
Alack, now there's my mantle torn! O Sir,
As you would hope for happiness, mind my cloak!

STRANGER: I scarcely can, but I will do my best.

PRAXINOE: Oh, what a crowd! They push like pigs.

STRANGER: Cheer up,
Dear madam, all's well now.

PRAXINOE: Oh, thanks indeed!
May all be well for ever and a day
With you, dear Sir, for shielding us! — What a good
Kind man! — Oh, there's poor Eunoë getting crushed!
Push, silly, push! That's right! "Now all are in,"
As cries the groomsman when he locks the door.

GORGO: Oh, come and look first at these broideries,
Subtle and lovely as the work of gods!

PRAXINOE: I wonder who the weaving-women were,
And who the draughtsmen that so deftly drew
These pictures! How like life they stand or move!
People, not pictures! Wonderful is man!
And there Adonis lies so fair to see
Upon his silver couch, youth's early down
Upon his tender cheek, the thrice-beloved,
Dead both to us and those that dwell below!

ANOTHER STRANGER: A plague upon your endless
   pigeon-prattle!
They'll kill a body with their Dorian brogue.

GORGO: Whence did this fellow come? What's that to you,
If we are prattlers? Lord it o'er the slaves
That you have paid for! Bully *us*, forsooth!
Ladies of Syracuse, who came of old
From Corinth, like Bellerophon — mark that —
And talk like people in the Peloponnese!
Since when may Dorians not talk Dorian, pray?

The range of the idylls, it will be seen, is really considerable.
Another describes a boxing match. Sidelights slant continually on
the intimate life of that old Græcised Egypt. You hear of their
banquets in humble life, where snails and truffles form the delica-

cies — a *menu* that might find favour in France. And over all is the lovely grace of an artful simplicity, the uncapturable something which is Theocritus. It is the best compliment to Mr. Hallard that a suggestion of this has been retained in his version.

MRS. BOYTHORN AND HER CANARY

[*Academy*, July 19, 1902]

In this triple review of Swinburne, Lang, and Dickens, Thompson is at his best. He might well be astride one of the hobby horses he describes, urged by his own *joie de vivre*, even in the musty business of book reviewing.

EVERYONE remembers how the canary sat on Mr. Boythorn's head while he described the Dedlock family as a nursery of pig-headed numskulls, and declared that nothing but ten thousand hundred-weight of gunpowder would avail to reform the Courts of Chancery. The canary knew the quiet heart of the man, and ruffled not a feather. Imagine a female Boythorn and a distrustful canary, and you have the counterparts of Mr. Algernon Charles Swinburne and Mr. Andrew Lang in the present dreadful affair of Charles Dickens.

Let us explain. A week ago it was whispered in heaven and muttered in hell, at any rate it was hinted in the *Academy*, that Mr. Swinburne was about to give Mr. Lang a piece of his mind. Thus is the wind tempered to a city shorn of Coronation flags. But a curious thing happened. Before we could realise it Mr. Lang was replying to Mr. Swinburne in the *Morning Post*. The fact that Mr. Swinburne had not yet spoken, that the rejoinder preceded the attack, was itself a cure for the lassitudes of July. Mr. Lang was not even sure that himself was the critic whom Mr. Swinburne meant to scourge, but pinning his faith to our statement, he acted with the consummate previousness of an old bird. Sure that he could not perch on Mrs. Boythorn's forehead with any comfort during the threatened eruption, and having no mind to flutter and burn in the intricacies of the chandelier, he flew to the *Morning Post*, and there chirped his defence. "I have followed," he said, "the advice of my country's proverb, 'Tak' the first word o' flyting,' and there ends my concern with the subject."

Mr. Lang was perhaps cleverer than even a Scotchman knew. Since he wrote those words the *Quarterly Review* has appeared; Mrs. Boythorn has screamed. Mr. Lang now knows that his article was a reply to ten incidental lines describing his introductions to the Gadshill series of Dickens as "the prefatory importunities of a writer disentitled to express and disqualified to form an opinion on the work of an English humorist. The intrusive condescension or adulation of such a commentator was perhaps somewhat superfluous in front of the reprinted Waverley Novels; the offence becomes an outrage, the impertinence becomes impudence, when such rubbish is shot down before the doorstep of Charles Dickens."

We do not know what term the "fancy" would give to this collapse of a first-class mill. We know that we are left alone with the most astonishing article that we have read, as America says, "in years." We were aware that Mr. Swinburne's prose had made the judicious grieve, as his poetry has caused the injudicious to rave; but we were as little prepared for the Heliogabalan roses of rodomontade which he heaps on Dickens' grave as for the feminine calling of names with which he degrades even that dubious ceremony. His first sentence exhibits his twin lacks of form and urbanity. Here it is:

> It is only when such names as Shakespeare's or Hugo's rise and remain as the supreme witnesses of what was highest in any particular country at any particular time that there can be no question among any but irrational and impudent men as to the supremacy of their greatest.

No doubt this sentence has a socket of sense into which one's intellect may drop with pleasing suddenness at any moment, but, for ourselves, we are still groping. Yet however difficult it is to read Mr. Swinburne's prose, it is not difficult to explain it. It is the energy of his poetry running *amok*. It is his violence without his viol. Mr. Swinburne's poetic door does not open, as a poet's should, on a gradual and verdant slope of beautiful prose; it precipitates him, every time he opens it, into the noisy street where the victory is to elbowish and vociferous persons. Yet the instincts of the poet survive, and the quality which Mr. Swinburne strives for in his prose is opulence. Unfortunately he seeks it in the wrong way. He appears to think that as that man is a benefactor who makes two blades of grass grow where only one grew before, so the writer is to be admired who crams two, three, or even four adjectives into the room of one. Add to this obsession his inability to praise or blame except in detonating superlatives and you describe the prose of the greatest poet of our day. Could violence be more misplaced than here: "There may possibly be some faint and flickering shadow of excuse for the dullards, if unmalignant, who prefer *Nicholas Nickelby* to the riper and sounder fruits of the same splendid and inexhaustible genius." Note the double adjectives: "faint and flickering," "riper and sounder," "splendid and inexhaustible." This duplicative and triplicative pother of words never stops. "No mortal man or woman, no human boy or girl, can resist the fascination of Mr. and Mrs. Quilp." . . . "The advance in tragic power is even more notable and memorable than this." . . . "Interest and sympathy are well-nigh superseded or overbalanced . . . ." "In immediate prospect of the imminent gallows . . . ." "Cannot mesmerise or hypnotise us." . . . "It is only by dunces that it is held improbable or impossible for a great writer to judge aright of his own work at its best, to select and to prefer the finest and fullest example of his active genius." . . . "It is not only by his masterpieces, it is also by his inferior works or even by his comparative failures that the greatness of a great writer may be reasonably judged and tested." So necessary are unnecessary words to Mr. Swinburne that he will employ them in automatic response to his physical craving for their rhythm. Take this sentence:

No son of Adam and no daughter of Eve on this God's earth, as his occasional friend Mr. Carlyle might have expressed it, could have imagined it possible — humanly possible — for anything in later comedy to rival the unspeakable perfection of Mrs. Quickly's eloquence at its best.

Here the words "humanly possible," and the pause for their entry, are amusing when you see what follows. It is melancholy, too, to observe the suffocation at birth of a fine sentence:

> Jonas Chuzzlewit has his place of eminence for ever among the most memorable types of living and breathing wickedness that ever were stamped and branded with immortality by the indignant genius of a great and unrelenting master.

Let us see what sane deletion will do for this sentence:

> Jonas Chuzzlewit is among the most memorable types of wickedness that ever were branded with immortality by indignant genius.

This is, at least, the cool embodiment of a thought of which Mr. Swinburne's sentence is the gesticulating fever.

Mr. Swinburne's love of noise and rotundity seems to preoccupy him to the extent of destroying his finer judgment, his sense of scale, and his eye for the architecture of his commentary. In a single paragraph he will deafen himself to his own voice, so that of Little Nell he can whisper that she would thoroughly deserve her fame "if she were but a thought more human and more credible," and then, on rising lungs, vociferate that "a child whom nothing can ever irritate, whom nothing can ever baffle, whom nothing can ever misguide, whom nothing can ever delude, and whom nothing can ever dismay, is a monster as inhuman as a baby with two heads."

Mr. Swinburne reserves to himself the right to blame Dickens. The objectors to the plot of *Bleak House,* as it affects Lady Dedlock, are "helots of culture whose brains may have been affected by the academic delirium of self-complacent superiority." The critics who find some parts of *A Tale of Two Cities* exaggerated and unreal share "the chattering duncery and the impudent malignity of so consummate and pseudosophical a quack as George Henry Lewes." Anon the lava-tide of adjectives overtakes "the blatant boobies who deny truthfulness and realism to the imagination or the genius of Dickens because it never condescended to wallow in metaphysics or in filth." Mr. Lang's gentle chidings of Dickens may have been a thin and unnecessary *sauce piquante* to the

Gadshill banquet, but we are quite unable to discover why they should infuriate a poet who screams the very same objections. It is he who finds the plot of *Dombey and Son* stupid, and the characters of the father and daughter "failures of the first magnitude." It is he who notes Dickens's "curious and seemingly incorrigible ignorance" of society; and whom the halting invention and the poor humour of *Little Dorrit* affect with "irrepressible irritation."

It may be that Mr. Swinburne resents the bestowal of warm instead of super-heated praise on the writer whom he can hardly refer to except under such phrase as "this magnificent and immortal benefactor." It is doubtful, however, whether the laudation contained in the following sentence has any meaning whatever: "*David Copperfield*, from the first chapter to the last, is unmistakeable by any eye above the level and beyond the insight of a beetle's as one of the masterpieces to which time can only add a new charm and an unimaginable value." Judgments like the following are more wonderful than the thing they wonder at: "To have created Abel Magwitch is to be a god indeed among the creators of deathless men." Even minor characters are described as "flashing into eternity across the stage of Dickens." It is but for a moment that we meet Bill Barley, but "eternity is in that moment." And so on, and so on. If Mr. Swinburne's aim were to do Dickens hurt by paralysing the praise of others it would perhaps explain his article though it would not effect his object. We can only compare the effect of his prose on our nerves with that of a relentless steam-organ braying in wafts of gas-heat, while the characters of Dickens ride round distractedly on hobby-horses, urged, as it seems, by the insupportable accompaniment.

FITZGERALD AND CALDERON *
[*Academy*, May 30, 1903]

The special merit of this review is its expression of Thompson's ideas on translations, keeping the *via media* between redactions and literal renditions. One would have expected a stronger note of regret at the omission of *Life Is a Dream*, in view of its appeal to Patmore, whose taste in literary matters Thompson so liberally shared.

THE ACTOR-MANAGER of the present day is at a loss for a good play, ancient or modern — apparently he is so hard-driven that he does not much care which. One has lately revived an eighteenth-century comedy which would be thought very far from brilliant were it produced by a modern dramatist. Another not so long ago fell back on a Spanish play of little merit. Even the society expressly devoted to remedying the regular theatre's want of enterprise seems itself to suffer under a deficiency of actable material. Or is it, in both cases, a contracted view that ails the searcher for plays actable yet unacted? Surely there are masterpieces begging to be acted. Why, for instance, should any manager risk his fortunes on a mediocre Spanish play when the whole theatre of Calderon lies before him? That is the question brought home to us by the issue of FitzGerald's — "Omar" FitzGerald's — *Six Dramas of Calderon*, edited by Dr. H. Oelsner. Allowing that the great Spaniard, as he stands, presents difficulties on the English stage, here are those difficulties removed. FitzGerald seems, indeed, to have had even an excessive eye on our own stage in the making of these versions; so that it would need little stage-editing of FitzGerald to place them bodily on the London boards. And such a play as *The Mayor of Zalamea* cries on the actor-manager, "Come, act me!" Were it sent in to him as a new piece, he must see the "fat" on every page. The situations (to maintain theatrical *parlance*) leap to the eye as we read. "How that would act!" we

* *Six Dramas of Calderon.* Freely translated by Edward FitzGerald. Edited by Dr. H. Oelsner.

exclaim involuntarily. But it is only a masterpiece written in Spain, quite two centuries or more ago; and — what would you? we do not act such things. Is there not farce still in Paris? yea, and musical comedy is much in the land. Vex us not with your Calderons.

It can scarce be accident, indeed, that FitzGerald's selection hardly at all displays the famed poetical quality of Calderon's drama. Manifestly (we think) he desired to commend the great Spaniard's fitness for the English stage; and therefore he chose pieces with the maximum of stage-quality, the minimum of that poetry which the modern theatre hates as the gates of Hades. This preoccupation with acting-possibilities is shown in more than one note. It is a pity, because his selection gives no complete suggestion of Calderon, does not even (from a literary standpoint) present the Spaniard at his highest. The more is our regret that the editor has not included the two plays which FitzGerald translated, but did not publish. What we have seen from one of them (*The Mighty Magician*) may stand beside Shelley's fragment of the same drama; and they would have represented precisely that high poetic side of Calderon which is here lacking.

But we must take Calderon as FitzGerald has chosen to give him us, and be glad to get him. FitzGerald's Omar was more Fitz-Gerald than Omar; and in a less degree, his Calderon suffers a FitzGeraldine change. If the Omar was FitzGerald-Omar, the Calderon is Calderon-FitzGerald. It was part of FitzGerald's strong personality to impose it on the authors he translated; and precisely from this process springs the vitality of his translations. Shelley's Goethe has the stamp of Shelley, Rossetti's Dante the stamp of Rossetti, Chapman's Homer the stamp of Chapman; and thereby they become English poems, and alive. Yet they have somewhat of the original, in so far as there was sympathy between translator and translated. By this dual process of re-creation metrical versions live or not at all. FitzGerald's Calderon is less changed from the original than his Omar. It is also less miraculous. But not because of the less freedom; rather because he had to do with a far greater master, on whom he could work no artistic improvement. He attempts such improvement — it was in the man; but it is countervailed by the inevitable loss of translation from a great genius. He attempts too much improvement, takes too much liberty; as when a Frenchman docks Shakespeare of all which — justly or unjustly — rasps a Gallic taste. Yet, with all that may rightly be brought against it, the translation remains a work of genius, vital as scrupulously respectful versions of Calderon are not vital. These are breathing English plays — and to compass that is a feat.

Calderon as revealed to us in these six plays (and we shall not go beyond them) is essentially a rhetorical dramatist. He does not come into competition with Shakespeare; he stands frankly on a lower plane — lower in kind. There is (with exceptions hereafter to be noticed) no attempt at realism of character — hardly at character at all, save in a generic and typical sort. The plot does not evolve (as in Shakespeare) through the interaction between fate or circumstance (which is a mode of fate) and character. It is a drama of skilful construction and striking "situation." Now "situation" is the proper instrument of rhetorical drama; for indeed situation is rhetoric in action. (We use "rhetoric" in its modern, not its true and ancient sense.) These plays are midway between the rhetorical French drama and the poetic naturalism of Elizabethan drama. In structure they are rhetorical and French, depending on unexpected and startling situation. In dialogue, they mingle a certain judicious element of rhetoric with a large proportion of naturalism. They are a mean between the two extreme kinds — English and French; though of course the Spanish theatre was earlier than either. And if in kind we must rank them below Shakespeare, they are above the French. The gay glitter of intrigue throughout these plays is admirably contrived and maintained. Gay it is in such excellent comedy as *Keep Your Own Secret*, or part of the *Mayor of Zalamea*. In other plays it is tragic and absorbing. For the devisal of sombrely terrible situation Victor Hugo does not surpass Calderon; only Calderon uses the device more sparingly. He confines it chiefly to the climax of his plays. In these dramas it turns invariably upon the famous "Point of Honour" — the right of the injured husband to take personal vengeance for his honour; nay, his duty to do so. *The*

Painter of His Own Dishonour is a well-known instance. The wife, carried off by her former lover, is confined unwillingly in a castle. The husband, an amateur painter, takes service as an artist with the Prince who is Governor of Naples, that he may search for her. The Prince, also in love with her, learns her presence in the castle, and commissions the disguised husband to paint her portrait for him. He bribes a servant to shut the painter in a grated room, whence he may see her. She enters, and falls asleep. Her abductor appears just as she wakes from a dream of her husband's vengeance; and, still under the influence of the dream, she flies to his arms, imploring him to save her from her husband. The husband, thus mistakenly convinced of her guilty complicity, unable to force the door, fires on them through the grating. They both fall, dying. The wife's father, the abductor's father (who is also the bosom friend of the avenging husband), and the Prince rush in at the report. "Open the door," cries the Prince; "but what is this?" "A picture," answers the emerging husband:

> Done by the Painter of his own Dishonour
> In blood.
> I am Don Juan Roca. Such revenge
> As each would have of me, now let him take,
> As far as one life holds. Don Pedro, who
> Gave me this lovely creature for a bride,
> And I return to him a bloody corpse:
> Don Luis, who beholds his bosom's son
> Slain by his bosom friend: and you, my lord,
> Who, for your favours, might expect a piece
> In some far other style of art than this:
> Deal with me as you list; 'twill be a mercy
> To swell this complement of death with mine:
> For all I had to do is done, and life
> Is worse than nothing now.

The Prince bids him fly; but the murdered man's father, Don Luis, asks "From whom?" He would himself have helped his friend to vengeance on his own son. According to the fierce Spanish code, Don Juan has done only what the fetish, Honour, compelled him to do. The girl's father, Don Pedro, bows to the

Prince's justice. "Be it so," says the Prince; "meanwhile" — but Don Juan interrupts him:

> Meanwhile, my lord, let me depart;
> Free, if you will, or not. But let me go,
> Nor wound these fathers with the sight of one
> Who has cut off the blossom of their age:
> Yea, and his own, more miserable than all.
> They know me; that I am a gentleman,
> Not cruel, nor without what seem'd due cause
> Put on this bloody business of my honour;
> Which having done, I will be answerable
> Here and elsewhere, to all for all.

"Depart," says the Prince, "in peace." "In peace!" groans the wretched husband. "Come, Leonelo"; and the curtain falls. The fine rhetorical point of all this, combined yet with a certain dignified truth to nature — Spanish nature; the reticent simplicity (quite Shakespearean) of that last despairing echo, "In peace!" and the impressive effect of the whole situation, are too evident that we should enlarge on them. Excellent, too, is FitzGerald's rendering. A more grimly terrible situation still is that which closes *Three Judgments at a Blow.* Something kindred is the close of *The Mayor of Zalamea;* and this play summarises in itself all the Calderonian qualities displayed in FitzGerald's selections, both comic and tragic. Its one and cardinal error, indeed, is that it breaks at the last, abruptly and without preparation or transition, from jovial comedy into the most harrowing tragedy. The farmer's daughter, hitherto the faintest figure of rural comedy, is suddenly revealed to us in a wood, mourning her violation by the Spanish captain. FitzGerald has transposed her speech from verse to prose, and even sought to de-poetize her language, though he avows it one of the finest poetic outbursts in Calderon. That is a mistake: since the poet chose to make this sudden change he did right to strike the altered keynote boldly at the outset. FitzGerald only spoils good poetry into vicious prose; still too raised for prose, while it misses the absolute heights of poetry. He does not remove the incongruity he desires to remove. But, for all this, the play is a masterpiece. The farmer (in the last scenes Mayor) and the old general, Don Lope de Figuerroa, are individual portraits of a distinctness unwonted in Calderon. Don Lope, in fact, is a portrait: Calderon personally served under him. The peppery obstinacy of Don Lope, the sturdy obstinacy of Pedro Crespo, the farmer, are admirably distinguished and contrasted: the scenes in which they alternately fraternise and clash are gems of comedy and deft stage effect. One can see an English audience in applauding laughter over them. No less splendidly written for stage effect are the tragic scenes; where Crespo, become Mayor, after vainly imploring the Captain, on his knees, to marry his outraged daughter, rises, grasps his official wand, and orders him to gaol. Standing before the prison, he refuses to surrender him, though Don Lope turns out his regiment and vows to burn down gaol and town. The King enters, Crespo presents the depositions; and — told that, though his sentence is just, he must give up the man to the military authorities — replies it is impossible. "What do you mean?" asks the astonished King; and the undaunted Crespo answers, "You will see." The prison gates unclose, revealing the Captain garrotted in a chair. Crespo is made perpetual Mayor of Zalamea; and, with a characteristic sturdy passage of arms between him and the choleric but good-natured Don Lope, this little masterpiece ends. But no description or extract could do justice to it: it must be read entire. It is not in bravura-passages, or anything quotable, that the power of these plays resides. It is in the gradually cumulative effect of the perfectly woven intrigue, the natural language, the masterly structure of the whole. And these are rendered in the freshest vernacular English, and blank verse handled with the skill of a poet. Let us, we say again, have the two unpublished plays.

THE SERAPHIC KEEPSAKE *
[Franciscan Annals, January, 1906]

This review of a study of two documents in the writing of the reviewer's patron saint shows Thompson's great care in examining the various theories propounded in the volume. The added theory which he himself proposes was thought by the author, in a subsequent "retort courteous," to be more ingenious than persuasive.

MR. REGINALD BALFOUR's *Seraphic Keepsake* is a very exhaustive study of two documents in the writing of St. Francis: a letter to Brother Leo, and the famous Blessing given by the Saint to that Brother, which has on the other side certain Divine Praises in Latin, written soon after the bestowal of the Stigmata. The first twice disappeared for long periods, and has been identified by comparison with the writing of the Blessing preserved at Assisi. With remarkable minuteness of knowledge and clearness of style, Mr. Balfour examines the history and authenticity of both documents, and his impartial study puts the matter beyond doubt. The book will be of great interest even to those not concerned with its main object: for the Blessing also gives the earliest account of the Miracle of the Stigmata, by Brother Leo himself.

It is, however, part of Mr. Balfour's purpose to advance a new theory concerning the design which St. Francis made at the foot of the Blessing. It consists of a *tau* (a capital T) arising from a figure so inefficiently drawn that what it represents is still in dispute. On either side the *tau* is written *Frater Leo, te dominus benedicat* ("Brother Leo, the Lord bless thee"), the *Leo* being divided by the stem of the *tau*. Brother Leo has made a memorandum at the foot of the page, that the Saint "with his own hand made the above sign *tau*, together with the head (*cum capite*)." There are but three views which count. One is Mr. Carmichael's, that the *tau* is a gallows, issuing from a hill which he thinks to resemble Alverna, and upon the gallows a head of St.

* *The Seraphic Keepsake*. By Reginald Balfour.

Francis. It seems answer enough to this that Leo says it is a *tau;* while the supposed head of the Saint Mr. Balfour says is a patch showing through. The second is the view of a writer in the *Civilta Cattolica* and of R. P. Edouard d'Alençon, Archivist General of the Capuchin Order, that the drawing represents a skull upon a small hill, surmounted by a *tau*, signifying the Cross on Calvary.

Mr. Balfour has a third view, argued with an ingenuity which must give to it general attention and respect. For its full force the reader must consult the book, but as well as we can briefly give it, it is this. He shows that the Saint's devotion to the *tau* was derived from the passage wherein Ezekiel is bidden to mark it on the brows of the men in Jerusalem who still mourned for its sins; and that the Saint was fond of signing it to his letters and even painting it on the walls of his cell. He even conjectures that Francis had a habit of marking with it the brows of men who mourned the vices of the time. Therefore he holds that the Saint meant to mark with the *tau* the brow of Brother Leo, that the drawing consequently represents the head of Leo; and this (he thinks) is emphasised by Leo's name being written on either side the *tau*, after the drawing was made. Nor could Leo have meant by *capite* anything but a head, not a skull. The argument is very arresting, much more so in the book than in my summary; and Mr. Balfour makes a strong case, which will have to be taken into account by future writers.

For my part I do not assent to Mr. Balfour's view. To indicate, he says, that the head was the head of Brother Leo, St. Francis wrote Leo's name on either side of the *tau* after the drawing had been made. (That this was done after the drawing had been made I do not dispute: I think it highly probable.) But if the Saint wrote Leo's name to show that the head was Leo's, why did he write on either side the *tau* and not on either side the head? Surely this would have been the natural way, if such was his purpose. St. Francis, says Mr. Balfour, intended to mark the *tau* on Leo's brow, following the injunction given to Ezekiel. But why, were this his design, did he not draw a head and write the *tau* on the forehead? If anything, it would have been easier than what he has done. He did not mark a *tau* on the brow, he made a *tau* growing out of the head, surely a different symbolism (whatever its intention) from the marking of a *tau* on the forehead. Again, the Praises and Blessing were written after the vision of the Seraph; the Saint's mind was evidently absorbed by his recent reception of the Stigmata, and the Cross, in this connection, has a special association with St. Francis, but not with Brother Leo. Were he to represent it as growing out of any one's head, it would surely be his own, rather than Leo's. It might plausibly be held, therefore, that the head was that of St. Francis. But this is a minor point, on which I lay no stress.

Lastly, Mr. Balfour dismisses points in favour of other views by the argument that it is strange Leo should have made no mention of them. But experience should tell us that in memoranda like this, made on a document for private reference, not for publication, nothing is commoner than to find points omitted, the docketing (as I may call it) not altogether explicit and complete: points, perhaps, too familiar at the time to the writer and his friends to seem necessary of explanation. One might as well argue that it is strange Leo should not have mentioned it was his own head — the most important point of all, on Mr. Balfour's theory. If we accept that theory, Leo must have omitted the point because it was so commonly known that it did not strike him as needful to record it. But the like reason will explain also the omission of points favourable to other theories. Mr. Balfour's argument, in fact, if we are to allow it weight, would tell as strongly against himself as against any of his predecessors.

My own view (let me say at the outset) I arrived at for myself from the examination of Mr. Balfour's reproduction, before I knew it had already been stated. It is the view of the Archivist General of the Capuchin Order, in part only supported by Mr. Carmichael; that the drawing represents a *tau* issuing from a skull within a hill. Against this Mr. Balfour has two arguments. One is that Brother Leo does not mention the hill or what the hill is intended for. With this argument I have already dealt. The other is that, if Leo meant a skull, he would have said a skull. He would have said *cum cranio*, not *cum capite*.

Now, asked if *caput* can mean a skull, I answer, No. Asked if a writer, in a memorandum never written for publication, might use *caput* to designate a skull, I must answer: One would not *à priori* expect him to do so, but it is not actually impossible. In a private memorandum we sometimes use expressions not strictly legitimate, for brevity's sake. He might casually say *caput* as an abbreviation for *caput mortuum* — formerly the common name for a death's dead or dead-head; just as we say a *post-mortem* (which means nothing) for a *post-mortem examen*. It is therefore a reasonable objection, but not a decisive objection. It could not weigh if otherwise we saw good reason to believe the object named was a skull.

Now the drawing is a very bad drawing, or there would be no dispute regarding it. But the fact stands out that, by Mr. Balfour's own confession, it has no resemblance to any conceivable human head. It has a rude resemblance to an inverted skull. Yet it is less easy to produce a recognisable semblance of a skull than a recognisable semblance of a head. Any nursery scrawler can produce what is at once seen to be meant for a head: a circle, two dots, a long-drawn stroke, and a short cross-stroke, are enough to make you smilingly say, "A head." Even in profile, some indication of nose, mouth, and eye is not beyond the nursery talent. I can scarce credit, therefore, that St. Francis could not have equalled the nursery, had he wished. But there is no possible indication of a feature. There is, however, the rough semblance of an inverted skull drawn in profile. And there is what might be meant for the jags and peaks of a hill. The skull is the common *caput mortuum* of the cell and hermitage, so often seen in pictures, a skull without the lower jaw-bone. But it is in profile, and inverted (that is, upside-down). I conclude that the drawing represents an inverted skull within a hill, with a *tau* issuing from the aperture in the base of the skull at which it joins the spinal vertebræ. The hill is Golgotha, "the place of the skull," and very likely Mount Alverna. That is, Alverna, where Francis received his Stigmata, as a type of Golgotha, where Christ received His Stigmata: the symbolism being, that through the mystical death to ourselves and the world must we attain the salvation of the Cross. We must die with Christ; the Cross has its roots in death.

Mr. Balfour says the *tau* is not truly a cross. But it is, on the contrary, the one true Cross. The Cross of Christ was *tau* surmounted by a wooden billet for the *titulus*. It is this wooden billet which (probably for symbolic reasons) has been exaggerated into the fourth limb of the conventional Cross.

Lastly, I think it possible (I must not use a stronger word) that St. Francis here employed a symbolism more or less known in his day. I recently saw a Russian cross of metal, evidently either itself antique or copied from an antique. It was full of subtle and ancient symbolisms, of which one feature only here concerns us. The cross (on which was graved a figure of the Crucified) grew out of a small conventional hill, and in the middle of the hill was a skull. If, as this would lead us to suspect, this symbolism of the Tree of Life arising from Death was in former times familiar, we can understand why Brother Leo did not think it required an explanation.

THE BLESSING OF THE BEAST *
[*Tablet*, London, October 27, 1906]

Here we find Thompson a master of gentle irony. The original manuscript of this review is in the Thompson Collection at Boston College.

THIS volume is a compilation — a kind of anthology — intended to show indirectly the mind of the Church regarding animals, by illustrating the spirit of the Saints, its most authentic exponents, in their relations with the lower creatures of God. For such a purpose, the author has freely and happily included legend no less than duly attested fact. Legend not only reveals the spirit of the Catholic faithful among whom it was believed and beloved, but often reveals also the spirit of the Saint about whom it was cherished, more intimately than do his attested deeds. Such "signs" in truth are more than "proofs." This volume, then, casts a wide net: the most varied sources are laid under contribution for stories of

* *The Church and Kindness to Animals*. By the Marquise de Rambures.

Saints the most various, from those known by every Catholic to those whose names themselves sound almost a legend, wild sea-fowl of the early Church, who built their nests in the cliffs of the desolate isles roughening the Northern seas, cave-dwellers who took their sacred prey in Gothic or Sarmatian fastnesses the very names of which are shaggy to our inward ear. It is a noteworthy collection, full of anecdotes which have a common fragrance of simple charity. It will end for ever the era under which it has been possible to accuse Catholics of callousness to the sufferings of the dumb creation; and the blessing which Pius X has bestowed upon it during its passage through the press will perpetuate and confirm the work that it is destined to accomplish. For, from its first page to its last, it is the Church's authentic blessing on the beast.

Nor is the enthralling record confined to romantic illustrations from the precepts and practices of the Saints. It opens with the big artillery of the Bishop of Nismes and Pope Pius V directed in no doubtful terms against bull-fights; and closes with the pronouncements of Cardinal Manning and other (chiefly) English-speaking Catholic ecclesiastics on vivisection. Yet it is to the practice of the Saints that we must mainly look for exposition of the Catholic attitude. The official Church, so far as it can be said to have spoken on the vexed theme of man's relation to lower creatures, has cautiously limited itself to pointing out the essential theological teaching affecting the question. It has need for caution. The advocates of animals include many minds with varying views and motives. One influential section obviously seeks to equalise man and the animals in regard to the possession — or lack — of soul; often leaning towards the Hindu view. To the moderate mind it seems clear that the taking of animal life is a necessity. The opposite view logically involves the infamy of all germicides, and the abominableness of murdering innocent microbes only seeking for a living. The greatest happiness of the greatest number obliges man to give place to the microbe; who, on any true principle of universal suffrage, would outvote him every time. But if he may inflict death for his own advantage, why not for his own advantage the lesser evil of pain? Obviously, it should seem, in these matters man is reduced to a practical compromise, as wise and forbearing as his wisdom may contrive. None the less, if he takes up a lordship of life and death, of pain and happiness, over these creatures committed to his rule, surely he therewith assumes duties towards the ruled, even as he looks to God for a merciful care of *his* life and death. As his control is less, so no doubt his duties are less and less defined: but they must be there for the searching. Hitherto, we fear, he has done very much as he felt inclined. The gentleman was gentle; the hasty man, who might refrain from striking his servants, made no scruple of kicking his dog.

This book of the Church's blessing on the beast is a practical protest against such unthinkingness of man, even more than against downright barbarity. It lets you into a beautiful world — a world of good fairies, so to speak; whose store of love, too full to be bounded by man, rains over upon all creatures God has made; who are ever kindling little fires of tenderness all over a blusterous earth, with great patience towards the rough and heedless breath that blows them out again. St. Philip Neri, says Cardinal Newman, "had great difficulty in keeping himself cool" at the sight of a butcher wounding a dog; and if a bird came into the room, would have the window opened lest it should be caught. There follows in these wide-spreading pages Newman's prayer to heaven to teach him to "love all God's works for God's sake." Numerous are the bird-stories in the volume; of Saint after Saint we are told how he would set free caged or trapped birds. There is one story where so charming an act was followed by as charming a repentance. Blessed Gerard of Majella liberated the bird of a little boy he was visiting, "after having caressed it." The small boy, of course, set up loud lamentation — small boys are still, it may be feared, slow to appreciate the saintly standpoint. Gerard went at once to the window: "Return, return, little bird, because the child is crying." And the bird came back to his hand, whence it was re-delivered to its childish master. Saint Bernard would, by the sign of the cross, save a hare almost in the jaws of the dogs; and (utterly destitute of the fine old sporting instinct!) tell the hunters that they would take no prey while *he* was there. But it needs not a Saint to feel compassion for trapped and uncarnivorous creatures. One remembers how deep-hearted Dr. Johnson set free the hare caught in his host's garden, hallooing it to speed its flight; and met complaint by solemnly arguing that the hare had put itself under the owner's protection by entering his garden, and was entitled to the rights of hospitality. We all know and appreciate that story. Similarly, let it be told, as it is here, of the great Anselm of Canterbury, when the boys he was training set the dogs on a hare. It fled under the belly of his horse, where the dogs surrounded it, without daring to attack it; and the hunters laughed in joy of the anticipated capture. Anselm burst into tears. "Ha! you laugh," he said, "but the poor animal does not"; and bidding them call off the dogs, he rode on, while the hare ran free. It is more difficult to emulate the feeling of the Ven. Joseph of Anchieta, who threw bananas to the panthers that prowled round his prayers; or Blessed Torello of Poppi, who replied to the wonder expressed that a solitary man should consume so much provisions. "It is true I live alone; but a friend of mine who has a large appetite will be here directly, he has only gone out into the wood." The bearer of the food hid himself to watch, and the friend with the large appetite presently arrived howling — being a wolf! Torello opened the door and gave it the meat; after which the wolf put its paws on his shoulders and licked him like a dog, until it was dismissed with the somewhat provincial charge to hurt no one — so far as the Abbey bell could be heard. Still more difficult were it for many irritated Londoners this last summer to follow St. Rose of Lima in her wrath with a sister-saint for "killing her guests" — gnats, no less, or probably mosquitoes. The other Saint observed the guest had too much of her blood for friendliness; but St. Rose promised that, if she would not hurt the gnats, the gnats should not hurt her — a compact they, of course, faithfully kept.

These are legends that carry their lessons, even when the examples are more possible of admiration than imitation. But the delightful little book is filled with examples capable of both. Nothing is perhaps more noteworthy, at this season, than the unanimous dislike of these Saints for sport — killing as an amusement — which we English carry almost into a vice. To hunt for pastime when it is no longer needful to hunt for a living, seems already to some of us moderns a barbarism well meriting saintly dislike. Many of the charming stories in the book concern sport, notably those of St. Joseph of Cupertino, a lover of animals *par excellence*, and a man after the heart of St. Francis. Beyond the line of sport lie such "pastimes" as the baiting of animals: and here the Church herself has spoken through her Head. The Bull of St. Pius V is given entire — a Bull which tossed bull-fights to the devil and declared all who attended them worthy of the censures of the Church. It was as little heeded as were Papal remonstrances against the Spanish Inquisition. But how many know of its existence? This, in fine, is a book to be read, a book to make Catholics reflect, a book to stimulate them that they shall not be hindmost in the movement for bringing man to a consciousness that charity does not end with his fellow-men. The man, in truth, who excuses apathy towards the sufferings of the brutes on the ground that there is so much human misery needing relief is probably a man who does not work himself to death in the cause of humanity.

Let us add, in conclusion, that the connexion between sanctity and kindness to beasts is emphasised by reproductions from a series of pictures by the great artists of Christendom.

BOOKS THAT HAVE INFLUENCED ME
[*Weekly Register*, January 26, 1900]

Although the material selected for these pages is Thompson's literary criticism, an exception has been made to include this article because of the light it throws upon his formation as literary critic as well as poet. That Sacred Scripture is one of the chief influences upon Thompson's prose, as well as his poetry, will scarcely have escaped even a superficial student of his work.

YOUNG Mr. Osbaldistone, you remember (if you are a reader of Scott's *Rob Roy*), grievously scandalised that devout rascal, Andrew Fairservice, by talking about the poetry of the Psalms. Yet apart from the direct religious value of the Scriptures, they may also enter into the category of books which, by their literary greatness, profoundly modify a writer's mind, or style, or both. And by "literary greatness" I mean not simply beauty of external form, but the whole content and soul of the book, approached from the literary rather than the moral and dogmatic side. In the one case you read to be taught, in the other you are taught, often insensibly, through the book's appeal to the sensitive side of your nature. Unlike most English writers, the Bible as an influence (from this standpoint) has a late but important date in my life. As a child I read it, but for its historical interest. Nevertheless, even then I was greatly, though vaguely, impressed by the mysterious imagery, the cloudy grandeurs, of the *Apocalypse*. Deeply uncomprehended, it was, of course, the pageantry of an appalling dream: insurgent darkness, with wild lights flashing through it; terrible phantasms, insupportably revealed against profound light, and in a moment no more; on the earth hurryings to and fro, like insects of the hearth at a sudden candle; unknown voices uttering out of darkness darkened and disastrous speech; and all this in motion and turmoil like the sands of a fretted pool. Such is the *Apocalypse* as it inscribes itself on the verges of my childish memories. In early youth it again drew me to itself, giving to my mind a permanent and shaping direction. In maturer years *Ecclesiastes* (casually opened during a week of solitude in the Fens) masterfully affected a temperament in key with its basic melancholy. But not till quite later years did the Bible as a whole become an influence. Then, however, it came with decisive power.

But not as it has influenced most writers. My style being already formed could receive no evident impress from it: its vocabulary had come to me through the great writers of our language. In the first place its influence was mystical. It revealed to me a whole scheme of existence, and lit up life like a lantern. Next to this, naturally, I was attracted by the poetry of the Bible, especially the prophetic books.

But beyond even its poetry, I was impressed by it as a treasury of *gnomic* wisdom. I mean its richness in utterances of which one could, as it were, chew the cud. This, of course, has long been recognised, and Biblical sentences have passed into the proverbial wisdom of our country. But the very finest, as too deep for popular perception, have remained unappropriated. Such is that beautiful saying in Proverbs: "As in water face answereth to face, so the heart of man to man." It is own sister to the lovely image in Rossetti's "Rose Mary."

> The mirrored souls shook each to each
> As the cloud-moon and the water-moon
> Shake each to each.

Again, that profound aphorism, also in Proverbs, "Wisdom is before him that hath understanding; but the eyes of a fool are in the ends of the earth." I associate it with Blake's pregnant utterance: "The fool sees not the same tree that a wise man sees." But the Biblical saying is deeper. The *Book of Wisdom*, which Protestants reject, is full of beauty and profundity of this kind. None of the Eastern and other heathen "sacred volumes" sometimes brought into comparison with it have anything like the same grave dignity of form or richness of significance in their maxims. Upon this single quality, I think, I finally would elect to take my stand in regard to the Bible; and by this it has firmest hold of me. And whoever opens it, learned or simple, equally finds something of this kind appropriate to his understanding; it is — and that is perhaps the final word about it — the most elastic of all books.

REVIEWS PRINTED FROM MANU-
SCRIPTS IN THE BOSTON COLLEGE
THOMPSON COLLECTION

OUR LITERARY LIFE *

This review of Catholic letters during the previous fifty years was written for the Jubilee Number of the *Tablet*, May 17, 1890. Possibly because the editor did not concur in Thompson's high praise of Coventry Patmore, the article was rejected. The essence of what is here said about Mrs. Meynell's poetry appears in Thompson's unsigned review of her *Poems*, in the *Tablet*, January 21, 1893.

Iᴛ is appropriate that the *Tablet*, which for fifty years has led the van of the Catholic press in the land that was once Mary's Dowry, should be pausing, to review the Catholic gains of those fifty strenuous years, now when Our Lady is mantling her in the May. What blossoms, more lasting than the blossoms of this pettish and April-like month, has Catholic literature yielded during that time? Fifty years ago it could hardly be said that we had a literature. Such little as we had was mainly controversial, and aimed more at hard knocks than at giving them with a grace. How indeed could it be otherwise? With our educational disabilities, our social disabilities, our political disabilities, our isolation, our fewness, our poverty, the marvel was, not that we were without a literature, but that we had still a faith. One great name survived to us from those days, the name of Lingard, first among our great historians to trace history back to its well-springs; and those fore-gone days had been illustrated also by the eminent naturalist, Waterton. But we had no press; the Graces cast no eye upon our literature; artists in style we had none, novelists were probably considered offspring of the Evil One, and poetry was a thing un-dreamed; it would have been as out of place as a polished helmet in

* *Our Literary Life*. Mᴀɴᴜsᴄʀɪᴘᴛ. Unsigned.

desert warfare. So that the great Protestant community about us grew to believe that Catholicism was inimical to culture; and it did indeed seem as if the culture which not Catholicism but themselves had withered up in us were beyond revival.

Catholic Emancipation had begun the era of religious equality. Among our French neighbours, as we know, religious equality means irreligious inequality. Ours was to be a happier experience. We had at length *la carrière ouverte aux talents;* the field was conceded, but wherefrom should come the seed to sow in it? Hardly in our own body could the impulse of renascence have been generated. We had among us men like Cardinal Wiseman, a man of wide knowledge, of great powers, and possessed of the literary mind, yet sharing with his fellows a misfortune fatal to purity of style — we mean foreign education. This it was, doubtless, which made the supposed original of Browning's "great bishop" write too often like a brilliant schoolboy. "They did not understand us when we spoke English to them," an eminent convert said of the Catholics born and bred. Such was the condition of things when the great flood of the Oxford Movement burst its Anglican banks, and rolling its waters over all the land of the Church, fertilised among others the thirsting fields of literature. It is impossible to overestimate the far-stretching influence exercised by the example of these brilliant pens. All of us who write are indirectly the children of the Oxford Movement. It swept into the Church, mediately or immediately, the style with which Newman had spread agitation amongst the minds of the Establishment and the lawn-sleeves of its episcopacy, the speech which was, in later days, to still those human waters by the London Docks, the song of Aubrey de Vere, the prose, which caught such radiance from song, of Faber, and Oakeley, and many a less practised writer exercising good influence in his minor sphere. From such a sowing much ought to come; and, bearing in mind what a minority we even yet are, it may justly be said that the seed fell on good ground.

When Frederick Lucas led his forlorn hope, we had no press; now, we have not only a press, but a worthy press. It has made way slowly, under oppressing difficulties: even within sufficiently recent memory, when it was otherwise ably conducted, there emanated from it, to the literary nostril, a teasing whiff of Philistinism. At the present day this is vanished: our leading papers may considerably more than vie in cultivation with the best Protestant religious weeklies. And along all lines of literature we have wonderfully advanced, are advancing, and, please God, will advance. Because religion is with us the primary fact of life, and because, too, of the men who have been our literary leaders, it is natural that round religion our greatest activity should have twined. In this department the name of Cardinal Newman dominates all others; a name *so* dominant that to the public at large it almost stands for Catholic literature. To record his name is in itself sufficient. To criticise him, to appraise him, even to laud him, is as superfluous as to estimate Tennyson: all that can be uttered has been uttered from the housetops; long since he has been placed by the consentient voice of his fellow-countrymen; he is a star whose height is taken. When we have said that the foremost minds among contemporary Protestants, from Mr. Gladstone to Mr. John Morley in his recent utterance, have recognised Cardinal Newman's mastery in letters, that he is accepted alike by Catholics and non-Catholics as one of the greatest prose-writers — by numbers as *the* greatest prose-writer — of the age; when we have said this, what is left to say? Simply to express one's gratification that his finest work, particularly the *Apologia* which is the cornerstone of his literary renown, has been composed in the bosom of the Church. The name of the one Cardinal naturally suggests the other Cardinal, the Cardinal of action. Manning's grand personality as a ruling Prince of the Church has eclipsed the excellence of his writings: nevertheless, he is the possessor of a manner cleaving like gold-leaf to its object, a manner which is, moreover, a singularly interesting example of *le style c'est l'homme*. A clear, severe, restrained, precise, tendinous style. A style macerated from all succulence. A mortified style; you can feel the hair-shirt through it. And yet a style with its own charm, worthy of the "silver-tongued archdeacon"; since silver, both in ring and gleam, is clear and cool. Faber, too, is ours; in some respects a Ruskin of the spiritual art, bringing home to the unlearned the teachings of spirituality through a style at times perhaps too *staccato*, but always fair and fresh with trickling rills of poetry. Ours too the famous author of the *Ideal of a Christian Church* [Dr. Ward]; no master of style, but commanding attention by his keen dialectic and uncompromising logic, no less than by the great part which he played among the Oxford secessionists; a man whose logic was at once his strength and his weakness, who had (as Mr. R. H. Hutton said some years ago) no half-lights in his mind; who held that two and two always and in all cases and in all things make four, and could by no means have been persuaded that in some cases and in some things two and two might possibly make four-and-a-half, or three-and-three-quarters. And though a little out of place, we may notice here for the sake of connection, his son, Mr. Wilfrid Ward, who has not only recently published an excellent biography of his father, but gives promise of following in that father's footsteps. Canon Oakeley was another clear and strong penman of the illustrious Tractarian band; while to-day we have such spiritual authors as Father Rawes, a writer with genuine style and poetic feeling, Father Dalgairns and Father Harper, the late Archbishop Ullathorne, whose *Groundwork of the Christian Virtues* combined great spiritual learning with literary ability in a high degree; the Rev. H. N. Oxenham, who was a *Saturday Reviewer* as well as a learned theologian; and many others. Among the earliest controversial writers of the period under review was Provost Husenbeth, whose antagonist was Faber's Anglican father. One may surmise that the service rendered by the son to the Church outweighed a hundredfold any damage that the father was capable of inflicting on her. In recent times we have had such men as Mr. Orby Shipley, the eminent convert, whose *Truthfulness and Ritualism* is well known, Father Lockhart, author of *The Old Religion*, and conspicuous besides as the translator of Rosmini's works, and indeed a host of others too numerous to mention. Among those who have given us valuable religious biographies are Father Coleridge, Mr. Edward Healy Thompson, Lady Herbert of Lea; and we may also notice the late Miss Kathleen O'Meara, and Lady Lovat's interesting *Life of Clare Vaughan*.

In history we have produced no new Lingard; but his example of research among original records has been followed by a

numerous band of students, who have produced volumes of historical research that will be priceless to future historians. Such is Fr.
Bridgett's *Our Lady's Dowry;* and our readers will have fresh in
their memories the controversy with Mr. Gladstone which the same
author's admirable *Life of Blessed John Fisher* recently gave rise
to in these columns. Mr. Joseph Gillow has earned the praise of
the Protestant no less than the Catholic press by his monumental
Bibliographical Dictionary of English Catholics, a work of prolonged research such as few have industry for in these superficial
days. Father Stevenson's record of Mary Stuart has added fresh
material to the unhappy and much-disputed history of that queen.
Then we have Father Amherst, the historian of Catholic Emancipation; Mr. Hubert Burke, who has given us valuable work on
the English monastic houses; Mr. Orlebar Payne, who has published interesting material showing the condition of English Catholics under the Penal Laws; Father Knox's *Records of the English
Catholics;* Father Morris's *Condition of English Catholics under
James the First;* Brother Foley, of the Jesuits, who has published
Records of the English Province: all storehouses for any future
master of history who may appear among us. And last, though not
least, we may cite Mr. Allies' *Formation of Christendom.* In the
philosophical treatment of the problems religious, social, or political suggested by modern thought, Mr. Lilly has made his mark
upon the non-Catholic world, and striven with all the power
of his wide knowledge and charm of style to make the Catholic
voice heard in the councils of the profane. The discussion created
by his last book, *A Century of Revolution,* is still of recent date.
And in science Dr. St. George Mivart has triumphantly refuted
the belief that Catholicism is incompatible with physical research,
by the high scientific position which his bitterest adversaries are
ready to concede to him. Nor in secular literature apart entirely
from religion are we less ably represented. In past years we have had
the elder Pugin, whose hard hitting in questions of art and architecture broke the ground for Ruskin; and Kenelm Digby, whose
Broad Stone of Honour, Mores Catholici, etc., with their presentation of Middle Age glories, had doubtless much influence on the
mediæval revival at Oxford. Sir George Bowyer is a distinguished

writer on law; Mr. Devas, known in the *Dublin Review*, is an able writer on economic subjects, and the Misses Clerke are *Edinburgh Reviewers* of the best type. Sir William Butler is well known for his records of travel, with their graphic word-pictures; and no less well known is Lady Anne Blunt's narrative of her own and her husband's wanderings among the Arabs of the Euphrates. Another woman-traveller who has companioned in his adventures a husband yet better known than herself is Lady Burton, author of the *Inner Life of Syria, Palestine, and the Holy Land*. Some of our peers have won literary laurels — without resorting to the *Nineteenth Century;* among them we may name Lord Bute and Lord Arundell of Wardour, who are learned in antiquarian by-ways. And in lighter literature Catholic writers are many. While the echoes of Mr. Gladstone's *Merry England* article [January, February, 1890] are still in the air, Lady Georgiana Fullerton, the authoress of *Ellen Middleton*, naturally comes most prominently to one's mind among our novelists: but besides her there are the but lately dead Mr. Edmund Randolph, author of two novels clever above the common, James Grant (though most of his novels were written when he was a Protestant), Mrs. Cashel Hoey, and Miss Rosa Mulholland. And to show, (if it were necessary) that Catholic piety does not involve long faces, the Church numbers or has numbered in her ranks the editor of *Punch*, first of punsters; Mr. T. W. Marshall, author of that clever satire *The Comedy of Convocation;* his successor Mr. Longueville, writer of the *Prig* series; and Mr. Arthur Sketchley, once famous as the creator of *Mrs. Brown*.

A sufficient bead-roll, surely, for those who, as we have said, are still a mere minority. But the Church which alone (in the West) retains the cult of the angels ought, one would think, to be a mother of song; and accordingly it is grateful to feel that in no department can English Catholics point to prouder results. The *doyen* of our Catholic poets, indeed of all English poets, is Mr. Aubrey de Vere. He has hung on the lips of Wordsworth, he has been in friendly intercourse with almost all the great poets since Wordsworth's day, and he survives now among a generation given over to newer ideals. Yet he has that public of the elect which he would probably choose if he had to choose, as did the great poet just dead. He has chosen Wordsworth for his master, and thereby deliberately submitted to the fate of not being supreme in his class. "Better than thee I cannot do," he might have said with Michelangelo; but unlike Michelangelo he has been nobly content to do only less well. Even Shakespeare left room for Fletcher, and Wordsworth assuredly has left room for Mr. de Vere. While, however, he has the grave, self-contained dignity of Wordsworth, a touch of the Shelleian influence sometimes differentiates him from his master by a gleam of lighter fancy. This is well seen in parts of the "Autumnal Ode," perhaps the very finest of his longer poems. The conclusion of it, however, is Wordsworth wholly, Wordsworth in his mood of most sustained majesty, and nothing finer of the kind has been written. No one that has once read them will forget such stately lines as

> On jacinth street and jasper parapet
> The unwaning light is light of deity;

or "That indeciduous forestry of spires." His best sonnets are equal to all but the supremest of Wordsworth's; and from them we may quote a beautiful one.

> For we the mighty mountain-plains have trod
> Both in the glow of sunset and sunrise;
> And lighted by the moon of Southern skies!
> The snow-white torrent of the thundering flood
> We two have watched together: in the wood
> We two have felt the warm tears dim our eyes
> While zephyrs softer than an infant's sighs
> Ruffled the light air of our solitude!
> O Earth, maternal Earth, and thou, O Heaven,
> And Night first-born, who now, e'en now, dost waken
> The host of stars, thy constellated train!
> Tell me if those can ever be forgiven,
> Those abject, who together have partaken
> These Sacraments of Nature — and in vain?

Father Faber's poems were often true poetry, though perhaps his best poetry is really his prose; and Adelaide Procter, one of the most popular female poets of her day, has doubtless exercised much religious influence over a multitude. The Reverend R. S. Hawker, who died a Catholic, would have been notable were it only for his "Song of the Western Men," which Macaulay noticed in his History under the impression that it was the genuine ballad sung by the Cornishmen who marched to free Trelawny from the Tower. Mr. Wilfrid Blunt has made himself a reputation of late days by his sonnets, — truly virile and original poems, often with a singularly Shakespearean sound. Miss Katharine Tynan and Miss Rosa Mulholland are unfortunately Irish poets, or they would merit a more extended mention; nor can we do more than mention a long list of lesser poets which testifies to the activity of Catholics in this branch of literature: Fathers Caswall, Christie, and Ryder, Lord Braye, Sir John Croker Barrow, Mr. Charles Kent, and Mr. John Charles Earle. The untimely dead Henry Patmore should be noted as a youth who gave promise of worthily following his father; and this brings us to the names of Alice Meynell and Coventry Patmore. Mrs. Meynell divides with Miss Christina Rossetti the honour of being the first among living female poets; indeed, in our opinion she is foremost of the two, because the more unique. It is always impossible to forget that Miss Rossetti is the sister of her brother. Mrs. Meynell's poetry is of a peculiar and most indescribably evanescing quality: it deals with emotions and aspirations which in their pensive spiritual sweetness it might have seemed no less impossible to express than to paint music. These nevertheless she conveys by a union of expression and suggestion absolutely adequate, yet so limpid in phrase that the choiceness is perceived only by its effects. It is diction rarefied to the vanishing point. In this respect she is a Coleridge of the feelings: her verse is volatilised feeling, as Coleridge's is volatilised imagination. And, like Coleridge's imagination, her emotion is wholly of the ethereal quality, you must not seek in it for ardour. It would be very false, however, to suppose her merely an emotional poet; on the contrary, she is penetratingly thoughtful; but feeling is the essence of her verse, it is feeling oozed through the pores of thought. In a bare two lines like the following her quality comes home to the reader:

> I touch not this day's secret, nor the thing
> That in the silence makes thy sweet eyes wild.

They grieve with their own exquisiteness, and pierce the heart with the incommunicableness of the beauty that aches in them. As a complete example we may give a sonnet, in which a mood is processed whose supremely subtle pencillings we had previously thought beyond the capabilities of poetic reproduction.

> Like him who met his own eyes in the river,
> The poet trembles at his own long gaze
> That meets him through the changing nights and days
> From out great Nature; all her waters quiver
> With his fair image facing him for ever;
> The music that he listens to betrays
> His own heart to his ears; by trackless ways
> His wild thoughts tend to him in long endeavour.
>
> His dreams are far among the silent hills;
> His vague voice calls him from the darkened plain
> With winds at night; strange recognition thrills
> His lonely heart with piercing love and pain;
> He knows his sweet mirth in the mountain rills,
> His weary tears that touch him with the rain.

What ineffable melancholy remoteness drifts down that line

> His dreams are far among the silent hills.

It is as the sound of distant water flowing under ice by night. Yet the diction is so seeming-innocent, that you are apt to think the spell enseated only in the feeling, and the phrases unsought, destitute of art. Try. Change one meanest word, and you will find that in lines like these each lightest phrase was as the single fatal hair of Ariosto's giant; you have plucked but one, yet the verse has paled and trailed in death. To say that Mrs. Meynell's name will ultimately stand far higher in public estimation than it stands at present, would be to keep within the straitest limits of the adage "Never prophesy unless you know"; it will probably stand higher than we ourselves at present feel competent to forecast. If there be faith in judgment, hers is emphatically poetry whose spiritual voice will become audible when the "high noises" of to-day have followed the feet that made them.

We turn lastly to the second of living poets (we say it unhesitatingly) and, were poetic greatness sufficient to ensure such a reversion, the heir-apparent to the Laureateship. But unfortunately, to say nothing of pettier requisites, reputation at once extended and high is needful for such a position; and the extended reputation of Mr. Coventry Patmore's less eminent work has almost completely distracted attention from his highest work. Since the success of *The Angel in the House*, he has been damned to irretrievable popularity: paradox though it sounds, he is obscured behind his own repute. Not upon *The Angel in the House*, with all its obvious beauties, but upon the Odes now collected in his reissue of the *Unknown Eros*, do we base our recognition of his greatness. It has been objected to him, as to Tennyson and Rossetti, that his verse is "all woman, woman, woman." This is approximately true, and anyone who finds in it an objection had better stand aside from Mr. Patmore's poetry. But had he not better also stand aside from the nineteenth century? because the nineteenth century is all woman, woman, woman. For good or for evil the woman of to-day is as different in point of position and influence from her last-century sister, as she is in point of attire from her Ancient British sister, who was clothed chiefly in woad and chastity. Look to what departments of modern life you will, the trail of the petticoat is over them all. Mr. Patmore, therefore, only realises the cardinal social fact of his age. Again, it has been objected that he is obscure; but (some casual lapses apart) he is intelligible enough to the poetically intelligent. It is at the same time tolerably certain, we admit, that the Odes can never be popular, because they cleave their way through regions in which the many cannot breathe; but it is equally certain that time, plucker-down of poets and up-builder of their monuments, will set these noble lyrics far beyond the poor mutabilities of popularity. Therefore the writer, all the more that with regard to Mr. Patmore he has in time gone dwelt among the tents of Philistia, gladly hails in this singer the great

Catholic poet whom it has been the desire of his life to see; and, being himself converted, would confirm his brethren. And it adds to our satisfaction that Mr. Patmore's muse (as regards the Odes) by both her main lines of ancestry is Catholic. Her lineage comes from Crashaw and the *Vita Nuova*. He is like Crashaw for his power of fusing translucent abstractions by a white flame of passion and blowing them into bubbled imagery; like the poet of the *Vita Nuova* for the lofty Platonism yet humanity of his love; at times like Milton for a certain proud majesty of diction. Hear the "Samson-Agonistes"-like ring of this:

> Listen: the warning all the champaign fills,
> And minatory murmurs, answering, mar
> The Night, both near and far,
> Perplexing many a drowsy citadel
> Beneath whose ill-watch'd walls the Powers of Hell,
> With armèd jar
> And angry threat, surcease
> Their long-kept compact of contemptuous peace!

With what fine, vibrant grate that "armèd jar" comes on the ear! In some things Crashaw, in some things Dante, in some things Milton; in all things Coventry Patmore. For while his Eros is Dantean in spirituality, it has a household bosom-closeness all its own, a warm mortality all its own: he girds with human ardours love "pinnacled dim in the intense inane"; into ethereal nectar he crushes the good grapes of the earth. Most high-Platonising singers leave us to pass through deserted household-rooms to seek the poet in his heavenward-lifted tower; and the outlook on the stars scarce compensates to all for the lack of kindly human fireside and refection.

But Mr. Patmore can scale the turret of the soul without relinquishing the dwelling-chambers of the body. That he is a singer of love — this, which some have cast upon him as a slur, should be set as a star upon his front. True, he sings of love; and how has he sung of love? For in this *how*, if you will consider it, lies the whole nobleness or ignobleness of the thing. He has sung of it so that all men and women to whom love shall be part of their allotted mortal course, may, reading him, love the more highly, the more lastingly, the more purely. In an age when too many have essayed, are yet essaying, to smirch and bedraggle man's conceptions of love, we can conceive few tasks more lofty for a poet than the making visible to men the immaculate fire wherewith love's feet are shod. This is the trumpet-challenge to the materialistic sensualism of the day; this, which peals against the assertion that love is a passion of the body, the assertion that love is a passion of the soul. The two principles front each other in primal, implacable antithesis; one the appointed winged destroyer of the other; one clad in light that purifies, one in light that sears. From the path of their encounter let dim half-theories swerve aside, for the unsunderable opposites will crush as between the hammer and the anvil all which delays their shock of onset. Mr. Patmore has made his choice, has taken his stand, with Eros, not Anteros; and in advancing to their haughty height the intemperable claims of Love, falls a sword as of eager lightning on the crest of Love's brute protagonist. He has added his minaret to the edifice of Dante, has preached Love to men: that he is worthy to be loved, for he is of the Eternal Love; that he is beautiful, for he is of the Eternal Beauty; that he is pure, for he is of the Eternal Purity; in words, in thoughts, in ways, in works, inevitably pure; that he but transfuses purity to passion, as the sunflower reflects the stainless sunlight, although she reflect it in flame.

SAINT BERNARD ON THE LOVE OF GOD *

St. Bernard's famous treatise, *On the Love of God,* was one of the chief sources of Patmore's inspiration in his Odes. Consequently, Thompson's review of this translation is important. Here, again, we find his ideas on Sanctity and Song.

THIS little translation, begun by Mrs. Patmore and completed by her husband, bears so much the stamp of a single mind that it might conceivably be throughout the work of Coventry Patmore. In that

* *Saint Bernard on the Love of God.* Translated by Marianne and Coventry Patmore. MANUSCRIPT. Unsigned.

beautiful saying regarding our divine Lord: "He is full of charm, of sweetness, and of mercy; clement, gay, affable, and gracious; liberal and royal"; the word "gay" is redolent of Coventry Patmore's choice. However countenanced by the original, your customary translator would have recoiled from its holy boldness. Besides the treatise on the Love of God which gives name to the book, it includes selected fragments from the Fragment which was St. Bernard's last work. Both have the Canticle of Solomon for their text; and it is uneasy to say which is the finer. They are not work for the lovers of devotional sentimentality, of those flowery French pieties which hold the modern religious market, and which the robust piety of Cardinal Manning had in such sound Saxon detestation. They are profound, contemplative, substantial, suggestive; demanding the thought which has gone to the writing of them. They exact digestion from the dyspeptic modern, apt to prefer a ready-digested food. St. Bernard has no flights of eloquence, crying — "Come, quote me!" It is a style serene and luminous; its very ardours have the austerity of white light; he thinks in his heart and feels in his brain.

His writing is loaden with Scripture — the Scripture which such mediæval teachers are impeached for neglecting. He is deeply perceptive of its symbolic meanings, scouted by the moderns; and his constant intuitional use of this symbolic imagery gives his work the quality of substantial poetry. In proportion to the height of their sanctity the Saints are inevitable poets. Sanctity is essential Song. Though literary charm appears, as a rule, only in the organic and cumulative effect of the whole; though St. Bernard seeks after truth, not beauty; now and again the sheer penetrative sincerity of that quest causes a passage to start forth by its pure literary beauty. Thus: "Intention is, as it were, the face of the soul." Or of union with God:

To attain to this is for the soul to be deified; as a small drop of water appears lost if mixed with wine, taking its taste and colour; and as, when plunged into a furnace, a bar of iron seems to lose its nature and assume that of fire; or as the air filled with the sun's beams seems rather to become light than to be illuminated. So it is with the natural life of the Saints; they seem to melt and pass away into the will of God.

But passages like this are rare: more often it is a single flash. As: "The word of God speaks not to the ear, but pierces the heart; He is not eloquent, but efficacious." In another passage, no less deep, than admirable in expression, he sets forth —

The great simplicity of His nature, which enables Him to regard many as one and one as many, without being Himself multiplied by multitude nor diminished by singularity, nor divided by diversity of objects, nor constrained by their likeness; so that He can belong utterly to one without being absorbed or prevented from belonging equally to many; and belong to many in such manner that He gives His whole heart to one.

Or let us finally quote that singly fervid utterance in the close of the Fragment, which asks what is the Soul compared to the fountain of Love?

The waters of the Lover and the Beloved, of the Soul and the Word, of the Bride and the Bridegroom, of the Creator and the creature, of her who thirsts and Him who assuages thirst, do not flow with the same abundance. But what then? Shall the prayers of the Spouse, her desires, her ardour, her trust, — shall they be lost because she cannot run with a giant, dispute sweetness with honey, mildness with the lamb, whiteness with the lily, splendour with the sun, love with Him who is Love?

But torn from their context, even these passages pale and seem null. Nor are such "beauties" characteristic and habitual, as with the honeyed Francis de Sales. What St. Bernard has for you is not beauty (as most understand beauty), not that mentally unexacting emotional luxury called "devotion," but holy wisdom — the blend of truth with the realised good of truth. It is exigent, requiring the active cooperation of the reader's meditative attention before it can transude into the blood of the soul (so to speak). It is no food for spiritual or mental *dilettantes*. You must take off your coat to it. Above all, assuming mere "virtue" as a stepping-stone, it treats of that personal embrace between Creator and creature which is not so much as dreamed by any form of Christianity save Catholicism; which is so wholly the secret and note of Catholicism that its language to the outer sects is unintelligibly fabulous — the strange bruit of an inapprehensible myth. This is not, therefore, a book for all; but for those (where should they be found but in the Church universal of range, Roman of obedience?) who quest beyond the trodden ways of common and all-bounden duty. For them it has treasure — the treasure of a Doctor and Saint, who leavens the teaching of knowledge with the personal sweetness of experience. To which is added the external suavity of pure and expert English.

POEMS OF ERNEST DOWSON *

One of the most important of Thompson's critical writings, this Manuscript is primarily an estimate of Dowson as a poet. But it is also a general criticism of the whole Decadence as a literary movement. An incomplete version of it appeared in *An Account of Books and Manuscripts of Francis Thompson*, edited by the present writer.

THIS tastefully produced volume contains the slight work of a frail and (in an artistic sense) faint minor poet. The four drawings by Aubrey Beardsley were originally made for and published with "The Pierrot of the Minute," which they here again illustrate. Besides Mr. Rothenstein's characteristic portrait of the author, the book has the advantage of a sympathetic memoir by Mr. Arthur Symons, himself a poet, a friend and appreciator of the poet he commemorates. To the few who share his interest in Dowson, this volume will be a welcome gift.

Dowson was a melancholy example of the decadent and (commercially) unsuccessful young poet, — an example more French than English. He has more affinity with the Quartier Latin than with Grub Street, with Verlaine than with Keats or even Savage, that eighteenth century decadent. The French influence was an evil thing in his career; though be it said that with him, at least, it

---

* *Poems of Ernest Dowson: with Memoir by Arthur Symons, Four Illustrations by Aubrey Beardsley, and Portrait by William Rothenstein.* Manuscript. Signed.

was no affectation, but the natural result of an early foreign up-bringing. Partly through native trend and affinities, partly (one fears) through the influence of a morbid Parisian tradition on an impressionable and imitative nature, he transplanted to the brutal atmosphere of the East End the worst follies associated with the literary cafés of Montmartre; from the *haschisch* of Baudelaire to the alcoholism of Verlaine. So he prematurely broke to pieces a fragile body and more fragile genius. A painful story, which we leave to be read in Mr. Symons' memoir.

He wrote prose, which does not here concern us; and verse, with which alone we have to do. Swinburne influenced him, and Verlaine clearly yet more, with the later modern French poets at large. But if, in substance and spirit, Verlaine be writ large on his work, it is not Verlaine's manner that he seems to us to have attained. We are reminded much more, in that respect, of *le divin Théo* and *Emaux et Camées*. The dainty sense of form, the diction delicately cut and graven, rather than (like Verlaine's and our own supreme lyrists') condensing from the emotion inevitably and freshly as dew; these features suggest Gautier or Gallic lyrism in general, not the spontaneous fluidity which Verlaine shares with so utterly different a lyrist as Hugo. It is the contrast between Greek artistry, reliant on the sculpturesque or architectural elements of form and structure; and Gothic or Celtic poetry, rooted in a peculiar spiritual intimacy, which we Goths distinctively recognise as poetry, and of which there are but the rarest examples in the classic poets (by "classic" meaning Greek and Latin). The French, as a nation, are classic and artistic rather than purely poetic. But Verlaine, with all his nation's instinct for external symmetry, had at his best the spiritual intimacy, both in substance and style, which is un-Greek and un-Gallic. Dowson, enamoured of Verlaine as an ideal, and evidently suggesting him in substance, is too natively Gallic to recall him in style. Paradox though it seem, with his devout endeavour he might have come nearer Verlaine had he been more English.

As it is, we have an admirable symmetry, a chosen and conscious diction, with a too conscious defect of absolute inspirational power. Not that Dowson was insincere, despite a morbidity which courted the suspicion of resolved imitativeness. So many modern poets have professed a Parisian morbidity at second hand that the thing is suspect. But here it was the too sincere outcome of a life influenced by what to him was a compatriot-atmosphere. Derivative he was in his morbidity; but as a Parisian poet might be. Nevertheless, this derivativeness condemns him, as it would a French writer, to the minor ranks. The major poet moulds more than he is moulded by his environment. And it may be doubted whether the most accomplished morbidity can survive the supreme test of time. In the long run Sanity endures: the finest art goes under if it be perverse and perverted art, though for a while it may create a life under the ribs of death.

Yet, with this great doubt, Ernest Dowson's work makes a present and delicate appeal to a generation itself sick of many ills. Not always of special originality or individuality, it is always dainty in form, finished in diction, and perfect in literary taste, with a sensitive avoidance of violence or exaggeration. Sensitiveness, indeed, is the precise word one would choose to indicate its leading quality. Not strong in imagination, emotion, or even fancy — lacking strength of any kind — it is always sensitive, responsive to the half-tones of emotion. It is altogether poetry of feeling, one might well-nigh say of a single feeling, or cast of feeling. Regret — the pathos of lost virtue, lost or at least ineffectual love, lost opportunities, lost virginalness in an æsthetic no less than ethical sense — informs these lyrics in monotone. An ineffectual regret, with not even a desire to regain what is lost, or a hope to attain effectual love. Inevitably, then, somewhat ineffectual (which is another matter from ineffective) poetry; for it is the poetry of disillusion. Read in bulk, the constant wail of regret and unsatisfied satiety becomes weak and weariful. But in single lyrics, when he touches his best, it has a frail and mournful charm.

This comes partly of a temperamental sweetness, which Mr. Symons noted also in his converse. And partly it is the entire classic grace, form, and sufficiency, the avoidance of the too much. His best, Mr. Symons thinks, is the poem with the refrain, "I have been faithful to thee, Cynara, in my fashion." Remembered love makes hollow present infidelities — that is the theme of it. Unwholesome, wistfully cynical, like the bulk of these lyrics, it is perfect in workmanship and a dainty symmetry contrasting with its sincere bitterness of regret. Mr. Symons, we think, is right. But in the superlatives of his praise we cannot join. Its grace, like that of all Dowson's poetry, is too hectic for supreme praise: nor has it the strange and penetrating power that makes Poe's "To Annie" haunting despite its opium-delirium. "This also is vanity" Dowson sings in many poems of a frail grace, sweetness, and slender completion of form. But the central defect of power keeps him still a lesser poet — a poet of the bitten apple, without the core of fire which made Rossetti, for instance, far more than a lesser poet. And then, too, unlike Rossetti, he has no brain, but just pure feminine sensibility.

BIBLIOGRAPHY

APPENDIX I

AN ESSAY TOWARDS A BIBLIOGRAPHY
OF FRANCIS THOMPSON'S UNCOLLECTED
BOOK REVIEWS AND LITERARY CRITICISM
CONTRIBUTED TO PERIODICALS

UNSIGNED articles or reviews are marked with an asterisk. Where a pseudonym was used, it is given. All unsigned articles and reviews here recorded have been identified by external evidence briefly cited in parentheses — a hitherto unpublished list by Everard Meynell; Thompson's notebooks or memoranda; signed articles; and correspondence with editors and friends. Four reviews are included on the authority of John Kingsley Rooker in his thesis on Thompson, presented at the University of Paris, 1912. In the preparation of his thesis, Rooker was assisted by Mr. Wilfrid Meynell and his son, Everard. References to the *Life* of Thompson by Everard Meynell are to the unabridged edition. "E. M.'s List" is Everard Meynell's list, seen at Greatham. Unless otherwise stated, notebooks to which reference is made are at Greatham, the Sussex residence of Mr. Meynell. "B. C." is an abbreviation for Boston College. Page references, in brackets, indicate the articles and reviews here reprinted.

I. THE ACADEMY

1896   Nov. 28   *Poems.* By Louisa Shore. (Letter in *Life*, p. 260.)

        Dec. 19   *MR. HENLEY'S "BYRON." *The Works of Lord Byron.* Vol. I. *Letters, 1804-1813.* Edited by William Ernest Henley. (Printed in part in *Essays of To-day and Yesterday.*)

1897   Feb. 27   ACADEMY PORTRAIT XVI. *Walter Savage Landor.* Signed.
                   [Page 177]

1897 (*Cont.*)   THE ACADEMY

Mar. 6   MR. HENLEY'S "BURNS." *The Poetry of Robert Burns*. Vol. III. Edited by W. E. Henley and T. F. Henderson. Signed.

Apr. 10   *WORDSWORTH AS PROSE WRITER. *Prose Works of Wordsworth*. Edited by William Knight. (Letter in *Life*, p. 260.)
             [Page 122]

Apr. 17   *CELTIC GLAMOUR. *Spiritual Tales; Barbaric Tales; Tragic Romances*. By Fiona Macleod. 3 Vols. (Letter in *Life*, p. 260.)

             ACADEMY PORTRAIT XXIII. *Tennyson*. Signed.
             [Page 240]

May 1   *The Secret Rose*. By W. B. Yeats. With Illustrations by J. B. Yeats. (E. M.'s List.)
             [Page 370]

May 8   ACADEMY PORTRAIT XXVI. *Robert Browning*. Signed.
             [Page 148]

May 29   *Handbook of English Literature*. By Austin Dobson and W. Hall Griffin. (E. M.'s List.)

             *A PEOPLE "RELIGIOUS TO EXCESS." *Religion of the Ancient Egyptians*. By Alfred Wiedemann. (Large Commonplace Book, B. C.)
             [Page 435]

June 5   *THE NOVELIST AND THE APOSTLE. *A Study of St. Paul*. By S. Baring-Gould. (E. M.'s List.)
             [Page 40]

Aug. 14   *COURTHOPE'S HISTORY OF POETRY. *A History of English Poetry*. Vol. II. By W. J. Courthope. (Signed review of Vols. III & IV, *Academy*, October 31, 1903.)
             [Page 275]

1897 (*Cont.*)   THE ACADEMY

Sept. 4   *Knight's "Wordsworth." *The Poetical Works of William Wordsworth.* Vol. VIII. Edited by William Knight. (E. M.'s List.)
[Page 125]

Sept. 25   James Clarence Mangan. *James Clarence Mangan: His Selected Poems.* Edited with an Introductory Study by Louise Imogen Guiney. Signed.
[Page 362]

Oct. 2   *Mr. Henley's "Burns." *The Poetry of Robert Burns.* Vol. IV. Edited by W. E. Henley and T. F. Henderson. (Signed review of Vol. III, *Academy*, March 6, 1897.)
[Page 96]

Oct. 23   The Withheld Poems of Tennyson. *Alfred, Lord Tennyson. A Memoir by His Son, Hallam, Lord Tennyson.* Signed.
[Page 245]

Oct. 30   Some Pamphlets. *Literary Pamphlets.* Vols. I and II. Edited by Ernest Rhys. Signed.

**Admirals All.* By Henry Newbolt. (*Life*, p. 269.)

Nov. 20   *Mr. Henley's Anthology. *English Lyrics.* By W. E. Henley. (E. M.'s List.)
[Page 497]

1898   Jan. 8   *Napoleon by Flashlights. *New Letters of Napoleon I.* Translated by Lady Mary Loyd. (E. M.'s List.)

Mar. 12   *Mr. Meredith's Ode on the French Revolution.* First of his "Odes in Contribution to the Song of French History." Signed.
[Page 185]

1898 *(Cont.)*   THE ACADEMY

Apr. 23   *A WOMAN AND BURNS. *Robert Burns and Mrs. Dunlop*. Correspondence now Published in Full for the First Time. With Elucidations by William Wallace. (Letter to Hind, *Life*, p. 261.)

May   14   ITALIAN LITERATURE. *A History of Italian Literature*. By Richard Garnett. Signed. [Page 419]

July   2   *MONTAIGNE. *Michel de Montaigne*. A Biographical Study. By M. E. Lowndes. (Notebook 101.) [Page 407]

July 30   *THE LIEBIG OF BIOGRAPHY. *Studies of a Biographer*. By Leslie Stephen. 2 Vols. (Subsequently printed privately in pamphlet form by Clement Shorter.) [Page 3]

Aug. 13   *A MODERN STUDY OF SANCTITY. *The Psychology of the Saints*. By Henri Joly. Translated by E. Holt. Preface and Notes by George Tyrrell, S. J. (Notebook 7.) [Page 446]

Aug. 27   *"THE PILGRIM'S PROGRESS" — AFTER TWO CENTURIES. *The Pilgrim's Progress*. By John Bunyan. Temple Classics. (Notebook 40.) [Page 47]

Sept. 3   *PASTORAL BURMAH. *The Soul of a People*. By H. Fielding. (Notebook 40.)

Sept. 10   *OF RALEIGH'S BREED. *The Poetry of Wilfrid Blunt*. Selected and Arranged by W. E. Henley and George Wyndham. (*Life*, p. 256.) [Page 137]

1898 (*Cont.*)   THE ACADEMY

Sept. 24   *THE SCANSION CASE. *Verdict and Sentence.* On Correspondence between Stephen Phillips and John Davidson in the *Star.* (E. M.'s List.) [Page 283]

Oct. 8   *ACADEMY PORTRAIT XXXVIII. *John Ruskin.* (E. M.'s List.) [Page 218]

HAMLET AND OPHELIA. Signed. [Page 482]

Nov. 19   *TIME: "WHAT YOU WILL." *Pan and the Young Shepherd.* A Pastoral in Two Acts. By Maurice Hewlett. (E. M.'s List.)

Dec. 17   *THE POETS AND LONDON. *London in Song.* Compiled by Wilfred Whitten. (Notebook 117, B. C.)

1899   Jan. 7   *MR. WATSON: A RETROSPECT. *The Collected Poems of William Watson.* (Telegram from Hind.)

Feb. 4   *THE LITTLE LANGUAGE. *Memoir and Correspondence of Susan Ferrier.* Edited by John A. Doyle. (Notebook B. C. 8.)

Feb. 11   *AN ADVENTURESS ON THE THRONE. *Marysiencka.* By K. Waliszewski. Translated by Lady Mary Loyd. (MS. at Greatham. Also, Notebook B. C. 8.)

Feb. 18   *LANDOR AND ROSE—WATER. *Letters of Walter Savage Landor, Private and Public.* Edited by Stephen Wheeler. (Notebook B. C. 8.) [Page 34]

Apr. 1   *DANTON. *Danton: A Study.* By Hilaire Belloc. *Life of Danton.* By A. H. Beesly. ("Fénelon" review, *Academy*, November 2, 1901.) [Page 387]

1899 (*Cont.*)   THE ACADEMY

Sept. 23   *THE DECADENCE OF FEMALE DECADENCE. *The Roman Empresses.* By Jacques Roergas de Serviez. Translated from the French. (E. M.'s List.)
[Page 13]

Oct. 7   *GUSTO. *Little Novels of Italy.* By Maurice Hewlett. (Galley Proof at Greatham.)
[Page 507]

Oct. 28   *ENGLISH SATIRISTS. *English Satires.* Edited by Oliphant Smeaton. (E. M.'s List.)
[Page 249]

*MISS LUCAS' POEMS. *Fugitives.* By Winifred Lucas. (Galley Proof at Greatham.)

Nov. 18   *THE REAL STEVENSON. *Letters to His Family and Friends.* By Robert Louis Stevenson. 2 Vols. (Telegram from *Academy* — No signature.)

1900   Jan. 13   *SOBER AND SUBSTANTIAL. *Tennyson, Ruskin, Mill, and Other Literary Estimates.* By Frederic Harrison. (E. M.'s List.)
[Page 130]

Feb. 3   *FLUENT AND UNSELECTIVE. *Rue.* By Laurence Housman. ("Little Land" review, *Academy*, June 17, 1899.)

Apr. 14   SOME MYSTICISMS AND A MYSTIC. *An Essay in Aid of the Better Appreciation of Catholic Mysticism.* By Algar Thorold. Illustrated from the Writings of Blessed Angela of Foligno. Signed.
[Page 441]

*EDWARD FITZGERALD'S "GREAT GUN." *The Poems of George Crabbe.* A Selection. Arranged and Edited by Bernard Holland. (Notebook 1.)

1900 (*Cont.*)   THE ACADEMY

Apr. 28   *"The Divine Chit-Chat of Cowper." *The Letters of Cowper*. Bohn's Libraries. *Cowper's Letters*. Golden Treasury Series. (Notebook in Mrs. Sowerby's possession.)

May 26   *"*The Shadowy Waters*." By William Butler Yeats. (A copy of the current — May, 1900, — *North American Review* sent by Whitten with note requesting review.)

June 2   *"And Yet — He Is a Master." *The Dead City*. By Gabriele d'Annunzio. Translated by Arthur Symons. (Galley Proof at Greatham.) [Page 429]

June 9   *Burton's Verse. *The Kasîdah* (*Couplets*) *of Hajî Abdû Al-Yazdi. A Lay of the Higher Law. Translated and Annotated by His Friend and Pupil, F.B.* By Capt. Sir Richard F. Burton. (Notebook 101.)

June 23   *The Newman of His Time. *The Confessions of St. Augustine*. In Ten Books. (MS. at Greatham.) [Page 16]

July 21   *Beatific Pot-Boilers. *Essays of John Dryden*. Selected and Edited by W. P. Ker. 2 Vols. (Notebook 101.) [Page 72]

July 28   *Byron in Venice. *Byron's Works: Letters and Journals*. Vol. IV. Edited by Rowland E. Prothero. (Undated letter from Whitten.)

Sept. 1   *A Criticism of Criticism. *Judgment in Literature*. By W. Basil Worsfold. (E. M.'s List. Also a letter from Whitten.) [Page 511]

1900 (*Cont.*) THE ACADEMY

Sept. 15   *MILTON's PROSE. *Areopagitica*. Temple Classics.
(Letter from Whitten.)
[Page 83]

Sept. 22   *AN EXPLOSION OF HUMANITY. *Rabelais: Gargantua and Pantagruel*. Translated by Sir Thomas Urquhart and Peter Le Motteux. With an Introduction by Charles Whibley. 3 Vols. (Thesis by J. K. Rooker.)

Oct. 27   *MR. MORLEY's "CROMWELL." *Oliver Cromwell*. By John Morley.(Letter fromWhitten.)

*SUN-CLOCKS. *The Book of Sun-Dials*. By Mrs. Alfred Gatty. Enlarged and Re-edited by H. K. K. Eden and Eleanor Lloyd. (Notebook 17).

Nov. 3   *COVENTRY PATMORE. *Memoirs and Correspondence of Coventry Patmore*. By Basil Champneys. 2 Vols. ("Patmore" review, *Academy*, November 24, 1900.)

Nov. 17   *"SOME OF THE BEST FIGHTING IN LITERATURE." *The Story of the Burnt Njal*. By Sir George Webbe Dasent. (MS. at Greatham.)

Nov. 24   *PATMORE's PHILOSOPHY. (Galley Proof at Greatham.)
[Page 212]

Dec. 22   *SOME EXCLUDED POETS. *The Oxford Anthology*. Chosen and Edited by A. Quiller-Couch. (Notebook 41 in Mrs. Sowerby's possession.)

1901 Jan. 12   *FOUR BOOKS OF VERSE. *Odes*. By Laurence Binyon. *The Professor, and Other Poems*. By A. C. Benson. *Love's Argument, and Other Poems*. By Ellen Thorneycroft Fowler. *Wings*. By Margaret Ethel Ashton.(Notebook B.C. 4.)

1901 *(Cont.)*   THE ACADEMY

July 27   **The Life and Times of Sydney Smith.* By S. J. Reid. (MS. at Greatham.)

Aug. 10   **AN HISTORICAL PAINTER. English Seamen in the Sixteenth Century.* Lectures Delivered at Oxford Easter Terms, 1893-94. By James Anthony Froude. (MS. at Greatham.)

*REAL LOVE LETTERS. *The Love-Letters of Abelard and Heloïse.* Temple Classics. (Marked as F. T.'s by Wilfrid Meynell.)

Aug. 17   *WHY? *A Commentary on Tennyson's "In Memoriam."* By A. C. Bradley. (E. M.'s List.)

Aug. 24   *A JOURNALIST'S APOLOGIA. *My Life's Record: A Fight for Justice.* By F. Reginald Statham. (Marked as F. T.'s by Wilfrid Meynell.)

Aug. 31   **Anselm and His Work.* By Rev. A. C. Welch. (MS. at Greatham.)

Sept. 7   **A Short History of the Hebrews.* By R. L. Ottley. (MS. at Greatham.)

Sept. 21   *A PRESCRIPTION FOR THE TWENTIETH CENTURY. *History of Intellectual Development.* Vol. III. By John Beattie Crozier. (Galley Proof at Greatham. Also Notebook B. C. 6.)

*MEREJKOWSKI'S "TREMENDOUS TASK." *The Death of the Gods.* By Dmitri Merejkowski. Translated by Herbert Trench. ("The Forerunner" review, *Academy*, August 16, 1902.)

*THE SERPENT IN LITERATURE. *The Life-History of British Serpents.* By Gerald R. Leighton. (A copy at Greatham.)

Sept. 28   *A DREAMER OF THINGS IMPOSSIBLE. (Galley Proof at Greatham.)
            [Page 317]

1901 (*Cont.*)   THE ACADEMY

Dec. 7   *PATRIOTISM AND POETRY. *Patriotic Song*. Edited
            by Arthur Stanley. (E. M.'s List.)
            [Page 254]

Dec. 14   *MR. HENLEY'S NEW POEMS. *Hawthorn and
            Lavender, with Other Verses*. By W. E. Hen-
            ley. (Notebook 117, B. C.)
            [Page 172]

Dec. 21   *A GREAT MINOR POET. *The English Poems of
            Richard Crashaw*. Edited, with Introduction
            and Notes, by Edward Hutton. (Notebook
            117, B. C.)
            [Page 62]

            *TO WHAT END? *The Thrush: A Book of Original
            Poems*. (Notebook 117, B. C.)

1902 Jan. 4   *Comments of a Countess*. Anonymous. (MS. at
            Greatham.)

            Ballads of the Fleet, and Other Poems. By Ren-
            nell Rodd. (Galley Proof at Greatham.)

Jan. 11   *THE OFFICIAL "LOWELL." *James Russell Lowell:
            A Biography*. By Horace Elisha Scudder. 2
            Vols. (E. M.'s List.)
            [Page 307]

            Insect Life. By J. H. Fabre. Translated from the
            French by the author of *Mademoiselle Mori*.
            With a Preface by David Sharp, and Edited
            by F. Merrifield. (MS. at Greatham.)

Jan. 25   *DECORATIVE VERSE. *The Collected Poems of A.
            Mary F. Robinson*. (Madame Duclaux.)
            (MS. at Greatham.)

            *MR. BRIDGES AND METRE. *Milton's Prosody*. By
            Robert Bridges. *Classical Metres in English
            Verse*. By William Johnson Stone. (E. M.'s
            List.)
            [Page 289]

1902 *(Cont.)*   THE ACADEMY

Feb. 1   *SIX VOLUMES OF VERSE. *The Moon of Leaves.* By
             Aristo. *A Palace of Dreams.* By Ada Bartrick
             Baker. *Sonnets of Empire.* By Laura Ackroyd.
             Songs of a Child. By "Darling" (Lady Flor-
             ence Dixie.) Part I. *Polyphemus.* By R. C.
             Trevelyan. *Poems by John Clare.* Selected
             and Introduced by Norman Gale. (Letter,
             Academy, January 4, 1902 and "The Thrush"
             review, *Academy,* December 21, 1901.)

Mar. 1   *A PLAIN MAN'S POET. *Ballads and Lyrics.* By
             Bliss Carman. (Galley Proof at Greatham.)

Mar. 15   *HINDOO LOVE-POEMS. *The Garden of Kama, and
             Other Love-Lyrics from India.* Arranged in
             Verse by Laurence Hope.(MS. at Greatham.)

Mar. 29   *HUGO IN ENGLISH. *Poems from Victor Hugo.* By
             Sir George Young. (Notebook 117, B. C.)
             [Page 403]

             *GOOD, FAIR, AND BAD. *The Hours of the Passion,
             and Other Poems.* By Harriet King. *Willie
             Winkie, and Other Songs and Poems.* By
             William Miller. *With Lead and Line.* By C.
             H. Webb. *A Mirror of Moods.* By G. F. Wil-
             son. *The Watchers of the Hearth.* By Benj.
             Sledd. *Marlowe: A Drama.* By Josephine P.
             Peabody. (MS. at Greatham.)

Apr. 5   *China and the Powers.* By H. C. Thomson.
             (Notebook 117, B. C.)

Apr. 12   *Leaves in the Road.* By Eric R. D. Maclagan.
             (Notebook 23.)

Apr. 19   *THE SOUL OF IRELAND. *With the Wild Geese.*
             By Emily Lawless. (Notebook 23.)

Apr. 26   *THE PERSISTENCE OF BYRON. (E. M.'s List.)

1902 (*Cont.*)   THE ACADEMY

May 17 *KAPELLMEISTER WAGNER. *Life of Richard Wagner.* Being an authorised English version by W. Ashton Ellis, of C. F. Glasenapp's *Das Leben Richard Wagners.* Vol. II. (Reference to review of Vol. I, *Academy*, February 2, 1901.)

June 7 *WHAT IS RUSSIA? *All the Russias.* By Henry Norman. (MS. at Greatham.)

*A PROPHET OF NIETZSCHE. *The Testament of an Empire-Builder.* By John Davidson. (MS. at Greatham.)

June 28 *MR. WATSON'S CORONATION ODE. *Ode on the Coronation of King Edward VII.* By William Watson. (E. M.'s List.)

July 12 **Some Ballads.* By Rose Haig Thomas. (Notebook 23.)

July 19 *THE PREFERENTIAL ANTHOLOGY. *Little Book of Life and Death.* By Miss Elizabeth Waterhouse. (Galley Proof at Greatham.)

*TWENTY-THREE VOLUMES OF VERSE. *Poems.* By Robert U. Johnson. *West Country Songs.* By Mark Guy Pearse. *In The Highlands.* By G. R. T. Ross. *Horæ Fugaces.* By W. A. Adams. *Life's Little Comedies.* By Hugh Bedwell. *Lyric and Other Poems.* By Harold Boulton. (Notebook 23.)

**Mrs. Boythorn and Her Canary.* An Article on the Swinburne-Lang Controversy concerning Dickens. (Prodigious Faint Ruled Notebook in Mrs. Sowerby's possession.)
[Page 523]

Aug. 9 *THE AMAZON. *The Warrior Woman.* By Edward Vizetelly. (MS. at Greatham.)

1902 (*Cont.*)   THE ACADEMY

Oct. 25   *Fiona Macleod on Mr. W. B. Yeats. A Review
            of an article in the *North American Review*,
            October 1902. (E. M.'s List. Also a letter from
            Hind.)
            [Page 373]

Nov. 1   *Cowley Redivivus. *Poems Selected from the
            Writings of Abraham Cowley*. Published by
            A. C. Curtis. (Notebook 101.)

Nov. 22   *Mother and Daughter, Too! *Hand-in-Hand*.
            Verses by a Mother and Daughter. (*Life*, p.
            268.)

            *Mr. Newbolt's New Poems. *The Sailing of the
            Long Ships*. By Henry Newbolt. ("Admirals
            All" review, *Academy*, October 30, 1897.)

            *An Agnostic of the Sixteenth Century.
            Essays of Montaigne. Translated by Charles
            Cotton. Edited by William C. Hazlitt. 4 Vols.
            (E. M.'s List.)
            [Page 413]

Dec. 6   *"Analysis, Order, Exactitude." *Studies of a
            Biographer*. Vols. III and IV. Second Series.
            By Sir Leslie Stephen. (Reference to review
            of Vols. I and II, *Academy*, July 30, 1898.)
            [Page 9]

1903 Jan. 10   *"Our Fathers Have Told Us." *Picturesque Old
            Houses*. By Allan Fea. ("King Monmouth"
            review, *Academy*, October 19, 1901.)

Feb. 21   *The Sun, etc. *Problems in Astro-Physics*. By
            Agnes M. Clerke. (Large Commonplace Book,
            B. C.)

            *The Sonnet. *Little Book of English Sonnets*.
            By Bowyer Nichol. (Galley Proof at Great-
            ham.)
            [Page 260]

1903 *(Cont.)*   THE ACADEMY

Feb. 28 *A Biblical Drama. *Absalom: A Chronicle-Play in Three Acts*. By T. Sturge Moore. (Galley Proof at Greatham.)

*The Preacher Poet. *Herbert's Poems*. A New Edition. With the Life of the Author by Izaak Walton. (Galley Proof at Greatham.)

Apr. 11 *A Rediscovered Poet. *The Poetical Works of Thomas Traherne*. Now First Published from the Original MS. Edited by Bertram Dobell. (Notebook 31, B. C.) [Page 89]

Apr. 18 *Living History. Carlyle's *French Revolution*. Edited by Holland Rose. (Galley Proof at Greatham.) [Page 163]

May 2   *A Poet's Table Talk. *Don Juan*. By Lord Byron. *Poetry*. Vol. VI. of *The Works of Lord Byron*. Edited by Ernest Hartley Coleridge. (Galley Proof at Greatham.) [Page 112]

May 9   *The Carlyle Pair. *New Letters and Memorials of Jane Welsh Carlyle*. Annotated by Thomas Carlyle. Edited by Alexander Carlyle, with an Introduction by Sir James Crichton-Browne. 2 Vols. (E. M.'s List.)

*Sane, Sensible, and Cautious. *Studies in Contemporary Biography*. By James Bryce. (E. M.'s List.)

May 16   *A Bewildered Poet. *James Clarence Mangan*. (Notebook 29, B. C.) [Page 367]

1903 (*Cont.*)   THE ACADEMY

May 30   *FitzGerald and Calderon. *Six Dramas of Calderon.* Freely Translated by Edward Fitz-Gerald. Edited by Dr. H. Oelsner. (Galley Proof at Greatham.)
[Page 528]

June 20   *The Last of It? *My Relations with Carlyle.* By J. A. Froude. (Reference to "Carlyle" review, *Academy*, May 9, 1903.)

June 27   *The Ways of Criticism. *Macbeth. New Variorum Edition.* By Horace Howard Furness, revised by his son, Horace Howard Furness, Jr. (Galley Proof at Greatham.)
[Page 477]

     *Language. *Two Lectures on the Science of Language.* By James Hope Moulton. (Galley Proof at Greatham.)

July 11   *Hudibras. Butler's *Hudibras.* With an Introductory Note by T. W. H. Crosland. (Thesis by J. K. Rooker.)

Aug. 1   *The Pre-Raphaelite Morris. *The Defence of Guenevere.* By William Morris. (Notebook 29, B. C.)
[Page 198]

Aug. 15   *"In the Dawn Before the Day-Star." *The Poems of John Dyer.* Edited by Edward Thomas. (Title considered by F. T. as possible title of *New Poems, Life,* p. 238.)

     *Mangan the Unhappy. *Poems of James Clarence Mangan.* Centenary Edition. Edited with Preface and Notes by D. J. O'Donoghue. (Signed "Mangan" review, *Academy*, September 25, 1897.)

Sept. 5   *The Early Patmore. (Thesis by J. K. Rooker.)

1903 (*Cont.*)   THE ACADEMY

Sept. 19   *THE INTERMINABLE DISPUTE. *The Nemesis of Froude: A Rejoinder to J. A. Froude's "My Relations with Carlyle."* By Sir James Crichton-Browne and Alexander Carlyle. ("Carlyle" review, *Academy*, June 20, 1903.)

Sept. 26   *ANCIENT KNOWLEDGE. *Ancient Calendars and Constellations.* By the Hon. Emmeline M. Plunket. (MS. at Greatham.)

*HINDU ASCETICISM. *The Mystics, Ascetics, and Saints of India.* By John Campbell Oman. (MS. at Greatham.)

Oct.   3   *COLERIDGE. *Select Poems of Samuel Taylor Coleridge.* Arranged in Chronological Order with Introduction and Notes by Andrew J. George. (Notebook 29, B. C.) [Page 117]

Oct. 10   CONCISE BUT ADEQUATE. *Crabbe.* By Alfred Ainger. Signed.

A LOVEABLE PERSONALITY. *The Life of Oliver Goldsmith.* By John Forster. Abridged and Newly Edited with Notes. Signed.

*POLITICS AND POETRY. *For England: Poems Written During Estrangement.* By William Watson. (Letter from V. Rendall mentioned this as having appeared in the *Academy*.)

Oct. 17   A MAN OF LAW AND ART. *William Wetmore Story and His Friends.* From Letters, Diaries, and Recollections. By Henry James. 2 Vols. Signed.

Platonism in English Poetry of the Sixteenth and Seventeenth Centuries. By John Smith Harrison. (E. M.'s List.)

1903 (*Cont.*)   THE ACADEMY

Oct. 31   ENGLISH POETRY. *A History of English Poetry.*
            Vols. III and IV. By W. J. Courthope. Signed.
            [Page 280]

Nov. 7   *The Responsibilities of the Novelist, and Other
            Literary Essays.* By Frank Norris. Signed.

Nov. 28   TWICE FORTUNATE. *Fanny Burney.* By Austin
            Dobson. Signed.

1904   Jan. 9   *POETRY. *A Survey of Poetry for the Year 1903.*
            (Letter from W. T. Shore.)

Jan. 16   *As the Sparks Fly Upward: Poems and Ballads.*
            By Dora Sigerson Shorter. Signed.

Feb. 13   A REVELATION. *The House of Quiet: An Auto-
            biography.* Edited by J. T. Signed.

Feb. 27   *The Kinship of Nature.* By Bliss Carman. Signed.
            [Page 296]

Mar. 5   POETRY AND POETICS. *Unseen Kings.* By Eva
            Gore-Booth. *Verses.* By Ruth Young. *The
            Knight's Tale of Palamon and Arcite.* Done
            into Modern English by Walter W. Skeat.
            Adonais. By Percy Bysshe Shelley. *An Intro-
            duction to the Poems of Tennyson.* By Henry
            Van Dyke. Signed.

Mar. 26   A ROMANTIC FANTASY. *Henry Brocken: His
            Travels and Adventures in the Rich, Strange,
            Scarce-Imaginable Regions of Romance.* By
            Walter J. De La Mare. Signed.

Apr. 23   *SOME MINOR VERSE. *Crumbs of Fancy.* By Lotte.
            St. John: a Poem. By Robert F. Horton.
            Poems. By W. E. Walkerdine. *The Poet's
            Child.* By Christie Finlayson. *Sidelights:
            Poems, Chiefly Local.* By E. Percy Schofield.
            Cornish Ballads and Other Poems. By R. S.
            Hawker. (Galley Proof at Greatham.)

1904 *(Cont.)*   THE ACADEMY

May 14   *Sweet Hours.* By Carmen Sylva. *An Elegy.* By
            Vivian Locke Ellis. *The Angel of Misfortune:
            a Fairy Tale.* By Nagesh Wishwanath Pai.
            (Galley Proof at Greatham.)

June 25   A. C. S. *The Poems of Algernon Charles Swin-
            burne.* Vol. I. *Poems and Ballads.* Signed.

July 30   *Dante and the English Poets, from Chaucer to
            Tennyson.* By Oscar Kuhns. (MS. at Great-
            ham.)

Aug. 27   THE POLITICAL SWINBURNE. *The Poems of
            Algernon Charles Swinburne.* Vol. II. *Songs
            before Sunrise* and *Songs of Two Nations.*
            Signed.

Sept. 17   A. C. S. *A Channel Passage, and Other Poems.*
            By Algernon Charles Swinburne. Signed.
            [Page 221]

Oct. 15   *POETRY. *The Works of Heinrich Heine.* Vol. IX.
            The Book of Song. Translated by T. Brooks-
            bank. Vol. X. *New Poems.* Translated by
            Margaret Armour. *To Leda, and Other Poems.*
            By T. Sturge Moore. *Lost Masterpieces, and
            Other Verses.* By St. John Hankin. *The Legend
            of St. Frideswide, and Other Poems.* By
            Florence Hayllar. (E. M.'s List.)

Nov. 26   *VERSES. *Vagabond Songs and Ballads of Scotland.*
            Edited by Robert Ford. *Egyptian and Other
            Verses.* By George Cookson. *The Tragedies
            of Seneca.* Rendered into English Verse by
            Ella I. Harris. *Hymns from the Greek Office-
            Books.* Rendered by the Rev. John Brownlie.
            (MS. at Greatham.)

Dec. 3   *PETRARCH. *The Secret of Petrarch.* By Edmund
            James Mills. (MS. at Greatham.)

1904 (*Cont.*)   THE ACADEMY

Dec. 17   SHELLEY. *The Complete Poetical Works of Shelley*. Edited by Thomas Hutchinson. Signed.

Dante's Divina Commedia. Translated into English Prose by the Rev. H. F. Tozer. (MS. at Greatham.)

1905   Jan. 7   *The Poems of William Watson*. Compiled by Mr. J. A. Spender. 2 Vols. Signed.

Studies in Prose and Verse. By Arthur Symons. (*Life*, p. 269.)
[Page 223]

Emerson, Poet and Thinker. By Elisabeth Luther Cary. (Prodigious Exercise Book in Mrs. Sowerby's possession.)

Feb. 11   *The Golden Bowl*. By Henry James. (E. M.'s List.)
[Page 298]

HUDIBRAS-BUTLER. Hudibras. By Samuel Butler. Edited by A. R. Waller. (Prodigious Exercise Book in Mrs. Sowerby's possession.)
[Page 57]

The Child Andrea. By Karin Michaëlis. Translated from the Danish by John Nilsen Laurvik. (Detached page of a notebook in Mrs. Sowerby's possession.)

Mar. 11   *Gossip*. A Novel. By Benjamin Swift. (Galley Proof at Greatham.)

Mar. 25   *APOPHTHEGMS. Life's Questionings: A Book of Experience*. By William R. Paterson. (MS. at Greatham.)

May 13   *Shining Ferry*. By "Q." (MS. at Greatham.)

The Grey Brethren: and Other Fragments in Prose and Verse. By Michael Fairless. (Prodigious Exercise Book in Mrs. Sowerby's possession.)

June 17   *PAMPERING THE STUDENT. Minor Poets of the Caroline Period*. Vol. I. (Containing Chamberlayne's *Pharonnida* and *England's Jubilee*, Benlowes' *Theophilia*, and the Poems of Katherine Philips and Patrick Hannay.) Edited by George Saintsbury. (Unnumbered Notebook at Greatham.)

Aug. 19   *Shelburne Essays*. Second Series. By Paul Elmer More. (Notebook 34, B. C.)
[Page 313]

Sept. 23   *MONTAIGNE. Michel de Montaigne*. By Edward Dowden. (Letter from *Academy*, July 6, 1905.)

ANDREW MARVELL. Andrew Marvell. By Augustine Birrell. English Men of Letters. (Letter from *Academy*, July 6, 1905.)

Sept. 30   *AN ELIZABETHAN POET. Michael Drayton. A Critical Study*. By Oliver Elton. (Letter from *Academy*, July 6, 1905.)

Oct. 7   *ABRAHAM COWLEY. Abraham Cowley. Poems*. Vol. I. Edited by A. R. Waller. (Letter from *Academy*, July 6, 1905.)

Nov. 4   *The Journals of Dorothy Wordsworth*. Edited by William Knight. (Notebook 29, B. C.)

Nov. 11   *LOST SIR LEWIS. The New Rambler: From Desk to Platform*. By Sir Lewis Morris. (Notebook 34, B. C.)

1905 (*Cont.*)   THE ACADEMY

Nov. 25   *A Lover of the English Tongue. *Lectures and Essays.* By Alfred Ainger. Edited by H. C. Beeching. 2 Vols. (Notebook 34, B. C. Also "Burns" review, *Academy*, January 20, 1906.)

1906   Jan. 20   *The Sun of Scotland. *Selected Poems of Robert Burns.* With an Introduction by Andrew Lang. (Reference to "Ainger" review, *Academy*, November 25, 1905.) [Page 102]

July 7   *An English Epic. *Drake. An English Epic.* Books I-III. By Alfred Noyes. (On list in letter dated October 23, 1906.)

July 14   *Towards Joy? *Vers la joi. Ames païennes, âmes chrétiennes.* Par Lucie Félix-Faure Goyau. (On list in letter dated October 23, 1906.)

Aug. 25   *The Growth of English Literature. *The Oxford Treasury of English Literature.* Vol. I. *Old English to Jacobean.* By G. E. Hadow and W. H. Hadow. (On list in letter dated October 23, 1906.)

Oct. 20   *The Complete Parson. *George Herbert and His Times.* By A. G. Hyde. (Notebook 19, B. C.)

*American Culture. *The Secret Life.* Being the Book of a Heretic. (On list in letter dated October 23, 1906.) [Page 323]

II. THE ATHENÆUM

1897   Sept. 18   *Nepenthe: A Poem in Two Cantos.* By George
Darley.With an Introduction by R. A. Streat-
feild. (Letter from *Athenæum*, August 25,
1897.)

1898   Aug. 6   *Poems and Sonnets of Henry Constable.* Edited
from Early Editions and Manuscripts by
John Gray. (E. M.'s List.)

Dec. 31   *A Dictionary of Proper Names and Notable
Matters in the Works of Dante.* By Paget
Toynbee. *Essays on Dante by Dr. Karl Witte.*
Selected, Translated, and Edited by C. Mabel
Lawrence and Philip H. Wicksteed. (Note-
book 117, B. C.)

1903   May 9   *The Love Letters of Dorothy Osborne to Sir
William Temple.* Newly Edited from the
Original MSS. by Israel Gollancz. (Unnum-
bered Notebook at Greatham.)

Aug. 1   *Skelton: A Selection from the Poetical Works
of John Skelton.* With Introduction, Notes,
Glossary, by W. H. Williams. (Notebook 40
in Mrs. Sowerby's possession.)

Aug. 15   *The Letters from Dorothy Osborne to Sir William Temple, 1652-54.* Edited by Edward
Abbott Parry. (Reference to previous article
in *Athenæum*, May 9, 1903.)

Dec. 12   *For England: Poems Written During Estrangement.* By William Watson. (Letter from V.
Rendall, November 20, 1903.)

The Wingless Psyche. By Morley Roberts. (Letter from V. Rendall, November 20, 1903.)

1904   June 11   *The Works of Sir Thomas Browne.* Vol. I. Edited
by Charles Sayle. (Reference in review of
Vol. III, *Athenæum*, October 19, 1907.)

Bibliography   589

1904 *(Cont.)*   THE ATHENÆUM

July 23   *_The Works of Sir Thomas Browne._ Vol. II. Edited by Charles Sayle. (Reference in review of Vol. III, _Athenæum_, October 19, 1907.)

Sept. 24   *_Richard Crashaw: Steps to the Temple, Delights of the Muses, and Other Poems._ Edited by A. R. Waller. (Letter from V. Rendall, July 15, 1904.)

*_The Defence of Poesie._ By Sir Philip Sidney. (Parallel passages in other Sidney article, _Academy_, December 21, 1901.)

*_Maria Edgeworth._ By Emily Lawless. (Letter from V. Rendall, August 24, 1904.)

Dec. 24   *_The Souls of the Streets, and Other Little Papers._ By Arthur Ransom. (Letter from V. Rendall, August 24, 1904.)

1905 Feb. 18   *_The Enchanted Woods and Other Essays on the Genius of Places._ By Vernon Lee. (Prodigious Exercise Book in possession of Mrs. Sowerby.)

Apr. 1   *_Coventry Patmore._ By Edmund Gosse. Literary Lives Series. (Prodigious Exercise Book in possession of Mrs. Sowerby.)

Apr. 8   *_Lhasa and Its Mysteries, with a Record of the Expedition of 1903-4._ By L. Austine Waddell. (Large Commonplace Book, B. C.)

June 3   *THE AUTHOR OF "JOHN INGLESANT." _Life and Letters of J. H. Shorthouse._ Edited by his Wife. 2 Vols. (Notebook B. C. 5.)

1906 Feb. 24   *_The Thread of Gold._ By the Author of _The House of Quiet._ (Notebook 34, B. C.)

*_Visionaries: A Book of Tales — Occult and Pagan, Mystical and Gothic._ By James Huneker. (Notebook 34, B. C.)

1906 (*Cont.*)   THE ATHENÆUM

Apr.   7   **The English Works of George Herbert, Newly Arranged and Annotated, and Considered in Relation to His Life.* By George H. Palmer. 3 Vols. (Notebook 34, B. C.)

June 30   **The Golden Book: Legends of Saints and Martyrs of the Church.* Translations from Mediæval Sources by Mrs. Francis Alexander. (Notebook 34, B. C.)

July   7   **The Poetry and Philosophy of George Meredith.* By George Macaulay Trevelyan. (Letter from V. Rendall, August 24, 1904.) [Page 181]

July 14   **Studies of English Mystics.* St. Margaret's Lectures, 1905. By William Ralph Inge. (E. M.'s List.) [Page 437]

1907   Jan. 19   **Thomas à Kempis: His Age and Book.* By J. E. C. de Montmorency. (E. M.'s List.) [Page 31]

Feb. 23   **Thomas Edward Brown, the Manx Poet: An Appreciation.* By Selwyn G. Simpson. With Preface by the Rev. J. M. Wilson. (E. M.'s List.) [Page 142]

Mar.   9   **The American Scene.* By Henry James. (E. M.'s List.) [Page 301]

Mar. 16   **George Herbert and His Times.* By A. G. Hyde. (Notebook 19, B. C.) [Page 79]

1907 *(Cont.)*   THE ATHENÆUM

May 11   *The Poetical Works of Wm. Strode.* Now first Collated from Manuscript and Printed Sources. Edited by Bertram Dobell, with a Memoir of the Author. *Thomas Stanley: His Original Lyrics.* Complete in their Collated Readings. Edited by Louise Imogen Guiney. (E. M.'s List.)

July 13   *The Blind Sisters of St. Paul.* By Maurice de la Sizeranne. Translated by L. M. Leggatt. (E. M.'s List.)

The Oxford Treasury of English Literature. Vol. II. *Growth of the Drama.* By G. E. and W. H. Hadow. (Notebook 31, B. C.)

Otc. 19   *The Works of Sir Thomas Browne.* Vol. III Edited by Charles Sayle. (E. M.'s List.)

III.   THE DAILY CHRONICLE

1899   May 26   *Poems.* By William Butler Yeats (Blue Notebook in Mrs. Sowerby's possession.)

1901   May 23   RECENT VERSE. *Verses Popular and Humorous.* By Henry Lawson. *At the Gates of Song.* By Lloyd Mifflin. *Ghost of Rosalys.* By C. Leonard Moore. *Poems of the Malay Peninsula.* By R. Greentree. *Poems.* By Alexander Blair Thaw. *Town and Country Poems.* By A. E. Legge. Signed.

June 29   *A THESIS IN VERSE. The Testament of a Vivisector.* By John Davidson. (Reference in "Testament of a Man Forbid" review, *Daily Chronicle,* December 13, 1901.) [Page 167]

1901 (*Cont.*)   THE DAILY CHRONICLE

Nov. 8   An Unreticent Poet. *The Complete Poetic Works of Robert Buchanan.* 2 Vols. Signed.

Dec. 13   *Pegasus in Harness. *The Testament of a Man Forbid.* By John Davidson. (Seen at Greatham.)

1902 May 22   *The Poetic Disciple of Nietzsche. *The Testament of an Empire-Builder.* By John Davidson. (Seen at Greatham with a letter from Davidson concerning the review, dated May 22, 1902.)

Aug. 21   *Heroes of Old. *Northern Hero Legends.* By Dr. Otto L. Jiriezek. Translated by Bentinck Smith. (E. M.'s List.)

1903 Nov. 12   *Poetry of Passion. *Stars of the Desert.* By Laurence Hope. (Seen at Greatham.)

1904 Feb. 20   *Week End Sussex. *Highways and Byways in Sussex.* By E. V. Lucas. With Illustrations by Frederick L. Griggs. (Notebook 40, at Greatham.)

IV. DUBLIN REVIEW

1889 Apr.   "Irish Minstrelsy." *Irish Minstrelsy. A Selection of Irish Songs, Lyrics, and Ballads.* Edited, with Notes and Introduction, by H. Halliday Sparling. *Vagrant Verses.* By Rosa Mulholland. *Louise de la Vallière, and Other Poems.* By Katharine Tynan. *Shamrocks.* By Katharine Tynan. Signed.
[Page 332]

July   The Macbeth Controversy. Signed.
[Page 456]

V. FRANCISCAN ANNALS

1893   July   *The Image of God.* Signed.
                 [Page 491]

1894   Jan.   SANCTITY AND SONG, II. *The Three Metrical
                 Canticles of St. Francis of Assisi.* Signed.
                 [Page 493]

1906   Jan.   "THE SERAPHIC KEEPSAKE." *The Seraphic Keep-
                 sake.* By Reginald Balfour. Signed.
                 [Page 534]

VI. MERRY ENGLAND

1889   Apr.   LITERARY COINCIDENCE. Signed.
                 [Page 451]

1891   Aug.   HEALTH AND HOLINESS. *The Letters of the Late
                 George Porter, S. J., Archbishop of Bombay.*
                 ("Francis Tancred.")

1892   Nov.   *ANDREW LANG AND LITERATURE AS A TRADE.
                 How to Fail in Literature.* By Andrew Lang.
                 (Seen at Greatham.)

1893   May   *Madame de Krudener.* By Clarence Ford.
                 ("Francis Tancred.")
                 [Page 22]

       July   MORE LETTERS OF CARDINAL NEWMAN. *Letters
                 and Correspondence of John Henry Newman
                 During His Life in the English Church, with
                 a Brief Autobiography.* Edited by Anne
                 Mozley. 2 Vols. ("Philip Hemans.")

       Sept.   A POET'S RELIGION. *Religio Poetæ.* By Coventry
                 Patmore. ("Francis Tancred.")
                 [Page 203]

MERRY ENGLAND

1894. Oct. THE RELIGIOUS RONDELEER. *Rondeaulx.* Translated from the black letter French edition of 1527 by John Richard Best. ("Philip Hemans.")
[Page 271]

Dec. A PARTNERSHIP IN SONG. *Songs from Vagabondia.* By Bliss Carman and Richard Hovey. Signed.
[Page 292]

VII. THE NEW REVIEW

1897 Nov. THE LIFE OF TENNYSON. *Alfred, Lord Tennyson, A Memoir by his Son, Hallam.* Signed.
[Page 225]

VIII. THE OUTLOOK (LONDON)

1898 Feb. 26 *MAETERLINCK'S ESSAYS. *The Treasure of the Humble.* By Maurice Maeterlinck. Translated by Alfred Sutro. With Introduction by A. B. Walkley. (Letter from F. T. submitting review.)
[Page 504]

*MR. HOUSMAN'S POEMS. *Spikenard: Devotional Love-Poems.* By Laurence Housman. (E. M.'s List.)

Apr. 16 *MR. LAURENCE IRVING'S DRAMATIC POEM. *Godefroi and Yolande.* By Laurence Irving. (E. M.'s List.)

1898 (*Cont.*) THE OUTLOOK (LONDON)

Apr. 30 *THE CASE AGAINST OMAR KHAYYAM. *The Rubá'iyát of Omar Khayyám.* Translated by E. Heron-Allen. (Notebook B. C. 7.)

May 7 THE NEW BYRON. *The Works of Lord Byron. A New Revised and Enlarged Edition with Illustrations. Vol. I.* Edited by Ernest Hartley Coleridge. Signed.
[Page 107]

Aug. 27 THE STUDY OF DANTE. *Dante at Ravenna.* By Catherine Phillimore. *The Ten Heavens of Dante.* By Edmund Gardner. Signed.
[Page 426]

Nov. 19 *SPANISH LITERATURE. *A History of Spanish Literature.* By J. Fitzmaurice-Kelly. (Letter from Hurd, October 22, 1898.)

IX. THE WEEKLY REGISTER

1890 Apr. 12 **A Century of Revolution.* By W. S. Lilly.
(*Life*, p. 124.)
[Page 484]

1891 Jan. 10 LOUIS LE BIEN-AIMÉ. *A Vision of Saints.* By Lewis Morris. Signed.
[Page 192]

1892 May 21 *MR. HENLEY'S NEW POEMS. *The Song of the Sword, and Other Poems.* By William E. Henley. (Parallel passages in *A Renegade Poet*, pp. 185-7.)

1893 Aug. 19 *LORD DE TABLEY'S POEMS. *Poems Dramatic and Lyrical.* By Lord de Tabley. (Unnumbered Notebook, Greatham.)

1900 Jan. 26 BOOKS THAT HAVE INFLUENCED ME. Signed.
[Page 542]

X. THE TABLET

1893   Jan.   21   *MRS. MEYNELL'S POEMS. *Poems*. By Alice
                    Meynell. (MS. at B. C.)
                    [Page 187]

1906   Oct.   27   *THE BLESSING OF THE BEAST. *The Church and
                    Kindness to Animals*. This is a translation of
                    L'Eglise et la Pitié envers les Animaux. By
                    "an anonymous English gentleman and the
                    Marquise de Rambures."(Signed MS. at B.C.)
                    [Page 538]

INDEX